Land Law Textbook

Land Law Textbook

SECOND EDITION

Roger Sexton, LLM, PhD
Senior Lecturer, Department of Academic Legal Studies,
Nottingham Trent University

OXFORD
UNIVERSITY PRESS

OXFORD

UNIVERSITY PRESS

Great Clarendon Street, Oxford OX2 6DP

Oxford University Press is a department of the University of Oxford.
It furthers the University's objective of excellence in research, scholarship,
and education by publishing worldwide in

Oxford New York

Auckland Cape Town Dar es Salaam Hong Kong Karachi
Kuala Lumpur Madrid Melbourne Mexico City Nairobi
New Delhi Shanghai Taipei Toronto

With offices in

Argentina Austria Brazil Chile Czech Republic France Greece
Guatemala Hungary Italy Japan Poland Portugal Singapore
South Korea Switzerland Thailand Turkey Ukraine Vietnam

Oxford is a registered trade mark of Oxford University Press
in the UK and in certain other countries

Published in the United States
by Oxford University Press Inc., New York

© Roger Sexton 2006

British Library Cataloguing in Publication Data
Data available

Library of Congress Cataloging in Publication Data
Data available

Typeset by Newgen Imaging Systems (P) Ltd., Chennai, India
Printed in Great Britain
on acid-free paper by
Ashford Colour Press Limited, Gosport, Hampshire

ISBN 0–19–928443–1   978–0–19–928443–6

10 9 8 7 6 5 4 3 2

PREFACE

Land law has a reputation for being a difficult and complex subject—a reputation that is only partly deserved. While part of land law is case-law derived, it has nothing like the number of cases encountered in subjects such as criminal law or tort.

The main problem with land law is that it is statute based, and many of the statutes derive from 1925. But society has radically changed since then. There has been a lot of piecemeal legislation over the last 80 years, and in the last ten years we have had two major Acts of Parliament, firstly the Trusts of Land and Appointment of Trustees Act 1996 and now the Land Registration Act 2002. But even these two pieces of quite far-reaching legislation did not give the law the total revamp which I believe it needs. We still need 'another 1925'.

In preparing this book my prime aim has always been to give a clear explanation of the subject, rather than a mass of detail. To cope with the difficulties of land law, I have divided the book up into 33 chapters. Some of these chapters conclude with an assessment question of similar length to that found in land law examinations. Within the chapters I have included a lot of *short* questions and other exercises to set the reader thinking.

In some universities, land law is a first year subject, whilst in others it is taught in the second or even final years. I hope that the more 'senior' students will forgive me when I say that I have written this book so that it can be used by first year undergraduates. I have assumed that the reader is in the process of studying contract, and has no knowledge of the law of trusts.

I firmly believe that land law can be fun, and I hope that my enthusiasm for this subject (which I have taught for 35 years) is apparent in the pages of this book. A lot of the enjoyment of any legal subject comes through discussion of the knottier points, so I would like to thank all those colleagues *and students* (past and present) who, with their ideas or their interest, have indirectly contributed to the content of this book. It would be impossible to name them all, so I shall not name anybody.

Land law used to be a subject which, in comparison to other legal subjects, changed only slowly. This is no longer true. I must therefore stress that I have endeavoured to state the law as of 1 November 2005.

Roger Sexton
Nottingham Trent University
November 2005

■ OUTLINE TABLE OF CONTENTS

■ CONTENTS

PART VI Leases

PART IX **Restrictive Covenants**

TABLE OF CASES

■ TABLE OF STATUTES

Page references in **bold** indicate that the text is reproduced in full.

■ SOURCE ACKNOWLEDGEMENTS

Grateful acknowledgement is made to all the authors and publishers of copyright material which appears in the book or on the accompanying Online Resource Centre, and in particular to the following for permission to reprint material from the sources indicated:

Extracts from *Law Commission Reports* (LCR) are Crown copyright material and are reproduced under Class Licence Number C01P0000148 with the permission of the Controller of HMSO and the Queen's Printer for Scotland.

Blackwell Publishing Ltd for extracts from *Modern Law Review*: P H Kenny: 'Constructive Trusts of Registered Land' 46 *MLR* 96 (1983).

Incorporated Council of Law Reporting for England and Wales, Megarry House, 119 Chancery Lane, London WC2A 1PP for extracts from *King's Bench Reports* (KB), *Queen's Bench Reports* (QB), *Appeals Cases Reports* (AC), *Weekly Law Reports* (WLR) and *Chancery Reports* (Ch); www.lawreports.co.uk.

Jordan Publishing Ltd: extracts from *Family Law Reports* (FLR).

Reed Elsevier (UK) Ltd trading as LexisNexis Butterworths for extracts from *All England Law Reports* (All ER) and from *Family Court Reports* (FCR).

Roger Sexton: extract from 'The Law Commission's Report on Trusts of Land: at last a law for contemporary society?', *Trust Law and Practice*, January 1989.

Every effort has been made to trace and contact copyright holders but this has not been possible in every case. If notified, the publisher will undertake to rectify any errors or omissions at the earliest opportunity.

■ HOW TO USE THIS BOOK

This book will give students of land law a good, clear, and accurate introduction to the subject. Our aim has been to make the material as accessible as possible for those students coming to the subject for the first time. To this end we have included a number of features throughout the text to allow for interactive use of the book by students, in testing their knowledge and checking their understanding.

The Online Resource Centre (www.oxfordtextbooks.co.uk/orc/sexton2e/) that accompanies this book features cases and materials that complement the textbook. These resources can be downloaded free of charge, and can be used either as individual features for independent study, or integrated into your institution's existing virtual learning environment. The Online Resource Centre also contains updates to the text.

Cases and Materials

Extracts from cases and materials that expand upon and support the primary sources and author commentary found in the textbook can be found on the Online Resource Centre (www.oxfordtextbooks.co.uk/orc/sexton2e/). Wherever there are cases or materials relating to the text, the following symbol appears in the margin of the textbook.

Chapter Objectives

Each chapter opens with a set of objectives to help students identify the areas they should understand by the end of the chapter

Question boxes

Questions are included throughout the text to encourage students to engage critically with the issues discussed. They also provide a useful means for students to test their knowledge while reading the chapter or during the revision process.

Exercises

Exercises are included throughout the text for students to test their understanding of the issues raised by key cases, and to encourage deeper reading and analysis of cases. Where the Online Resource Centre (www.oxfordtextbooks.co.uk/orc/sexton2e/) contains cases or materials relating to an exercise the symbol will appear in the exercise box.

Chapter Summaries

Chapters end with a summary of the main issues discussed in the chapter. This is not intended as a substitute for reading the chapter, but rather as a section to refresh the student's memory on the key issues discussed.

Further Reading

Sources recommended in the text for additional reading assist the student to understand the important issues, and encourage a broader knowledge of the subject.

Assessment Exercises

Many chapters end with an 'Assessment Exercise' that asks a question or sets up a scenario for the students to assess and answer using the knowledge gained through reading the chapter. Full specimen answers to the Assessment Exercises appear in the Appendix.

Glossary

A glossary ensures students are able to understand the terminology specific to land law.

Updates

Updates to the text can be found on the Online Resource Centre (www.oxfordtextbooks. co.uk/orc/sexton2e/). This indispensable resource allows students to access changes in the law that have occurred since publication of the book: students can keep up to date with new developments without buying a new book. Updates are available in pdf format, so can be printed for easy reference.

PART I

Underlying Principles

1 Introduction to the types of property rights in land

1.1 Objectives

By the end of this chapter you should:

1 Have some appreciation of the enormous variety of property rights which can exist with respect to land

2 Be able to explain in outline the fundamental concept of the 'fee simple estate'

3 Be familiar with the concept of a lease

4 Be able to recognize the important types of property right which can exist in favour of third parties against land the fee simple in which is owned by someone else.

1.2 Introduction

In this chapter I aim to give you an **introduction** to certain basic concepts of land law. I should stress that you are not expected at this stage to learn the detailed rules governing (say) leases, easements, or restrictive covenants. Rather, I am trying to give you a broad overview of those property rights in land which are so important that we will be meeting them constantly throughout this text.

Before embarking on this broad overview, there is just one other preliminary point. In English law, 'land' includes not just the surface of the earth, but also buildings and things 'underground' as well. If you own an open site upon which a house is then built, the house becomes part of the land and is therefore yours.

Elitestone v *Morris* [1997] 1 WLR 687 concerned the legal status of a wooden bungalow which rested by its own weight on concrete pillars embedded in the ground. Unlike a 'Portakabin', the bungalow could only be removed by demolition. The House of Lords therefore held that the bungalow had become part of the land. It followed that the lease which the defendant Morris had taken of the land included both the area upon which the bungalow stood and the bungalow itself.

The wooden bungalow in *Elitestone* should be contrasted with the houseboat involved in *Chelsea Yacht and Boat Co.* v *Pope [2000]* 1 WLR 1941. The houseboat was moored on a tidal stretch of the river Thames. It had connections to the shore for electricity, fresh water, and other services. The tidal nature of the Thames meant that it was actually floating for (on average) about half the day. The houseboat was held not to have become 'land'.

1.3 Property rights which give immediate use and enjoyment of land

If a man is occupying land which he regards as 'his', this will almost certainly be because either:

(a) he owns a **fee simple** estate in that land; or

(b) he holds a **lease** of that land.

(There are other possibilities which need not concern us yet.)

1.3.1 Fee simple estate

In everyday conversation we say things like, 'Farmer Giles owns all those fields over there'; 'Fannie Bloggs owns that cottage'; 'Big Company plc owns that hideous looking factory'. As a matter of strict legal theory such statements are incorrect. Ever since the Norman Conquest (1066), all English (and Welsh) land has been vested **theoretically** in the Crown (the monarch for the time being)!

The persons who are colloquially referred to as 'owners' of a piece of land (Giles, Fannie, Big Company) technically own not the land itself but a 'fee simple estate' in the land. They hold this fee simple estate from the Crown under **freehold** tenure. (We might sometimes say in ordinary conversation things like, 'Fannie owns the freehold to her cottage' or 'Giles has got the freeholds to [of/in] those fields'.)

Nowadays the idea that everybody holds 'their land' off the Crown is nothing more than an amusing historical relic. Since 1925 there has been no practical difference between ownership of a fee simple estate in land and ownership of all other types of property, such as furniture, jewellery, other types of goods, money, stocks and shares, bank accounts, etc. Ownership of a fee simple does not now involve performing any special obligations to the Crown.

Ownership of a fee simple, just like ownership of goods and chattels, money, etc., is in principle perpetual. There is just one problem which occurs very occasionally. If an owner of property dies intestate (i.e., without having made a will), all his property passes (after debts etc. have been paid) to his **statutory next-of-kin**. The deceased's widow(er) and children obviously qualify as 'statutory next-of-kin'. Failing them, other close blood relatives such as parents, siblings, uncles/aunts, and first cousins qualify as 'statutory next-of-kin'. If, however, the deceased left no close relatives, his property is in effect now without an owner. We use the Latin phrase *Bona Vacantia* to describe such property. *Bona Vacantia* (ownerless property) passes to the Crown.

> **?** **QUESTION** 1.1
>
> Jack owns the fee simple estate in a 5,000 acre farm, 'Bigtrees'. He is a bachelor and has no close relatives whatsoever. He is 30 years old and in excellent health. Why should he make a will?

Recent surveys show that two-thirds of people die intestate. For people who own very little property this perhaps does not matter. But if Jack dies intestate, the valuable fee simple in Bigtrees (together with all other property he owns) will pass to the Crown. I think Jack would prefer his wealth to go to his friends and/or his favourite charities.

1.3.2 Leases

If somebody has a lease over a piece of land then he has the right to use and enjoyment of that land for the duration of his lease. It must be stressed that a lease is itself a property right. Leases can (as a general rule) be bought and sold, given away, or left by will.

? QUESTION 1.2

If an owner of a lease died intestate, what would happen?

Like the rest of his property, the lease would pass to his statutory next-of-kin.

A lease may (depending on the circumstances) be extremely valuable. Suppose you owned a 999-year lease of a 5,000 acre farm; the rent payable is just one pound per year; there are no other obligations on you, the lessee. You would consider yourself quite a wealthy person!

Leases are basically of two types:

(a) fixed term; and

(b) periodic tenancies.

1.3.2.1 Fixed-term leases

A fixed term lease may be for any period of time, provided the maximum duration is fixed. Thus, for example, one could have a lease for one day, one week, five years, twenty-one years, ninety-nine years, 999 years, or any other **definite** period. (Very short fixed-term leases are, however, unusual.)

You cannot create a lease for an uncertain period such as 'so long as there is a Labour Government', or 'while Manchester United play in the Premier Division'. However, a fixed term lease often includes a forfeiture clause entitling the lessor to terminate the lease prematurely if the lessee breaks any terms of the lease (e.g., fails to pay the rent). Such a clause does not infringe the rule that a lease must have a definite maximum duration.

1.3.2.2 Periodic tenancies

These comprise, for example, weekly, monthly, quarterly, or yearly tenancies. A periodic tenancy is technically a lease for one period, which goes on extending itself automatically until either landlord or tenant gives notice to terminate the tenancy. (The period of notice is usually one period.)

Suppose you have a monthly tenancy of the private lock-up garage in which you keep your car. As a matter of **technical law** you have a lease for one month, then another, then another . . . and so on, until either you or your landlord give one month's notice to terminate the arrangement. In **practical terms**, however, a periodic tenancy goes on indefinitely until one or other party gives notice.

1.4 Property rights against land owned by other people

One of the factors which makes land law both interesting and complicated is the fact that while Bloggs may own the 'fee simple estate' in a piece of land, 'Blackacre', all sorts of other people may have rights against that fee simple. We have just mentioned leases. But there are all sorts of other property rights which could affect the fee simple in Blackacre. One practical effect of the existence of a lot of 'third party' rights against a fee simple would be to reduce the value of that fee simple.

The first of these 'third party' rights is one with which many of you (particularly older readers) may have **some** acquaintance.

1.4.1 Mortgages

How many times have you heard a couple (call them Mr and Mrs Average) say something like, 'We are buying our house with the assistance of a mortgage given us by the Bruddersford Building Society'? You may have said it yourself. If you have, you were wrong, but I will forgive you. The correct legal analysis is as follows:

Mr and Mrs Average own the fee simple estate in the house. In order to finance their purchase they borrowed a lot of money from the Building Society. The moment they acquired the fee simple in the house the Averages **granted to the Building Society** a mortgage, i.e., the Averages are the **grantors** of the mortgage; they are the **mortgagors**. The Building Society did not 'give' the mortgage. It lent the money, and **was granted** the mortgage. It is the **mortgagee**.

The Building Society does not own the fee simple in the house; it owns its 'mortgage'. The mortgage gives the Building Society security. If the Averages fail to repay the loan the Society can enforce its mortgage. This will usually involve taking possession and selling the house over the heads of the Averages. (Mortgages may of course exist with respect to all types of property, not just houses. Any person, not just Building Societies and Banks, can be a mortgagee.)

> **? QUESTION** 1.3
>
> Adverts in banks often say 'mortgages available here'. What is really meant by such advertising?

Such advertising should not be taken literally. The bank is really saying, 'We are willing to lend you (our customers) money provided **you grant us** a mortgage of your house (or other property) to secure the loan'.

1.4.2 Restrictive covenants

This is another type of right in land which you may have already come across, particularly if your house is in a relatively 'posh' area. A restrictive covenant is a promise by one landowner in favour of a neighbouring landowner(s) that he will **not** do certain things upon his land. For example, a farmer promises a neighbouring farmer not to develop his own land but to keep it for agricultural purposes only; or a shopowner promises a neighbouring house-owner that he will not sell takeaway food. In each of these two cases the land restricted is the **servient** land; the land benefited is the **dominant** land.

A more complicated example is as follows. A developer sells off a new housing estate. Each house on the estate is subject to a set of similar restrictive covenants:

(a) Houses shall not be used for any trade, profession, or business.

(b) Front fences must not be more than one foot high.

(c) Caravans and boats must not be kept on the properties.

(d) There must be no outside TV aerials or satellite dishes.

Each purchaser is granted (by the developer) the right to enforce these covenants. Thus every house on the estate is both servient and dominant.

1.4.3 **Easements**

Only a very vague definition of this concept is possible. An easement is a right of one landowner to make use of another nearby piece of land for the benefit of his own land. A mere glance at any textbook's chapter on easements will show that a wide variety of rights come under that general heading.

The most commonly encountered kind of easement, and the one which is easiest to envisage, is the private right of way. For example, Farmer Smith, current owner of High Farm, has the right to use a track across Farmer Brown's Low Field in order to get from the public road to High Farm. We say that the easement is 'appurtenant' to High Farm: High Farm is the **dominant** land; Low Field is the **servient** land.

Another easement of considerable modern importance relates to drains. There may be a right 'appurtenant' to a building to run the drains from that building under neighbouring land (owned by someone else) to the public sewer. Similar easements can exist in relation to gas-pipes, electric and telephone cables, etc.

1.4.4 **Profits à prendre**

A quite extraordinary mixture of rights come under the general heading of profits à prendre ('Profits'). A loose definition of a 'profit' is a right to go on to somebody else's land and to remove from that land something which exists there naturally.

The concept of a 'profit' includes, for example:

(a) a right to extract minerals such as gravel or chalk;

(b) a right to cut peat;

(c) a right to go hunting or shooting over somebody else's land;

(d) a right to fish in someone's lake/river/pond;

(e) a right of a farmer to graze sheep or other animals on land which does not belong to him.

We have already noticed that with easements and restrictive covenants, in addition to the **servient** land over which the right exists, there must also always be **dominant** land benefited by the right. A profit can and usually does exist 'in gross', i.e., as a totally separate right not attached to any dominant land. A profit may, however, exist 'appurtenant' to dominant land, and one important example should be mentioned. The fee simple estates in our great moorlands such as Dartmoor, the Northern Peak District, etc. belong not to the government but usually to some big private landowner. The sheep (and possibly other animals) which we see grazing on the moors do not (normally) belong to that 'big private landowner'. Rather, they belong to farmers who own farms on the edge of the moor.

> **? QUESTION** 1.4
>
> If I bought a farm on the edge of (say) Dartmoor, what sort of 'profit' would almost certainly be an automatic part of my purchase?

I would expect that 'appurtenant' to the farm would be a right to graze a fixed number of sheep (or other animals) upon the moor.

1.4.5 **Rentcharges**

This is a type of property right which many find difficult to understand. Rentcharges, for historical reasons, are very common in the Manchester and Bristol areas, but are relatively uncommon in all other parts of the country.

   If you own a rentcharge, you have the right to receive payment of a regular (usually annual) sum of money. That sum of money is charged upon a fee simple estate in a piece of land. You are **not** landlord of that land. Now this probably does not mean much to you. Things should become clearer if I explain what used to happen in the Bristol area from (about) 1950 to 1977 on the sale of new houses.

   Imagine it is 1960. Bloggs is a builder of houses operating in the Bristol area. He builds new houses on land which he owns. He then sells each house for £10,000 **and** a perpetual rentcharge of £100 per annum. (These figures are realistic.) Smith buys one of these new houses from Bloggs. He pays £10,000 and acquires the fee simple estate in his house. Despite having the freehold, not a lease, Smith must still pay £100 per annum to Bloggs. If Smith sells the house to Thompson, Thompson must now pay the £100 per annum.

> **? QUESTION** 1.5
>
> What happens if Thompson now sells the fee simple in the house to Unwin?

Bloggs has a property right in the house—the right to £100 per annum—which he can claim from the current owner of the fee simple. So Unwin must pay the rentcharge, until he, Unwin, disposes of the fee simple in the house.

   Rentcharges have never been popular with the ordinary public. The Rentcharges Act 1977 did not abolish them, but:

(a) (subject to exceptions) it prohibited the creation of new ones;

(b) it provided that existing rentcharges (which usually are perpetual, i.e., for ever) should terminate after a further 60 years.

1.4.6 **Rights of occupation under the Matrimonial Homes Acts, now renamed matrimonial home rights**

Where one spouse has sole title to the matrimonial home (whether he/she has a fee simple or a lease), the other spouse has a statutory right to occupy the home. This kind of property right was first created by Parliament by the Matrimonial Homes Act 1967. Sections 30 to 32 of the Family Law Act 1996 renamed these rights 'Matrimonial Home Rights'. Viewed from a land law point of view, this is purely a change in terminology; there is no change in the nature of the right, which lawyers sometimes also call (for reasons which will emerge at 8.3.3.3) 'Class F land charges'.

Matrimonial home rights ('rights of occupation') have no application where the legal title to the home is in the joint names of both husband and wife. Nor do matrimonial home rights apply to cohabitees. They apply only to couples who have had a proper ceremonial marriage.

A further point of extreme importance is that matrimonial home rights are entirely independent of any equitable share in the home which the spouse without legal title may have by virtue of a constructive trust.

(The Civil Partnerships Act 2004, which came into force in December 2005, gives civil partners (in appropriate cases) rights analogous to matrimonial home rights. See Sch. 9, para. 1.)

1.4.7 **Interest under a constructive trust**

Detailed examination of constructive trusts forms part of the law of trusts. For present purposes you need only a basic understanding of the one aspect of constructive trusts which affects land law. This point is best explained by reference to an example.

Alfred owns the fee simple in a house, Chenu. Bertha makes substantial contributions to Chenu in one or more of the following ways:

(a) she directly pays a large part of the price of Chenu;

(b) (the most likely possibility) Chenu is bought with the assistance of a mortgage, and Bertha contributes substantially to the mortgage repayments;

(c) Bertha makes substantial improvements to Chenu, e.g., by personally renovating the house, or by paying for contractors to build an extension.

In this sort of situation the courts will normally infer that Bertha was intended to have a share in the property approximately proportionate to her contributions. Suppose in (a) above the house cost £90,000. Alfred paid 'cash down', i.e., he did not have to borrow. £30,000 was in fact provided by Bertha. In principle Bertha will acquire a one-third (equitable) share in the property under a constructive trust. Calculating the size of Bertha's share is going to be more difficult in situations (b) and (c) above; for the purposes of a **land law** course, we need not worry too much about this problem.

You may have noticed that I have not told you whether Alfred and Bertha are married. It does not matter! Nor would it matter if Bertha had the legal title to the property and it was Alfred who made substantial contributions. Nor would it matter if the property were not a house but some other kind (say a farm).

In *Lloyds Bank* v *Rosset* [1991] 1 AC 107, the husband had been given money to buy a derelict house on the understanding that the house should be in his name alone. The wife did a limited amount of work helping the renovation of the house; in particular she helped with the interior decorations. The vast bulk of the work was done by contractors employed and paid for by the husband. The House of Lords held that the wife had not acquired a constructive trust interest. The result would undoubtedly have been different if she had done the renovation work herself, or she had paid the contractors.

> **? QUESTION** 1.6
>
> Horace and Wendy were married in 1956. They have always lived in Grey House. Horace is sole owner of the fee simple in Grey House. Wendy has just come into your office in great distress. Between sobs she explains that Horace has just left her. Consider the land law aspects of this situation. She certainly has one, perhaps two, property rights against the home.

You should have concluded that Wendy will **automatically** have matrimonial home rights, and this will be so even if her role throughout the marriage has been purely as a housewife making no financial contributions to the family income. She **may** also have a constructive trust interest, but that would (normally) depend upon her having made a substantial contribution to the acquisition or improvement of the house.

1.4.8 Licences by estoppel

In *Inwards* v *Baker* [1965] 1 All ER 446 the Court of Appeal (led by Lord Denning) appeared to invent a new type of property right in land, i.e., licences by estoppel (sometimes called 'proprietary estoppel').

Baker junior was keen to build himself a bungalow, but he could not afford the price of an empty site. His father had some spare land. Baker senior said to his son, 'Why not put the bungalow on my land and make the bungalow a little bigger?' Baker junior did exactly that, and made the bungalow his permanent home.

Baker senior retained ownership of the fee simple to the land, and so the house also became **Baker senior's** property. All was well while both senior and junior were still alive, but when Baker senior died his will (made long before the bungalow was built) left the land in question not to Baker junior but to Inwards. Inwards brought proceedings to recover possession of the bungalow. These proceedings failed.

The Court of Appeal held that where a landowner (L) encourages a third party (T) to expend money and/or effort on L's land, and T reasonably assumes that he will have some degree of permanence on the land, T acquires some sort of right with respect to the land. This right is (in principle) binding on third parties. This is now confirmed by s. 116 of the Land Registration Act 2002.

There have been many other cases since, but the exact nature of the proprietary estoppel right is still subject to much debate. It seems that T acquires such right in the land as the court thinks just in all the circumstances. In *Inwards* v *Baker* the son was allowed to live (rent-free) in the bungalow for the rest of his life. That sounds fair enough. But the Court of Appeal surely went too far in *Pascoe* v *Turner* [1979] 1 WLR 431 when it awarded T a full fee simple in the house which was the subject matter of the dispute.

1.4.9 **Estate contracts**

As anyone who has bought a house or other land may well know, the purchase of a piece of land **may** be a long-drawn-out process. From a legal point of view, the purchase of a piece of land normally takes place in two stages:

(a) The vendor and the purchaser enter into a contract under which it is agreed that the land should be sold by V to P (the 'contract stage').

(b) The vendor transfers the fee simple in the land to the purchaser by conveyance or land transfer (the 'completion stage').

The time interval between stages (a) and (b) is normally only a few weeks. The important point to remember is that, during this time interval, the purchaser does not own the fee simple in the land. But he does own an interest in the land known as an **estate contract**.

1.4.10 **Options**

An option is a right under which the grantee (i.e., owner) of the option can at any time during a fixed period (not exceeding twenty-one years) exercise the option and insist that the land the subject matter of the option is sold to him.

Suppose, during my travels, I come across Purple House, a very attractive country residence. I immediately react, 'What a smashing place; one day I might want to buy it!'. I approach Valerie, the owner of Purple House, and we do the following deal.

Valerie grants to me an option exercisable at any time within the next ten years. I pay her £5,000 **for the option**. The option agreement includes a clause that should I exercise the option the price for Purple House itself is to be negotiated between us. If we cannot agree a figure, the price is to be fixed by an arbitrator appointed by the President of the Royal Institution of Chartered Surveyors.

It is important to note the following points:

(a) If at any time in the next 10 years I exercise the option, Valerie cannot turn round and say, 'But I don't want to sell'. I can sue if she refuses to comply.

(b) Valerie has in effect granted me a valuable right over Purple House. Hence the price of £5,000 which I paid **for the option**.

(c) An option should not be confused with **a right of first refusal** (sometimes called a right of pre-emption). A right of first refusal is much less valuable than an option. Suppose that Valerie had granted me a right of first refusal instead of an option. All that would mean is that **if she decided to sell** she would have to offer the property to me before she put it on the open market. I don't think that I would pay very much for a right of pre-emption over Purple House.

(d) The clause in the option agreement regarding the fixing of the price if I do exercise the option reflects standard modern practice.

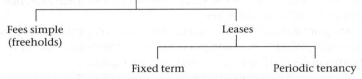

CONCLUDING REMARKS

If somebody is occupying a piece of land, his right to be there will (normally) stem from the fact that he either owns the fee simple ('freehold') in the land, or he has some form of lease (fixed term or periodic) over the land.

Fees simple and leases are not, however, the only property rights which can exist in land. There is a wide variety of property rights which people can enjoy over land which they do not themselves in any sense 'own'. Some of these rights, e.g., restrictive covenants and options, can come about only as a result of some formally agreed transaction. But others, notably interests under constructive trusts and licences by estoppel, can arise informally as a result of a course of conduct. As you will see as you work through this text, much of the difficulty (but also the fascination) of land law lies in the rules governing rights against other people's land, whether those rights are created formally or informally.

SUMMARY

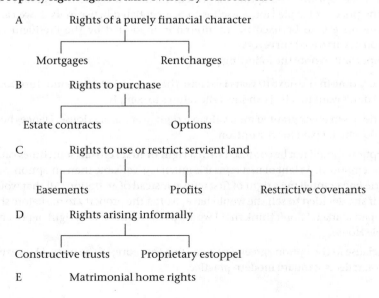

Property rights giving immediate enjoyment of land

Fees simple (freeholds)

Leases

Fixed term

Periodic tenancy

Property rights against land owned by someone else

A   Rights of a purely financial character

Mortgages

Rentcharges

B   Rights to purchase

Estate contracts

Options

C   Rights to use or restrict servient land

Easements

Profits

Restrictive covenants

D   Rights arising informally

Constructive trusts

Proprietary estoppel

E   Matrimonial home rights

■ **FURTHER READING**

For the 'vertical extent' of land ownership, see Kevin Gray, 'Property Rights in Thin Air', [1991] Cambridge Law Journal 252, especially at 292–294.

For an extended consideration of the question 'what is land?' see Gray and Gray, *'Elements of Land Law'*, fourth edition, pages 1–65.

2 Some basic concepts of property law

2.1 Objectives

By the end of this chapter you should:

1 Be familiar with the basic features of a trust

2 Be aware of the types of trust which can exist with respect to land

3 Be able to explain the fundamental differences between unregistered and registered title

4 Be able to explain what are 'title deeds'

5 Be able to distinguish between 'real property' and 'personal property'

2.2 Introduction

This chapter is necessarily something of a miscellany. In it we will examine in outline three matters of which you need some basic understanding before we proceed further with land law. These three matters are the concept of the trust and how it applies to land law; unregistered and registered title; and the (fortunately now relatively unimportant) distinction between real and personal property.

2.3 The trust

2.3.1 The concept of the trust

The concept of the trust is fundamental to English property law, and has been so for hundreds of years. You have probably already learnt that historically the **common law** had the biggest influence on the evolution of English law. But the system of rules known as **equity**, developed by the Court of Chancery, has also been and remains of profound importance. The concept of the trust is equity's biggest contribution to the English legal tradition.

A trust normally involves three parties or groups of parties:

(a) the **settlor** who creates the trust;

(b) the **trustees** who manage the trust property but do not keep any income (rents, interest, dividends, etc.) derived from the property;

(c) the **beneficiaries** who are entitled to the income from the trust property.

The structure of a trust is illustrated by **Figure 2.1**.

SETTLOR ——————————————————— TRUSTEES
(They hold the legal title)

BENEFICIARIES
(They hold the equitable title)

Figure 2.1 Structure of a trust

The references in **Figure 2.1** to 'legal title' and 'equitable title' can be properly explained only by going back a long way in history to about 1300. The following story is typical of that era.

Sir Richard Goodbody is going abroad for a long period of time, quite probably on a Crusade or some other warlike activity. He is concerned that, in his absence:

(a) his land ('Widetrees Manor') should be properly managed;

(b) the income from the land should be used to support his wife and children.

He makes the following arrangement with Thomas and Terence, two old friends whom he thinks he can trust:

(a) He transfers the ownership (i.e., the 'fee simple') in Widetrees Manor to Thomas and Terence.

(b) They agree—
   (i) to manage the land;
   (ii) to pay the income from the land to Lady Goodbody and the children;
   (iii) to transfer the land back to Sir Richard on his return;
   (iv) should Sir Richard be killed, to transfer the land to Sir Richard's eldest son Stephen on his attaining the age of 21.

Now, with the vast majority of trusts created over the last 700 years, the trustees faithfully carry out their trust and the beneficiaries are perfectly happy. You have, however, perhaps already guessed that Thomas and Terence turn out to be a couple of rogues. They manage Widetrees Manor, but keep all the profits from the land for themselves. Lady Goodbody and the children (the 'beneficiaries') are left destitute. They resort to litigation.

Lady Goodbody first tries to bring proceedings against Terence and Thomas in one of the common law courts (the Court of King's Bench, Common Pleas, or Exchequer). These proceedings are dismissed. The court rules that, under the common law, Thomas and Terence are the **legal** owners of Widetrees Manor, and they can do what they like with the land. The claims of Lady Goodbody and the children are purely **moral** ones.

Lady Goodbody now goes to the Lord Chancellor, who until about 1550 was usually a distinguished clergyman rather than a lawyer. He is very concerned that Thomas and Terence carry out their moral obligations. He thus orders them to carry out the terms of the trust, and to pay the profits from the land to the Goodbody family. If they disobey his order, they are locked up for contempt of court, the 'court' being the Court of Chancery.

As a result of many cases similar to the example we have just considered, it became apparent that where a trust is created:

(a) the trustees (Thomas and Terence in my example) are recognized **by the common law** as the owners of the property—they are the **legal** owners of the property;

(b) the beneficiaries (the Goodbody family in my example) are recognized **by equity** as the owners of the property—they are the equitable owners. Each beneficiary has a separate equitable interest in the trust property.

Until the reorganization of English courts in 1875, if trustees committed a breach of trust, the beneficiaries could not bring a successful claim in a common law court. They could only enforce their claim in the Court of Chancery. Although the courts were merged in 1875, the distinction between common law and equity has continued. In particular, it is still correct to refer to trustees as **legal owners** and to beneficiaries as **equitable owners**.

? QUESTION 2.1

Imagine that it is 1850. Tim and Tom hold a large farm, Blackacre, in trust for Anne, Betty, and Cath. Tim and Tom are in breach of trust by keeping the profits from Blackacre for themselves. In which court should the women commence proceedings?

Since the example occurred before 1875, they would of course sue in the Court of Chancery. If the example happened today, they would sue in the High Court. But note that the case would be allocated to the Chancery Division of the High Court!

2.3.2 Modern trusts

2.3.2.1 The trust property

Any type of property can be subjected to a trust, even items such as antiques or valuable paintings. As we shall see later at 2.4, land is still often subjected to a trust. However, in most modern trusts the trust property is stocks and shares, or other investment assets such as company debentures or government bonds. Usually trustees of investment assets have wide powers to vary the investments; see Trustee Act 2000, s. 3.

2.3.2.2 The settlor

The settlor's motivation in creating the trust may well even today be to benefit members of his family, or perhaps his friends or employees; or he may wish to benefit 'charity'. With a charitable trust the trust has charitable purposes; there are no human beneficiaries.

Trusts may be created 'inter vivos', i.e., while the settlor is still alive. Alternatively, a settlor may create a trust by his will, though I must stress that a will only takes effect when the testator (the person who has made the will) actually dies.

(It is usual to think of the settlor, trustees, and beneficiaries, as three distinct persons or groups of persons. This is not always the case. For example, a settlor may appoint himself as one of the trustees, or, rather paradoxically, some of the beneficiaries may also be trustees.)

2.4 Trusts of land

This area of law has been subjected to major changes introduced by the Trusts of Land and Appointment of Trustees Act 1996. This Act, henceforth referred to as the 'Trusts of Land etc. Act' came into force on 1 January 1997.

Prior to the Trusts of Land etc. Act 1996, trusts of land came in three basic forms:

(a) Strict settlements.

(b) Trusts for sale.

(c) Bare trusts.

2.4.1 Strict settlement

This is a type of trust which could be applied only to land. Strict settlements used to be extremely important. It is estimated that even as late as the end of the nineteenth century, 50% of all land in England was subject to a strict settlement! Nowadays strict settlements are rare but not unknown. For reasons which will emerge later in this text, modern lawyers discouraged their clients from creating strict settlements.

A strict settlement was usually created where the settlor hoped that the land would remain 'in the family' from generation to generation, e.g., land was granted to A for life, remainder to A's eldest son (B) for life, remainder to A's eldest grandson (C) in fee simple.

Do not worry at this stage about the technical word 'remainder'. What is important is to understand:

(a) that A, B, and C are the beneficiaries of a trust;

(b) that A enjoys the benefits from the land for his lifetime;

(c) that on A's death the right to enjoy the benefits from the land passes to B for his lifetime;

(d) that on B's death, C becomes entitled to the land outright, and can do what he likes with the land.

You may well be asking the question, 'If a strict settlement is a form of trust, and A, B, and C are the beneficiaries, who then are the trustees of the land?' I have to answer that strict settlements are such a big anomaly in this respect when compared to all other trusts that it is better not to try and answer this question **at this stage**!

2.4.2 **Trust for sale**

Almost all trusts of land in existence immediately prior to 1997 were trusts for sale. For example, Greenacres is conveyed by X to Tim and Tom as trustees with a direction that they must sell the property and invest the proceeds; the investments are to be held in trust for X's children.

You will no doubt immediately realize that:

(a) X is the settlor;

(b) Tim and Tom are the trustees;

(c) X's children are the beneficiaries.

What is rather more surprising is the fact that Tim and Tom do not in fact have to sell the land immediately. Trustees for sale nowadays invariably have 'a power to postpone sale'. This means that they can put off selling the property indefinitely. This is an important, if rather paradoxical, point which you will have to get used to!

One other point to make at this stage is that while a strict settlement could be applied **only** to land, any type of property can be made the subject of a trust for sale.

? **QUESTION** 2.2

In the example above of a trust of Greenacres, who holds the legal title to the land, and who owns equitable interests under the trust?

I hope you found this question very easy. Tim and Tom hold (jointly) the legal title, while X's children own equitable interests under the trust.

2.4.3 **Bare trust**

This is also a form of trust which can be applied to any type of property. It is rare in practice. A bare trust is any trust where the legal ownership of the property is vested in trustees, but:

(a) there is only one beneficiary;

(b) he/she is of full age; and

(c) he/she is entitled to all the benefits from the trust property.

2.4.4 **Trusts of land post-1996**

The Trusts of Land etc. Act 1996 governs:

(a) all trusts of land created **after** 1996;

(b) all trusts of land existing on 1 January 1997, **except strict settlements**.

Except for the (very few) strict settlements which survive into the new era, there will be now just one type of trust of land. This one type I call **'the new-style trust of land'**. Put in a slightly different way, all existing trusts for sale and bare trusts of land, and all new trusts of land, take effect as new-style trusts of land. It is no longer possible to create a strict settlement.

Where a new-style trust of land exists, the situation is like the 'old' trust for sale, but with one difference. As with a trust for sale, the trustees hold the legal title and the beneficiaries own equitable interests. The difference is that with the new-style trust, there is no longer the paradox of a duty to sell coupled with a power to postpone sale. Instead, the 'new-style' trustees have the power to sell at any time they choose.

2.5 Proof of title to land

2.5.1 Importance of proof of title

As you probably already know, buying a piece of land (be it a house, field, factory, or anything else) can be a painfully slow process. One of the reasons for the slowness is that the purchaser needs to make all sorts of enquiries about the land he is intending to buy.

Above all, if you are buying a piece of land from (say) Victor, you want to be absolutely sure that Victor does in fact own the land in question. In technical terms, you want to be sure that Victor has a 'good title' to the 'fee simple' in the land which you are buying. Think what a disaster it would be if you paid Victor £300,000 for the house of your dreams, only to find out later that Victor was a fraudster and the house really belonged to somebody else.

2.5.2 Methods of proving that a vendor has good title

In the English legal system it is up to the vendor to prove to the purchaser that he has got a 'good title' to the land being sold. All fees simple and leases in England and Wales are either **unregistered** title or **registered** title.

Until 1897 unregistered title was the only system operating in this country. It can be fairly described as the 'traditional system' for proving that a vendor has a title to his land.

2.5.2.1 Unregistered title

Title deeds

Where land is unregistered title, the vendor produces 'title deeds' to the purchaser. That sounds rather mysterious, but the basic idea is really quite simple. The title deeds are simply those documents which have been used in the past to carry out transactions with the land. The popular conception of 'title deeds' is as a bundle or pile of old, perhaps even ancient, documents. Subject to the point about 'root of title' which I will explain later, this popular conception is correct.

When a vendor produces title deeds to a purchaser, the vendor is demonstrating that he and his **predecessors in title** have been in control of the land for such a long time that no one could possibly dispute their claim to ownership. By 'predecessors in title' I mean the person (let's call her Penny Predecessor) from whom the vendor obtained the property, the person from whom Penny obtained the property, and so on back in time.

Title deeds will include:

(a) **Conveyances**, 'conveyance' is the name given to the formal document, which must be a deed, which is used to transfer a fee simple from one person to another, whether the transfer is a sale or gift.

(b) **Legal mortgages**, even after the mortgage has been paid off. (Do not worry about the complex historical reasons why mortgages form part of the title deeds.)

(c) **Grants of probate** to executors.

(d) **Grants of letters of administration** to administrators.

(e) **Assents** from personal representatives.

Devolution of ownership on death

The matters mentioned in (c), (d), and (e) above have probably left you rather puzzled. They are all to do with what happens to a person's property on his/her death. After a person dies there will be a need for **personal representatives** (who may be either **executors** or **administrators**) to wind up the deceased's affairs. There are three possibilities:

(a) The deceased has made a will (we say he has died 'testate'), and that will appoints executors who are able and willing to act. The executors will obtain from the court a grant of probate and then—
  (i) gather together all the deceased's property;
  (ii) from that property pay any debts owed by the deceased;
  (iii) pay any inheritance tax or other taxes which become payable on the deceased's death;
  (iv) (once they are sure that all debts and taxes have been paid) distribute the property according to the terms of the deceased's will.

(b) The deceased died '**intestate**', i.e., without making a will. In such a case close relative(s) of the deceased obtain **letters of administration**. The administrators (as they are called) then proceed as in (a) above, except that when they get to stage (iv) they transfer the deceased's property to his **statutory next-of-kin**.

(c) The deceased made a valid will, but that will either fails to appoint executors, or those appointed are either unable or unwilling to act. In such a case close relative(s) of the deceased obtain **letters of administration with the will annexed**. The administrators then proceed exactly as in (a) above.

Assent

Here we have a rather awkward example of the law taking a perfectly ordinary little English word and giving it a technical meaning. In the context of documents relating to land, an 'assent' is the document signed by executors or administrators transferring the land to the person entitled, either under the deceased's will or as statutory next-of-kin.

Investigating title deeds back to the root of title

As we shall learn later when we come to consider the topic of **adverse possession** (see **Chapter 21**), if somebody (and/or his predecessors) has been in control of a piece of unregistered land for a long period of time (usually 12 years is enough), all rival claims to the land are automatically destroyed by lapse of time. In investigating title deeds it is not therefore necessary to wade through huge mountains of paper right back to the proverbial 'year dot'.

Normally the purchaser investigates only as far back as the 'root of title'. Usually the root of title is the most recent conveyance which is at least 15 years old. For example:

- In 1938 A conveyed Purpleacre to B.
- In 1987 B conveyed Purpleacre to C.
- In 1988 C conveyed Purpleacre to D.
- Imagine that we are back in 2001. D (in 2001) is selling Purpleacre to E.

The 1938 conveyance from A to B will be the root of title.

? **QUESTION** 2.3

What if in the above example the conveyance from B to C had been seven years earlier, in 1980?

That conveyance would be the root of title, as it is the most recent conveyance which is at least 15 years old.

(The **Land Charges Register**, which is kept on a computer situated at Plymouth, is an adjunct to the system of unregistered title. It is not to be confused with the Register of Title, which we consider in 2.5.2.2.)

2.5.2.2 Registered title

The vendor proves his title to the purchaser by reference to a register kept by the government at various centres. Registered title is gradually taking over from unregistered title. Compulsory registration of title started in Central London in 1897. It was extended to the rest of (modern) London in 1926. In the 1950s it was extended to parts of the South-East of England south of the Thames. In the 1960s and 1970s it was extended to **most** of the heavily populated areas of the country. There was then a lull from 1978 to 1985. From 1985 to December 1990, new compulsory areas were created every six months, with the result that, as from December 1990, the whole country is covered.

The Land Registry has had to be considerably expanded to meet the growth of registration of title. The registers are kept at 22 District Registries scattered around England and Wales.

The fact that the whole country is now 'compulsory' does not mean that all titles to land are now in fact registered. When an area was designated 'compulsory' that did not mean that everybody had immediately to rush off to the District Registry and register the land they owned. That would have been hopelessly impractical. Ever since 1897 and until recently the basic principle has been that a title to land must be registered the first time it is **sold** after the area in which it is situated is designated a compulsory area. This point will become even clearer if I tell you that there is in Central London ('compulsory' for over 100 years) a large amount of land the fee simple titles to which have not been registered.

 EXERCISE 2.1

Why do you think there is a lot of unregistered land in Central London?

As you may well know, a lot of land in London is owned by long-established companies, the government, the Church, big charities, and family trusts of people such as the Duke of Westminster. Such people/organizations may own the fees simple for (literally) hundreds of years.

Under the Land Registration Act 1997, registration became compulsory where a fee simple passes by a gift, or by an assent from personal representatives.

? QUESTION 2.4

Will this extension of compulsory registration ensure that all fees simple are registered within (say) 100 years?

Unfortunately not. It will not affect land owned by charities, companies, or government agencies (local or national). Such organizations 'never die'.

Registration of leases

One possibly confusing feature of the English system of land registration is that it extends not just to fees simple ('freeholds') but also to long leases. Basically, as the law stood prior to 13 October 2003:

(a) if a new lease was created which was to last more than 21 years, that lease had to be registered;

(b) if an existing long lease was 'assigned' (i.e., transferred from one person to another) the title to the lease had to be registered if the lease had more than 21 years still unexpired.

Leases under the Land Registration Act 2002

When the Land Registration Act 2002 came into force on 13 October 2003 the rules for registration of leases were changed so that all new leases lasting more than **seven** years and all assignments of existing leases with more than **seven** years unexpired have to be registered. This is a simple but far-reaching change in the law, which means that many more leasehold estates will have to be registered than hitherto.

Note that if the appropriate rules for registration of a lease are satisfied, the lease must be registered even if the fee simple out of which the lease is derived is unregistered title.

Voluntary registrations

Prior to 1990, provided the land was situated **within** a compulsory area, it was always possible for somebody with an unregistered title to register that title voluntarily, thus not waiting for the next time the land was sold.

With the whole country now a 'compulsory area', this general right to register voluntarily now extends throughout England and Wales. An existing owner with an unregistered title may wish to voluntarily register. Registration may make the land easier to sell, particularly if the owner intends to subdivide his land and sell it in lots of small units. The Land Registration Act 2002 creates a new incentive to voluntarily register a title; a registered proprietor will under the 2002 Act have much greater protection against the claims of 'squatters' than an unregistered proprietor. (See **Chapter 21**.)

You may perhaps be surprised to learn that prior to 1990 it was not uncommon for registered titles to be found in non-compulsory areas. This was (usually) the result of voluntary registration by builders of new housing estates, such registrations being encouraged by the Land Registry.

In 1973 my parents and I jointly bought a bungalow in Hitchin (North Hertfordshire). The title was registered, and had been since 1958, when the bungalow (and its neighbours) was first built. North Hertfordshire did not become an area of compulsory registration of title until November 1985.

Transactions with a registered title

Once a title has been registered, all subsequent transactions with that title must be registered. When registered land is sold a 'land transfer' is executed by the parties. However, ownership of the land does not pass until that transfer is registered.

2.6 Real property and personal property

Most foreign legal systems divide property (and rights in property) into two types: moveable property and immovable property. The distinction is a perfectly logical one. All land (including buildings) is immovable; all other property is moveable. Unfortunately, English law (and other legal systems such as Australian law and Jamaican law which are derived from English law) draws a less logical distinction. English law distinguishes between real property and personal property.

2.6.1 Real property

All property rights relating to land (fees simple, mortgages, easements, profits, etc.) are real property, **except leases**.

2.6.2 Personal property

This concept includes:

(a) rights in all types of property except land (so things as diverse as goods and chattels, money, stocks and shares, patents and copyrights are all personal property);

    and

(b) leases.

It will be immediately apparent that the big anomaly is leases. The reason for the anomaly is purely historical. In the Middle Ages a lease was regarded as a purely contractual right enforceable only against the landlord, not as a property right against the land itself.

Happily, the distinction between real property and personal property became much less important after 1925. Prior to 1926, if someone died intestate (without making a will) there was one set of rules governing the succession to his real property, and another different set of rules governing the succession to his personal property. After 1925, if someone dies intestate, the same rules of succession apply to both types of property.

There is one situation where the distinction between real property and personal property remains of some significance. This is where a legal document such as a will or trust is drawn up using the phrases 'real property' and 'personal property'. In interpreting the will or other document, these phrases must be given their technical legal meaning.

 QUESTION 2.5

Suppose that Charley Proper makes his own will, without getting any form of legal advice. The will reads: 'I leave my real property to my dear wife Florinda and my personal property to my son David'.

Charley was quite wealthy, and his assets included a 99-year lease over 'Greenroof', the former matrimonial home. Who will inherit the lease?

His son would inherit that lease, though that was probably not what Charley really intended.

CONCLUDING REMARKS

We have just discussed the distinction between real and personal property, a distinction which fortunately is not of great significance today. But other matters dealt with in this chapter are of vital importance. As we shall see in later chapters (especially **Chapter 10**) the results of cases with apparently similar facts may well be different depending upon whether the land in dispute is registered or unregistered title.

Trusts of land is also a vitally important topic. Although strict settlements are (fortunately) largely things of the past, trusts for sale were, prior to the Trusts of Land etc. Act 1996, very common. For reasons which will not become apparent until we reach **Chapters 14** to **16**, there were (prior to the 1996 Act) literally millions of trusts for sale in existence in England and Wales. From 1 January 1997, there are no longer millions of trusts for sale of land. Instead there are millions of 'new-style trusts of land'.

■ SUMMARY

Trusts of Land

Prior to 1997 there were three types of trust of land—strict settlements, trusts for sale, and bare trusts. Since 1996, with the exception of the few strict settlements which still exist, all trusts of land are 'new-style' trusts of land governed by the Trusts of Land and Appointment of Trustees Act 1996.

Proving Ownership

Unregistered land: The owner proves ownership by producing title deeds, i.e., the past transactions with the land. A purchaser of land investigates title back to the 'root of title'. The root of title is the most recent transaction which is at least fifteen years old.

Registered Land: In effect the state keeps records as to who owns which piece of land.

Classification of Property Rights

Real Property: All property rights in land, **except leases**.

Personal Property: Leases, and rights in all other types of property except land.

■ FURTHER READING

For a concise discussion of the meaning of real property, see *Megarry and Wade: The Law of Real Property*, sixth edition by Charles Harpum, at pages 5–7.

For a **short** book explaining the basic principles of trusts (not a full textbook!), read *Understanding Equity and Trusts* by Alastair Hudson (Cavendish Publishing).

For a concise explanation of the differences between registered and unregistered title, see Gray and Gray, *Elements of Land Law*, fourth edition, pages 155–168.

3 Tenures (including commonhold)

3.1 Objectives

By the end of this chapter you should:

1 Be able to explain the concept of tenures

2 Appreciate why it is of rather limited significance today

3 Understand the basic principle of the newly created tenure of 'Commonhold'

3.2 Introduction

In medieval times, there were two legal concepts of fundamental importance to English land law. These concepts were 'tenures' and 'estates'. Where a person lawfully occupied a piece of land, he held that land under a tenure for the duration of an estate. (We will be considering estates in **Chapter 4**.)

Originally there were many different types of tenure. Where a person occupied land his **tenure** indicated the type of **conditions** upon which he held his land. His estate indicated **the length of time** for which he held his land. Theoretically, this is still true today.

3.3 Feudal tenures

What I am about to say may remind you of school history lessons! We have already referred to the fact that in strict legal theory somebody who 'owns' a piece of land in fact holds a fee simple estate off the Crown under 'freehold tenure'. In the days of the feudal system (approx 1066–1300) there were lots of different tenures. As you may know, after the Norman Conquest the King and other feudal lords granted land in **fee simple** to their supporters in return for the supporters rendering various types of services to the King or the other feudal lords. A man's tenure indicated the kind of services he had to perform. For example if a man held land under a 'military tenure', he had to supply troops for the army. If he held under 'socage' tenure, he had to help farm his lord's land. If he held in 'frankalmoigne' tenure, he had to pray for the salvation of his lord's soul!

Happily for England, the system of holding land in return for rendering physical services began to die out as early as the thirteenth century. By a statute called 'Quia Emptores' passed as early as 1290 (and still in force), Parliament banned further 'subinfeudation', i.e., a fee simple can no longer be granted in return for the grantee rendering services.

Existing obligations on fee simple owners to perform services continued after 1290, but these obligations gradually disappeared as a result of a mixture of economic and historical factors. Many tenures also just disappeared, but some were abolished by Act of Parliament. In particular the Tenures Abolition Act 1660 (part of the agreed compromise which led to the restoration of Charles II) abolished military tenure. 'Copyhold' tenure (a form of tenure originally very important for small-scale farmers) was not abolished until 1925.

The result of all this is that today there is only one tenure left which has its origins in feudalism, namely freehold tenure. (Freehold tenure is actually the modern name for 'socage' tenure.) If somebody owns land, he (in technical terms) holds that land off the Crown under freehold tenure for a fee simple estate. Thankfully, though, he does not have to render any services to the Crown!

? **QUESTION** 3.1

Old Joe Bloggs has owned 'Greytrees' for a very long time. You are trying to explain basic land law to him. He suddenly interjects, 'Does this all mean that I don't really own Greytrees, but the Queen does and that I am merely her tenant and I have to do a lot of work for her?'. How do you reassure Joe?

I think you will say something like this: 'You, Joe, are in the same position as every other landowner in England and Wales. You are technically a "tenant" of Her Majesty, but you are not a lessee. You hold your land for a fee simple estate, a right to the land which goes on forever. You hold that fee simple estate under a "freehold" tenure. Once upon a time freehold tenure meant that a landowner had to work hard for his land, but nowadays the obligation to work for your land has disappeared'.

3.4 Leasehold tenure

Leases did not exist under the feudal system of medieval times. The practice of granting land **for a fixed period** in return for a regular money payment (i.e., rent) only commenced about 1450.

Where there is a lease the **tenant** holds the land off his **landlord**, and (normally) the tenant must pay for holding the land. The position of a tenant holding a lease from his landlord for a rent has been regarded as analogous to a medieval fee simple owner holding his land off the King or other feudal lord in return for rendering services. (I am somewhat sceptical of this analogy, but I am very much outvoted!)

The practical result of drawing this (somewhat strained) analogy between leases and feudal tenures is that 'leasehold' is today regarded by both textbook writers and Parliament as a form of tenure. For example, legislation sometimes refers to 'land of any tenure'.

3.5 Commonhold—a new tenure for the twenty-first century

3.5.1 The problem commonhold is designed to solve

Suppose I own a fee simple estate in Blue House, a four-storey building in a quite desirable area of Nottingham. The building is empty, and I convert it into four one-storey flats. I now want to sell each of the flats, though I might retain ownership of 'the common parts' such as the hallway, stairs, and lift.

As some readers may already know, under the law prior to the introduction of Commonhold, I would not 'sell' a fee simple estate to each of the four flat purchasers. Rather I would grant to each of them a long lease, probably for 99 years. Why?

Each 99 year lease would include promises ('positive covenants') by the lessee to keep the part of Blue House leased to him in good repair. Such covenants were essential because otherwise Blue House might fall down because of the neglect of (say) the ground-floor lessee. More important still, these positive covenants to repair would 'run with the land'. I.e., the landlord of Blue House for the time being (**I or my successors**) would be able enforce the promises to repair against **the current owner** of the 99 year lease. (These rules regarding covenants in leases are discussed in depth in **Chapter 19**.)

Could not a fee simple in a flat be sold subject to a promise by the purchaser of the fee simple that he would keep the flat in good repair? In practice, the answer to this question was 'No!' Unfortunately, if a purchaser of a fee simple made a positive promise regarding his land, that promise was enforceable against him, **but not against his successors in title**. (See *Rhone* v *Stephens* [1994] 2 AC 310.)

Suppose I (foolishly) sold in fee simple the ground-floor flat in Blue House to Fred. Fred covenanted to keep the ground floor in good repair. Fred then sold the ground floor to George. I could not enforce the repairing covenant against George. Now that could be literally disastrous for the owners of the upper floors.

3.5.2 Commonhold tenure to the rescue

Parliament has used the ancient concept of Tenure to solve this problem of the inability to sell flats in fee simple. The Commonhold and Leasehold Reform Act 2002 creates a new Tenure, 'Commonhold' which will allow residential flats to be owned in fee simple. (The new Act is not by its terms confined to flats. Commonhold could be applied, e.g., to a block of offices.) The Act came into force on 27 September 2004.

The 2002 Act enables a person ('The Developer') building a new block of flats (or creating a block of flats out of an existing building as in my Blue House example) to use the new Commonhold system. (Somewhat simplified), Commonhold will operate in the following way.

The developer of the flats will create a special form of limited company known as a 'Commonhold Association' or 'ChA'. The ChA will be registered at the Land Registry as the owner of a normal fee simple in the building held off the Crown in freehold tenure. The ChA is, in this respect, no different from any other landowner.

The big novelty is when somebody comes to buy a flat in the Commonhold building. The purchaser of a flat will buy, not a lease, but a fee simple held off the ChA **in Commonhold Tenure**.

Let us suppose I decide to organize Blue House as a Commonhold. (The minimum size of a Commonhold is just two flats.) I will create the Blue House ChA, which will be registered at the Land Registry as owner in fee simple of Blue House as a whole. I will also register a 'Commonhold Community Statement' ('CCS'). This CCS will contain a detailed set of rules regarding the use and upkeep of the whole building. The CCS is likely to make the individual flat owners liable for repair of their flats, but make the ChA responsible for common parts such as the lifts, stairs, and corridors.

Suppose I sell the four flats in Blue House in 2006 to Penny, Queenie, Rita, and Steph. I cease to have any rights (or responsibilities) with respect to the building. The legal position will now be as follows.

The four ladies each have a fee simple estate in their respective flats (called 'units' by the Act). Those estates will be held under Commonhold Tenure, and will be registered as separate titles at the Land Registry. (There will therefore now be **five** files at the Registry regarding Blue House.)

The four ladies (and only them) will be the members of the ChA. When (say) Rita sells her flat, the new purchaser will automatically become a member of the ChA instead of Rita.

The four ladies will of course be subject to the detailed rules laid down in the CCS. The ChA will remain owner of the common parts. The expenses of the ChA will be met by its members applying the rules laid down in the CCS.

3.5.3 Common parts in a commonhold

When I talk of 'common parts' in a commonhold, I naturally think of the stairs, lifts, and corridors in a block of flats. However s. 25(1) of the new Act defines 'common parts' simply as, 'every part of the commonhold which is not for the time being a commonhold unit in accordance with the commonhold community statement'. It will therefore be perfectly possible to have commonholds where the common parts (in the direct ownership of the ChA) includes 'communal areas' such as a garden, gym, or swimming pool! (Experience in jurisdictions such as Germany which already have the legal equivalent to commonhold suggests that there will be a demand for commonholds at the 'luxury' end of the property market.)

 CONCLUDING REMARKS

From 1926 until 2004, only two tenures were possible in modern land law, namely Freehold and Leasehold. But now there is a third Tenure. Just as a 'freeholder' holds his land off the Crown, and a lessee holds his land off his landlord, so a Commonholder will (in effect) hold his flat off his Commonhold Association.

It remains to be seen how many Commonholds will be created in practice. It is perhaps unfortunate that there is no compulsion on the developers of new blocks of flats to use the Commonhold system. Developers may therefore still choose to build a block and then lease the flats to tenants.

■ SUMMARY

There are now effectively three tenures:

Freehold—derived from feudalism;

Leasehold—derived from (ancient) common law;

Commonhold—created by modern legislation.

■ FURTHER READING

If you would like to know more detail as to how Commnoholds are set up, see the two-page article by Robin Grove, 'A developer's guide to commonhold' in 2005 New Law Journal 208–209.

For a more detailed (but not overlong) consideration of Commonhold see Sparkes, '*A New Land Law*' (second edition, Hart Publishing) Chapter 4, entitled 'Houses, Flats and Commonhold'.

For details on feudal tenures, see *Megarry and Wade: Law of Real Property*, sixth edtion by Charles Harpum, chapter two.

4 Estates

4.1 Objectives

By the end of this chapter you should:

1 Be able to explain the concept of a fee simple estate, both in its pre-1926 form and in its post-1925 form

2 Be able to distinguish between a fee simple upon condition subsequent and a determinable fee simple

3 Be familiar with the (archaic) rules which govern the duration of a fee tail estate

4 Have a basic idea of the (anachronistic) rules governing the barring of entails

5 Be familiar with the various forms which can be taken by a life estate

6 Be able to distinguish between an estate in possession, an estate in remainder, and an estate in reversion

4.2 Introduction

We have already seen that in modern law the concept of **tenures** is of very limited significance. By contrast, the concept of **estates** remains of prime importance. If a person holds a piece of land, his 'estate' indicates the period of time over which he (and his successors) can continue to hold that land. Some of the basic rules regarding estates are easy to follow; but I must also warn you that there are also some complex and confusing anachronisms.

   At common law there were four types of estates:

- Fee simple ⎫
- Fee tail   ⎬   estates of freehold
- Life estate ⎭
- Lease

The three 'estates of freehold' are far more ancient in origin than the leasehold estate, and they are discussed below.

4.3 Fee simple

The fee simple estate in land has always been the most valuable and the most important of the estates. It has always been an 'estate of inheritance', i.e., an estate which can pass on from generation to generation. Indeed, a fee simple has always been capable of lasting indefinitely.

Since the very early days, the owner of a fee simple has been able to sell it. He has also been able, on his death, to leave the fee simple by his will to whomever he chooses, even though that might mean that his 'heir' (who would have inherited the land on intestacy) was disappointed.

The 1925 legislation made quite important changes to the nature of a fee simple, and you still need to know the pre-1926 nature of a fee simple, as well as the modern position.

4.3.1 Fees simple pre-1926

Prior to 1926 the fee simple was dominated by the (old-fashioned) concept of the 'heir'. This dominance manifested itself in two ways.

In the first place, a fee simple estate continued indefinitely, subject only to the possibility of 'natural determination'. Natural determination occurred where the present owner of a fee simple died intestate without leaving any traceable **heir**. In the (rare) event of there being no traceable heir, there was an 'escheat'. The fee simple terminated and the Crown became entitled to the land.

Secondly, if you wanted to convey a fee simple to a human being you had to include the magic words 'and his heirs' in the conveyance. Thus to convey to John Smith a fee simple in Blackacre, the conveyance had to grant Blackacre 'To John Smith and his heirs'. If a conveyance said 'To John Smith' or 'To John Smith forever', John would get only a life estate. Prior to 1882, even saying 'to John Smith in fee simple' would not work to convey a fee simple.

This rule, that you had to add 'and his heirs' after the name of the grantee, looks even sillier when you remember that the heir of the owner of a fee simple had no guarantee that he would actually inherit the estate. In my example of a grant of Blackacre to John Smith, John is free to sell or give away his fee simple at any time, or he can leave it by his will to whomever he chooses.

4.3.1.1 Rules for identifying the heir

The following rules, which to us now may seem rather archaic, had to be applied if somebody died **intestate** owning a fee simple in land. As a general rule the closest blood relative of the deceased was his heir. If the deceased left children, the eldest son was the heir. If the deceased left no son, but daughters, the daughters jointly constituted the heir. If the deceased left neither children nor remoter descendants (grandchildren, etc.) then a collateral relative (such as a brother, an uncle, or a cousin) could inherit the fee simple as heir.

You should not attempt to learn the detailed rules set out in some larger textbooks. Just remember the following points, which show the rather antique nature of the rules for identifying heirs:

(a) The rules always preferred males over females.

(b) Amongst males (only), the rules preferred the eldest over the others.

(c) The deceased's surviving spouse could never be heir, even if the deceased had only very remote blood relatives, or no blood relatives at all.

> ### ? QUESTION 4.1
>
> John died intestate in 1920. His main asset was a fee simple estate in Vastacres, worth £500,000. He left a widow with no financial resources of her own. He also left a sister aged 80, and two brothers aged 75 and 70. The brothers emigrated to Australia in 1900 and John never saw them again. Both became extremely prosperous. Who inherited the fee simple?

Applying the rules set out above, the widow cannot be heir, males are preferred over females, and between males the eldest takes. Thus the 75-year-old brother inherits the fee simple to Vastacres.

4.3.2 Fees simple after 1925

For purposes connected with fees simple (though not for certain other purposes) the old rules relating to heirs have been abandoned. The old concept of escheat for want of heirs was also abolished.

As you may well remember from **Chapter 1**, a fee simple estate is now in principle eternal, and owning a fee simple is really no different from owning any other type of property. If a person dies intestate all his property passes to his **statutory next-of-kin**. The rules relating to next-of-kin give preference to surviving spouses, do not discriminate between the sexes, nor do they discriminate between elder and younger children. If someone dies intestate without statutory next-of-kin then all his property vests in the Crown as 'bona vacantia' (ownerless property).

With regard to the wording of a conveyance of a fee simple after 1925, the law on this point has been brought into line with common sense. To convey a fee simple after 1925 to John Smith it is sufficient to say 'To John Smith': Law of Property Act 1925, s. 60.

4.3.3 Modified fees simple

So far, we have assumed that all fees simple are **absolute**, i.e., that in principle they go on for ever, subject to the (remote) possibility of the current owner dying intestate without any relatives capable of inheriting the estate. Now, in the twenty-first century, the overwhelming majority of fees simple are absolute. Unfortunately it is still just possible to come across 'modified fees simple'. No doubt you will quickly agree that modified fees should have been abolished in 1925. They are anachronisms, just like fees tail (see 4.4).

A fee simple is modified if it may come to a premature end for some specified reason other than lack of people to inherit. Just to confuse matters further, there are two types of modified fee simple, the **determinable fee simple** and the **fee simple upon condition subsequent**.

4.3.3.1 Determinable fee simple

This can be defined as a fee simple which terminates automatically on the occurrence of a specified event which may never happen. For example:

(a) To John Smith in fee simple until he marries Fanny Bloggs.

(b) To the X charity in fee simple while my grave remains in good condition.

(c) To Ann Green in fee simple during the time that she remains a faithful Protestant.

4.3.3.2 **Fee simple upon condition subsequent**

This can be defined as a fee simple where the grantee is given an apparently absolute fee simple, but a clause is then added to the effect that if a stated condition is broken, the estate shall be forfeit. For example:

(a) To John Smith in fee simple provided that he never marries Fanny Bloggs.

(b) To the X charity on condition that my grave remains in good condition.

(c) To Ann Green in fee simple unless she forsakes the Protestant religion.

(d) To David Brown in fee simple, but not if he marries a Roman Catholic.

 EXERCISE 4.1

What do you think was the motivation of the grantor in the two examples '(a)' in 4.3.3.1 and 4.3.3.2 above?

It is fairly obvious that the grantor (who is perhaps John's father) does not want John to marry Fanny. He is in effect saying to John, 'If you marry that wretch of a woman you lose your land!'

4.3.3.3 **'It's all a matter of words'**

It is very easy to identify a modified fee simple, but it is not always so easy to tell whether it is a determinable fee or a fee on condition subsequent. It depends on the kind of wording used by the grantor. If he uses words of a **temporal** nature, such as 'until', 'during the time that', 'whilst', etc., then there is a determinable fee. If he uses words of a **conditional** nature, such as 'provided that', 'on condition that', or 'unless', it is a fee simple upon condition subsequent.

4.3.3.4 **The differing rights of the grantor**

With a determinable fee, the grantor retains a **possibility of reverter**. If the determining event takes place, the possibility of reverter automatically takes effect and revests an absolute fee simple in the grantor. Consider example (a) in 4.3.3.1. If John marries Fanny then he loses the fee simple as soon as the marriage takes place. The grantor regains the fee simple without having to make any claim for it.

With a fee simple upon condition subsequent the grantor retains a **right of entry**. (The phrase 'right of entry' is really a euphemism for a 'right to forfeit'.) If the condition is broken the fee simple remains vested in the grantee until the grantor chooses to exercise the right of entry.

 QUESTION 4.2

Consider example (a) in 4.3.3.2. If John marries Fanny, when (if at all) does he lose the land?

Now when the priest/registrar says 'I hereby pronounce you man and wife' John retains the fee simple until the grantor chooses to reclaim the land. (The grantor has got 12 years to get the fee simple back. He will, normally, get the fee simple back by repossessing the land. If the grantor allows 12 years to elapse without reclaiming the land, John can breathe again! He keeps the fee simple.)

One reason why modified fees should be abolished is that they are out of line with modern ideas of freedom, particularly religious freedom. Amazingly, modified fees limiting freedom to marry and freedom of religion have been held valid. In 1975 the House of Lords unanimously **upheld** a condition subsequent which provided for forfeiture on the grantee becoming a Roman Catholic: (*Blathwayt* v *Cawley (Baron) and Others* [1976] AC 397.)

The Law Lords stressed the freedom of landowners to give away their land on whatever conditions they saw fit. It is nevertheless submitted that *Blathwayt* v *Cawley (Baron) and Others* needs reconsideration in the light of the Human Rights Act 1998 and Article 9 of the European Convention on Human Rights guaranteeing freedom of religion.

On a few occasions (mainly in the nineteenth century) the courts have held a particular modified fee to infringe public policy. Notably, modified fees which discourage entry into the armed forces (e.g., to X provided he does not join the Navy) are ineffective. Modified fees are (thank goodness) virtually obsolete.

4.4 Fee tail

The fee tail is a strange legal relic which has somehow survived into the twenty-first century. Fees tail were first recognized as an estate in land in 1285. Until the nineteenth century land (particularly the large country estate) was often subject to a fee tail. Very few fees tail exist today. They should have been abolished in 1925; they are totally out of place in the twenty-first century. A fee tail cannot be bought or sold, or given away or left by will. (However, as we shall see at 4.4.2, a fee tail can often be converted into a fee simple by the process of 'barring the entail'. This possibility should be ignored for the moment.)

A fee tail is an 'estate of inheritance', i.e., it can pass on from generation to generation within the same family. **It is an estate which lasts as long as the original grantee or any of his lineal descendants are still alive**. If all the descendants of the original grantee die out the fee tail will terminate. Consider the following example:

Whiteacre is granted to Brian in fee tail. His 'family tree' is as in Figure 4.1

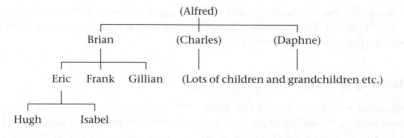

Figure 4.1 Example: Alfred's family free

When an owner of a fee tail dies, the old rule regarding 'heirs' still has to be applied, **even after 1925**. Thus:

- When Brian dies the fee tail passes to Eric.
- When Eric dies the fee tail passes to Hugh.
- When Hugh dies he is childless; the fee tail passes to Isabel.
- When Isabel dies she is childless. The fee tail can pass to Frank or Gillian, if either is still alive.

> **? QUESTION** 4.3
>
> What happens to the fee tail if Frank and Gillian both die childless?

The answer is that the fee tail is at an end, as Brian's descendants have now all died out. (Applying rules discussed at 4.6.2, the right to the land will revert to the person who granted the fee tail.)

A fee tail cannot pass to the collateral relatives (e.g., brothers, sisters, cousins) of the **original grantee** (Brian in my example). This is a big difference between a fee tail and a (pre- or post-1925) fee simple. If, in my example, Brian had had a fee simple, that could pass to Charles, Daphne, and their families. But the fee **tail** granted to Brian cannot pass to them.

4.4.1 The inalienability of fees tail (as such)

As already mentioned, fees tail were popular from about 1300 to the late nineteenth century. They were employed by large country landowners (usually members of the aristocracy) anxious that the family lands should remain in the family from generation to generation.

Suppose Baron Blogtown owns Wideacres in fee simple. By his will, Baron Blogtown left Wideacres 'to my elder son Stephen in fee tail, remainder in fee simple to my younger son Keith'. Now it must be stressed that a fee tail is 'inalienable', i.e., it cannot be sold or given away, nor could it be left by will. Thus, in my example, Stephen is stuck with Wideacres for his lifetime. On Stephen's death the fee tail estate **must** pass to his heir, who is of course equally incapable of selling or giving away the fee tail. (And so on when the heir dies.)

A lot of fees tail were created in medieval times. That meant that a lot of land was 'frozen', as it were, to a particular family, and could not be bought and sold. This was not good for the prosperity of England. English lawyers found a solution to the problem when, in about 1450, they invented the process of 'barring an entail'.

4.4.2 Barring an entail

Anybody of full age who owns a fee tail estate in possession can 'bar' the entail. Prior to 1833, the barring of an entail was a complex and expensive process; since then it has been cheap and simple. All the fee tail owner (Stephen in my Wideacres example) has to do is to execute a document called a 'disentailing assurance'.

If a fee tail is 'barred' the following consequences ensue:

- the fee tail is converted into a fee simple;
- any fee simple existing in remainder or reversion to the fee tail being barred is destroyed.

Thus in my Wideacres example, Stephen will probably want to bar the entail. If he executes a disentailing assurance that will convert his unsaleable fee tail into a fee simple which he can dispose of in any way he chooses. Moreover, the disentailing assurance will also destroy Keith's fee simple in remainder.

You may be thinking, 'That's rough upon Keith. His rights are destroyed by Stephen signing a simple document. Does he get any compensation?' The answer is a firm 'No!' (If you were Keith, would you seriously expect that the land would ever come to you?)

4.4.3 Barring a fee tail by will

As barring an entail is now so easy and cheap, almost everybody of full age who acquires a fee tail in possession will bar it immediately. That, of course, is the major reason why fees tail are almost extinct.

Suppose, however, that somebody acquires a fee tail, wishes to keep the land during his lifetime, but then wants to be free to leave the land to the person of his choice. Since 1925 a fee tail can be barred by will. All that is required is that the will specifically refers to the land subject to the fee tail.

Suppose in my Wideacres example Stephen wishes to keep the land until he dies, but he wants the land to then pass to his beloved daughter Florence rather than to his scoundrel eldest son Roger. If, when he died, his will simply read, 'I leave all my property to my daughter Florence', that would not bar the entail. Roger would inherit the fee tail in Wideacres under the old rules about heirs. Moreover, Roger could then bar the entail!

If, on the other hand, Stephen's will had read, 'I leave all my property including Wideacres to my daughter Florence', there is a specific reference to Wideacres, so the entail would be barred. Florence would get a fee simple in Wideacres, and Roger would get nothing.

4.5 Life estates

While fees tail are exceedingly rare today, property rights which last 'for life' are still quite common. As you can probably guess, the essential feature of a life estate is that its duration is governed by the length of the life of a named person or persons. A life estate is bound to come to an end sooner or later!

Life estates can take various forms, e.g.,

(a) Property is granted 'To Jane Brown for life'.

This is the simplest and commonest form of life estate. Jane enjoys the property for her own lifetime. Her rights terminate on her death, and she will have nothing which she can pass on by her will. Other forms of life estate can be a little more complex, e.g.,

(b) Property is granted to 'Jane and John Brown for their lives', or

(c) Property is granted to 'Jane and John Brown for their joint lives'.

The second example lasts as long as **either** Jane or John is alive. The third example is not so good; it lasts only as long as they are **both** alive.

The form of life estate which people sometimes find difficult is the estate 'pur autre vie', e.g.,

(d) Property is granted to 'Ann Green for the life of Karen White'. This means that the estate comes to an end when Karen dies, not when Ann dies. If Ann dies before Karen the estate continues until Karen dies, and the right to enjoy the property until Karen's death will pass to Ann's successors under her will. If there is no will it will pass according to the normal intestacy rules.

I should mention one other complication with life estates. Go back to my first example (a) above. Let us suppose that Jane sells (or gives) her life estate to Penny Pink. Penny acquires the right to enjoy the property for **Jane's** lifetime, not for her own. (Put another way, Penny acquires an 'estate pur autre vie' lasting for Jane's life.) If you stop and think for a moment, no doubt you will agree that this result is both logical and fair.

> **? QUESTION** 4.4
>
> In 1985 Whiteacre was granted 'to Tom, Dick, and Harriet for their joint lives'. Tom, Dick, and Harriet have just executed a deed transferring to you their rights in Whiteacre. Tom is on his deathbed. Is it worth your moving into Whiteacre?

I think that you had better start praying for a miracle to restore Tom to full health! You have acquired an estate pur autre vie which will terminate when the **first** of Tom, Dick, or Harriet dies.

4.6 Estates in possession, reversion, and remainder

In the preceding discussion we have often assumed one thing which is not always true. We have assumed that all estates are 'in possession'. In fact, while most estates are 'in possession', estates in reversion and in remainder can also exist.

4.6.1 Estate in possession

This is almost self-explanatory. An estate in possession is one which confers on its owner an immediate right to occupy the relevant land.

4.6.2 Estate in reversion

An estate in reversion arises where the owner of a greater estate (usually a fee simple) grants out of that estate a lesser estate. For example, Alfred owns fees simple in Blueacre, Greenacre, and

Redacre. He grants Blueacre 'to Brian for life'. He grants Greenacre 'to Charles in tail'. He grants Redacre 'to David for 99 years'.

In each case, during the time that the life estate, fee tail, and lease are in possession, Alfred retains an estate **in reversion**. When the life estate, fee tail, and lease expire, the right to actual enjoyment of the land returns to Alfred. But what if, in the meantime, Alfred has died? An estate in reversion (also an estate in remainder) can be inherited just like any other property. So it will be Alfred's successors under the law of succession who will be able to claim possession of the land.

Two other points should be noted about reversions. First, sub-leases. Suppose David (in the example just considered) sub-leased Redacre to Edward for 50 years. David would also now have an estate in reversion. Secondly, unlike estates in remainder (see 4.6.3 below), an estate in reversion arises **by implication**. It arises whenever the owner of a greater estate creates a lesser estate but does not make express provision for what is to happen when the lesser estate expires.

4.6.3 Estates in remainder

An estate in remainder arises where the owner of a fee simple grants a life estate (or possibly a fee tail) and then in the same document grants a further estate to follow on after the termination of the life estate or fee tail. For example:

(a) Frank owns the fee simple in Purpleacre. He grants Purpleacre 'to George for life, remainder to Henry in fee simple'. This means that on George's death the land will not revert to Frank. Rather it will pass on to Henry. If Henry died before George, the land would pass on to Henry's successors under the law of succession.

It is possible to have a series of 'remainders', one after another. For example:

(b) Frank owns the fee simple estate in Mauveacre. Prior to 1997 he grants Mauveacre 'to Ian for life, remainder to John in fee tail, remainder to Keith in fee simple'.

   Notice that Keith (or more likely his successors) will have to wait for John's fee tail to expire before he/they can enjoy the land. They may be waiting a very long time!

(c) Frank owns the fee simple estate in Orangeacre. He grants Orangeacre 'to Norma for life, remainder to Olivia for life, remainder to Philippa for life . . . remainder to Wendy in fee simple'. This sort of thing is possible, but highly unlikely.

Note that one thing Frank cannot do is to grant land 'to Leonard in fee simple, remainder to Malcolm in fee simple'. Having granted the fee simple to Leonard, he has given all his rights away. Malcolm gets **nothing**.

> **? QUESTION** 4.5
>
> Frank owned Greenacre in fee simple. Prior to 1997 he executed a deed granting the land 'to Quentin for life, remainder to Richard in fee tail'. There are now three estates in Greenacre; what are they?

Applying the rules set out above, you should conclude that Quentin has a life estate in possession and Richard has a fee tail in remainder. But Frank also still has an estate, as he retains a fee simple in reversion.

4.7 Interests under trusts

For the purposes of **land law** you need only understand the general idea of interests under trusts. Details can wait until you study the law of trusts.

Equitable interests under a trust (of any type of property) may be in possession or in remainder. Suppose Peter owns 10,000 shares in ICI:

(a) He transfers 6,000 of those shares 'to Tim and Tom as trustees, on trust for Quentin for life, remainder to Richard absolutely'. This means that during Quentin's lifetime he will get the (net) dividends from the shares. When Quentin dies, Richard (or if he is dead his successors) will have outright ownership of the shares.

(b) He transfers the other 4,000 shares 'to the National Westminster Bank plc, on trust for Stephen for life, remainder to Thomas for life'. The obvious question is, 'What happens to the shares after both Stephen and Thomas are dead?' The answer is that Peter retains an interest under **a resulting trust**. This resulting trust will take effect after the death of Stephen and Thomas, so that Peter (or his successors) will regain outright ownership of the shares.

(One other point about the above example: It is quite common nowadays to appoint as trustee a bank, or (say) accountants or solicitors. Why do you think this practice has become common?)

 CONCLUDING REMARKS

The cornerstone of English land law has been, for hundreds of years, the fee simple estate. The 1925 legislation changed (somewhat) the nature of the fee simple, but (as we shall see from ensuing chapters) the cornerstone status of that estate was enhanced.

Life estates (and also life interests under trusts) have been important for hundreds of years. Though they occur less frequently than in the past, no one doubts their continued utility to property law generally (not just land law). The same cannot be said regarding fees tail and modified fees simple. In 1989, the Law Commission produced a report which contained proposals for reform of 'Trusts of Land'. This topic included settled land and a wide variety of related issues, including fees tail and modified fees.

The Trusts of Land etc. Act 1996 is (largely) an enactment of the 1989 Law Commission report. The Act forbids the creation of new fees tail. Any attempt to create a fee tail will mean that the grantor declares himself to be a trustee for the grantee who will acquire an equitable fee simple. (See Sch. 1, para. 5 of the 1996 Act.)

All existing fees tail are unaffected by the 1996 Act. Disappointingly, the Act makes no provision banning modified fees. I still adhere to the views which I expressed in an article which appeared in the autumn of 1989 in *Trust Law and Practice*:

____As every law student knows, land law is still cluttered up with strange devices such as fees tail, determinable fees and fees upon condition subsequent. The Commission does propose that no new entails should be created; any attempt to create an entail would in future result in a fee simple being transferred. This proposal does not, however, go far enough.

In its working paper, the Commission proposed to convert all existing fees tail into fees simple, but this is another proposal which has disappeared (without any explanation) from the final report. The Commission should have stuck by its original proposal. Indeed it should have gone further. Modified fees should also be banned, and any existing ones converted into absolute fees simple. (Many modified fees where the 'modification' relates to marriage or religion must surely infringe the European Convention on Human Rights.)

■ SUMMARY

At common law there were three types of freehold estate in land.

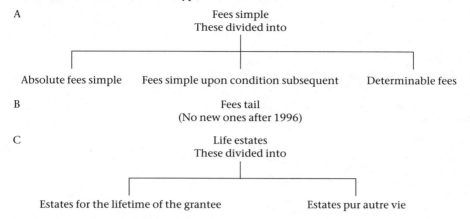

A   Fees simple
These divided into

Absolute fees simple   Fees simple upon condition subsequent   Determinable fees

B   Fees tail
(No new ones after 1996)

C   Life estates
These divided into

Estates for the lifetime of the grantee   Estates pur autre vie

Any estate in land can exist
(i)   in possession
(ii) in remainder
(iii) in reversion.

 CHAPTER 4: ASSESSMENT EXERCISE

'As every law student knows, land law is cluttered up with strange devices such as fees tail, determinable fees, and fees upon condition subsequent. In 1989, the Law Commission merely proposed that no new entails should be created. This proposal, now enacted as part of the Trusts of Land and Appointment of Trustees Act 1996, does not go far enough.'

Critically examine this statement.

See Appendix for a specimen answer.

■ FURTHER READING

Regarding entails and modified fees, see Law Commission Report no. 181, Transfer of Land—Trusts of Land, sections 16.1 and 17.1. Compare these views with my views expressed above.

For an exhaustive account of the common law regarding estates in land, see *Megarry and Wade: Law of Real Property*, sixth edition by Charles Harpum, chapter three, pages 37–86.

5 Legal and equitable rights in land

5.1 Objectives

By the end of this chapter you should:

1 Appreciate that property rights in land fall into two classes, 'legal' and 'equitable'

2 Have firmly grasped that there are more **types** of equitable property right in land than there are **types** of legal property right

3 Be able to explain how **legal** property rights are created

4 Be able to explain the many various ways in which **equitable** property rights are created

5 Be familiar with the concept of an 'estate contract', and the consequences which flow from the existence of an estate contract

5.2 Introduction

The rules of modern English land law are derived from three sources, common law, equity, and (increasingly in the twentieth and twenty-first centuries) statute. All three sources are represented in this (lengthy) chapter, which is mainly concerned with how property rights in land are created. You will see that the common law contributed a (relatively) straightforward set of rules, while the contribution of equity is altogether much more complex. You will also see that a modern statute, the Law of Property (Miscellaneous Provisions) Act 1989, has also contributed to this area of law.

5.3 Legal and equitable property rights

5.3.1 Legal property rights

As you saw from reading **Chapter 1**, there is a wide range of property rights which can exist with respect to land. Most (but not all) of these property rights were recognized by the common law. Property rights recognized by the common law were (and still are) classified as either **legal estates** (e.g., fees simple or leases) or **legal interests** (e.g., easements, profits, or rentcharges).

Prior to 1875, if somebody had a legal property right, he could protect that right by proceedings in either the common law courts or in the Court of Chancery. Suppose in 1840, Harold, owner in fee simple of Westacre, executed a deed granting Ian, owner in fee simple of neighbouring Eastacre, a right of way across Westacre to get to Eastacre. Ian has a **legal easement** over Westacre.

Suppose that in 1845 Kevin buys Westacre, and then blocks the right of way. Ian's **legal** property right binds everyone, not just Harold. Ian can sue Kevin in a common law court for the remedy of **damages**. He can also sue Kevin in the Court of Chancery for the equitable remedy of an **injunction** prohibiting the obstruction of the right of way.

5.3.2 Equitable property rights

From a very early stage in the history of the Court of Chancery, it became clear that it was possible to create property rights which **were not** recognized by the common law courts, but which **were** recognized and enforced by the Court of Chancery. These rights became known as **equitable interests**.

In **Chapter 2** we have already (briefly) considered the most important type of equitable interest, namely the right of a beneficiary under a trust. We have also seen that if the beneficiaries of a trust tried to enforce their rights in a common law court they were sent away disappointed (see 2.3.1). If, however, they went to the Court of Chancery, their (**equitable**) property rights were enforced.

Another very important type of equitable interest in land, never recognized by the common law, is the restrictive covenant. (We mentioned restrictive covenants at 1.4.2.) Suppose in the Westacre/Eastacre example just considered, Harold, in the deed granting the easement, had also promised not to build upon Westacre. When Kevin bought Westacre in 1845 he knew of this 'covenant'. He nevertheless started to build on Westacre.

? QUESTION 5.1

If Ian sued Kevin in a common law court, what would be the result of the case?

His action would fail. The common law regarded the 'no buildings' promise as binding only on the original covenantor (Harold in the example). But if Ian sued Kevin in the Court of Chancery, he would win and obtain an injunction. The Court of Chancery regarded a restrictive covenant as an equitable property right over the servient land which, subject to certain limitations, was binding on subsequent purchasers of the land.

5.3.3 Legal and equitable property rights after 1875

As you should already know from your studies of the development of the English legal system, common law and equity, have, ever since 1875, been administered by a unified court system.

However, the 1875 court reform legislation did not abolish the distinction between legal property rights and equitable property rights. (Nor did the 1925 property reform legislation.) As we shall see (especially in **Chapter 6**), important consequences flow from whether property rights are 'legal' or 'equitable'.

5.4 Creation and transfer of legal property rights

The common law has always been keen on formalities. It was long ago laid down that to transfer an existing legal property right, or to create a new one, a **deed** was required. This rule has now been embodied in s. 52(1) of the Law of Property Act 1925 which states:

All conveyances of land or of any interest therein are void for the purpose of conveying or creating a legal estate unless made by deed.

(There are certain exceptions to this rule that a deed is required to create or transfer a legal estate or interest, but these exceptions can for present purposes be ignored.)

5.4.1 Formalities for a deed: the traditional rule

(Unfortunately, we must make a slight digression and discuss this issue.) **The traditional rule** is applicable to all deeds executed up to 30 July 1990. The traditional rule was that for a document to be a deed it must be signed, sealed, and delivered. A document is (normally) 'delivered' when it is handed over with the intention that it should take legal effect.

As for sealing, special sealing wax used to be used, but in modern times almost everybody executing a deed 'sealed' it by attaching a small piece of adhesive red paper. Under the traditional rule there was no legal requirement for the signature(s) on the deed to be witnessed, though usually they were.

5.4.2 Formalities for a deed: the modern rule

The **modern rule** is applicable to all deeds executed on or after 31 July 1990. It is set out in section 1 of the Law of Property (Miscellaneous Provisions) Act. Subsections 2 and 3 provide:

(2) an instrument shall not be a deed unless—
    (a) it makes clear on its face that it is intended to be a deed by the person making it or, as the case may be, by the parties to it . . . and
    (b) it is validly executed as a deed by that person or, as the case may be, one or more of those parties,
(3) An instrument is validly executed as a deed by an individual if, and only if,—
    (a) it is signed—
        (i) by him in the presence of a witness who attests the signature; . . .
    (b) it is delivered as a deed by him or a person authorised to do so on his behalf.

The effect of section 1 is that as from 31 July 1990 to be a deed a document need not be sealed. The document must, however:

(a) be 'clear on its face that it is intended to be a deed'; and

(b) be validly executed.

For a deed to be 'validly executed' by a person it must;

(i) be signed;

(ii) (a new requirement) that signature must be witnessed by **one** witness;

(iii) the deed must be 'delivered'.

> **?** **QUESTION** 5.2
>
> What ought to happen to the hallowed English phrase, 'signed, sealed and delivered'?

I hope you agree with me that amongst lawyers, it **ought** to have fallen into disuse. We **ought** now to use some sort of phrase such as 'signed as a deed, witnessed, and delivered'. But of course old habits die hard! Moreover, I expect we will still be using the phrase 'signed, sealed and delivered' when, as is very likely within the next few years, legislation takes effect allowing deeds to be executed in electronic form, without there being any 'hard copy'.

5.5 Creation of equitable interests in land

While, as we have just seen, legal estates and legal interests can normally be created only if a deed is used, equitable interests in land can be created in a wide variety of different ways:

(a) by express trust;

(b) by a contract to convey or create a legal estate or interest;

(c) by the granting of an estate or interest which is void at common law for want of the correct formalities;

(d) by a grant of an estate or interest by a person who owns only an equitable interest;

(e) by a grant of an interest which can exist only in equity;

(f) by constructive trust or proprietary estoppel.

Before we look at these headings in more detail, there is one other potentially confusing point which we must consider carefully.

5.5.1 'Equity follows the law' as to types of property right

Although you have probably been studying the law only for a brief period, you should have already realized that the system of rules known as equity was developed by the Lord Chancellors to correct some of the harsh injustices of the common law. We have already considered the concept of the trust (see **Chapter** 2). The rigid and inflexible common law refused to accept the trust as imposing legal duties on the trustees; but equity ruled otherwise and enforced trusts.

The maxim 'equity follows the law' simply means that equity **copied the various types of property right** recognized by the common law. Put another way, one can say that for every kind of legal estate or legal interest in land recognized by the common law there is an equivalent equitable interest capable of existing.

Thus, as legal fees simple can exist, so can equitable fees simple. As you can have legal leases, so also you can have equitable leases (a particularly important example, as we shall see). There are legal mortgages, and so there are also equitable mortgages. There can be legal easements and legal profits, so therefore there can be equitable easements and equitable profits. And so on . . .

On the basis of what I have just said, you might conclude that the list of types of equitable property rights in land would be identical to the list of the types of legal property rights in land. This of course would be wrong, as there are (as I have already hinted) certain types of equitable interests which have no legal equivalents. These include (as well as interests arising under an express trust):

(a) restrictive covenants;

(b) licences by estoppel (proprietary estoppel);

(c) constructive trusts;

(d) estate contracts.

It is because of the existence of restrictive covenants, constructive trusts, etc. that the list of types of equitable interest is longer than the list of types of legal estate and interest.

5.5.2 Creation of equitable interests in land by express trust

Though express trusts of land are of enormous importance, there is only one point we need to note at this stage—s. 53(1)(b) of the Law of Property Act 1925. This provides:

A declaration of trust respecting any land or any interest therein must be manifested and proved by some writing signed by some person who is able to declare such trust or by his will.

So you cannot create an express trust of land simply by word of mouth. It can only be done by an **inter vivos** written document (which strictly speaking does not have to be a deed, though it is normal to use a deed) or by a will. (Remember that a will takes effect only on the death of the testator.)

5.5.3 Creation of equitable interests by a contract to convey or create a legal estate or interest

Before we can discuss this heading it is necessary for us to engage in a very lengthy digression.

5.5.3.1 Contracts for the sale of estates or interests in land

As we saw in **Chapter 2**, if land is being bought or sold it is normal for the transaction to take place in two stages. There is first the 'contract stage', followed (normally a few weeks later) by the 'completion stage'. A deed is executed only at the completion stage, **so it is only at completion that the legal estate passes to the purchaser.**

This two-stage process is not obligatory, but it is normal when purchasing a fee simple. It is also usual to have the two stages when a lessee is taking a new long-term lease, or where an existing long lease is being sold. It is also possible (though unusual) to have the two stages where other property rights such as easements, profits, or rentcharges are being created.

5.5.3.2 Formalities for contracts to sell estates or interests in land

As you have probably already learnt from your studies of the law of contract, in English law, **as a general rule**, no special formalities are required for a valid contract. Contracts to sell property rights in land are **the big exception** to this general rule.

Just to complicate matters, the law on formalities for land contracts has been changed relatively recently. Contracts entered into before 27 September 1989 are governed by s. 40 of the Law of Property Act 1925 (a statutory provision which was first enacted in 1677). Contracts entered into on or after 27 September 1989 are governed by s. 2 of the Law of Property (Miscellaneous Provisions) Act 1989.

Law of Property Act 1925, s. 40 provided as follows:

(1) No action may be brought upon any contract for the sale or other disposition of land or any interest in land, unless the agreement upon which such action is brought, or some memorandum or note thereof, is in writing, and signed by the party to be charged or by some other person thereunder by him lawfully authorised.

(2) This section . . . does not affect the law relating to part performance . . .

The practical effect of s. 40 was that if a contract relating to land was to be enforceable and so create rights, one of the following three conditions had to be satisfied:

(a) The contract was in writing, signed by the person (usually the vendor) promising rights over his land, or by his agent.

(b) The contract was purely oral, but subsequently a document came into existence evidencing the contract. This 'note or memorandum' had to be signed by the person promising rights over his land, or by his agent.

(c) The contract was purely oral, but the person claiming rights under the contract (e.g., the purchaser or prospective tenant) did some act of 'part performance'. 'Part performance' meant some conduct which indicated the existence of a contract between the parties. For example, (in particular) if the contract envisaged transfer of possession of the land to (say) a tenant or even a purchaser, that tenant/purchaser taking possession of the land was considered an act of part performance: see *Steadman* v *Steadman* [1974] 2 All ER 977.

It should be stressed that a contract which did not comply with s. 40 was not void, but merely **unenforceable**. If, with respect to such a contract, conditions (b) or (c) above were **subsequently** fulfilled, the contract **became enforceable**. (There is a sharp contrast with s. 2 of the 1989 Act, which we will be discussing shortly.)

? QUESTION 5.3

Suppose (pre-1989) Victor entered into a purely oral contract to sell Brownacre to Percy. At that stage the contract was unenforceable and Percy had no rights. But what if Victor subsequently signed a document recording the terms of the contract?

Surprising as it may seem, the contract became enforceable and Percy acquired rights. (See rule (b) above.)

? **QUESTION** 5.4

Suppose, in the example we are currently considering, Victor never signed anything, but after the oral agreement allowed Percy to take possession of Brownacre. What then?

I hope you realized that the taking of possession was 'part performance' by Percy, and the contract became enforceable by virtue of that fact. (See rule (c) above.)

Law of Property (Miscellaneous Provisions) Act, s. 2

Section 2 of the 1989 Act came into force on 27 September 1989, over 10 months before the coming into effect of s. 1, which we have already discussed at 5.4.2. Section 2 repealed s. 40 of the Law of Property Act 1925, and also abolished the rules about part performance. All contracts for the sale of estates and interests in land must now be **in writing and signed by the parties**. The first three subsections of section 2 are crucial:

(1) A contract for the sale or other disposition of an interest in land can only be made in writing and only by incorporating all the terms which the parties have expressly agreed in one document or, where contracts are exchanged, in each.

(2) The terms may be incorporated in a document either by being set out in it or by reference to some other document.

(3) The document incorporating the terms or, where contracts are exchanged, one of the documents incorporating them (but not necessarily the same one) must be signed by or on behalf of each party to the contract.

Although few lawyers were sad at the repeal of the old s. 40, the new provision is a strict one which must be complied with carefully. The crucial point about the new provision is that the contract **itself** must be in writing and signed by the parties. Any contract which is oral, or in writing but not signed by **all** the parties is **void**, and there are no obligations on the parties. Moreover, subsequent events such as the creation of a document recording the 'contract' or acts of 'part performance' cannot validate the void contract. Lawyers brought up in the 'old school' find this hard medicine to swallow!

? **QUESTION** 5.5

If the events set out in **Question 5.3** and **Question 5.4** were to occur today, would Percy be able to claim any rights under the agreement?

The answer is no. The purely oral contract between Victor and Percy is totally void, and nothing which happens subsequently can give Percy rights **under the void agreement**. If however Percy nevertheless took possession of the property **and spent a lot of money and/or effort improving the property**, that **expenditure** would create a constructive trust interest in his favour. See *Yaxley* v *Gotts* [2000] Ch 162.

5.5.3.3 Exchange of contracts

Section 2 leaves one hallowed land law tradition untouched. You will notice that both s. 2(1) and (3) refer to 'where contracts are exchanged'. It has always been possible for parties to contract to sell property rights in land by them both signing a single document setting out the agreed terms of the sale. However, solicitors have, on the sale of a fee simple, traditionally preferred to use an alternative method. Two identical documents are prepared, each setting out **all** the expressly agreed terms of the contract. The vendor signs one copy; the purchaser signs the other. Agreement is signified by 'exchanging contracts', i.e., there is a swap. The purchaser gets the copy signed by the vendor and vice versa. Contracts in this form are valid under the new law, and solicitors have (since 1989) generally stuck to the traditional practice of 'exchanging contracts'.

We can now at last return to the discussion of how equitable interests are created.

5.5.3.4 Estate contracts

Once a contract for the sale of a fee simple has been made, equity regards the purchaser as owning an equitable interest known as an estate contract. This equitable interest is normally of only short duration, as it comes to an end 'on completion', i.e., when the legal estate is conveyed to the purchaser. Despite the short duration of estate contracts, the whole concept is important and we need to examine it in a little more depth.

I should first mention the reasoning which gave rise to the concept of an 'estate contract'. The Lord Chancellors developed the broad maxim, 'Equity looks on that as done which ought to be done'. Applying this maxim to contracts to sell land, the Chancellors reasoned that the purchaser should be regarded as having a right to the land once the contract had been signed **without having to wait for the conveyance of the legal estate**. Moreover, the Chancellors backed up this argument with a weapon. **Contracts for the sale of land, or rights in land, are always in principle enforceable by the decree of specific performance**.

'Specific performance' is a remedy which prior to 1875 was available only in the Court of Chancery, and is therefore even today referred to as an 'equitable remedy'. As its name perhaps implies, it is an order of the court that the contract actually be carried out.

For most types of contract, the remedy of specific performance is **not** available. Suppose I have contracted to purchase a ton of potatoes from Farmer Giles, and he fails to deliver. I can always get potatoes elsewhere, so for this breach of the contract the court would not grant specific performance. I would have to be content with the usual remedy for breach of contract, namely **damages**.

Suppose, by contrast, I contracted to buy a field, Highacre, from Giles. Now each piece of land is unique, a fact which equity recognized. If Giles refuses to convey Highacre to me, I cannot buy Highacre from anyone else. I may well be able to buy a field of similar dimensions and value, but that replacement field will inevitably be in a different location. I may well not want that location. I will therefore seek a decree of specific performance compelling Giles to convey Highacre to me. In principle the court (pre-1875 it would have been the Court of Chancery) will grant me that decree.

The consequences of an estate contract

It is often said that in the period between contract and completion the vendor is a 'trustee' for the purchaser. This is rather misleading. If the vendor were a 'trustee' in the usual sense of that word, the **purchaser** would become immediately entitled to enjoy all the benefits of the land. Yet between contract and completion the **vendor** retains the right to enjoy all benefits from the land. Thus he can occupy the land until completion.

> **? QUESTION** 5.6
>
> What if the land which has been contracted to be sold is currently leased to a tenant. Who is entitled to the rent?

It is the vendor who is entitled to the rent up to the date the legal estate is conveyed to the purchaser, 'the date of completion'.

There are, however, two important consequences which **do** flow from creation of an estate contract:

(a) The vendor must take good care of the property and consult the purchaser before taking any managerial decisions regarding the property.

Between contract and completion the vendor cannot (unless the purchaser agrees) demolish, alter, or reconstruct the property. Other important decisions about the property can be taken only with the agreement of the purchaser.

In *Abdullah* v *Shah* [1959] AC 124 the vendor owned a row of three shops. At the time the contract of sale for the shops was signed all three of them were leased to tenants. Between contract and completion one of the tenants (unexpectedly) terminated his tenancy. The vendor, **without asking the purchaser**, immediately relet the shop. The purchaser would have preferred the shop to have been left empty.

The Judicial Committee held that the vendor should have consulted the purchaser about the proposed reletting. In consequence the purchaser (who was willing to go through with the deal) was, as compensation, entitled to a reduction in the agreed price.

(b) The risk of anything untoward happening to the property passes to the purchaser when the contract is signed.

In this context, the 'estate contract' concept **usually** works to the purchaser's disadvantage. There are two kinds of 'disaster' which can befall a property between contract and completion. The first is actions taken by a public authority.

In *Hillingdon Estates Co.* v *Stonefield Estate Ltd* [1952] 1 All ER 853 the local authority, after the contract was signed, slapped a compulsory purchase order on the property. The court held that the vendor was entitled to insist on completing the sale, even though the purchaser would then have to convey the land to the local authority. (The purchaser would of course get the compensation payable on compulsory purchase.)

In *Amalgamated Investment & Property Co. Ltd* v *John Walker & Sons Ltd* [1976] 3 All ER 509 the plaintiffs contracted to buy an old building which they planned to demolish and replace with modern offices. The local authority then 'listed' the building as one of special historical interest, thus effectively preventing the redevelopment. The court held that the plaintiffs must nevertheless complete the purchase.

Unexpected action by a public authority can improve the value of a property.

> **? QUESTION** 5.7
>
> Suppose last week I contracted to purchase a petrol station. Today the local authority announces new traffic plans which will take more traffic past my petrol pumps! Can I insist that the vendor completes the deal?

The answer is of course yes, and at the original price, even though the land is more valuable than it was a week ago.

Destruction of the property

The second kind of 'disaster' which might occur is destruction of the property. The traditional position has been that, unless the parties agree otherwise, the purchaser of land must bear the risk of destruction once a contract of sale has been made. Suppose last week I contracted to buy a house. Yesterday the house was destroyed by fire (or hurricane or earthquake). I must still complete the deal at the agreed price even though I am now getting a bare site with perhaps some useless ruins on it!

The moral of this little tale is that a purchaser of a building (unless he intends to demolish) should insure the building immediately he agrees the contract to purchase. One fairly recent change should however be noticed. In March 1990, the Law Society published new 'Standard Conditions of Sale'. It is intended that these Standard Conditions will be used by solicitors when drafting contracts to sell land, though **their use is not obligatory**. Clause 5 reads:

5.1.1 The seller will transfer the property in the same physical state as it was at the date of the contract (except for fair wear and tear) which means that the seller retains the risk until completion.

5.1.2 If at any time before completion the physical state of the property makes it unusable for its purpose at the date of the contract: (a) The buyer may rescind the contract, . . .

(The rest of Clause 5 does not really help the present discussion.)

Thus **provided the contract is drafted using the new Standard Conditions**, the traditional rule that risk of physical destruction passes to the purchaser on the contract of sale being made no longer applies. In practice, most contracts for sale of residential properties follow the new Standard Conditions, but contracts for sale of commercial properties often do not use the Standard Conditions.

5.5.3.5 A contract to create rights in land itself creates an equitable interest in the land

The preceding discussion has focused on contracts to **transfer** an **existing** fee simple estate in land. We must now consider the situation where an owner of a fee simple estate contracts to create out of that estate some property right such as a lease, mortgage, easement, or profit.

In practice the problem is most likely to arise in the context of leases, because, as indicated earlier, where a long-term lease is to be created the transaction often proceeds in two stages.

The parties sign a contract for the lease, followed by a formal deed a few weeks later. The leading case of *Walsh* v *Lonsdale* (1882) 21 ChD 9 concerned a situation where the parties had made a **contract** for a seven-year lease of a mill in Oldham, the tenant had gone into possession and had (literally) started weaving, but the parties had forgotten to execute the formal deed needed for a valid legal lease.

The crucial issues were the legal consequences (if any) of the contract, and the clause in that contract regarding the payment of rent. This clause (in effect) provided that under the lease the rent should be £X per year payable in advance, i.e., at beginning of each year.

Despite the absence of a deed granting a legal lease, the landlord demanded the rent in advance. The tenant claimed that as there was no deed, and therefore no proper lease, any rent should be payable in arrear. The Court of Appeal decided in the landlord's favour.

The Court held that the contract created an **equitable lease** enforceable between the parties. Moreover, the terms of the contract formed the terms of the equitable lease, and therefore the landlord was entitled to have the rent paid in advance. In the circumstances of the case, it did not really matter that the parties had forgotten to execute the deed.

As a result of *Walsh* v *Lonsdale*, a contract for a lease creates an equitable lease. Similar reasoning can be applied to all other types of right in land. A contract for an easement will create an equitable easement. A contract for a profit will create an equitable profit.

? **QUESTION** 5.8

What will a contract for a mortgage create?

It will create an equitable mortgage. (But never lose sight of the fact that a contract relating to rights in land must now comply with s. 2 of the 1989 Act. I will return to this point at 5.5.4.1.)

5.5.4 An informal grant of rights in land is treated as a contract and so creates an equitable interest in land

One thing may have struck you about the preceding discussion. There is **in logic** a difference between saying 'I promise to grant you this land' and 'I grant you this land'; between 'I promise to give you a lease' and 'I grant you this lease now'. Nevertheless, equity, with decisions such as *Walsh* v *Lonsdale*, has blurred over this logical distinction. The following discussion contributes further to this blurring.

In *Parker* v *Taswell* (1858) 2 De G & J 559 the landlord and tenant signed a document which purported to **grant** a lease to the tenant. The document did not bear a seal, and therefore was not a deed. It therefore could not create a **legal** lease. (Remember that for legal property rights a deed is required.)

The Court of Chancery held that a purported **grant** of property rights in land which lacked the necessary formality (i.e., a deed) to create a legal estate should be deemed to be a **contract**, which could be enforced by a decree of specific performance. The court indeed awarded the plaintiff specific performance of the transaction deemed to be a contract.

Although this may not have been realized in 1858 (when *Parker* v *Taswell* was decided), the effect of that decision is that if a grantor purports to create property rights informally (i.e., other than by deed) the informal grant creates an equitable interest. Put simply:

[informal grant = deemed contract = equitable interest]

A fairly modern example of this reasoning is the House of Lords decision in *Mason* v *Clarke* [1955] AC 778 at 797 (Lord Morton's speech). SM Ltd granted a legal lease of a farm to Clarke. As is common in leases of agricultural holdings, the lease included a clause whereby the landlord retained the right to hunt and/or trap wild animals roaming over the leased land.

In 1950, the land in question (in common with much of the rest of England) was plagued by rabbits. In October 1950, SM Ltd granted to Mason (a specialist rabbit-catcher) the right for one year to catch all rabbits on the farm. This transaction was purely oral. Mason paid £100 for the right, and entered the land and set traps. Clarke interfered with the traps. The House of Lords gave judgment for Mason.

It was held that the oral grant of the right to catch rabbits should be deemed a contract; that entering the land and setting the traps should be considered to be part performance (see 5.5.3.2, remembering that this is a pre-1989 case); and that therefore Mason had an equitable profit to catch rabbits for one year.

5.5.4.1 Limits on the principle that a contract or informal grant creates an equitable interest

There are two limitations to the broad principle that a contract or informal grant of rights creates an equitable interest. The first limitation is the formalities required for a **contract** to transfer or create rights in land.

Position prior to 27 September 1989

For a contract or an informal grant (which, remember, is deemed to be a contract) to be enforceable and thus create an equitable interest, the contract/informal grant must be:

(a) in writing, or

(b) evidenced in writing, or

(c) oral, but with part performance.

In *Mason* v *Clarke* (above) the transaction was originally purely oral. If nothing more had happened, Mason would not have been able to claim an equitable interest. However, the crucial fact was Mason's entering the land and setting his traps. This constituted 'part performance' and therefore he could claim an equitable profit.

Position after 26 September 1989

Contracts to create or transfer interests in land are now governed by s. 2 of the Law of Property (Miscellaneous Provisions) Act 1989. It follows from this that for a contract or informal grant to create an equitable interest in land the contract or informal grant **must be in writing signed by both parties**. A contract or other transaction with land which is oral, or which is unsigned writing will be **void**. Moreover, subsequent events cannot validate the contract. This conclusion regarding s. 2 of the 1989 Act is confirmed by the Court of Appeal decision in *United Bank of Kuwait plc* v *Sahib* [1996] 3 All ER 215; discussed at 29.7.3.

QUESTION 5.9

What if the facts of *Mason* v *Clarke* were to recur today. Would Mason acquire an equitable profit?

No he would not. The purely oral grant would be void, and Mason's entering and setting his traps would be a trespass. Moreover such trivial activities could not give rise to a constructive trust interest.

EXERCISE 5.1

Change the facts of *Mason* v *Clarke* so that even today an equitable profit would be created.

The agreement between SM Ltd and Mason would have to be in writing, signed by both parties.

EXERCISE 5.2

It would appear that as a result of s. 2 of the Law of Property (Miscellaneous Provisions) Act 1989, fewer equitable interests arise by 'informal' grant. Consider why this is the case.

(See the conclusion to this chapter.)

The second limitation on the principle that contracts/informal grants create equitable interests is that **the right to treat a contract or an informal grant as creating an equitable interest depends on the availability of specific performance**. This second limitation is long standing, and fortunately unaffected by modern statute.

As we saw earlier in this chapter (at 5.5.3.3), all contracts (and transactions deemed to be contracts) for the transfer or creation of rights in land are in principle enforceable by the equitable remedy of specific performance. However, you may have already come across the maxim that 'All equitable remedies are discretionary', and also perhaps the quaintly worded maxim that 'He who comes to equity must come with clean hands'. It is not appropriate at this point to give you all the detailed ramifications of these two maxims. What matters now is their practical application in the context of the current discussion.

If somebody enters into a contract (or a transaction deemed to be a contract) to acquire rights in land, but he is then in **substantial** breach of his own obligations under that contract, he will be said to have 'unclean hands'. The court will consequently refuse to order specific performance of the contract. Moreover, because he is not entitled to the remedy of specific performance to compel completion of the transaction, the party with 'unclean hands' cannot claim that the contract or informal transaction has created an equitable interest in his favour.

The point is best illustrated by the case of *Coatsworth* v *Johnson* [1886–90] All ER Rep 547. Johnson entered into an agreement to lease a farm to Coatsworth for 21 years. The agreement contained a clause (even today to be found in agricultural leases) to farm 'in a good and husband-like manner', i.e., Coatsworth promised to farm efficiently and to take good care of the land.

Coatsworth took possession of the farm without a formal deed being executed. Within a few months of his taking possession he had allowed the condition of the land to deteriorate very badly. Johnson evicted Coatsworth from the farm.

Coatsworth sued for wrongful eviction, contending that the agreement created an equitable lease lasting 21 years. Now if Coatsworth had taken good care of the farm he would have undoubtedly won the case. However, his failure to take good care of the farm meant that (metaphorically) he had 'unclean hands'. If he had claimed specific performance of the agreement it would not have been granted because of his substantial breach of his side of the bargain. The Court of Appeal therefore held that as Coatsworth was not entitled to specific performance he could not contend that the agreement created an equitable lease. That in turn meant that Coatsworth had no right to be on the land, and so his action for wrongful eviction failed.

(It is worth noting that if Coatsworth had had a legal lease, he could not have been summarily booted off the land, however bad a farmer he had been!)

> **? QUESTION** 5.10
>
> In 1990, Lenny and Terry signed a written contract (not a deed) under which Lenny agreed to lease a corner shop to Terry for 20 years. Lenny is a fundamentalist Christian, and the contract therefore included a clause that Terry must not open on Sundays. For the last year, Terry has opened on a Sunday, and done a roaring trade. Can Lenny argue that, like the tenant in *Coatsworth* v *Johnson*, Terry has lost his right to claim that he has an equitable lease?

You will probably agree that the answer is not clear-cut. Terry will argue that in the light of the changes in the Sunday trading laws his breach of contract was **trivial**, and not such as to amount to 'unclean hands' depriving him of the right to specific performance, and therefore of his equitable lease. Lenny will argue that although Terry's conduct is no longer an offence, his activities still constitute, from Lenny's point of view, a **substantial** breach of contract.

5.5.5 Grant of an estate or interest by a person who owns only an equitable interest

Somebody who owns only an equitable interest in land has no rights recognized by the common law. Therefore, if he executes a deed purporting to create a right derived from his equitable interest, that right is itself only equitable. A brief example should suffice.

Suppose Leonora owns the fee simple in Yellowacre. Last year she and Teresa sign a document which is not a deed, under which Leonora leases Yellowacre to Teresa for 10 years. The lease will, under principles just discussed, be only an equitable lease. This year Teresa executes a **deed** under which she sub-leases Yellowacre for five years to Stephen. Although a deed has been used, this sub-lease will also only be equitable. At common law Teresa's lease does not exist, and of course it follows that she cannot create a legal right from something which does not exist!

5.5.6 **Grants of interests which can exist only in equity**

Restrictive covenants and express trusts are usually created by using a formal **deed**. Yet, as has already been mentioned, restrictive covenants and interests under trusts are recognized only by equity.

5.5.7 **Constructive trusts and proprietary estoppel**

These are (in terms of history) relatively new types of equitable interest. In **Chapter 1** we saw (in outline) how these interests arise. The thing particularly to note in the present context is that these interests normally arise as a result of the **conduct** of the parties, rather than as a result of some document (whether or not a deed). The recent case of *Yaxley* v *Gotts* [2000] Ch 162, underlines this point.

 CONCLUDING REMARKS

We have seen that to create **legal** property rights in land a formal deed is required. **Equitable** property rights in land can (by contrast) arise in a number of different ways, even by conduct of the parties.

In the past many equitable interests arose as a result of contract (5.5.3.3) or 'informal grant' (5.5.4). But the limiting effect of s. 2 of the 1989 Act must be carefully noted. A contract or 'informal' grant, to be valid and therefore create an equitable interest, must now (slightly paradoxically) have a degree of formality! While a deed is not required, the transaction must be in writing and signed by both parties.

■ SUMMARY

A   Legal Property Rights.
To create legal property rights, a deed is required.

1 Prior to 1990, a deed had to be signed, sealed, and delivered.

2 After 1990, a deed has to be clear on its face that is intended to be a deed; signed, **witnessed**, and delivered.

B   Equitable Property Rights
These can arise in a wide variety of ways:

1 By express trust.

2 By a contract to create a property right. Prior to 1989 this contract must comply with s. 40 of the Law of Property Act 1925. After 1989 it must comply with s. 2 of the Law of Property (Miscellaneous Provisions) Act 1989.

3 By an informal grant void at common law. But this 'informal' grant had prior to 1989 to comply with s. 40—after 1989 it must comply with. s. 2.

4 By grant of an estate or interest created out of an equitable interest.

5 By creation of an interest (such as a restrictive covenant) which can only exist in equity.

6 By conduct giving rise to a constructive trust or a proprietary estoppel.

 CHAPTER 5: ASSESSMENT EXERCISE

(a) Norma owns the legal fee simple estate (unregistered title) in 'Ramsey House'. Two months ago she entered into a written agreement (not in the form of a deed) to let Ramsey House to Matthew for five years. The agreement specifically stated that the house should be used for residential purposes only.

Matthew has just been made redundant, and is now considering using Ramsey House for a business repairing bicycles. He has heard rumours that Norma is about to sell the house.

Advise Matthew, who is concerned that, as his lease is not in the form of a deed, he might be evicted by Norma.

And

(b) Last week, by a written contract, Teresa agreed to sell 'Taylor Cottage' to Henry, the sale to be completed in six weeks' time.

Unfortunately yesterday, a bus crashed into Taylor Cottage causing considerable damage.

This morning Teresa demolished a small outhouse which stood at the bottom of the garden of Taylor Cottage.

Advise Henry, who wants either to rescind the contract or at least obtain a reduction in the previously agreed price.

See Appendix for a specimen answer.

■ FURTHER READING

For a detailed discussion of the formal requirements for a deed, see Sparkes, '*A New Land Law*' (second edition) chapter seven.

For an extended discussion of estate contracts and equitable leases under *Walsh* v *Lonsdale*, see Gray and Gray *Elements of Land Law* (fourth edition) chapter nine, pages 741–777.

For the reasoning behind the enactment of s. 2 of the Law of Property (Miscellaneous Provisions) Act 1989, see Law Commission Report no. 164 (1987) 'Transfer of Land—Formalities for Contracts for sale etc. of Land'.

For a discussion of the rule that the risk passes on signing a contract to sell land, see Law Commission Report no. 191, 'Transfer of risk on sale'.

PART II

Unregistered Land

6 Differences in validity between legal property rights and equitable property rights

6.1 Objectives

By the end of this chapter you should be able to:

1 Demonstrate why legal property rights are 'stronger' than equitable property rights

2 Appreciate that legal property rights are good against the whole world

3 Appreciate that, by contrast, equitable property rights are (traditionally) subject to the doctrine of notice

4 Explain the elements of the equitable doctrine of notice, especially constructive notice and imputed notice

5 Explain the maxim 'first in time, first in right', and the implications of that maxim for equitable property rights

6.2 Introduction

In order to explain this topic in a comprehensible way, I have to make (for the moment) two very big assumptions which are not in fact true: (i) that all land remains **unregistered** title; (ii) that this area of law was unaffected by the reforms made in 1925.

I must also make a broad assertion which, just for the moment, may not seem to make much sense. This assertion underlies much of what is said in this chapter. I assert that from the point of view of somebody who owns a property right, it is better that the right should be legal rather than equitable. This is because **legal property rights are good against the whole world; equitable property rights are subject to the doctrine of notice.**

6.3 Legal and equitable property rights: the tale of High Chimneys

Before going any further, you must familiarize yourself with the facts of a story designed to illustrate most of the points which we will encounter in this chapter. Imagine that last winter I purchased the fee simple in a large country house, High Chimneys, together with its quite extensive garden. I bought the house from Vanessa, a wealthy and elderly spinster. Before completing the purchase, I, my solicitor, and my surveyor made very careful enquiries regarding High Chimneys. There was a careful examination of the title deeds going back to a root of title in 1964, which was when Vanessa had bought the property. My surveyor and I made a very careful physical inspection of both the house and garden.

As a result of these careful enquiries I concluded that the land was not subject to any third party rights such as easements, profits, restrictive covenants, mortgages, etc. I therefore completed the purchase in March.

The last few months have been quite traumatic. First of all I had a visit from Norman, owner of neighbouring Low Stacks. He produced a deed dated 1910. By that deed the then owner of High Chimneys granted to the then owner of Low Stacks a right of way across the garden of High Chimneys. This right of way was expressly granted for the benefit of Low Stacks, and was to last in perpetuity. Norman explains that the right of way has not been used for five years (which is why my surveyor did not detect any sign of a worn path or track), but that now he intends to use it every day as a short cut to the nearest station.

Soon after Norman came Philip, owner of Smokey Farm, which adjoins the foot of my garden. He produced a deed dated 1920. By that deed the then owner of High Chimneys granted to the then owner of Smokey Farm a right to graze 15 sheep in the large garden. This right was expressly granted for the benefit of Smokey Farm, and was to last in perpetuity. Philip explains that he has not owned any sheep for about the last eight years, but now he has acquired some and intends to graze them in my garden. (I hope you have noted that Norman owns a **legal** easement, while Philip owns a **legal** profit.)

Lastly, George arrives. He explains that from 1964 to 2005 he was Vanessa's 'gentleman-friend', but they have now split up. He further explains that he contributed a substantial amount of money both to the original purchase of High Chimneys and to its subsequent renovation. He therefore has a constructive trust interest in the property. That interest is **equitable**. George claims that his equitable interest in the land binds me. He is very anxious to claim against me because Vanessa has taken the whole price I paid to her and emigrated to Bolivia.

Do the rights of Norman, Philip, and George bind me?

6.3.1 The legal property rights of Norman and Philip

Here the position is very simple, and I am afraid that I am the loser. I am going to have to put up with Norman tramping across my land and with Philip's sheep. Each of these two rights is a **legal** property interest.

It is a fundamental principle that **legal** property rights are 'good against the whole world'. That means that, once a legal property right has been created with respect to a piece of land, that right binds everybody else who later acquires that land or other rights in that land.

Put another way, legal rights are in principle indestructible. I must particularly stress that I am stuck with Norman's easement and Philip's profit even though, at the time I bought High Chimneys, neither I nor my advisers knew or could have known of these rights. (Remember that we had all made careful enquiries. Incidentally, as my solicitor and surveyor exercised all due care, there is no possibility of my suing them for professional negligence.)

? **QUESTION** 6.1

Suppose that John owned the legal fee simple in Blackfields. In September 2003, John granted a legal lease of Blackfields to Kenneth for 20 years, but Kenneth has not as yet taken any steps to occupy Blackfields. John has now sold the fee simple in Blackfields to Leonard, who knew nothing of Kenneth's lease. Is Leonard bound by the lease?

Now it may well strike you that as a matter of simple moral justice Leonard should not be bound by Kenneth's lease. Leonard probably had no way of knowing that there was a lease, and Kenneth could not even be bothered to take possession of Blackfields. Yet the law is that Kenneth's lease does bind Leonard. It is a legal property right, and (like Norman's easement and Philip's profit) will bind everybody who later acquires the relevant land or rights in that land. It is no good Leonard saying, 'Kenneth was not in possession, so how could I know that there was a lease'.

6.3.2 The equitable property right of George

Now here, for me, things are a lot more hopeful. Equitable rights are not totally indestructible. An equitable interest is good against the whole world **except** a bona fide purchaser for value of a legal estate or legal interest who took without notice of the equitable interest. Thus to be free of George's interest I must prove four things. I must prove that at the time I purchased High Chimneys:

(a) I acted 'bona fide', i.e., in good faith; and

(b) I was a purchaser for value; and

(c) I acquired a legal estate or legal interest; and

(d) I had no notice of George's equitable interest.

Before examining the four elements of the doctrine of notice listed above, I want us to recall a point made previously: 'From the point of view of somebody who owns a property right, it is better that the right should be legal rather than equitable'. Put slightly differently, legal property rights are stronger than equitable property rights.

? **QUESTION** 6.2

Consider the story of High Chimneys from the points of view of Norman and Philip on the one hand, and George on the other. Norman and Philip can sleep soundly in their beds, while George's position may not be so comfortable. Why is that?

The crucial point for Norman and Philip is that they have **legal** interests (as had Kenneth in **Question 6.1**). They can therefore relax. They can rest assured that whatever happens to High Chimneys, and whoever buys High Chimneys their rights will still continue. They will continue even against me, who knew nothing of their rights. Their rights are (in effect) indestructible.

George's position is not quite so comfortable. His right will bind somebody who is given or inherits the land. It will bind somebody who buys the land **with notice** of George's interest. But it has one weakness. It will not bind a bona fide purchaser for value of a legal estate or interest who took without notice of George's interest. If I am such a purchaser then George's rights will not bind me. His only claim will be against Vanessa for cash compensation. It will be his tough luck that she has just emigrated to Bolivia!

6.4 The elements of the doctrine of notice

All four elements set out at 6.3.2 must be proved by a purchaser (me in the High Chimneys story) if he is to take a piece of property free from an equitable interest affecting that property.

6.4.1 Bona fide

When talking about the doctrine of notice, lawyers usually use the Latin phrase '**bona fide**'. This simply means '**good faith**'. A person acts in good faith if he acts honestly and without any fraudulent intent. In disputes which arise involving the doctrine of notice, it is usually easy for a purchaser to establish that he has acted in good faith. (As we shall see at 6.4.4, it may be much more difficult for him to prove that he is 'without notice'.)

6.4.2 Purchaser for value

If a person acquires a piece of land as a result of an inter vivos gift, or if he inherits it from somebody, he is clearly not a purchaser for value. He will always be bound by any equitable interests affecting the land.

? **QUESTION** 6.3

What would be the result if in my High Chimneys story Vanessa had given me the property; or if she had died and left me the property by her will?

I hope you realized that in both cases I would always be bound by George's equitable interest. It would be no use my protesting that I had no 'notice' of George's interest. If you think about it, that is only fair. It would be wrong that he should lose his rights to somebody who has not had to do or pay anything for the property.

6.4.2.1 The meaning of 'value'

Suppose, in my High Chimneys story, I had paid a price for High Chimneys, but Vanessa was so anxious to get a quick sale that she sold it to me at a bargain price which did not represent the real value of the land. Would I be a purchaser for value? The answer is '**Yes**'. Suppose I had paid only a nominal price of £1 for High Chimneys. Would I be a purchaser for value? The answer (you may be perhaps surprised to learn) is still 'Yes'!

In your studies of the law of contract you are probably already encountering the 'doctrine of consideration'.

> **EXERCISE** 6.1
>
> Refer to your contract textbook, and quickly re-read the chapter on what constitutes 'consideration'. It may help if you list the more important points.

In contract you learn that even the tiniest payment, or the most minimal 'detriment' may constitute consideration. As I hope you have guessed, anything which constitutes 'consideration' in the law of contract will be 'value' for the purposes of the law of property.

6.4.2.2 Marriage as 'value'

This may seem a rather obscure point, but it is of some significance to the historic development of property law. Until 1970, an engagement to marry was a legally enforceable contract. (You have probably heard of actions for breach of promise of marriage!) As a result of the Law Reform (Miscellaneous Provisions) Act 1970, engagements to marry are no longer legally enforceable. It follows that a promise to marry is no longer 'consideration'; nor is it 'value' for the purposes of the doctrine of notice.

Suppose Vanessa conveyed High Chimneys to me. In return, I did not pay a cash price, but I **promised** to marry her. She then disappeared to Bolivia before we could have a ceremony. I would not be a 'purchaser for value' of High Chimneys. Had the facts occurred before 1970 (say, in 1965), I would have been a purchaser for value.

> **QUESTION** 6.4
>
> Change the story in a slightly different way. Suppose Vanessa conveyed High Chimneys to me in March 2006 in return for my actually marrying her. Would I be a purchaser for value? (Put another way, is my actually marrying her consideration?)

The crucial point in answering this question is to realize that the actual act of marrying is a 'detriment' suffered by me. (I have given up the freedom of my single status.) It is 'consideration' and therefore it is 'value'; thus (on this version of the story) I am, even today, a purchaser for value!

6.4.3 Purchaser of a legal estate or legal interest

This may strike you as a rather technical and arbitrary aspect of the doctrine of notice. Under this rule, a purchaser of an equitable interest cannot claim the benefit of the doctrine of notice. If you buy only an equitable interest in Blackacre, any existing equitable interest(s) in Blackacre is/are automatically binding on you.

Suppose in my High Chimneys example I did not buy the legal fee simple; instead I **entered into a contract** with Vanessa under which she agreed to lease me the property for 99 years. I paid her an agreed 'premium' (capital lump sum) of £100,000, and took possession. Vanessa then ran off to Bolivia without executing a deed in my favour. On these facts I have 'purchased' only an equitable lease. I will therefore be bound by George's equitable interest, even if I can establish that I had no notice of that interest.

Suppose (by contrast) that Vanessa did execute a deed leasing the property to me before she disappeared westwards. Now on this version of the story **I am a purchaser of a legal estate**. I therefore will not be bound by George's interest if I can prove the other elements of the doctrine of notice. (Note that this last illustration confirms the proposition that legal property rights are 'better' than equitable property rights.)

Another way of looking at the same point is that if there are two or more equitable interests affecting the same piece of land the rule is '**first in time, first in right**'. The first equitable interest to be created has the first claim, the second equitable interest has the second claim, and so on. Suppose that in 2004, Xerxes, the owner of Greenacre, granted an equitable lease for 10 years of Greenacre to Yorick. In 2005, while Yorick was absent from Greenacre because of a lengthy hospitalization, Xerxes granted an equitable lease for 10 years of Greenacre to Zebedee.

Yorick has just come out of hospital, and we now have Yorick and Zebedee arguing as to who can occupy Greenacre. Yorick will win the argument. His equitable interest was created first, therefore he has first claim to the land. His right has **priority** over any later-created equitable interest(s).

Let us now add just one more twist to this Greenacre story. Suppose that in 2007 Yorick has no more use for Greenacre, so he assigns (i.e., transfers) his equitable lease to his friend Albert. Can Zebedee come along and say, 'I got my interest before Albert got his; I am first in time and should now be allowed to occupy Greenacre!'?

Zebedee's claim to occupy Greenacre will still fail. It is the order of **creation** of interests which matters, not the order of **acquisition**. Albert's interest was, of course, **created** before Zebedee's. It was **created** when, in 2004, it was granted to Yorick. It would be very strange if, when Yorick disposed of his equitable interest to Albert, that interest lost its priority.

? **QUESTION** 6.5

In 1989, Harry acquired West House. In 2001, his lady-friend, Letitia, acquired a constructive trust interest in West House. (She paid substantial sums to renovate the house.) Harry has now left, and has just granted an equitable lease of West House to Martha for 6 years. Does Letitia's right bind Martha?
  Would your answer be different if Martha's lease was a legal lease?

On the first version of the facts, we have two competing equitable interests with respect to the same piece of land. It follows that we must apply the 'first in time, first in right' rule. Letitia's right will have 'priority' and will bind Martha.

If, however, Martha's lease was a legal lease, she would be a purchaser of a legal estate. Thus, if she acted in good faith, gave value (e.g., agreed to pay rent), and was without notice of Letitia's right, Martha would not be bound by Letitia's interest.

6.4.4 **Without notice of the equitable interest**

In any dispute involving the equitable doctrine of notice, the most likely cause for arguments is the question of whether the purchaser has notice of the relevant equitable interests. In my High Chimneys story, the crucial question will be, 'Did I, Roger Sexton, at the time the fee simple estate in High Chimneys was conveyed to me, have notice of George's equitable interest?'

As purchaser I will have the task of proving that I was without **any form** of notice of George's interest. Notice comes in three forms:

(a) actual notice;

(b) constructive notice;

(c) imputed notice.

A purchaser has actual notice if, at the time of the purchase, he **actually knew** of the existence of the equitable interest.

A purchaser has constructive notice if, at the time of the purchase, he **ought to have known** of the existence of the equitable interest.

A purchaser has imputed notice if, at the time of the purchase, his agent (solicitor, surveyor, etc.) knew or ought to have known of the existence of the equitable interest.

(This threefold division of notice is confirmed by section 199(1) of the Law of Property Act 1925, which provides that a purchaser shall not have notice of an equitable interest unless:

(a) it is within his own knowledge, or would have come to his knowledge if such inquiries and inspections had been made as ought reasonably to have been made by him; or

(b) in the same transaction with respect to which a question of notice to the purchaser arises, it has come to the knowledge of his counsel, as such, or of his solicitor or other agent, as such, or would have come to the knowledge of his solicitor or other agent, as such, if such inquiries and inspections had been made as ought reasonably to have been made by the solicitor or other agent.[ )]

6.4.4.1 **Actual notice**

This is, of course, of considerable importance, but requires no further explanation.

6.4.4.2 **Constructive notice**

A purchaser has constructive notice of any equitable interest which **he would have discovered** had he made those enquiries which a reasonable purchaser would make.

As you already know, when somebody buys a piece of land he needs to make all sorts of careful enquiries with respect to that land. Some of these enquiries may relate to the physical condition of the land (e.g., is it liable to subsidence or flooding?), but many of these enquiries relate (at least in part) to property law matters.

When buying a piece of land the wise purchaser always checks:

(a) whether the vendor has a good title to the land;

(b) whether there are any third party rights (legal or equitable) such as easements, profits, or restrictive covenants affecting the land.

As you have probably already guessed the constructive notice rule in effect places a duty upon the purchaser to act wisely. The rule requires a purchaser to make those enquiries which a reasonable man, **with competent legal advice**, would make. (Rightly, in my view, the rule makes no concessions to 'do-it-yourself' conveyancers who buy land without taking legal advice.)

Legal interests, you will recall, always bind the purchaser, whether he discovers them or not. So a wise purchaser always looks very carefully for legal interests. Under the constructive notice rule he is expected to look just as carefully for equitable interests. In particular, there are two types of enquiry which every purchaser is expected to make:

(a) inspect the land; and

(b) investigate the vendor's title.

Inspect the land

When the wise purchaser inspects the land, some of the things he is on the look out for will relate to the physical condition of the land, e.g., is there evidence of subsidence? But the wise purchaser will also be on the alert for matters such as worn tracks or grazing sheep. Their presence might indicate the existence of easements or profits. He will also want to establish whether anybody other than the vendor is occupying the whole or part of the land. Such a person might have a lease (perhaps legal, perhaps equitable), or might claim a constructive trust interest in the land or possibly some other right in the land.

If anyone (other than the vendor) is in possession of the land or part of it, the 'rule' in *Hunt* v *Luck* applies. (The case is reported [1902] 1 Ch 428, but, contrary to what you might expect, a consideration of the details of the case is not a great deal of help.) Under this rule, the purchaser must look for person(s) in possession, and if he finds anybody he must ask that person what interest he claims in the land. If the purchaser fails to discover a person who is in possession, or fails to ask such a person whether he claims any interest in the land, he has not made adequate enquiries. The purchaser is deemed to have constructive notice of any equitable interest owned by that person.

Put another way, a purchaser has notice of any equitable interest owned by a person in possession (of whole or part of the land) unless enquiry is made of that person and he does not reveal his interest.

Suppose that in my High Chimneys example Harry was living in the house last winter (when I bought it). Harry is another 'gentleman-friend' of Vanessa. He too made substantial contributions to the purchase and renovation of the property. He too therefore has an interest in High Chimneys under a constructive trust.

Suppose, further, that on my visit to High Chimneys I somehow failed to realize that Harry was there. Or perhaps I saw him, but I assumed that he was some kind of servant so I asked no questions. Either way, I have not made proper enquiries. I will have constructive notice of Harry's equitable interest.

Let us now suppose that I did see Harry, and I went up to him and said, 'Excuse me sir, do you claim any kind of right or lease over this house?'. If he tells me that he has made substantial contributions to the house, or words to that effect, I have actual notice of his interest. But if he replies, 'Mind your own business!', or something similar but perhaps even less polite, I have sufficiently pursued this line of enquiry. I will not have notice of Harry's interest.

> **? QUESTION** 6.6
>
> In 1990, Norma bought East House. In 2004, Oswald started to cohabit with her in East House. He acquired a constructive trust interest in East House by paying off the bulk of the mortgage on the house.
>
> The relationship has now broken up, and Oswald is living alone in East House. This morning a couple of surveyors called wanting to inspect the house. Oswald told them to '* * * * off!' The surveyors left saying, 'We will be back tomorrow'.
>
> Advise Oswald.

I hope you may have concluded that Oswald is a very lucky man, as he will get a second chance to tell the surveyors about his constructive trust interest. The surveyors are probably acting on behalf of a potential purchaser or mortgagee. Oswald should tell them of his interest, so that the purchaser/mortgagee will have notice of his interest. If, on the other hand, Oswald continues to be rude, then the purchaser/mortgagee will be able to say that he had made adequate enquiries and that he had no notice of Oswald's interest.

Investigate the title

As was explained in **Chapter 2**, a purchaser should always investigate the vendor's title. The deeds and other documents relating to the land must be inspected going back to the **root of title**, which is normally the most recent conveyance which is at least 15 years old, i.e., the purchaser should inspect the root of title and all **later** documents. There is no duty to inspect documents which are dated before the root of title. (These documents are said to be 'behind' the root of title.)

If a purchaser fails to inspect a document which he should have inspected, then he has constructive notice of the contents of that document. In particular, he has constructive notice of all equitable interests **created or revealed** by that document.

The primary purpose of a conveyance is to transfer legal ownership from the vendor to the purchaser. But conveyances often do more than that. A conveyance will often also **create** third party rights such as easements, profits, and restrictive covenants. For example, let us suppose that Edwina owned two adjoining fields, Green Field and Yellow Field. She recently sold Green Field to Frank. As well as transferring ownership, the conveyance:

(a) grants Frank a right of way (easement) over Yellow Field to get to Green Field;

(b) contains a restrictive covenant entered into by Frank that he will use Green Field for agricultural purposes only.

Conveyances **creating** third party rights are commonplace. You may be more puzzled by the reference to conveyances **revealing** third party rights. The point is really a simple one: Where land is sold, that land may already be subject to third party rights such as easements or restrictive covenants. These may have been created some time ago, perhaps a hundred years or more. If land is sold subject to existing third party rights it is normal practice, though not absolutely obligatory, for the conveyance to mention ('recite') those existing rights.

Example of constructive notice through failure to investigate

The recent history of Purple House is as follows:

• In 1956 Norma sold Purple House to Malcolm.

- In 1973 Malcolm sold Purple House to Leonard.
- In 1989 Leonard sold Purple House to Keith.
- In 2001 Isobel purchased Purple House from Keith.

When Isobel bought the land in 2001, the correct root of title should have been the 1973 conveyance from Malcolm to Leonard. (It was the most recent document which was **at least** 15 years old.) Isobel should therefore have inspected both the 1973 and the 1989 conveyances. She (foolishly) inspected only the 1989 conveyance.

The 1973 conveyance, which Isobel did not inspect, revealed a restrictive covenant (not mentioned in the 1989 conveyance) in favour of a neighbouring property. That covenant, entered into as long ago as 1910, limited Purple House to residential purposes only.

Isobel, who intended to convert Purple House into offices, is bound by the restrictive covenant. She should have inspected the 1973 conveyance, and that would have revealed the 1910 covenant. She has constructive notice of that equitable interest.

Suppose, however, that the 1910 restrictive covenant was mentioned in the 1956 conveyance from Norma to Malcolm, but not in any later conveyances. Under the rule about 'root of title' Isobel did not have to investigate the 1956 conveyance. Therefore (whether or not she looked at the 1973 conveyance) she would not have had constructive notice of the covenant.

> **? QUESTION** 6.7
>
> In 1922, Peter sold North House to Quentin. The 1922 conveyance contained a restrictive covenant under which Quentin promised to use the house for residential purposes only.
> In 1989, Quentin sold North House to Richard.
> Stephen bought North House from Richard in 2002. Did he have notice of the restrictive covenant?
> Would your answer be different if the conveyance from Quentin to Richard took place in 1980?

On the basis that the sale from Quentin to Richard took place in 1989, there can be no doubt that Stephen would have notice of the restrictive covenant. The root of title, the most recent conveyance **at least 15 years old**, is that executed in 1922. If Stephen looked at the 1922 conveyance he would have actual notice. If he did not bother to look at the 1922 conveyance, he would have constructive notice.

If the conveyance from Quentin to Richard took place in 1980, then that conveyance would be the root of title. If that (1980) conveyance **recited** the (1922) restrictive covenant, then Stephen would still have notice of the restrictive covenant. But if the 1980 conveyance did not mention the restrictive covenant, then there would not be notice. The only mention of the covenant would be in a document 'behind the root of title', which Stephen had no duty to investigate.

6.4.4.3 Imputed notice

(See also s. 199(1)(b) of Law of Property Act 1925, already quoted at 6.4.4 above)

In most purchases of land, agents such as solicitors and/or surveyors are employed. The purchaser does not personally make the necessary enquiries. In view of this fact, a rule of 'imputed notice' is essential if the doctrine of notice is to operate fairly. If an agent, while acting for a particular purchaser with respect to a particular transaction, receives actual or constructive notice of an equitable interest, that notice is ascribed to the purchaser himself. This rule applies to all forms of agent, and is not just confined to solicitors and surveyors.

Suppose that in my example at 6.4.4.2, of Isobel purchasing Purple House, Isobel had employed a solicitor, Bloggs, to investigate the title to the house. Bloggs did look at the 1973 conveyance, noticed the 1910 restrictive covenant, but omitted to tell Isobel. Isobel will have imputed actual notice of the covenant.

What if Bloggs looked only at the 1989 conveyance, and failed to look at the 1973 conveyance? In that case Isobel would have imputed constructive notice of the restrictive covenant.

In either of these two situations Isobel would be justifiably annoyed with Bloggs! She would be bound by the restrictive covenant. But she would have one consolation. She could sue Bloggs for damages for professional negligence.

For a further example let us go back to one version of my High Chimneys story. In one version of the story (see 6.4.4.2, page 70) Harry, a gentleman-friend of Vanessa with a constructive trust interest in the property, is living in the property at the time of my purchase.

Let us now suppose that I did not visit High Chimneys prior to the purchase but left inspection of the property to my surveyor, Muggins. When Muggins visited the property, Harry was out. Vanessa made no mention of Harry, but there were male clothes lying around in some of the rooms. Muggins never reported this fact to me, nor did he take up with Vanessa the presence of the male clothing. It appears that I would have imputed constructive notice of Harry's interest.

This last example is rather loosely based on *Kingsnorth Finance Ltd* v *Tizard* [1986] 1 WLR 783, a case which repays close study.

Mr Tizard ('H') owned the legal title to the matrimonial home 'Willowdown', but Mrs Tizard ('W') had contributed substantially to the cost of acquisition and therefore had a constructive trust interest. The marriage broke down and W then spent most of her time with her sister nearby. However, W returned to Willowdown daily to help care for the couple's teenage children who still lived there. If H was away, W spent the night at Willowdown. W still kept personal clothes and belongings at Willowdown, shut up in a wardrobe.

H decided to remortgage Willowdown to Kingsnorth Finance. Kingsnorth (acting through local mortgage brokers) instructed a surveyor, M, to inspect the property. Because of his unusual family situation, H arranged for M to visit on a Sunday afternoon. H also cunningly arranged for W to take the children out for the day.

When M called, his suspicions were aroused when he spotted various items belonging to the children. H had described himself as single on the application form for the mortgage loan, but now admitted to M that he was 'separated'. M made no further inquiries, and M's report to Kingsnorth did not mention his suspicions that there might be a wife/mother with some kind of claim on the house.

Kingsnorth lent H a large sum of money on the security of a mortgage of Willowdown; H later defaulted on the payments. Kingsnorth tried to enforce the mortgage, but the deputy High Court judge (Judge Finlay) held that W's constructive trust interest had priority over the mortgage.

When confronted by the suspicious circumstances on the Sunday afternoon, M, as a reasonable man, should have carried out further enquiries independent of H. In particular, while it would have been wrong to have gone around opening up cupboards etc., M should have called around unannounced in the hope of catching the mystery woman. Kingsnorth therefore had imputed constructive notice of W's constructive trust interest.

(I do not know whether Kingsnorth sued M for professional negligence, but (reverting to my example) I would certainly be suing Muggins!)

6.5 Position of successors in title to a purchaser without notice

If a purchaser of a legal estate to which an equitable interest was subject takes his estate free from the equitable interest because of the doctrine of notice, all persons who derive title from that purchaser take free from the equitable interest as well.

To explain this point I must go back to the original version of my High Chimneys story (see 6.3, where George left in 2005). In my dispute with George I shall contend that I am a bona fide purchaser for value of a legal estate without notice of George's interest. George does not accept this, and sues me in a court case which is splashed all over the local papers. I win. I succeed in proving:

(a) I was acting bona fide;

(b) I was a purchaser for value;

(c) that I purchased a legal estate;

(d) that I was without notice of George's interest. (Remember that in the **original** version of my story both my agents and I made very careful enquiries which did not reveal even George's existence.)

Although I have won the case, I am sick of High Chimneys. I put it up for sale. Beatrice is the first prospective purchaser to visit the property. Luckily, she does not mind the sheep, nor does she mind Norman cutting across the garden. But suddenly she says, 'Is this not the house there was that big court case about? A fellow called George came along and claimed he had some sort of share in it. I read all about it in the *Maxwellshire Sun*'.

'Yes', I reply, 'but I won the case.'

'Congratulations', says Beatrice, 'but is there a risk that his claim will bind me? I seem to remember that you won because at the time you purchased you neither knew nor could have known of George's claim. **I do know** that George has a claim!'

? **QUESTION** 6.8

Why has Beatrice no need to worry?

Beatrice need not worry, for the reason given in the first paragraph of this section: once an equitable interest is void against a purchaser for value without notice, it is void against everybody else who **derives title** from that purchaser. This is so even if (like Beatrice) a successor in title has actual knowledge of the equitable interest.

This is both logical and fair. It would be illogical if an invalid equitable interest could in effect revive against a later purchaser. Such a revival would also be grossly unfair to somebody in my position. I (personally) would not be bound by George's claim. But nobody would want to buy from me for fear that George would claim against them.

One final point. I have referred to 'persons who derive title' from the purchaser without notice. 'Persons who derive title' is not just confined to later purchasers. It extends to anyone whose rights are derived directly or indirectly from the original purchaser without notice. So if Beatrice does buy, all her successors are also protected from George's claim. If I decide not to sell, but to lease, or perhaps even to give away the property, the lessee or donee is not bound by George's claim.

 CONCLUDING REMARKS

Before you became a law student, you probably already knew that buying land (a house or any other type of land) was time-consuming. You now know one of the major reasons for the delays. It is essential that if you are buying land you make very careful enquiries regarding easements, profits, constructive trust interests, etc. Moreover, if you fail to discover a **legal** property right (e.g., a legal easement) you are stuck with it. You are bound by the right even though the most careful of enquiries would not have revealed its existence.

But if you fail to discover (say) a constructive trust interest, you may yet escape. You will not be bound by the interest if you are what old-fashioned lawyers sometimes call 'equity's darling', i.e., a bona fide purchaser for value of a legal estate or interest without notice of the equitable interest.

■ SUMMARY

Will a purchaser of land which is unregistered title be bound by third party property rights which exist against that land?

Legal Property Rights If the third party property right is a **legal** property right, then 'it is good against the whole world'. This means it will bind the purchaser even if the purchaser neither knew of the right nor had any means of finding out about the right.

Equitable Property Rights If the third party property right is an **equitable** property right, then it will bind everybody else who acquires rights in the land except a bona fide purchaser for value of a legal estate or interest who had no notice of the equitable interest ('equity's darling').

Thus a purchaser escapes from an equitable interest provided neither he nor his agents knew or ought to have known of that interest.

As *Kingsnorth Finance* v *Tizard* demonstrates, it is crucial that purchasers (and people acting on their behalf) carry out all enquiries which a reasonable person would make.

■ FURTHER READING

For a detailed discussion of the equitable doctrine of notice, see *Megarry and Wade* (sixth edition by Harpum) chapter five, pages 136–150.

7 The impact of the 1925 legislation

7.1 Objectives

By the end of this chapter you should:

1 Appreciate fully that the 1925 legislation reduced quite drastically the number of types of **legal** property right

2 Be able to explain the concepts 'fee simple absolute in possession' and 'term of years absolute'

3 Be able to identify the various types of property interest in land which can still exist as **legal** interests

4 Appreciate that all 'estates' and interests which fall outside s. 1(1) and (2) of the Law of Property Act 1925 can now exist only as equitable interests

5 In particular, appreciate that life 'estates', fees tail, and fees simple in remainder can exist only as equitable interests

7.2 Introduction

In the previous chapter we deliberately ignored changes made by the great reforming legislation of 1925. We must now start to consider these changes. Before going into matters of detail, it will help if I state, in general terms, what the 1925 legislators were trying to achieve in this field. They had two main objectives:

(a) to reduce the number of types of legal estates and legal interests;

(b) to reduce substantially the importance of the equitable doctrine of notice.

In this chapter we will be looking at how the first objective was achieved; the second objective will be considered in **Chapter 8**.

7.3 Legal estates and interests and the 1925 legislation

7.3.1 The number of types of legal estates and interests prior to 1925

Prior to 1925 there was a quite wide variety of types of right in land recognized by the common law. But (as explained in **Chapter 5**) there was an even wider variety of types of right recognized by equity. Expressed diagramatically, as in **Figure 7.1**, you should think of two lists:

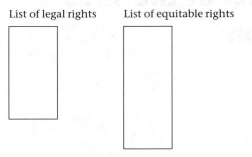

Figure 7.1

(I hope that you have remembered that all types of property right recognized by the common law are also recognized by equity. But there are some types of right, e.g., restrictive covenants and estate contracts, which have never been recognized by the common law. That is why the list of equitable rights is longer.)

7.3.2 The effect of the 1925 legislation

As a result of the 1925 reform, the length of the list of types of legal right is reduced, as shown in **Figure 7.2**, below. The list of types of equitable right remains the same length.

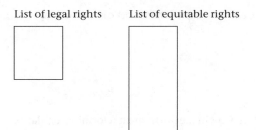

Figure 7.2

The 1925 legislators did not totally abolish any type of property right. (It might have been better had they done so!) Rather they (in effect) provided that certain types of right which previously were recognized by **both law and equity** are now recognized **by equity alone**. Property rights which were treated in this way include, e.g., fees tail, determinable fees, life estates, and fees simple in remainder. You may well be wondering why this was done.

It was hoped that, by limiting the number of types of legal right, land law would be simplified, and that conveyancing transactions (buying and selling land, leasing, etc.) would be made easier. It is debatable whether these ends have in fact been achieved.

7.3.3 Law of Property Act 1925, section 1

The Law of Property Act 1925 does not contain a long list of rights which used to exist at law but which can now only exist in equity. Instead, s. 1(1) and (2) set out those types of property right which are still capable of existing **at law** after 1925.

Legal estates and equitable interests

(1) The only estates in land which are capable of subsisting or of being conveyed or created at law are—

    (a) An estate in fee simple absolute in possession;

    (b) A term of years absolute.

(2) The only interests or charges in or over land which are capable of subsisting or of being conveyed or created at law are—

    (a) An easement, right, or privilege in or over land for an interest equivalent to an estate in fee simple absolute in possession or a term of years absolute;

    (b) A rentcharge in possession issuing out of or charged on land being either perpetual or for a term of years absolute;

    (c) A charge by way of legal mortgage;

    (d) . . . and any other similar charge on land which is not created by an instrument;

    (e) Rights of entry exercisable over or in respect of a legal term of years absolute, or annexed, for any purpose, to a legal rentcharge.

Section 1(3) then provides: 'All other estates, interests and charges in or over land take effect as equitable interests.'

If a particular property right is one of the two 'estates' listed in s. 1(1), or falls into one of the five categories of legal interest listed in s. 1(2), then it can be a legal property right. But if it falls outside all seven headings then (applying s. 1(3)) it can only be an equitable interest.

?   **QUESTION** 7.1

If you now look at s. 1(1) and (2) above, you will find no reference to fees tail. What follows from the fact that these subsections do not mention fees tail?

It follows that any fee tail existing after 1925 exists only as an equitable interest.

7.4 Legal estates existing after 1925

(Remember that an 'estate' is a right to enjoy possession of a piece of land for a period of time.)

By s. 1(1) of the Law of Property Act 1925 there are now only two legal estates:

(a) fee simple absolute in possession;

(b) term of years absolute.

7.4.1 Term of years absolute

The statutory phrase 'term of years absolute' is very misleading. Worse still, the phrase is given a very elaborate definition by s. 205(1)(xxvii) of the Law of Property Act 1925 which many people (myself included) do not find very helpful. This elaborate definition is as follows:

(xxvii) 'Term of years absolute' means a term of years (taking effect either in possession or in reversion whether or not at a rent) with or without impeachment for waste, subject or not to another legal estate, and either certain or liable to determination by notice, re-entry, operation of law, or by a provision for cesser on redemption, or in any other event (other than the dropping of a life, or the determination of a determinable life interest); but does not include any term of years determinable with life or lives or with the cesser of a determinable life interest, nor, if created after the commencement of this Act, a term of years which is not expressed to take effect in possession within twenty-one years after the creation thereof where required by this Act to take effect within that period; and in this definition the expression 'term of years' includes a term for less than a year, or for a year or years and a fraction of a year or from year to year . . .

Term of years absolute' can, however, be explained much more simply than is done in s. 205(1)(xxvii). **To all intents and purposes 'term of years absolute' is synonymous with 'lease'!** The concept of a lease has been explained at 1.3.2, and in particular I stress there that leases come in two forms, 'fixed term' and 'periodic tenancies'. It may prove useful to read that explanation again.

I can now go on to tell you that all forms of lease (including a fixed term for, say, just six months, or a weekly periodic tenancy) are technically 'terms of years absolute'. (I said the phrase was misleading!) The conclusion is thus very simple. All forms of lease (even very short ones) are still capable of existing as a legal estate.

7.4.2 Fee simple absolute in possession

You may recall from **Chapter 4** that fees simple, fees tail, and life estates were, at common law 'estates of freehold'. Leases were not.

The basic plan underlying s. 1(1)(a) of the 1925 Act and its concept 'fee simple absolute in possession' is easy to understand. It was that the only estate of freehold to be recognized by law is one which:

(a) in principle goes on for ever; **and**

(b) gives its owner an immediate right to enjoy the land.

'Absolute' (in this context) means going on for ever. 'In possession' means giving a right to immediate enjoyment. We must now consider the phrases in greater detail.

7.4.2.1 'In possession'

In **Chapter 4** we considered 'estates in possession, remainder, and reversion' (see 4.6). I then said that an estate in possession is one which confers on its owner an **immediate** right to occupy the relevant land. In the context of a general discussion on the nature of estates, that definition is, I insist, perfectly sound; but in the context of the present discussion we need to add a qualification to this definition. First, though, an example:

Suppose Roger owns a legal 'fee simple absolute in possession' in Blueacre. He leases Blueacre to Tamsin for six months at £10 per week rent. In a literal sense, Roger will not be 'in possession' of Blueacre for the next six months; Tamsin will be. Nevertheless it would be very strange if, having had a legal estate in Blueacre, Roger should lose it, only to regain it after just six months. Moreover, if this were correct, nobody would seem to 'own' Blueacre during the six months of the lease.

The answer to this puzzle is tucked away in s. 205(1)(xix) of the Law of Property Act 1925. This states that for the purposes of the 1925 Act, ' "Possession" includes receipt of rents and profits or the right to receive the same, if any; . . .'

Now you may find this wording strange and archaic. What it really means is that a right to receive rent with respect to a piece of land (even a nominal rent or one which is not in fact collected) is deemed to be possession of that land. A slightly different way of putting it is to say that the right to receive rent from a piece of land is 'constructive possession' of that land. It follows that a fee simple **in reversion to a lease** counts as 'in possession' for the purposes of s. 1(1) of the Act. So in my Blueacre example Roger retains a legal fee simple estate during the six months of the lease.

? QUESTION 7.2

Leonora owns the legal fee simple absolute in possession with respect to Greenacre. She executes a deed leasing Greenacre to Tamsin for 7 years. Almost immediately Tamsin executes a deed sub-leasing Greenacre to Susan for five years. How many legal estates now exist with respect to Greenacre?

There are three. Leonora, despite what has happened to Greenacre, retains her legal fee simple absolute in possession. Tamsin and Susan **both** own terms of years absolute.

One other complication. You may well recall from 4.6.2 that a fee simple can exist in reversion, not just to a lease, but also to a life estate or fee tail. Now when somebody grants a life estate or fee tail, in practice he does so gratuitously. Unlike when he grants a lease, he does not charge a rent. A fee simple in reversion to a life estate or fee tail is therefore not, even under the wide statutory definition, 'in possession' and can exist only as an equitable interest. (Who owns the **legal** fee simple to the land in this situation will emerge later in 7.6.)

7.4.2.2 'Absolute'

The original plan in 1925 was that **all** modified fees simple should merely be equitable interests. Unfortunately two exceptions have been made to this principle.

Statutory determinable fees simple

In 4.3.3.1, when discussing determinable fees simple, I gave illustrations: 'To John Smith in fee simple until he marries Fanny Bloggs'; 'To Ann Green in fee simple during the time that she remains a faithful Protestant'. Such determinable fees **are not absolute**. After 1925, a determinable fee simple granted to a human being must be an equitable interest.

The complication is not with determinable fees of the kind we have just considered. Rather it is with those fees simple which are made determinable by statute. In the first half of the nineteenth century, a lot of land was taken by way of compulsory purchase for railways and canals. To soften the blow for the expropriated landowners the relevant legislation (usually the Lands Clauses Acts) provided that should a railway or canal close down, the land taken should revert to its original owner or his heirs.

The facts of a case which you learn about in constitutional law illustrate this point. In *Pickin* v *British Railways* [1974] AC 765, land had in effect been granted 'to the Bristol and Exeter

Railway in fee simple until the Clevedon to Yatton railway is abandoned'. The railway in this case (and in countless other similar situations) obtained a statutory determinable fee simple.

In 1925, Parliament was well aware of these special fees simple, and decided that they should not be downgraded to equitable interests. Section 7(1) of the Law of Property Act 1925 therefore provides:

A fee simple which, by virtue of the Lands Clauses Acts, the School Sites Acts, or any similar statute, is liable to be divested, is for the purposes of this Act a fee simple absolute, and remains liable to be divested as if this Act had not been passed . . .

As a result of this provision, a statutory determinable fee simple remains a legal estate.

School Sites Acts

You will notice that the School Sites Acts are also mentioned in s. 7(1). These Acts were passed in the nineteenth century. They were designed to encourage (but **not compel**) wealthy landowners to donate land for schools, village halls, etc. The School Sites Acts provided for the land to revert from the trustees of the school to the original grantor or his heirs should the school close.

As you may have guessed, problems arose in the late twentieth century where a school had closed, but it is difficult to trace the original grantor's heirs, the grantor having died a long time ago. The problem was considered in two modern cases (*Re Clayton's Deed* [1980] Ch 99 and *Re Rowhook Mission Hall* [1985] Ch 62) which came to conflicting solutions. The problem was solved by the Reverter of Sites Act 1987.

You need not worry about the cases or the 1987 Act, except to note that the cases **agreed** on one point. A fee simple liable to be divested under the School Sites Act or similar legislation is a special type of determinable fee simple and, unlike determinable fees generally, it continues to exist as a legal estate after 1925.

Fees simple subject to a right of entry

'Right of entry' is a rather misleading phrase we have already come across and will encounter again at 7.5.5. It is not a right simply to go on somebody else's land. It is much more drastic than that. It is a right for a grantor of land to forfeit the grant and reclaim the land should the grantee break some condition.

Rights of entry (i.e., forfeiture) are commonplace in leases; leases usually provide that the landlord can terminate the lease prematurely if the tenant breaks the terms of the lease. In contrast, rights of entry attached to the conveyance of a fee simple are fortunately relatively rare. 'Fortunately', because clearly for an owner to lose a fee simple back to the original grantor is a disaster. In practice there are two possible situations where a right of entry attached to a fee simple may be encountered:

(a) Where there is a fee simple upon condition subsequent. (Refer back to the discussion in 4.3.3.2 and examples such as 'to John Smith in fee simple provided he never marries Fanny Bloggs'.)

(b) Where land has been conveyed in return for a rentcharge, and a right of entry for non-payment of that rentcharge has been imposed.

Situation (b) takes a little bit of explaining. In about 1900 a rather strange way of selling land enjoyed a period of popularity in and around Manchester. Land was sold not for a capital price (say £200, a tidy sum in those days), but in return for a rentcharge.

Rentcharges were discussed at 1.4.5, and I suggest that you refer back for a moment to remind yourself of what a rentcharge is. We have already looked at an illustration drawn from the (fairly modern) **Bristol** practice. We will now consider an example of the old **Manchester** practice.

In 1905, Tatlock sold the fee simple in Raineyacre to Sharples in return for a rentcharge of £12 per annum. (This figure is realistic.) As a result of this transaction **three** property rights existed:

(a) a **fee simple** estate in Raineyacre vested in Sharples;

(b) a **rentcharge** for £12 per year charged on Raineyacre, payable to Tatlock;

(c) a **'right of entry'** (i.e., forfeiture) in favour of Tatlock which he could exercise if the rentcharge was not paid.

It was the inclusion of this 'right of entry' in the old Manchester transactions (rights of entry were not normally included in the more modern Bristol transactions) which caused a problem when the 1925 legislation was enacted.

January 1926—panic in Manchester

It is clear that the 1925 legislators originally intended that fees simple upon condition subsequent should, like non-statutory determinable fees simple, in future exist only as equitable interests. But they totally overlooked fees simple subject to a right of entry for non-payment of a rentcharge. As a result of this oversight, there was in early 1926 worry and confusion amongst solicitors and landowners in the Manchester area. It appeared that any person who owned a fee simple subject to **a right of entry** for non-payment of a rentcharge no longer had an **absolute** fee simple. They therefore no longer owned a legal estate but only an equitable interest.

To meet this problem, the Law of Property Amendment Act 1926 hastily added a further clause to s. 7(1) of the Law of Property Act 1925: 'a fee simple subject to a legal or equitable right of entry or re-entry is for the purposes of this Act a fee simple absolute'. This provision was made retrospective to 1 January 1926. It ensured that a fee simple subject to a right of entry for non-payment of a rentcharge can still exist as a legal estate. But this provision also has one (probably unintended) side effect.

As we have already seen, a fee simple upon condition subsequent is (by its nature) also a fee simple subject to a right of entry. Thus it appears that, contrary to the original 1925 plan, a fee simple upon condition subsequent is 'absolute' for the purposes of the 1925 Act and can therefore still exist as a legal estate.

> **? QUESTION** 7.3
>
> Janet owns the legal fee simple absolute in possession in Broadacre. She executes a deed conveying Broadacre, 'To my daughter Karen in fee simple on condition that she does not marry a professional footballer'. Has Karen acquired a legal estate?

Karen has of course only a fee simple (in possession) upon condition subsequent. The original intention in 1925 was that such a modified fee should be an equitable interest only. But as Karen's fee simple also fits the description 'a fee simple subject to a right of entry', it is caught by the 1926 amendment and will be a legal estate.

7.5 Legal interests existing after 1925

As already indicated, under s. 1(2) of the Law of Property Act 1925, there are five categories of legal interests. The categories are lettered (a) to (e). In the case of categories (a), (b), and (d) (see 7.5.1, 7.5.2, and 7.5.4), the actual wording of the legislation, set out at **7.3.3** leaves something to be desired.

7.5.1 (a) Easements and profits

This category covers any easement or profit, provided its duration is equivalent to a fee simple absolute in possession or a term of years absolute. Thus rights such as private rights of way (an easement) and grazing rights (a profit) are normally going to be legal interests. However, carefully note the requirement regarding duration. If, for example, I granted my neighbour Charley a right 'for the rest of his life' to cross my land to get to his own house, Charley would have an easement for life. That right, even if granted by deed, could exist only as an equitable interest.

7.5.2 (b) Rentcharges

A rentcharge which in its duration is either 'perpetual' or for 'a term of years absolute' (i.e., lasts for a fixed period) is capable of being a legal interest. Again note the duration requirement. At one time rentcharges granted for the life of the recipient of the payments were quite common. If any such rights survive today, they **must** be equitable interests.

As we saw in 1.4.5, the Rentcharges Act 1977 prohibits (subject to exceptions) the creation of new rentcharges. It also provides that existing perpetual rentcharges can endure for only another 60 years (i.e., they will all expire in the year 2037). The 1977 Act, while it ensures the gradual decline in number of rentcharges, does not affect the question whether a particular rentcharge is a legal interest or an equitable interest.

7.5.3 (c) 'A charge by way of legal mortgage'

The 'charge by way of legal mortgage' is the standard modern form of 'legal mortgage'. There must be literally several million of this type of legal interest in existence today.

7.5.4 (d) All interests in land which arise by operation of statute

In this text we have so far assumed that all rights against a piece of land are created by action of the relevant parties. This is not entirely correct. Some rights arise against a piece of land by operation of an Act of Parliament. The owner of the rights will in practice be some form of government department.

In modern law, there are two (very contrasting) rights arising by statute which are sufficiently important for them to be mentioned as part of a land law course.

7.5.4.1 The charge for inheritance tax

When a person dies owning a lot of property, the Revenue will claim what is often still loosely referred to as 'death duties'. With a very wealthy person, the bill for 'death duties' is substantial. 'Death duties' has, however, never been the official name for this tax. Prior to 1971 it was estate duty. From 1971 to 1984 it was capital transfer tax. Since 1984 it has been inheritance tax.

The important point for our purposes is that where inheritance tax is payable with respect to a piece of real property, that tax becomes a 'charge' on the land in favour of the Revenue. (The same used to be true of estate duty and capital transfer tax.) The Revenue has (in effect) a legal interest in the land.

7.5.4.2 Legal services commission charge—usually still known as the 'legal aid charge'

Where a legally aided litigant 'recovers or preserves' land, the costs of the litigation (in so far as they are not recovered from the other side) become a charge on the land in favour of the Legal Services Commission. This rule is particularly important where former spouses or cohabitees have been litigating about who owns their former home. The winner may find that she or he gets the house, but encumbered by a substantial charge (in effect a legal interest rather akin to a mortgage) in favour of the Legal Services Commission (formerly the Legal Aid Board).

7.5.5 (e) Rights of entry

Section 1(2)(e) of the 1925 Act covers 'Rights of entry exercisable over or in respect of a legal term of years absolute, or annexed, for any purpose, to a legal rentcharge'.

As explained earlier, 'right of entry' is synonymous with 'right to forfeit'. The practical effect of s. 1(2)(e) is that:

(a) a landlord's right to forfeit a lease if the tenant breaks the terms of the lease;

(b) a rentcharge owner's right (if any) to reclaim the land if the money is not paid,

can both be legal interests.

? | **QUESTION** 7.4

In the example given in **Question 7.3**, Janet will retain a right of entry exercisable *for breach of a condition subsequent*. Is that right legal or equitable?

A right of entry for breach of a condition subsequent is not within s. 1(2)(e), nor of course is it within any other paragraph of s. 1(1) and (2). Therefore such a right of entry can **only be an equitable interest**, even though the fee simple upon condition subsequent can still (thanks to the 1926 amendment) be a legal estate.

> **? QUESTION** 7.5
>
> Which of the following can exist as legal property rights after 1925?
>
> (a) An easement to last for 10 years.
> (b) A profit to last for the lifetime of the grantee.
> (c) A determinable fee simple, 'To John in fee simple until he marries Fanny'.
> (d) A restrictive covenant.
> (e) A weekly periodic tenancy.

Only (a) and (e) come within s. 1(1) or (2), and they (alone) **can** be legal property rights. Right (a) comes within s. 1(2)(a); contrast (b), which does not come within the same paragraph, as it lasts for a lifetime, not for a 'term of years'. Right (e) **can** be a legal property right because (paradoxically) it is a 'term of years absolute' within s. 1(1)(b).

7.6 Equitable interests after 1925

The first point to remember is that if a property right falls within one of the seven headings in s. 1(1) and (2) of the Law of Property Act 1925, it **can** be a legal right; it does **not** follow that it **must** be a legal right. In particular remember that at 5.4 it was stressed that to create or convey legal property rights a deed is required. Thus let us suppose that Len owns Blue Field. He and Tom sign a document which is not a deed, under which Len leases Blue Field to Tom for 10 years. They have created a 'term of years absolute' within the meaning of s. 1(1)(b), but the transaction is, of course, only an equitable lease as it is not in the form of a deed.

7.6.1 The status of fees tail, fees simple in remainder, determinable fees, life estates

Fees tail, fees simple in remainder, determinable fees, and life estates can now exist only as equitable interests. Any legal fees tail, legal life estates, etc. existing on 1 January 1926 were automatically downgraded to equitable interests.

Suppose that in 1900, land had been granted by deed, 'To Alfred for life, remainder to Brian in fee tail, remainder to Charles in fee simple'. Until 1925, Alfred, Brian, and Charles would each have a legal estate in the land. The legal ownership of the land was said to be divided up into 'temporal slices'. One legal estate followed on after another. Since 1925 it has been impossible to divide up the legal **freehold** ownership of land into 'temporal slices'. **For every piece of land in the country there must now be just one legal freehold estate, a fee simple absolute in possession.**

Suppose that at some time between 1926 and 1996 Blackacre was granted by deed, 'to Alfred for life, remainder to Brian for life, remainder to Charles in fee simple'. Such a grant created a 'strict settlement'. (Refer back to 2.4.1.) The life interests of Alfred and Brian, and the interest of Charles, are equitable interests only.

As we also saw at 2.4.1, the strict settlement is a form of trust peculiar to land. As you may have been able to guess, the legal fee simple absolute in possession in Blackacre will therefore be held by a trustee or trustees in trust for Alfred, Brian, and Charles.

Now comes the surprising point. Thinking back to **Chapter 2**, and/or just applying some common sense, you may be thinking that the legal fee simple estate in Blackacre must be vested in independent trustees (for the sake of argument, let us call them Tim and Tam). You would be wrong to think this.

As a result of the **Settled Land Act 1925**, where, as in our Blackacre example, there is a 'strict settlement' of land, the trustee(s) of the legal fee simple estate will not normally be independent people such as Tim and Tam. Rather the **'life tenant in possession'** will be the sole trustee. Thus in our Blackacre example, Alfred (remember he has a life interest in possession) will hold the legal estate on trust for himself, Brian, and Charles. Do not panic if this seems very strange. Particularly, remember that in **Chapter 2** it was said that strict settlements were a legal anomaly, and that they are rare today.

Moreover, under the Trusts of Land etc. Act 1996 no new strict settlements can be created. If, after 1996, Blackacre is granted by deed to Alfred for life, remainder to Brian for life, remainder to Charles in fee simple, the life interests of Alfred and Brian, and the interest of Charles, are (as before) equitable interests only. But, instead of there being a strict settlement, there will be a 'new-style trust of land'. As we shall see in **Chapter 12**, where there is a new-style trust, the legal estate in the trust land will not be vested in the life tenant but will be vested in independent trustees.

?   **QUESTION** 7.6

Prior to 1997, Vastacres was granted to Leonard for life, remainder to Malcolm in fee tail, remainder to Norma in fee simple.

(a) Are the rights expressly granted to Leonard, Malcolm, and Norma legal or equitable?

(b) Who will own the legal 'fee simple absolute in possession' to Vastacres?

The right expressly granted to Leonard is an equitable life interest in possession, while Malcolm has an equitable fee tail in remainder, and Norma has an equitable fee simple in remainder. Leonard will also own the legal 'fee simple absolute in possession', holding it in trust for himself, Malcolm, and Norma.

✳   **CONCLUDING REMARKS**

In this chapter we have examined the seven categories of property right which can still exist as legal property rights after the quite fundamental changes made by the 1925 property legislation. No property rights were abolished by s. 1 of the Law of Property Act 1925, but some rights were 'downgraded' (as it were) so that they could exist only as equitable interests. Prominent among those 'downgraded' are rights the duration of which is measured by the life or lives of person(s), including life estates, an easement or profit for life, and even a rentcharge to last for the life of a person.

This downgrading meant that when the new legislation came into force (1 January 1926) there was **an immediate increase in the absolute number of equitable property rights**. This increase led to other consequences which we examine in the next chapter.

■ SUMMARY

In the law which has existed since 1925, it is possible to identify four 'families' of property right in land.

A   **Legal Estates**. This family has only two members:

  (i)   A fee simple which goes on for ever and which gives its owner either immediate personal enjoyment of the land or the right to collect rent from the land.

  (ii)   Leases. But this 'member' includes both fixed-term leases and periodic tenancies.

B   **Legal Interests.** The most important members of this family are:

  (i)   Easements which last for ever or for a fixed period

  (ii)   Profits which last for ever or for a fixed period

  (iii)   Charges by way of legal mortgage

  (iv)   'Legal aid' charges

  (v)   Inheritance tax charges.

C   **Equitable interests which arise by agreement or by conduct**

The most important members of this family are:

  (i)   Easements and profits which last for the lifetime of the grantee

  (ii)   Easements and profits which are created by a signed agreement, rather than by a formal deed

  (iii)   Restrictive covenants (even if created by deed)

  (iv)   Constructive trust interests

  (v)   Licences by estoppel, sometimes known as proprietary estoppel.

D   **Equitable Interests which exist under deliberately created express trusts**

The most important members of this family are:

  (i)   Life estates/life interests

  (ii)   Fees simple in remainder

  (iii)   Fees tail (but remember that there can be no new ones).

■ FURTHER READING

For a discussion of the impact of s. 1 of the Law of Property Act 1925, see *Megarry and Wade* (sixth edition by Harpum) chapter four, pages 107–117.

<table>
<tr><td>

8

</td><td>

Status of equitable
interests after 1925

</td></tr>
</table>

8.1 Objectives

By the end of this chapter you should:

1 Appreciate why and how the 1925 property legislation reduced the importance of the equitable doctrine of notice

2 Be able to explain how the system of land **charges** registration operates

3 Be able to list those important property rights which are registrable as land charges

4 Be able to explain the concept of overreaching, and how it operates

5 Be able to list those equitable interests which are still subject to the equitable doctrine of notice

8.2 Introduction

As I hinted at the end of **Chapter 7**, the effect of s. 1 of the Law of Property Act 1925 in statistical terms was that, at the stroke of midnight on 1 January 1926, the number of **legal** rights in land decreased sharply, and the number of equitable interests increased sharply. Now, as the number of equitable interests dramatically increased, you might be thinking that the equitable doctrine of notice (discussed at 6.4) became post-1925 even more important than it was prior to the great reforms. For reasons which will now be explained, this is a wrong conclusion.

8.2.1 The desire to reduce the importance of the doctrine of notice

As I noted at **7.2**, the 1925 legislators actually aimed to **reduce** the importance of the doctrine of notice. This policy aim is easy to understand. If somebody owns an equitable interest he can never be 100% sure that his rights will remain enforceable against the land. There is always the risk that a purchaser of the land will come along who is a bona fide purchaser for value of a legal estate without notice of the equitable interest.

Prior to 1926 almost all equitable interests were subject to the doctrine of notice. Since 1925 only a minority are subject to the doctrine. The 1925 legislation divides equitable interests which exist with respect to land which is **unregistered title** into three groups:

(a) equitable interests registrable as land charges;

(b) equitable interests which are 'overreachable';

(c) equitable interests which are neither registrable as land charges nor overreachable, and are therefore still subject to the doctrine of notice.

8.3 **Registration of land charges**

As we shall shortly see, a wide variety of equitable interests are registrable as land charges. A person who owns an equitable interest which is registrable as a land charge is well advised to register it. Why?

(a) If the interest is registered then s. 198(1) of the Law of Property Act 1925 provides that the registration shall constitute actual notice to the whole world of the equitable interest. Thus if you register your right as a land charge, you can be sure that it will be binding on a purchaser.

(b) If an interest is registrable as a land charge, but it is not registered, then by the Land Charges Acts 1925 and 1972, the interest is void against a purchaser for value (whatever the state of that purchaser's knowledge).

The important case of *Hollington Brothers Ltd* v *Rhodes* is a dramatic illustration of the second principle. H 'leased' some offices to R for seven years by a document which was not a deed. R therefore acquired only an equitable lease. An equitable lease is (since 1925) **registrable as a land charge** (see 8.3.3.1). R took possession of the premises, but omitted to register his lease as a land charge.

The equitable lease was valid against H, but H then sold its estate in reversion to D. This sale was expressly 'subject to and with the benefit of such tenancies as may affect the premises'. There can be no doubt that D had 'notice' of R's equitable lease. Nevertheless D was not bound by it. The Court of Appeal emphasized that where an equitable interest is registrable as a land charge, **the doctrine of notice is irrelevant**.

The moral of this case (and the case of *Midland Bank Trust Co. Ltd* v *Green* discussed at 8.3.5.1) is clear. If you have an equitable interest which is registrable as a land charge, register it! If you do not, you will lose your rights if the land is sold. You will lose your rights even if the purchaser knew of your interest and/or could see you were occupying the land.

? **QUESTION** 8.1

In 2000, Lenny granted an equitable lease of his house 'Broomtrees' to Tommy for 10 years. Tommy lives in the house. The house is unregistered title. Recently Lenny sold the fee simple in the house to Percy. Percy knew of the equitable lease, because both Lenny and Tommy told him about it. Is Percy bound by Tommy's equitable lease?

Percy will be bound by Tommy's equitable lease **only if** Tommy had registered it as a land charge. If Tommy has not so registered, then his equitable lease will be void against a purchaser such as Percy. It is irrelevant that Percy knew of Tommy's lease.

8.3.1 The operation of the Land Charges Register

Before examining this topic, remember that the Land Charges Register is relevant only where the **title** to land is **unregistered**. The Land Charges Register must not be confused with the Register of Title. As more and more titles are registered, the Land Charges Register is becoming less and less important.

The decline in importance of the Land Charges Register is very welcome, as it operates in a rather strange way. A person who owns a registrable interest registers it not against the land, but against the **name** of the owner (at the time the interest was created) of the legal estate out of which the interest is derived.

The Land Charges Register is basically an immensely long list of names of landowners. It used to be a gigantic card-index system, kept at Kidbrooke in south-east London (one name, one card!). For a long time critics predicted that the register would grow so large that it would become unmanageable. By the early 1970s, so many entries had been made that the crisis point seemed to be upon us. The situation was saved (in 1974) by transferring the Land Charges Register on to a computer kept at Plymouth. One of the clear defects in the 1925 property legislation was (largely) solved, not by legislation but by a technology unheard of in 1925!

I said a moment ago that an owner of a registrable interest must register against the name of the owner of the legal estate out of which the interest is derived. To be more accurate, registration must be against the name **as shown in the title deeds**. Suppose I own Pinkacre, and someone wishes to register a land charge against me. The conveyance of Pinkacre to me names me as 'Rodger Norman Sexton'. Registration must be against 'Rodger Norman Sexton', even though on my birth certificate and in every day life I am 'Roger' without the 'd'.

Suppose, however, that you want to register a land charge, but you do not have access to the relevant title deed(s) to see how the name has been written. What do you do then? The answer (strange as it sounds) is that you register against all possible alternative versions of the name. (This quite often happens with 'Class F' rights of occupation (matrimonial home rights), discussed below at 8.3.3.3.)

?   **QUESTION** 8.2

Wendy comes into your office in a flood of tears. She explains that her husband of nearly 50 years has just left her. She is still in the matrimonial home, which her husband bought in his sole name in 1956. The house is unregistered title. She is frightened that her husband will sell the house and she will be out on the street. She tells you, 'He usually called himself Stuart Pearse, but I am not sure that is the correct spelling. On the marriage certificate it says "Stewart Pierce" '.

In this situation every good lawyer will 'drop everything' and immediately register a land charge. But what do you do about the names problem?

I would register against **six** versions; the two versions of the husbands' first name multiplied by the three possible spellings of the surname (remember 'Pearce' is very common).

8.3.2 Searches of the Land Charges Register

As a result of s. 198 of the Law of Property Act 1925, all interests which have been correctly registered are automatically binding upon a purchaser. You should therefore have already realized that when a purchaser is buying land which is unregistered title, one enquiry he always should make is a 'search' of the Land Charges Register. He needs to know what (relevant) entries there are on the register.

The computerization of the Land Charges Register does not alter the fact that when a purchaser is buying unregistered land he 'searches' by supplying the Land Charges Registry with a list of the names of the past owners of the land, if possible going back to 1925. For reasons already indicated, those names should be supplied as they have been spelt in the relevant deeds.

8.3.2.1 The complexities of a names-based register

The cases of *Oak Co-operative BS* v *Blackburn* [1968] Ch 730 and *Diligent Finance Co. Ltd* v *Alleyne* (1972) 23 P & CR 346 illustrate just how awkward and cumbersome this system of registration against names can be!

In *the Oak Co-operative* case:

1 A man whose real name was Francis David Blackburn agreed to sell his house to Ms Caines;

2 She registered her 'estate contract' land charge against the name Frank David Blackburn;

3 Later, Blackburn mortgaged the house to the building society, who searched the Land Charges register against the name of Francis Davis Blackburn. This search did not reveal Caines' estate contract.

Blackburn defaulted on the mortgage repayments, so the courts had to decide whether Caines' estate contract was binding on the building society.

The Court of Appeal held in favour of Ms Caines. It ruled that a registration against a version of the owner's name was valid and binding on anyone who searched against the wrong name, or who did not search at all. But Ms Caines' estate contract would not have been binding on the building society if it had searched against the correct name as it appeared in the title deeds and Caines' interest had not been revealed.

In *Diligent Finance Co. Ltd* v *Alleyne* (1972) 23 P & CR 346 a house was conveyed to 'Erskine Owen Alleyne', and used by himself and his wife as their matrimonial home. When the marriage broke down, Mrs Alleyne registered her 'Class F' matrimonial home rights against the name of Erskine Alleyne. Mr Alleyne later mortgaged the house to the claimants, who searched against the correct name of Erskine Owen Alleyne. Applying what had been said in *Oak Co-operative*, Foster J held that the wife's land charge did not bind the claimants.

8.3.3 Equitable interests registrable as land charges

The Land Charges Act 1925 (now replaced by the Land Charges Act 1972) introduced a system of classes of land charge. For our purposes these classes are discussed below in order of importance, rather than alphabetical order.

8.3.3.1 Class C(iv): estate contract

'Estate contract' I defined at 5.5.3.4 as the equitable interest which a purchaser of land acquires in the (usually fairly brief) period which elapses between the contract for sale and its completion by conveyance of the legal estate. This may be called the traditional definition. The definition of 'estate contract' contained in the Land Charges Act 1972 (see s. 2(4)(iv)) is far wider than the traditional definition. In consequence, quite a wide variety of rights are registrable under the general heading 'estate contract':

(a) any contract to create or convey a legal estate;

(b) equitable leases arising under contracts or informal grants (hence the need to register the lease in *Hollington* v *Rhodes*);

(c) options;

(d) rights of pre-emption (i.e., first refusal).

8.3.3.2 Class D(ii): restrictive covenants

Any restrictive covenant entered into after 1925 (except one contained in a lease) is registrable as a land charge. Restrictive covenants entered into before 1926 (of which there is a tremendous number) are not registrable as land charges. They remain subject to the doctrine of notice.

? QUESTION 8.3

Pippa recently purchased Snooty House. Snooty House was unregistered title. When Pippa investigated title, the root of title was a conveyance dated 1981. That conveyance revealed a large number of restrictive covenants affecting Snooty House. Some were imposed on the house in 1910; others were imposed in 1940. When Pippa had a search made of the Land Charges Register, the official search certificate revealed no restrictive covenants. Is Pippa bound:

(a) by the 1940 covenants?

(b) by the 1910 covenants?

Provided she searched against the correct name(s) she will not be bound by the 1940 covenants, even though she knew about them. She will be bound by the 1910 covenants. The doctrine of notice applies to these 'old' covenants, and Pippa had notice of them because they were recited in the root of title.

8.3.3.3 Class F: spousal rights of occupation; 'matrimonial home rights'

Where one spouse (or civil partner) has the legal title to the matrimonial home in his/her sole name, the other spouse (or civil partner) **automatically** has a statutory right of occupation with respect to the home. This right of occupation, renamed 'matrimonial home rights' by the Family Law Act 1996, is registrable as a land charge.

The 'Class F' right is **in addition** to any right under a constructive trust which the spouse (or civil partner) who does not have the legal title **may** have by virtue of having contributed substantially to the cost of acquisition of the matrimonial home. Confusingly, a constructive trust interest is an equitable interest which is still subject to the doctrine of notice!

8.3.3.4 Class C(iii): general equitable charge

'General equitable charge' can be defined as an equitable charge for money where the owner of the charge does not take possession of the title deeds to the legal estate affected by the charge. You may not find that particularly meaningful. What really matters is that there are two significant equitable interests covered by this concept:

(a) an equitable mortgage where the mortgagee does not take the title deeds to the property mortgaged;

(b) an 'unpaid vendor's lien'.

(An unpaid vendor's lien arises where a vendor of land conveys the land to a purchaser, but allows the purchaser to delay paying part or the whole of the price. It is a kind of equitable interest in the land which exists in favour of the vendor until he is paid in full.)

8.3.3.5 Class D(iii): equitable easements and profits

This class of land charge is relatively rare as most easements and profits are legal interests, and like legal interests generally they bind purchasers whatever the circumstances.

Equitable easements and equitable profits are registrable under Class D(iii) if created after 1925. (Equitable easements and equitable profits created pre-1926 are not registrable as land charges. They are still subject to the doctrine of notice.)

8.3.3.6 Class C(ii): a 'limited owner's charge'

This form of equitable interest is relatively rare nowadays. It arises in favour of a person who has only a life interest in a piece of land, but he pays off out of his own pocket a financial incumbrance burdening the fee simple, such as a mortgage, or a charge for inheritance tax, or the taxes now replaced by inheritance tax.

8.3.3.7 Class E: annuities

This class is totally obsolete, and we need not bother with it.

8.3.4 Legal interests registrable as land charges

We now come to an annoying anomaly in the law, actually the result of the 1925 reforms. The vast majority of property rights registrable as land charges are equitable interests which otherwise would have been subject to the doctrine of notice. Rather strangely, a few legal interests are also registrable as land charges.

To put the matter bluntly, the rights we are about to consider are **called** 'legal interests', as they fall within s. 1 of the Law of Property Act 1925. But ironically, as they are registrable as land charges, they are deprived of the all-important characteristic of legal interests, which is that they bind purchasers of the land whatever the circumstances. If an interest of one of the types discussed below is not registered as a land charge, it will be void against a purchaser in the usual way. It will even be void against a purchaser who actually knew of the unregistered interest. (*Cf. Hollington Brothers* v *Rhodes*.)

8.3.4.1 Class C(i): puisne mortgage

('Puisne' is pronounced 'puny'.) A puisne mortgage is a legal mortgage where the mortgagee does not take possession of the title deeds.

Where land is mortgaged, the mortgagee (i.e., the lender) normally takes possession of the title deeds relating to the land mortgaged. However, as you may already know, a piece of land may be mortgaged more than once, so that there are (simultaneously) two or more mortgages with respect to the same piece of land. Where this is the case, the first mortgagee (i.e., the lender whose mortgage was created first) will in practice have taken the deeds to the land. The later mortgagees (second, third, etc.) will therefore not be able to take any deeds.

This in turn means that if a second or later mortgage is a legal mortgage, it will be a 'puisne' mortgage and registrable as a Class C(i) land charge. (If a second or later mortgage is an equitable mortgage, it will constitute a general equitable charge registrable as a Class C(iii) land charge: see 8.3.3.4.)

If these points regarding mortgages have left you somewhat baffled, do not worry unduly. We will return to them when we study the law of mortgages in **Chapter 32**.

8.3.4.2 Class D(i): charge for inheritance tax

This charge was mentioned at 7.5.4.1 when discussing types of legal interest. The inheritance tax (in earlier days the capital transfer tax or estate duty) which may be payable with respect to a piece of real property is a charge on that real property. It is a legal interest, **but it is registrable as a land charge, Class D(i)**. The charge can arise only in favour of the Revenue, and the taxpayer (the person who has inherited the land) is permitted to pay off the tax by annual instalments over 10 years.

Strangely, it is the practice of the Revenue to register a Class D(i) charge only in exceptional cases where it anticipates having difficulty getting its money.

> **? QUESTION** 8.4
>
> Harold recently died. He owned, *inter alia*, Hugeacres (unregistered title), worth about £10 million. His will appointed the National Westminster Bank to be his sole executor, and it (as it is entitled to) has put Hugeacres up for sale. Your wealthy friend Leonard is thinking of buying, but in conversation he asks, 'Hugeacres must be subject to a whopping bill for inheritance tax. If I bought Hugeacres, could the taxman claim the money from me?' Advise Leonard.

Although the inheritance tax is a 'legal' interest against Hugeacres, it is registrable as a land charge. It would bind a purchaser such as Leonard only if the Revenue registered its claim on the computer at Plymouth. The Revenue would be confident of getting its money from National Westminster Bank, so it would not bother to register.

8.3.4.3 Classes A and B: certain types of right created by Act of Parliament

We need not bother with the details of these charges, which are nowadays mostly unimportant. There is, however, one very important type of Class B charge—the 'legal aid charge'—which was discussed briefly at 7.5.4.2. This arises in favour of the Legal Services Commission for the costs of litigation involving a legally aided person in which a piece of land is 'recovered or preserved' for that person. It is the policy of the Commission (and was the policy of the Legal Aid Board which used to administer legal aid) to register all Class B charges arising in its favour.

8.3.5 Consequences of failure to register a land charge

I have been saying that an unregistered land charge is void against a purchaser for value of the land. This is something of an oversimplification. The exact consequences of failure to register a land charge depend on the type of charge involved.

8.3.5.1 Failure to register an estate contract, restrictive covenant, inheritance tax charge, or equitable easement/profit

A failure to register as a land charge one of these types of interest will mean that it is void against a purchaser for money or money's worth of a legal estate or legal interest. It must, however, be stressed that the interest will still be valid against the original grantor, donees from him, and people who inherit the land from him.

The case of *Midland Bank* v *Green* [1981] AC 513 defined what was meant by a purchaser for 'money or money's worth'. In that case a father owned a farm. He granted his son an option to purchase the farm at any time in the next 10 years. The son should have registered the option as an estate contract, but omitted to do so.

Father and son later fell out. In order to spite the son, the father sold the farm (worth about £40,000) to his wife for just £500. The wife, of course, knew all about the option. Was she bound by it? The Court of Appeal, presided over by Lord Denning, found that the wife was bound by the option. That court said that 'money or money's worth' meant a fair price, which £500 clearly was not.

Lord Denning offered no definition of the concept 'fair price'. To the great relief of property lawyers, the Court of Appeal decision was overturned by the House of Lords. The House of Lords held that 'money or money's worth' was synonymous with the traditional concept of 'value', except that marriage does not count as money or money's worth. Thus the wife was not bound by the option.

> **? QUESTION 8.5**
>
> Would the wife have been bound if she had paid just £1 or some other nominal consideration?

The answer is, of course, 'No'. As we saw at 6.4.2.1, even a nominal consideration constitutes 'value'.

8.3.5.2 Failure to register other land charges

Midland Bank v *Green* demonstrates what may be described as a 'tough' rule; tough, that is, on people who forget to register land charges such as estate contracts and restrictive covenants. An even tougher rule applies where there is a failure to register land charges of a type not mentioned in the previous heading. The charges subject to the even tougher rule include Class F rights and general equitable charges, as well as less important matters such as limited owner's charges.

This even tougher rule is that failure to register makes the interest in question void against a purchaser for value of any estate or interest in the land, **legal or equitable**. A particular point should be made about the Class F matrimonial home rights. In statistical terms, the number of Class F rights has been in decline ever since they were first invented in 1967. This is because nowadays almost all married couples buy their matrimonial homes in their joint names. However, there are still some marriages where the legal title to the home is in the husband's sole name. This is particularly true of marriages contracted in the 1940s and 1950s. In these cases the wife has 'Class F' rights.

In practice, however, the wife probably has not registered her right. Class F rights are usually registered only when the marriage gets into difficulties and the wife goes to see a solicitor. The solicitor will immediately (while the wife is still in the office) register the Class F charge, but it may be too late. The husband may have already sold, leased, or mortgaged the home, or contracted to do so.

8.3.6 Other registers associated with the Land Charges Register

There are four specialized registers (one of them now obsolete, but the other three of some significance) which are closely associated with the Land Charges Register. These registers used to be incorporated into the card-index system at Kidbrooke, and are now on the computer at Plymouth.

8.3.6.1 The Register of Pending Actions

If any court proceedings are brought which in any way relate to a piece of land, those proceedings should be registered as a 'pending action' (whether or not any proprietary rights are being claimed). This ensures that the outcome of the proceedings will bind any purchaser of the land.

You need not worry about the detailed law relating to 'pending actions', except that you do need to have a basic understanding of one point. This point involves another instance where land law and family law overlap. Where divorce proceedings are commenced, it is common for the less wealthy spouse (usually but not necessarily the wife) to claim a **property adjustment order** under ss. 23 to 25 of the Matrimonial Causes Act 1973. The divorce courts are given by these sections virtually unlimited powers to, in effect, redistribute property (of all kinds) belonging to one or other, or both of the spouses. *Inter alia*, the court can order:

(a) property to be transferred from one spouse to the other;

(b) property solely owned by one spouse to be shared between the spouses;

(c) property jointly owned by the spouses to be transferred into the name of one spouse;

(d) property jointly owned by the spouses to be sold and the proceeds divided as the court sees fit.

If an application for a property adjustment order does, or even may possibly, relate to a piece of land (the ex-matrimonial home or any other land), it should be registered as a pending action. In practice, in divorce proceedings where the legal title to the home is in the husband's name, the wife usually seeks a property adjustment order with respect to that home. This claim is **in addition** to:

(a) her Class F matrimonial home rights, which (anyway) cease on decree absolute of divorce;

(b) any constructive trust interest she may have by virtue of having made a substantial contribution to the cost of the matrimonial home.

The issue of property adjustment orders will crop up again in later chapters of this book. The case of *Perez-Adamson* v *Perez-Rivas* [1987] 3 All ER 20, [1987] 3 WLR 500 is instructive and shows the potential importance of a divorcing spouse registering a pending action. In that case the matrimonial home was in the sole name of the husband. The wife petitioned for a divorce, and in the petition requested a property adjustment order in her favour. She registered this application as a pending action. While the divorce proceedings were pending, the husband mortgaged the house to a bank. The Court of Appeal held (applying s. 198 of the Law of Property Act 1925) that the wife's claim had priority over the mortgage. Any property adjustment order made by the divorce court would therefore be binding on the bank.

8.3.6.2 The Register of Writs and Orders Affecting Land

Any judgment or court order which affects a piece of land should be placed in this register. Though there are others, two kinds of order are commonly found in this register:

(a) **An order charging land with a judgment debt.** A judgment debt arises where a court has awarded damages, but they have not been paid. Suppose you have successfully sued Charley Farnsbarn for damages for (say) breach of contract, and the court has awarded you £60,000 damages. He still refuses to pay, so you wish to enforce your judgment by 'execution' on Farnsbarn's property. Suppose Farnsbarn's most valuable asset is Highacre, worth £100,000. You should get a charging order against Highacre, and register it in the register of writs and orders. If Farnsbarn still does not pay the £60,000, you can force a sale of Highacre, and get your money out of the proceeds.

(b) **A receiving order in bankruptcy.** (When somebody goes bankrupt all his property is vested, by court order, in his 'trustee in bankruptcy'.)

8.3.6.3 Register of Deeds of Arrangement

A few hundred such deeds (at most) are entered into every year. If somebody cannot pay all of his debts, we say that he is 'insolvent'. Normally, somebody who is insolvent goes bankrupt. If, however, an insolvent person has a limited number of creditors, all of whom are willing to accept payment of only a percentage of their debts, a 'deed of arrangement' is a simpler way out. The costs and stigma of bankruptcy are avoided. A deed of arrangement usually transfers most/all of the insolvent person's assets to a trustee who holds the property for the benefit of the creditors.

8.3.6.4 The Register of Annuities

This is now totally obsolete.

8.3.7 Searches of the Land Charges Register—the importance of the official search certificate

The usual method for a solicitor to request a search is by post, but it is also possible to telephone. Though telephoned replies are given, you should always wait to receive the official search certificate through the post. (Searches requested by post take only a few days. During the crisis period at the beginning of the 1970s delays of six weeks were not unknown.)

8.3.7.1 **The official search certificate is conclusive in favour of an intending purchaser**

Provided the purchaser has searched against the correct names, if by some accident a correctly registered charge has been omitted from the search certificate, the purchaser will take free from the omitted charge. The search certificate is conclusive (see Land Charges Act 1972, s. 10(4)). The registry's error will (in effect) destroy the rights of the owner of the charge. Such errors are, fortunately, extremely rare, and it appears that the registry would pay compensation to the owner of the charge which they had accidentally destroyed.

8.3.7.2 **The official certificate 'priority period'**

When buying land, a purchaser needs in practice to search the register a few days before completing the purchase. The priority period rule (s. 11 of the Land Charges Act 1972) gives the purchaser protection against charges which are registered in the period between search and completion. A purchaser is not bound by a charge registered between search and completion provided:

(a) the purchase is completed within 15 working days from the date of the search certificate; **and**

(b) the charge registered in the intervening period was not registered in pursuance of a 'priority notice'.

Priority notices

It would appear that not much use is made in practice of this legal device. A priority notice can be used by someone who contemplates a land charge being created in his favour in the near future, and he wishes to ensure that his charge has priority over and is binding upon other transactions which happen to the relevant land.

For example, Xerxes is selling Greenacre to Yorick. It is envisaged that the conveyance will grant to Xerxes an option to repurchase Greenacre. Xerxes knows that Yorick intends to mortgage Greenacre to Zebedee to secure funds for the purchase price. Xerxes wishes to ensure his option binds Zebedee. He therefore enters a priority notice.

For the priority notice device to work:

(a) there must be an interval of at least 15 working days between the entry of the priority notice and the creation of the land charge; **and**

(b) the charge must be created and registered within 30 working days of the entry of the priority notice.

If these conditions are satisfied then registration of the charge is deemed to have taken place at the moment the charge was created.

Working days

Any day when the registry is open counts as a working day. Thus 15 working days is normally approximately three weeks, as the registry is open Monday to Fridays, excepting Bank and statutory holidays. There will usually be **three working days** between Christmas and New Year.

8.4 Overreachable equitable interests

Prior to the commencement of the Trusts of Land etc. Act 1996 on 1 January 1997, those equitable interests which were overreachable fell into two related categories:

(a) interests under a strict settlement;

(b) interests under a trust for sale.

After the commencement of the 1996 Act, equitable interests under the new-style trusts of land are also overreachable.

Beneficiaries who acquire equitable interests under trusts of land ('old-style' or 'new-style') have usually not paid for them; they probably have to thank the generosity of the settlor. Having been given rights in the land, they should not have too much of a sense of grievance if they find that those rights are converted from being rights in land to rights in something else.

8.4.1 The essence of overreaching

The essence of overreaching is that if the land is sold the rights of the beneficiaries of a strict settlement, trust for sale, or new-style trust cannot bind the purchaser. Provided the purchase price is paid to the correct persons, the purchaser, irrespective of whether he had notice of the beneficiaries' rights, will take the land free from those rights.

The rights of the beneficiaries are not totally lost, however. These rights are transferred to the purchase price. This money will form a trust fund which must be invested. The beneficiaries will now have equitable interests in the trust fund.

8.4.2 Overreaching where there is a strict settlement

In 7.6.1 I gave you an example where land was granted at some time between 1926 and 1996, 'to Alfred for life, remainder to Brian for life, remainder to Charles in fee simple'. I also explained (the possibly surprising point) that under the Settled Land Act 1925, Alfred ('the life tenant in possession') is trustee of the legal estate in the land for himself and the other beneficiaries. Now we meet another possibly surprising point arising from the Settled Land Act 1925. By virtue of his status as 'life tenant', Alfred can sell the land, and the rights of Brian, Charles (and Alfred) **will be overreached**.

There is one condition, which may at this stage strike you as slightly odd. To achieve overreaching, the purchaser must pay the purchase price not to Alfred (who might squander the money) **but to independent people**, called 'trustees of the settlement for the purposes of the Settled Land Act'.

These 'SLA trustees' (who will have been appointed by the settlor in case there is a sale) must invest the proceeds of sale. In effect, a trust fund is created with those proceeds, **and the fund is regarded as representing the land**. During his life, Alfred, instead of enjoying the benefits from the land, will get the income from the trust fund. On Alfred's death, Brian will be entitled to the income from the fund. When Brian dies, Charles (or his successors if Charles is dead) will be entitled to the 'fee simple' in the fund. The fund will be claimed from the SLA trustees, and the trust will be at an end.

> **? QUESTION** 8.6
>
> In 1985, 'Widetrees' (a very attractive Nottinghamshire farm) was made the subject of a strict settlement. The land was granted 'to Richard for life, remainder to Winifred for life, remainder to Yorick in fee simple'. Last month Richard sold Widetrees to Philip. Philip paid the purchase price to Tam and Tom, who were the 'trustees for the purposes of the Settled Land Act'. Richard died last week.
>   Winifred and Yorick feel hard done by: 'We have been defrauded of our land,' they complain. What would you say in answer to their complaint?

You would first remind them that they were **given** their interests under the settlement, perhaps citing the old proverb, 'Don't look a gift-horse in the mouth'. Then you would stress that the law expressly allowed Richard to sell the land, **but did not allow him to keep the proceeds.** Tam and Tom must now invest the proceeds and pay the income from the investments to Winifred. When Winifred dies, Yorick will become outright owner of the investments.

8.4.3 Overreaching where there is a trust for sale

At 2.4.2 we had a basic explanation of the trust for sale. We also considered an example: Greenacres was conveyed by X to Tim and Tom as Trustees with a direction that they must sell the property and invest the proceeds; the investments are to be held in trust for X's children. Where there is a trust for sale the process of overreaching is very simple to follow. When the trustees actually decide to sell, the purchase price is paid to the trustees themselves. The only condition is that there must be at least two trustees. In the example just given, any purchaser will get the land free from the rights of X's children provided they pay the money to Tim and Tom. Tim and Tom then invest that money and hold the fund for the benefit of X's children. What could be simpler!

8.4.3.1 Overreaching where there is a new-style trust of land

This is in essence very simple, and works in the same way as overreaching worked with a trust for sale. As with 'old' trusts for sale, there must be a minimum of two trustees.

Suppose in 2003 Samuel conveys Whiteacre to Terry and Tammy, to hold on trust for Flossy (his lady-friend) for life, remainder to their child Lavinia. Under the new-style trust which arises, Terry and Tammy have the **power** to sell the land at any time. Any purchaser of Whiteacre will buy the land from the trustees and pay the purchase price to the trustees. On paying the price to the trustees, the equitable interests of Flossy and Lavinia will be overreached.

8.4.4 Overreaching on a sale by personal representatives

This is a point where land law and succession law overlap, and it need be dealt with only briefly. As I explained in 2.5.2.1, where a person dies his affairs are wound up by personal representatives, who will be either executors or administrators. Almost all deceased persons leave some debts (even if it's only the gas and electricity bills). Moreover, if the deceased was wealthy, there may be a huge taxation bill to pay. The personal representatives of the deceased have a completely free hand to sell whatever assets of the deceased they like so that they can pay the debts and/or taxes.

If the personal representatives sell any land owned by the deceased, the purchaser will always get a good title. The rights of people left property by the will are always overreached. Moreover, a purchaser from personal representatives is under no duty to check whether a sale is really necessary.

Suppose George (a fairly wealthy widower) has just died. His will appoints Eddie and Edwina to be his executors. He leaves his large house, 'High Manor', to his son Alfred. The 'residue' (i.e., the rest) of his property he leaves to be divided equally between his three daughters, Betty, Cath, and Diana.

Eddie and Edwina need to sell something in order to pay debts/taxes. The 'residue' consists almost entirely of shares in small family private companies. Such shares are not easy to sell. They therefore sell High Manor. Alfred cannot object to the sale. He will however, be able to claim compensation (the value of High Manor) out of the residue.

Suppose, however, that the residue consists of shares in large public limited companies ('PLCs') quoted on the stock exchange. Such shares are very easy to sell. Eddie and Edwina still choose to sell High Manor. They are perfectly within their powers to do so. The purchaser (who, remember, need not check whether a sale is necessary) will get a good title and Alfred will still have to claim compensation out of the residue.

8.4.5 Overreaching on a sale by a mortgagee of mortgaged land

This point can be left until we deal with the law of mortgages in **Chapter 30**.

8.5 Equitable interests still subject to the doctrine of notice

Quite a few such interests remain, indeed rather more than was anticipated by the 1925 legislators:

(a) An equitable fee simple under a bare trust.

(b) An equitable mortgage where the mortgagee does take the title deeds. (We will come back to this one later; there will be very few, if any of these rights **created** after 1989.)

(c) A restrictive covenant created before 1926.

(d) A restrictive covenant contained in a lease.

(e) An equitable easement or equitable profit created before 1926.

(f) A right of entry for breach of a condition subsequent.

(g) A licence by estoppel (proprietary estoppel).

(h) A right under a constructive trust.

With respect to categories (g) and (h) above, the decision of the Court of Appeal in *Lloyds Bank* v *Carrick* [1996] 4 All ER 630, should be noted. B contracted to sell a long lease of a maisonette to S. A deed transferring the lease was never executed. However S paid the price, took possession, and (it appears) spent a lot of money upon the property. B later mortgaged the lease to the Bank.

S had never registered her 'estate contract' to purchase the lease as a class C(iv) land charge. Her estate contract was therefore void as against the Bank. However S claimed that, in addition to her estate contract, she also had a constructive trust or proprietary estoppel interest which would be binding on the Bank under the doctrine of notice as it had not made adequate enquiries.

The Court of Appeal rejected S's claim. It held that if a person acquires an estate contract to purchase a property, that person cannot in addition claim a constructive trust or proprietary estoppel interest, however much money and/or effort he/she has expended.

Lloyds Bank v *Carrick* should be contrasted with *Yaxley* v *Gotts* [2000] Ch 162; [2000] 1 All ER 711; [1999] 3 WLR 1217. In *Yaxley* v *Gotts* P entered into a purely oral 'contract' to purchase a building. This contract was rendered void by s. 2 of the Law of Property (Miscellaneous Provisions) Act 1989, so **P had no estate contract interest in the land**. Nevertheless, on the faith of the supposed 'contract', P spent a lot of money and effort on reconstructing the building. P was held to have acquired a constructive trust interest! Note that P, who never had a valid contract to buy, ends up better off than S in *Carrick*, who did have a contract!

 CONCLUDING REMARKS

In this chapter we have seen that, in an endeavour to reduce the importance of the equitable doctrine of notice, the 1925 legislators decreed that several important equitable interests should be registrable as land charges, and that other interests (especially interests under a trust of land) should be overreachable. But the doctrine of notice **was not abolished**.

As we have just seen, there are quite a few rights still subject to the doctrine. It is particularly worth noting that (statistically) there are still a lot of 'old' (pre-1926) restrictive covenants in existence. However, it is the explosion of rights in the last two categories just listed ((g) and (h)) which (more than anything) accounts for the continued importance of the doctrine of notice. Indeed, constructive trust interests occur so frequently that they can be described as 'commonplace'. I should add, though, that rights under a constructive trust can sometimes be overreached. How this can come about will have to wait until we consider the law of co-ownership (see 16.4).

■ SUMMARY

Third party rights which may exist against land which is unregistered title can be divided into five categories:

A   Legal interests which are good against the whole world. The vast majority of legal interests still fall into this category.

B   Legal interests which are (anomalously) registrable as land charges. There only three types of right in this category—pusine mortgages; legal aid charges; charges for inheritance tax.

C   Equitable interests registrable as land charges. The most important types of right in this category are post-1925 restrictive covenants and matrimonial home rights. Note also post-1925 equitable easements and post-1925 equitable profits come into this category.

D   Equitable interests which are overreachable. This category includes not only rights of beneficiaries under 'new-style' trusts of land but also rights of beneficiaries under 'old-style' trusts for sale and strict settlements.

E   Rights subject to the doctrine of notice. This (in particular) includes pre-1926 restrictive covenants, constructive trust interests, and licences by estoppel (proprietary estoppel).

Where a right is registrable as a land charge, the doctrine of notice does not apply. If the right has been registered on the land charges register computer at Plymouth against the correct name, it will bind all purchasers, mortgages, etc. If it has not been correctly registered, then it will be void against purchasers (and mortgagees), **even though the purchaser may know of the right from some other source.** It is the state of the computer which matters—not the state of mind of the purchaser.

 CHAPTER 8: ASSESSMENT EXERCISE

In 1960 Ruth purchased the fee simple in Grand Villa, a large country house with two acres of grounds. The title was unregistered in an area which did not become an area of compulsory registration until 1988. Grand Villa was conveyed to Ruth in her sole name.

Four weeks ago William purchased Grand Villa from Ruth. Since the execution of the conveyance, the following matters have come to light.

(a) Martin, Ruth's husband, has returned from an extended business trip to Malaysia, and is alarmed to discover that Ruth has sold Grand Villa to William. Martin claims that, since in 1980 he paid £200,000 for a total reconstruction of Grand Villa, he has 'rights' which bind William.

(b) David has arrived at Grand Villa and has produced a document (not in the form of a deed) which Ruth and David signed six months ago. The document is a lease for fifteen years of part of the grounds of Grand Villa.

(c) Harry, owner of neighbouring Blackview, has arrived at Grand Villa and produced a deed executed some time in the 1920s. (The exact date is difficult to read.) This deed was executed by the then owner of Grand Villa, and contains a restrictive covenant in favour of the owners of Blackview to the effect that Grand Villa is to be used for residential purposes only. William plans to convert Grand Villa into a conference centre.

Advise William as to whether any of these matters will affect him.

See Appendix for a specimen answer.

■ **FURTHER READING**

For an excellent collection of materials relating to the complexities of **Land Charges** registration see Maudsley and Burn, *Cases and Materials on Land Law*, eighth edition, pages 29–51.

For a discussion of the modern relevance of overreaching, *see Megarry and Wade: Law of Real Property* (sixth edition by Charles Harpum) pages 125–130.

PART III

Registration of Title

9 Registration of title—the basic principles

9.1 Objectives

By the end of this chapter you should:

1 Be able to explain the circumstances in which the title to a fee simple estate must be registered

2 Be able to explain the circumstances in which the title to a leasehold estate must be registered

3 Appreciate what happens when there is a first registration of an estate

4 Be able to distinguish between the various 'grades of title' granted by the Land Registry

9.2 Introduction

The discussion in **Chapters 6, 7,** and **8** focused exclusively on the legal principles which relate to land which is unregistered title. In view of the fact that the whole country is now an area of compulsory registration this may seem a rather artificial approach. However, you should always remember two things. First, there is still a lot of land which is unregistered title. Secondly, in order to understand the principles of registered land, some understanding of the principles governing unregistered land is essential. Unless there is further radical reform in English land law, I cannot see it ever being possible for land law teachers to ignore the principles governing unregistered title.

The Land Registration Act 2002 certainly makes major changes to the law, **but does not make the principles governing unregistered title obsolete.** The Land Registration Act 2002 received the royal assent in February 2002 and came into force on 13 October 2003.

The 2002 Act makes major changes to the law which I deal with in this chapter, and also impacts on **Chapters 10, 21, 22, 24, 25,** and **33.** The Act is meant to pave the way for the eventual introduction of 'electronic conveyancing'. When this system is introduced, land will no longer be bought and sold through paper documents such as contracts and deeds. Instead everything will be done through computers. In effect, computers in lawyers' offices and the Land Registry's own computers will be linked up to form a gigantic electronic conveyancing network.

No definite date has been set for the commencement of this futuristic system of electronic conveyancing. In the meantime, we must grapple with the substantive law, as amended by the

2002 Act. In this chapter we will be dealing with the basic principles which govern the substantive registration of **estates** in land.

The position of 'third party rights' (restrictive covenants, constructive trust interests, etc.) will be discussed in **Chapter 10**.

9.3 Categories of rights in registered land

With registered land, the division of property rights into legal rights and equitable rights is (while not irrelevant) of less importance than with unregistered land. For most purposes rights in registered land divide into four categories: Employing the terminology of the Land Registration Act **1925**, they are:

(a) **Estates and interests capable of substantive** registration (i.e. the estate registered has a separate file at the registry with a separate title number).

  (i) Prior to 13 October 2003. Fees simple and leases over 21 years;

  (ii) After 12 October 2003. Fees simple; leases over seven years; expressly created profits whether or not the servient land is registered title; expressly created easements where the servient land is registered title.

(b) **Overriding interests:** for example, short legal leases; easements arising by prescription. These interests bind the registered proprietor and any purchaser from him irrespective of:

  (i) whether they are entered on the register in any way;

  (ii) whether the proprietor knew or ought to have known of them.

(*Cf*. **legal interests** in unregistered land.)

(c) **Minor interests**: for example, restrictive covenants; estate contracts. These interests bind the purchaser of a registered title only if they are 'protected' in some way by an entry on the **register of title**. (Rather confusingly, overreachable equitable interests are also classified as 'minor' interests. They are, as with unregistered title, overreached provided the purchase price is paid to the correct trustees.)

(d) **Mortgage by registered charge**: the standard form of registered land mortgage.

9.3.1 The (clumsy) terminology used by the Land Registration Act 2002

The four-fold classification of property rights just discussed existed under the Land Registration Act 1925, and continues to exist under the Land Registration Act 2002. However, the 2002 Act has made two clumsy changes in terminology.

With respect to category (b) above, the new Act does not talk of 'overriding interests', but rather of '**Unregistered interests which override registered dispositions**'. See (in particular) the heading to Sch. 3 of the new Act. We have six words to denote an absolutely crucial concept, where two words used to suffice.

With respect to category (c) the position is even worse. The two word phrase 'minor interests' does not appear in the LRA 2002. Officially, we should now talk of '**Third party rights which need to be protected by an entry on the register**'—14 words in place of two.

I hope readers (including fellow land law teachers) will not be surprised to find that I am continuing to stick with the old terminology. Apart from the obvious point, 'the old phrases are simpler', there is another strong argument for adhering to the old terminology. All the cases I will be referring to in **Chapter 10** were decided under the old 1925 Act, and those cases use the old terminology.

9.4 Circumstances in which registration is compulsory

Though we touched on this in **Chapter 2**, it would be a good idea if we recapped, and added one or two new points.

9.4.1 Compulsory registration

9.4.1.1 The position prior to the commencement of s. 2 of the Land Registration Act 1997

The estate transferred (or created) had to be registered if there had been:

(a) a conveyance on sale of a fee simple;

(b) a grant of a lease for more than 21 years, even if the estate in reversion was not registered;

(c) an assignment of a lease with more than 21 years unexpired, even if the estate in reversion was not registered.

9.4.1.2 Land Registration Act 1997, s. 2

Section 2 (amending s. 123 of the Land Registration Act 1925) came into force on 1 April 1998. In addition to the transactions mentioned in 9.4.1.1, the following transactions with a fee simple estate or with a lease with more than 21 years to run rendered the fee simple or lease subject to compulsory registration:

(d) a deed of gift;

(e) an assent executed by personal representatives;

(f) a first legal mortgage where the mortgagee takes possession of the title deeds.

9.4.1.3 The impact of the Land Registration Act 2002 (see esp. s. 4)

The 2002 Act makes TWO significant extensions to the principle of compulsory registration.

Leases granted for more than seven years; leases with more than seven years to run

To understand this change, you must know the economic background. Leases of commercial premises such as shops, offices, and factories have always been a major feature of English commercial and industrial life. Until relatively recently, the typical commercial lease was for at least 25 years. However, particularly in the last 20 years, the length of commercial leases has reduced considerably. Neither business landlords nor business tenants want to commit themselves for long periods. The average length of a commercial lease is now only (about) 10 years.

The Law Commission, the Land Registry, and the Government all felt that medium length commercial leases should be subject to compulsory registration. Therefore, as from 13 October 2003:

(a) any grant of a new lease for more than seven years;

(b) any assignment (or first legal mortgage) of an existing lease with more than seven years to run,

is subject to compulsory registration.

These changes (which apply to all types of properties not just commercial properties) mean a lot more work for the Land Registry. But two things should be noted. Firstly, the business community may try to avoid the new rules by making new commercial lettings last **exactly** seven years. Secondly, except in situation (b) above, existing leases for between seven and 21 years will not be subject to compulsory registration.

Express grants of easements and profits

This change, tucked away in s. 27(2)(d) of the new Act, is a completely new departure. Hitherto, easements and profits have usually been overriding interests incapable of substantive registration. Hitherto, if (say) by agreement with your neighbour he granted you by deed a perpetual right of way over his land to improve the access to your land, you did not have to register the easement at the district Land Registry.

Now, under the new law, if (after the commencement of the new Act):

(a) there is an **express** grant by deed of an easement or profit to last for ever or for a term of years; and

(b) the **servient** land is already registered title;

then the easement or profit will have to be substantively registered.

This (untrumpeted) major change creates a lot more work for dominant owners, their legal advisers, and for the Land Registry.

To complicate matters yet further not all easements (and profits) arise by deliberate conscious agreement between the dominant and servient owners—not all easements are expressly spelt out in a deed. As we shall see in **Chapter 24**, easements can arise by implication—the creation of a new easement is inferred from the circumstances of the sale (or lease) of what becomes the dominant property. Easements (and profits) can also arise by prescription (see **Chapter 25**)—created by the **conduct** of the dominant owner.

Crucially, the compulsion to register new easements and profits does not extend to those created by **implied** grant or by prescription. Worse still, these easements and profits are still normally overriding interests, automatically binding on a purchaser even though they do not appear anywhere on the register.

9.5 Voluntary registration

Prior to 1966, voluntary registration was possible at any time, whatever the circumstances and wherever the land was situated. After 1966, voluntary registration was still permitted without restriction in **compulsory** areas.

In **non-compulsory** areas the Land Registration Act 1966 and rules made under that Act limited voluntary registration to:

(a) exceptional situations such as lost title deeds;

(b) developments where a large area of land was being sold off in at least 20 units. (This used to apply only to housing estates, but in 1982 the rule was extended to all developments.)

With the whole country being now a compulsory area, we are in effect back to the pre-1966 position. Moreover, since 1997 the Land Registry has charged reduced fees for voluntary registrations. It is hoped that landowners (especially those owning large tracts of land) will take advantage of this 'special offer', thus getting a lot of land on to the register sooner than otherwise would be the case. Moreover, as I said in **Chapter 2**, voluntary registration may make the land easier to sell, particularly if the owner intends to subdivide his land and sell it in lots of small units. Furthermore, the Land Registration Act 2002 creates a new incentive to voluntarily register a title; a registered proprietor will under the 2002 Act have much greater protection against the claims of 'squatters' than an unregistered proprietor. (See **Chapter 21**.)

9.6 Register of estates not register of plots

Most foreign systems of land registration (e.g., the much-admired German and Swedish systems) work on the basis that for each plot of land there will be just one file kept at the registry. That file will show who owns the plot of land, all leases of the plot, and all third party rights affecting the plot.

The English system is not as efficient. There are very good geographical 'index maps', but each **estate** in a plot of land (except leases for not more than seven years which cannot be registered) has a separate file.

> **?** **QUESTION** 9.1
>
> Suppose Leonard owns the fee simple in Blue House, situated in central London. He grants a lease of Blue House to Teresa for 100 years. Teresa sub-leases Blue House to Susan for 50 years. How many files will there be in relation to Blue House?

Each of the three estates must be registered separately, and therefore there will be three files. Those files used to be 'hard copy', but nowadays are usually in electronic form.

Another curiosity of the English system of land registration is that one (quite commonly) encounters a situation where a lease is registered, but the fee simple out of which it is derived is not.

> **?** **QUESTION** 9.2
>
> How could this situation arise?

Under the Land Registration Act 2002 this situation arises whenever the owner of an unregistered freehold grants a lease for more than seven years.

(This situation arose under the Land Registration Act 1925 where the landlord purchased his fee simple **before** the relevant area became compulsory, but granted a lease for more than 21 years **after** the area became compulsory. It could also arise where the landlord purchased his fee simple before the relevant area became compulsory, granted a long lease **before** the date set for compulsory registration, and then that lease was assigned with more than 21 years unexpired **after** the area became compulsory.)

The general expansion in the registration of freehold titles will eventually mean that this situation of a registered lease created out of an unregistered freehold will become extremely rare. However, a side effect of the expansion of the registration of leases by the Land Registration Act 2002 is that, in the short term, there will be an increase in the number of cases of a registered lease created out of an unregistered freehold.

9.7 Procedure where a sale or lease gives rise to first registration

The transaction goes through basically as an unregistered transaction, but with additional stages at the end:

(a) The purchaser investigates the title deeds, inspects the land, and searches the Land Charges Register.

(b) The legal title passes on the execution of the conveyance.

(c) The purchaser must apply for first registration within two months of the execution of the conveyance.

(d) If he fails to do so, the legal title revests in the vendor on trust for the purchaser.

(e) The purchaser can then apply for late registration, but he may have to pay a late fee.

9.7.1 Applications for first registration

Failure to register within two months is (unfortunately) not that unusual. The sanctions for failure to register within two months (which are not changed by the 2002 Act) may strike you as both strange and rather weak.

As I have just stated, the legal title revests in the vendor on trust for the purchaser. Yet the vendor has almost certainly moved away, and has no idea of his trustee status! Equally, when the purchaser does belatedly register, the legal title revests in the purchaser without the vendor ever knowing (or needing to know) that he has lost his trustee status!

The only real sanction against late registrations is that the registry **may** charge a late fee.

> **EXERCISE** 9.1
>
> Dumphouse is unregistered title. Joe Gormless now purchases Dumphouse. Joe does his own conveyancing. Dumphouse is conveyed to Joe, but he omits to register his title. Consider when (and by whom) the error is likely to be discovered.

There are I think three possibilities. First, when Joe comes to sell Dumphouse, the new purchaser's solicitor will discover the error. Secondly, if Joe wants to mortgage Dumphouse, the potential lender will investigate Joe's title and discover the error. Thirdly, when Joe dies, his personal representatives will probably discover the error.

On an application for first registration, the purchaser produces all the title deeds to the registry. The Land Registry then conducts its own (very thorough) investigation of title. It decides what grade of title to grant (see 9.8). When in the course of its investigations it discovers (in the deeds or on the Land Charges Register) 'minor interests' such as restrictive covenants, it enters the appropriate notices on the register. ('Notices' will be explained in **Chapter 10**.)

On first and later registrations under the Land Registration Act 1925, the registry issued a **land certificate** to the **registered proprietor**. However, the Land Registration Act 2002 effectively abolishes land certificates.

9.7.2 **What third party interests bind a first registered proprietor?**

When a purchaser buys an unregistered title and then registers that title, his title will, on first registration, be subject only to those third party interests (e.g., easements, restrictive covenants, constructive trust interests) still existing with respect to the land and which are either:

(a) protected by the entry of a notice on the register; or

(b) an overriding interest within Schedule **one** of the Land Registration Act 2002.

It should, however, be stressed that a purchase of an unregistered title which triggers first registration is an **unregistered** transaction with an extra stage tacked on the end. Suppose a purchaser buys an unregistered title which was subject to a third party right, but that right has become void against the purchaser either under the doctrine of notice (**Chapter 7**) or under the Land Charges Act (**Chapter 8**). That right cannot be revived. It will be void, even if either

(a) the registry erroneously enter a notice to 'protect' the right; or

(b) the right, were it still in existence, would be an overriding interest within Sch. 1.

9.7.3 **Procedure on transfer of a registered title**

(a) The vendor proves his title by reference to the register. Note that the purchaser will still have to check whether there are any overriding interests, as these bind him even though they are not usually mentioned on the register.

(b) The vendor executes a document known as a **land transfer**. This must be a deed. It is, for the purposes of the 1925 property legislation, a 'conveyance'. However, unlike a conveyance of unregistered land, a land transfer does not vest the legal title in the purchaser.

(c) The purchaser applies for registration, producing the land transfer. (Prior to the Land Registration Act 2002 the land certificate also had to be produced.)

There is no time limit within which the application must be made. The changing of the files at the registry passes the legal title, though the change in legal ownership is retrospective to the date when application for registration was made. (Prior to 2003, a new land certificate was issued to the new registered proprietor.)

9.8 Grades of title

This is governed by Land Registration Act 2002, ss. 9 and 10.

9.8.1 Freeholds

Once the registry has investigated the title of an applicant for first registration, it can grant to him as registered proprietor one of three grades of title. In almost all cases an **absolute** grade is granted. However, in a significant minority of cases (about 1 per cent of all titles) only a **possessory** grade is granted. A **qualified** grade is also possible, but they are extremely rare.

9.8.1.1 Absolute title

This is the grade of title which is granted where the applicant's title is sound, i.e., the title deeds are in order and it appears that nobody else could possibly claim the land. Where an absolute title is granted, the government (through the agency of the Land Registry) is in effect saying to the registered proprietor (and anybody who wants to buy the land from him) 'We guarantee that you own this land'.

Nevertheless, a fee simple registered with absolute title is subject to:

(a) overriding interests;

(b) minor interests protected by entry on the register;

(c) if the registered proprietor is a trustee, equitable interests under the trust of which he has notice.

9.8.1.2 Possessory title

This is the grade of title which is granted where the applicant for registration's claim to ownership is debatable. It particularly occurs where the title deeds he can produce are inadequate, or if he cannot produce any at all. The applicant may even admit that the land was not originally his, but claim that he now has a title by virtue of 'adverse possession'. (As we saw in 2.5.2.1 when discussing investigation of title, the adverse possession rule means that if somebody has been in control of a piece of land for 12 years, all rival claims are normally automatically destroyed by lapse of time.)

When it is first granted, a possessory title is of only limited comfort to the registered proprietor. The registry is merely accepting that the proprietor is currently in control of the land; it does not guarantee that he is owner. Any rival claimant to the land whose rights have not been time-barred under the adverse possession rule can still reclaim the land.

The great value of a possessory title is in the long term. If somebody is registered with a possessory title to a piece of land and remains in undisputed possession of that land for 12 years after registration, his title will normally be upgraded to 'absolute'. He then (just like any other proprietor with an absolute title) will have a clear guarantee that he is undisputed owner of the land.

9.8.1.3 Qualified title

This grade of title is extremely rare. It is granted where there is some minor question mark over an otherwise sound claim to ownership.

A qualified title is in effect 'absolute but for such-and-such'. A qualified title is the same as absolute, apart from a specified exception against which the proprietor is not guaranteed. This exception (qualification) can be either:

(a) with respect to claims arising before a certain date; or

(b) with respect to claims arising under a specified instrument.

For example, if a document of title was only partly legible, the registry might qualify a grant of title, saying that the proprietor is not protected from claims arising under the partially legible document.

(The paucity of qualified titles may perhaps be explained by the Land Registry's policy on technical defects of title. If there is an application for registration of a title, but there is some technical defect in the documents, e.g., documents going back 13 but not 15 years, the registry usually deliberately ignores the technical defect and grants an absolute title.)

9.8.2 Leaseholds

There are four grades of title which may be granted to a lease: absolute, 'good leasehold', qualified, and possessory. **Possessory leasehold** is granted where the landlord's reversion to the lease is registered with a possessory title. **Qualified leasehold** is virtually unknown. That leaves absolute leasehold and good leasehold, both of which are common, though the percentage of 'good leasehold' should gradually decline.

9.8.2.1 Good leasehold

The existence of the good leasehold grade of title is really an unfortunate by-product of an outdated common law rule which ought to be abolished. That rule is that when a tenant takes a lease (even a very long lease) he is not entitled to examine the landlord's title deeds; neither is he entitled to insist that the deeds be produced to third parties such as the Land Registry. In effect, the tenant must take a chance that the landlord owns the land!

Where a lease for more than seven years is granted out of a reversion which is not registered, the lease must be registered. Normally it can only be registered with good leasehold title, as neither the Registry nor the tenant will have access to the landlord's title deeds. The granting of a good leasehold title guarantees that the lease is valid and that the tenant is owner of that lease, **but only on the assumption** that the lessor's title to the reversion is sound. If it turns out that the landlord was leasing out land which was not his, there is no come-back against the registry!

9.8.2.2 Absolute leasehold

This is an out-and-out guarantee that the lease is valid and that the tenant is owner of the lease. It is in practice granted where either:

(a) the landlord's reversion is already registered with absolute title; or

(b) (rare in practice) the tenant has been able to persuade the landlord to produce his title deeds to the registry. (This may happen if the tenant is some large organization which has made it clear that it will take a lease of the property only if it has access to the title deeds.)

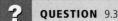 **QUESTION** 9.3

I said at 9.8.2 that 'the percentage of good leasehold should gradually decline'. Why is this so?

Good leasehold is designed for the (currently quite common) situation where the lease is registered but the freehold from which it is derived is not registered. As more and more freeholds are registered, there will be proportionately **fewer** registered leases created out of unregistered freeholds. (See also point (a) below under the heading 'Upgrading of Title'.)

9.8.3 Upgrading of title

This area of law was simplified by the Land Registration Act 1986, and this simplified law has been carried forward into the Land Registration Act 2002. (See ss. 62–64 of the 2002 Act.) In appropriate cases the registered proprietor may apply for an upgrading of his title; but the registrar can (and often does) act without waiting for an application.

Of the four situations listed below, (a) and (b) occur frequently, while (c) and (d) are (in the nature of things) rare.

The registrar may upgrade a title in the following cases:

(a) A good leasehold may be upgraded to absolute if the registrar 'is satisfied as to the title to the freehold and the title to any intermediate leasehold'. In practice, where a registered lease has been created out of an unregistered fee simple, and that fee simple is **later** registered with an absolute title, the lease will be immediately upgraded from good leasehold to absolute.

(b) A possessory freehold may be upgraded to absolute if the title has been registered for 12 years, or the registrar is for some other reason satisfied that the proprietor's title is sound. As indicated at 9.8.1.2, if a possessory title has been registered without challenge for 12 years, it will be upgraded to absolute more or less automatically.

(c) A possessory leasehold may be upgraded to good leasehold if the title has been registered for 12 years.

(d) A qualified title may be upgraded to absolute (or good leasehold) if the registrar is now satisfied that the title is sound.

9.9 The form of the register

 EXERCISE 9.2

The Land Registry has a specimen register entry on its web-site. The easiest way to access this specimen is by going to www.landregisteronline.gov.uk/resources/example_register.pdf. Please study this specimen. You will see that it displays the various characteristics discussed below.

The current form of the Land Register is a file for each title (estate) registered. The file, which is nowadays held electronically, consists of at least four pages. The file is divided into three parts, called:

(a) The Property Register;

(b) The Proprietorship Register;

(c) The Charges Register.

The use of the word 'Register' is in this context very unfortunate. When I first came across it as a student I was totally confused! I thought there were **three** files for each **title** registered! But in fact there is only one file, divided into three **parts**, which I will call the Property Part, the Proprietorship Part, and the Charges Part.

9.9.1 The property part

In this part of the Land Register there is a verbal description of the land, and a reference to the 'file plan'. The boundaries shown on this file plan are normally only 'general', i.e., approximate. (Another feature of English land registration strange to foreign eyes is that our system does not fix the exact boundaries of each plot. The Land Registry like to boast that their plans are **in fact** accurate to within a few inches. No doubt they usually are, but in *Lee* v *Barrey* [1957] Ch 251, there was a discrepancy of eight feet (2.5 m) between the plan and the actual boundary on the ground!)

The property part indicates the estate registered, and in the case of a lease the duration of the lease. In the case of a lease created out of a registered reversion, it will contain a reference to the 'title' (i.e., file) number of that reversion.

If the land is 'dominant' with respect to any easements or restrictive covenants (i.e., benefited by such rights), the existence of such rights may be 'noted' in this section, but unfortunately this 'noting' is not mandatory. (Why 'unfortunately' will become apparent when we deal with the law of restrictive covenants.)

9.9.2 The proprietorship part

This part of the Land Register states the grade of title. It gives the name and address of the registered proprietor(s) and it indicates the 'restrictions' affecting the right to deal with the land. (We consider 'restrictions' in **Chapter 10**.)

9.9.3 **The charges part**

This part of the Land Register contains 'notices' of minor interests such as restrictive covenants. It contains a note of any mortgage by registered charge created out of the estate registered and a note of any other registered estate (i.e., a lease) created out of the estate registered.

9.10 **Land certificates**

Under the pre-2003 law, this was a copy of the relevant register file, which was issued whenever an estate was first registered or was subsequently transferred to a new owner. In principle it was issued to the registered proprietor, but if the estate was mortgaged by registered charge the land certificate was kept at the registry. (In practice, as a result of the rule which operated when the land was mortgaged, an enormous number of certificates were kept at the registry.)

The land certificate was not a 'title deed' or a 'document of title'. As a new certificate was created only when the estate in question was transferred, it might not accurately reflect the current state of the register. A wise purchaser would never therefore rely on the certificate, but would always search the register.

As already noted, the Land Registration Act 2002 **makes no provision for** land certificates.

 CONCLUDING REMARKS

In this chapter we have discussed the rules governing which estates must be registered, what grades of title can be granted, and the form of the register. These rules may be rather dull and mechanical, but they are extremely important. Perhaps the most crucial point is that to talk of 'registered **land**' is, strictly speaking, inaccurate. A piece of land (i.e., the physical area upon which you can walk) is never registered. It is the 'estate(s)' in that land which is or are capable of registration. The extension of compulsory registration to leases for more than seven years, and to express grants of easements and profits, makes this point of even greater importance.

■ **SUMMARY**

Compulsory First Registration

Freeholds. First registration is compulsory when an unregistered freehold is sold, given away, passes by an assent executed by personal representatives, or where there is a first legal mortgage.

New legal leases must be registered if the duration is for more than seven years.

An existing lease must be registered if it is assigned when there is more than seven years of the lease to run.

New legal easements and legal profits must be registered if the servient estate out of which the new right is created is already registered.

Grades of Title

Freeholds are normally granted absolute title. Possessory freehold title is occasionally encountered; freeholds with qualified title are very rare.

Leaseholds will normally be granted absolute leasehold title where the landlord's reversion is registered with absolute title, but only good leasehold title if the landlord's reversion is not registered.

Upgrading of titles

The two common cases of upgrading are:

(a) where a possessory freehold is upgraded to absolute freehold after the registered proprietor has been in possession for 12 years;

(b) where a good leasehold is upgraded to absolute leasehold on the registration of the landlord's reversion with absolute freehold title.

The form of the register

Each registered **estate** has a separate file. That file is in three parts.

The property register identifies the land and indicates the estate registered.

The proprietorship register indicates the name(s) of the registered proprietors.

The charges register indicates mortgages and certain other property rights derived from the registered estate.

■ FURTHER READING

For the thinking which led to the enactment of the Land Registration Act 2002, see Law Commission report no. 271, 'Land Registration for the Twenty-First Century'. This runs to just over 300 pages. However, only parts I, II, III, IV, and IX of the report are relevant to what I have just discussed in chapter 9.

For a highly critical analysis of the Land Registration Act 2002, see the short book by Professor Elizabeth Cooke, '*The New Law of Land Registration*'. Her chapter three is particularly relevant to the matters just discussed.

10 Overriding interests and minor interests

10.1 Objectives

By the end of this chapter you should:

1 Be familiar with the important concept of 'overriding interests' ('unregistered interests which override registered dispositions')

2 Be able to explain the 'actual occupation' overriding interest which used to be governed by Land Registration Act 1925, s. 70(1)(g), and is now governed by Sch. 3, para. 2 of the Land Registration Act 2002, which replaces s. 70(1)(g)

3 Appreciate that 'minor interests' (third party rights which need to be protected by an entry on the register) have an important role to play in registered land

4 Be familiar with the concepts 'notices' and 'restrictions', and be able to distinguish between them

10.2 Introduction

In the previous chapter we saw that with the commencement of the 2002 Act, substantive registration now extends to leases for more than seven years, together with expressly granted easements and profits. What then is the position of short leases, and third party rights such as restrictive covenants, constructive trust interests, and matrimonial home rights?

Leaving aside mortgages of a registered estate (a topic we consider in **Chapter 33**), all third party rights against a registered estate and all short-term leases are either **overriding** or **minor** interests. If a third party right against a registered estate is 'overriding' then it automatically binds all purchasers of that estate. (This is roughly comparable to a legal interest against an unregistered title.) If a third party right is not overriding then it will be a minor interest, and it will be binding on purchasers of the estate only if protected by some kind of entry on the register. (This is roughly comparable to a registrable land charge.)

10.3 Overriding interests

It is extremely important to know whether a third party right (such as a constructive trust interest) is overriding or minor. Overriding interests are a major hazard for any purchaser of a registered title. Such interests do not appear on the register, yet a purchaser is bound by overriding interests affecting the title purchased whether he knew about them or not.

The Land Registration Act 1925 listed out the 'old law' overriding interests in s. 70(1). Section 70(1) consisted of a number of lettered paragraphs. Many of the types of interest listed in s. 70(1) were unimportant; in practice there were five important categories of overriding interest.

One of the avowed purposes of the 2002 Act is to reduce the number of overriding interests which are binding upon the purchaser of a registered title. However, in my view, the 2002 Act achieves this purpose only to a very limited degree.

The 2002 Act further complicates matters by containing **two**, slightly differing, lists of overriding interests. Schedule 1 lists 'unregistered interests which override first registration', while schedule 3 lists 'unregistered interests which override registered dispositions'. The limited practical significance of schedule 1 has already been discussed, see 9.7.2 above.

It is Sch. 3 which is of overwhelming long-term importance, and I will focus my discussion on that schedule. The new list of overriding interests set out in Sch. 3 of the 2002 Act, consists of 14 numbered paragraphs. Schedule 3 is almost as long as the 'old' s. 70(1) of the 1925 Act.

A number of unimportant overriding interests have been abolished. However, of the five important categories of overriding interests in the 1925 Land Registration Act, only one is abolished. The one abolished is that in the old s. 70(1)(f) 'rights acquired or in the course of being acquired under the limitation acts'. How the law of adverse possession applies to registered land both before and after the 2002 Act will be explained in the latter part of **Chapter 21**.

Of the remaining four important overriding interests, one, **Local Land Charges**, is retained unchanged. (See Sch. 3, para. 6.) The other three categories are:

(a) **Easements and Profits;**

(b) **Short-Term Legal Leases;**

(c) **Property Rights of a Person in Actual Occupation.**

These have all been reduced in their scope but will continue to be of fundamental importance.

The discussion in the following sections will be confined to the four (remaining) important categories of overriding interest. For reasons which will become apparent it will be necessary (except with Local Land Charges) to first explain the 'old' law and then consider the 'new' law.

10.3.1 Local land charges

(Previously Land Registration Act 1925, s. 70(1)(i), now Land Registration Act 2003, Sch. 3, para. 6.)

Local land charges have not been mentioned before, as they are a matter peripheral to a study of pure land law. Each District Council in England and Wales keeps a register of local land charges, and the system of local charges operates irrespective of whether title to the land is registered or unregistered. Thus, when buying land, the wise purchaser always 'does a local search'.

What sort of matters are local land charges? Basically they cover 'public law' rights such as the special charge which sometimes exists for the making up of a road; the 'listing' of a building as of historic interest; tree preservation orders, and many other matters connected with town and country planning.

10.3.2 Easements and profits (old law)

The relevant 'old' provision is Land Registration Act 1925 s. 70(1)(a). As far as material, this read, '. . . profits à prendre, . . . and easements not being equitable easements required to be protected by notice on the register'.

The wording of s. 70(1)(a) was somewhat archaic, but certain consequences were clear:

(a) A legal profit was an overriding interest.

(b) An equitable profit was also an overriding interest. (Contrast unregistered land, where an equitable profit is registrable as a land charge.)

(c) A legal easement was an overriding interest.

That left equitable easements. Now on the wording of paragraph (a) you are probably thinking, as everybody used to think, that equitable easements were not overriding interests but minor interests, and that to be binding upon a purchaser they needed to be protected by an entry on the register. However, in *Thatcher* v *Douglas* (1996) 146 NLJ 282, the Court of Appeal, by some rather strained logic, managed to hold that an equitable easement was an overriding interest within s. 70(1)(a).

10.3.3 Easements and profits (new law)

Perhaps the most difficult feature of the whole of the 2002 Act is its treatment of easements and profits.

10.3.3.1 All easements and profits already existing against a registered estate at the commencement of the new Act

Easements and profits already existing against a registered title (and there must be a huge number of such rights) will continue to be governed by the old LRA 1925, s. 70(1)(a) and the case law interpreting that provision. (See Sch. 12, para. 9 of the LRA 2002.) So (subject to the doubts regarding *Thatcher* v *Douglas*) all 'old' easements and profits, however they were created, and whether they are legal or equitable, continue to be overriding interests after 12 October 2003. However, after 12 October 2006 these 'existing easements and profits' will be subject to the 'permanent' rules which I discuss in 10.3.3.4 part (b). In certain (very limited circumstances) an easement existing on 13 October 2003 could, as from 13 October 2006, lose its overriding status.

10.3.3.2 Easements and profits expressly granted after the commencement of the new Act

As already explained in the previous chapter, s. 27(2)(d) (in effect) requires all new **express grants** of easements and profits (created out of a registered title) to be substantively registered. If a dominant owner of an easement or profit fails to substantively register his right, the easement or profit will take effect only as an equitable interest.

10.3.3.3 Equitable easements and equitable profits created after the commencement of the new Act are always minor interests

Schedule 3, para. 3 refers only to legal easements and legal profits. So an equitable easement or an equitable profit which arises either:

(a) because there is an **express grant** which the dominant owner fails to substantively register; or

(b) because the easement or profit is to endure only for the life or lives of a person(s); or

(c) because a written contract not in the form of a deed creates the right,

cannot be an overriding interest.

It follows that all equitable easements arising after the commencement of the 2002 Act will be minor interests, which will only bind a purchaser if the dominant owner has entered a 'Notice' on the register protecting his right.

10.3.3.4 Legal easements and profits created by implied grant or prescription

As indicated in the previous chapter, easements may arise **by implication**—the creation of an easement is inferred from the circumstances of the sale (or lease) of what becomes the dominant property. Easements (and profits) can also arise **by prescription**—created by the **conduct** of the dominant owner.

(a) Transitional period of three years from the commencement of the LRA 2002

As a result of Sch. 12, para. 10 of the LRA 2002 all **new** legal easements and profits arising by implication or by prescription in this transitional period of three years will automatically be overriding interests for the transitional period. Once that transitional period is over (in October 2006) these implied or prescriptive easements or profits will become subject to the permanent rules set out under (b) below.

(b) Permanent provisions for easements and profits arising by implied grant or prescription

The Law Commission, in its consultations which preceded the 2002 Act, was very concerned about the plight of a purchaser who buys a piece of land and then discovers that the land is subject to easements and/or profits which have not been exercised for some years.

Refer back to **Chapter 6** (at 6.3 and 6.3.1) where I tell a story of my buying High Chimneys and then finding that the land is subject to a right of way which has not been exercised for five years and a profit of pasture which has not been exercised for eight years. High Chimneys was unregistered title, but unfortunately (for me) the result would be the same if Vanessa had been the registered proprietor. Norman's easement and Philip's profit would both be overriding interests under schedule 3 and therefore (in principle) binding on me.

The new 'permanent rules' for easements and profits are set out in LRA 2002, Sch. 3, para. 3. In principle, a legal easement or profit arising by implied grant or prescription will only be overriding if any one of the following three conditions is fulfilled.

(a) the purchaser had 'actual knowledge' of the easement or profit on the date of the land transfer in his favour; or

(b) the existence of the right would have been apparent 'on a reasonably careful inspection of the land over which the easement or profit is exercisable' (e.g., a worn track leading to the dominant land); or

(c) if the easement or profit has been exercised at least once in the year prior to the land transfer. (So one journey at 0300 in the morning would be enough to preserve the overriding status of a right of way!)

EXERCISE 10.1

The new rules as to when easements and profits will be overriding interests are being trumpeted as a major reform 'which will make life easier for purchasers of registered land'. I do not agree with this view—why do I not agree?

Firstly, I am sure you will agree that the 'new' rules are extremely complicated.

Secondly, as a result of these new rules, only a very few legal easements and profits will be excluded from being overriding interests. The new rules exclude from being overriding only an (undiscovered) legal easement or profit which has neither:

(a) left physical evidence on the land of its existence; nor

(b) been exercised at least once in the year before the land transfer.

? **QUESTION** 10.1

Go back to my High Chimneys example in 6.3 and 6.3.1. Assume that I purchase in 2008, that Vanessa was registered proprietor of High Chimneys, but the facts regarding Norman's easement and Philip's profit are the same as before. Will I be bound by their rights even though:

(a) I had no knowledge of their rights; and

(b) I could not have possibly discovered those rights by inspecting the land; and

(c) Those rights have not been exercised for several years?

I will not be bound. But note that I would be bound by the easement if Norman had used his right of way just once (perhaps at the dead of night) in the year before my purchase. Similarly, I would be bound by the profit if Philip, in the last year, had left just one sheep in the garden for perhaps a few hours, perhaps while Vanessa was away on holiday.

10.3.4 Short-term legal leases (old law)

The 'old law' overriding interest was set out in Land Registration Act 1925, s. 70(1)(k), which read, '**leases granted for a term not exceeding twenty-one years**'.

Section 70(1)(k) was an enormously important category of overriding interest, and there are a number of points which must (still) be noted carefully.

First, the Land Registration Act 1925, s. 70(1)(k) must not in any circumstances be confused with s. 70(1)(g) of the same Act, which we will be considering shortly! (Depending on the circumstances a lease might have come within both paragraphs, one but not the other, or neither!)

Secondly, it is clear that paragraph **(k)** was confined to legal leases. An equitable lease could **never** be overriding within s. 70(1)(k) (though, as we shall see, it may well have come within s. 70(1)(g)).

Thirdly, and perhaps most importantly, a legal lease for not more than 21 years (and that includes periodic tenancies) was automatically an overriding interest within s. 70(1)(k). This was so even if the tenant was **currently not occupying** the property. It was also so even if the tenant refused to tell enquirers what his rights were with respect to the land.

10.3.5 Short-term leases (new law)

The old s. 70(1)(k) is replaced by Sch. 3, para. 1, which makes overriding all legal leases for a duration not exceeding **seven** years. As before, the short **legal** lease will be overriding irrespective of whether the tenant is occupying the property and irrespective of whether or not the tenant tells any enquirers that he has rights in the land.

The reduction of the short lease period from 21 to seven years is the natural corollary of the decision to make all leases **over seven years** substantively registrable. But two special points should be noted. Firstly, legal leases for between seven and twenty-one years already in existence on the day the new Act commences will continue to be overriding interests. (Sch. 12, para. 12.) Put another way, on the commencement date (13 October 2003) there was no need for lessees with leases between seven and 21 years to rush off and substantively register.

Secondly, what happens if, after the commencement of the new Act, a lease is granted by deed for (say) **ten** years and the lessee takes possession but fails to substantively register the lease? The lease will not be totally void; it will take effect in equity, and (ironically) it might well still be an overriding interest under Sch. 3, para. 2 (property rights of a person in actual occupation).

10.3.6 Property rights of a person in actual occupation—a very different kind of overriding interest

The Land Registration Act 1925, s. 70(1)(g) set out the following overriding interest:

The rights of every person in actual occupation of the land or in receipt of the rents and profits thereof, save where enquiry is made of such person and the rights are not disclosed.

The Society of Legal Scholars (the University Law Lecturers' professional association) recommended to the Law Commission that the s. 70(1)(g) overriding interest should be repealed **without replacement**. That would have meant a considerable simplification in the law. But the Commission (and Parliament) rejected this advice. Instead, they have replaced s. 70(1)(g) with a new provision, LRA 2002, Sch. 3, para. 2 (set out in **10.3.8**), which is similar to but more complex than s. 70(1)(g).

I propose to consider s. 70(1)(g) in some depth, even though it has now disappeared from the statute book. The 'new' more complex provision cannot be understood without a knowledge of the old law. In particular, a large amount of case law has developed around the 'old' provision especially as to the meaning of 'actual occupation', and there can be no real doubt that (with one exception) this old case law will equally be applicable to the new provision.

Even 30 years ago, the extreme importance of s. 70(1)(g) was not fully realized by many lawyers. Indeed, some did not really see its significance until the decision of the House of Lords in *Williams and Glyn's Bank Ltd* v *Boland* [1980] 2 All ER 408. Before we consider *Boland's* case, the following story illustrates the impact of s. 70(1)(g). (Although written with reference to the old law, the new law Sch. 3 para. 2 would produce the same result.)

10.3.6.1 **A tale of two fields**

Letitia owned in fee simple two adjoining fields, Upper Field and Redwood Field. Because she acquired Upper Field a long time ago and Redwood Field only recently, Upper Field is **unregistered** title, while Redwood Field is **registered** title.

In 2001 Letitia met Terri. They signed an agreement under which Letitia agreed to lease both fields to Terri for 10 years. Terri took possession of both fields, and has remained in possession, cultivating both fields assiduously. However, as the agreement was not in the form of a deed, Terri had only an equitable lease of the two fields. Moreover, Terri had not taken any legal advice, and therefore she had not taken any steps to register her equitable lease as a land charge.

In 2002 Letitia sold both fields to Rachel for £30,000. Rachel knew that Terri was occupying the fields, but did not ask Terri what right(s) she (Terri) claimed over the fields. Rachel wanted to evict Terri as quickly as possible.

QUESTION 10.2

Did Terri's equitable lease bind Rachel?

Your answer to this question may have required some thought. The answer is both 'No' and 'Yes'. The answer with respect to Upper Field is 'No'. Terri should have registered her equitable lease as a land charge. As she did not, it was void against a purchaser for money or money's worth. It was void even against a purchaser who knew of her equitable lease. (Remember *Hollington* v *Rhodes* and *Midland Bank* v *Green* at 8.3.)

The answer with respect to Redwood Field is 'Yes'. Terri was in 'actual occupation' of that field. Rachel never asked her what her rights were. Thus she had an overriding interest within s. 70(1)(g). (Under the new law she would have an overriding interest under Sch. 3, para. 2.)

If Terri had not been occupying Redwood Field, her equitable lease would have been only a 'minor interest' which would have needed protection by an entry on the register of title. But as she was occupying the field, s. 70(1)(g) promoted her interest into an overriding interest. If, however, Rachel had, before buying Redwood Field, made enquiries of Terri, and Terri had replied, 'Go to B . . .!', Terri's rudeness would have deprived her of her overriding interest.

10.3.7 **Case law under the old s. 70(1)(g)**

10.3.7.1 *Williams and Glyn's Bank Ltd* v *Boland* [1981] AC 487

The material facts of this case are very simple. Mr Boland ('H') bought a house, registered title, in his sole name. His wife ('W') made substantial contributions to the cost of acquisition, and therefore acquired a constructive trust interest in the house.

While H and W were living happily together in the house, H decided to borrow some more money. Without telling his wife, he borrowed it from the bank. He granted the bank a mortgage by registered charge. The bank did not bother to send an employee to the house, and certainly did not ask W any questions.

H defaulted on repaying the loan, and the bank wished to enforce its mortgage by taking possession of the house and selling. Was W's interest binding on the bank? If it was, the bank was effectively prevented from enforcing its security.

To almost audible groans from all the big banks (*Boland* was very much a test case) the House of Lords unanimously held that W's constructive trust interest was an overriding interest by virtue of s. 70(1)(g) of the Land Registration Act 1925 and was therefore binding on the bank.

Their Lordships, in a judgment given by Lord Wilberforce, clarified a number of points about s. 70(1)(g) and related matters. The first two points should be noted in particular, as they may come as a bit of a surprise:

(a) Their Lordships pointed out (what land lawyers already knew) that the equitable doctrine of notice had no application to registered land.

(b) It therefore followed that, as 'the rule in *Hunt* v *Luck*' (see 6.4.4.2) is part of the equitable doctrine of notice, s. 70(1)(g) is not 'the rule in *Hunt* v *Luck*'. Section 70(1)(g) is a rule for registered land akin to (but not necessarily identical with) *Hunt* v *Luck*.

(c) The word 'rights' in s. 70(1)(g) should be construed to cover every proprietary interest in land. Every type of property right in land can be an overriding interest provided there is actual occupation at the relevant time by its owner. The only exception was rights of occupation under the Matrimonial Homes Acts, which were expressly excluded from the scope of s. 70(1)(g) by s. 2(8)(b) of the Matrimonial Homes Act 1983. (Similarly, s. 31(10)(b) of the Family Law Act 1996 excluded 'matrimonial home rights' from the scope of s. 70(1)(g).)

(d) As 'rights' in s. 70(1)(g) includes all proprietary rights (except matrimonial home rights), the word 'rights' includes an equitable interest arising by way of constructive trust where Y has contributed substantially to the cost of acquisition of property the legal title to which is registered in X's name. Thus, although Mrs Boland's rights of occupation (matrimonial home rights) under the Matrimonial Homes Act 1983 could not be overriding, her **entirely separate** constructive trust interest could be overriding within s. 70(1)(g).

(e) The words 'actual occupation' must be construed literally.

(f) Consequently, if a registered proprietor is occupying the property but members of his family (or even strangers) are living there too, these members of the family or strangers **are 'in actual occupation'**. Their Lordships rejected the argument that where the registered proprietor is in actual occupation, nobody else can be.

(g) Their Lordships very strongly disapproved *Caunce* v *Caunce* [1969] 1 All ER 722. The material facts of that case were identical to those in *Boland*, except that the title to the house was unregistered. The judge held that, for the purposes of the rule in *Hunt* v *Luck*, W was not in occupation of the home and that therefore the mortgagee did not have constructive notice of her equitable interest. *Caunce* has never been formally overruled, but everybody (particularly legal advisers to purchasers and mortgagees) acts on the assumption that it is wrong.

10.3.7.2 *Abbey National Building Society* v *Cann* [1991] AC 56

This more recent House of Lords case further clarified s. 70(1)(g), especially the meaning of 'actual occupation'. The essential facts of the case are as follows. George Cann purchased a maisonette in his sole name. His mother (who lived with him) made a substantial contribution to the cost of acquisition and thus was entitled to a constructive trust interest.

At about 11.45 a.m. on 13 August ('the date of completion') furniture removers acting on behalf of Mrs Cann started laying carpets and bringing in her furniture. (She was on holiday in the Netherlands.) At 12.20 p.m. the same day, a land transfer was executed in favour of George. As is normal in these situations, he immediately executed a mortgage in favour of the building society. The society were of course lending a substantial proportion of the purchase price, and were taking the mortage as security for the loan.

Both the land transfer and the mortgage were registered on 13 September ('the date of registration'), by which time Mrs Cann was living in the maisonette with her son. (A delay of one month before registration is by no means excessive.)

As you have probably guessed, George defaulted in repaying the loan. Mrs Cann then claimed that her constructive trust interest was an overriding interest under s. 70(1)(g) binding on the building society.

The first issue which their Lordships had to decide was, on what date a person must be in 'actual occupation' to have an overriding interest under s. 70(1)(g) binding upon a purchaser/mortgagee. Was it the date of completion of the sale or mortgage, or was it the (inevitably later) date of registration? Their Lordships held in favour of the 'date of completion'; on the facts of the case, 12.20 p.m. on 13 August.

The second issue then had to be considered. Was Mrs Cann in occupation at that time (after all, men were fitting her carpets and bringing in her furniture)? Their Lordships found that this activity did not amount to 'actual occupation'.

10.3.7.3 The meaning of actual occupation

Lord Oliver, who delivered the only reasoned speech in *Abbey National* v *Cann*, elaborated on the issue of what constitutes 'actual occupation':

It is, perhaps, dangerous to suggest any test for what is essentially a question of fact, for occupation is a concept which may have different connotations according to the nature and purpose of the property which is claimed to be occupied. It does not necessarily, I think, involve the personal presence of the person claiming to occupy. A caretaker or the representative of a company can occupy, I should have thought, on behalf of his employer. On the other hand, it does in my judgment, involve some degree of permanence and continuity which would rule out mere fleeting presence.

10.3.7.4 *Strand Securities* v *Caswell* [1965] 1 Ch 958

This relatively old case highlights how quirkish s. 70(1)(g) could become. Caswell took a 39-year lease of a London flat. As the lease was for over 21 years, it should have been registered. Caswell did not register the lease. The practical effect of this failure to register the lease was that it took effect only as an equitable lease. The reversion was sold to Strand, who would be bound by Caswell's lease only if it was an overriding interest within s. 70(1)(g).

Caswell did not personally live in the flat, but did drop in for the night from time-to-time when he was in London. The permanent occupant of the flat was his step-daughter. He let her live there **rent-free**, as her marriage had broken down.

The Court of Appeal held that Caswell was not in actual occupation and therefore he had no overriding interest within s. 70(1)(g). Later cases, especially *Abbey National* v *Cann*, underline the correctness of this conclusion. Two startling points should however be noticed:

(a) If Caswell had charged his step-daughter a rent (even a nominal rent) he would have been 'in receipt of rents' and therefore would have had an overriding interest under s. 70(1)(g).

(b) Alternatively, if he had employed her as his caretaker, he would (as *Cann* confirms) have been **through her agency** 'in actual occupation' and therefore have an overriding interest under s. 70(1)(g).

> **? QUESTION** 10.3
>
> In 2001 Leonard was the registered (freehold) owner of two adjoining houses, Alpha House and Beta House. He granted an *equitable* lease of the two houses to Tony. Tony was going abroad, so he sub-let Alpha House to Susan and arranged for his friend Charley to live in Beta House as caretaker. In 2002, Leonard sold both houses to Rowena. Was Rowena bound by Tony's equitable lease?

Applying the principles discussed above, Rowena was bound by the equitable lease with respect to both houses, unless she asked **Tony** what rights he claimed and he refused to reveal his lease. With respect to Alpha House, Tony's equitable lease was overriding within s. 70(1)(g) because he was 'in receipt of rents . . .'. With respect to Beta House, Tony's lease was overriding because **he** was 'in actual occupation' through the agency of Charley.

10.3.7.5 *Webb v Pollmount* [1966] 1 Ch 584

This case is perhaps the most surprising of all the s. 70(1)(g) cases. It is, however, undoubtedly correct (and is equally applicable to the new law in Sch. 3, para. 2). It is the clearest illustration of the proposition that 'Every type of property right in land can be an overriding interest provided there is actual occupation at the relevant time by its owner'.

L granted to Webb a legal lease to last for seven years. This lease was overriding under s. 70(1)(k) (see 10.3.4). The lease also granted to Webb an option to purchase the fee simple reversion. Options to purchase land are normally 'minor interests', and therefore should be protected by entering a notice on the register. No notice was entered to protect Webb's option. The fee simple was sold to Pollmount Ltd, who claimed that the option was not binding on it. Section 70(1)(g) came to Webb's rescue. He was actually occupying the leased property at the time of the sale, therefore his **option** was an overriding interest within s. 70(1)(g).

Webb was of course occupying the property by virtue of his **lease**, but that was held not to matter. 'Rights of a person in actual occupation' is not to be confined to the right by virtue of which that person occupies the land. Section 70(1)(g) makes overriding all his property rights in the land!

10.3.7.6 *Ferrishurst v Wallcite* [1999] 1 All ER 977

This case pointed out yet another strange quirk of s. 70(1)(g). The facts (slightly simplified) were that the plaintiffs had a lease of **part** of an office block, but the lease included an option to purchase the **whole** of the block. The Court of Appeal held that if a person had a right relating to the whole of a piece of registered land, then actual occupation of **part** of the land was sufficient to make the right an overriding interest with respect to the **whole** of the land.

10.3.7.7 *Malory Enterprises* v *Cheshire Homes* [2002] EWCA Civ 151; [2002] Ch 216; [2002] 3 WLR 1

How do you actually occupy derelict land?

The derelict land was part disused buildings, part open land. The crucial findings of the trial judge are summarized at para. 10 of the Court of Appeal judgment. (The land under dispute is referred to as the 'rear land'.)

Originally there was a concrete panel on the rear boundary and on the east boundary. The west boundary was open and there was no fence between the rear land and the front land on the boundary where they abutted. However, in September 1996 the openings on the west boundary were closed up by a Mr Neil Donald, a joiner [employed by the claimants]. In addition, in August 1996 Mr Donald boarded up the openings on the ground floor of the rear building and put up 'No trespassing' signs. In December 1996 he erected a low fence between the buildings: a post and rail fence with wooden uprights about three feet high. The rear land was, however, subject to vandalism and the wooden fence proved inadequate. Accordingly, in July 1997 Mrs Chang arranged for the erection of a high security steel fence in the gap between the buildings and in front of the low wooden fence. This was almost six feet high and was topped with razor wire. At a later stage, a gate was put into the fence held by a latch on the inside and locked in place by a padlock.

Both the trial judge and Court of Appeal found that the claimants (who had organized all these things) were in actual occupation of the derelict land (both open land and buildings) at the time of the Land Transfer in January 1999.

The Court of Appeal said at para. 80.

What constitutes actual occupation of property depends on the nature and state of the property in question, and the judge adopted that approach. If a site is uninhabitable, as the rear land was, residence is not required, but there must be some physical presence, with some degree of permanence and continuity.

10.3.8 Rights of persons in actual occupation—the new law— Schedule 3, paragraph 2

It should first be stressed that this new rule will be applicable to all cases where the **land transfer is executed** after the 12 October 2003. For example, suppose that Alfie and Bertha agreed back in 1990 that Bertha should have an equitable lease over Alfie's field, Pinkacre. Bertha has made regular use of Pinkacre. In late 2003, Alfie sold Pinkacre to Charley. The Land Transfer was executed on the **fourteenth** of October. In deciding whether Bertha has an 'actual occupation' overriding interest binding on Charley, the new Sch. 3, para. 2 rules must be applied, not the old s. 70(1)(g). Put bluntly, in the context of the 'actual occupation' overriding interest (and unlike short-term leases) 'old' rights **are** subject to the new law.

The important parts of para. 2 read as follows:

An interest belonging at the time of the disposition to a person in actual occupation, so far as relating to land of which he is in actual occupation, except for—

(a) an interest under a settlement under the Settled Land Act 1925;

(b) an interest of a person of whom inquiry was made before the disposition and who failed to disclose the right when he could reasonably have been expected to do so;

(c) an interest—
   (i) which belongs to a person whose occupation would not have been obvious on a reasonably careful inspection of the land at the time of the disposition, and
   (ii) of which the person to whom the disposition is made does not have actual knowledge at that time; . . .

The new law preserves the basic principle underlying the old s. 70(1)(g)—

Every type of property right in land can be an overriding interest provided there is actual occupation at the relevant time by its owner.

Matrimonial Home Rights remain an exception to this rule—see LRA 2002, Sch. 11, para. 34(2)(b). A further (unimportant) exception is created by para. 2(a). An interest under a strict settlement (very few of these exist today) cannot be an overriding interest.

10.3.8.1 Three features of Schedule 3, paragraph 2

Three other features of para. 2 should be immediately noted. Firstly, the new law (as enacted) contains no definition of 'actual occupation'. We can only assume that existing case law on the meaning of this phrase (in particular the decisions in *Boland* and in *Cann*) will apply to the new provision.

Secondly, the decision in *Webb* v *Pollmount* discussed at 10.3.7.5 remains good law.

Thirdly, under the old law an interest lost its overriding status—'where enquiry is made of such person [in actual occupation] and the rights are not disclosed'. Contrast this very blunt old wording with the new sub-para. (b), which excludes from being overriding—

an interest of a person of whom inquiry was made before the disposition and who failed to disclose the right **when he could reasonably have been expected to do so;**

10.3.8.2 When is it reasonable to expect that an interest will be revealed?

Under the old law, if:

(a) X occupied Blackacre in which he had a property interest; and

(b) enquiry was made of X about his interest; and

(c) X did not reveal his interest;

the non-revelation automatically meant that X's property right forfeited its overriding status.

Under the new law X's property right will only forfeit overriding status if X **could reasonably have been expected to reveal his (or her) right**. The new law envisages that there will be situations where it is not reasonable to expect someone to respond to an inquiry by revealing their right.

Sub-paragraph (b) is likely to generate litigation.

EXERCISE 10.2

It is 2006 and the new law has been in force for three years. Geraldine owned Grey House. She lived there with her semi-literate 'boyfriend' Harold. Harold's one great talent was do-it-yourself. While Geraldine was out at work, Harold totally renovated Grey House, doubling its value. 'Constructive trust interest!' we all shout.

Geraldine recently (2006) sold Grey House to Keith. When Keith visited the house, he saw Harold, and Keith asked Harold (both orally and in writing) 'Do you claim any share, interest, or property right in this house?' Harold did not reply as he did not understand the question. Has Harold's constructive trust interest lost its overriding status?

Those readers who tend to favour the underprivileged 'underdog' will answer, 'It was not reasonable to expect Harold to reveal his interest'. Others who think that purchasers like Keith should be protected if they make proper enquiries will say, 'Harold's lack of education (low intelligence?) should be irrelevant. The reasonable "boyfriend" would have answered Keith's enquiry'.

At least if the 'underdog' interpretation of sub-para. (b) is adopted, sub-para. (b) does have the effect of actually **increasing** the number of overriding interests, and thus increasing the hazards for purchasers of registered land. However, in three respects the new Sch. 3, para. 2 is **narrower in scope** than its predecessor s. 70(1)(g).

10.3.8.3 The owner of a property interest who (sub)leases that interest

Under the old s. 70(1)(g) it was clear that if the owner of some property right such as an equitable lease did not occupy the land himself but sub-let that land to a third party, the owner of the property right could still claim the benefit of s. 70(1)(g) as a person 'in receipt of rents'. See 10.3.7.4 and **Question 10.3**.

Schedule 3, para. 2 is, by contrast to the old law, confined to the owners of property interests who are in 'actual occupation'. The new provision cannot make overriding the property interest of somebody who is merely in receipt of rents.

10.3.8.4 The owner of a property interest who occupies only part of the relevant land

It is clear from the wording of Sch. 3, para. 2 that the decision in *Ferrishurst* v *Wallcite* (10.3.7.6) will not apply to the new law. If X has a property interest in the whole of Blackacre, but is in actual occupation of only of part of Blackacre, then his interest will be overriding only in relation to the part of the land he is occupying.

? **QUESTION** 10.4

Same facts as in Question 10.3, but the facts occur in 2007, after the commencement of the new Act.

Tony's equitable lease will be overriding with respect to Beta House, but not with respect to Alpha House.

10.3.8.5 The owner of a property interest whose occupation is not obvious on reasonably careful inspection

Sub-paragraph (c) contains an important new limitation on the 'actual occupation' overriding interest. Sub-paragraph (c) excludes from being overriding:

(c) an interest—
  (i) which belongs to a person **whose occupation would not have been obvious on a reasonably careful inspection of the land** at the time of the disposition, and
  (ii) of which the person to whom the disposition is made does not have actual knowledge at that time; . . .

Thus, the property interest of somebody whose **occupation** was **not obvious on reasonably careful inspection** will not be overriding, unless the purchaser of the registered title **actually knew of the interest** from some other source.

 EXERCISE 10.3

Same facts as in Exercise 10.2, except that during the period Geraldine was negotiating and completing the sale to Keith, Harold was in hospital for lengthy treatment. Geraldine locked all Harold's belongings away in cupboards. Keith, very reasonably, assumed that Geraldine was the sole occupant of Grey House. Keith knew nothing of Harold, or of his constructive trust interest. Does Harold have an overriding interest binding on Keith?

The answer to this question (contrast **Exercise 10.2**) is clear cut. Harold's occupation was not obvious on reasonably careful inspection, so Harold does not have an overriding interest. While the **Exercise 10.2** scenario raises a difficult point which might well be litigated right up to the House of Lords, the answer to the **Exercise 10.3** scenario is crystal clear.

10.4 Minor interests

Minor interests are all proprietary interests in registered land which are not:

(a) capable of substantive registration; or

(b) overriding interests, or

(c) mortgages by registered charge.

Rights which are **normally** minor interests include:

(a) estate contracts, restrictive covenants, unpaid vendor's liens, and matrimonial home rights (rights of occupation under the Matrimonial Homes Acts);

(b) overreachable interests arising under a strict settlement, trust for sale, or new-style trust of land.

It should be remembered, though, that with the exception of matrimonial home rights and interests under a strict settlement, all minor interests are capable of being promoted to 'overriding' by operation of Sch. 3, para. 2 of the 2002 Act, if the owner of the interest is in actual occupation (see 10.3.7 and 10.3.8).

This is even true of overreachable equitable interests arising under a trust for sale or new-style trust of land. However, if an owner of an overreachable equitable interest is in actual occupation of the land, his rights can still be overreached provided the purchase price is paid by the purchaser **to the correct trustees**. The House of Lords so decided in *City of London Building Society* v *Flegg* [1987] 3 All ER 435. If you do not follow this point yet, do not worry. I shall deal with *Flegg's* case when we consider the law of co-ownership. (See 16.4.2.)

10.4.1 **Protection of minor interests**

As I have already said several times, the owner of a minor interest should always protect it by entry on the register. By s. 20(1) of the Land Registration Act 1925 and by s. 29(1) of the LRA 2002, a purchaser for valuable consideration of a registered title takes free from minor interests which have not been properly protected. This will be so, even if he knew of the unprotected minor interest. (Compare this point with the House of Lords decision in the unregistered land case of *Midland Bank* v *Green*, see 8.3.5.1.)

However, the decision in *Lyus* v *Prowsa Developments* [1982] 1 WLR 1044 in effect creates a possible slight exception to the above principle. There a land transfer was executed, expressly subject to a minor interest which had not been protected by entry on the register. The purchaser was held to be bound by the minor interest, **because it had expressly undertaken to give effect to the unprotected minor interest**. Though 'justice may have been done', the case is questionable. It makes a very odd contrast with the unregistered land case of *Hollington Brothers* v *Rhodes* (see 8.3). Unfortunately the new 2002 Act does not clear up the uncertainty created by *Lyus*.

10.4.2 **Protection of minor interests under the Land Registration Act 1925**

Under the Land Registration Act 1925 there were effectively three types of entry which could be placed on the register to protect a minor interest; these were notices, cautions, and restrictions.

In practice restrictions were entered where a registered title was subject to equitable interests arising under a trust for sale, new-style trust, or strict settlement. All other minor interests (including an interest under a **constructive** trust, see *Elias* v *Mitchell* [1972] 2 All ER 153) were protected by the entry of either a notice or a caution.

From the point of view of the owner of a minor interest, the entry of a notice was and is the best method of protecting that minor interest. Entry of a notice automatically ensures that the minor interest is binding on a purchaser. Once a notice has been entered, the owner of a minor interest can sleep easy in his bed, confident that his rights cannot be destroyed. (Compare this point with the registration of a land charge in unregistered land, discussed at 8.3.)

There was, however, one significant limitation which was put upon the entry of notices on to the register by the Land Registration Act 1925. For the owner of a minor interest to be able to enter a notice, **the consent of the registered proprietor** was required. I should immediately add that proprietors often did agree to the entry of notices. However, under the 'old' Land Registration Act 1925, if the registered proprietor did not agree to the entry of a notice, the person claiming a minor interest could only enter a caution.

10.4.3 'Old law' cautions

This still needs to be briefly mentioned, as all cautions on the register on 13 October 2003 will continue to be valid and governed by the old law. (See LRA 2002, Sch. 12, para. 2(3).) **As a matter of law** the entry of a caution gave the person entering the caution only limited protection. (See *Clarke* v *Chief Land Registrar* [1994] 4 All ER 96.) But in practical reality, the presence of a caution entered against a registered title was effective to protect the minor interest. The presence of a caution on the register would put off all but the most foolhardy purchaser.

10.5 **Protection of minor interests under the 2002 Act**

In this respect, the 2002 Act makes an enormous improvement over the old law. The new law on protection of minor interests is remarkably straightforward.

The 2002 Act abolishes cautions as a means of protecting minor interests. All minor interests must be protected by the entry of a notice (see s. 32), except that interests arising under a trust of land (expressly created **or constructive**) will be protected by the entry of a restriction. Moreover (and this is a crucial change) both notices and restrictions may in future be entered **without the consent of the registered proprietor**.

So what now happens if a notice is entered to protect a claim to a minor interest, but that claim to an interest is disputed by the registered proprietor? In this situation, the registered proprietor can do two things.

Firstly, he can challenge the notice under the procedure sketched out in s. 36 of the new Act. If the dispute as to the existence (or otherwise) of the minor interest cannot be settled by negotiation, the dispute will be referred to a new type of 'judge' called a 'Land Registry Adjudicator'. If the Adjudicator decides that the person who has entered the notice has a valid interest in the land, he will order that the notice should remain on the register. If the Adjudicator decides that the person who entered the notice does not have an interest, the notice will be deleted.

Secondly, the registered proprietor could claim damages under s. 77(2) of the 2002 Act. A person who enters a notice 'without reasonable cause' (e.g., where he wrongly claims to have a minor interest) will be liable to pay damages to cover any loss suffered by the registered proprietor (e.g., the loss of a sale at good price!).

10.5.1 **Restrictions**

Under the Land Registration Acts 1925 and 2002, a restriction is entered on the register where there is some special limit on the registered proprietor's freedom to dispose of the land. For example, a few 'corporate persons' (a corporate person is an artificial entity such as a limited company or local authority) do not have complete freedom to dispose of their land. If such a 'person' is a registered proprietor, an appropriate restriction should be entered.

The important point for the purposes of this text is that a restriction should be used where registered land is subject to a strict settlement, trust for sale, or new-style trust. (The equitable interests under such trusts are technically minor interests, but they are overreachable as with unregistered land. Refer back to 8.4.) It follows that:

(a) Where land is subject to a strict settlement, the life tenant is owner of the fee simple and is therefore the registered proprietor. A restriction should be entered indicating that 'capital money' (e.g., in particular the purchase price when the land is sold) must be paid not to the registered proprietor but to the trustees of the settlement for the purposes of the Settled Land Act.

(b) Where land is held under a trust for sale or new-style trust, the trustee(s) are of course the registered proprietors. A restriction should be entered, however, requiring there to be at least two trustees for a valid disposition. (The significance of this point will emerge in **Chapters 15** and **16**.)

10.5.2 Protecting constructive trust interests under the 2002 Act

Under the 1925 Land Registration Act, an owner of a constructive trust interest could protect his interest in the land by lodging a caution. (See *Elias* v *Mitchell* [1972] 2 All ER 153.) However, it appears from the wording of the LRA 2002, s. 33(a) that, under the new law, the owner cannot use a notice, but will have to ask the registry to enter some kind of restriction.

This change is of limited practical significance. The owner of a constructive trust interest is unlikely to know about the desirability of making an entry on the register. But he/she may well be (like Mrs Boland) in 'actual occupation' and therefore (in normal circumstances) the constructive trust interest will be overriding by virtue of Sch. 3, para. 2.

10.6 Searches of the register

The tradition of English land registration (to be contrasted with foreign systems) had been until relatively recently one of privacy. The registry was not open to the public, and to inspect a particular registered title you needed the permission of the registered proprietor. However, a person who had contracted to buy a registered title was automatically entitled to receive permission to inspect the register.

The Land Registration Act 1988 came into force in December 1990, and this Act allowed any person to inspect any registered title on the payment of an appropriate fee. This principle of a register freely open to public inspection is now set out in s. 66 of the Land Registration Act 2002. Nevertheless, the wise purchaser of a registered title will not rely on a personal inspection, but will ask the registry to make an 'official search' of the register.

In practice, a purchase of registered land is not completed on the day of the official search, but only after a few days have elapsed. Once an official search certificate is issued the purchaser has a priority period of 30 working days (though the length of this period may be altered by the Land Registration Rules). Provided the purchaser lodges the land transfer for registration within this priority period, he is not bound by entries (notices, restrictions, etc.) made on the register in the intervening period.

CONCLUDING REMARKS

When you read the introduction to this chapter, you may well have thought, 'This is going to be easy. I learn the list of overriding interests; every right not on that list is a minor interest which you enter on the register much as you enter a land charge on the computer at Plymouth if the title to the land is unregistered'.

I hope that you now see that matters are not nearly as straightforward as that. In particular s. 70(1)(g) of the Land Registration Act 1925 created enormous problems (three House of Lords cases since 1980!) which have not been solved by Sch. 3, para. 2 of the 2002 Act.

The Land Registration Act 2002 does simplify matters by abolishing cautions and allowing notices and restrictions to be entered without the consent of the registered proprietor. But the 'rights of a person in actual occupation' problem has been made worse. The Society of Legal Scholars (the professional association for University Law Lecturers) recommended to the Law Commission that s. 70(1)(g) should be abolished **without replacement**. Instead, the devil we lecturers knew (and understood) has been replaced by an even worse devil, Sch. 3, para. 2.

I personally would go much further than the majority of my professional colleagues. But first, I would like to recount two matters which have occurred during my teaching career which I think illustrate the need for reform going far beyond the fiddly changes introduced by the 2002 Act. About twenty-five years ago there was an enormous public clamour regarding the cost of conveyancing. During that period I was at a meeting addressed by a Member of Parliament who obviously thought that anybody (not just legally qualified people) could easily undertake transactions with registered land: 'What is the big difficulty? Everything you need to know is on the register'. 'What about overriding interests?' somebody asked.

  EXERCISE 10.4

Think for a moment about what the MP's answer might have been.

As the questioner (a fellow land law teacher) expected, the MP was unable to give an answer. He did not understand the question! Now in my view, what our MP friend should be advocating (he is still an MP) is that this country should abolish all overriding interests and go over to German-style land registration.

Some years ago, I had in my land law classes a very good student of Austrian extraction. She already had an Austrian law degree. Now Austrian law is heavily influenced by German law; in particular Austria has adopted the German system of land registration. Under this system **all** property rights with respect to a piece of land must to be valid be entered in the land register (*Grundbuch*). My Austrian student found the whole idea of overriding interests (but particularly s. 70(1)(g) and *Boland*) absolutely ridiculous: 'In Austria, every schoolchild knows that if you claim a right in land you must enter it on the *Grundbuch*'.

I would abolish overriding interests, making all third party rights minor interests. Then we would be at least approaching the position which already exists in some countries within the European Union, where it is actually true that, 'Everything you need to know is on the register'.

■ SUMMARY

Overriding Interests

Under the Land Registration Act 2002, the following are (normally) overriding interests automatically binding on purchasers.

A Easements and profits already existing on 12 October 2003

B Easements and profits created after 12 October 2003 by implied grant or by prescription

C Legal leases for a duration of not more than seven years

D Local land charges

E Property rights which are 'upgraded' by the operation of Sch. 3, para. 2—see below.

Minor interests

The following rights are minor interests which should be protected by entry of a 'notice' on the register.

F Matrimonial home rights

G Restrictive covenants

H Equitable leases

I Estate contracts

J Options to purchase

K Licences by estoppel (proprietary estoppel).

But with the exception of matrimonial home rights, all these interests could be 'upgraded' to overriding by operation of Sch. 3, para. 2.

The following rights are minor interests which should be protected by an entry of a 'restriction' on the register.

L Equitable interests arising under a strict settlement

M Equitable interests under an (old) trust for sale

N Equitable interests under a new-style trust of land

O Constructive trust interests.

But with the exception of equitable interests under a strict settlement, all these interests could be 'upgraded' to overriding by operation of Sch. 3, para. 2.

The operation of Schedule 3 paragraph 2

First remember that matrimonial home rights and interests under a strict settlement cannot be upgraded by the operation of this provision. All other property rights may be 'upgraded' by this provision.

If you are considering whether somebody ('the claimant') has an overriding interest within Sch. 3, para. 2, go through the following multi-stage process:

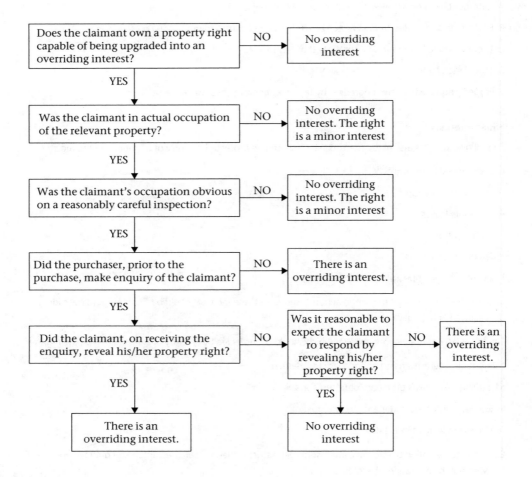

CHAPTER 10: ASSESSMENT EXERCISE

'Brecklands', is a detached house with garden situated in Derby. It has been registered title since 1985. Seema purchased Brecklands in November 2005, and became registered proprietor.

In December 2005 she signed an agreement (not in the form of a deed) with her neighbour Ursula, allowing Ursula and her family to use the inside toilet in Brecklands. Ursula pays £10 per month for this right. In practice this right is 'exercised' about twice a day.

In February 2006 Seema signed another agreement (not in the form of a deed) with Ursula, under which she leased a part of Brecklands' garden to Ursula for six years. The agreement also granted to Ursula an option to purchase the whole of the garden for £12,000.

In April 2006 Seema married Pritesh, who moved into Brecklands. Pritesh had no income of his own, but he looked after the house, cooked the meals, and did very small do-it-yourself jobs.

In July 2006 Seema left Pritesh to go and live with Harun. Last week she sold Brecklands to Ahmed. Ahmed bought the property without taking any professional advice, and did not even visit the property.

On arriving at Brecklands Ahmed finds Pritesh still living in the house, and refusing to move out. He also found Ursula digging the garden, and insisting that she has a right to use the toilet. Moreover Ursula announces her intention of exercising the option to buy the whole of the garden.

Advise Ahmed.

See Appendix for a specimen answer.

■ **FURTHER READING**

Law Commission report no. 271, 'Land Registration for the Twenty-First Century', Part IX which deals with the operation of the register itself, Part VIII which deals with overriding interests, and Part VI which deals with notices and restrictions. Note the very strange order in which the report is set out!

For a highly critical and stimulating analysis of the Land Registration Act 2002, see a short book, '*The New Law of Land Registration*' by Professor Elizabeth Cooke, published by Hart Publishing in 2003. See especially chapter five which deals with overriding interests and related matters, and chapter nine, which looks at foreign systems of land registration.

PART IV

Trusts of Land

11 Old-style trusts of land

11.1 Objectives

By the end of this chapter you should:

1 Be able to explain and distinguish between the three forms of trust of land which existed prior to 1997

2 In particular, appreciate the problems caused by accidental strict settlements

3 Be able to explain the paradoxical nature of a trust for sale, especially trusts for sale subject to consents

4 Appreciate why the law in this area was ripe for reform

11.2 Introduction to the Trusts of Land and Appointment of Trustees Act 1996

Prior to the Land Registration Act 2002, the Trusts of Land and Appointment of Trustees Act 1996 constituted the biggest single change in property law since the momentous changes made in 1925. For reasons which only become fully apparent when we consider the law of co-ownership, trusts of land (and therefore the 1996 Act) is a legal concept which affects most of the adult population of England and Wales.

Despite that fact, the Trusts of Land etc. Act 1996 went through Parliament with a minimum amount of bother. An obvious contrast is the furious and morally-charged debates in and out of Parliament over the Family Law Act 1996, which was intended to make drastic and highly controversial changes to the law on divorce. Why the lack of excitement over trusts of land? I think there are three reasons for this.

First, the Trusts of Land etc. Act 1996 concerns highly technical 'lawyers' law' unlikely to arouse much interest either in the press or amongst back-bench Members of Parliament. Secondly, the Act, taken as a whole, both simplified the law and created a law suited to conditions in modern Britain. Thirdly, while the Trusts of Land etc. Act 1996 made quite substantial changes in technical legal concepts, the Act is unlikely to change the outcome of many legal disputes. Moreover, most property law is **not** about settling disputes; rather it is concerned with facilitating people to manage their own affairs. The Trusts of Land etc. 1996 Act allows people to arrange their land ownership in ways suited to the new Millennium, rather than to the 1920s.

11.2.1 **Introduction to Chapters 11 to 13**

In **Chapter 11** I discuss those aspects of the **old** law ('old-style trusts') which I consider will aid you in understanding the law of 'new-style trusts'. In the new **Chapter 12** I explain in some detail the wide range of trusts to which the new legal regime applies, and in the new **Chapter 13** I set out the extensive and complex powers of trustees of new-style trusts of land.

11.2.2 **Introduction to Chapter 11**

In this chapter I explain the three types of express trust of land which existed prior to the commencement of the 1996 Act. I call these 'old' forms, 'old-style' trusts of land. I set out the characteristics of each of the three old-style forms and discuss the problems associated with each of them. At the end of the chapter, I discuss trusts for sale subject to consents, a (paradoxical) concept of great importance to the 'old' law.

11.3 **The three types of trust under the old law**

Under the old law which operated prior to the commencement of the Trusts of Land etc. Act 1996 there were three types of ('old-style') trusts of land which could exist.

11.3.1 **The bare trust**

In practice, such a trust of land is fairly rare. A bare trust exists where there is a trust, but there is only one beneficiary, and that beneficiary is of full age. For example, Blackacre is conveyed to Tim and Tom as trustees for Alfred in [equitable] fee simple.

One special use of bare trusts—'purchase in the name of a nominee'—should be noted.

 EXERCISE 11.1

Suppose Jack Bloggs is intending to buy a great deal of land in Muddletown. He wants to conceal this fact, perhaps to avoid sending prices up when existing owners discover that there is somebody very keen to own property in the town. Consider how he goes about his plan of concealment, and how the 'bare trust' concept will assist him.

He employs a whole series of agents to act on his behalf. For example, with money provided by Jack, Albert buys Green House, Betty buys Yellowfield, Charles buys Black Factory, and so on. By private arrangements known only to the trustee and beneficiary, Albert will hold Green House on bare trust for Jack, Betty will hold Yellowfield on bare trust for Jack, and Charles will hold Black Factory on bare trust for Jack.

11.3.2 **The strict settlement**

Where there is a strict settlement, the settlor envisages that the land will be retained and enjoyed as such by successive beneficiaries. **He wants the land to be kept, not to be sold.** Such strict settlements were very common until about 1900, but nowadays are very rare.

For example, Greenacre (a large country estate) was granted (prior to 1997), 'To X for life, remainder to Y in fee tail, remainder to Z in fee simple'.

Since 1925 all strict settlements must involve a succession of equitable interests and **must** involve a trust. (This is a consequence, of course, of s. 1 of the LPA 1925.) The Settled Land Act 1925 requires that the legal title to the land be held not by independent trustees but by the life tenant, acting as a trustee for himself and the other beneficiaries. Thus in the Greenacre example X holds the legal fee simple in Greenacre in trust for X, Y, and Z.

11.3.3 **The trust for sale**

The essence of a trust for sale is that land is conveyed to trustees who are placed under a 'duty' to sell the land. (If land was prior to 1997 conveyed to trustees who were given merely a **power** to sell the land, then a (highly irregular) strict settlement was created.)

For example, Whiteacre is conveyed to Tim and Tom as trustees for sale to sell Whiteacre and hold the proceeds in trust for Wendy for life, remainder to her children in equal shares.

Where there is a trust for sale, the trustees have a power to postpone sale. In practice, this power to postpone sale is extremely important. If the power to postpone is exercised (and this often does happen) the beneficiaries (in the example Wendy and after her death her children) get the income or other benefits from the **unsold** land.

11.4 **Criticism of the old law governing bare trusts of land**

Where there is a trust for sale or strict settlement, the equitable interests of the beneficiaries are **overreached** on a sale or other disposition of the land, provided any 'capital money' (e.g., the price paid by the purchaser) is paid to at least **two** trustees. (See 8.4 to 8.4.3 above.)

Under the 'old' law operating prior to 1997, an equitable fee simple under a bare trust of land could not be overreached; if the land was unregistered the equitable fee simple was subject to the doctrine of notice.

11.5 **Criticisms of strict settlements and the Settled Land Act 1925**

11.5.1 **An anomalous form of trust**

With every other type of trust, ancient or modern, the trustees hold the legal title to the trust property—the trustees are boss. With a strict settlement, there is a big anomaly—the life tenant is boss. In the Greenacre example at 11.3.2, X (not independent trustees) holds the legal title, and he decides whether the land should be sold, leased, etc.

With a strict settlement, there are independent 'trustees for the purposes of the Settled Land Act'. However, they have only limited functions. In particular, any 'capital money' arising on a sale or lease is paid to the SLA trustees, not to the life tenant. But the SLA trustees have no say in whether the land should be sold, leased, etc.

11.5.2 Limited powers of disposition of life tenants

The Settled Land Act 1925 gives the life tenant unlimited power to sell the land, but some of the other powers of the life tenant are limited by antiquated restrictions. Subject to certain exceptions, he cannot lease the land for more than 50 years. He cannot grant options where the price on exercise of the option is to be fixed by an arbitrator, even though this is the only type of option which makes sense in modern economic conditions. Mortgaging the land to pay for improvements (very important when the first Settled Land Acts were passed in the late nineteenth century) can only be done subject to complex and outmoded conditions.

 EXERCISE 11.2

Purely for amusement, and if you get the opportunity, look up Sch. 3 of the Settled Land Act 1925. You will get some idea from this schedule how antiquated the 'old' law is.

11.5.3 Complex documentation

There had to be at least two documents to create a fully effective strict settlement. There was the 'vesting deed' transferring the legal estate to the life tenant, and the 'trust instrument' setting out the details of the equitable interests under the settlement. Mistakes were often made with the documentation. The situation when one life tenant died and was succeeded by another life tenant was particularly complex.

11.5.4 Accidental strict settlements

Modern competent lawyers **never** created strict settlements. But they could arise by accident.

11.5.4.1 Home-made wills

The testator said something like, 'I leave my house to my wife Betty for the rest of her life, and after her death it is to go to our daughter Andrea'. This created a strict settlement, with Betty as life tenant. (A testator who was properly advised would never create a strict settlement. Rather he would create a trust for sale similar to the one I will be setting out in **Question 11.2**.)

11.5.4.2 Conveying land subject to a right to reside

 In *Binions* v *Evans* [1972] 1 Ch 359, the trustees of the Tredegar Estate owned a cottage in which there resided rent-free Mrs Evans, the widow of an employee of the Estate.

The trustees sold the cottage to Binions, expressly on the condition that Mrs Evans should be allowed to live there for the rest of her life. Binions paid a reduced price because of this condition. Binions nevertheless tried to evict Mrs Evans; he claimed that she had no proprietary interest in the land. Not surprisingly Binions found no sympathy in the Court of Appeal. The majority of the Court of Appeal (Megaw and Stephenson LJJ) held that the conveyance to Binions created a life interest in favour of Mrs Evans. Therefore the land was 'settled land' within the meaning of the 1925 Act, with Mrs Evans as life tenant. (The reasoning of Lord Denning MR in this case is generally considered not to be correct.)

The majority view in *Binions* v *Evans* was applied in the more recent case of *Ungurian* v *Lesnoff* [1990] Ch 206. This case concerned a cohabiting couple who eventually split up. Mr Ungurian bought a house in Muswell Hill (North London). Ms Lesnoff moved in, and spent an enormous amount of time, energy, and money renovating the house. The judge **found as a fact** that this money was spent on the understanding that Ms Lesnoff should be able to occupy the house **for the rest of her life**. The judge therefore held that Lesnoff had a life interest in the house (rather than a constructive trust share in the house) and that meant the house was settled land. Ms Lesnoff was life tenant. The judge even ordered that a vesting deed should be executed in her favour.

11.5.4.3 Trusts with a *power* to sell the land

For example, Whiteacre is conveyed to Tim and Tom as trustees to hold the land in trust for Wendy for life, remainder to her son John in fee simple. The trustees are given a **power** to sell the land, but are not placed under any **duty** to sell the land.

Under the 'old' law this disposition created a strict settlement. Wendy was the life tenant and 'the boss' holding the legal estate and the power to dispose of the land. That was not what the settlor intended.

11.5.4.4 Conveying land to a minor

A minor (i.e., a person under 18 years of age, formerly 21) cannot own a legal estate in land. Any attempt to grant a minor a legal estate is not however totally void. The minor will acquire an equitable interest equivalent to the legal estate intended to be granted. Thus if Fred Idiot conveys the fee simple in Blackacre to his son George, aged 15, George acquires only an equitable fee simple. The legal fee simple remains with Fred.

The Settled Land Act 1925 provided that where there was an attempt to grant a minor a legal estate, the land was settled land, and thus governed by the complex provisions of the Act.

11.6 Criticisms of the trust for sale

11.6.1 The artificial nature of the *duty* to sell

For reasons which will become more apparent when we consider the law of co-ownership, there have been literally millions of trusts for sale of land created since 1925.

In all these trusts the trustees were under a notional duty to sell the land. In the vast majority of cases, trustees for sale exercised their power to postpone sale, and went on postponing sale for an indefinite period. Thus legal theory was out of touch with the practical reality.

11.6.2 The archaic doctrine of 'conversion'

The Court of Chancery applied its maxim 'equity looks on as done that which ought to be done' to trusts for sale of land, and reasoned:

The trustees should be deemed to have sold the land the moment the trust is set up. The equitable interests of the beneficiaries of a trust for sale of land are **personal** property not **real** property.

> **?** **QUESTION** 11.1
>
> In a case which arose shortly after 1925, a solicitor was the owner of an absolute ('fee simple') interest *under a trust for sale* of a piece of freehold land, i.e., he was a beneficiary of the trust for sale. He made his own will, which in effect said, 'I leave my real estate to X and my personal property to Y'. Who received the interest under the trust for sale?

The answer is that Y was held entitled to the interest under the trust for sale.

11.6.3 Doubts as to whether beneficiaries have a right to occupy the land

This difficulty also stemmed from the doctrine of conversion. Traditionalist lawyers argued:

The interests of beneficiaries under a trust for sale of land are interests in money not interests in land. So the beneficiaries have no right to occupy the trust land.

However, in 1955, the Court of Appeal (led by Denning LJ) held that where land subject to a trust for sale has in fact been acquired for personal occupation by the beneficiaries, then the beneficiaries do indeed have the right to occupy the land. This decision, *Bull* v *Bull* [1955] 1 All ER 253 (unlike some of Lord Denning's other ideas) gained almost universal support from his colleagues. The House of Lords in *Boland* expressly approved *Bull* v *Bull*.

11.6.4 Limited powers of trustees for sale

Unless the trust provided otherwise, trustees for sale had the same limited and outdated powers of disposition as life tenants.

11.6.5 The anomalous concept of a trust for sale subject to consents

Under the old pre-1997 law land could be conveyed to trustees for sale, but subject to a clause that the consent of named person(s) be obtained to the sale. For example, land was conveyed, 'to Tim and Tam on trust for sale for X for life, remainder to Y. The sale shall only take place if W and X agree to it'. This was a valid trust for sale, even though Tim and Tam could not carry out their 'duty' to sell unless W and X agreed.

Although a trust for sale subject to consent was a paradoxical concept, much use has been made of such trusts.

QUESTION 11.2

Assume that the Trusts of Land etc. Act 1996 was never enacted. Tom owns a large house. He has a wife, Wendy, and a son Simon. Tom is in poor health, and wishes to make a will under which Wendy would have the right to occupy the house for the rest of her lifetime, but without any power to sell or lease the house. On Wendy's death the house would pass to Simon absolutely.

Why is it that Tom would be advised to create, not a strict settlement, but a trust for sale and what sort of provisions would that trust contain?

There are two reasons why Tom would not create a strict settlement. First, we would not want his family to get entangled in the highly complex law of strict settlements. Secondly, if a strict settlement were created, Wendy would be life tenant, and she would have a power to sell the house which could not be taken away from her.

Tom would create a trust for sale and appoint as trustees people who are sympathetic to his wishes; he would also include clauses:

(a) requiring that any sale be with the consent of **both** Wendy and Simon;

(b) requiring the trustees to permit Wendy to live in the house pending sale.

CONCLUDING REMARKS

Arguably the most important part of this chapter is **Question 11.2**, and my suggested answer to it. The 'old' law of trusts of land was full of anachronisms, and pitfalls for the unwary, but competent solicitors knew how to deal with that law. They avoided the creation of strict settlements and (by careful drafting) used the trust for sale to achieve their clients' wishes. As we shall see, the 'new' law gets rid of the anachronisms and the pitfalls but drafting of new-style trusts of land may still require care.

■ SUMMARY

Prior to the Trusts of Land and Appointment of Trustees Act 1996 there were three types of trust of land:

A **Bare Trust** The equitable fee simple which existed under such a trust was still subject to the doctrine of notice. It was not overreachable.

B **Strict Settlement** This was an anachronism even in 1996. Where there is a strict settlement:

1 The life tenant (not independent trustees) acts as trustee of the land, has the legal title to the land, and can even sell the land;

2 If the life tenant sells the land, the price is paid by the purchaser to independent 'Trustees for the purposes of the Settled Land Act';

3 Strict settlements involved very complicated conveyancing documents.

C **Trust for Sale**

1 The trustees held the legal title and were theoretically under a duty to sell the land and invest the proceeds.

2 In reality, most trustees for sale postponed the sale of the land—often indefinitely—and allowed the beneficiaries to enjoy the land.

3 The (rather paradoxical) concept of trust for sale where the sale could only take place with the consent of named persons proved very useful, particularly when creating a trust of the family home.

■ **FURTHER READING**

For the historical background to trusts of land, see chapter one of a small book *Settlements of Land* published in 1973 by Sweet and Maxwell and written by Professor Brian Harvey.

For the intricacies of the old-fashioned strict settlement, see Harvey's chapter two.

For details of the law governing pre-1997 strict settlements and trusts for sale, see *Megarry and Wade: Law of Real Property* (sixth edition by Harpum) chapter eight, pages 373–434.

12 New-style trusts of land defined

12.1 Objectives

By the end of this chapter you should:

1 Be able to explain the various situations in which a new-style trust of land will arise

2 Be able to explain what will happen in future to transactions which, in the past, would have given rise to 'an accidental strict settlement'

3 Be familiar with the basic rules for the appointment, retirement, and removal of trustees

12.2 Introduction

As you may already have noticed, I constantly talk of **new-style** trusts of land. The Trusts of Land and Appointment of Trustees Act 1996 itself simply talks of 'trusts of land'. I have added the words **'new-style'** to emphasize the fact that we are dealing with a new (all-embracing) concept very different from what has gone before.

In this chapter I endeavour to identify all those trusts and other dispositions which are caught by the new legal regime. There is, however, one important exception from this otherwise comprehensive coverage. I do not consider co-ownership. This area of law is not considered until **Chapters 14** to **16**.

At the end of this chapter I explain certain basic principles regarding the appointment, retirement, and removal of trustees. I should warn you that you will need to know more about these topics when you come to study the law of trusts.

12.3 The definition in section 1

Section 1 of the 1996 Act contains a sweeping definition of the new-style 'trust of land':

(1) In this Act—
    (a) 'trust of land' means (subject to subsection (3)) any trust of property which consists of or includes land, and
    (b) 'trustees of land' means trustees of a trust of land.

(2) The reference in subsection (1)(a) to a trust—

    (a) is to any description of trust (whether express, implied, resulting or constructive), including a trust for sale and a bare trust, and

    (b) includes a trust created, or arising, before the commencement of this Act.

Subsection (3) then excludes (existing) 'settled land' from the definition of 'trust of land'.

Thus right at the outset, the 1996 Act makes it clear that, with the exception of existing strict settlements, its new legal regime is to apply to every conceivable type of trust of land, whether created before or after the commencement of the Act. It will be useful if we consider various possible types of trust, and how the all-embracing new legal regime applies to them.

12.3.1 Existing trusts for sale

These are subject to the new legal regime, in particular:

(a) the trustees have the unlimited powers of disposition granted by s. 6 of the 1996 Act;

and

(b) the (much improved) provisions for sorting out disputes contained in s. 14 are applicable.

Two further specific points should be made. First, if the existing trust for sale includes any restriction on the trustees' power to postpone sale, that restriction is invalidated by s. 4(1) of the 1996 Act.

Secondly, the awkward doctrine of 'conversion', by virtue of which interests under a trust for sale were regarded as personal property not real property, is abolished by s. 3 of the 1996 Act.

12.3.2 Trusts for sale arising after 1996

Any trust for sale created after the commencement of the new Act is of course perfectly valid. However, it is governed by the new legal regime and takes effect as a new-style trust of land. Moreover, s. 4(1) of the 1996 Act invalidates any provision which restricts or removes the trustees' power to postpone sale.

 EXERCISE 12.1

In 1995 James owned a large farm, Spreadacres. He had five children, who were and are constantly quarrelling. He was diagnosed as terminally ill. He told his solicitor, 'I want to leave all my property to my children in equal shares. But to avoid them falling out over the management of Spreadacres, I want the farm sold within (say) four years and the proceeds split between them'.

'Easy!' replied the solicitor; 'we will create a trust for sale, but include a clause restricting the power to postpone sale to four years from the date of your death'.

Consider this scenario on the assumption that:

(a) James died shortly before the commencement of the 1996 Act.

(b) James died shortly after the commencement of the 1996 Act.

If James died before the commencement of the 1996 Act, the restriction on the power to postpone would initially be valid. However (assuming the trustees have not been able to sell in the meantime), the restriction on the power to postpone sale would be invalidated by the commencement of the Act on 1 January 1997.

If James died after the commencement of the 1996 Act, his (undoubtedly well-meant) restriction on the power to postpone sale would be invalid from the outset.

12.3.3 Deliberately created trusts of land after the commencement of the 1996 Act

Note that in the (b) version of the scenario just considered James made his will before 1 January 1997 but died after that date. In such a case, the 'trust for sale' which the testator intended takes effect as a 'new-style' trust of land.

It will be perfectly possible for a post-1996 trust of land to be **drafted** as a trust for sale. But there seems to be no point in so doing. As the doctrine of conversion disappears, and as all trustees of land have a power to postpone sale indefinitely which cannot be excluded, a 'trust for sale of land' will be no different from any other new-style trust of land.

In the past, numerous settlors creating trusts of land for the benefit of their families have employed the trust for sale. But they have done so, not because of any desire to see the land sold in the near future, but rather because the trust for sale was the only sensible way of achieving their wishes. (See, for example, the answer to **Question 11.2** at **11.6.5** above.) The trust for sale, with its highly artificial 'duty to sell' was the lesser of two evils. The greater evil, to be avoided at all costs, was the strict settlement.

The 1996 Act eliminates the greater evil of the strict settlement and simultaneously renders unnecessary the use of trusts for sale. Solicitors have quickly realized this and largely ceased employing trusts for sale. Instead, they simply convey the legal estate in the land to the chosen trustees, in trust for the chosen beneficiaries.

 EXERCISE 12.2

Re-read 8.4.3.1 above. Samuel clearly had a good solicitor who knew the implications of the 1996 Act.

12.3.4 Bare trusts after 1996

 EXERCISE 12.3

Re-read what I say about bare trusts at 2.4.3, 11.3.1, and 11.4.

A 'bare trust' of land is expressly brought within the definition of a new-style trust of land (see s. 1(2)(a)). This is a point of some significance. Prior to the commencement of the 1996 Act, an equitable interest under a bare trust, unlike interests under a strict settlement or trust for sale, could not be overreached.

As a bare trust of land is now simply one form of new-style trust of land, it is clear that the equitable interest of the sole beneficiary can now be overreached, provided the sale (or other disposition) is made by **at least two trustees**.

12.3.5 Constructive trusts affecting land

 EXERCISE 12.4

Go back to 1.4.7 of this text, and re-familiarize yourself with the Chenu-Alfred-Bertha story set out in that section.

As we saw at 1.4.7, where somebody (Bertha) makes a substantial contribution to the acquisition or improvement of a piece of property (Chenu), that person (Bertha) acquires a constructive trust interest in the property.

It follows from s. 1(2)(a) of the 1996 Act that where land is subject to a constructive trust interest, a new-style trust of land will automatically exist. The ramifications which flow from this are quite complex; it is better if we ignore the application of the new Act to constructive trusts until we are dealing with co-ownership.

12.3.6 Treatment of transactions which would have been strict settlements

As we have seen in **Chapter 11** (see 11.5.4), there are a number of situations where, prior to 1997, a strict settlement would arise 'by accident'. How are these situations dealt with by the new law?

12.3.6.1 One document creating equitable interests

Suppose Joe Idiot owns Blueacre. He executes a single deed which purports to grant Blueacre, 'to Adam for life, remainder to Betty in fee simple'. Prior to 1926 this grant would have been a classic strict settlement, with Adam holding a legal life estate in possession, and Betty holding a legal fee simple in remainder.

If this grant took place at any time between 1926 and 1996 it would still be a valid strict settlement. However, Adam's life interest and Betty's fee simple in remainder were (and are) both equitable interests. More importantly, for reasons we need no longer consider, the use of a single deed was an error on Joe's part. The Settled Land Act 1925 provided a complicated rigmarole which had to be gone through before the land could be sold or dealt with in any other way. That rigmarole need not concern us.

If Joe executes his single deed after 1996 there is no great difficulty. He has (unwittingly) created a new-style trust of land. Adam and Betty (as before) acquire equitable interests.

Joe retains the legal estate in Blueacre; it therefore follows that **he** is the (sole) trustee of the new-style trust.

12.3.6.2 Post-1996 attempt to create a fee tail

Although the 1996 Act does not abolish existing fees tail, it does provide that no new fees tail can be created. Schedule 1, para. 5(1)(b) provides that any document which purports to grant a fee tail:

operates instead as a declaration that the property is held in trust absolutely for the person to whom an entailed interest in the property was purportedly granted.

Suppose Joe Idiot owns Redacre. After 1996 he executes a deed which purportedly conveys Redacre to 'my son Charles in fee tail'. This deed will create a 'new-style' (bare) trust of land, with Joe as a sole trustee and Charles as the sole beneficiary.

? QUESTION 12.1

Suppose Joe Idiot owns Yellowacre, and in 2006 he executes a single deed which states, 'I grant Yellowacre to Adam for life, remainder to Chris in fee tail, remainder to Donald in fee simple'. What is the result?

There will be a new-style trust. Joe will be sole trustee of that trust. The equitable interests under the trust will be (in effect) to Adam for life, remainder to Chris **in fee simple**. Donald does not acquire any interest in the land.

12.3.6.3 Conveyance to a minor

A minor (a person under 18 years of age) cannot own a legal estate in land. What then happens if someone purported to convey a legal estate to a minor or minors? Amazingly, under the old law the minor acquired an equitable interest **and** the land became settled land subject to all the complexities of the Settled Land Act 1925.

Schedule 1, para. 1(1) of the 1996 Act will in future govern an attempted conveyance to a minor:

(1) Where after the commencement of this Act a person purports to convey a legal estate in land to a minor, or two or more minors . . . the conveyance—

   (a) is not effective to pass the legal estate, but

   (b) operates as a declaration that the land is held in trust for the minor or minors . . .

? QUESTION 12.2

Joe Idiot owns Pinkacre. In 2006 he purports to convey Pinkacre to his daughter Edwina, then aged 15. What is the effect of this conveyance?

Joe has created a new-style trust of land with himself as (sole) trustee of Pinkacre and Edwina as the sole beneficiary. (Technically this is not a 'bare' trust, as Edwina is under age. It will become a bare trust on her eighteenth birthday.)

12.3.6.4 Accidental trusts of land: conveying land subject to a right to reside

 EXERCISE 12.5

Re-read what I said about the cases of *Binions* v *Evans* and *Ungurian* v *Lesnoff* at 11.5.4.2 and consider how these cases would be decided if the relevant events all occurred after the commencement of the Trusts of Land etc. Act 1996.

In *Binions* v *Evans* the majority in effect ruled that there was a strict settlement with the effect that the cottage was granted by Tredegar Estates 'to Mrs Evans for life, remainder to Binions in fee simple'. Under the new law there is therefore a new-style trust, with Tredegar Estates as the (sole) trustee and Mrs Evans and Binions as the beneficiaries. (Compare this with the Joe Idiot Blueacre example I gave at 12.3.6.1 above.)

In *Ungurian* v *Lesnoff* the judge in effect held that the house was subject to a strict settlement, 'To Lesnoff for life, remainder to Ungurian in fee simple'. Under the 1996 Act there is a new-style trust, with Ungurian (he created the trust) as (sole) trustee of the legal estate, holding the house in trust for Lesnoff for life and then on 'resulting trust' to himself.

12.3.6.5 Accidental trusts in home-made wills

John Knowall (perhaps a friend of Joe Idiot) thinks all solicitors charge extortionate fees, so he drafts his own will. He left his house, 'To my dear son Edward, but on condition that he allows my beloved wife Hilda to occupy the house for the rest of her life'. It appears that such a will under the old law would create a strict settlement, with Hilda as the life tenant, and Edward entitled to a fee simple in remainder.

 EXERCISE 12.6

Consider what the outcome would be applying the Trusts of Land etc. Act 1996 to John Knowall's will.

The will would create a new-style trust of land, in effect, 'To Hilda for life, remainder to Edward in fee simple'. As John has not appointed any trustees, his personal representatives would act as the first trustees of the trust.

12.4 The need for two trustees for a new-style trust of land

I hope that you have noticed that in a number of the examples we have just been discussing there is only one trustee. It should be stressed that a new-style trust of land (just like an 'old' trust for sale) is perfectly valid even though there is only one trustee. However, as I have already pointed out at 8.4.3 and 8.4.3.1 above, for a sale (or other disposition) by trustees to 'overreach' the equitable interests of beneficiaries, there **must be at least two trustees**.

This rule of minimum of two (in s. 27 of the LPA 1925) has always applied to trusts for sale, and now applies to new-style trusts of land. It follows that where there is a sole trustee of a new-style trust, that trustee should appoint a colleague before selling the land or making any other disposition. What happens if he tries to sell (or mortgage or lease) the trust land acting on his own is a difficult question. I will postpone considering that question until we reach 16.4.1.

12.5 Appointment, retirement, and removal of trustees

You will need to consider these topics in more depth when studying the law of trusts. What follows are certain basic principles you need to know for the purposes of land law.

12.5.1 The original trustees

The general rule is that the settlor appoints the original trustees by the document(s) setting up the trust. A person appointed at the outset can 'disclaim' the trust, i.e., refuse to act. Equity has always ruled that, **unless the trust instrument provides otherwise**, trustees are not allowed to charge for their services, though they may claim the expenses of running the trust out of trust income. However s. 29 of the Trustee Act 2000 allows professional trustees (solicitors, accountants, banks, etc.) to charge for their services even if the trust instrument says nothing about charges.

With a trust of land there is a **maximum** of four trustees. As we shall see in **Chapters 15** and **16**, this rule is important. If a document purports to appoint more than four trustees, the first four named are the trustees.

Suppose a deed conveys Greenacre to Alfred, Bernard, Charles, David, and Eric on trust for sale. (All are of full age.) Eric will not be a trustee. Suppose that Bernard dies shortly after the trust is set up. Alfred, Charles, and David continue as trustees, but Eric **does not become a trustee**. As we shall see, Alfred, Charles, and David can now appoint a colleague, **who can be anybody they wish**. There is no obligation on them to appoint Eric.

A minor cannot be appointed to be a trustee, though an attempt to do so will not invalidate the trust. Suppose a trust instrument appointed Angela, Betty, and Cathy to be trustees, but Betty was only 17. Angela and Cathy will be the trustees. Betty **would not become a trustee** on her attaining 18. As you may have guessed, Angela and Cathy can appoint up to two colleagues, who can be **whoever they wish**. There is no obligation on them to appoint Betty after her eighteenth birthday.

> **? QUESTION** 12.3
>
> A settlor creates a trust of land, with George, Harriet, Isobel, John, Karen, Leonard, and Marina as trustees. Five of these people are over 40 years old, but Harriet and Karen are both only aged 16. Who will be the trustees?

The first four named of full age. They will be George, Isobel, John, and Leonard. Moreover those four will still be the trustees when Harriet and Karen attain 18.

12.5.2 Appointing fresh trustees to an existing trust

This is governed by section 36 of the Trustee Act 1925, as amended.

There are basically four rules.

(a) New appointments may be made by the person(s) nominated by the trust instrument as having the power to appoint new trustees. It is, however, relatively rare for a family trust to make provision for appointments by an 'outsider'. Such a provision is sometimes found in charitable trusts, and is normal in pension fund trusts.

(b) If there is no provision for appointment by an outsider(s), or the outsider(s) refuse to act, the existing trustee(s) appoint new trustee(s). In practice this rule that existing trustees appoint new trustees is the rule which operates in the vast majority of cases. It is particularly important to realize that this rule operates even where (for whatever reason) there is currently only one trustee. That one trustee can appoint up to three colleagues!

(c) Suppose all the trustees of a trust die. The rule then is that the personal representatives (executors or administrators) of **the last trustee to die** are automatically temporary trustees of the trust and have the power to appoint permanent trustees. It is perfectly permissible, indeed it is quite common, for the personal representatives to appoint themselves permanent trustees.

(d) The court may have to appoint trustees, though this will in practice happen only in cases of special difficulty, e.g., where all the trustees are incapacitated by mental illness.

12.5.3 When may new appointments be made?

12.5.3.1 Additional trustees

These may be appointed at any time provided the number of trustees is not increased above the maximum of four.

12.5.3.2 Replacement of trustees

A new trustee may be appointed to replace an existing trustee if the existing trustee:

(a) remains outside the United Kingdom for more than 12 months continuously;

(b) desires to retire from the trust;

(c) becomes unfit to act (due to bankruptcy, criminal conviction, etc.);

(d) becomes incapable of acting by reason of lunacy, old age, infirmity, or other reason;

(e) is removed under a power contained in the trust instrument.

(A trustee who is retiring may participate in the appointment of a replacement trustee.)

12.5.4 Removal of trustees

A trustee may be removed:

(a) under heads (a), (c), (d), and (e) in 12.5.3.2 above;

(b) by the court;

(c) where the beneficiaries, all being of full age and in agreement, desire the removal of a trustee.

12.5.4.1 The rule in *Saunders* v *Vautier* and s. 19 of Trusts of Land etc. Act 1996

In order to explain point (c) above I need to explain the rule in *Saunders* v *Vautier* (1841) 10 LJ Ch 354. This rule remains of fundamental importance to both land law and the law of trusts. The rule is that if the beneficiaries of a trust (of any type of property) are all of full age and in unanimous agreement, they can (in effect) dictate what is to be done with the trust property.

Suppose Tim and Tam are the trustees of a trust fund invested in stocks and shares. They hold the fund in trust for A for life, remainder to B absolutely. A and B are of full age. A would like to get his hands on some capital. B would also like some capital, but does not want to wait until A dies. They therefore agree to end the trust, and split the fund (say) 50–50. A and B have the right to do so under *Saunders* v *Vautier*. The rule in *Saunders* v *Vautier* has now been reinforced by s. 19 of the Trusts of Land etc. Act 1996. This section applies to all trusts of any type of property; it is not confined to trusts of land. Under s. 19, if the beneficiaries of a trust are all of full age and in unanimous agreement, they can by written direction:

(a) require a trustee or trustees to retire from the trust (i.e., sack the trustee(s)); and/or

(b) require the existing trustees to appoint a new trustee or trustees chosen by the beneficiaries.

> **? QUESTION** 12.4
>
> Suppose, in the imaginary trust discussed above, A and B are happy with their existing equitable interests under the trust, but do not like Tim and Tam as trustees. They would prefer Tom and Terri. Advise A and B.

A and B should invoke s. 19. They will send Tim and Tam a written direction that they must execute a deed which appoints Tom and Terri as trustees and then 'retires' Tim and Tam from the trust.

12.5.5 Retirement of trustees

A trustee may retire:

(a) if another trustee is appointed in his place;

(b) if after his retirement there will be at least two persons continuing as trustees;

(c) by employing an express power to retire granted by the trust instrument;

(d) by getting the unanimous consent of all the beneficiaries;

(e) by getting the court's consent.

12.5.6 Situations where a trustee is also a beneficiary

As we shall see more clearly in **Chapters 15** and **16**, there are certain situations where a trustee is also a beneficiary under the trust. Indeed, where there is co-ownership it is quite normal for a person to have dual roles as both trustee and beneficiary.

The point to get **now** is that if somebody is both trustee and beneficiary and he sells or gives away his equitable interest, he nevertheless remains a trustee of the legal title. The disposal of his equitable interest is not to be treated as a resignation or retirement from the trust, nor is it as such grounds for removing him from the trusteeship.

12.6 Method of appointment of trustees

An appointment of a new trustee must be in writing; in practice it is normally made by deed in order to take advantage of s. 40(1) of the Trustee Act 1925. If the deed contains a declaration that the trust property shall vest in the new trustee(s), it conveys the legal title in the trust property from the existing trustees to the persons who will be the trustees after the appointment.

For example, suppose A, B, and C are the existing trustees, and they appoint D to replace C who is retiring from the trust, the declaration conveys the legal title from A, B, and C to A, B, and D.

 EXERCISE 12.7

What I have just said rather assumes that any land involved is unregistered title. What do you think happens if (as is very likely) new trustees are appointed to a trust where the land involved is registered title?

The trustees prior to the new appointment(s) are the registered proprietors until the deed of appointment is presented to the Land Registry. The necessary change(s) are then made to the register.

12.7 Unanimity of trustees

It is a general rule of the law of trusts that trustees can act only if there is unanimous agreement. Thus if there are four trustees of a trust for sale of land, and the land is to be sold, **all four** trustees must sign both the contract and the conveyance. Please remember this point, particularly when answering examination questions.

? **QUESTION** 12.5

If there are three trustees of a trust of land, and the land is to be sold, how many trustees must sign both the contract and the conveyance?

The answer is, of course, three. Why am I labouring this point that all the trustees must sign? This is because every year I read exam answers which either expressly state or assume that where there are three or four trustees, the signatures of any two will suffice to make a transaction valid.

12.7.1 Exceptions to the unanimity rule

The exceptions are:

(a) If the trust instrument provides for decisions to be taken by a majority. (Such a provision is today not uncommon.)

(b) If land is held subject to a charitable trust. In the case of such a trust the law permits there to be more than four trustees but it also provides that decisions may be taken by majority of the trustees of the charity.

 CONCLUDING REMARKS

In the first part of this chapter I considered the various situations where a new-style trust of land will exist. I would again stress the all-embracing nature of the new concept.

In the last few pages I have been dealing with certain rules which are common to all types of trust (e.g., trusts of stocks and shares); these rules are not confined to old-style or new-style trusts of land. This serves to underline a very important point. The old trust for sale of land and the new-style trust of land are merely two species of a very large family of 'animals' all of which are classified as 'trusts'. Remember that, as I said in **Chapter 2**, 'any type of property can be subjected to a trust'.

Land is however a very different type of asset from, say, shares or debentures. It cannot be moved, but it can be put to all sorts of uses and made subject to a wide range of transactions. It therefore necessarily follows that trustees **of land** need wide powers of disposition and management which will be irrelevant to trusts of abstract assets such as shares or debentures. It is these powers of disposition which we will be considering in **Chapter 13**.

■ SUMMARY

Scope of the 1996 Act

With the sole exception of the relatively few strict settlements in existence on 1 January 1997, all trusts of land are now governed by the Trusts of Land and Appointment of Trustees Act 1996.

In particular the 1996 Act extends to:

A   Trusts for sale existing on 1 January 1997

B   Trusts for sale created after 1996

C   All trusts of land deliberately created after 1996

D   All trusts of land accidentally created after 1996

E   All bare trusts of land, whenever created

F   All attempts to convey land to a minor.

Appointment of Trustees

1   The settlor should appoint the original trustees;

2   A minor cannot be a trustee;

3   As a general rule, the existing trustees appoint new or replacement trustees;

4   (Important to Land Law) Where a trustee is also a beneficiary, and that trustee disposes of his equitable interest under the trust, that disposal is not a resignation from the trust.

Saunders v _Vautier_ and s. 19 of the Trusts of Land and Appointment of Trustees Act

Where the beneficiaries of a trust are of full age and in total agreement, they can do what they like with the trust property. They can also dismiss the existing trustees and replace them with their own choices.

■ FURTHER READING

For the thinking which led to the enactment of the 1996 Act, see Law Commission report no. 181 'Transfer of Land—Trusts of Land' pages 1–16. (Part I and Part IIA.)

For a concise summary of the continuing importance of trusts of land and why people create them, see April Stroud, '_Making Sense of Land Law_' chapter six, entitled 'The use of trusts in land'.

13 The powers of new-style trustees of land

13.1 Objectives

By the end of this chapter you should:

1 Be familiar with the basic functions and duties of new-style trustees of land

2 Be able to explain the circumstances in which s. 12 of the Trusts of Land etc. Act 1996 creates a right to reside on the trust property

3 Appreciate the problems created by s. 8 of the Trusts of Land etc. Act 1996

4 Be able to explain the rules governing the trustees' power to delegate their functions to a beneficiary, including an important change made by the Trustee Act 2000

13.2 Introduction

This chapter is, necessarily, a rather long one. In it, I examine the detailed workings of the new legal regime. It will help if I first remind you of one of the weaknesses of the old law. In section 12.3 of the first edition of this text I introduced the topic of the powers of the life tenant under the Settled Land Act 1925 by stating:

The thinking in 1925 was **not** to give the life tenant totally unrestricted powers over the settled land. Rather it was to give him only those powers which a 'reasonable landowner' would want.

Hence, for example, the fact that a life tenant of a strict settlement can normally only lease the land for a maximum of 50 years. This 50-year limit is too short in modern conditions.

As there are very few strict settlements left, it might be thought that the restrictions on the powers of the life tenant are of no great consequence. However, s. 28(1) of the Law of Property Act 1925 provided that **trustees for sale** of land should have the same powers of disposition as life tenants. So in principle the same (somewhat inadequate) powers of disposition of life tenants also applied to the trustees of the many millions of trusts for sale set up in England and Wales since 1925.

In recent times, lawyers became increasingly aware of the inadequacy of the statutory powers of trustees for sale. In many (but not all) modern trusts for sale one sees included a clause giving to the trustees the same powers of disposition as would be enjoyed by an outright owner.

13.3 **The powers of disposition of new-style trustees of land**

In the light of what I have just said, s. 6(1) of the 1996 Act is not a very surprising provision. It states, quite baldly:

For the purposes of exercising their functions as trustees, the trustees of land have in relation to the land subject to the trust all the powers of an absolute owner.

It should be stressed that this new provision extends to **all** new-style trusts of land, whether created before or after the commencement of the 1996 Act. (Regrettably, it has not been applied to life tenants under the few strict settlements which still exist.) Thus trustees of 'new-style' trusts of land can, unlike life tenants under a strict settlement, lease the trust land for any period they and the prospective tenant consider appropriate. Similarly, unlike life tenants, the trustees can grant an option to purchase the trust land at a price to be fixed by an arbitrator.

Life tenants of strict settlements do have power, under the Settled Land Act 1925, to mortgage the settled land to pay for improvements to the land, e.g., land drainage. However, the power under the SLA 1925 is subject to complex and antiquated restrictions which need not now concern us. By contrast, 'new-style' trustees of land are, as a result of s. 6 of the 1996 Act, able to mortgage the trust land to raise funds for any purpose which benefits the land in the long term. In particular, the trustees are not subject to the outdated rules regarding improvements contained in Sch. 3 of the 1925 Act.

13.4 **The trustees' duties on exercising their powers**

Ever since the Court of Chancery invented the concept of the trust in medieval times (remember 2.3.1 and Sir Richard Goodbody), trustees of all forms of trust have been under a duty to get the best financial return from the trust property obtainable by reasonable methods. This duty does of course apply to new-style trustees of land.

This traditional duty on trustees to get the best return from the trust property is now both codified and amplified by s. 1 of the Trustee Act 2000, an Act which applies to all trustees of all types of trust when exercising their various powers and functions.

(1) Whenever the duty under this subsection applies to a trustee, he must exercise such care and skill as is reasonable in the circumstances, having regard in particular—

    (a) to any special knowledge that he has or holds himself out as having, and

    (b) if he acts as trustee in the course of a business or profession, to any special knowledge or experience that it is reasonable to expect of a person acting in the course of that kind of business or profession.

You should however carefully note para. 7 of Sch. 1 of the 2000 Act:

The duty of care does not apply if or in so far as it appears from the trust instrument that the duty is not meant to apply.

Thus a trust deed can include a clause exempting trustees from liability for negligence in carrying out any or all of their powers and functions. The Unfair Contract Terms Act 1977 and similar legislation designed to protect consumers does not (unfortunately) apply to Trusts. (Paragraph 7 is merely restating the existing law—see the alarming case of *Armitage* v *Nurse* [1998] Ch 241; [1997] 3 WLR 1046; [1997] 2 All ER 705.)

13.4.1 Specific duties of trustees of land

If new-style trustees of land decide to sell all or part of the trust land, they are under a duty to get the best price reasonably obtainable. If trustees sell at less than the best price, then provided the **purchaser** has acted in good faith the sale will be valid and the **purchaser** cannot be sued. However, the trustees who sold at the cheap price will be in breach of trust, and the beneficiaries can insist that the trustees make up the shortfall.

Similarly, trustees who lease all or part of the trust land to a tenant must charge the full market rent. (The trustees can however charge a premium on the grant of a lease, even though this has the effect of reducing the 'market' rent the tenant is willing to pay.) If the trustees decide to grant an option over the trust land, it must be on terms similar to those which would be obtained by an outright owner acting in his own financial best interests.

Suppose, however, the trust land is farm land and the trustees decide to retain the land in their own possession. They will be under a duty to farm the land efficiently, so as to get the best financial return obtainable by reasonable farming methods.

 EXERCISE 13.1

Darren and Sharon, two city-dwellers who know nothing about agriculture, are appointed trustees of Purpleacre, a large farm. Advise Darren and Sharon.

Clearly they would be fools to try and run the farm themselves. They might well end up having to pay damages for breach of trust. On what I have already told you, I hope you have spotted two possible courses of action. Darren and Sharon could lease Purpleacre to a tenant farmer who did have the requisite expertise. Alternatively, they could simply sell Purpleacre and invest the proceeds in stocks and shares, etc.

A rather different solution would be to appoint a person who is an expert in agriculture to manage the farm on their behalf. The manager's salary (and the wages of his employees) will be a legitimate expense of the trust which Darren and Sharon will be able to deduct from the **gross** revenue of the farm. The **net** income will be payable to the beneficiary(ies) with current equitable interest(s) under the trust.

A yet further alternative may be to delegate their powers to a beneficiary under s. 9 of the 1996 Act. This power of delegation is considered at 13.6 to 13.6.3 below.

13.4.2 Placing trustees of land under a duty to consult the beneficiaries

One of the criticisms often made of the Settled Land Act 1925 is that it makes the life tenant 'boss' of the settled land. Although a Settled Land Act life tenant is a (rather peculiar) type of trustee, subject to the general duty to get the best financial return for any disposition he makes, he is not under any duty to consult other beneficiaries about proposed dispositions.

Suppose Hugeacres is subject to a strict settlement, 'To John for life, remainder to [John's son] Keith for life, remainder to [Keith's son] Leonard in fee simple'. John is life tenant and now wants to sell Hugeacres as he feels that he is getting too old to manage the land properly. Under the Settled Land Act 1925 John can sell Hugeacres without even consulting Keith and Leonard, who may well be disappointed that they do not 'inherit' what they regard as the family estate.

Where there is a trust for sale, then normally independent trustees are 'bosses' of the trust land. It was possible, under the law operating prior to the Trusts of Land etc. Act 1996, for a person creating a trust for sale to include an express clause that the trustees should consult the beneficiaries regarding the running of the trust, including the decision whether to carry out the 'duty' to sell. However, it seems that such a clause was included only in a minority of express trusts for sale.

Against this background of (usually) no duty to consult beneficiaries, s. 11 of the Trusts of Land etc. Act 1996 does represent a small but not insignificant change in the law. Section 11(1) provides:

(1) The trustees of land shall in the exercise of any function relating to land subject to the trust—
   (a) so far as practicable, consult the beneficiaries of full age and beneficially entitled to an interest in possession in the land, and
   (b) so far as consistent with the general interest of the trust, give effect to the wishes of those beneficiaries, or (in case of dispute) of the majority (according to the value of their combined interests).

A number of more detailed points should be made about this provision; all of these points tend to demonstrate that the duty created by s. 11(1) is somewhat restricted in character.

First, the duty is to consult the beneficiary or beneficiaries 'entitled to an interest in possession'. Suppose, in 1998, Blueacre is conveyed, 'To Timmy and Tammy in trust for Mr and Mrs Smith for their lives, remainder to their [eight] children in equal shares'. Timmy and Tammy will be under a duty to consult Mr and Mrs Smith, not the children. This would be the case even if Mr and Mrs Smith were elderly and in poor health.

Secondly, it is a duty **to consult** not a duty **to obey**. True, paragraph (b) talks of giving effect to the wishes of the beneficiaries, but only 'as far as consistent with the general interest of the trust'. It is the trustees who decide what is in the general interest of the trust.

Thirdly, unlike most of the Trusts of Land etc. Act 1996, s. 11(1) only applies to trusts coming into effect after the commencement of the Act. Moreover, where a trust of land is created by will, s. 11(1) only applies if the will was **made** after the commencement of the Act. A will is made when it is signed and witnessed. It takes effect when the testator dies, perhaps many years later.

? QUESTION 13.1

Suppose that Jack *made* his will in 1996, but died in 2005. The will creates a trust which was phrased as a trust for sale but which will now take effect as a new-style trust of land. Will the s. 11 duty to consult beneficiaries be applicable?

The answer is 'No', as the will was **made** before the Act commenced.

Finally, a purchaser of trust land is not under any duty to enquire whether the beneficiaries have been consulted. If beneficiaries have not been consulted when they should have been, the conveyance (or other transaction) is valid.

13.4.3 Personal occupation of trust land by beneficiaries

Prior to the coming into force of the Trusts of Land etc. Act 1996 there were numerous **trusts for sale** displaying the following characteristics:

(a) The property involved was not some vast estate but a house, cottage, flat, or (occasionally) small business premises.

(b) It was the intention of the people creating the trust that the property should be used by beneficiaries of the trust as their home, or (where appropriate) their place of business.

(c) Despite the trust for sale, there was no intention that the property be sold in the foreseeable future. In technical terms, the trustees exercised their power to postpone sale.

These trusts for sale, numerous as they were, caused problems for traditionalist land lawyers. They pedantically and zealously applied the old doctrine of conversion—'How can beneficiaries who have not got an interest in land but only an interest in proceeds of sale have a right to live on the land?'

Fortunately these traditionalists lost the argument long before 1996. Back in 1955 Lord Denning held that where property subject to a trust for sale was acquired for occupation by the beneficiaries, the beneficiaries did have a right to occupy the land, notwithstanding the doctrine of conversion. This view was adhered to in later cases, and the House of Lords in *Williams and Glyn's Bank* v *Boland* [1981] AC 487 accepted that it was correct.

The 1996 Act sweeps away the doctrine of conversion and transforms all trusts for sale into 'new-style' trusts. Further, to make matters crystal clear regarding occupation of trust land by beneficiaries, it includes a specific provision on the issue, s. 12.

13.4.3.1 Section 12 of the Trusts of Land and Appointment of Trustees Act 1996

This section provides:

(1) A beneficiary who is beneficially entitled to an interest in possession in land subject to a trust of land is entitled by reason of his interest to occupy the land at any time if at that time—

(a) the purposes of the trust include making the land available for his occupation (or for the occupation of beneficiaries of a class of which he is a member or of beneficiaries in general), or

(b) the land is held by the trustees so as to be so available.

(2) Subsection (1) does not confer on a beneficiary a right to occupy land if it is either unavailable or unsuitable for occupation by him.

In short, a beneficiary (subject to s. 12(2)) has the right to occupy the trust land if either:

(a) the trust was set up to provide land for his occupation, either solely or jointly with others; **or**

(b) the trustees subsequent to the creation of the trust acquired the land for his occupation, either solely or jointly with others.

I should at this stage make two supplementary points. First, if in pursuance to s. 12(1)(a) a beneficiary or beneficiaries exercise his/their right to occupy the trust land, the trustees are of course exempted from their normal duty to maximize the financial return from the land.

Secondly, for reasons which will emerge in **Chapters 14** to **16**, there will be numerous trusts where two or sometimes more beneficiaries have simultaneously the right to occupy the trust land. If the beneficiaries fall out with each other the extensive provisions in the 1996 Act for settling disputes will come into play. These provisions (ss. 13, 14, and 15) are discussed in **Chapter 16**.

13.4.4 Investment (or other use) of 'capital money' by trustees of land

If trustees of land sell all or part of the land, the sale will of course give rise to a payment of capital money (the price!). Capital money may also be generated by other transactions falling short of an outright sale, e.g., if a lease is granted at a premium, that premium is capital money. If an option is granted, the price **paid for the option** is capital money.

Any capital received by the trustees cannot just be left in a current bank account. It must be put to good use by the trustees for benefit of the beneficiaries. To what sort of uses can trustees of land put capital which they have in their hands?

The trustees could, subject to the duty of care in s. 1 of the 2000 Act, invest spare capital in any kind of investment, e.g., stocks and shares or government bonds (s. 3 of the Trustee Act 2000); or they could spend the money on improving any land which they retain; or they could exercise the very broad power originally granted by s. 6(3) and (4) of the Trusts of Land etc. Act 1996 but now contained in s. 8 of the Trustee Act 2000. Section 8 provides:

(1) A trustee may acquire freehold or leasehold land in the United Kingdom—
  (a) as an investment,
  (b) for occupation by a beneficiary; or
  (c) for any other reason.

The reference in s. 8(1) to 'freehold or leasehold land' means that trustees of land can buy a fee simple **or a lease of any duration**. Under the old law in force prior to the commencement of the 1996 Act, trustees for sale of land could purchase a fee simple or a lease **with at least 60 years to run**. Trustees of a new-style trust of land can now invest in a short-term lease. However, bearing in mind the duty of trustees to act in the interests of the trust as a whole, it would surely be a breach of trust for trustees of a trust expected to endure for many years to invest capital in buying short-term leases.

The reference in s. 8(1)(c) to 'any other reason' may at first sight be puzzling. Again we must read it against the background of the trustees' duty to act in the best interests of the trust. 'Any other reason' clearly must mean 'any other reason which benefits the trust or the beneficiaries'. For example, suppose the main trust land is Blackacre. Neighbouring Whiteacre comes up for sale. The trustees fear that Whiteacre will be purchased by someone who will use that land for an undesirable purpose which will depreciate the value of Blackacre. The trustees can use any spare capital they have to purchase Whiteacre.

13.4.4.1 Sale of the whole of the trust land followed by purchase of 'replacement' land

At the beginning of 13.4.3 I made the point that prior to the coming into force of the 1996 Act, there were numerous **trusts for sale** where the trust property consisted of just one house, cottage, or even flat. What if the trustees sold the house/cottage/flat—could the trustees then redeploy the proceeds on the purchase of a 'replacement'?

Amazingly, a judge in 1945 (*Re Wakeman* [1945] Ch 177) held that trustees for sale, once they had sold all the land they held, could not go out and buy replacement land. Instead, the money had to be put into investments such as stocks and shares. This highly inconvenient ruling could however be avoided by putting an express clause in the trust for sale authorizing the trustees to buy replacement land.

Happily, the *Re Wakeman* principle has now been reversed by legislation, first by s. 17(1) of the 1996 Act and now by s. 8(1) of the Trustee Act 2000.

13.5 Restrictions on trustees of land powers of disposition

We now come to that part of the Trusts of Land etc. Act 1996 which I find the most troublesome. Section 8 effectively allows settlors creating trusts of land to restrict the wide powers of disposition conferred by s 6. (Note that s. 7 referred to in s. 8 is a very minor provision not considered in this text.) Section 8 provides:

(1) Sections 6 and 7 do not apply in the case of a [new-style] trust of land created by a disposition in so far as provision to the effect that they do not apply is made by the disposition.

(2) If the disposition creating such a trust makes provision requiring any consent to be obtained to the exercise of any power conferred by section 6 or 7, the power may not be exercised without that consent.

Section 8(1) thus allows what I call '**takeaway clauses**', under which the settlor deprives the trustees of powers of disposition which they would otherwise have. Section 8(2) (less radically) provides for '**consent clauses**', under which a disposition requires the consent of named person(s).

13.5.1 Takeaway clauses

Section 8(1), unlike s. 8(2), represents a radical new departure in the law. Under the old and hopelessly outmoded Settled Land Act 1925 the life tenant was given somewhat restricted powers of disposition, but those powers of disposition were then zealously guarded by s. 106 of the Act. Under s. 106, any attempt to directly or indirectly limit the life tenant's statutory powers was void.

Contrast the 1996 Act. Section 6 gives the trustees unlimited powers of disposition, but s. 8 then tells settlors, 'you can take away any or all of the trustees' powers of disposition'. There can be both '**partial takeaway clauses**' and '**total takeaway clauses**'. A settlor could say, for example, 'the trustees shall have no power to lease the land for more than 50 years', or 'the trustees shall not grant any options to purchase with respect to the trust land'. Alternatively, there seems absolutely nothing to stop a settlor imposing a total takeaway. He can now include in his trust of land a clause, 'The trustees shall have no power to create or convey any estate or interest in the land held in trust under this deed'.

13.5.2 **The problem posed by total takeaway clauses**

By using a clause like the one just quoted above, the settlor will have achieved, in the third millenium, the great ambition of generations of old-fashioned settlors of land. He will have rendered the land in question (for the duration of the trust) inalienable.

It may be argued that no **sensible** settlor of a trust of land would ever, in modern economic conditions, create a trust with a total takeaway clause. That may be so. But the history of land law (and the law of trusts) is littered with **eccentric** settlors trying to impose their conditions for holding property on succeeding generations of their families. A lot of the thinking behind the Settled Land Acts 1882 and 1925 was to curb such eccentric settlors. By contrast, s. 8 of the 1996 Act is an open invitation to such settlors to impose their eccentric wishes.

13.5.3 **Dispositions infringing takeaway clauses**

What if the trustees attempt to make a disposition which exceeds their powers because the relevant power has been removed by a takeaway clause? For example, what if the trustees 'sell' the fee simple despite the trust specifically stating that there shall be no power of sale?

13.5.3.1 **Where the land is registered title**

The limits on the trustees' powers will presumably be entered on the register in the form of a formal 'restriction'. (I use the word 'restriction' in its technical land registration sense; see 10.5.1 above.) Any transaction in breach of the 'restriction' would be void, and the registry would obviously refuse to register it.

If, for some reason, no 'restriction' has been entered on the register, then any sale in breach of the takeaway clause would (applying general principles of land registration law) be valid.

13.5.3.2 **Where land is unregistered title**

The problem of dispositions by trustees which exceed their powers is dealt with by s. 16(3) of the 1996 Act:

(3) Where the powers of trustees of land are limited by virtue of section 8—
    (a) the trustees shall take all reasonable steps to bring the limitation to the notice of any purchaser of the land from them, but
    (b) the limitation does not invalidate any conveyance by the trustees to a purchaser who has no actual notice of the limitation.

Thus a disposition in favour of a purchaser who has **no actual notice** of the takeaway clause will be valid.

 EXERCISE 13.2

Consider whether a purchaser is likely to have actual notice of a restriction on the trustees' powers.

I think almost all (potential) purchasers will have notice of restrictions on the trustees' powers. I do not place any faith in the trustees complying with s. 16(3)(a). Rather, I look to the fact that the limits on the trustees' powers will almost certainly be set out in the conveyance to the trustees. It follows that the only sort of purchaser who is likely to be 'protected' by s. 16(3)(b) is one who never even looked at the title deeds. Put a slightly different way, a conveyance in defiance of a takeaway clause is likely to be **valid** in favour of a grossly negligent do-it-yourself purchaser who never even looked at the deeds. Vis-à-vis a purchaser who did look at the deeds, the conveyance will be **void**, as the purchaser is bound to have seen the takeaway clause.

13.5.4 Are there ways of escaping from a takeaway clause?

In the light of the previous discussion, this is an important question. Suppose, for example, there is a partial takeaway clause forbidding the trustees from leasing the land for more than 50 years. A potential tenant comes along, offering to take a lease for 99 years. The terms he is offering to the trustees regarding premium, rent, tenants' covenants, etc. are in economic terms absolutely irresistible. What can be done?

There are three possibilities which need to be considered, though in my view only the first of these possibilities is of any help, and then only in limited situations.

13.5.4.1 Invoke the rule in *Saunders v Vautier*

If all the beneficiaries of the trust are of full age and in total agreement, they can terminate the trust containing the takeaway clause, and set up another trust without the offending clause. Too much faith should not be placed in this solution to the problem which Parliament has created by s. 8. In most trusts there is usually at least one non-adult beneficiary. Even when all the beneficiaries are adults, getting unanimity may not be easy.

13.5.4.2 Invoke the statutory disputes jurisdiction of the court

Section 14 of the 1996 Act contains very wide powers for the courts to settle disputes arising regarding a trust of land. The details of this provision we will consider in **Chapter 16**. By s. 14(2)(a) the court is empowered to make an order:

relating to the exercise by the trustees of any of their functions (including an order relieving them of any obligation to obtain the consent of, or to consult, any person in connection with the exercise of their functions). . .

Ignoring for a moment the words in brackets, I find it difficult to believe that the key phrase 'the exercise by the trustees of any of their functions' extends to cover 'functions' which the settlor has deliberately said the trustees shall not have.

Then when we do look at the words in brackets we see that if a settlor has, pursuant to s. 8(2), included a consent clause, then the need for consent(s) can be overridden by court order. The very presence of these words in brackets allowing a consent clause under s. 8(2) to be overridden by a s. 14 order strongly suggests that a takeaway clause under s. 8(1) cannot be overridden.

13.5.4.3 Invoke the inherent jurisdiction of the court to deal with 'emergencies'

There is a line of cases in the law of trusts which says that if some 'emergency' arises in the administration of a trust, the court can authorize trustees to carry out transactions which would otherwise be beyond the trustees' powers. The leading (and seemingly most recent) case dates from 1901 (*Re New* [1901] 2 Ch 534 at 544). In that case the Court of Appeal stressed that the emergency must arise 'from some peculiar state of circumstances for which provision is not expressly made by the trust instrument'. The case must be one where 'it may reasonably be supposed to be one not foreseen or anticipated by the author of the trust'.

I do not think that a takeaway clause could be overridden using this 'emergency' jurisdiction. A settlor who insists on inserting a takeaway clause has presumably been advised by his solicitor of the risks involved, e.g., that the takeaway clause will prevent the trustees from seizing some golden economic opportunity to exploit the land. The 'emergency' can hardly be described as 'unforeseen'.

Nor has the settlor failed to expressly provide for 'some peculiar state of circumstances'. He has made **express** provision. He has, exercising the **right** given to him by the 1996 Act, provided that the trustees shall have no power to deal with the situation.

13.5.5 Consent clauses

While s. 8(1) of the 1996 Act is a radical new departure in the law (contrast s. 106 of the Settled Land Act 1925) the same cannot be said for s. 8(2). That subsection provides:

If the disposition creating such a trust [of land] makes provision requiring any consent to be obtained to the exercise of any power conferred by section 6 or 7, the power may not be exercised without that consent.

 EXERCISE 13.3

Re-read 11.6.5 above, including **Question 11.2**.

Under the old law we had the (somewhat paradoxical) concept of a trust for sale subject to consents. Under the new law we have the (in practical reality) very similar concept of a 'new-style' trust of land subject to consents.

 EXERCISE 13.4

At 11.6.5 above I gave an example of a trust for sale:

To Tim and Tam on trust for sale for X for life, remainder to Y. The sale shall only take place if W and X agree to it.

Redraft this example so that it complies with the new law.

The land is conveyed, 'To Tim and Tam on trust for X for life, remainder to Y. If the trustees wish to create or convey any estate or interest in the land held in trust under this deed, they must obtain the consent of W and X'.

The close similarity of the new-style trust of land subject to consents to the old trust for sale subject to consents is further demonstrated by the following two points. The first point is s. 10(1) of the 1996 Act, equivalent to s. 26(1) of the Law of Property

Act 1925, which provides:

If a disposition creating a trust of land requires the consent of more than two persons to the exercise by the trustees of any function relating to the land, the consent of any two of them to the exercise of the function is sufficient in favour of a purchaser.

Suppose land is conveyed to Tim and Tom as trustees, 'Any sale or other disposition of the land to take place only with the consent of A, B, C, D, E, F, G, H, I, J, K, L, M, N, O, P, Q, R, S, T, U, V, W, X, Y, and Z'. The settlor has **not** been very smart. The consent of any two of A to Z will be sufficient to validate a sale or other disposition, e.g., a lease. By supplying a long list of names, rather than confining himself to two, the settlor has (ironically) made it easier to dispose of the land.

The second point I have already touched upon. Under the old law, where there was a trust for sale subject to consent, but a transaction was being blocked by a refusal of consent, the trustees (or beneficiaries) could invoke the court's jurisdiction under s. 30 of the Law of Property Act 1925. Under s. 30 the court could (*inter alia*) authorize a proposed transaction to go ahead despite the absence of consent(s).

The position is effectively the same under new-style trusts of land subject to consents. At 13.5.4.2 above I referred to s. 14(2)(a) of the 1996 Act. While under this provision the court cannot (it seems) authorize a transaction in defiance of a 'takeaway clause', it can authorize a transaction to go ahead without the consent(s) required by the trust deed.

13.5.5.1 A likely use for a new-style trust subject to consents

 QUESTION 13.2

Reconsider **Question 11.2** (at 11.6.5) on the assumption that the new law applies to Tom's will.

The answer is now more straightforward. Tom cannot, of course, create a strict settlement. His **only** option is to create a new-style trust. He should appoint as trustees people who are sympathetic to his wishes. They will hold the large house in trust for Wendy for life, remainder to Simon. He should also include clauses:

(a) requiring that any disposition affecting the land should be with the consent of both Wendy and Simon;

(b) stating that a purpose of the trust is that the large house should be available for Wendy to live in.

(By clause (b) he will confer on Wendy a right to occupy the house under s. 12 of the 1996 Act.)

13.6 Delegation of trustees' powers to beneficiaries

13.6.1 The old law background

Where a strict settlement exists (and there are still a few) the position regarding both ownership of the legal estate and powers of disposition is very anomalous when compared with every other type of trust, whether ancient or modern. One of the **beneficiaries** of the trust, the life tenant, is very much 'the boss'. He holds the legal title to the trust property. He also has wide (though not unlimited) powers of disposition over the settled land.

Where there is a strict settlement, there will be 'trustees for the purposes of the Settled Land Acts'. But 'SLA trustees' do not hold the legal title or indeed (speaking generally) have much to do until the land is sold. The most important role of SLA trustees is that when a transaction by the life tenant gives rise to a capital payment (e.g., the price on a sale or the premium on the grant of a long lease), the SLA trustees receive and invest that capital payment.

Where a trust for sale of land was created under the 'old' law, the trustees were 'boss'. They held the legal estate to the land and they had the powers of disposition over the trust land. The trustees (for sale) were in control, just like every other type of trust except the strict settlement.

Section 29 of the Law of Property Act 1925 constituted a relatively small exception to the rule that 'the trustees are "bosses" of a trust for sale of land'. Under the old s. 29, trustees for sale had power to delegate certain of their functions to a beneficiary currently entitled to the income from the land.

The following two points regarding the old s. 29 are worth noting:

(a) The power to delegate was confined to the day-to-day management of the land and the leasing of the land. Other functions of the trustees (e.g., sale!) could not be delegated.

(b) If the trustees delegated management and/or leasing, and the beneficiary failed to exercise his (delegated) powers with proper care, it was the beneficiary, never the trustees, who was liable for any loss suffered.

13.6.2 **Delegation by trustees under section 9 of the 1996 Act**

Section 9 of the Trusts of Land etc. Act 1996 is a far-reaching provision, much wider in its scope than s. 29 of the Law of Property Act 1925, which it 'replaces'. However, in one material respect s. 9 is narrower than the old s. 29. Under s. 29, a delegation could be made by a simple written document. Under the new s. 9 the trustees (acting jointly) must, in order to delegate their functions, use a 'power of attorney'. (A power of attorney is a formal deed appointing the 'donee of the power' to act as an agent of the donor of the power.)

The far-reaching nature of s. 9 should be apparent if you study the terms of subsections (1) and (5):

(1) The trustees of land may, by power of attorney, delegate to any beneficiary or beneficiaries of full age and beneficially entitled to an interest in possession in land subject to the trust any of their functions as trustees which relate to the land.

. . .

(5) A delegation under subsection (1) may be for any period or indefinite.

Suppose Tim, Tom, and Tam hold Highacres farm on trust for Leonard for life, remainder to Matthew in fee simple. At one extreme Tim, Tom, and Tam could simply delegate the management of the farm to Leonard for a short period, say one year. At the other extreme they could execute a power of attorney saying, 'We delegate all our functions in relation to Highacres to Leonard for an indefinite period'. This latter sort of delegation I will refer to as '**total delegation**'. The trustees retain the legal estate to the land, but will have absolutely no functions **in relation to the land**. (Note that there cannot be any delegation to Matthew—he is not a beneficiary entitled to an interest in possession.)

13.6.2.1 **The revocation of a section 9 power of attorney**

First, note that it is a characteristic of a power of attorney that it ceases to be valid if the donee of the power (Leonard in the example just given) dies or becomes incapable of acting. Of greater importance is s. 9(3):

A power of attorney under subsection (1) shall be given by all the trustees jointly and . . . may be revoked by any one or more of them; and such a power is revoked by the appointment as a trustee of a person other than those by whom it is given (though not by any of those dying or otherwise ceasing to be a trustee).

Two specific points should be carefully noted about this provision:

(a) While all trustees must sign a delegation, a revocation can be achieved by one trustee on his own. Suppose in my Highacres example, Tim, Tom, and Tam all sign a total delegation. Tim subsequently becomes concerned about the way Leonard is dealing with Highacres. He can unilaterally revoke the delegation, even though Tom and Tam still have complete confidence in Leonard.

(b) If a trustee dies or resigns from the trust, that does not revoke a s. 9 delegation. However, if a new trustee is appointed, that does revoke the delegation! Suppose in my Highacres example, Tim, rather than force the issue regarding Leonard's competence, resigns from the trust. This resignation will not end the s. 9 delegation. But if Tom and Tam then appoint another trustee, Tem, that **appointment** will revoke the delegation.

13.6.2.2 **Liability if a delegatee beneficiary proves to be incompetent**

My Highacres example raises the perhaps obvious question, 'What if Leonard really is incompetent to run the farm? Who must compensate the trust for losses which it suffers because of Leonard's incompetence?'

Liability of the delegatee(s)

This is governed by s. 9(7), which provides:

Beneficiaries to whom functions have been delegated under subsection (1) are, in relation to the exercise of the functions, in the same position as trustees (with the same duties and liabilities) . . .

Thus a delegatee under s. 9 becomes a kind of quasi-trustee. A delegatee will be under the usual duty of a trustee to take good care of the trust property and to get the best financial return from the land obtainable by reasonable methods. For example, if a delegatee with a 'total delegation' decides to sell the land, he must get the best price reasonably obtainable. If he fails to get that 'best price', the other beneficiaries (and presumably the real trustees) could sue to compel him to make up the difference.

Liability of the trustees—the 1996 rule

The original Trusts of Land etc. Bill, as drafted by the Law Commission, provided that trustees who delegated their functions would (in principle) be liable for the acts and defaults of the delegatee(s). In my 1989 article I therefore wrote:

> Under the new scheme trustees of land will not want to delegate their powers to a beneficiary whose competence is open to question. Moreover, once they have delegated powers to a beneficiary, they will need, in their own interests, to keep the beneficiary under close supervision.

However Parliament in 1996 decided to enact a different rule, much more favourable to trustees than that proposed by the Law Commission. Section 9(8) provided:

> Where any function has been delegated to a beneficiary or beneficiaries under subsection (1), the trustees are jointly and severally liable for any act or default of the beneficiary, or of any of the beneficiaries, in the exercise of the function if, and only if, the trustees did not exercise reasonable care in deciding to delegate the function to the beneficiary or beneficiaries.

Thus it was the **decision** to delegate which mattered. If that decision to delegate was taken with reasonable care, but the delegatee messed things up and caused a loss to the trust, the trustees were not liable.

Liability of the trustees—the stricter rule in the Trustee Act 2000

The generous rule to trustees in s. 9(8) of the Trusts of Land etc. Act did not survive very long. Any delegation under s. 9 made after the commencement date of the Trustee Act 2000 (1 February 2001) is governed by a new s. 9A of the Trusts of Land etc. Act, inserted by Sch. 2, Part II, para. 45 of the 2000 Trustee Act.

(Do not be confused by the reference to irrevocable delegations in s. 9A(2)(b). With the kinds of trusts we are concerned with in a Land Law course, a delegation is always revocable.)

Under this new section the trustees are under a duty to take reasonable care to keep an active watch on the delegatee beneficiary, and to 'intervene' under subsection (4) if things appear to be going wrong. The trustees could 'intervene' by revoking (or at least threatening to revoke) the delegation or could give directions to the delegate beneficiary. If trustees failed to keep a careful eye on the beneficiary, and/or failed to 'intervene' when things seemed to be going wrong, the trustees could be liable to compensate the **other** beneficiaries for any loss suffered.

The practical effect of this new s. 9A (unfortunate in my view) is that trustees of land may be less keen to delegate the running of the land to the relevant beneficiary(ies) for fear of incurring liability under the new section. Suppose, then, that you are drafting a new trust of land where the settlor is in fact keen that the life beneficiary (Leonard in my Highacres example) should actually run the land? I would suggest that in drafting the new trust, a clause should be inserted excluding the trustees' duty under s. 9A. This can be done under Sch. 1, para. 7 of the Trustee Act 2000, a provision which I mentioned at 13.4, and which allows trusts to include 'exemption clauses' limiting or excluding the trustees' liability for negligent acts.

13.6.3 Total delegation almost settled land

You may find this heading puzzling, but I do believe that, where the new-style trustees of land make a total delegation, the situation becomes somewhat analogous to 'old-fashioned' settled land. Why do I say that?

I say that because of two factors. First, when there is a total delegation, the delegatee beneficiary, like a life tenant of settled land, becomes the effective 'boss' of the trust land. The second factor is an important point which I have not previously mentioned. The trustees can delegate those functions 'which relate to the land'. That phrase does not include the receiving and investing of any 'capital money' payable by a purchaser if the delegatee makes a disposition over the land. So if the delegatee-beneficiary sells the land, the purchaser must pay the price to the **trustees**. If he pays the price to the delegatee, the equitable interests of the other beneficiaries will not be overreached. Similarly, if land is leased at a premium, the premium must be paid by the tenant to the trustees, not the delegatee who granted the lease.

There are, of course, significant differences between settled land and total delegation under a new-style trust. In particular, even though there is a total delegation, the legal estate to the trust land remains with the trustees. When the delegatee sells, he is actually (validly) conveying a legal estate he has not got.

I should also remind you that a total delegatee, unlike a life tenant, will have unlimited powers of disposition over the trust land. On the other hand, a life tenant cannot (normally) have his powers revoked. A delegatee's powers can be revoked by one trustee, perhaps acting in opposition to his colleagues who wish the delegation to continue. Moreover, there is no duty to give any reason for the revocation.

?   **QUESTION** 13.2

John is a farmer aged 65. He wishes to retire from farming. He wishes to create a trust over his farm, Widefields, with equitable interests 'to my daughter Linda [aged 35] for life, remainder in fee simple to her son Sam [aged 5]'. Linda has helped her father run the farm since graduating from agricultural college. John tells you proudly: 'She is a first-rate farmer, and with excellent business sense. I want her to have total control of Widefields. It is of course too early to say how Sam will turn out. He might not want to be a farmer. So when Linda in her turn retires, I want her to have the power to sell Widefields.' Advise John.

John cannot, of course, create a strict settlement. He should create a new-style trust of land, appointing as trustees people who fully understand his intentions. (He should perhaps select younger members of 'our' firm of solicitors.) He should include in the trust the following three provisions:

(a) a statement that a purpose of the trust is to allow Linda to occupy Widefields farm (he thus invokes s. 12 of the 1996 Act, which, I should stress, is not confined to residential premises);

(b) a paragraph setting out his views as to his daughter's capabilities as a farmer and businesswoman, and strongly recommending that the trustees make a 'total delegation' in her favour;

(c) a clause exempting the trustees from the duty under s. 9A.

(The trustees could make a total delegation confident that an accusation of negligence against them would get short shrift from a court.)

CONCLUDING REMARKS

We have now considered most of the important provisions of the Trusts of Land and Appointment of Trustees Act 1996. We have not, however, considered ss. 13, 14, and 15, though s. 14 has received a brief mention. These three sections provide for the settling of any disputes which may arise regarding a trust of land. While these sections are in principle applicable to all trusts of land, they are likely to be of particular importance where the trust of land exists in favour of co-owners. We have not yet considered the law of co-ownership. It is therefore sensible to deal with ss. 13 to 15 in **Chapter 16**.

The provisions we have considered in this chapter are certainly not immune from criticism. The biggest problem is of course s. 8(1). This is a charter for eccentric settlors to saddle their families with unsaleable land. It seems to put the clock back to before 1882. Moreover, we should contrast eccentric settlors who impose total takeaway clauses with James in **Exercise 12.1** at 12.3.2. He proposes an eminently sensible solution to the problems of his family but he is not allowed to adopt that solution because the power to postpone sale cannot be excluded. James cannot **insist** that the land be sold within a defined period.

Another serious defect with the 1996 Act is what I called in my 1989 article, 'the lingering death of settled land'. Existing strict settlements could have been brought within the new regime in the following way. On the commencement of the new Act:

(a) the legal title would automatically be taken from the life tenant and vested in the SLA trustees;

(b) there would be an automatic total delegation to the ex-life tenant of all the trustees' functions in relation to the land;

(c) by way of exception to the general rules in s. 9, the delegation would be irrevocable;

(d) again by way of exception to the general rules in s. 9, the trustees should not in any circumstances be liable for the delegatee's defaults.

SUMMARY

Right to Occupy Trust Land Section 12 of the Trusts of Land etc Act gives the current beneficiary(ies) a right to occupy the land if either

(a) the trust was set up with a view to personal occupation by the beneficiary(ies) or

(b) the land was acquired by the trustees with a view to personal occupation by the beneficiary(ies).

Trustees' Powers In principle, trustees have all the powers of an outright owner of land, but those powers can be limited, either by

(i) a partial or total takeaway clause restricting those powers;

(ii) a consent clause allowing some or all powers to be only exercised if the consent of named person(s) is obtained.

Delegation of Trustees Powers Section 9 of the 1996 Act allows the trustees to delegate any or all of their powers to the current beneficiary. But the trustees must be sure that the initial decision to delegate is a wise one. Furthermore, the trustees must now supervise the delegate beneficiary, and intervene if things start going wrong.

CHAPTER 13: ASSESSMENT EXERCISE

Samantha owns two houses, Black House and White House. She is critically ill and wishes to make a new will.

With respect to Black House, she wants to leave it to her son Thomas for life, remainder in fee simple to her grandsons Luke and John. 'I am very keen that Luke and John should inherit Black House after Thomas's death. I don't want the house disposed of during Thomas's lifetime.'

With respect to White House, she wants to leave it to her cousin Norman for life, remainder in fee simple to Norman's two children Philip and Philippa. 'White House is rather large and a long way from the shops. It may prove unsuitable for Norman. If that proves to be the case, would it be possible for him, or somebody on his behalf, to sell White House and buy (say) a lease of a smaller house on the edge of the town centre?'

Advise Samantha as to the drafting of her will.

See Appendix for a specimen answer.

■ **FURTHER READING**

For the thinking behind the various provisions of the 1996 Act discussed in this chapter, see Law Commission report no. 181 'Transfer of Land—Trusts of Land', pages 16–25. (Part IIB of the report.)

For possible ways round the problems created by s 8(1) of the 1996 Act, see Gary Watt, 'Escaping s 8(1) provisions in "new style" trusts of land', (1997) 61 Conveyancer 263.

PART V

Co-ownership

14 Co-ownership of land—the basic concepts

14.1 Objectives

By the end of this chapter you should:

1 Be able to explain the crucial concepts of 'joint tenancy' and 'tenancy in common', **and the differences between them**

2 Appreciate the problem which existed at the beginning of the twentieth century caused by tenancies in common existing with respect to a legal estate

3 Appreciate why the 1925 legislators chose to impose a trust for sale upon all co-owners

4 Have very firmly in your mind that a tenancy in common cannot now exist with respect to a legal estate

5 Be able to apply the rules which determine whether co-owners are joint tenants or tenants in common of their equitable interests under the trust (for sale) which must exist in all cases of co-ownership

14.2 Introduction

The law of co-ownership is a topic which directly affects the private lives of many of the readers of this text. Most married (and unmarried) couples co-own the fee simple of the house in which they live. Alternatively, they co-own a fixed-term lease or periodic tenancy of the house or flat in which they are living. I should, however, stress that co-ownership is not confined to domestic/family situations. For example, (in particular) business partners may well be co-owners of the premises from which they conduct their business.

This chapter (the first of three on co-ownership) will focus on certain basic principles. It has two main themes. The first is that there are **two (very distinct) forms** of co-ownership in modern English property law. The second is the way Parliament, in 1925, endeavoured to solve problems which existed at that time in relation to co-ownership.

14.3 Unity of possession—the cornerstone of co-ownership

Co-ownership exists with respect to a piece of land only if 'unity of possession' between two or more people exists with respect to that piece of land. There is unity of possession if two or more people have concurrent rights to enjoy the **whole** of the relevant piece of land. For example,

Jack and Jill Smith own Dream House. Like all normal (married or unmarried) couples they each have rights to possess and enjoy the whole of the house. There is unity of possession and therefore co-ownership.

Contrast Dream House with Hollowtree Field. Farmers Dan and Giles 'own' Hollowtree Field. To the ordinary passer-by it appears to be a perfectly normal field. However there is an imaginary line running north-south across the field. Dan and Giles know where this boundary line is. Everything to the east of that line belongs exclusively to Dan, and Giles has no rights. Everything to the west belongs to Giles, and Dan has no rights. Is there co-ownership in this situation? Of course not. There is no unity of possession and therefore no co-ownership. There are two separate individual ownerships.

14.4 The two forms of co-ownership existing today

There were at common law four forms of co-ownership, but only two forms of co-ownership exist today:

(a) **Joint tenancy** Extremely common today; it is the usual (but not obligatory) form of co-ownership where the co-owners are members of the same 'family'.

(b) **Tenancy in common** Common today. It is usual (but not obligatory) where the co-owners are in a business relationship. Sometimes found within a 'family'.

(Note that in this context the words 'tenant' and 'tenancy' are used in their older, **broader**, sense. In that older sense the word 'tenant' connotes anybody who holds an estate in land, whether a fee simple, fee tail, life estate, or lease.)

14.5 Joint tenancy

Joint tenancy, at least in modern circumstances, is the simpler of the two forms of co-ownership. Its crucial distinguishing feature is the right of survivorship.

14.5.1 Right of survivorship

On the death of a joint tenant his interest does not pass under the law of succession, but rather passes to the surviving joint tenant(s).

Suppose Alf, Ben, and Chris are joint tenants of Green Field in fee simple. Alf dies. His will leaves 'all my property to my sister Diana'. Diana acquires no interest in Green Field. Ben and Chris are now joint tenants of Green Field. This would even be true if Alf's will had said, 'I leave all my property including my interest in Green Field to Diana'.

Suppose that Ben now dies intestate, with his widow Elspeth as his sole 'statutory next-of-kin'. Elspeth acquires no interest in Green Field. Chris will be the sole outright owner in fee simple of Green Field. (When he dies normal succession laws will apply.) To put the matter crudely, there is a sort of 'survival of the fittest'. Where there is a joint tenancy, the joint tenant who lives longest gets outright ownership!

This survivorship rule is the main reason why husband and wife co-owners (and other co-owners who are in a close family-type relationship) usually choose to be joint tenants rather than tenants in common. They genuinely wish the land to go to whoever lives longest.

The survivorship rule also explains why people who are **trustees** of property (whether land or any other type of property) are always joint tenants of that property. There are no complications when a trustee dies. The legal title to the trust property automatically passes to the remaining trustee(s).

?   **QUESTION** 14.1

Humphrey and Wendy Smith are joint tenants of Bugthorpe Manor, worth about £500,000. Humphrey is killed in a road accident. He dies intestate. His assets (apart from Bugthorpe Manor) are worth £120,000. He leaves two children, Jack and Jill. On intestacy a surviving spouse is always entitled to the first £125,000 of the deceased's assets. Above that figure, and the children get a share.

Do the children inherit anything on their father's death intestate?

The children inherit nothing, and that would be true even if Bugthorpe Manor were worth not £500,000 but (say) £5,000,000. In working out who gets the deceased's assets on a death intestate, the fact that the deceased was a joint tenant of a (possibly valuable) piece of property must be totally ignored. Thus Wendy is entitled to the £120,000 'other' assets left by her husband.

14.5.2 **The 'four unities'**

Wherever there is a joint tenancy, it necessarily follows that 'the four unities' exist between the co-owners:

- **Unity of possession.**
- **Unity of interest.**
- **Unity of title.**
- **Unity of time.**

'Unity of possession' I have already explained (see 14.3), and it is of course an essential prerequisite of all forms of co-ownership. (*Cf.* my Dan and Giles, owners of Green Field, example.) For co-owners to be joint tenants, the unities of interest, title, and time must also be present. If any of these three unities is absent, the co-owners will be tenants in common.

14.5.2.1 **Unity of interest**

For there to be unity of interest, each co-owner must have absolutely identical rights over the land in question. This subdivides into two separate points:

- **Each co-owner must have the same estate** It is of course possible for two or more people to be joint tenants of (say) a 10-year lease. What is not possible is a joint tenancy between (say) somebody with a 10-year lease and somebody with a 20-year lease.

- **Each co-owner must have an equal right to enjoy the land** Where there is a tenancy in common it is possible for the co-owners to have unequal shares. But where there is a joint tenancy, each joint tenant must have an equal interest in the land.

Suppose Len, Mike, Norman, and Ossie are joint tenants in fee simple of Blue Field. They lease Blue Field to Terri. Each of the four joint landlords is entitled to 25 per cent of the rent. (Note that it is technically **wrong** to talk of joint tenants having '**shares**' in land. One should rather talk of joint tenants having '**interests**' or '**rights**'.)

14.5.2.2 Unity of title

This means that each joint tenant must have acquired his interest from the same document or transaction. (As we shall see later when talking about 'severance' (see **Chapter 15**), it is possible to have a situation where there is co-ownership but the co-owners have acquired their rights under different transactions. Such co-owners must necessarily be tenants in common.)

14.5.2.3 Unity of time

For there to be a joint tenancy, the rights of each joint tenant must 'vest in interest' at the same time. Put in more every-day language, the rights of each joint tenant must commence at the same moment.

It is relatively rare to come across situations where the rights of co-owners commence at different times. But sometimes land is left by will (or granted by deed) in terms such as 'to the children of X as each attains 21'. Now (unless all the children are twins/triplets/quads, etc.) each child will attain 21 on a different date. There will be no unity of time. The children will therefore be tenants in common.

> **?** **QUESTION** 14.2
>
> What if land were granted 'to the children of X when the youngest attains 21'. Could the children in this example be joint tenants?

There would be unity of time, and the children therefore could be joint tenants.

14.6 Tenancy in common

14.6.1 The concept of undivided shares

Where a tenancy in common exists, the co-owners are said to own the property in 'undivided shares'. Each co-owner is regarded as having a distinct share in the property. The use of the adjective 'undivided' emphasizes that there is unity of possession. The land in question has not been physically divided up between the owners.

When a tenant in common dies there is no right of survivorship. His share passes under the normal law of succession. Let us suppose that Alf, Ben, and Chris, the same people mentioned at 14.5.1 as being joint tenants of Green Field, are also tenants in common in equal shares of Yellow Field. When Alf dies his one-third share in Yellow Field passes according to the terms of his will to his sister Diana. When Ben dies intestate his one-third share passes under the normal rules of intestacy to his widow Elspeth.

? **QUESTION** 14.3

Humphrey and Wendy Smith are tenants in common in equal shares of Bugthorpe Manor, worth about £500,000. Humphrey is killed in a road accident. He dies intestate. His assets (apart from Bugthorpe Manor) are worth £120,000. He leaves two children, Jack and Jill. On intestacy a surviving spouse is always entitled to the first £125,000 of the deceased's assets. Above that figure, and the children get a share.

  Do the children inherit anything on their father's death intestate?

This time, the answer is 'Yes'. On his death, Humphrey's assets are worth £370,000, his half share in Bugthorpe Manor plus his 'other' assets. Wendy will be entitled (outright) to the first £125,000. The remaining £245,000 is split between her and the two children employing a rather complex formula the details of which we need not consider.

14.6.2 **Unequal tenancies in common**

As has already been stressed, unity of possession is an essential feature of a tenancy in common. The other three 'unities' (interest, title, and time, see 14.5.2) **may** be present in a tenancy in common, **but are not essential**.

  It is particularly important to note that there can be a tenancy in common in **unequal** shares. Suppose Len, Mike, Norman, and Ossie are tenants in common of Red Field, Len with a one-third share, Mike and Norman with a quarter share each, and Ossie with one-sixth. They must share the benefits of the field in the appropriate proportions.

? **QUESTION** 14.4

Suppose the four men lease Red Field to Toni at £1,200 per annum rent. How should the rent be divided between them?

The rent should be divided £400 to Len, £300 each to Mike and Norman, and £200 to Ossie.

14.6.3 **The problems with tenancies in common in the early twentieth century**

At the beginning of the twentieth century **joint tenancies** were far less common than they are today. The idea (so prevalent today) of members of a family buying a home as joint tenants was almost unknown. On the other hand, there were a lot of tenancies in common, probably far more than exist today. At the turn of the twentieth century, if a family 'owned' a farm, or a small business such as a shop, then usually the individual members of the family owned the land as tenants in common.

Nowadays, if a family 'owns' a farm or business premises, one usually finds (on closer examination) that the farm, shop, or whatever is owned by a limited company bearing some title such as 'Bloggs Brothers **Limited**'. Bloggs Brothers Limited is in law **one person**, therefore the land is not co-owned. The individual brothers will be shareholders **in the company**. They will also probably be directors of the company, though that is not essential. (There is no legal limit on the maximum number of directors a company can have.)

Reverting to talking about co-ownership of land, you may have already noticed a practical conclusion to be drawn from my 'Alf, Ben, and Chris' examples at 14.5.1 and 14.6.1. Where there is a joint tenancy, the number of joint tenants will gradually decline by a process of natural wastage until the last survivor emerges as sole owner. Where there is a tenancy in common the fact that the shares of each co-owner pass according to the law of succession means that the number of co-owners is unlikely to decline, and the co-ownership is unlikely to come to an end.

I am at last getting to the problem which existed in the first part of the twentieth century. Suppose that in 1900 four brothers, Alan, Brian, Charles, and David, were tenants in common in equal shares of the fee simple in Streamfield Farm. In 1901, Giles, a neighbouring farmer, offered to buy a field which is inconveniently remote from the rest of Streamfield. The brothers accepted the offer and conveyed the field to Giles. For the conveyance to be valid all four brothers had to sign, as all four had a share in the legal fee simple in the field. (Getting four signatures on a document is not that difficult, particularly if the four people live in close proximity. But let us continue the story of Streamfield Farm.)

In 1905 Alan died. His will said 'My share in Streamfield is to be divided in equal shares between my three children'. In 1910 Brian died. His will said 'My share in Streamfield is to be divided in equal shares between my four children'. In 1915 Charles died. His will said 'My share in Streamfield is to be divided in equal shares between my five children'. In 1920 David died. His will said 'My share in Streamfield is to be divided in equal shares between my six children'.

Thus in the early 1920s no fewer than 18 people were tenants in common of Streamfield Farm. This sort of situation was not uncommon. A whole host of people would be tenants in common of a piece of land. Some might have an extremely small share.

In 1921 Giles offered to buy the rest of Streamfield Field at a price which all 14 tenants in common still in Britain thought was irresistible. The problem was the four who were abroad. Eleanor, Alan's daughter, had married and gone to Australia; Frank, one of Brian's sons, was a sheep farmer in New Zealand; George, one of Charles's sons, was a 'Mountie' in (remote) north-west Canada; Harriet, one of David's children, had gone exploring in the Amazon jungle.

For a valid conveyance of the legal fee simple in Streamfield Farm, all 18 would have had to have signed. Some of the signatures could not be obtained. Reluctantly, Giles had to withdraw his offer. Effectively, Streamfield Farm was unsaleable. Stories like the one of Streamfield Farm were commonplace in 1925. Remember that 1925 was in an era of large families and the far-flung British Empire. Passenger planes and telecommunications were in their infancy. Parliament therefore decided that a drastic remedy was needed to solve the problem caused by tenancies in common. This remedy also affected joint tenancies.

14.7 **The reform of co-ownership in 1925—the main objective**

Parliament was desperate to ameliorate the problem illustrated by our Streamfield Farm story at **14.6.3**. It thus passed reforms (to be found in ss. 34–36 of the Law of Property Act 1925) which ensured that where land is co-owned a maximum of four signatures is required on any conveyance or other transaction affecting that land.

14.7.1 **Drastic treatment for tenancies in common**

It would clearly have been impossible to abolish completely tenancies in common. Parliament did, however, enact the Law of Property Act 1925, s. 34. Subsection 2 provides (as amended in 1996):

Where, after the commencement of this Act, land is expressed to be conveyed to any persons in undivided shares and those persons are of full age, the conveyance shall (notwithstanding anything to the contrary in this Act) operate as if the land had been expressed to be conveyed to the grantees, or, if there are more than four grantees, to the four first named in the conveyance, as joint tenants [in trust for the persons interested in the land.]

The actual wording of this provision may strike you as obscure or even intimidating. But Parliament is **in effect** saying, 'A tenancy in common can no longer exist with respect to a legal fee simple or other legal property rights. A tenancy in common can still exist with respect to an equitable interest'.

Does this mean that land cannot be 'owned' by tenants in common? No—land can still be 'owned' by tenants in common. Section 34(2) of the 1925 Act is, however, crucial. This provision in effect lays down that where an estate or interest in land is conveyed to co-owners as tenants in common, a 'statutory' trust (for sale) is **imposed** upon those co-owners. Prior to the commencement of the Trusts of Land etc. Act 1996 the imposed trust was a trust for sale. After the commencement of the 1996 Act, the imposed trust is a new-style trust of land. (Whenever in **Chapters 14** to **16** you read the phrase 'trust (for sale)', I am referring to a situation where prior to the commencement of the 1996 Act there was a trust for sale, but after its commencement there is a new-style trust.) An example should explain how s. 34(2) operates.

Suppose that in 1990 the fee simple in Highfields Farm was conveyed 'to Keith, Leonard, Michael, and Norman as tenants in common in equal shares'. This conveyance would (in 1990) have the following consequences:

(a) Highfields Farm is subject to a trust for sale.

(b) (Provided they were of full age at the time of the conveyance) Keith, Leonard, Michael, and Norman are the trustees of the trust for sale.

(c) (Like all other trustees) they hold the legal fee simple in Highfields Farm as **joint tenants**.

(d) Keith, Leonard, Michael, and Norman are also the beneficiaries of the trust (for sale). Each has a quarter share of the equitable interest under the trust as **tenants in common**. While the land remains unsold, each is entitled to a quarter of any income derived from the land. ('Income' includes profits from personal cultivation or rent from tenants.) When the land is sold, each will be entitled to a quarter of the proceeds of sale.

(e) (Like trustees for sale generally) Keith, Leonard, Michael, and Norman have the power to postpone the sale of land.

(f) (In practical terms perhaps the most important point) the four 'trustees' will almost certainly not want to sell the land immediately. They will therefore exercise their power to postpone sale. Indeed, the four men may not know that there is a trust for sale! If that is the case, they will be subconsciously exercising the power to postpone.

(g) From 1 January 1997, Highfields is subject to a new-style trust of land. It is (happily) no longer necessary to talk of the four men subconsciously exercising the power to postpone sale.

14.7.2 Why impose trusts (for sale) on tenants in common?

Take our Highfields Farm example a little further. Let us suppose that Keith died in 1992. His will read, 'all my property I give to my four daughters Olive, Penny, Quennie, and Rose in equal shares'. The ownership position regarding the farm is as follows:

(a) **The legal estate** This, of course, was held by the four men as trustees and as joint tenants. When Keith died there was a survivorship in the usual way. Thus Leonard, Malcolm, and Norman are now trustees of the legal title.

(b) **The equitable interests under the trust (for sale)** Leonard, Malcolm, Norman, Olive, Penny, Quennie, and Rose are now all beneficiaries under the trust. The three men each have a quarter share. The four women each have a one-sixteenth share.

Suppose that Stephen is now keen to buy Highfields Farm, and is willing to pay an attractive price. He should make his offer to the three trustees. If the trustees do decide to sell, **they alone need sign the contract and conveyance**. When the sale takes place the rights of all seven beneficiaries will be overreached.

 EXERCISE 14.1

Just pause for a moment, think about this Highfields Farm example, and consider why the imposition of the trust (for sale) on the tenants in common was a wise change in the law.

I hope you can now see the advantage gained by imposing the trust (for sale) upon the tenancy in common. The usual rule limiting the number of trustees of land to four applies; thus the number of owners of the legal title is strictly limited. Moreover it is the trustees who decide on whether the land should be sold, leased, etc. The 'overreaching' device ensures that the trustees' decisions bind the non-trustee beneficiaries.

The usual rules for the appointment, retirement, and removal of trustees (discussed at 12.5) apply to imposed trusts (for sale). Thus if in my Highfields Farm example Leonard, Michael, and Norman **wish** to appoint **one** additional trustee they **may** do so. Moreover they can choose anybody. They are not obliged to pick from Olive, Penny, Quennie, and Rose.

(The usual rule that where there is a sale by trustees (for sale) **a minimum of two trustees** is required to effect an overreaching also normally applies to imposed trusts (for sale). However, as we shall see at 16.4.1, there is a significant exception to this 'minimum of two' rule. Under this exception a sale by a sole trustee will in certain circumstances be valid.)

(I must also again stress that if there are three trustees (for sale) of a piece of land, **all three** must sign conveyances and other transactions with the land. If there are four trustees (for sale), **all four** must sign conveyances and other transactions with the land.)

14.7.3 What if there are more than four tenants in common to start with?

Suppose land is conveyed 'to A, B, C, D, E, F, and G as tenants in common'. You may have already noticed that s. 34(2) of the 1925 Act provides an answer to this problem. There is a somewhat arbitrary rule that the first four people (of full age) named in the conveyance will be the trustees (for sale).

Suppose that in my example C is only 17 at the date of the conveyance. A, B, D, and E will be the original trustees. They will of course remain the trustees when C attains 18. If (say) B dies, A, D, and E will continue as trustees. They **may** appoint a fourth trustee. If they do, they can appoint anybody. They are not obliged to pick C, F, or G.

> **?** **QUESTION** 14.5
>
> In 1975 the fee simple in 'Faracres' was conveyed 'to Anthea, Betty, Camilla, Devina, Emily, and Florence as tenants in common'. Camilla was then aged only 16, but the other five women were of full age. You are now buying Faracres. All six 'owners' are still alive. For a valid sale, which of them should sign the conveyance?

Anthea, Betty, Devina, and Emily should sign the conveyance.

14.8 Joint tenancies in the early twentieth century

Because of the convenience of the survivorship rule, trustees of property (land or any other property) have always been made joint tenants of the legal title to the property. Prior to 1925, joint tenancies of land were quite common. However, where such a joint tenancy existed with respect to a piece of land it usually transpired that the joint tenants held the land not for their own benefit but as trustees for other people.

In the early part of the twentieth century **beneficial joint tenancies**, i.e., joint tenants holding land for their own personal enjoyment rather than as trustees, were relatively rare. This is in very marked contrast to the position today. There must be now several million 'beneficial' joint tenancies. Most (but not all) of these joint tenancies will exist where husband and wife jointly own the matrimonial home.

14.8.1 Imposition of trusts (for sale) on beneficial joint tenants

In 1925, Parliament (at a time when beneficial joint tenancies were rare) decided to impose a trust (for sale) on beneficial joint tenants. (See the Law of Property Act 1925, s. 36(1).) As with tenancies in common the joint tenants are themselves the trustees (for sale). In the unusual event of there being more than four joint tenants, the first four named in the conveyance (of full age) will be the trustees.

Suppose John and Jane Smith decide to buy the fee simple in Dreamhouse as joint tenants, a kind of transaction which today is extremely commonplace. The fee simple in Dreamhouse is conveyed 'to John and Jane Smith as beneficial joint tenants'. A trust (for sale) is imposed upon John and Jane and the ownership position regarding Dreamhouse is as follows.

- **The legal estate** This is vested in John and Jane as joint tenants and as trustees (for sale).
- **The equitable interests under the trust (for sale)** John and Jane are of course also joint tenants of the equitable interest under the trust (for sale).

 EXERCISE 14.2

Consider whether John and Jane Smith are likely to realize that they are trustees (for sale).

The truth of the matter is that John and Jane (and countless people like them) do not know that a trust (for sale) has been thrust upon them. Moreover, there can be no doubt that John and Jane (and countless people like them) have been, prior to the commencement of the 1996 Act, subconsciously exercising 'the power to postpone sale' and enjoying the benefits of the trust by living in the house.

14.8.2 Why impose a trust (for sale) on joint tenants?

I hope you have already been asking yourself this question. After all, we have already seen that, because of the survivorship rule, it is a natural characteristic of a joint tenancy that the number of joint tenants gradually dwindles to one. Moreover, although joint tenancies are far more common today than they were in 1925, modern joint tenancies usually start with only two joint tenants.

The answer to the question lies in the fact that Parliament in 1925 had to take into account the possibility of 'severance' of a joint tenancy. Every joint tenant has the right to 'sever' the joint tenancy. If a joint tenant does this, he converts his interest as joint tenant into a share as tenant in common. That share becomes subject to the normal law of succession.

Prior to 1925 a joint tenant could sever his right in the legal estate. Since 1925 this has not been possible. Since 1925 any severance affects only the equitable interest under the trust (for sale). It is not necessary at this stage to explain how a severance is achieved (nowadays, as we shall see in the next chapter, it is easy to achieve). What I do need to give is an example of the effects of severance.

Let us suppose that in 1990 three close friends, Rachel, Sally, and Tanya, decided to buy Easthouse. The fee simple in Easthouse was conveyed to them as joint tenants. They consciously chose to be joint tenants as they wished the survivorship rule to operate. The result of the 1990 conveyance was that there was a trust (for sale), but with the three women as both trustees of the legal title and joint tenants of the equitable interest under the trust.

Now suppose that in 1994 Tanya quarrelled with Rachel and Sally. She consequently severed the joint tenancy. The position as to ownership of Easthouse would now be as follows:

- **Legal estate** There would be no change. The three women would remain trustees and joint tenants of the legal fee simple estate in Easthouse.
- **Equitable interests under the trust (for sale)** Tanya now has a one-third share as tenant in common. The other two-thirds (note this carefully) are owned by Rachel and Sally as joint tenants.

Suppose now that Tanya has just died. Her will leaves all her property 'to be divided in equal shares between my gentlemen friends Unwin, Victor, Willy, Xerxes, and Yorick'. The position as to ownership of Easthouse is now as follows:

- **Legal estate** By virtue of survivorship, Rachel and Sally are the only trustees of the legal title.
- **Equitable interests under the trust (for sale)** Rachel and Sally are still joint tenants of two-thirds. Each of the five men has a one-fifteenth share as tenant in common. I hope you realize that this Easthouse example has now reached a position rather similar to my Highfields Farm example at 14.7.2. The number of co-owners of Easthouse has grown, but the legal estate is vested in the two surviving women as trustees (for sale).

? **QUESTION** 14.6

You want to buy Easthouse. To whom do you make the offer?

You make the offer to Rachel and Sally only. As trustees (for sale) they can sell (or lease, etc.) Easthouse, and the rights of all seven beneficiaries will be overreached.

14.9 The modern conveyancing practice to create an express trust (for sale)

All modern property lawyers have been brought up knowing that wherever there is co-ownership of land there must be a trust (for sale). They know that there is no escaping the effects of ss. 34–36 of the Law of Property Act. This has brought about a change in conveyancing practices.

Where land is conveyed to co-owners it is nowadays good conveyancing practice (followed by most but not all solicitors) to create an **express** trust (for sale). The co-owners will be made the trustees (except in those cases, very rare nowadays, where there are more than four). The 'express declaration of trust' will make it clear whether the equitable interests under the trust are held as joint tenants or as tenants in common. If the co-owners are tenants in common the size of the shares is spelt out. (After the commencement of the 1996 Act, the modern conveyancing practice is to create an **express** new-style trust of land. The only

practical difference is that solicitors are spared the problem of having to explain 'trust for sale' to those (more intelligent) clients who actually read the conveyancing documents put in front of them!)

The express declaration of trust is usually contained in the conveyance or (if the land is already registered title) in the land transfer. Unfortunately, details of the express declaration of trust are not recorded on the register of title. The solicitor acting for the co-owners should therefore keep a copy of the conveyance or transfer.

By employing an express declaration of trust solicitors avoid the problems which we are about to discuss in the next section of this chapter. Moreover the practice of having an express declaration of trust has been endorsed by the Court of Appeal in two fairly modern cases which deserve to be better known.

In *Walker* v *Hall* (1984) 5 FLR 126, the Court of Appeal expressed the view that it might well be professional negligence for a solicitor acting for co-owners to fail to draw up an express declaration of trust. The point their Lordships were making is that if there is an express declaration of trust, that prevents later arguments between co-owners as to whether they are joint tenants or tenants in common, and if tenants in common, the size of their respective shares.

(In *Goodman* v *Gallant* [1986] 2 WLR 236, the Court of Appeal held that if there is an express trust for sale declaring the co-owners to be joint tenants in equity, any severance must produce a tenancy in common **in equal shares**.)

14.10 Co-owners—joint tenants or tenants in common?

First, an elementary point rather overlooked by some textbooks. The rules which I am about to discuss **apply only where there is no express declaration of a trust (for sale)**. Where there is an express trust (for sale), that trust (for sale) is conclusive as to whether the co-owners are joint tenants or tenants in common. Furthermore, where the beneficiaries hold their equitable interests as tenants in common, the express declaration is conclusive as to the size of their shares. (*Re Pavlou* [1993] 3 All ER 995, which conflicts with these principles, must be regarded as wrongly decided.)

With a co-ownership where there is **no** express declaration of trust (nowadays very much the minority of cases) the following rules apply. There is an initial presumption that the co-owners are joint tenants.

This presumption in favour of joint tenancy can be **rebutted** in favour of a tenancy in common in the following situations.

(a) (Rather obviously) where the conveyance (or will) expressly describes the co-owners as tenants in common.

(b) Where the conveyance (or will) uses 'words of severance', e.g., 'I convey Blackacre to A, B, and C in equal shares', 'I grant Blackacre to be divided between my sons Tom, Dick, and Harry'. Any words in a conveyance (or will) which indicate that the co-owners are to have distinct shares in the property, albeit those shares are geographically undivided, are 'words of severance'.

As you may have guessed, this rule about 'words of severance' is nowadays important only where lay people draft their own conveyances or wills. I should also add that you must not confuse 'words of severance' with the concept 'severance of a joint tenancy' which we shall be considering in the next chapter.

(c) Where either unity of time, unity of title, or unity of interest is absent. (This of course follows from the very nature of joint tenancies and tenancies in common.)

(d) Where the co-owners contribute to the purchase price in unequal shares. For example, Yorick and Zebedee buy Purple House for £120,000. Purple House is conveyed to Yorick and Zebedee. There is **no** express declaration of a trust (for sale). Yorick contributed £90,000; Zebedee £30,000. Yorick and Zebedee will be tenants in common of the equitable interest under the trust (for sale). Their shares will be proportionate to their contributions. Thus Yorick will have a three-quarters share and Zebedee will have a one-quarter share.

The example just given is a simple one, but rather unrealistic as Yorick and Zebedee paid 'cash down'. Consider now Andrea and Bobby. They decided to cohabit rather than get married. They bought 'Lovenest' (what I call a 'quasi-matrimonial home') for £100,000, of which £80,000 was borrowed from Bloggs Bank. They granted a mortgage to the Bank to secure the loan. The house was conveyed to them in their joint names **but there was no express declaration of a trust (for sale)**. Andrea paid the initial £20,000 deposit out of her savings, and she also paid some of the instalments. Bobby paid the rest of the instalments. They did not keep a detailed record as to who paid what. The relationship has now broken down.

In this kind of situation (which is quite frequent and was similar to the situation in *Walker* v *Hall*) calculating the size of Andrea's and Bobby's shares as tenants in common will be very difficult; I would say more-or-less guesswork! However, if there had been an express declaration of trust, arguments as to who contributed what **would not have arisen**. As I keep on repeating, if there is an express declaration of a trust (for sale) that declaration is conclusive as to the co-owners' equitable interests.

(e) Where the property is acquired for use by a business partnership. For example, Alf, Bert, and Charles buy High Tower for £300,000 to use as the office for their accountancy practice. They each contribute £100,000. High Tower is conveyed to them, **but there is no express declaration of a trust (for sale)**. (To save money, they do their own conveyancing.) Alf, Bert, and Charles will be tenants in common of the equitable interest under the trust (for sale) imposed by the Law of Property Act 1925, s. 34. Each will have a one-third share.

The reason behind this 'business partners are tenants in common' rule is as follows. Equity always considered that the very hit and miss 'survival of the fittest' survivorship rule which applies to joint tenancies is inappropriate in a commercial context. A businessman would (in most cases at least) want his interest in land held for use in the business to pass under his will. There is nothing, of course, to stop business partners making themselves joint tenants. Since 1925 they do so by creating an express trust (for sale) with the partners as **joint tenants** of the equitable interests under the trust.

(f) Where there is a 'joint mortgage'. Of the six rules under which a tenancy in common can arise, this rule is perhaps the least important, but perhaps the most difficult to understand. A joint mortgage can arise if there are joint **lenders**. A joint mortgage has the following features:

   (i) There is (normally) just one borrower.

   (ii) There are two or more lenders who pool the money they are willing to lend.

   (iii) They lend the pooled money as one loan.

   (iv) The borrower grants the lenders a **single** mortgage.

(v) The lenders are co-owners **of the mortgage**.

(vi) (Since 1925) the lenders hold their title **to the mortgage** on trust (for sale) for themselves as tenants in common.

When in practice might there be a joint mortgage? Suppose Greg owns Broadacres, worth something over £1,000,000. He wants to borrow £1,000,000, and is offering Broadacres as security. He approaches Alex's Bank, which says, 'Sorry we would like to lend the full sum but we have only £500,000 available'. He approaches Clive's Bank, which gives a very similar reply. A joint mortgage will satisfy everyone. The two banks pool their respective half millions. Greg gets a single loan for £1,000,000 and grants a joint mortgage to the two banks.

 QUESTION 14.7

Greenacre is conveyed to Anne and Bertha. There is an express declaration of a trust (for sale) for themselves as joint tenants in equity. The price was £90,000. Anne contributed £60,000; Bertha contributed £30,000. Anne dies. Her will leaves all her property to Charles. Does Charles inherit any interest in Greenacre?

The answer is of course, 'No'. The express declaration of trust stating that Anne and Bertha are joint tenants in equity is conclusive. Thus when Anne dies, her equitable interest in Greenacre passes by survivorship to Bertha.

QUESTION 14.8

Alf, Barry, and Charles (all of full age) have just bought High Farm for £240,000. Alf contributed £120,000, Barry £80,000, and Charles £40,000. The land has been conveyed to them, but there has been no express declaration of a trust (for sale). What is the end result?

In these circumstances all three men are trustees (for sale) of the legal estate. But their equitable interests under the trust will be that Alf owns a half, Barry owns a third, and Charles a sixth.

CONCLUDING REMARKS

At the beginning of this chapter we discussed the basic characteristics of joint tenancies and tenancies in common. This involved our considering very long-standing common law-derived rules. At the end of this chapter the rules for determining whether co-owners are joint tenants or tenants in common were considered. Many of these rules are also of some antiquity.

The central part of this chapter was therefore something of a contrast. There we dealt with one of the fundamental changes made by the 1925 property legislation, namely the imposition on co-owners of a trust for sale. This cured one major problem thrown up by the common law—that of multiplicity of co-owners. But, it brought with it other problems, which, as we shall see in **Chapter 16**, have now been largely solved by the Trusts of Land etc. Act 1996.

■ SUMMARY

English law recognizes two forms of co-ownership:

Joint tenancy The co-owners have equal **interests** in the land, and if one joint tenant dies, his **interest** passes to the survivors.

Tenants in common The tenants in common have **shares** in the land which may or may not be equal. When a tenant in common dies, his share passes according to the normal rules of succession.

The 1925 reforms mean:

(i) that a tenancy in common cannot exist with respect to a legal estate. A tenancy in common can only exist with respect to equitable interests under a trust;

(ii) that whenever land is conveyed to co-owners, there must be a trust (for sale) of the land. The co-owners are the trustees of the legal title, unless there are more than four, in which case the first four named will be the trustees.

Determining whether co-owners are joint tenants or tenants in common

In the vast majority of co-ownerships which have been created in modern times, there is no problem, as the conveyance (or land transfer) contains an express declaration of trust.

In the small minority of cases **where there is no express declaration of trust**, there is presumption in favour of joint tenancy, but that presumption will be rebutted if:

the owners are described as tenants in common;
the conveyance uses phrases such as 'in equal shares';
the owners contributed unequal amounts to the purchase price;
the owners were business partners.

■ FURTHER READING

For an extended discussion of the matters dealt with in this chapter, see *Megarry and Wade: Law of Real Property*, sixth edition, chapter nine, pages 475–490 and 501–505.

An even more detailed discussion is in Gray and Gray, *Elements of Land Law*, fourth edition, chapter eleven, pages 1022–1052 and 1082–1092.

Note the careful way the authors explain that in any co-ownership situation, the legal ownership of the trustees must be kept separate from the equitable ownership of the beneficiaries, even if the trustees and beneficiaries are the same people!

15 Severance of joint tenancies

15.1 Objectives

By the end of this chapter you should:

1 Be able to explain the effects of severance of a joint tenancy

2 Be thoroughly familiar with the various methods by which a joint tenancy can be severed

15.2 Introduction

As you are probably aware, there has been over the last (about) 50 years an enormous growth in the number of joint tenancies. This has come about as a result of two factors; firstly the growth in owner occupation, and secondly women's equality. Most (but not all) joint tenancies exist between married couples or between parties to a stable unmarried cohabitation.

The great attraction of a joint tenancy for married (and unmarried) couples is the automatic right of survivorship which operates on the death of one of the co-owners. But this advantage of a joint tenancy may disappear if the joint tenants fall out with each other. It is thus fortunate that the law provides for severance of joint tenancies, i.e., a process whereby a joint tenancy is converted into a tenancy in common.

15.3 Severance of a legal joint tenancy impossible

Since 1925, a legal joint tenancy cannot be severed. Any severance affects only the equitable interests under the trust (for sale).

Suppose that Blackacre has been conveyed to A, B, and C as joint tenants on trust (for sale) for themselves as joint tenants. Later A severs the joint tenancy by sending a written notice of severance to B and C. (We will consider details of this method of severance at 15.4.5.1.) The position will now be:

- **Legal title** This will be still vested in A, B, and C as joint tenants and as trustees (for sale).

- **Equitable interest** A will have a one-third share as tenant in common; B and C will have the other two-thirds share as (between themselves) joint tenants.

> **?** **QUESTION** 15.1
>
> Suppose that C dies. What is the position now?

The legal title is vested in A and B as joint tenants and as trustees (for sale).

The equitable interests will be that A has a one-third share as tenant in common while B has a two-thirds share as tenant in common.

15.4 Methods of severance

Under the post-1925 law, severance can be achieved in a variety of different ways.

15.4.1 Total alienation

If a joint tenant sells (or gives away inter vivos) his equitable interest, that effects a severance.

Suppose Blackacre was conveyed to Debbie, Ena, Felicity, and Gillian as joint tenants on express trust (for sale) for themselves as joint tenants. Later, Gillian sells her interest in Blackacre to Henry. The position now is as follows:

- **Legal title** This is unchanged. The four women remain joint tenants and trustees of the legal title. The fact that Gillian has sold her equitable interest does not mean that she has resigned as a trustee.
- **Equitable interest** Henry has a quarter share as tenant in common. The other three-quarters are held by Debbie, Ena, and Felicity as (between themselves) joint tenants.

> **?** **QUESTION** 15.2
>
> Let us now suppose that Felicity, Gillian, and Henry all die. Henry's will leaves 'all my property to my old pal Keith'. What is the position now?

- **Legal title** By virtue of survivorship, Debbie and Ena are the trustees. (Though there is no need for them to do so, they may appoint one or two additional trustees. Do you remember the discussion at 12.5?)
- **Equitable interest** Keith has a one-quarter share as tenant in common. The other three-quarters belongs to Debbie and Ena as (between themselves) joint tenants.

15.4.2 Bankruptcy

If a joint tenant goes bankrupt, his equitable interest vests in his trustee in bankruptcy, to be held for the benefit of all his creditors. This compulsory transfer automatically severs the joint tenancy.

In modern conditions this is a short but not unimportant point. Suppose Harry and Winny Brown are joint tenants of Highroofs. Harry goes bankrupt. The position will now be:

- **Legal title** This will still be held by Harry and Winny.
- **Equitable interest** Winny and Harry's trustee in bankruptcy will be tenants in common in equal shares.

15.4.3 **Partial alienation**

A partial alienation would occur where a joint tenant mortgaged or leased his interest. If a joint tenant wished to sever the joint tenancy without his fellow joint tenant(s) knowing, he could do so by mortgaging his interest to a friend to secure a loan of a nominal amount (say £5)!

15.4.4 **Contract to alienate**

If a joint tenant contracts to sell, lease, or mortgage his interest that will effect a severance.

15.4.5 **Written notice and informal severance under the Law of Property Act 1925**

These two forms of severance depend upon the rather opaque wording of the second paragraph of s. 36(2) of the Law of Property Act 1925. Stripped to its bare essentials, this provides:

. . . where a legal estate . . . is vested in joint tenants beneficially, and any tenant desires to sever the joint tenancy in equity, he shall give to the other joint tenants a notice in writing of such desire

or do such other acts or things as would, in the case of personal estate, have been effectual to sever the tenancy in equity, . . .

As well as leaving out non-essential words, I have split the paragraph into two parts. The first part relates to severance by written notice; the second part relates to informal severance.

15.4.5.1 **Severance by written notice**

For a severance under this heading to be effective:

(a) the notice must be received by the other joint tenant(s) or be deemed to have been received; **and**

(b) it must use the wording appropriate to effect a severance.

Thus a joint tenant can sever by sending a written notice to each of the other joint tenants saying, 'I am severing our joint tenancy' (or words to that effect). The notice of severance can be handed to the intended recipient. It is inadvisable to send the notice by ordinary post, as that may lead to disputes as to whether the notice has been received or not.

If the notice is sent through the post, registered post or recorded delivery should be used and the letter addressed to the recipient's residence or (where appropriate) place of business. This will take advantage of s. 196(4) of the Law of Property Act 1925. Under that provision a notice sent by recorded delivery or registered post to the correct address will be deemed to have been received by the addressee unless it is returned through the post office undelivered.

The case of *Re 88 Berkeley Road* [1971] 1 All ER 254 dramatically demonstrates the impact of s. 196(4). Two unmarried ladies, Miss Eldridge and Miss Goodwin, were joint tenants of their home, 88 Berkeley Road. Eldridge (who was 'a generation younger') announced that she was getting married. Goodwin consulted solicitors, who advised her to sever the joint tenancy. The solicitors drafted a notice of severance, and this was sent **recorded delivery** to Eldridge at her 'residence', 88 Berkeley Road.

When the postman called, Eldridge had already gone to work. Goodwin signed for the letter! Goodwin died soon afterwards. In the ensuing court case, Eldridge swore that she had never seen the letter. Had there been an effective severance of the joint tenancy? The judge held that there had been a severance. The letter had not been 'returned undelivered'.

What if a notice is sent ordinary post?

If a notice of severance is sent **ordinary** post, then provided that **it can be proved** that the letter was actually put through the letterbox at the intended recipient's address, then it seems that the severance will be effective under s. 196(3) of the LPA 1925. Section 196(3) states 'any . . . notice shall be sufficiently served if it is left at the last known place of abode . . . of the person to be served'. In *Kinch* v *Bullard* [1998] 4 All ER 650 a letter of severance sent ordinary post and which had undoubtedly arrived at the recipient's home was held to be effective as it had been 'left at' that home.

15.4.5.2 What sort of wording is required in a notice of severance?

In the last 30 years there have been a number of cases where events have followed the following pattern:

(a) Two people (usually but not always husband and wife) buy a house as joint tenants.

(b) The relationship breaks down.

(c) One of the two makes a statement, writes a letter, or commences divorce proceedings, or another form of litigation.

(d) Before matters can be resolved, one of the parties suddenly dies.

(e) There is litigation as to whether event (c) above has brought about a severance.

The surviving partner is of course arguing (as Eldridge argued in *Re 88 Berkeley Road*) that there has been no severance. The personal representatives of the deceased argue that there has been a severance.

In my opinion the Court of Appeal has in two modern decisions laid clear rules for resolving these cases. The cases are *Burgess* v *Rawnsley* (discussed at 15.4.6) and *Harris* v *Goddard*.

In *Harris* v *Goddard* [1983] 1 WLR 1203, the Court of Appeal ruled that any written statement by a joint tenant either expressly indicating or implying that he wishes **immediately** to end the joint tenancy relationship will sever that joint tenancy, provided the statement is received (or is deemed to have been received under s. 196(4) or (3)).

The Court of Appeal in *Harris* v *Goddard* expressly approved the decision in *Re Draper's Conveyance* [1967] 3 All ER 853, where a wife applied under s. 30 of the Law of Property Act 1925 for an order for sale of the jointly owned matrimonial home. This application was held to have severed the joint tenancy. By demanding that the property be sold and the proceeds of sale split, the wife demonstrated that she wished an immediate end to the joint tenancy arrangement.

The Trusts of Land etc. Act 1996 repeals s. 30 of the Law of Property Act 1925 and replaces it with its own even more far-reaching s. 14 (see **Chapter 16**). A direct application for an order of sale made under the new s. 14 would undoubtedly sever any equitable joint tenancy in the relevant land.

15.4.5.3 *Harris v Goddard*

Before considering *Harris* v *Goddard*, re-read what I said at 8.3.6.1 regarding 'property adjustment orders' under ss. 23–25 of the Matrimonial Causes Act 1973. You certainly do not need to know the details of ss. 23–25, but you do need to understand the basic idea of a property adjustment order.

In *Harris* v *Goddard*, husband and wife were joint tenants of the matrimonial home. The marriage broke down, and the wife petitioned for divorce. The petition included an application for a property adjustment order under s. 24 of the Matrimonial Causes Act 1973. The application was (as is quite usual) in very general terms:

That such order may be made by way of transfer of property and/or settlement of property and/or variation of settlement in respect of the former matrimonial home . . . as may be just.

(By 'variation of settlement' is meant, in this context, varying the terms of the existing trust for sale.)

While the divorce proceedings were pending, the husband was killed in a car crash. The wife successfully argued that the application in her divorce petiton was not a severance. The Court of Appeal held that for a document sent by one joint tenant to amount to a severance it must show an intention to end **immediately** the joint tenancy arrangement. The application for an order of sale made in *Re Draper* satisfied that test, but the application in *Harris* v *Goddard* itself did not.

15.4.6 **Informal severance**

The gist of the last part of s. 36(2) of the Law of Property Act 1925 (see 15.4.5) is that a joint tenant can sever by doing 'such other acts or things as would, in the case of personal estate, have been effectual to sever the tenancy in equity'.

Prior to 1926 it was possible to sever a joint tenancy in **personal** but not **real** property by informal conduct. The intention behind the last part of s. 36(2) was to extend the pre-1926 rules regarding informal severance by conduct to real property.

Unfortunately, the 1925 legislators rather overlooked the fact that the pre-1926 rules regarding informal severance were far from clear cut. Even today some textbooks go into great depth regarding certain nineteenth-century 'informal severance' cases in an effort to establish the rules for informal severance. This is totally unnecessary. The job has been done for us by Sir John Pennycuick in *Burgess* v *Rawnsley* [1975] 1 Ch 429, CA. (If you read this case, bear in mind that Lord Denning's judgment gives a graphic account of the facts, but his views as to the applicable law are incorrect. For the correct law, study Sir John Pennycuick's judgment noting his numbered propositions.)

In *Burgess* v *Rawnsley* Mr Honick (a widower) and Mrs Rawnsley (a widow) met at a scripture rally in Trafalgar Square. They became close friends. They bought as joint tenants the fee simple to the house in Waltham Cross of which Honick had hitherto been a lessee. They later fell out. It was orally agreed that Honick should buy out Mrs Rawnsley's interest for just £750. Before matters could finally be resolved, Honick died.

The Court of Appeal held that the oral agreement (though not an enforceable contract) was sufficient to sever the joint tenancy. After analysing the older cases Sir John Pennycuick concluded that there were three forms of informal severance:

(a) an oral agreement that the joint tenancy should be severed;

(b) an oral agreement that one joint tenant should buy the other out;

(c) '[A]cts of the parties, including, it seems to me, negotiations which, although not otherwise resulting in any agreement, indicate a common intention that the joint tenancy should be regarded as severed'.

15.5 Matters which are not a severance

15.5.1 Unilateral oral statements

Lord Denning in *Burgess* v *Rawnsley* took the view that even a unilateral oral statement by one joint tenant to the other(s) could amount to a severance. This view is not shared by any other judge (ancient or modern) and is clearly wrong.

 EXERCISE 15.1

I have always considered the view taken by Lord Denning in *Burgess* v *Rawnsley* as hopelessly impractical. Why? (There are two reasons.)

First, if Lord Denning were correct, then angry unilateral statements made in haste during a family quarrel would be effective to sever the joint tenancy. Secondly, there would be problems proving what exactly had been said in the heat of argument.

15.5.2 Subsequent use of property for business purposes

In *Barton* v *Morris* [1985] 2 All ER 1032 a farm was conveyed to two cohabitees on express trust for themselves as joint tenants in equity. 'The property was run as a guest house and small farm on a partnership basis and Miss Barton kept partnership accounts which showed the farm as a partnership asset'. This use of the property for the purposes of a partnership was held not to sever the joint tenancy.

15.5.3 'Severance by will'

I should just remind you that you cannot sever a joint tenancy by will.

CONCLUDING REMARKS

It is obviously extremely important for you to understand fully the various ways in which a joint tenancy can be severed. Some of these methods (e.g., written notice) are the result of the deliberate actions of the parties. Others (e.g., in particular severance by bankruptcy) come about automatically, irrespective of any intention.

It is also very important to remember that certain matters **do not** constitute severance. The principle recognized in *Barton* v *Morris*, that **subsequent** business use of premises does not sever an expressly created joint tenancy, should always be kept very firmly in mind.

■ SUMMARY

A   A legal joint tenancy cannot be severed.

B   A joint tenant in equity can sever the joint tenancy, whether or not he is a trustee of the legal title.

C   Where one of three or more equitable joint tenants severs, his interest becomes a share as a tenant in common. The other parties remain equitable joint tenants vis-à-vis each other.

D   **Methods of severance**

1   Total alienation, whether by sale, gift, or on bankruptcy;

2   Partial alienation—by lease or mortgage;

3   A contract for total or partial alienation;

4   Written notice under s. 36(2) of LPA. The notice must demand an immediate end to the relationship, and must reach (or be deemed to have reached) the intended recipients;

5   Informal severance by mutual agreement (*Burgess* v *Rawnsley*) or by a mutual course of conduct.

NOT severances

Gift in a will;

Unilateral oral statements;

Subsequent use of premises for business purposes.

■ FURTHER READING

For an extended discussion of severance, see either *Megarry and Wade: Law of Real Property*, sixth edition, chapter nine, pages 491–501, or

alternatively, see Gray and Gray, *Elements of Land Law*, fourth edition, chapter eleven, pages 1052–1081.

16 Co-ownership—the problems when co-owners fall out

16.1 Objectives

By the end of this chapter you should:

1 Appreciate fully the problems which arise where a tenancy in common exists because there is a constructive trust interest

2 Be able to explain the legal position if a sole trustee of a trust of land attempts to make a disposition

3 Be familiar with the workings of ss. 13 to 15 of the Trusts of Land etc. Act 1996, and how these provisions enable courts to settle disputes between co-owners and other disputes affecting trusts of land

4 Be able to explain why the Trusts of Land etc. Act 1996 has solved previous controversies as to whether rights of co-owners are interests in land or interests in money

5 Appreciate the (limited) significance of the Law of Property (Joint Tenants) Act 1964

16.2 Introduction

By imposing a trust for sale upon all co-owners, Parliament (in 1925) solved the problem of the saleability of land belonging to a multiplicity of co-owners. But this 'solution' to the problems set out at 14.7 brought with it a whole crop of new difficulties. These difficulties related to the exact legal nature of the rights of co-owners (e.g., does a co-owner have the right personally to occupy the land?) and as to what happens if co-owners disagree regarding the fate of the property. Happily these problems are now (largely) solved by the Trusts of Land etc. Act 1996.

The issues discussed in this chapter are of a fundamental importance to contemporary England and Wales. I say this because the **amount** of co-ownership has shown enormous growth since 1925. This growth is due not just to an increase in number of expressly agreed co-ownerships but also to the growth in tenancies in common arising because someone has acquired a constructive trust 'share' in a piece of land.

16.3 The effect of imposing a trust (for sale) upon co-owners

Before I launch into perhaps the biggest problem created by the decision made in 1925 to impose a trust (for sale) upon all co-owners, I need to remind you of two points:

(a) A 'co-ownership trust (for sale)', like any other trust (for sale), is subject to the 'maximum of four' limit on the number of trustees.

(b) While a co-ownership trust (for sale) can validly **exist** with only one trustee, a disposition (sale, lease, mortgage, etc.) requires two trustees if it is to 'overreach' the rights of non-trustee co-owners. (As we shall see in a moment, there is however an important exception to this 'minimum of two' rule.)

16.4 Tenancy in common arising because there is a constructive trust

(This is the heading I prefer, but some people have in the past preferred the heading, 'The problem of the undisclosed trust for sale'. Now they prefer to talk about 'the problem of the undisclosed [new-style] trust of land'. An even better alternative heading (in my view) would be 'the new-style trust of land which is not apparent from the documents or the land register'.)

Refer back to 1.4.7 and the example of 'Chenu', Alfred, and Bertha. You will recall that Alfred owns the legal fee simple estate in Chenu. However, Bertha (who may or may not be his wife) acquired an '(equitable) share in the property under a constructive trust'. You will also recall that Bertha acquired her **share** by paying £30,000 cash down towards a price of £90,000. She would equally have acquired a **share** (under a constructive trust) if she had made substantial contributions to mortgage instalments, or had made a substantial contribution to the improvement of Chenu.

 EXERCISE 16.1

Consider what my next point is going to be.

As Bertha acquires a **share** in Chenu, she and Alfred become tenants in common! Consequently, as a result of ss. 34–36 of the Law of Property Act 1925, there was a trust for sale, or after the commencement of the 1996 Act, a new-style trust. Alfred will be a trustee (for sale), in trust for himself and Bertha. This trust (for sale) will be irregular in two respects:

(a) there will be only one trustee;

(b) the people involved (Alfred, Bertha, and later potential purchasers or mortgagees of Chenu) will probably not realize that a trust (for sale) exists. (Hence the phrase, 'undisclosed trust (for sale)'.) They will, therefore, probably not realize that a second trustee should be appointed before any disposition takes place.

You will not be surprised to learn that this problem of an irregular ('undisclosed') trust (for sale) is a frequent occurrence in contemporary legal practice. It arises frequently simply because cases of 'a constructive trust share' arise frequently.

16.4.1 Dispositions by a single trustee

It will help your understanding if we continue to develop the 'Chenu' example. Suppose Albert sells, leases, or mortgages 'Chenu' acting entirely on his own. Put in more technical language, he makes a disposition without appointing a second trustee. Will Bertha's interest be overreached despite the absence of a second trustee? Or (and this is the only alternative) will it be binding upon the purchaser? ('Purchaser' in this context includes a mortgagee or lessee.)

16.4.1.1 Unregistered title

First, I should stress that where the relevant land is unregistered title, a constructive trust share is **not registrable as a land charge**. It is now well established that where a disposition is made by a sole trustee such as Alfred, the doctrine of notice must be applied. This was the approach taken, e.g., in *Kingsnorth Finance Co. Ltd* v *Tizard* [1986] 2 All ER 64 (see 6.4.4.3 at page 66).

If a purchaser from Alfred had notice (actual, constructive, or imputed) of Bertha's interest (call it a 'share' if you like), he will be bound by Bertha's interest. Bertha's interest will not bind a purchaser only if that purchaser is a bona fide purchaser for value of a legal estate without notice of Bertha's interest.

In *Caunce* v *Caunce* [1969] 1 All ER 722, H had sole ownership of the matrimonial home. However, W paid a substantial part of the purchase price, and therefore had a constructive trust 'share'. Thus H held the legal title on trust for sale for H and W. While they were happily living together in the home, H decided to borrow some money from Lloyds Bank. Lloyds lent the money and H mortgaged the home to the bank to secure the loan. H never told W about the mortgage. **Lloyds neither visited the house nor made any enquiries of W.**

 EXERCISE 16.2

Consider how a court would decide this case *today*.

The court would reason in the following way:

(a) The doctrine of notice must be applied.

(b) Lloyds (or rather a representative acting for Lloyds!) should have visited the house.

(c) Lloyds' representative should have seen W living in the home.

(d) The representative should have therefore asked her whether she claimed any interest in the home.

(e) As Lloyds made no such enquiries, they have constructive notice of the wife's interest ('share') applying the rule in *Hunt* v *Luck* and are therefore bound by it.

Amazingly, I have to tell you that back in the dark ages of 1969 the judge (Stamp J) decided otherwise. He laid down a special exception to the *Hunt* v *Luck* rule. A purchaser (mortgagee or lessee) need not make enquiries of persons occupying the land if the vendor (mortgagor or lessor) is himself in possession. He thus held that Lloyds were a 'purchaser without notice' and were not bound by the wife's interest. In practical terms that meant that W could not stop Lloyds enforcing the mortgage and selling the home 'over her head'.

It is now clear that the decision in *Caunce* to create an exception to *Hunt* v *Luck* was totally wrong. (See my earlier comments at 10.3.7.1.)

? **QUESTION** 16.1

Charley is owner in fee simple of Superhouse (*unregistered title*). His cohabitee, Dinah, has contributed substantially to the cost of acquisition, and has therefore acquired a share under a constructive trust. The relationship has now broken down and Dinah is contemplating the possibility of leaving. However she wants to be sure that her interest will bind a purchaser of Superhouse. Advise Dinah.

First of all, I hope you realized that **there is no land charge** which Dinah can register. Rather, her constructive trust interest is subject to the equitable doctrine of notice. However, provided she stays put in Superhouse **and** reveals her interest to anybody who asks whether she has a share in the home, the rule in *Hunt* v *Luck* will (normally) protect her. If Dinah follows this advice, a purchaser from Albert will have notice of her equitable interest and be bound by it. (I should however add that I am temporarily ignoring the effect of the decision of the House of Lords in *City of London Building Society* v *Flegg*, which I will be discussing at 16.4.2.)

16.4.1.2 Registered title

Reverting to my 'Chenu' example, if the house is registered title then the decision of the House of Lords in *Williams and Glyn's Bank Ltd* v *Boland* will apply. (I have already discussed this case at 10.3.7.1 and you should re-read that text.) It follows from *Boland* that if Chenu is registered title, Bertha, provided she is in 'actual occupation' of Chenu at the relevant time, will have an overriding interest within Sch. 3, para. 2 of the Land Registration Act 2002, unless either her occupation is not obvious on a reasonably careful inspection or enquiry is made of her and she (unreasonably) fails to reveal her interest.

The owner of a constructive trust interest/share in a registered title who is not 'in actual occupation' (e.g., Bertha has gone to live with another man) will have a minor interest. This minor interest can (under the Land Registration Act 2002) be protected by entering a restriction. Prior to the 2002 Act it could be protected by a caution.

In *Elias* v *Mitchell* [1972] 2 All ER 153, two business partners had fallen out. One was the sole registered proprietor of their business premises, but both had 'shares' (as tenants in common) in the premises. The partner who was not the registered proprietor had left those premises. His interest was held to be a minor interest which could be protected by lodging a caution. There can be no doubt that this decision can be applied to 'domestic' situations such as my Chenu example; however under Land Registration Act 2002, s. 33(a), a restriction will now have to be used. See 10.5.2.

> **?** **QUESTION** 16.2
>
> It is 2006, Charley is owner in fee simple of Superhouse (*registered title*). His cohabitee, Dinah, has contributed substantially to the cost of acquisition, and has therefore acquired a share under a constructive trust. The relationship has now broken down, and Dinah is contemplating the possibility of leaving. However, she wants to be sure that her interest will bind a purchaser of Superhouse. Advise Dinah.

Provided she stays (visibly) put in Superhouse **and** reveals her interest to anybody who asks whether she has a share in the home, Dinah's interest will be an overriding interest under Sch. 3, para. 2 and a purchaser from Albert will be bound by it.

If Dinah moves out her position is better than in **Question 16.1**. She should (*cf.* the partner in *Elias* v *Mitchell*) protect her minor interest by entering a restriction. (Prior to 2003 she would have used a caution. I should again add that I am temporarily ignoring the effect of the decision of the House of Lords in *City of London Building Society* v *Flegg*, which I will be discussing at 16.4.2.)

16.4.2 What if Alfred did appoint a second trustee?

Suppose that in my Chenu example Alfred does realize that there is a co-ownership and that therefore he is a lone trustee (for sale). If he wants to make a disposition (sale, lease, or mortgage) Alfred can appoint a friend as co-trustee. The appointment of a second trustee changes the position dramatically:

(a) If the title to Chenu is **unregistered**, Bertha's interest will be overreached in the usual way.

(b) If the title to Chenu is **registered**, a disposition by two trustees will similarly overreach Bertha's interest, notwithstanding the operation of Sch. 3, para. 2 or the entering of a restriction. This is because it is an inherent characteristic of Bertha's interest (remember it is an interest under a trust (for sale)) that it can be overreached by a disposition made by two trustees.

16.4.2.1 *City of London Building Society v Flegg* [1988] 1 AC 54, HL

Mr and Mrs Flegg both contributed to the purchase of a house; the title to the house was registered in the names of their daughter and son-in-law (the Maxwell-Browns). The Fleggs, as a consequence of their contributions, each had an interest as a tenant in common under a constructive trust. All four lived in the house, and were therefore in 'actual occupation'. The house was **subsequently** mortgaged to the building society.

The building society successfully argued (in the House of Lords) that the mortgage, being executed by **two** trustees, overreached the rights of Mr and Mrs Flegg. They could thus sell the house 'over the heads' of the Fleggs.

16.4.2.2 The erroneous rulings of the Court of Appeal

The Court of Appeal had held that the mortgage did not overreach the rights of Mr and Mrs Flegg. It ruled that the decision in *Boland* meant that the Fleggs each had an overriding interest under s. 70(1)(g) of the Land Registration Act 1925 which could not be overreached even by a disposition made by two or more trustees.

> ### ? QUESTION 16.3
>
> A, B, C, and D are the trustees for sale of a very large house. It is the residence of: A, B, C, D, E, F, G, H, I, J, K, L, M, N, O, P, Q, R, S, T, U, V, W, X, Y, and Z. All of them contributed to the purchase price. If the decision of the Court of Appeal in *Flegg* had been upheld, how many signatures would have been required on any conveyance of the house?

The answer is of course 26!

16.4.2.3 The decision of the House of Lords

The House of Lords in *Flegg* unanimously overruled the Court of Appeal. The ruling in *Boland* that a non-trustee co-owner had an overriding interest if she/he was in actual occupation did not mean that such an interest could not be overreached by a disposition made by **two** (or more) trustees. It was an inherent characteristic of an interest under a trust for sale that it could be overreached by a disposition made by two trustees.

(It also held that s. 14 of the Law of Property Act 1925 did not mean that the rights of co-owners in occupation could not be overreached.)

There can be no doubt the decision in *Flegg* also applies to new-style trusts of land, and continues to apply after the Land Registration Act 2002.

> ### ? QUESTION 16.4
>
> Charley is owner in fee simple of Superhouse. His cohabitee, Dinah, has contributed substantially to the cost of acquisition, and has therefore acquired a share under a constructive trust. The relationship has now broken down, and Dinah is contemplating the possibility of leaving. However she wants to be sure that her interest will bind a purchaser of Superhouse. Charley has just appointed his friend Edward to be a second trustee of Superhouse. Advise Dinah.

First, I hope you realized that with this question, it makes no difference whether Superhouse is registered or unregistered title. Secondly, and this is the crucial point, as a result of *Flegg* there is **nothing** Dinah can do 'to be sure that her interest will bind a purchaser of Superhouse'. If she gets the Land Registry to enter a restriction, that restriction will require the purchase price to be paid to two trustees. But there are two trustees, and therefore any sale (lease or mortgage) of Superhouse by the two trustees Charley and Edward will automatically overreach Dinah's interest.

16.4.3 Other trusts of land where there is only a single trustee

This is a slight digression from the law of co-ownership, but it is appropriate to make it at this point. If you refer back to 12.3.6 to 12.4 you will see that in those sections I identify a number of situations where a new-style trust of land may arise with only one trustee. At 12.4 I make the point that:

It follows that where there is a sole trustee of a new-style trust, that trustee should appoint a colleague before selling the land or making some other disposition. What happens if he tries to sell (or mortgage or lease) the trust land acting on his own is a difficult question.

 EXERCISE 16.3

Now try and answer this 'difficult' question.

I hope that you have realized that you apply to this question the discussion contained in 16.4.1 to 16.4.1.2.

In summary, the position where there is a new-style trust of land but a disposition is made by only one trustee is as follows.

16.4.3.1 **Where the trust land is unregistered title**

Apply the doctrine of notice. Where the purchaser from the sole trustee has no notice of the new-style trust, then the rights of the beneficiary(ies) under the trust will be overreached, notwithstanding there being only one trustee.

Where the purchaser has notice of the new-style trust (e.g., under the rule in *Hunt* v *Luck* because a beneficiary is occupying the property) he will be bound by the equitable interests under that trust.

16.4.3.2 **Where the trust land is registered title**

Apply the usual rules about overriding and minor interests.

The only way an equitable interest under a new-style trust can be an overriding interest is by virtue of Sch. 3, para. 2 of the Land Registration Act 2002. Thus the purchaser from a **sole** trustee will be bound by an equitable interest under a new-style trust if the owner of that equitable interest is in obvious actual occupation. If the owner of an equitable interest under a new-style trust is not in obvious actual occupation, his interest will be a minor interest, not normally binding on a purchaser from a sole trustee. (The minor interest could however be 'protected' by entering a restriction.)

16.5 **Sections 13 to 15 of the Trusts of Land and Appointment of Trustees Act 1996**

Where under the 'old' law a dispute arose regarding a trust for sale of land then, whether the dispute was '*beneficiary* v *trustees*' or '*trustee* v *trustee*' or even '*beneficiary* v *beneficiary*', s. 30 of the Law of Property Act 1925 provided a procedure for the court to settle the dispute. Section 30 applied to all trusts for sale, not just those arising on a co-ownership. However most litigation under s. 30 (and certainly most **reported** cases) involved co-owners who had fallen out with each other.

Section 30 is repealed by the Trusts of Land etc. Act 1996 and is replaced by ss. 13 to 15 of the new Act. These sections are applicable to all new-style trusts of land. However, although not confined to co-ownership trusts, there can be little doubt that most litigation invoking these sections will (as with the old s. 30) involve co-owners who have fallen out with each other. There can also be no doubt that, for reasons I will explain at **16.6**, it is highly unlikely that these new sections will be invoked in a husband against wife dispute.

16.5.1 The basic pattern of sections 13 to 15

Section 13 is relatively narrow in scope. Where two or more beneficiaries have **simultaneously** the right to occupy trust land, the **trustees** are given power to regulate that occupation and even to decide who can occupy and on what conditions.

Section 14 is the main provision. Under this provision the court can settle any dispute amongst trustees and/or beneficiaries of a trust of land.

Section 15 sets out the factors which the court should take into account when making an order settling a dispute brought before it under s. 14.

16.5.2 Section 13—disputes regarding occupation of trust land

Two points should be made before I quote you the important parts of this section. First, s. 13 is a natural continuation from s. 12. Refer back to 13.4.2 and 13.4.3. Section 12 confirms the common sense proposition that if trust land is acquired for personal occupation by the current beneficiary(ies) then the beneficiary(ies) do indeed have a right to occupy that land.

Secondly, s. 13 in effect allows the **trustees** to sort out arguments between **beneficiaries** over occupation of the trust land. But, with co-ownership trusts of land, the trustees and beneficiaries are usually (though not always) the same people! Section 13 is clearly of no **direct** use where the people in dispute over occupying land (e.g., over who should live in a house) are both trustees and beneficiaries. Such people, unless they can settle matters by negotiation, will have to resort to litigation under s. 14. Under s. 14 the court can (*inter alia*) **order** anything which the trustees could have decided under s. 13.

Against this background, I think you will agree that the provisions of s. 13, though quite lengthy, are largely self-explanatory. Section 13 provides:

(1) Where two or more beneficiaries are (or apart from this subsection would be) entitled under section 12 to occupy land, the trustees of land may exclude or restrict the entitlement of any one or more (but not all) of them.

(2) Trustees may not under subsection (1)—
    (a) unreasonably exclude any beneficiary's entitlement to occupy the land, or
    (b) restrict such entitlement to an unreasonable extent.

(3) The trustees of land may from time to time impose reasonable conditions on any beneficiary in relation to his occupation of land by reason of his entitlement under section 12.

(4) The matters to which the trustees are to have regard in exercising the powers conferred by this section include—
    (a) the intentions of the person or persons (if any) who created the trust,
    (b) the purposes for which the land is held, and

(c) the circumstances and wishes of each of the beneficiaries who is (or apart from any previous exercise by the trustees of those powers would be) entitled to occupy the land under section 12.

(5) The conditions which may be imposed on a beneficiary under subsection (3) include, in particular, conditions requiring him—

(a) to pay any outgoings or expenses in respect of the land . . .

(6) Where the entitlement of any beneficiary to occupy land under section 12 has been excluded or restricted, the conditions which may be imposed on any other beneficiary under subsection (3) include, in particular conditions requiring him to—

(a) make payments by way of compensation to the beneficiary whose entitlement has been excluded or restricted . . .

 EXERCISE 16.4

Tim and Tom are trustees of Smallhouse in trust for three brothers, Alan, Bert, and Chris in equal shares. The trust was created by the brothers' parents, 'to provide a home for our three boys'. Chris has fallen out with his brothers. As the other two are constantly arguing with him, he has found a flat of his own. Advise Tim and Tom.

They can make a decision under s. 13(1) excluding Chris from Smallhouse. But under s. 13(5), they could require Alan and Bert to pay all the outgoings on the house. Under s. 13(6) they could also require Alan and Bert to make regular payments to Chris (almost like a 'rent') for their exclusive use of the house. These payments, I would suggest, should not exceed one-third of the rent the house would fetch if it was leased out to a tenant.

Section 13(7) also needs to be considered:

(7) The powers conferred on trustees by this section may not be exercised—

(a) so as to prevent any person who is in occupation of land (whether or not by reason of an entitlement under section 12) from continuing to occupy the land . . . unless he consents or the court has given approval.

Suppose in our Smallhouse example Alan and Bert want Chris to leave, but he resolutely refuses to go. Tim and Tom cannot make a decision ordering him to vacate the house. If they want to 'evict' Chris, they will have to get a court order authorizing his eviction.

16.5.3 Section 14—courts settling disputes regarding trusts of land

Section 14 is a relatively short section, but of crucial importance. It is drafted in very straightforward language. I set out the first two subsections verbatim:

(1) Any person who is a trustee of land or has an interest in property subject to a trust of land may make an application to the court for an order under this section.

(2) On application for an order under this section the court may make any such order—

(a) relating to the exercise by the trustees of any of their functions (including an order relieving them of any obligation to obtain the consent of, or to consult, any person in connection with the exercise of their functions), or

(b) declaring the nature or extent of a person's interest in property subject to the trust,
as the court thinks fit.

Section 14 seems to cover almost every conceivable dispute which might arise regarding a trust of land. I would suggest that most cases brought under s. 14 are likely to fall into one of four categories.

16.5.3.1 Disputes regarding size of co-ownership interests

These disputes can be settled under s. 14(2)(b). Refer back to the discussion at 14.10, especially the first paragraph and **Question 14.7**. If a conveyance to co-owners does **not** contain an express declaration of trust, that omission leaves room for all sorts of arguments as to who owns what interests. Those arguments can be settled in proceedings brought under s. 14.

16.5.3.2 Disputes regarding occupation of the trust land

If the trustees cannot settle a dispute between beneficiaries regarding the occupation of trust land (s. 13), then the court can do so under s. 14. Moreover if the trustees have made a decision under s. 13 trying to settle an occupation dispute, then a beneficiary disgruntled with the trustees' decision could challenge that decision by proceedings under s. 14.

16.5.3.3 Authorizing transactions without requisite consent(s)

I have already mentioned this aspect of s. 14 in the last two paragraphs of 13.5.4.2.

16.5.3.4 Disputes as to whether co-owned land should be sold

Almost all cases under the 'old' s. 30 of the Law of Property Act 1925 seemed to be in the following pattern. Two or more people buy a house or some other type of land. They fall out. One (or more) of the co-owners wants the land sold so that he can 'cash in his share'. The other(s) want to retain the land. We will return to consider how this type of dispute may be settled after we have considered s. 15.

16.5.4 Section 15—factors to be considered in settling disputes

The drafting of this section is relatively simple, and I set out a (slightly edited) version below.

(1) The matters to which the court is to have regard in determining an application for an order under section 14 include—
  (a) the intentions of the person or persons . . . who created the trust,
  (b) the purposes for which the property subject to the trust is held,
  (c) the welfare of any minor who occupies or might reasonably be expected to occupy any land subject to the trust as his home, and
  (d) the interests of any secured creditor of any beneficiary. [Paragraph (d) will apply in those relatively rare cases where a co-owner has mortgaged his **share** in the property.]

(2) In the case of an application relating to the exercise in relation to any land of the powers conferred on the trustees by s. 13, the matters to which the court is to have regard also include the circumstances and wishes of each of the beneficiaries who is (or apart from any previous exercise by the trustees would be) entitled to occupy the land under section 12.

(3) In the case of any other application [i.e., not one relating to section 13] . . . the matters to which the court is to have regard also include the circumstances and wishes of any beneficiaries of full

age and entitled to an interest in possession in property subject to the trust or (in case of dispute) of the majority (according to the value of their combined interests).

16.5.5 Settling disputes as to whether the trust property should be sold

The old s. 30 of the Law of Property Act 1925 gave rise to quite a lot of case law on the issue as to whether co-owned property should be sold when the co-owners fall out. This case law is of assistance as we now consider how courts will settle similar disputes arising under the new s. 14.

In the situation described at 16.5.3.4, the court has (it seems) five types of order open to it:

(a) refuse a sale

(b) refuse a sale but make an order regulating the right to occupy the property

(c) order a sale

(d) order a sale but suspend the order for a short period

(e) (only possible in exceptional cases) partition the co-owned property.

16.5.5.1 Refuse a sale

Re Buchanan-Wollaston [1939] 1 CL 738, CA

In this case there was a piece of open ground at Lowestoft in Suffolk separating four houses from the sea. This land was for sale, and the owners of the four houses clubbed together to buy it as tenants in common. They were anxious to preserve their view of the sea. One of the four subsequently sold his house and moved away. He then applied to the court for an order that the open ground should be sold and the proceeds divided. He argued that as the land was held on trust for sale it followed that if any of the four asked for a sale, a sale must take place.

This argument was firmly rejected by the Court of Appeal. Where land was bought for a specific purpose and that purpose could still be fulfilled, the courts should normally refuse to order a sale. This decision was sensational back in 1939. Nowadays it appears as plain common sense. The Court of Appeal recognized (as most later courts have recognized) that the imposition of a trust **for sale** on co-owners was pure 'legal machinery' and it should not affect co-owners' substantive rights.

There can of course be absolutely no doubt that if a case similar to *Re Buchanan-Wollaston* arose under s. 14 of the Trusts of Land etc. Act 1996, the courts would refuse a sale. (See especially s. 15(1)(b) of the 1996 Act.)

Re Evers [1980] 3 All ER 399

The facts of this case are very different, but involve the same principle as in *Re Buchanan-Wollaston*. A cohabiting couple bought a house as joint tenants, in order to house themselves and the three children for whom they had responsibility. The relationship broke up, and the man left. The other four members of the family continued to live in the house.

The Court of Appeal refused the man's application for an order of sale. The greater part of the purpose of acquiring the house (housing the family of five) could still be fulfilled. The Court did, however, indicate that if or when circumstances changed (e.g., the children grow up and leave home) a renewed application by the man would probably receive a sympathetic hearing.

16.5.5.2 Refuse a sale but make an order regulating the right to occupy the property

Dennis v *McDonald* [1982] Fam 63, [1982] 2 WLR 275, and [1982] 1 All ER 590 was a controversial decision under s. 30. A cohabiting couple bought a house as tenants in common in equal shares. They eventually had five children. The relationship broke up because of the man's violence. The woman left home, but had care only of the two youngest children. The three older children continued to live with their father in the house. The Court of Appeal refused to order the sale of the house, but ordered the man to pay a 'rent' to the woman. This was fixed (logically enough) at **half** a 'fair rent' for the premises.

> **EXERCISE** 16.5
>
> Study ss. 13 to 15 of the 1996 Act as set out in previous sections of this chapter, and consider how *Dennis* v *McDonald* would be decided under the 1996 Act.

The case would obviously be decided in a similar way to before. The court would refuse an order of sale, but make an order under s. 14 that the man make payments to the woman to compensate her for the fact that she is no longer occupying the home. (Note also s. 15(1)(c).)

I would further submit that a similar solution (refuse a sale but order payments to compensate the co-owner(s) excluded from possession) should be adopted in every case where:

(a) it is socially undesirable to order the property sold; **and**

(b) it is unfair that the co-owner(s) not in occupation should be excluded from all benefit from the property.

Such a solution could be used, e.g., where the co-owned property houses a flourishing business which might have to close if a sale were ordered. (An alternative compromise solution is that set out at 16.5.5.4 below.)

16.5.5.3 Order a sale

Applying the old s. 30, this solution is the one normally adopted where the purposes for which the property was acquired have clearly failed. For example, the property was acquired for use in a business, and that business has ceased. I feel sure that the courts will adopt a similar attitude when applying the new s. 14.

In *Jones* v *Challenger* [1961] 1 QB 176, the husband and wife bought their matrimonial home as joint tenants. The marriage broke down and the wife went to live with another man. The husband was left alone in the house. Despite protests from the husband that the wife's adultery was being 'rewarded', the Court of Appeal ruled that the purpose of acquisition of the house had failed and a sale should be ordered.

On a rather different point, I am sure that a court would normally also order a sale if there were a large number of co-owners and a clear majority **by value** wanted a sale. See now s. 15(3) of the 1996 Act.

16.5.5.4 Order a sale but suspend the order for a short period

The possibility of making an order in this form was expressly recognized by the Court of Appeal in *Jones* v *Challenger*. The court can (under the old s. 30 or the new s. 14) suspend the order of sale for a few months so as to give a co-owner wishing to retain the property a chance to buy the other(s) out. He will have, of course, to pay the appropriate fraction of a fair value of the property.

 EXERCISE 16.6

If co-owners fall out, what is a sensible compromise solution which can be achieved *without litigation*?

The parties agree that the co-owner(s) wanting to keep the property buy out the co-owner(s) who 'want the cash'. (Arrangements will, of course, have to be made for the property to be valued.)

16.5.5.5 Partition

Partition, i.e., geographically splitting up co-owned property, is governed by Trusts of Land etc. Act 1996, s. 7. **Only in very rare cases is partition going to be a practical remedy**. (Try partitioning an ordinary semi-detached house!) Partition was possible in *Rodway* v *Landy* [2001] 2 WLR 1775; [2001] Ch 703, esp. at para. 27. This case involved a doctor's surgery which was capable of being split into two separate surgeries, each with its own consulting rooms, waiting areas, and toilets.

16.6 The modern position of husband and wife co-owners on a marriage break-up

The next few paragraphs arguably represent something of a digression into family law. I would stress that what follows is all you need to know for the purposes of a land law course. There is no need to learn the detailed 'property adjustment' rules in ss. 23–25 of the Matrimonial Causes Act 1973.

Where husband and wife are co-owners of **any property** (usually it will be the matrimonial home) and the marriage has broken down, one spouse could still (in theory) invoke s. 14 of the Trusts of Land etc. Act 1996. Alternatively, a spouse could (in theory) still invoke a special procedure available only for inter-spousal property disputes laid down in s. 17 of the Married Women's Property Act 1882.

Neither under s. 14 of the 1996 Act nor under s. 17 of the 1882 Act do the courts have any power to **vary** the property rights of the spouses.

? **QUESTION** 16.5

How is this last point, in the context of s. 14, relevant to cohabitees who co-own their home?

While under s. 14 the court can regulate the cohabitees' rights to occupy the property (as was done in *Dennis* v *McDonald*), it could not order one (ex-)cohabitee to transfer part or all of his/her interest to the other (ex-)cohabitee.

By contrast, as I explained earlier at 8.3.6.1, the divorce court does have nowadays very wide powers (under ss. 23–25 of the Matrimonial Causes Act 1973) to make 'property adjustment orders'. The co-owned property of divorcing couples is nowadays invariably dealt with under ss. 23–25. If a divorcing spouse tried to invoke s. 14 (or s. 17 of the 1882 Act) the court should refuse the application and order that the matter be dealt with by the divorce court under ss. 23–25: see *Williams J.* v *Williams M.* [1977] 1 All ER 28, where a divorcing spouse attempted (unsuccessfully) to invoke the old s. 30 of the Law of Property Act 1925.

Under ss. 23–25 of the Matrimonial Causes Act 1973 the divorce court is particularly careful where young children are still living in the ex-matrimonial home. (Usually, of course, a parent is there with them.) In such cases the divorce court is unlikely to order an immediate sale of the home. Rather, the normal practice is to **refuse** an order for immediate sale of the home and to make some kind of order which will ensure that the children can continue to live in the home until they have grown up: see *Mesher* v *Mesher* [1980] 1 All ER 126 (a case actually decided in 1973). Orders designed to protect children in this way are sometimes referred to as '*Mesher* orders'.

It is instructive to study the story behind the case of *Thompson* v *Thompson* [1985] 2 All ER 243. The order of the divorce court, made in 1981, directed that the ex-husband and the ex-wife, who remained the trustees for sale, should postpone sale of the home 'until the youngest child of the family...reaches the age of 17 years or finishes further education, whichever is later, or further order'. The ex-wife continued to live in the home with the two children, the youngest of which was (in 1985) aged 11. The ex-wife wanted to move from the home; ironically the ex-husband would not agree to a sale. She sought and obtained an order of sale, which was granted under s. 24A of the Matrimonial Causes Act 1973.

Another instructive divorce case is *Allen v Allen* [1974] 3 All ER 385. There the matrimonial home had been in the husband's name alone. The Court of Appeal (varying the order of the divorce court judge) ordered:

that the former matrimonial home should be transferred to the husband and the wife, to be held on trust for sale, with a direction that the sale should not take place until the younger child had attained the age of 17 years, or had finished his full-time education, whichever date should be the earlier, without either the consent of both the parents or under an order of the court, and that during that limited period the property should be held in trust for the wife to the exclusion of the husband for the purpose of her providing a home there for the children of the family, and, in particular, the two boys, and that at the expiration of that limited period it should then be held on trust for the two spouses in equal shares. (Per Buckley LJ)

Thompson, Allen, Harvey v Harvey [1982] 1 All ER 693 (and many other divorce cases I could cite) are striking for a number of reasons.

(a) The court continues as trustees (or, as in *Allen*, appoints as trustees) two people who are estranged from each other.

(b) The court inserted into the trust for sale provisions (such as that in *Thompson* and *Allen*) designed to ensure that the land would not be sold!

(c) These modern divorce cases demonstrated the highly artificial nature of the trust for sale which the 1925 legislation forced upon all co-owners. They thus underlined the good sense now embodied in the Trusts of Land etc. Act 1996.

(It is also worth noting that solutions such as those adopted in *Allen* and *Harvey* are often reached by divorcing couples **by negotiation,** without the need for the divorce court to **impose** an order. However, one unfortunate side effect of the Child Support Act 1992 is that it discourages divorcing spouses from settling their differences on the basis that the spouse with care of the children gets **possession** of the former matrimonial home.)

16.7 Rights of co-owners in equity—are they interests in land?

At 11.6.2 I discussed the 'archaic' doctrine of conversion. Under this doctrine, the equitable interests of beneficiaries under a trust for sale are personal property not real property. This 'conversion' doctrine gave rise to complex case law on the issue of whether equitable rights of co-owners were or were not 'interests in land'. The conclusion to be drawn from these cases was that for **most** (but not all) purposes equitable interests of co-owners, despite the doctrine of conversion, were interests in land. We need not now bother with this complex case law.

> **? QUESTION** 16.6
>
> Under the Trusts of Land etc. Act 1996, are the equitable interests of co-owners interests in land?

The answer is of course 'yes', as s. 3 of the 1996 Act abolishes the doctrine of conversion.

16.8 Law of Property (Joint Tenants) Act 1964

(This Act applies only to unregistered titles and is thus of declining importance.)

Where two or more people are joint tenants at law and in equity, the joint tenancy of course comes to an end the moment there is only one joint tenant left, i.e., on the death of the 'penultimate' joint tenant. It follows that the moment there is only one owner, the trust for sale (after the commencement of the 1996 Act, the new-style trust) also ends. The sole survivor can deal with the land as an absolute owner and does not have to appoint another trustee to effect a sale, lease, etc.

Prior to 1964 there was, however, a practical difficulty if a last surviving joint tenant wanted to sell the land without appointing a second trustee. A purchaser from a last surviving joint tenant might well ask, 'How do I know that the joint tenancy has not been severed?' (If there has been a severance there will be a tenancy in common and the trust (for sale) will still continue and a second trustee is needed for a sale.)

Just think for a moment. It is now easy to sever a joint tenancy. Indeed it can be done without the knowledge of fellow joint tenants. Consequently, it is impossible for the 'last survivor' to prove objectively that there has been no severance and that the trust (for sale) is at an end.

Prior to 1964, purchasers therefore insisted that the last survivor appointed a co-trustee before selling the property. This was a source of annoyance to solicitors and their clients, and the 1964 Act is designed to end the annoyance. Under the 1964 Act a purchaser from the last surviving joint tenant can assume that there has been no severance unless either:

(a) a memorandum of severance has been endorsed upon the conveyance to the joint tenants; or

(b) a bankruptcy petition or receiving order has been registered as a pending action.

Thus, unless one or other of the above conditions is fulfilled, a conveyance by a last surviving joint tenant acting on his/her own will convey a good title to a purchaser.

It should be noted that a 'memorandum of severance' is not another way of severing a joint tenancy. Rather it is something which can be endorsed on the conveyance to 'tell the world' that a severance has already taken place.

16.9 Co-ownership of registered land

The co-owners are registered as joint proprietors, but as the register does not indicate any trusts affecting registered titles, the register will not indicate whether the co-owners are joint tenants or tenants in common; if the latter it will not indicate the size of the shares. Thus (as mentioned at 14.9) a solicitor acting for co-owners should retain in his files a document expressly declaring the **equitable interests** of the co-owners.

There is, however, one further point which should be noted. If the registered co-proprietors are tenants in common in equity or if they are trustees (for sale) for other beneficiaries, then a 'restriction' will be entered in the proprietorship register in the following terms:

No disposition by a sole proprietor of the land (not being a trust corporation) under which capital money arises is to be registered except under an order of the registrar or of the court.

If co-proprietors are registered without such a 'restriction' being entered, that conclusively indicates that at least originally they were joint tenants in equity (*Re Gorman* [1990] 1 WLR 616). It is safe for a purchaser to deal with a last survivor if there is no such 'restriction', even if he suspects that there has been a severance.

A joint tenant who severs an equitable joint tenancy in a piece of registered land should also enter a restriction on the register.

CONCLUDING REMARKS

The 80 years which have elapsed since the compulsory imposition of a trust for sale on co-owners have seen both an enormous increase in the amount of co-ownership and the realization that the 1925 legislators in solving one problem (multiplicity of co-owners) created several others.

Until 1996, Parliament's contribution to the solution of the problems had been minimal—the rather technical Law of Property (Joint Tenants) Act 1964, which despite its grandiose title tackled but one minor problem which is anyway confined to unregistered land.

In contrast, the judiciary have (usually) worked very hard to sort things out. The senior judiciary have brought an enormous amount of common sense into this socially important area of law. As long ago as 1939 the Court of Appeal (in *Re Buchanan-Wollaston*) refused to be blinded by the existence of the trust for sale imposed on all co-owners. It saw that the compulsory trust for sale was merely legal machinery which should not affect the substantive rights of the parties. Subsequent generations of judges, with minor exceptions, have endorsed that approach.

In 1996, common sense, at long last, reached the legislature. In the field of co-ownership the Trusts of Land etc. Act 1996 in effect both adopts and adapts the common sense which shines through the pre-existing case law.

For example, in 1955, Lord Denning held that where property is acquired by co-owners for personal occupation, then the co-owners do indeed (notwithstanding the existence of a trust) have the right to occupy the land. This was a sensation in 1955. However, Lord Denning's colleagues went along with him on this point (e.g., in *Boland*) and now we see the same point in s. 12 of the 1996 Act.

Judges also made great efforts to sort out the cumbersome s. 30 of the Law of Property Act 1925. These efforts are now reflected in the new ss. 14 and 15. The factors listed in s. 15 are largely (though not completely) derived from existing case law. Section 13 is also very welcome; especially as, when read with ss. 14 and 15, it clearly vindicates the bold decision in *Dennis* v *McDonald*.

Finally, judges tried to circumvent (or simply ignore) the ridiculous doctrine of conversion. Section 3 of the 1996 Act abolished the doctrine.

■ SUMMARY

Does a constructive trust share belonging to a claimant (C) bind someone (A) who acquires the relevant land?

To answer this question go through the following multi-stage process

STAGE ONE

Did A acquire the land from one person acting alone, or from two or more vendors (in effect acting as trustees)?

If the land is acquired from two or more vendors, C's interest is overreached (*Flegg*) and will not bind A. Neither the doctrine of notice nor Sch. 3, para. 2 has any application.

Stop here!

If A acquired the land from one person, go to stage two.

STAGE TWO

Is the relevant land unregistered or registered title?

If unregistered go to stage three

If registered go to stage **five**

STAGE THREE (unregistered title)

Was A a purchaser for value of a legal estate or interest?

If no, e.g. A is a donee, C's interest binds A

Stop here!

If yes, go to stage four

STAGE FOUR (unregistered title)

Did A have notice of C's interest?

If yes (as in *Tizard*) A is bound.

If no, A is not bound.

STAGE FIVE (Registered title)

If the land was acquired from one person, consider whether C has an overriding interest under Sch. 3, para. 2. Apply the multi-stage process set out in the summary at the end of Chapter 10!

Five possible solutions where co-owners fall out.

(All five can be achieved either by negotiation or by court order.)

1 Sell the property and divide the proceeds.

2 Those wanting to retain the land buy out the interest(s) of those wanting sale.

3 As in *Buchanan-Wollaston and Evers* just let those who want to enjoy the land continue to enjoy the land. (Unlikely to be achieved by negotiation!)

4 Let those who want to enjoy the land continue to enjoy the land, but subject to conditions.

   Likely conditions are (a) that the occupiers pay the outgoings (see s 13(5)(a)); (b) that the occupiers pay 'rent' to those not in occupation (see s. 13(6)(a)).

5 (Only possible in a minority of cases) Geographically divide ('partition') the land between the co-owners.

CHAPTER 16: ASSESSMENT EXERCISE

In 1989 four friends, Steven, Julia, Mark, and Tracey, purchased a cottage called 'The Retreat' for the purpose of a holiday home. The Retreat was unregistered title situated in an area which had not yet become an area of compulsory registration of title. The conveyance to them contained no express declaration of a trust for sale. The purchase money was provided equally and at the time of the purchase Tracey was only 17 years of age.

In January 2005 Julia became short of cash and therefore obtained a bank loan which was secured on her interest in The Retreat.

Some months later, Steven also found himself in financial difficulties. However his solution to the problem was to create frequent arguments with the others in which he would demand that they 'buy him out'. These outbursts were ignored by the others and Steven eventually stopped using The Retreat.

In October 2005 Steven and Julia were killed in a car accident. By their wills Steven left all his property to his mother Violet, and Julia left all her property to her sister, Karen.

Mark is keen to sell The Retreat and has just found a purchaser who wants an early completion. Tracey vehemently opposes the proposed sale as since the deaths of Steven and Julia she has been living at The Retreat permanently. Violet is in agreement with Mark, but Karen is uncertain.

Advise Mark as to:

(a) exactly who owns The Retreat and in what proportions;

(b) his prospects of forcing a sale.

See Appendix for a specimen answer.

■ FURTHER READING

The decision in *Flegg* did not (initially) find universal approval, and the Law Commission provisionally proposed that it should be overruled. See The Law Commission, Working Paper No. 106, 'Trusts of Land: Overreaching'. In enacting the 1996 Trusts of Land etc. Act, Parliament firmly rejected this suggestion.

For the thinking behind s. 12 to 15 of the Trusts of Land and Appointment of Trustees Act, see Law Commission report no. 181, 'Transfer of Land—Trusts of Land' pages 21–24.

PART VI

Leases

17 Leases—the basic requirements

17.1 Objectives

By the end of this chapter you should:

1 Be able to list the basic requirements for a valid lease

2 Be fully conversant with the rules governing the duration of fixed-term leases and periodic tenancies

3 Appreciate the importance of the distinction between a lease and a licence

4 Be able to explain how the law determines whether a transaction is a lease or a licence

5 Be familiar with and be able to distinguish between the formalities required for the creation of (i) legal and (ii) equitable leases

6 Appreciate how periodic tenancies may arise by operation of law

17.2 Introduction

As is obvious if you visit any law library, whole textbooks have been written on the law of leases, or 'landlord and tenant law' as it is often called. In this text (designed for a land law course where only three or four weeks are spent studying leases) we have space to consider only basic principles. It should therefore in particular be stressed that the following legislation is outside the scope of this text.

• **The Rent Acts** These Acts (the history of which goes back to the First World War) grant special security to and control the rents of most residential tenants whose leases were granted before the Housing Act 1988.

• **Housing Acts 1988 and 1996** These Acts remove **new** residential leases from the scope of the Rent Acts.

• **Agricultural Holdings Acts**, and the **Agricultural Tenancies Act 1995** which replaces those Acts. The Agricultural Holdings Acts gave special protection to tenant farmers. The 1995 Act removes most of that special statutory protection.

- **Landlord and Tenant Act 1954, Part II** This legislation grants special protection to lessees of business premises (e.g., shops, offices, and factories). In particular when the lease of a business tenant (e.g., a shopkeeper) runs out, he can usually insist that the lease be renewed.

- **Leasehold Reform Act 1967 and later similar legislation** This legislation allows long lessees of certain types of houses compulsorily to purchase the freehold reversions of their houses from **private** landlords.

- **Leasehold Reform, Housing and Urban Development Act 1993** This statute (*inter alia*) gives the lessees of long leases living in certain types of flats the right compulsorily to purchase the freehold reversion of their block of flats from **private** landlords.

- **The Commonhold and Leasehold Reform Act 2002** This Act, as well as creating the new Commonhold Tenure (briefly outlined in **Chapter 3**), gives further rights to lessees holding long leases of certain types of flats. Note that this Act does NOT give tenants of a block of flats the right to insist that the ownership of the block be converted to the Commonhold system.

I have to warn you that this chapter is rather a bulky one, and contains rather a large quantity of complex technical concepts. Much of the technicality stems from one simple fact: if the owner of a fee simple estate allows another person to make use of his land, that transaction **may** be a lease; alternatively it may be only a licence. Differentiating between leases and licences has given rise to a quite considerable amount of case law.

Other causes of the complexity of this chapter stem from matters we have already touched upon. In **Chapter 1** we noted the differences between fixed-term leases and periodic tenancies, while in **Chapter 5** we considered *Walsh* v *Lonsdale* and noted that leases may be either legal leases or equitable leases. These matters must now be considered in greater depth.

17.3 The essential requirements for a lease

There are three essential requirements:

(a) The estate must be of a duration permitted for a leasehold estate.

(b) The grant must give exclusive possession.

(c) The grant must have the correct formalities.

In *Street* v *Mountford* [1985] 2 All ER 289, the House of Lords held that (subject to minor exceptions) a transaction which fulfils these three requirements **must be a lease** even if the parties say (in the relevant document) that the transaction is something else, e.g., a licence.

17.4 Duration of leases

Leases can either be for a **fixed term**, or they can be **periodic tenancies**.

17.4.1 **Fixed-term leases**

Here we are talking of leases for periods such as one month, three years, 99 years, 999 years. The vital feature of a fixed-term lease is that there is a fixed **maximum** duration. It is perfectly possible (indeed normal) for a lease to contain a forfeiture clause under which the landlord can terminate the lease prematurely if the tenant breaks any of the terms of the lease.

Some fixed-term leases also contain a 'break clause', which can be invoked by the tenant. Under such a clause the tenant has a right unilaterally to terminate the lease before it has run its full course. For example you will sometimes see '21-year leases with seven year breaks'. The lease in principle lasts 21 years, but the tenant has the option to terminate the lease after seven or 14 years.

Leases for **uncertain maximum periods** are not permitted. In *Lace v Chantler* [1944] KB 368 leases 'for the duration of the war' were held to be invalid. This caused widespread panic, as such grants were (at the time) common. Parliament therefore rushed through an ingenious piece of legislation, the Validation of Wartime Leases Act 1944. This Act was retrospective, and converted grants 'for the duration of the war' into leases for a fixed term of 10 years, with a proviso that either landlord or tenant could terminate the lease once the war ended by giving a month's notice.

The House of Lords applied the *Lace v Chantler* principle in *Prudential Assurance v London Residuary Body* [1992] 2 AC 386. The former London County Council had, in 1930, granted a lease of property fronting the busy Walworth Road. The lease was on terms that 'the tenancy shall continue until the . . . land is required by the council for the purposes of the widening of [the road]'. The rent was £30 per annum. The road widening never took place. The House of Lords held that there was not a valid fixed-term lease. For reasons which will appear at 17.4.2, the House found that there was a yearly periodic tenancy.

> **?**   **QUESTION** 17.1
>
> Alan has just been appointed manager of Bruddersford Town football club. He knows that he is likely to be sacked if the team plays poorly. He wants to take a lease of a house in Bruddersford from Charley, a keen Bruddersford supporter. Alan and Charley envisage that the lease will be for 'as long as Alan remains manager'. What sort of lease would meet their requirements? (A clue is the Validation of Wartime Leases Act 1944!)

Alan and Charley should agree on a fixed-term lease for some very long period (e.g., 40 years), but include a clause that should Alan cease to be manager either party can terminate the lease by (say) one month's notice.

17.4.2 **Periodic tenancies**

Here we are talking of weekly, monthly, yearly, quarterly tenancies, etc. The practical effect of a periodic tenancy is that it continues indefinitely until terminated by one or other side giving the appropriate notice. Why, then, do periodic tenancies not infringe the rule that a leasehold estate must have a fixed maximum duration? At least three different explanations have been given:

(a) A periodic tenancy is a lease for one period which goes on renewing itself automatically.

(b) A periodic tenancy is a lease for one period which goes on extending itself automatically.

(c) A periodic tenancy is a lease because its maximum duration is 'capable of being rendered certain' by the giving of the appropriate period of notice.

In *Prudential Assurance* v *London Residuary Body* (see 17.4.1) the House of Lords clearly favoured explanation (a), **so this must be regarded as the correct one**.

The period of notice to terminate a periodic tenancy is prima facie one period, to expire at the end of a period. Thus, e.g., suppose on 1 January Les grants a monthly tenancy to Tom. Tom now decides he wants to leave. He must give (at least) one month's notice to expire on the last day of a calendar month.

? **QUESTION** 17.2

Suppose today is 15 February. If Tom gives Les one month's notice that he is quitting the property, when will that notice expire?

The answer is that the notice will expire at midnight at the end of 31 March. You should note that in practical terms this means that if Tom in fact moves out on (say) 16 February, he must still pay the rent until the end of March.

The parties to a periodic tenancy can agree that the requisite notice should be less than one period, but not more. Thus, e.g., in a half-yearly tenancy they could agree to it being terminable on giving three months' notice. They could not agree to a year's notice.

A special rule operates for yearly tenancies. In the absence of contrary agreement the period of notice is (anomalously) six months, though the parties can expressly agree to any period of notice up to one year.

It **used to be thought** that a party to a periodic tenancy could agree to conditions restricting his right to terminate the tenancy. See *Re Midland Railway's Agreement* [1971] 1 All ER 1007.

However this case, and another very confusing case, *Ashburn Anstalt* v *Arnold* [1988] 2 All ER 147, were both (on this point) overruled by the House of Lords in the *Prudential Assurance* case. In *Prudential Assurance* the Court of Appeal had held that the tenants had a yearly tenancy, but subject to a condition that the tenancy could not be terminated until the land was required for the road-widening scheme. The House of Lords held that parties to a periodic tenancy cannot restrict their basic right to terminate the tenancy by giving the appropriate notice.

17.4.3 Special problems connected with the duration of leases

17.4.3.1 'Leases for lives'

Traditionally life estates were created, for no consideration, as part of a strict settlement, and were governed by the Settled Land Act 1925, considered briefly in **Chapter 11**. If after the commencement of the Trusts of Land etc. Act 1996 a life estate is created for no consideration, a new-style trust of land will automatically arise.

Back in 1925 the legislators had a problem with a practice which existed in some parts of the country. Landlords in some areas used to grant to tenant-farmers not fixed terms, but a life estate in return for the tenant paying a rent and/or premium. (A premium is a capital sum paid for the grant of a lease.) Clearly it would have been totally wrong to bring such transactions within the Settled Land Act 1925.

Section 149(6) of the Law of Property Act 1925 is designed to convert such 'leases for life' transactions into fixed-term leases, but unfortunately s. 149(6) is drafted in an unnecessarily wide way, and catches:

(a) a lease at a rent and/or premium granted for life or lives;

(b) a lease for a fixed period determinable on life or lives;

(c) a lease for a fixed period determinable on marriage.

All the three types of transaction are converted into leases for a fixed term of 90 years. However, once the relevant death or marriage has occurred either the landlord or the tenant (or their personal representatives) can terminate the lease by giving a month's notice to expire on one of the traditional quarter days. The 'traditional quarter days' are Lady Day (25 March), Mid-Summer (24 June), Michaelmas (29 September), and Christmas.

Section 149(6) works perfectly well when applied to transactions of type (a) above. (Remember the Validation of Wartime Leases Act 1944 and **Question 17.1**.) However, the applicability of s. 149(6) to transactions of types (b) and (c) creates a trap for the foolish landlord.

Suppose in 2000 Laurie leases Blackacre to Terry at £500 per year rent, 'for 10 years or until Terry's death, if earlier'. Terry is a healthy young man of 20. Laurie expects the lease to expire in 2010. But it is converted by s. 149(6) into a 90-year term, and Laurie will not be able to give notice to terminate the lease until Terry dies, which may not be for a very long time. (And the rent remains fixed at £500 per year!)

> **? QUESTION** 17.3
>
> In 2005, Harry leased a house to Wassilla, a spinster aged 22, 'for five years or until her earlier marriage'. Harry is looking forward to getting the house back in 2010. Wassilla has just joined a religious group which required her to take a vow that she would never marry. Advise Harry.

Harry is caught by s. 149(6). He will have to hope that Wassilla changes her religious views, as otherwise he (or his personal representatives) will not be able to terminate the lease until either Wassilla dies or she achieves the age of 112!

17.4.3.2 Perpetually renewable leases

The essence of such a lease **was** that the tenant took a fixed term of X years, but every time X years expired he had the option to renew the lease for a further X years. Thus **provided the tenant remembered** to renew every time X years expired, he could keep the land indefinitely.

Prior to 1926 a perpetually renewable lease would be created by including in a fixed-term lease a clause like the following: 'This lease shall be renewable by the tenant at his option on exactly the same terms and conditions, including this provision.' The crucial words are of course, 'including this provision'. Had they been omitted, the lease would have been renewable just **once**.

As a result of s. 145 of the Law of Property Act **1925**, a perpetually renewable lease is not possible after 1925. Section 145 does not, however, invalidate leases containing the kind of clause just quoted. Far from it! Section 145 converts any purported grant of a perpetually renewable lease into a lease for 2,000 (sic) years. The tenant (not the landlord) has the option to terminate the lease by 10 **days'** notice every time the lease would have been due for renewal had it been allowed to take effect as a perpetually renewable lease.

In *Caerphilly Concrete* v *Owen* [1972] 1 All ER 248 the landlord granted the tenant a lease stated to last for five years. However, the lease granted the tenant the option to renew the lease for a further five years 'at the same rent and containing the like covenants and provisos as are herein contained (including the option to renew such lease for a further term of five years at the expiration thereof)'.

The words in brackets proved fatal for the landlords. Those words (prior to 1926) would have created a perpetually renewable lease. But the transaction took place in 1963, so the landlords discovered that they had leased their land for 2,000 years, and at a very low rent!

17.4.3.3 **Tenancy at will**

A tenancy at will is a very insecure arrangement, because either side can terminate it at a moment's notice. It is particularly unattractive from the point of view of the tenant at will, as he can be thrown out without any prior warning.

In modern conditions, tenancies at will are relatively rare. One does, however, exist where a landlord has allowed somebody to take possession of his land intending him to be a tenant, but, probably because the execution of a formal lease has been forgotten, or the formal lease is for some reason invalid, no estate or interest has been granted to the tenant. (It is, however, also possible deliberately to create a tenancy at will, as in *Manfield* v *Botchin* [1970] 2 QB 612.)

If a tenant at will starts paying rent on a regular basis, the tenancy at will is automatically converted into a periodic tenancy. This rule, which we consider at 17.7.2 and which the House of Lords applied in the *Prudential Assurance* case, goes a long way to mitigating the extremely insecure position of tenants at will.

 One other point. In *Heslop* v *Burns* [1974] 3 All ER 406, a fairly wealthy person allowed two friends to occupy rent-free a house he owned. The Court of Appeal held that such a friendly arrangement (made without intent to create legal relations) regarding the occupation of a house or flat is nowadays to be treated as a **licence**, not as a tenancy at will.

17.5 **Some concepts related to the law of leases**

It is convenient to deal with certain miscellaneous points at this stage. I would stress that what follows is a bare outline of certain matters which you need to know to be able to understand the basic principles of the law of leases and also certain of the cases on the distinction between leases and licences.

17.5.1 **Tenancy at sufferance**

This occurs where a tenant's lease has expired but he (**unlawfully**) continues in possession without the landlord's express agreement or express disagreement. The tenant is said to 'hold over'. If the landlord **expressly disagrees** with the ex-tenant staying, the ex-tenant is simply a trespasser, who should leave immediately. If the landlord **expressly agrees** to the tenant staying in possession, he is a tenant at will.

(Like a tenancy at will a tenancy at sufferance will automatically be converted into a periodic tenancy if the 'tenant' starts paying rent on a regular basis.)

17.5.2 **Protected tenancy**

This is a lease (granted prior to 15 January 1989) of a 'dwelling house' (which concept includes a flat) within the scope of the Rent Acts. If the lease terminates (even after 15 January 1989) then normally the tenant can lawfully stay in possession as a **statutory tenant**. (He will not be a tenant at sufferance.)

17.5.3 **Statutory tenancy**

A statutory tenant technically has no estate or interest in the house or flat he is still occupying. He has a right given **by the statute** (a right which cannot be transferred) to continue to occupy the property notwithstanding the termination of his lease. Statutory tenancies are usually thought of as arising under the Rent Acts. It is worth noting that they could also arise under the Agricultural Holdings Acts, when a lease of a farm terminated but the tenant-farmer was allowed by the Acts to retain possession.

17.5.4 **Secure tenancies**

Under the Housing Act 1980 public sector lettings such as council houses are **secure tenancies**; they are outside the Rent Acts and the Housing Act 1988, but the public sector secure tenant enjoys similar security of tenure to his private sector counterpart under the old Rent Acts. For lettings after 14 January 1989, the public sector tenant is better off.

17.5.5 **Assured tenancies**

Under the Housing Act 1988 (as a general rule), no new protected tenancies can arise. All private landlords of houses or flats were empowered by the 1988 Act to grant **assured tenancies**. The assured tenant has some degree of security of tenure, but there are no controls on the rent charged. Since the commencement of the Housing Act 1996, new assured tenancies are still possible, but rather unlikely.

17.5.6 **Assured shorthold tenancies**

Under the Housing Act 1988 a private landlord could grant an **assured shorthold tenancy**. Under the 1988 Act, an assured shorthold was a fixed-term lease of a house or flat for at least six months. The tenant has no security of tenure once the fixed period expires; there are rather weak controls on the amount of rent. This form of letting proved to be very popular with landlords, especially those who let to undergraduate students.

Assured shorthold tenancies are now even more common. Subject to minor exceptions such as holiday lettings, the Housing Act 1996 provides that all residential lettings are assured shortholds. It does not matter whether the residential letting is for a fixed term or is a periodic tenancy. If the letting is a periodic tenancy, then by way of exception to the usual common law rules about termination by notice, a landlord cannot terminate the tenancy before six months have elapsed from the date of the original grant. (This six months rule is the only provision for security of tenure. There are still weak controls on the rent which can be charged.)

17.6 The distinction between leases and licences

The distinction is very important because:

(a) As leases are property rights (an estate or interest in land), they are in principle freely alienable, i.e., they can be sold, given away, or left by will. A licence is a right personal to the licensee and cannot be assigned. (Suppose I was going away, for a few weeks, and allowed a friend of mine to occupy my flat rent-free in my absence. That would be a 'licence'. It would obviously be wrong for my friend to transfer his right to a third party.)

(b) As leases are property rights, they in principle bind third party purchasers of the landlord's reversion. Licences generally do not bind purchasers of the land over which the licence is exercisable. (Exceptionally a licence could bind a purchaser if a licensee acquired by his activities on the land a proprietary estoppel or a constructive trust interest. See 1.4.7 and 1.4.8.)

(c) Leases are subject to security of tenure legislation such as the Rent Acts; licences are generally outside the scope of such legislation.

As you will see if you quickly flip through the next few pages of this text, there have been a lot of cases on the lease/licence distinction. Almost all of them relate to point (c) just mentioned. In almost all of them a landowner has granted a right to occupy his land, but tried to make the arrangement a licence, not a lease, so that he avoids the Rent Acts or other similar legislation.

17.6.1 Exclusive possession as the foundation of the lease/licence distinction

17.6.1.1 *Street* v *Mountford* [1985] 1 AC 809

Most land law teachers welcomed the decision of the House of Lords in *Street* v *Mountford*, as it both simplified and clarified the law. Most of the essential facts of this case are set out in the opening paragraph of Lord Templeman's speech:

By an agreement dated 7 March 1983, the respondent Mr Street granted the appellant Mrs Mountford the right to occupy the furnished rooms numbers 5 and 6 at 5, St Clements Gardens, Boscombe, from 7 March 1983 for £37 per week, subject to termination by 14 days written notice and subject to [quite elaborate] conditions set forth in the agreement.

I need only add that the agreement was called a 'licence', but nevertheless undoubtedly granted Mrs Mountford exclusive possession. When the case was decided by the Court of Appeal, it held that as 'the [subjective] intention of the parties' was that there should be a licence, that was all Mrs Mountford had. She did not have any form of lease protected by the Rent Acts.

This decision of the Court of Appeal was blasted off the face of the earth ('overruled' is too mild a word) by the unanimous decision of the House of Lords. (Lord Templeman gave the only reasoned speech.) The House held that whether a transaction is a lease or a licence depends (with minor exceptions) entirely on whether or not there is **exclusive possession**. The 'intent of the parties' and the label the parties attach to the transaction is irrelevant. As none of the minor exceptions was applicable, Mrs Mountford had a lease which was protected by the Rent Acts.

The House of Lords has fairly recently reaffirmed *Street* v *Mountford* in *Bruton* v *London and Quadrant Housing Trust* [1999] 3 All ER 481. The defendant housing association had granted to Bruton the exclusive possession of a flat, but under a transaction carefully described as a licence. Their Lordships held that a lease had been created. (See also *Addiscombe Gardens* v *Crabbe* [1958] 1 QB 513, a Court of Appeal decision which is clearly correct in the light of the later House of Lords decisions.)

17.6.2 **The meaning of exclusive possession**

If there is no exclusive possession granted to the 'grantee' then the transaction is a licence. The test for exclusive possession is:

Has the grantee been given the general control of the property?

This test stems from the nineteenth-century case of *Wells* v *Hull Corporation* (1875) LR 10 CP 402. In that case Hull Corporation owned a 'dry dock' used by shipowners to repair their ships. The corporation 'let' the dock to shipowners on terms which included provisions:

(a) that the corporation was responsible for opening and shutting the dock gates to allow ships to sail in and out;

(b) that the shipowner should clean out the dock at the end of each day's work under the supervision of the corporation's employees.

The court held that the shipowner was not granted 'general control' of the dock. Therefore the 'letting' to the shipowner was in fact only a licence.

17.6.2.1 *Shell-Mex* v *Manchester Garages* [1971] 1 All ER 841

In this case Shell granted the use of a filling station it owned to the garage company for one year. The agreement included a provision under which Shell retained control over the layout of the premises. It could move the pumps and the (extensive) underground storage tanks. The arrangement was held to be only a licence. (Although this case and *Marchant* v *Charters*, discussed next, are still correct in their result, some of Lord Denning's remarks in them about 'intent of the parties' are clearly wrong in the light of *Street* v *Mountford*.)

17.6.2.2 *Marchant v Charters* [1977] 1 WLR 1181, CA

It has always been accepted that a 'lodger' does not have exclusive possession and therefore is only a licensee. In *Marchant* v *Charters* the 'grantee' was not a lodger in the traditional sense but occupied a 'service flat'. The grantor provided daily cleaning and regular changes of bed linen. The grantee was found to be only a licensee.

17.6.3 Retention of keys by the grantor

The mere fact that a grantor retains keys to the premises does not as such negate the existence of a lease. Lord Donaldson, MR, in *Aslan* v *Murphy* [1990] 1 WLR 766, CA explained:

It is not a requirement of a tenancy [i.e., lease] that the occupier shall have exclusive possession of the keys to the property. What matters is what underlies the provision as to keys. Why does the owner want a key, want to prevent keys being issued to the friends of the occupier or want to prevent the lock being changed?

A landlord may well need a key in order that he may be able to enter quickly in the event of emergency; fire, burst pipes or whatever. He may need a key to enable him or those authorised by him to read meters or to do repairs which are his responsibility. None of these underlying reasons would of themselves indicate that the true bargain between the parties was such that the occupier was in law a lodger [i.e., licensee]. On the other hand, if the true bargain is that the owner will provide genuine services which can only be provided by having keys, such as frequent cleaning, daily bed-making, the provision of clean linen at regular intervals and the like, there are materials from which it is possible to infer that the occupier is a lodger [licensee] rather than a tenant.

17.6.4 Possessory licences after *Street* v *Mountford*

The constantly recurring theme of the decision in *Street* v *Mountford* is that whether a transaction is a lease or a licence depends on whether exclusive possession is granted. However, almost at the end of his speech, Lord Templeman says this:

Sometimes it may be difficult to discover whether, on the true construction of an agreement, exclusive possession is conferred. Sometimes it may appear from the surrounding circumstances that there was no intention to create legal relationships. Sometimes it may appear from the surrounding circumstances that the right to exclusive possession is referable to a legal relationship other than a tenancy. Legal relationships to which the grant of exclusive possession might be referable and which would or might negative the grant of an estate or interest in the land include occupancy under a contract for the sale of the land, occupancy pursuant to a contract of employment or occupancy referable to the holding of an office. But where as in the present case the only circumstances are that residential accommodation is offered and accepted with exclusive possession for a term at a rent, the result is a tenancy.

In practice it therefore appears that there are, after *Street* v *Mountford*, four types of situation where somebody can have 'exclusive possession' of property but have only a licence. Put another way, there are four exceptions to the general rule laid down in *Street* that 'exclusive possession means that there is a lease'.

17.6.4.1 Acts of generosity, charity, or friendship where there is no intent to create legal relations

We have already noted *Heslop v Burns* [1974] 3 All ER 406, where a licence was held to exist (see 17.4.3.3). I do not think there is any doubt that that decision is still correct after *Street*.

Slightly more debatable is the decision of the Court of Appeal in *Rhodes* v *Dalby* [1971] 2 All ER 1144.

Two men were **long-standing friends**. One owned a bungalow, but was going abroad for two years. The two men signed a document, described as 'a gentleman's agreement' not intended to create legal relations. Under that agreement the friend staying in this country took possession of the bungalow during the two-year absence. He agreed to pay a quite high 'rent' for being able to live in the bungalow. This arrangement was found to be a licence. I think this decision is correct. The crucial fact was that the two men were friends **before** they signed the agreement.

The fairly recent decision of the Court of Appeal in *Gray* v *Taylor* [1998] 4 All ER 17 is entirely consistent with *Street* v *Mountford*. The trustees of some almshouses granted Mrs Taylor exclusive possession of a flat within the almshouses. She did not pay rent, but was required to pay a (small) contribution towards the upkeep of the building. She was held to have only a licence.

17.6.4.2 Service occupancies

It is perfectly possible for an employer to grant to an employee a formal lease over a house situated close to the place of work. However (and this is unaffected by *Street* v *Mountford*), if an employer, without executing a formal lease, allows an employee to live in the employer's accommodation so that he can readily be available for work at any time, the employee has a form of licence known as a 'service occupancy'. This is the case whether or not the employee is obliged by his contract of employment to live in the accommodation: *Crane* v *Morris* [1965] 3 All ER 77.

EXERCISE 17.1

Can you think of types of workers who often have service occupancies?

Caretakers, agricultural workers, and members of the police, armed forces, and fire brigade often have 'service occupancies'. A rather more unusual case is *Norris* v *Checksfield* [1991] 1 WLR 1241. In that case a coach mechanic had been granted the use of a bungalow close to the depot. The Court of Appeal held that he was a service occupier, not a tenant!

17.6.4.3 Occupancy by virtue of an office

This point is most likely to affect clergymen, who (you may be surprised to learn) do not usually have contracts of employment. Clergymen are only licensees of their manses, vicarages, presbyteries, etc.

17.6.4.4 Occupancy prior to the completion of a contract for sale

From time to time a purchaser who has **contracted** to buy a piece of land is allowed by the vendor to take possession of the property even though the sale has not yet been completed by a conveyance or land transfer.

In the past, it was sometimes said that such a purchaser in possession 'ahead of completion' was a tenant at will. *Street* v *Mountford* confirms that this view is not correct. Rather, the purchaser is to be regarded as a licensee.

17.6.5 **Flat-sharing agreements**

In recent years there have been a number of cases where the facts have followed a similar sort of pattern. Two (or more) people are together looking for a flat or house to share. They find a 'landlord', who refuses to grant them a lease. Instead he grants each of them a separate 'non-exclusive' licence. Each licence includes a clause under which the grantor can introduce into the property other person(s).

17.6.5.1 **Somma v Hazelhurst [1978] 2 All ER 1011**

In this case H and S (a cohabiting couple) had each signed on the same day a separate agreement granting each the use of a bed-sitting room to be shared with a person 'to be introduced'. The Court of Appeal rejected the argument that the two transactions should be read together, and should be regarded as together granting exclusive possession and therefore creating a lease. In the view of the Court of Appeal, two licences had been created.

In the light of later cases, this decision is undoubtedly wrong. It was disapproved of in very strong terms by the House of Lords in *Street* v *Mountford*. Lord Templeman said of *Somma* v *Hazelhurst*:

The agreements [sic] signed by H and S constituted the grant to H and S jointly of exclusive possession at a rent for a term for the purposes for which the room was taken and the agreement [sic] therefore created a tenancy.

17.6.5.2 **The 1988 cases**

In 1988 the House of Lords gave judgment on the same day in two cases raising the 'non-exclusive licence' issue.

Antoniades v *Villiers* [1990] 1 AC 417

In this case V1 and V2 (a cohabiting couple) each signed on the same day an agreement giving them the right to use a **small** flat. Clause 16 of each agreement provided: 'The licensor shall be entitled at any time to use the rooms together with the licensee and permit other persons to use all of the rooms together with the licensee'.

The House of Lords, led by Lord Templeman, took a very robust approach. The practical realities had to be looked at. The two documents read together granted exclusive possession and therefore created a lease. Moreover clause 16 should be ignored. It had been inserted by the grantor as a 'pretence', in an effort to show that V1 and V2 did not together have exclusive possession. Nobody would expect the grantor to exercise the 'right' conferred on him by clause 16.

 EXERCISE 17.2

In a radio interview some years ago, Lord Templeman (whose first name is Sydney) admitted that he had been given the nickname 'Sid Vicious' by some lawyers. He mentioned, as one of the reasons for the nickname, his judgments in lease/licence cases. Why then 'Vicious'? (His judgment in *Billson* v *Residential Apartments*, see 20.6.2, is further evidence of why he got the nickname.)

After reading some of his judgments on the lease/licence issue, you will realize that Lord Templeman is very tough on landlords who try to get round legislation designed to protect tenants.

AG Securities v *Vaughan* [1990] 1 AC 417

AGS owned a four-bedroomed flat. Each of the four occupiers had signed a non-exclusive licence. Each licence was signed on a different date, was for a different period, and was at a different rent. Was this one lease or four licences?

The House of Lords held that a lease had **not** been created. There were four separate licences.

? **QUESTION** 17.4

You own a house, the use of which you are willing to grant to full-time students. In mid-September you are approached by a group of four respectable law students, who want accommodation for the forthcoming academic year. They want a lease to last to the following early July. You would rather give them 'non-exclusive licences'. How do you achieve your objective?

To achieve your objective you grant them four separate non-exclusive licences, to begin and end on different dates. For example:

(a) Licence A would run from 20 September to 1 July.

(b) Licence B would run from 23 September to 4 July.

(c) Licence C would run from 18 September to 6 July.

(d) Licence D would run from 25 September to 5 July.

17.6.6 'Pretence' clauses designed to negate exclusive possession

We have already seen that in *Antoniades* v *Villiers* (17.6.5) the grantor inserted the highly artificial clause 16 in an effort to fool the courts into thinking that V1 and V2, even taken together, did not have exclusive possession. The robust approach taken by Lord Templeman in *Antoniades* was applied by the Court of Appeal in two cases it decided together in 1989, *Aslan* v *Murphy* and *Duke* v *Wynne* [1990] 3 All ER 130.

In the first case, A granted to M the use of a tiny basement room. The licence included a term that A could introduce another occupant. It also included another provision that M had no right to use the room between 1030 and 1200 hours. Both these clauses were found to be 'pretences', and M was held to be a tenant.

In the second case D granted to Mr and Mrs W (who had two children living with them) a three-bedroom house for two years. D again reserved the right to introduce other occupiers to the property. This clause was found to be a 'pretence'. D had no genuine intention of introducing other person(s) to the house. The Ws were held to have a lease.

17.7 Formalities for leases

There are three kinds of formality possible for a lease:

(a) legal leases arising by express grant;

(b) legal leases arising by operation of law;

(c) equitable leases arising by virtue of a contract or an informal grant.

17.7.1 Legal leases by express grant

Normally to create a lease which is valid as a **legal lease** a deed is required. Section 54(2) of the Law of Property Act 1925 creates an important exception. Under this provision no special formality is required to create a legal lease if it satisfies **all** the following conditions (even an oral grant will suffice):

(a) The lease is for a period not exceeding three years. (This includes periodic tenancies.)

(b) The lease is at the best rent reasonably obtainable.

(c) No premium ('fine') is charged for the grant of the lease.

(d) The lease takes effect in possession immediately.

17.7.2 Legal leases by operation of law

This applies only to periodic tenancies. A periodic tenancy will arise automatically where a tenant at will (or at sufferance) commences paying rent calculated on a periodic basis. (It is in effect presumed that the parties intended a periodic tenancy; see, e.g., the case of *Martin* v *Smith* (1874) LR 9 Ex 50.)

What the 'period' (weekly, monthly, etc.) is for the periodic tenancy depends on the period by reference to which the rent is calculated, looking at all the evidence available. Usually the period by reference to which the rent is calculated is also the period by reference to which it actually has to be paid: £x per week will mean a weekly tenancy; £y a month will mean a monthly tenancy, and so on. In *Prudential Assurance* v *London Residuary Body* [1992] 3 All ER 504 (see 17.4.1), the House of Lords held, applying the principle we are currently considering, that as the rent had been fixed at £30 per annum, a yearly tenancy had arisen.

A problem might seem to arise if, for example, the evidence shows that informally the parties had agreed to a rent of £600 per annum, payable in monthly instalments. As the rent is **calculated** on an annual basis, there would in this example be a yearly tenancy.

A periodic tenancy by operation of law will not arise if the parties have expressly agreed that the arrangement between them should remain a tenancy at will. Neither will one arise where a prospective lessee has been let into possession, starts paying rent, but continues to negotiate with the landlord for the grant of a fixed-term lease: *Javad* v *Aqil* [1991] 1 All ER 243.

Hitherto I have never owned a car. I have therefore allowed Tom to keep his car in the garage attached to my house. There is nothing in writing, but Tom pays me £100 per month rent. I have now bought a car, and therefore want Tom out of my garage. How much notice must I give?

Assuming that Tom has had exclusive possession, he will have a monthly periodic tenancy. He will therefore be entitled to a month's notice to quit.

17.7.3 Equitable leases

    EXERCISE 17.3

Re-read 5.5.3.5 and 5.5.4 regarding the creation of equitable leases. Note particularly the rulings in *Walsh* v *Lonsdale* and *Parker* v *Taswell*.

As a result of *Walsh* v *Lonsdale* it is sometimes said that 'an agreement for a lease is as good as a lease'. This is rather misleading, as there are in fact important differences between legal leases and equitable leases:

(a) A person's right to treat an agreement or an informal grant as an equitable lease depends on his being able to obtain specific performance. (Remember *Coatsworth* v *Johnson* at 5.5.4.1.)

(b) Where the reversion is unregistered title, the equitable lease is registrable as a land charge. (Class C(iv) estate contract.)

(c) Where the reversion is registered title, an equitable lease could not be an overriding interest within LRA 1925, s. 70(1)(k), nor can it be an overriding interest within LRA 2002, Sch. 3, para. 1, but it could of course have come within LRA 1925, s. 70(1)(g) and can now come within LRA 2002, Sch. 3, para. 2. If not within Sch. 3, para. 2, the equitable lessee can protect his interest by entering a notice.

(d) An equitable lessee is not a 'purchaser of a legal estate' for the purposes of the Land Charges Acts or the old doctrine of notice. (A legal lessee is a 'purchaser of a legal estate'.)

(e) An assignee of a pre-1996 equitable lease is apparently not directly bound by the obligations in the lease. (It seems that the doctrine of 'privity of estate', which we consider in **Chapter 19**, does not apply to pre-1996 equitable leases.)

(f) Section 62 of the Law of Property Act 1925 (which relates to the implied grant of easements and profits and which we discuss in **Chapter 24**) does not apply to equitable leases.

17.7.4 **Equitable lease and legal periodic tenancy existing concurrently**

I now come to a point which students often find puzzling. As a result of a single informal trans-action, a tenant may actually have **simultaneously both a legal periodic tenancy and an equitable lease** over the same piece of land.

Suppose L and T informally agree (in a document which does not amount to a deed) to a 10-year lease of Blackacre at £500 per annum rent. T takes possession and pays the rent. **At law** T will have a yearly periodic tenancy by operation of law; **in equity** T will have a 10-year lease. Applying the usual principle that where law and equity are in conflict, equity should prevail, it is the equitable lease which will govern the rights of the parties.

The legal periodic tenancy will not be totally invalid; **rather it will lie dormant**. If, the equitable lease should fail for any reason such as 'unclean hands' (remember *Coatsworth* v *Johnson*) or non-registration as a land charge, the legal periodic tenancy will become operative.

? **QUESTION** 17.6

In 2002 Carolyn and Dinah entered into a written agreement (which was not in the form of a deed) whereby Carolyn agreed to let to Dinah a field in which Dinah proposed to keep rabbits. The agreement was to last for 10 years. The rent was fixed at £60 per month. The field is unregistered title.

Dinah promised that she would not allow her rabbits to escape into neighbouring fields remaining in Carolyn's possession. Numerous rabbits have escaped into Carolyn's fields, causing damage to her crops of lettuces and carrots. Recently Carolyn sold all her fields, including the one occupied by Dinah, to Edwina. Advise Edwina, who wants Dinah to vacate the field immediately.

Dinah originally had an equitable lease, but it certainly will not be binding on Edwina. Even assuming that Dinah registered her equitable lease as a land charge, she clearly has 'unclean hands', and therefore has now lost her claim to an equitable lease. However, Dinah still has her monthly **legal periodic tenancy**. Edwina will therefore have to give her a month's notice before she can gain possession of the field.

✳ **CONCLUDING REMARKS**

In this rather lengthy and involved chapter I hope to have achieved two things. First, you should now have enough understanding to be able to decide whether a particular transaction is a lease or whether it is something else. If it is a lease, you should be able to identify what type it is. Secondly, you should have a foundation of knowledge upon which we can build in the next three chapters.

■ SUMMARY

Types of Leases

The law recognizes two types of lease—fixed term lease and periodic tenancy.

The following transactions cannot (in modern law) be valid leases.

(a) a lease for an uncertain period (e.g. so long as Manchester United play in the premier league);

(b) a 'lease for life'—this is converted into a 90-year fixed term;.

(c) A perpetually renewable lease—this is converted into 2000 year fixed term.

The law does recognize 'Tenancies at will' and 'Tenancies at sufferance', but these arrangements are **not** leases.

The lease/licence distinction

A lease is a property right which can (in principle) be sold, given away, or inherited. A lease (in principle) binds third party purchasers of the reversion.

A licence is purely personal to the licensee. It cannot be sold or given away. Unless there is an estoppel, it cannot bind third party purchasers.

A transaction which grants the grantee **exclusive possession** is (subject to exceptions) a lease.

A grantee has exclusive possession if he has general overall control of the property.

A grantee of a flat will normally have exclusive possession, even though the landlord retains a key for emergencies and/or so that he can inspect the property.

A 'lodger' does not have exclusive possession.

Possessory licences

The following are licensees, despite having exclusive possession:

A person who occupies land because of the generosity of (or friendship to) the land owner;

A person who occupies his employer's house/flat so that he can be readily available for work;

A person who occupies a house/flat by virtue of his office (e.g, the prime minister's occupation of no. 10).

Formalities for leases

To create a legal lease, a deed is normally required. (A legal lease for not more than three years at the full market rent can be created without any special formality.)

A legal periodic tenancy can arise 'by operation of law'—this happens without formality if somebody possessing land starts paying a regular rent to the landowner.

An equitable lease can arise applying the principles in *Walsh* v *Lonsdale* and *Parker* v *Taswell*.

CHAPTER 17: ASSESSMENT EXERCISE

'Whether a transaction under which someone acquires the right to use another's property is a lease or a licence depends largely, but not exclusively, on whether the transaction grants "exclusive possession" '. Discuss.

See Appendix for a specimen answer.

FURTHER READING

For a comprehensive discussion of the essential requirements for a valid lease, see *Megarry and Wade: The Law of Real Property* (sixth edition by Harpum) chapter 14, pages 758–779.

For an in-depth consideration of how to distinguish between leases and licences, see Waite, AJ, 'Leases and Licences: The True Distinguishing Test' (1987) 50 MLR 226.

For a discussion of flat-sharing agreements, see Hill, J 'Shared Accommodation and Exclusive Possession' (1989) 52 MLR 408.

18 Obligations in leases

18.1 Objectives

By the end of this chapter you should:

1 Be familiar with the concept of a rent review

2 Be familiar with the various rules which govern the liabilities of landlords and tenants to repair leased premises

3 Be able to explain the wide range of remedies which a tenant can deploy against a landlord who is in breach of an obligation to repair the leased property

4 Be able to explain the law applicable where the landlord wishes to sue the tenant for breach of a tenant's covenant to repair

5 Be familiar with the rules governing qualified covenants against assigning, sub-letting, and parting with possession of premises, and in particular how the Landlord and Tenant Act 1988 has made things (in this area) easier for tenants

18.2 Introduction

This is another chapter in which I necessarily have to paint with a rather broad brush. Leases (particularly long leases of commercial properties such as shops, offices, and factories) are often very elaborate documents containing pages and pages of detailed obligations, many imposed on the tenant, some imposed on the landlord. We cannot possibly consider all the possible duties which a lease might impose. Instead we will concentrate on the three most common (and important) kinds of obligations in leases, namely rent, repairs, and covenants relating to assigning and sub-letting.

18.3 Rent—certain basic points

18.3.1 Form and payment of rent

Rent need not be in money, but could be in kind, such as 'five hundred bottles of champagne a year'. In practice, the rent agreed upon at the commencement of a lease almost always takes the form of a regular money payment (£600 per year, £20 per week, etc.). Unless the parties agree otherwise, rent is payable 'in arrear', i.e., at the end of each year, week, etc. However, landlords almost always insist on payment in advance, at the beginning of each year, week, etc.

18.3.2 **Rent reviews**

Whole encyclopaedias have been written on this topic! Ask anyone who is a surveyor. The first point to realize is that, **unless the parties agree otherwise**, the rent agreed on at the beginning of a lease remains the same throughout its duration. Nowadays, of course, long-term leases usually contain a provision to protect landlords from the ravages of inflation. It is possible to put in a clause 'index-linking' the rent, but this is relatively rare.

EXERCISE 18.1

Consider why index-linking of rents has never really caught on.

The value (and changes in value) of a property (and therefore the rent it will fetch) can vary widely according to the type of property and its location. Even in a recession, there may be local 'booms' for particular kinds of property. Imagine that Blogtown gains a reputation for small-scale high-tech industry. There is consequently a shortage of small factory units. Rents for such units go up, even though elsewhere in Blogtown there are offices and shops standing empty.

Usually, in long fixed-term leases, there is a 'rent review clause'. Most modern rent review clauses provide for the landlord to claim a higher rent every five years, though there is no special magic in 'five' years; other periods, such as every seven years, are encountered.

Rent review clauses usually operate in the following way:

(a) The landlord must serve notice on the tenant claiming a higher rent, and proposing what the new rent should be. The lease usually provides that this notice must be served some time (e.g., six months) before the new rent becomes payable.

(b) The tenant can accept the new rent, or make a counter-proposal.

(c) If the parties cannot agree a new rent, the matter is referred to an arbitrator. Usually the lease provides for the arbitrator to be appointed by the president of the Royal Institution of Chartered Surveyors (RICS).

In the 1970s there was a lot of litigation involving landlords who had been late in claiming a rent review. In some cases landlords claimed a review even though the first date for payment of the new rent was past, and the tenants were continuing to pay the old rent.

The House of Lords ended the controversy with a very pro-landlord decision, *United Scientific Holdings Ltd* v *Burnley Borough Council* [1977] 2 All ER 62. Their Lordships held that 'time is not of the essence' with a rent review clause. This means that if the landlord is late in claiming a rent review, prima facie that does not matter. The landlord can still insist on a higher rent, and if necessary have it fixed by the arbitrator, even though he forgetfully allowed the review date to slip by. Their Lordships reasoned that in modern economic conditions, tenants with long leases of shops, offices, factories, etc. expect the rent to go up every few years. It would be wrong to allow tenants to benefit from landlords' forgetfulness.

There are two exceptions to the general principle in *United Scientific Holdings Ltd* v *Burnley Borough Council*:

(a) The parties can always expressly agree in the lease that 'time shall be of the essence'; if the landlord is late claiming the review, that is his hard luck. This point is illustrated by *Weller* v *Akehurst* [1981] 3 All ER 411.

(b) There could be an **estoppel**. If a landlord delayed a very long time in claiming a review and the tenant reasonably assumed that the old rent would remain in force and acted on that assumption, then the landlord could be estopped from claiming a review. But mere delay does not give rise to an estoppel.

In *Amherst* v *James Walker Goldsmith and Silversmith Ltd* [1983] 1 Ch 305, CA, Amherst was the landlord of a shop, and James Walker Ltd, the well-known 'High Street Chain', was the tenant. Amherst claimed a rent review four years late. Amherst succeeded in his claim. The crucial point was that the rent on one shop was 'a drop in the ocean' for a big firm like James Walker.

 EXERCISE 18.2

Consider how you would alter the facts in *Amherst* v *James Walker* to produce a situation where the court would hold that there was an estoppel preventing a late claim for a rent review.

Suppose 'big' James Walker own the freehold to a spare shop which they lease to 'little' Mr Amherst. Walkers forget to claim a rent review. After waiting two years Amherst (reasonably) concludes that the rent is not going to go up. So in fixing the prices he charges customers in his shop, he (very reasonably) assumes that his rent is going to stay the same until the next review date. This would estop Walkers from presenting a late claim for a rent review.

18.4 **Repairs**

18.4.1 **Liability to repair—general**

Usually the lease itself will contain a clause, either:

(a) placing liability to repair the property on the landlord; or

(b) (common in long leases) placing liability to repair on the tenant; or

(c) dividing the responsibility between landlord and tenant. For example, it is quite common to see leases where the landlord promises to do 'external' repairs and the tenant promises to do 'internal' repairs.

The form of repair clause adopted is a matter for negotiation between the parties. If the parties have not expressly agreed on the issue of repairs then (except where the Landlord and Tenant Act 1985 applies) the following (rather inadequate) common law rules apply:

(a) A fixed-term lessee is liable for 'permissive waste', i.e., he must maintain the property in the condition it was in at the commencement of the lease.

(b) A periodic tenant is under no liability to repair, but must use the property in a responsible manner.

You should note that except where the Landlord and Tenant Act 1985 applies, there are normally no implied duties to repair placed on the landlord. However in *Barrett* v *Lounova (1982) Ltd* [1990] 1 QB 348, the Court of Appeal was faced with a lease of a dwelling house (dating from 1941) under which the tenant covenanted to do all **internal** repairs. The Court held that, in order 'to give business efficacy to the agreement', there was an implied obligation on the landlord to do **external** repairs.

Nevertheless, it is still possible to have a situation where, because of the drafting of the lease, when a particular type of defect arises in the leased premises neither landlord nor tenant is under a duty to the other party to repair it. For example, in long fixed-term leases you will often see a covenant under which the tenant agrees to do the repairs 'fair wear and tear excepted'. If a defect arises in the premises which **is** fair wear and tear (see 18.4.4 on that issue), the tenant is not liable to repair the defect; but neither is the landlord liable to make good the defect.

18.4.2 The Landlord and Tenant Act 1985

The Housing Acts 1957 and 1961 imposed on landlords of 'dwelling houses' (i.e., houses and flats) obligations which applied **notwithstanding any agreement to the contrary**. These Acts have now been consolidated into the Landlord and Tenant Act 1985.

18.4.2.1 Sections 8 to 10 of the 1985 Act (derived from 1957 Act)

Sections 8 to 10 of the 1985 Act are of extremely limited significance, because they apply only to lettings at not more than £52 per annum (£80 per annum within London). They do not apply to lettings for three or more years. (The £52/£80 per week rent limit was laid down in 1957! Despite repeated criticism from courts, law reform bodies, and academics, the limit has never been raised.)

Section 8 provides that the dwelling must be kept 'fit for human habitation'. The standards are strict, detailed matters being set out in the Act. However, as the rent limits for ss. 8–10 are so absurdly low, these provisions have only limited relevance today. Nevertheless, carefully consider the following question:

> **? QUESTION** 18.1
>
> I own a derelict house in Nottingham. Four students desperate for accommodation approach me. (As it happens, two are studying building, one is studying quantity surveying, and the other interior design.) They say, 'Lease your house to us for two years at one penny a week rent, and we will do it up for you. We can put up with the discomfort!' Advise me.

At first sight, it seems like a very good idea for all five of us. However, if I charge only one pence a week I will caught by ss. 8 to 10 of the 1985 Act and **I will be liable to do all the repairs!** I must therefore ensure that I charge at least one pound and a penny per week rent. We would also need to get the consent of the county court to exclude ss. 11–14: see below.

18.4.2.2 **Sections 11–14 of the 1985 Act (derived from 1961 Act)**

Sections 11 to 14 of the 1985 Act apply to all lettings of dwellings for not more than seven years; also to lettings for more than seven years if the landlord has an option to terminate within the first seven years. (It is possible for the parties to agree that ss. 11 to 14 shall not apply, but only if the consent of the county court is obtained in advance. Applications to the court for such consent are relatively rare.)

Under ss. 11 to 14, the landlord must:

(a) keep in repair the structure and exterior of the house (including drains, gutters, and external pipes) (*Quick* v *Taff Ely BC* [1985] 3 All ER 321 indicates complications which can arise);

(b) keep in repair and proper working order the installations in the home for the supply of water, gas, and electricity, for space heating, and the heating of water;

(c) (added by s. 116 of the Housing Act 1988) in the case of blocks of flats, keep in repair 'common parts' such as lifts and staircases.

18.4.3 **The crucial principle in** *O'Brien* v *Robinson*

The principle in this case applies whenever a landlord is under an obligation to do repairs, whether that obligation is imposed by the terms of the lease or by the Landlord and Tenant Act 1985.

In *O'Brien* v *Robinson* [1973] AC 912 a tenant was injured when the ceiling of his flat suddenly and unexpectedly caved in upon him. His claim for damages was dismissed by the House of Lords. Their Lordships held that a landlord can be liable for disrepair only if either:

(a) he knows of the need for repair; or

(b) he has 'had information about the existence of a defect . . . such as would put him on enquiry as to whether works of repair were needed'.

? **QUESTION** 18.2

What is the moral of this case for tenants who are concerned about the condition of their premises?

If your landlord is liable to do the repairs, tell him of any defect or possible defect the moment it arises. Until he has been told of the defect, the landlord cannot be made liable for any damage suffered by the tenant as a result of the disrepair.

(If a landlord is liable to do repairs he will in practice expressly reserve a right to enter the premises to carry out the repairs. The House of Lords has assumed that such an express right entitles a landlord to take complete possession temporarily, if temporary complete possession is necessary to carry out the repairs: *Heath* v *Drown* [1972] 2 All ER 561.)

18.4.3.1 **Landlord's covenant to repair common parts**

The Court of Appeal has held that where a landlord covenants with a tenant to repair property which the landlord retains **in his possession** (e.g., in particular he promises to repair the common parts of a block of offices or flats) the principle in *O'Brien* v *Robinson* does not apply.

A landlord must make good defects in the property he retains, whether or not he knew that there might be a defect and whether or not the tenant(s) have complained (*British Telecom* v *Sun Life Assurance* [1995] 4 All ER 44).

18.4.4 Meaning of express covenants to repair

(The same principles apply whether it is a landlord's covenant or a tenant's covenant.)

Leases often use phrases such as 'good tenantable repair', 'substantial repair', 'satisfactory repair', etc. However, it seems that the adjectives are superfluous, and add nothing to the basic meaning of 'repair'.

The duty to repair was expressed thus by Professor Cheshire:

After making due allowance for the locality, character and age of the premises at the time of the lease, he must keep them in the condition in which they would be kept by a reasonably minded owner. (*Cheshire and Burn*, 15th edn., p. 404.)

The standard of repair is fixed at the commencement of the lease. In *Anstruther-Gough-Calthorpe* v *McOscar* [1924] 1 KB 716, a 95-year lease was granted in 1825 of three houses. They were, in 1825, brand new, and in a very pleasant position on the then edge of the built-up area of London. By the time the lease expired in 1920 the area (in the vicinity of Kings Cross station) had become very 'run down'. In an action by the landlord against the tenant for breaking the covenant to repair, the Court of Appeal held that **even in 1920** the tenant should have maintained the property to the **1825** standard!

 EXERCISE 18.3

Just pause for a few moments and consider the possible financial implications of *Anstruther-Gough-Calthorpe* v *McOscar* for tenants who hold under long leases.

The rule applied in that case is of course extremely harsh on tenants of long leases who have covenanted to repair. That is why a tenant's promise to repair is nowadays often subject to the proviso **'fair wear and tear excepted'**. If such a proviso is included the tenant will not have to make good the natural ageing of the premises.

However, as Talbot J explained in *Haskell* v *Marlow* [1928] 2 KB 45 at 59, the 'fair wear and tear exception' may not be much protection for tenants in some kinds of situations:

The tenant is bound to do such repairs as may be required to prevent the consequences flowing originally from wear and tear from producing others which wear and tear would not directly produce. For example, if a tile falls off the roof, the tenant is not liable for the immediate consequences, but if he does nothing and in the result more and more water gets in, the roof and walls decay and ultimately the top floor, or the whole house, becomes uninhabitable, he cannot say that it is due to reasonable wear and tear.

18.4.5 The repair/reconstruction distinction

An obligation to 'repair' extends to replacing defective subsidiary parts of a building, but not to complete reconstruction of the building. In *Ravenseft Properties* v *Davstone Ltd* [1979] 2 WLR

897, QBD, Forbes J restated the test thus:

> ... it is always a question of degree whether that which the tenant[/landlord] is being asked to do can properly be described as repair, or whether on the contrary it would involve giving back to the landlord[/tenant] a wholly different thing from that which he [leased].

In *Lister* v *Lane* [1893] 2 QB 212 the tenant did not have to reconstruct the whole house when the foundations became unsafe. However, in *Lurcott* v *Wakely* [1911] 1 KB 905, the tenant had to replace the front wall of a house, and in *Ravenseft Properties* v *Davstone Ltd* [1979] 1 All ER 929 a property company had to replace the external stone cladding on the whole of a block of flats.

'Repair' includes painting only in so far as painting is necessary to prevent deterioration of woodwork.

18.4.6 Remedies for breach of landlord's express covenants to repair

(In the following discussion, you should never forget the principle in *O'Brien* v *Robinson* that a landlord becomes liable only if he knew or ought to have known of the defect: see **18.4.3**.)

If a landlord is in breach of a covenant to repair, then the most usual remedy for the tenant is to sue for damages. However, in the last 30 years both the courts and Parliament have been busy expanding the remedies available to tenants against recalcitrant landlords who fail to do repairs which they know need doing.

18.4.6.1 No rent-strikes, *but* . . .

A tenant cannot simply go on 'rent-strike'. He cannot say to the landlord, 'I am not paying the rent until you do the repairs'. The tenant can, however, carry out the repairs himself (or employ contractors to do the work) and deduct the cost from future instalments of rent: *Lee-Parker* v *Izzet* [1971] 1 WLR 1688, ChD.

? QUESTION 18.3

Suppose that the rent is £50 per week. The tenant spends £1,000 on repairs. If he invokes *Izzet's* case, what does he say to the landlord or his rent-collector?

He can say, 'See you in 20 weeks' time'.

I must, however, warn you that this **'do-it-yourself'** remedy has its limitations. First, a tenant contemplating employing builders to do the repairs should ensure that he gets several quotations before engaging contractors to do the repairs. Secondly, this remedy is not much good where a landlord has allowed a whole block of offices or flats, leased to individual tenants, to fall into a bad state of disrepair. Repairing the whole block is likely to be beyond the resources of an individual tenant, and even beyond the resources of the tenants acting jointly.

18.4.6.2 Specific performance for breach of a repairing obligation

Where the property is a dwelling house the Housing Act 1975, s. 125 specifically authorizes the courts to award specific performance of the landlord's obligation to repair. (This is notwithstanding the fact that the tenant is still in possession of the property to be repaired.)

In any proceedings in which a tenant of a dwelling alleges a breach on the part of his landlord of a repairing covenant relating to any part of the premises in which the dwelling is comprised, the court may, in its discretion, order specific performance of that covenant, whether or not the breach relates to a part of the premises let to the tenant and notwithstanding any equitable rule restricting the scope of that remedy, whether on the basis of lack of mutuality or otherwise

(If the facts of *Jeune* v *Queen Cross Properties* [1973] 3 All ER .97 were to recur today, the tenants would undoubtedly seek an order under s. 125. In *Jeune* a York Stone balcony at the front of a house had partially collapsed, spoiling the appearance of the whole of a Georgian terrace. The judge (applying general principles of equity) decreed specific performance of the landlord's obligation to repair the balcony.)

18.4.6.3 **Appointing a receiver**

In recent years there have been increasing problems with recalcitrant private landlords of blocks of flats and blocks of offices failing to carry out their repairing obligations. Often the premises involved are 'up-market'.

In 1983 somebody hit upon the bright idea of invoking s. 37 of the Supreme Court Act 1981 to appoint a receiver: *Hart* v *Emelkirk* [1983] 3 All ER 15. Mention of the word 'receiver' probably makes you think of insolvent companies; but 'receivers' have their uses in land law! We shall come across them again in the law of mortgages (**Chapter 30**).

In the present context, 'appointing a receiver' works as follows:

(a) The court appoints a responsible professional person to act as receiver.

(b) The landlord must hand over management (though not of course ownership) of the block to the receiver.

(c) Rents are now payable to the receiver, not to the landlord.

(d) The receiver uses the money from the rents to pay for the repairs.

The remedy under s. 37 of the 1981 Act does unfortunately have its limitations as illustrated by the facts of *Evans* v *Clayhope Properties Ltd* [1987] 2 All ER 40. Suppose the block requires very extensive repairs, costing more than the total of several years' rent. Such a situation is far from unknown. Appointing a receiver under s. 37 is no good. The receiver cannot enter into long-term repair contracts binding on the landlord. Neither can he mortgage the block to finance the repairs.

(On a rather different point, s. 37 cannot be invoked against a local authority landlord which fails to repair its housing stock: *Parker* v *Camden LBC* [1985] 2 All ER 141. This is because s. 111 of the Housing Act 1957 unequivocally vests the management of local authority housing in the local authority.)

18.4.6.4 **Appointing a receiver-manager**

The tenants of a privately owned block of flats (but not offices) have been given a new stronger 'receiver' remedy against landlords who fail to do repairs. They can apply for the appointment of a receiver-manager under ss. 21 to 24 of the Landlord and Tenant Act 1987. This application for a receiver-manager used to be made to the county court, but must now be made to the

Leasehold Valuation Tribunal. It would **appear** that under s. 24 the tribunal could (unlike the courts under the 1981 Act):

(a) authorize the receiver-manager to mortgage the block to pay for repairs; and/or

(b) require the landlord to pay repair bills incurred by the receiver-manager.

18.4.6.5 Local authorities taking action against private landlords

Where a house, flat, or block of flats is in disrepair, the local district council can serve a notice on the landlord requiring specified repairs. If the landlord fails to comply, the council can enter the property, carry out the repairs, and charge them to the landlord. (See the Housing Acts 1957 and 1988.)

18.4.6.6 Measure of damages against landlords

If a tenant sues the landlord for damages, he can recover, in addition to the cost of repairs actually done by the tenant:

(a) compensation for any injury to health suffered;

(b) the cost of alternative accommodation if the disrepair is such as to render the premises uninhabitable.

See the Court of Appeal decision in *Calabar Properties* v *Stitcher* [1984] 1 WLR 287, where the condition of the tenant's flat was so bad she became ill and had to rent alternative accommodation.

 EXERCISE 18.4

> What would be the position if landlords were in breach of a covenant to repair a shop, with the result that (potential) customers considered the premises unsafe?

I think that the tenant could sue for loss of profits.

18.4.7 Damages against a tenant in breach of repairing obligations

You should remember that in some leases, particularly long-term ones, the tenant undertakes to do the repairs. If the tenant fails to do repairs he has promised to do, then normally the landlord can recover from the tenant the cost of repairing the property. However, the landlord's right to damages may be limited or eliminated by s. 18 of the Landlord and Tenant Act 1927:

Damages for a breach of a covenant to repair . . . shall in no case exceed the amount (if any) by which the value of the reversion in the premises is diminished . . . In particular no damage shall be recovered for a breach of covenant to repair if it is shown that the premises would at or shortly after the termination of the tenancy have been or be pulled down . . .

Thus if on the expiry of the lease the landlord is going to demolish the premises, or reconstruct the premises to such an extent that their state of repair is immaterial, the landlord will not be able to claim any damages from the tenant for his breach of the covenant to repair.

A rather disturbing situation faced the judge in *Hibernian Properties* v *[A Very Bad Tenant]* [1973] 2 All ER 1117. The very bad tenant (VBT) leased a row of houses in Liverpool from Hibernian. VBT undertook to do the repairs. VBT failed so miserably in this task that Liverpool City Council public health officials came along, condemned the properties as unfit for human habitation, and made the houses the subject of a compulsory purchase order. The houses were then demolished.

Hibernian were paid compensation by Liverpool City Council limited to 'the site value'. That meant that they received no compensation for the buildings. They therefore sued VBT for damages. VBT pleaded the second sentence of s. 18 of the 1927 Act as a defence: 'The property has been pulled down. Therefore no damages are payable'. The judge boldly rejected this defence, holding that the words 'by the landlords' must be implied into s. 18 after the words 'pulled down'.

The identity of VBT is **totally irrelevant to this decision**. The decision would have been the same if VBT had been a big plc, or Charley Farns-Barnes, or you or me.

 EXERCISE 18.5

Can you guess the identity of VBT?

In fact VBT was Liverpool City Council itself.

(The Leasehold Property Repairs Act 1938 is also relevant to cases where the tenant is liable to do repairs. It can be properly understood only after I have explained forfeiture of leases, which I will do in **Chapter 20**.)

18.5 Covenants against assigning, sub-letting, and parting with possession

18.5.1 Introduction

A lease is of course a property right, an estate in land. It therefore follows that, prima facie, a lessee can:

(a) assign his lease, i.e., transfer the lease to somebody else, retaining no rights whatsoever;

(b) sub-lease (when a person sub-lets he creates a lease out of his lease—refer back to my Redacre example at 4.6.2);

(c) part with possession to a licensee, e.g., to a friend, or to an employee occupying the property under a 'service occupancy' (see 17.6.4.2).

However, I should immediately add that modern leases often restrict the lessee's right to assign, sub-let or part with possession. **As a generalization**:

(a) Short-term leases and periodic tenancies (particularly of flats/houses) usually contain 'absolute covenants' under which the tenant is totally banned from assigning, sub-letting, or parting with possession.

(b) Medium-term lettings (say 10 to 50 years) usually contain a 'qualified covenant', under which the tenant can assign, sub-let, or part with possession (the whole or part of the premises) only if the landlord gives his consent.

(c) Very long-term leases (e.g., a 99-year lease of a flat) usually contain no restrictions on the right to assign, sub-let, or part with possession.

It must be stressed that 'qualified covenants' are particularly common where the premises are of a commercial nature, e.g., shops, offices, or factories. Landlords of commercial premises have found that **it is not a good idea** to insert into a commercial letting an 'absolute covenant'. The insertion of an absolute covenant into a commercial letting would substantially reduce the amount of rent the tenant was willing to pay.

18.5.2 **Absolute covenants**

The covenant creates an absolute ban on all transactions. However, an assignment or sub-letting in defiance of the ban **does** convey or create an estate in the land. Breach of the covenant will merely entitle the landlord to damages, and to forfeit the lease, assuming the lease contains a forfeiture clause: *Peabody Fund* v *Higgins* [1983] 3 All ER 122.

A landlord can **waive** observance of an absolute covenant so as to permit a transaction in favour of a person he considers desirable. But a decision by a landlord to withhold his waiver cannot be challenged, however unreasonable, sexist, or racist the landlord is being.

Suppose in 2004 I leased a house to Hamish Macdonald (Scots**man**) for five years. The lease contained an absolute covenant against assigning, sub-letting, or parting with possession. Hamish has now decided to buy a house. He comes to me with Trudi Jones, a perfectly respectable Welsh**woman**: 'Please can I assign my lease to Trudi?'

Now I **can** say 'Yes', and waive the absolute covenant. But if I say, 'No, I don't like the colour of her hair' or 'I don't like the Welsh' or 'I don't like women as my tenants', my decision to withhold my waiver cannot be challenged. (As we will see in a moment, the position would be very different if I had inserted only a 'qualified covenant' into the five-year lease.)

18.5.3 **Qualified covenants**

Where there is a qualified covenant, a tenant can assign, sub-let, or part with possession only if he gets the landlord's consent.

The Landlord and Tenant Act 1927, s. 19(1)(a), is applicable to qualified covenants but not to absolute covenants. It provides:

[A covenant against] assigning, underletting [i.e., sub-letting], charging or parting with possession of demised premises without licence or consent . . . shall . . . be subject to a proviso that such licence or consent is not to be unreasonably withheld.

Section 19(1)(a) operates 'notwithstanding any express provision to the contrary'. Thus a landlord who wants to retain the freedom to veto assignments or sub-lettings on whatever grounds he pleases (colour of hair, etc.) should insert an absolute covenant. But always remember that tenants of commercial premises are unlikely to accept an 'absolute covenant', or do so only in return for a considerable reduction in rent.

18.5.4 **When is a consent unreasonably withheld?**

There is not much statutory guidance on this issue. However:

(a) The Race Relations Acts and the Sex Discrimination Act provide that a consent withheld on grounds of race or sex is unreasonably withheld.

(b) The House of Lords has recently held (clarifying earlier conflicting case law) that it is (in principle) reasonable for a landlord to prohibit an assignment where it reasonably believes that an assignee may break a covenant in the lease relating to the use of the property. *Ashworth Frazer Ltd* v *Gloucester City Council* [2001] 1 WLR 2180.

(c) The Law of Property Act 1925, s. 144 prohibits the charging of a premium for the giving of consent to an assignment or a sub-letting.

? **QUESTION** 18.4

What, then, if a landlord said to a tenant, 'I will agree to your proposed transaction if you give me £10,000 pounds', but the tenant says 'I will not pay'?

The landlord would be threatening to break s. 144, and therefore withholding consent because the £10,000 was not forthcoming would clearly be unreasonable.

Apart from the matters just discussed, whether or not the landlord's veto is reasonable is primarily a question of fact. That has not prevented an enormous amount of case law developing, the effect of which was summarized and clarified in *International Drilling Fluids Ltd* v *Louisville Investments (Uxbridge) Ltd* [1986] 1 Ch 513, CA. Except in one (obvious) respect, this case appears unaffected by the Landlord and Tenant Act 1988 (an Act we will discuss after we have considered the case).

The Court came up with seven numbered propositions. My comments on those propositions I have placed in square brackets:

1. The purpose of a covenant against assignment [sub-letting, etc.] without the consent of the landlord, such consent not to be unreasonably withheld, was to protect the lessor from having his premises used or occupied in an undesirable way, or by an undesirable tenant or assignee.

[(a) It is clearly reasonable for a landlord to veto a proposed assignee/sub-tenant/licensee who is of bad character, e.g., one who has a criminal record.

(b) It is clearly reasonable for a landlord to object to a transaction which will depreciate the value of his reversion. The leading cases are *Norfolk Capital Group* v *Kitway Ltd* [1976] 3 All ER 787, and *Bickel* v *Duke of Westminster* [1975] 3 All ER 801. In both cases a long lease of a house was vested in a limited company. It was proposed to assign the lease to a human tenant who would be able to take advantage of various pieces of protective legislation not available to 'artificial persons'. This fact would have the effect of reducing the value of the landlords' fees simple in reversion. It was held that the landlords were reasonable in vetoing the assignments.

(c) It is clearly reasonable for the landlord to object where the proposed assignee/sub-tenant proposes using the premises for unsuitable purposes. For example, using a house in a narrow street for a business which will create a lot of parking problems. Refer also to the court's proposition number 5.]

2. As a corollary to [proposition 1], a landlord was not entitled to refuse his consent to an assignment on grounds which had nothing whatever to do with the relationship of landlord and tenant in regard to the subject matter of the lease. [For example, 'I don't want the lease assigned to him because he has just run off with my wife'. Such an attitude would clearly be unreasonable.]

3. (**Overruled by the Landlord and Tenant Act 1988.**) The onus of proving that consent had been unreasonably withheld was on the tenant.

4. It was not necessary for the landlord to prove that the conclusions which led him to refuse consent were justified, if they were conclusions which might be reached by a reasonable man in the circumstances.

5. It might be reasonable for the landlord to refuse his consent to an assignment on the ground of the purpose for which the proposed assignee intended to use the premises, even though that purpose was not forbidden by the lease. [Refer back to note (c) under proposition 1.]

6. On the question whether it was permissible to have regard to consequences to the tenant if consent to the proposed assignment was withheld there was a divergence of authority. . . . A proper reconciliation of the two streams of authority could be achieved by saying that while a landlord needed usually only to consider his own relevant interests, there might be cases where there was such a disproportion between the benefit to the landlord and the detriment to the tenant if the landlord withheld his consent to an assignment that it was unreasonable for the landlord to refuse consent.'

[There have been a lot of cases in recent years where a tenant of business premises has been anxious to sell the **business**. The lease of the premises is of course an important asset **of the business**. If a landlord is unwilling to approve a particular prospective purchaser of the business as assignee of the lease, the prospective purchaser is not going to buy the business.]

7. Subject to the preceding propositions, it was in each case a question of fact, depending upon all the circumstances, whether the landlord's consent was being unreasonably withheld.

 EXERCISE 18.5

Consider whether it would be reasonable for a landlord to object to a proposed assignee on the ground that the assignee would use the premises for a business which competes with a similar business carried on by the landlord. (For example, 'Your proposed assignee is a greengrocer; so am I'.)

This point is controversial. The (first instance) case of *Premier Confectionery* v *London Commercial Sale Rooms* [1933] Ch 904, suggests that the landlord would be in the right. But I would argue that this case is wrong, as the landlord's reason for the veto has nothing to do with the landlord and tenant relationship (proposition 2 in *International Drilling*).

18.5.5 **Seeking the landlord's consent to a proposed transaction**

If a tenant has a proposed transaction (assignment, sub-letting, or parting with possession) he must always first ask the landlord for his consent (in writing), even if he thinks that there could not possibly be any reasonable objection. If the landlord vetoes a proposed transaction (or fails to reply in writing within a reasonable time) there are four courses of action open to the tenant:

(a) to concede that the landlord has a good argument and abandon the proposal;

(b) to abandon the proposal, but claim damages under the Landlord and Tenant Act 1988 (this is what happened in *Design Progression Ltd v Thurloe Properties ltd* [2005] 1 WLR 1);

(c) to go ahead with the proposed transaction, risking proceedings for damages (and forfeiture if the lease contains a forfeiture clause);

(d) to seek a declaration from the court that the consent is being withheld unreasonably (the tenant may well add a claim for damages under the 1988 Act).

18.5.6 **Landlord and Tenant Act 1988**

The Landlord and Tenant Act 1988 represents a shift in the law in favour of tenants. Until 1988, the onus of proof that the landlord was withholding his consent unreasonably was on the tenant. Moreover landlords frequently delayed their decisions for inordinate periods. Landlords who did eventually say 'Yes' often imposed stringent conditions. The overall effect of the 1988 Act is:

(a) to put pressure on landlords to make a decision on the tenant's application without unreasonable delay;

(b) to ensure that landlords who veto transactions have really good grounds for doing so;

(c) to ensure that landlords, if they impose conditions, impose only sensible ones.

Section 1 of the 1988 Act provides:

. . .

(3) Where there is served on the [landlord] a written application by the tenant for consent to [a] transaction, he owes a duty to the tenant within a reasonable time—

(a) to give consent, except in a case where it is reasonable not to give consent,

(b) to serve on the tenant written notice of his decision whether or not to give consent specifying in addition—

(i) if the consent is given subject to conditions, the conditions,
(ii) if the consent is withheld, the reasons for withholding it.

(4) Giving consent subject to any condition that is not a reasonable condition does not satisfy the duty under subsection (3)(a) above.

. . .

(6) It is for the [landlord]—

(a) if he gave consent and the question arises whether he gave it within a reasonable time, to show that he did,

(b) if he gave consent subject to any condition and the question arises whether the condition was a reasonable condition, to show that it was,

(c) if he did not give consent and the question arises whether it was reasonable for him not to do so, to show that it was reasonable,

and, if the question arises whether he served notice under that subsection within a reasonable time, to show that he did.

Section 4 places further pressures on landlords. It makes a landlord who breaks any of the duties laid down in the Act liable in damages to the tenant. Thus, for example, a tenant who was unable to sell his business because of his landlord's delaying tactics in giving consent might have a claim for hefty damages.

The Law Commission says of these reforms:

Reversal of the burden of proof should have the effect in practice that the landlord will have to concentrate his mind on his reasons before he makes his decision on the tenant's application for consent. This, together with our recommendation that the tenant should be given a written statement of reasons and that the landlord should be liable in damages for delay or unreasonable witholding, should have the conveyancing advantage of reducing considerably the delays that are liable to occur at present in dispositions of tenancies.

The courts have been very firm in implementing the policy behind the 1988 Act. See the article by Dr H W Wilkinson at (1999) New Law Journal 1039. In *Norwich Union* v *Shopmoor* [1998] 3 All ER 32, Sir Richard Scott, V-C held that if a tenant's application for consent has not received a written reply within a reasonable time, then consent was deemed to be unreasonably withheld. This case was then followed by Neuberger J in *Footwear Corp* v *Amplight* [1998] 3 All ER 52, who added that any purely **oral** objections from the landlord must be ignored. Moreover, it is clear from the *Footwear* case and other cases cited by Dr Wilkinson that courts are being strict with landlords on the issue of how long is a reasonable time for replying. It seems that, at most, landlords have three months in which to reply to a tenant's request for permission.

This strict approach of the lower courts has now been confirmed by the Court of Appeal in *Go West Ltd* v *Spigarolo* [2003] 2 WLR 986. Moreover, in that case the Court held that if the landlord's refusal of consent is challenged by the tenant as being unreasonable, the landlord can rely only on reasons set out in the written reply to the tenant's request. Other reasons cannot be relied on when the dispute reaches court. In the *Go West* case, the landlord vetoed a proposed assignment on the grounds (in effect) that it was unsure of the financial soundness of the proposed assignee. In ensuing litigation, the landlord was not entitled to rely on the state of repair of the premises as grounds for withholding consent.

A further blow against recalcitrant landlords is the decision of Peter Smith J in *Design Progression Ltd* v *Thurloe Properties Ltd* [2005] 1 WLR 1. In that case the existing tenant (the claimants) wanted to assign the lease of a shop to a very successful businesswoman. There could be no possible reasonable objection to her being tenant.

The landlords nevertheless withheld their consent, hoping that the claimants would (in desperation) surrender their lease to the landlords. The landlords would then be able to let to the successful businesswoman at a much increased rent. Put another way, the landlords unlawfully withheld their consent hoping to make a profit from their unreasonable and unlawful actions. Peter Smith J awarded the claimants not only £75,000 compensatory damages (the premium the businesswoman was willing to pay for the assignment), but also £25,000 exemplary ('punitive') damages.

> **EXERCISE** 18.6
>
> Consider why the Landlord and Tenant Act 1988 makes it easier for tenants of business premises (e.g., a shop) to sell their businesses.

With shops and other small businesses, the (long) lease over the shop or other premises is often the business's most valuable asset. If a shopkeeper who wants to sell up and retire cannot sell (i.e., assign for consideration) his lease, he obviously will not be able to sell his business. The 1988 Act makes it easier to sell the lease.

18.6 Section 22 of the Landlord and Tenant (Covenants) Act 1995

(The main provisions of this new Act, most of which are pro-tenant, are dealt with in the next chapter.) Section 22 of the 1995 Act is a pro-**landlord** provision, which applies to qualified covenants against assignment of leases of commercial properties (offices, shops, factories, etc.) commencing **after** 1995. It has no application to sub-letting or parting with possession.

Section 22 was inserted into the 1995 Act at the insistence of big commercial landlords (property companies, institutional investors, etc.) who are very concerned that leases should not be assigned to tenants who will be unable to pay rent, do repairs, etc. Where s. 22 applies, a landlord can tighten his control over the assignment of a lease by including in the lease a specific clause stipulating that the landlord is entitled to withhold his consent in given circumstances. A withholding of consent in those circumstances will not be unreasonable.

For example, the lease states 'The Landlord will not consent to an assignment if the assignee fails to provide a bankers' reference that he will be able to pay the rent'. A potential assignee who is in fact financially very sound forgets to provide the reference. The landlord's veto will automatically be reasonable and not open to challenge under the 1927 and 1988 Landlord and Tenant Acts.

However, there are limits on what I call 'section 22 clauses'. The clause cannot leave the decision as to whether circumstances exist justifying a landlord's veto to the landlord's subjective opinion. For example, a clause 'The Landlord will not agree to an assignee unless he is satisfied that the assignee can pay the rent' is not allowed. However it is permitted to have a clause which entrusts a decision to an independent third party, e.g., 'The landlord will not agree to an assignee unless the assignee can produce satisfactory evidence that he can pay the rent. In the event of a dispute as to whether the evidence is satisfactory, the matter shall be resolved by an arbitrator appointed by the president of the RICS'.

CONCLUDING REMARKS

The law relating to obligations between landlord and tenant is often attacked as being too heavily biased in favour of landlords. Critics point to decisions such as *United Scientific Holdings, O'Brien* v *Robinson*, and *Anstruther-Gough-Calthorpe* v *McOscar*. They also cite the rule banning rent-strikes should the landlord fail to do the repairs, pointing out that in many American states such strikes are permitted.

My own view is that pro-landlord bias is gradually disappearing. Over the last 30 years, both the courts and Parliament have done a lot to redress the balance. See, for example, the Landlord and Tenant Act 1988, and the rigorous way in which it has been applied by the courts. And just look again at the sections in this chapter dealing with the greatly expanded remedies which tenants (particularly of residential properties) have if their landlords are in breach of a duty to repair. The decision in *Calabar* v *Stitcher* is perhaps of particular importance (see18.4.6.6).

The real problem with the law discussed in this chapter is, in my view, the piecemeal way in which it has been developed. This produces anomalies. For example, why on earth should the 'receiver' remedy created by ss. 21 to 24 of the Landlord and Tenant Act 1987 be confined to residential properties?

What is needed is a complete and organized statutory code of obligations between landlord and tenants. The Law Commission has been proposing something along these lines ever since 1975. But like many other proposals for major structural reform of land law, this proposal just gathers dust.

■ SUMMARY

Rent Fixed term leases usually contain rent review clauses, to ensure that rent keeps pace with the inflation of property prices. A typical clause allows a review every five years. A landlord may make a late claim for review, unless it is clear from the terms of the lease that time is of the essence.

Repairs Subject only to the Housing Act 1985, the parties are free to negotiate who should be responsible for repairs.
Where the tenant of a fixed-term lease covenants to repair, he must keep the premises in the condition they were in at the beginning of the lease. If the tenant breaks his obligation, the landlord can recover the cost of the repairs; but not if the landlord is going to demolish the premises at the end of the lease.

Landlord's Obligations to Repair These may be derived from the Housing Act 1985 or from an express covenant in the lease. The landlord is only liable to repair defects he either knows about or would have known about had he acted on information suggesting that there might be a need for repair.

Remedies for breach of the Landlord's obligation to repair
do a *Lee-Parker* v *Izzet*;
sue for damages, including (where appropriate) injuries to health and cost of alternative accommodation;
sue for specific performance under s. 125 of Housing Act 1975;
seek appointment of a receiver under the general powers of the court;
seek appointment of a receiver-manager from the Leasehold Valuation Tribunal (blocks of flats only).

Qualified covenants against assigning, sub-letting, etc.

These covenants are common in commercial lettings. The tenant (normally) needs consent to an assignment or sub-letting, but the landlord must have reasonable grounds if he withholds consent. Such reasonable grounds (normally) should relate to the assignee/sub-tenant's character or proposed use of the premises.

If the tenant wants to assign or sub-let he should ask (in writing) for permission. If the landlord:

does not reply within about three months; or
gives consent but on unreasonable conditions; or
unreasonably withholds consent;

then the tenant should either:

(a) go ahead and assign or sub-let or

(b) sue the landlord for damages and/or a declaration.

In any litigation, the onus will be on the landlord to prove that his grounds for objection are reasonable. Moreover he can rely only on grounds which he advanced when first asked for permission.

■ FURTHER READING

For a very full explanation of the thinking which led to the Landlord and Tenant Act 1988, see Law Commission report no. 141 (1985) 'Covenants restricting dispositions, alterations and change of user'.

For an exhaustive discussion of right and duties between landlord and tenant, see *Megarry and Wade: Law of Real Property* (sixth edition by Harpum) chapter fourteen, part five, pages 860–917.

19 The running of covenants in a lease

19.1 Objectives

By the end of this chapter you should:

1 Be familiar with the concepts of 'privity of contract' and 'privity of estate', and be able to explain how they apply to the law of leases

2 Be able to distinguish between covenants which 'touch and concern the land' and those which do not touch and concern

3 Appreciate the position of a sub-tenant vis-à-vis a head landlord

4 Appreciate the new principles laid down in the Landlord and Tenant (Covenants) Act 1995 and applicable to leases granted after 1995

19.2 Introduction

In the preceding chapter we rather assumed one point which is often not in fact true. We assumed that the persons involved in any disputes or potential disputes over obligations in a lease were the **original** landlord and tenant. Especially with long-term leases, this is often not the case.

As we saw at 18.5, a tenant who no longer wants to use the land he has leased can (subject to the terms of his lease) assign (i.e., transfer) that lease to a third party. Alternatively, he can sub-let the whole or part of the property to a sub-tenant, provided the sub-tenancy is shorter in duration than the head lease. One day shorter will suffice. Equally a landlord is free to sell his fee simple reversion, though (except in unusual situations such as in *Hollington* v *Rhodes*) the purchaser will take the fee simple subject to the tenant's leasehold estate.

The issues discussed in this chapter can be summarized in the form of a question. If a tenant assigns his lease, or sub-lets, and/or a landlord sells his fee simple, who is now entitled to enforce the various terms of the lease, and against whom can they be enforced?

Before addressing these questions I must warn you that the Landlord and Tenant (Covenants) Act 1995 makes important changes in the law. But (subject to one minor exception) the changes only apply to leases granted on or after the commencement date of the new Act, which is 1 January 1996. I am therefore going to start by explaining the 'old' law which will continue to govern all pre-1996 leases. I will then turn to consider the 'new' law.

19.3 Privity of estate—introduction

Figure 19.1 (you will see similar diagrams in textbooks) sets out the story of the letting of Black House. We will need to consider that story in some detail.

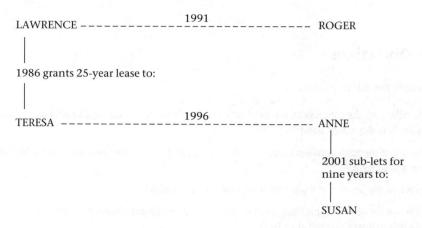

Figure 19.1 The letting of Black House

There are four stages in the recent history of Black House:

(a) In 1986, Lawrence leased the house to Teresa for 25 years.

(b) In 1991, Lawrence sold the fee simple reversion to Roger.

(c) In 1996, Teresa assigned the lease to Anne.

(d) In 2001, Anne sub-let the house to Susan.

By the terms of the lease agreed back in 1986, Lawrence covenanted to keep the property in good repair.

Teresa covenanted:

(i) to pay £500 per annum rent;

(ii) to use the property only for residential purposes;

(iii) to paint the landlord's portrait every five years.

I will immediately add that covenant (iii) is a very odd one to find in a lease. It really has nothing to do with the lease. In technical phraseology, it does not 'touch and concern the land'.

Suppose that today the following problems have arisen:

1. Roger is very vain and wants Teresa and/or Anne to paint his portrait.

2. The rent is a long way in arrears. Can Roger sue for that rent (logically the answer should be 'Yes') and, if so, whom can he sue—Anne, Teresa, or Susan?

3. To the great annoyance of Anne and Susan, the property is in disrepair. Who can enforce the repairing covenant? Who can the covenant be enforced **against**?

4. Susan is using the house for business purposes. Can anyone stop her from doing so?

19.3.1 The basic principles of the running of covenants in pre-1996 leases

The following basic principles are applicable to the questions posed above:

A If the landlord and tenant are in **privity of contract** then all the covenants in the lease will be enforceable between them. However, only the original parties to a lease are in 'privity of contract'. (In my story of Black House the original parties were Lawrence and Teresa. Between 1986 and 1991 all the terms of the lease were enforceable between them. Since 1991 a lot has happened. Privity of contract will not provide the answer to three of the four questions just posed.)

B If the landlord and the tenant are not in privity of contract but are in **privity of estate**, then those covenants which 'touch and concern the land' (but only those covenants) are enforceable between them.

C Privity of estate exists where two persons are in a **direct relationship** of landlord and tenant.

Thus in my little story:

(a) Between 1991 and 1996 there was privity of estate between Roger and Teresa.

(b) Between 1996 and 2001 there was privity of estate between Roger and Anne.

(c) From 2001 onwards there is (still) privity of estate between Roger and Anne; in addition there is a separate privity of estate (and contract) between Anne and Susan.

? QUESTION 19.1

Why is there no privity of estate between Roger and Susan?

Roger and Susan are not in a **direct** landlord and tenant relationship. Anne (as it were) is in the way! The point I am trying to illustrate in this **Question** is absolutely crucial. If you did not get it right, think very carefully before proceeding to **Exercise 19.1**.

🚶 EXERCISE 19.1

Try to apply the principles A, B, and C set out above to the four problems (numbered 1 to 4) which have now arisen regarding the lease of Black House:

1.

2.

3.

4.

I hope your answers are similar to what now follows.

1. **The portrait painting** As indicated earlier, the covenant to paint the portrait does not 'touch and concern the land'. A covenant which does not touch and concern is called 'a personal covenant'. Personal covenants which have been inserted into a lease normally remain enforceable only between the original parties. Thus Roger cannot insist on having his portrait painted. Assuming that Lawrence has remembered what was agreed 20-odd years ago, he could insist that Teresa paint his (Lawrence's) portrait.

2. **The arrears of rent** A covenant to pay rent does touch and concern the land. It follows that as there is privity of estate between Roger and Anne, Roger can (and normally would) sue Anne for those arrears. (For reasons which I will mention later at 19.5, he could alternatively sue Teresa, assuming he can find her.)

3. **The repairing covenant** A repairing covenant also touches and concerns the land. At the current time it is Susan who is personally suffering from the disrepair of the house. However, there is no privity of estate between Susan and Roger. It is only Anne who can enforce the repairing covenant against Roger.

4. **The use of the house for business purposes** As there is privity of estate between Roger and Anne, but not between Roger and Susan, you are probably thinking that Roger can sue Anne, but not Susan, on the covenant to use the house for residential purposes only.

On the basic principles of the law of leases, this would be correct. Unfortunately there is an added complication which will work to Roger's advantage. Roger, although he cannot sue Susan under the basic **law of leases**, may have a case against her under **the law of restrictive covenants**. I will return to this point at 19.9.2.

19.4 Which covenants touch and concern the land?

The tests traditionally applied are:

'Does the covenant affect the landlord **qua** landlord or the tenant **qua** tenant?' ('Qua' means 'in his capacity as'.)

or

'Does the covenant have some direct connection with the landlord and tenant relationship?'

If you are thinking that these tests are somewhat vague and uncertain in their operation, then I agree with you. Moreover, the courts have not always been consistent in applying these tests. If confronted with some new covenant not covered by existing case law you should apply the tests, but you should also consider whether the covenant is analogous to a covenant on which there is already a court decision. I summarize below the important court decisions.

19.4.1 Covenants by landlords which do touch and concern

(a) A covenant to repair, also to reconstruct or repaint.

(b) A covenant granting the tenant an option to renew the lease.

(c) A covenant to supply the land with fresh water. (I would suggest that this decision would apply to covenants to provide 'services' such as gas and electricity.)

19.4.2 Covenants by landlords which do not touch and concern

(a) A covenant granting the tenant an option to purchase the freehold reversion.
(b) A covenant in the lease of a public house under which the landlord brewery promised not to supply beer to other pubs within a half-mile radius: *Thomas* v *Hayward* (1869) LR 4 Ex 311.

19.4.3 Covenants by tenants which do touch and concern

(a) Covenants to pay rent.
(b) Covenants to pay rates or other taxes payable with respect to the land leased.
(c) Covenants to repair, repaint, etc.
(d) Covenants relating to the use for which the premises may be put.
(e) 'Tie clauses' under which the tenant of a pub or filling station can sell only the landlord's brand of beer or petrol. (See *Clegg* v *Hands* (1890) 44 Ch 503, which makes an ironic contrast with *Thomas* v *Hayward*.)

19.4.4 Covenants by tenants which do not touch and concern

Interestingly, examples are hard to find. One which is noteworthy is *Gower* v *Postmaster-General* (1887) 57 LT 527. This was a covenant by a tenant to pay rates on land **not comprised** within the lease. (This case could perhaps be extended by analogy to, say, a covenant to carry out building work on land other than that comprised in the lease.)

19.5 Liability of original parties after assignment

It is extremely important for you to realize that in all leases granted prior to 1996 the original contractual liability of a party to a lease lasts for the full duration of the lease. That is why in my Black House story at 19.3, Roger could sue Teresa, the original tenant, for the arrears of rent.

An original tenant of (say) a 50-year lease can be sued for arrears of rent run up by an assignee many years after he has parted with the lease. Or he can be sued for 'breaching' a repairing covenant, even though he has now no control over the premises. This point is of particular concern to small traders who 'sell up and retire'. They sometimes find that a peaceful retirement is rudely interrupted by a hefty claim for damages.

In *Arlesford Trading* v *Servansingh* [1971] 3 All ER 113, Arlesford were not the original landlords, but, like Roger in the Black House story at 19.3, purchasers of the reversion. The Court of Appeal, confirming earlier cases, held that a purchaser of a reversion automatically acquires the right to enforce the original tenant's contractual liability for covenants which touch and concern the land. Thus people like Servansingh (or Teresa in our story) can be chased for damages by landlords of whom they may well have never heard.

19.5.1 Indemnities between assignees of a lease

The rules I am about to discuss go **a little way** towards mitigating the harshness on original tenants of the rules set out above.

In various contexts (including the present one) the law gives to a **defendant** to legal proceedings a 'right of indemnity'. This is a right, having paid damages to the claimant, to reclaim those damages from a third party.

```
L
|
|
1957
|
|
A — 1967 — B — 1967 — C — 1987 — D — 1997 — E  (who is not paying the rent)
```

Figure 19.2 Assignments of a lease

Figure 19.2 represents the following story:

(a) In 1957, L granted a 99-year lease to A.

(b) In 1967, A assigned the lease to B.

(c) In 1977, B assigned the lease to C.

(d) In 1987, C assigned the lease to D.

(e) In 1997, D assigned the lease to E.

(f) E has now run up arrears of rent.

In this situation L has a choice of whether to sue A (on the original tenant's contractual liability) or E under the privity of estate rule. L can recover only one lot of compensation; he will choose to sue whoever has the most money. **Suppose L decides to sue A.**

A, having paid L, will have two, alternative rights of indemnity:

(a) At **common law** a right against the tenant in possession at the time of the breach (E in this story).

or

(b) Under the **Law of Property Act 1925, s. 77(1)**, a right against the person to whom he assigned the lease (B in this story).

Suppose A decides to claim indemnity from B. B pays up:

(a) B can then claim indemnity from C (s. 77(1)) or E (common law).

(b) B decides to claim indemnity from C. C pays up.

(c) C can then claim indemnity from D or E.

(d) C decides to claim indemnity from D. D pays up.

(e) D can claim indemnity from E.

QUESTION 19.2

Will it be worth while D taking proceedings against E?

I very much doubt it. **E** is the one who is behind with the rent, and everyone else has avoided suing him, so it looks as though he has got little or no money.

EXERCISE 19.2

It follows from the answer just given to **Question 19.2** that D will (probably) end up footing the bill. Do you think this is fair?

I personally think that this is fair. It was **D** who brought the financially unsound party (**E**) into the story, so it is D who should bear the loss.

19.6 Position of covenants which do not touch and concern

Suppose that Toni is the tenant of the Spotted Cow. She holds the property on a 21-year lease granted in 1992 from Lovely Ales plc. The lease includes a covenant under which Lovely Ales promise not to supply their beer to other pubs within a quarter-mile radius. As mentioned at 19.4.2, such a covenant does not 'touch and concern' the land.

Alice is contemplating taking an assignment of the lease of the Spotted Cow. She wants to get the benefit of the 'local monopoly' in Lovely Ales beer. As the 'local monopoly' does not 'touch and concern the land', it will not **automatically** pass to Alice on the assignment of the lease. But it will pass if the deed assigning the lease **includes a special express clause** assigning the benefit of the 'local monopoly' covenant. So Alice should ensure that such a special clause is inserted into the assignment.

Alice should, however, be warned of one thing. If Lovely Ales sell their business to another brewery, the successor brewery will not be bound by the 'local monopoly' covenant.

The point of this Spotted Cow story is this. The benefit of a covenant which does not touch and concern the land can be passed on to an assignee of a lease, but only if there is a separate express assignment of the benefit of the covenant. However, the burden of a covenant which does not touch and concern is enforceable only against the original covenantor, Lovely Ales plc in my example.

19.6.1 Position of options to purchase the reversion

Anybody who is an assignee of a lease which contains an option to purchase the landlord's reversion is almost certainly going to want to obtain that option as well as the lease itself. A covenant by the landlord granting a tenant an option to purchase the reversion does **not**, however, touch and concern the land. Nevertheless, the assignee can get what he wants, provided he remembers that the option (as well as being a covenant) is an independent equitable interest in the land. Consequently:

(a) If the reversion is unregistered title, the option should be registered as a land charge. It comes within the very broad definition of an 'estate contract', Class C(iv). Registering the option as a land charge will make the option binding on a purchaser of the reversion.

(b) If the reversion is registered title, then it will usually be an overriding interest, previously under the Land Registration Act 1925, s. 70(1)(g) and now under Land Registration Act 2002, Sch. 3, para. 2. (*Webb* v *Pollmount*).

(c) If you are purchasing a lease which includes an option to purchase the reversion, you should ensure that the deed assigning the lease also includes a separate clause assigning the option.

19.6.2 **Position of options to renew the lease**

A covenant by a landlord giving a tenant an option to renew the lease **does** touch and concern the land. However, in *Phillips* v *Mobil Oil* [1989] 3 All ER 97, the Court of Appeal created a yet further complication by holding that, if the reversion is unregistered title, such an option is registrable as a Class C(iv) land charge. A tenant of a filling station who had not registered his option to renew as a land charge was thus not able to exercise it against a purchaser of the freehold reversion.

? **QUESTION** 19.3

What if the fee simple in reversion to Phillips's lease had been *registered* title?

If the reversion were registered, the tenant's option would normally be an overriding interest within s. 70(1)(g) or Sch. 3, para. 2, applying the principle in *Webb* v *Pollmount*. (Provided Phillips had been 'in actual occupation' there would be no need for him to enter a notice.)

? **QUESTION** 19.4

Lion Petrols plc owns the freehold in Blogford Garage. Its title is unregistered. In 1995 it granted a 20-year lease of the garage to Tony. The lease contains a clause giving the tenant a right to purchase the freehold. Ali now wants to take an assignment of the lease; he particularly wants to ensure that he will (if he can raise the finance) be able to exercise the option. Advise Ali. (There are two points you should make.)

First, Ali should ensure that the option has been registered as a land charge. Secondly he should insist that the deed assigning him the lease includes a separate provision assigning to him the benefit of the option.

? **QUESTION** 19.5

The 1995 lease of Blogford Garage (predictably) includes a clause that the tenant must not sell brands of petrol other than Lion's. Will Ali be bound by this 'tie clause'?

Of course he will. There will be privity of estate between Lion and Ali, and courts consistently have held that 'tie clauses' touch and concern the land (see 19.4.3). (See also *Regent Oil* v *Gregory (Hatch End)* [1965] 3 All ER 673.)

19.7 **The Landlord and Tenant (Covenants) Act 1995**

It is only now that the major changes introduced by this Act are beginning to have a large-scale impact, as they only apply to post-1995 leases. In the years prior to 1996, the press (even the tabloids) were full of sob stories about former original tenants who have assigned their leases but who many years later have been sued for breach of covenant (e.g., arrears of rent) by the landlord under what has (perhaps misleadingly) been dubbed the 'privity of contract' rule. There were widespread calls for the law to be changed so that the original tenant would not be liable for breaches of covenant which happened after he had assigned the lease.

The 1995 Act was eventually passed against opposition from landlords. They argued that they carefully select **original** tenants, and let only to persons of sound financial standing who will be able to pay the rent for the full duration of the lease. An assignee of a lease is selected by the assignor. An assignee may not be of the same sound financial standing as the original tenant.

Landlords did, however, extract two important concessions from Parliament. The first was s. 22, already discussed in the previous chapter (see 18.6). The second is 'authorized guarantee agreements' (discussed below in 19.7.3).

19.7.1 **All covenants in a lease now 'touch and concern the land'**

I will start with perhaps the most surprising change made by the 1995 Act. Section 2 effectively abolishes the distinction between covenants which 'touch and concern' and those 'personal covenants' which do not. **Any covenant** entered into by a tenant **actually written into a lease** granted after 1995 will be enforceable by the current landlord against the current tenant under the doctrine of privity of estate, and similarly **any** covenant entered into by a landlord and written into the lease will be enforceable by the current tenant against the current landlord under the doctrine of privity of estate.

EXERCISE 19.3

Reconsider the 'Spotted Cow' example I gave earlier in 19.6, on the assumption that the lease to Toni commenced in 1996. What would be the position when Toni assigns the lease to Alice?

If Toni assigns the lease to Alice, Alice will now automatically get the benefit of the 'local monopoly' clause. A separate assignment of this clause is no longer required. More important still, if Lovely Ales sell their business to another brewery, the local monopoly **will be enforceable** against the successor brewery.

Reconsider also the situation in **Question 19.4** on the assumption that the lease of Blogford Garage was granted in 1996. Ali need no longer insist that there be a special clause in the assignment transferring to him the option, but he should still ensure that it has been registered as a land charge.

19.7.2 Original tenant's liability ceases on assignment

Section 5 is the key provision in the 1995 Act. It basically provides that an original tenant cannot be liable for breaches of covenant which occur after he has assigned the lease. However, an original tenant will still be liable if the assignment is itself in breach of covenant, or if the assignment occurs 'by operation of law' on death or bankruptcy of the original tenant.

19.7.3 Authorized guarantee agreements

This is a major concession to landlords, spelt out in s. 16 of the Act. If a tenant needs a landlord's consent to assignment (whether under an absolute or qualified covenant against assigning) then the landlord can give his consent on condition that the tenant guarantees that the person to whom he is assigning will perform the tenant's covenants in the lease.

It must be stressed that this guarantee, when given by the assignor tenant, lasts only as long as the original assignee is the tenant of the property. Suppose:

(a) L in 2001 grants a 99-year lease to T.

(b) In 2003 T assigns the lease to U, with T entering into an authorized guarantee agreement.

(c) In 2005 U assigns to V, who in 2010 falls into arrears of rent or breaks some other kind of covenant.

T is not liable on the guarantee. His liability ceased in 2005, when U assigned to V.

19.7.4 Cessation of original landlord's liability

A landlord of a post–1996 lease who disposes of his reversion still remains liable on the covenants he entered into (e.g., relating to repair). However, ss. 6 to 8 of the new Act provide a procedure under which he can be released from this continuing liability. The ex-landlord must serve notice on the tenant at the latest four weeks after he has assigned his reversion. The landlord is automatically released from his covenants once four weeks have elapsed from service of the notice, unless the tenant objects. If the tenant does object, the landlord is only released if a county court decides that such a release would be reasonable.

19.7.5 Notice to tenant or guarantor of arrears

Section 17 is the one significant provision which applies to pre-1996 leases as well as new leases. If a landlord wants to recover arrears of rent (or service charges) from an original tenant or somebody who has entered into an authorized guarantee agreement, then the landlord must serve a warning notice within six months of the arrears arising.

19.8 Position of equitable leases

19.8.1 Pre-1996 equitable leases

A tenant under an equitable lease can assign the lease and the rights thereunder. However, the court in *Purchase* v *Lichfield Brewery* [1915] 1 KB 184 held that the doctrine of privity of estate did not apply to equitable leases. In consequence, an assignee of an equitable lease could not be sued by the landlord for rent or breach of other obligations in the lease. Liability for the rent and other obligations in the lease remained solely with the original tenant.

EXERCISE 19.4

An assignee of an equitable lease was nevertheless well advised to ensure that the tenant's obligations in the equitable lease were carried out. Why?

If there were any substantial breach of these obligations, the right to specific performance would be lost and consequently there would no longer be any equitable lease. (Remember *Coatsworth* v *Johnson* discussed at 5.5.4.1).

19.8.2 Post-1995 equitable leases

As a result of a provision tucked away in the definition section of the 1995 Landlord and Tenant (Covenants) Act (s.28(1)), it appears that the 1995 Act DOES apply to equitable leases. It therefore follows that where a post-1995 equitable lease is assigned, the original tenant ceases to be liable on the obligations on the lease; the assignee is liable instead.

19.9 Position of sub-tenants and head landlords

As we have already seen, there is no privity of estate between a head landlord and a sub-tenant. In my story at 19.3, there was no privity of estate between Roger and Susan. It follows that the terms of the head lease are not, as a general rule, enforceable by or against a sub-tenant. A sub-tenant should, however, be wary of the two points discussed below.

19.9.1 Forfeiture clauses

A sub-tenant should as far as possible ensure that all terms of the head lease which are enforceable by **forfeiture** are in fact observed. If the head lease is forfeited, any sub-lease derived from it is automatically destroyed as well. But you should note the possibility of the sub-tenant claiming relief under s. 146(4) of the Law of Property Act 1925. I will discuss s. 146 in **Chapter 20**.

19.9.2 Restrictive covenants in the head lease

Here we have another awkward anomaly in the law. In my story at 19.3 it was indicated that Roger may be able to enforce the 'residential purposes only' covenant against Susan under the law of restrictive covenants. I want to stress two points:

(a) A landlord's reversionary estate counts as 'dominant land'.

(b) A restrictive covenant contained in a lease which is unregistered title is not registrable as a land charge. **Whenever created** such a covenant is subject to the doctrine of notice.

The practical consequence of this is that a head landlord can enforce restrictive covenants in the lease against a sub-tenant, despite the absence of privity of estate, where:

(a) the **lease is unregistered title and the sub-tenant has notice** of the restrictive covenants (usually the sub-tenant will have notice of the restrictive covenants in the head lease as the head tenant will, for his own protection, at least tell the sub-tenant about them); or

(b) **the lease is registered title.** Restrictive covenants in registered leases are seemingly automatically binding on sub-tenants by virtue of the Land Registration Act 2002, s. 29(2)(b).

CONCLUDING REMARKS

The best way of concluding this chapter is to return to the Black House example at 19.3.

? QUESTION 19.6

What difference would it make to the four problems listed at 19.3 if, instead of sub-letting to Susan, Anne had assigned the lease to Susan? (The diagram now looks as shown in **Figure 19.3**.)

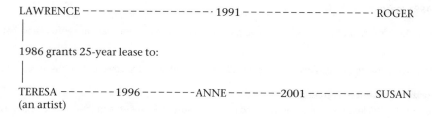

Figure 19.3   The letting of Black House with assignment to Susan

1. With respect to the 'purely personal' portrait painting covenant, the answer is as before. The covenant remains enforceable by Lawrence (only) against Teresa (only).
2. Roger can sue either Teresa or Susan (but not Anne) for the arrears of rent. But you should note that if he chooses to sue Teresa, Teresa can claim an indemnity from Anne (s. 77(1)) or Susan (common law).
3. On our revised version of the story, Susan is in privity of estate with Roger, and this will work to her advantage. Susan can sue Roger for the disrepairs.
4. Roger can sue Susan invoking the privity of estate principle. There is no need for him to invoke the (rather technical) rule regarding restrictive covenants.

If you now compare the answers to the four problems with those following **Exercise 19.1**, you will see that a lot does turn on whether the transaction between Anne and Susan is a sub-letting (a lease created out of a lease) or an assignment (a transfer of the existing leasehold estate).

In answering examination problems in the area of law covered in this **and/or the next chapter**, some students often get confused between assignments and sub-lettings. This is fatal to their chances of getting good marks. To help avoid the confusion, here are two tips:

(a) As we did with Black House, always draw a diagram to illustrate the facts of the problem.
(b) In that diagram **always** use **vertical** lines for leases and sub-leases, and **horizontal** lines for assignments and sales of freehold reversions.

■ SUMMARY

Successors in title to the original landlord and to the original tenant may be liable to each other on the covenants in the lease if there is 'privity of estate'. Privity of estate exists between two parties if they are in a direct landlord and tenant relationship.

Pre-1996 leases

1 Where there is privity of estate but not privity of contract between two parties, only covenants which 'touch and concern the land' are enforceable between them.

2 The original tenant is liable on all covenants in the lease for the full duration of the lease. If a later assignee of the lease breaks a covenant but the original tenant is sued, the original tenant has a common law right of indemnity against the person breaking the covenant, and a statutory right of indemnity aganst the person to whom he assigned the lease.

Post-1995 leases

1 Where there is privity of estate between two parties, **all** covenants in the lease are enforceable between them.

2 When an original tenant assigns the lease he ceases to be liable on the covenants in the lease.

Authorized Guarantee Agreements.

Where a post-1995 lease contains a qualified covenant against assignment, and the current tenant asks for permission to assign, the landlord may, if it is reasonable to do, ask the assignor to enter into an 'authorized guarantee agreement'. Under such a guarantee, the assignor (A1) guarantees that the assignee (A2) will perform the covenants. The guarantee only lasts so long as A2 remains owner of the lease.

Sub-tenants are generally not liable on covenants contained in the head lease. However, restrictive covenants are (normally) directly enforceable by the head landlord against the sub-tenant.

A sub-tenant should (where possible) ensure that covenants in the head lease which are enforceable by forfeiture are performed.

 CHAPTER 19: ASSESSMENT EXERCISE

In 1980 Lisa leased (by deed) a house to Tommy for 40 years. The lease includes the following covenants:

(a) the tenant should pay £2,000 per year rent;

(b) the tenant should not use the house for any purpose other than as a private dwelling;

(c) the tenant should not assign, sub-let, or part with possession except with the landlord's consent.

The lease does not contain a forfeiture clause.

Lisa believes that Tommy intends to assign or sub-let to Percy. She is alarmed at that prospect, as Percy uses a number of houses in the area as branches of his very extensive accountancy practice.

   Advise Lisa:

(i) as to the possible legal consequences if she withheld her consent to an assignment or sub-letting to Percy;

(ii) as to her position if she gave her consent to an assignment or sub-letting, but subsequently wishes to enforce covenants (a) or (b).

See Appendix for a specimen answer.

■ FURTHER READING

For the thinking which led to the Landlord and Tenant (Covenants) Act 1995, see Law Commission report no 174, 'Landlord and Tenant—Privity of contract and estate'.

For a very thorough treatment of 'running of lesehold covenants' see *Megarry and Wade: Law of Real Property* (sixth edition by Harpum) chapter fifteen.

20 Termination of leases

20.1 Objectives

By the end of this chapter you should:

1 Appreciate the various ways in which a lease may be terminated
2 Be able to both explain and distinguish between the two very different concepts of **waiver** of forfeiture and **relief** from forfeiture
3 Be familiar with the basic principles of s. 146 of the Law of Property Act 1925
4 Be able to explain the basic principles of the Leasehold Property (Repairs) Act 1938.

20.2 Introduction

There are various ways in which a lease can come to an end (see 20.3). Most of the ways in which a lease can terminate (e.g., notice or expiry) are self-explanatory; only one of them, forfeiture, requires extended consideration.

As you have probably guessed, forfeiture of a lease occurs where the landlord cancels a lease because the tenant has broken a provision in that lease. If a long-term lease is forfeit, that could be a disaster for the tenant, particularly if the rent is low relative to the value of the property. It is therefore not surprising that the law has placed quite severe restrictions on a landlord's right to forfeit a lease. However, as we shall see, those restrictions have become rather complex, and (possibly) too protective of tenants.

20.3 Ways in which leases may terminate

20.3.1 Natural expiry

This occurs where a fixed-term lease runs out and requires no further explanation here.

20.3.2 **Giving of notice**

A lease may be terminated:

(a) by either the landlord or the tenant giving notice to terminate a periodic tenancy; or

(b) by the tenant invoking a 'break clause' in a fixed-term lease. A 'break clause' is in effect an option to terminate the lease early.

20.3.3 **Merger**

A merger occurs where the tenant buys the landlord's reversion. The former lease then comes to an end.

20.3.4 **Surrender**

A lease is surrendered where it is terminated by mutual agreement between landlord and tenant. (I should stress that, except where there is a break clause or the lease has been 'frustrated' (see 20.3.5), a tenant cannot unilaterally give up a fixed-term lease he no longer wants.)

20.3.5 **Frustration**

 EXERCISE 20.1

If you have not yet studied the doctrine of frustration, or are perhaps 'rusty' as to what it involves, read the relevant Chapter in your contract textbook. Concentrate on the issue of what sorts of events do/do not constitute frustration. There is no need for you to consider the consequences of a contract being frustrated.

 A contract is 'frustrated' when something unanticipated happens, the fault of neither party, which makes the performance of the contract radically different from that which was originally agreed. In *National Carriers* v *Panalpina* [1981] 1 All ER 161, the House of Lords ended many years of controversy by holding that this law of contract rule of 'frustration' **does apply** to leases.

In January 1974, the defendants took a 10-year lease of a warehouse. In May 1979 the local authority closed the only access road to the warehouse. The closure was likely to last 20 months. The tenants refused to pay any further rent, arguing that the lease was frustrated by the lack of road access. Their Lordships held that:

(a) the doctrine of frustration did apply to leases; but

(b) a 20-month interruption in the enjoyment of a 10-year lease was not such a drastic change in the rights of the parties as to amount to a frustrating event terminating the lease.

Unfortunately their Lordships did not indicate how long an interruption there would have to have been to have terminated the lease.

EXERCISE 20.2

Traditionalist land lawyers (like me) do not like *Panalpina*, and would have preferred the House of Lords to have followed old cases (going back to the seventeenth century) which held that leases cannot be frustrated. Consider why we think like this.

The *Panalpina* decision is productive of a lot of uncertainty. Suppose that the blockage of the access road had lasted several years. The lease would be frustrated, but **exactly when**? This question is important as the lease, and therefore the tenant's liability for rent, would terminate on the **exact date** of frustration.

20.3.6 **Repudiatory breach by the landlord accepted by the tenant**

It is of course trite **contract** law that if one party to a contract commits a serious breach of contract going to the root of the contract, the other party can accept that repudiation and regard that contract as terminated. It seems that this doctrine can also be applied to breaches of terms of leases committed by landlords, though currently there is only a very limited amount of case law on the point. See *Nynehead Developments* v *Fireboard* [1999] Conveyancer 150. I would submit the introduction of this contract rule into the law of leases is highly unwelcome. It will generate a lot of disputes as to whether the landlord's conduct was sufficiently grave so as to justify the tenant treating the lease as terminated.

20.3.7 **Forfeiture**

This is a topic which requires extended consideration.

20.4 **Forfeiture of leases**

20.4.1 **The need for a forfeiture clause**

Obligations in leases are usually phrased as covenants, e.g., T covenants to pay the rent or T promises to do the repairs. Where the tenant's obligations in a lease are phrased as covenants, the landlord has the right to forfeit for breach by the tenant of one of his obligations only if the lease contains an express forfeiture clause ('right of entry'). Moreover, that forfeiture clause must extend to the breach which has in fact occurred.

I should immediately add that virtually every lease in existence today except some very long term leases includes a very widely drawn express forfeiture clause which can be invoked if the tenant breaks **any** of his obligations. In the case of non-payment of rent, it is usual for the forfeiture clause to allow a period of 'grace'. For example, it is common for a lease to provide that the landlord can forfeit for non-payment of rent, but only if the rent is 30 days (or one month) in arrears.

(If, which nowadays is unlikely, an obligation in a lease is phrased as a condition, e.g., 'I grant you this lease provided that the premises are kept in good repair', no forfeiture clause is necessary. The landlord automatically has a right of entry for breach of the condition.)

20.4.2 Modes of forfeiture

Traditionally there have been two alternative ways in which a landlord can forfeit a lease:

(a) **Peaceable** re-entry. This should be resorted to only if the property has been abandoned, or if it is absolutely clear that the tenant will leave of his own free will.

(b) Court proceedings for forfeiture. Such proceedings are usually essential because the Criminal Law Act 1977, ss. 6 to 13 (replacing the Forcible Entry Act 1381), makes it a crime to re-possess property by force.

'Peaceable re-entry' is not often used to forfeit a lease. In giving the leading speech in the House of Lords in *Billson* v *Residential Apartments* [1992] 2 WLR 15, Lord Templeman described peaceable re-entry as a 'dubious and dangerous method of determining [a] lease'. The decision of the House in this case (see 20.6.2) further discourages the use of peaceable re-entry, except in cases of commercial premises abandoned by the tenant.

For reasons which will emerge at 20.4.3, peaceable re-entry should never be used to forfeit a lease of an occupied dwelling house.

20.4.3 Forfeiture of a lease of a dwelling house

First, a little bit of a digression. In the last 40 or so years, there has been an enormous problem with landlords 'harassing' tenants (cutting off electricity, creating loud noises at night, etc.) in an effort unlawfully to drive those tenants out of the houses or flats they have leased.

The 'harassment' of tenants is made **criminal** by the Protection from Eviction Act 1977, s. 1, but that provision did not create a civil claim for damages or an injunction. (But see s. 2 below.) However, under ss. 27 and 28 of the Housing Act 1988, a statutory tort has been created of harassing a 'residential occupier'.

The central point, though, for our present purposes is s. 2 of the Protection from Eviction Act 1977:

Where any premises are let as a dwelling on a lease which is subject to a right of re-entry or forfeiture it shall not be lawful to enforce that right otherwise than by proceedings in the court while any person is lawfully residing in the premises or part of them.

This section effectively renders it impossible to forfeit a lease of an occupied dwelling by peaceable re-entry.

20.5 Waiver of forfeiture

Waiver of forfeiture must not be confused with **relief** from forfeiture. The essence of 'waiver' is that the **landlord**, because of his conduct, is deemed to have forgiven the tenant and renounced his claim to forfeiture. (The landlord can still pursue a claim for damages.)

Relief from forfeiture (discussed at 20.6) occurs where **the court** decides that although the tenant has broken the terms of the lease, he (the tenant) should be allowed to keep the lease. In effect **the court** shows mercy and forgives the erring tenant.

Waiver will occur where:

(a) the landlord knows of the breach; and

(b) with that knowledge, he does some unequivocal act, known to the tenant, which would indicate to a reasonable onlooker that he (the landlord) regards the lease as still subsisting.

The most frequently occurring 'unequivocal acts' are where the landlord either demands or accepts rent for a period after the breach. If the landlord distrains for rent, that is an 'unequivocal act' irrespective of when the rent in question was due. Another example of an 'unequivocal act' would be where the landlord enters into negotiations to renew the lease on its expiry, or offers to vary the terms of the existing lease.

A landlord has knowledge of facts constituting a breach if they come to his attention, or to the attention of any of his agents. If agent One has knowledge of a breach and agent Two sends out a rent demand, there is a waiver. The case of *Central Estates (Belgravia)* v *Woolgar (No. 2)* [1972] 3 All ER 610 illustrates many of the points just discussed.

Woolgar, an OAP and a First World War veteran, was tenant of a long lease (due to expire in 1993) of a sizeable house in central London. He had a fall from grace, and was convicted of using the premises as a (homosexual) brothel. In view of his past exemplary record he was granted a conditional discharge by the magistrates.

The landlords decided to forfeit the lease for breach of the covenant in the lease prohibiting illegal user, and served on Woolgar the warning notice required by s. 146 of the Law of Property Act 1925. (We will discuss this section later: see 20.6.2.) The landlords were anxious to forfeit the lease as the property would be **much more valuable** to them with vacant possession. (Sometimes property used as brothels or drug-dens gets stigmatized. That does not seem to have happened in *Woolgar's* case.)

A minor official of the landlords then made a fatal mistake—he sent to Woolgar a rent demand for a future instalment of rent. The Court of Appeal unanimously found that this rent demand waived the breach, even though:

(a) it was sent out in error;

(b) Woolgar had not been in any way misled by the demand. Even after the demand was sent he still personally believed that he was going to be thrown out of his home. The Court stressed that the test for an 'unequivocal act' was not what the tenant subjectively thought; rather it was an objective test of what a **'reasonable onlooker'** would think. The reasonable onlooker always considers rent demands as indicating that the landlord intends to allow the lease to continue.

In *Blackstones Ltd* v *Burnetts* [1973] 3 All ER 782 Burnetts had a lease from Blackstones of premises in central London. There was a qualified covenant against sub-letting. Burnetts obtained Blackstones' consent to sub-let to two people, A and D, trading in partnership. However Burnetts actually sub-let to a **different** person, Flat Finders Ltd. (A and D were the directors of that company.)

The landlords' solicitors heard of what had happened. The solicitors seem to have been ignorant of the very basic principle of company law that a company is a **separate person** from its shareholders and directors. They sought counsel's opinion as to whether there had been breach of the qualified covenant against sub-letting. (Clearly there had been such a breach.) While this opinion was awaited, a clerk in the landlords' office sent out a rent demand for the next quarter's rent. The rent demand was held to have waived the breach.

> **?** **QUESTION** 20.1
>
> What is the moral for landlords of the two cases just discussed?

If you want to forfeit a lease, give clear instructions to all your agents (and not just to your specialist rent-collectors) that they must neither send out rent demands nor accept rent paid without a demand being sent. (If the landlord's rent files are computerized, the computer should be programmed to warn that no rent should be demanded/accepted. If he still has manual files, a red warning marker should be placed in the file.)

20.6 Relief from forfeiture

Where a tenant claims relief from forfeiture, he will normally do so by counterclaiming for relief in the landlord's proceedings to terminate the lease. The tenant could bring a separate action 'for relief', but that is unlikely as it would mean unnecessary additional costs.

20.6.1 Relief from forfeiture for non-payment of rent

Such relief from forfeiture was traditionally governed by equity, but has now been incorporated into statute (currently the Supreme Court Act 1981, s. 38).

Three conditions must be fulfilled for relief to be granted:

(a) the tenant must pay all the arrears of rent;

(b) the tenant must pay all the landlord's costs;

(c) it must appear just and equitable to grant relief.

You may already know that it is a general rule of English litigation that the loser of court proceedings pays both sides' costs. Point (b) above is a perfectly sensible **exception** to this rule. The tenant 'wins' relief, but he must pay the landlord's legal costs as part of the price of winning.

It is fair to say that if points (a) and (b) above are satisfied the court will in normal circumstances automatically conclude that it is 'just and equitable' to grant relief. Point (c) really means that the court has a discretion to refuse relief even though the tenant pays off all the arrears of rent and the landlord's costs.

> **EXERCISE** 20.3
>
> Can you think of situations where a court might refuse relief despite the fact that the tenant has cleared the arrears and paid all the landlord's costs?

The court might well refuse relief if the circumstances are such that the tenant is very likely to fall into serious arrears of rent again. It might also refuse relief if the tenant is in serious breach of other obligations in the lease as well as rent, e.g., had broken covenants regarding the user of premises.

Another (related) aspect of 'condition (c)' above is that in exceptional cases the court can grant relief on conditions which do not relate to payment of rent. Suppose the tenant is rather neglecting the property. The court could grant relief on condition that the property be put into good repair: *Belgravia Insurance* v *Meah* [1964] 1 QB 436.

Relief against forfeiture for non-payment of rent has one further oddity. Unlike relief where court proceedings have been taken under s. 146 of the Law of Property Act 1925 (see 20.6.2) the court has the power to grant relief to the tenant even **after** the landlord has repossessed the property! The tenant can claim this 'late relief' up to six months after the landlord's repossession. But I should stress that this late relief requires the expense of separate court proceedings brought by the tenant, and that the court would not grant this late relief if the landlord had already let the property to a new tenant.

20.6.2 Forfeiture for breach of covenant other than rent

This is governed by s. 146 of the Law of Property Act 1925. Section 146(1) provides:

A right of re-entry or forfeiture under any proviso or stipulation in a lease for a breach of any covenant or condition in the lease shall not be enforceable, by action or otherwise, unless and until the lessor serves on the lessee a notice—

(a) specifying the particular breach complained of; and

(b) if the breach is capable of remedy, requiring the lessee to remedy the breach; and

(c) in any case, [where the landlord wants compensation] requiring the lessee to make compensation in money for the breach;

and the lessee fails, within a reasonable time thereafter, to remedy the breach, if it is capable of remedy, and to make reasonable compensation in money, to the satisfaction of the lessor, for the breach.

Section 146(2) provides that the court can, in its discretion (in the landlord's forfeiture proceedings or in separate proceedings commenced by the tenant), grant relief from forfeiture. The general rule under s. 146(2) is that a tenant cannot claim relief once a landlord has actually repossessed the property. But this general rule applies only if the landlord forfeits **by court proceedings**.

In *Billson* v *Residential Apartments* [1991] 3 All ER 265, the defendant was lessee of an empty building. It broke a covenant against altering the building without the landlord's consent.

The landlord served a s. 146 notice. After waiting a reasonable time, the landord, instead of commencing court proceedings for possession, peaceably re-entered the building early one morning, changed the locks, and assumed control of the building.

The Court of Appeal held that once a landlord had peaceably re-entered, the tenant had no right to claim relief. However, this decision was overruled by the House of Lords, which held that where the landlord forfeited a lease by **peaceable re-entry**, the tenant could, **after** the landlord has re-occupied the property, commence court proceedings to get the property back. Their Lordships stressed that there is no fixed time limit on such an application for relief after peaceable re-entry. However, if the tenant delayed a long time before claiming relief, that would be a factor to be considered by the court when exercising its discretion whether or not to grant relief.

?   **QUESTION** 20.2

Why does the decision in *Billson* further discourage the use of peaceable re-entry to forfeit leases?

If a landlord forfeits by court proceedings under s. 146, he knows that once he has taken possession under the court order there is no possibility of the tenant's lease being restored. If he forfeits by peaceable re-entry, he is subject to the risk that (perhaps years later) the court will give the lease back to the tenant.

20.6.2.1 The four stages required by s. 146 for forfeiture by court proceedings

(a) The landlord must serve a carefully drafted warning notice on the **current** tenant: *Old Grovebury Estates* v *Seymour Plant Sales (No. 2)* [1979] 3 All ER 504.

(b) The landlord must then wait 'a reasonable time' before commencing forfeiture proceedings. If during this time the tenant 'remedies' the breach, the landlord cannot claim forfeiture.

(c) Assuming (as is usually the case) the breach is not remedied within a 'reasonable time', the landlord can issue a claim form demanding forfeiture.

(d) When the landlord's forfeiture case reaches court, the tenant can beg the court to grant him relief. The court is most likely to grant relief either where the breach (e.g., disrepair) has now at last been put right, or where the landlord has not been substantially harmed by an 'irremediable' breach.

20.6.2.2 The s. 146 notice must be drafted correctly

The notice must spell out in detail what breaches the landlord is relying on. For example, it is not sufficient to say, 'the property is in disrepair'. If the breach is capable of remedy, the landlord must specifically include a clause in the notice demanding the breach be put right.

If the s. 146 'warning' notice has not been drafted correctly, any court proceedings commenced by the landlord will be abortive, even if the tenant is clearly a sinner who should be thrown out. In such a case the landlord would have to serve another (this time correctly drafted) s. 146 notice and start all over again.

20.6.2.3 **Remediable or irremediable breaches?**

This is a very important distinction for three reasons:

(a) The need to draft the s. 146 notice correctly. (There have been a number of cases where the landlord has drafted his s. 146 notice on the assumption that the breach is irremediable, but the court has ruled that the breach was 'remediable'. The landlord's forfeiture proceedings were therefore dismissed.)

(b) The length of the 'reasonable time' which must elapse between service of the s. 146 notice and the commencement of proceedings for possession.

   (i) Where the breach is remediable, then the landlord must wait at least three months.

  (ii) Where the breach is irremediable, a fortnight's delay between service of notice and commencement of proceedings generally suffices. Two days was held to be insufficient in *Horsey Estates* v *Steiger* [1899] 2 QB 79, at 91.

(c) The court is **more likely** to grant relief where the breach is capable of remedy.

Breaches of **positive covenants**, e.g., repairing and painting covenants, are generally capable of remedy. This is confirmed by the decision in *Expert Clothing* v *Hillgate House* [1985] 2 All ER 998, especially at 1008. In that case the breach consisted of a failure to reconstruct the premises by an agreed date. The Court of Appeal held that the breach was 'remediable' by the tenant belatedly doing the reconstruction. Slade LJ said:

Nevertheless, I would, for my part, accept the submission of counsel for the defendants that the breach of a positive covenant (whether it be a continuing breach or a once and for all breach) will ordinarily be capable of remedy. As Bristow J pointed out in the course of argument, the concept of capability of remedy for the purpose of s. 146 must surely be directed to the question **whether the harm that has been done to the landlord by the relevant breach is for practical purposes capable of being retrieved**. In the ordinary case, the breach of a promise to do something by a certain time can for practical purposes be remedied by the thing being done, even out of time. (Emphasis added.)

In the past, breaches of **negative** covenants have generally been regarded as incapable of remedy. In particular, it has long been accepted that breaches of covenants against assigning, sub-letting, and parting with possession are incapable of remedy. See *Scala House* v *Forbes* [1973] 3 All ER 308.

However, the Court of Appeal in *Savva* v *Houssein* (1996) 73 P & CR 150, a case involving the breach of a covenant not to alter a building without consent, expressed the view that **all** breaches of **negative** covenants, except those within the *Scala House* principle, were to be regarded as **capable of remedy**. This view (arguably *obiter*) is controversial, and further confuses this area of law. **If correct**, it represents a major shift in the law.

The case of *Glass* v *Kencakes* [1964] 3 All ER 807, which involved a breach of covenant against illegal and/or immoral use, is anyway still difficult. In *Glass*, L let to T and the lease included a covenant against illegal/immoral user. T sub-let to S, who, without T's knowledge, used the premises for prostitution. L served a s. 146 notice on T in terms which assumed the breach was incapable of remedy. T in turn served a s. 146 notice on S. The **sub**-lease was declared forfeit. The judge then held that T had remedied his (arguably technical) **breach** of the head lease by getting rid of S **before the property became tainted with a stigma**.

20.6.3 Relief for breaches which are incapable of remedy

Glass v *Kencakes* was decided before the Court of Appeal's decision in *Central Estates* v *Woolgar*. I have already told you the facts of that case (see 20.5) and the court's ruling on the waiver issue. Woolgar also (in the alternative) claimed relief from forfeiture. The Court of Appeal broke new ground by holding that relief could be granted even where the breach was **irremediable**. (In *Central Estates* v *Woolgar*, all three judges of the Court of Appeal assumed that a breach of a covenant against illegal/immoral user was normally a breach **incapable** of remedy. I believe this to be still correct, and that *Savva* v *Houssein*, in so far as it might suggest otherwise, is wrong.)

A majority of the court (had it not already decided the waiver issue in Woolgar's favour) would have granted Woolgar relief. The majority was clearly impressed by three facts: (i) Woolgar's hitherto exemplary character; (ii) his genuine repentance; (iii) the fact that if there was a forfeiture the landlord's fee simple (now with 'vacant possesion') would substantially **increase** in value.

> **? QUESTION** 20.3
>
> If a case like *Glass* v *Kencakes* recurred today (an innocent head tenant prejudiced by the nefarious activities of a sub-tenant) how do you think that the court would deal with the case?

I think that even after *Savva* v *Houssein*, the court would deal with the matter by granting relief from forfeiture, without worrying whether the breach was capable of remedy.

20.6.4 Relief to sub-tenants

If a head lease is forfeited, then all sub-leases created out of that head lease are destroyed as well. Situations thus arise from time to time where a sub-tenant who has faithfully fulfilled all the conditions of the sub-lease is nevertheless imperilled by the failure of the head tenant to perform an obligation in the head lease. (Contrast *Glass* v *Kencakes* at 20.6.2.3.)

A sub-tenant who is imperilled by the head tenant's failure to pay the rent under the head lease can (in theory) claim relief in equity. This remedy is unlikely to be invoked nowadays for two reasons:

(a) The lease of the (unsatisfactory) head tenant is preserved by the sub-tenant's efforts in paying off the arrears, yet the head tenant may well again fall into arrears.

(b) If the sub-lease is of part of the property, relief cannot be confined to that part. (In one old case the head lease consisted of 100 houses. Each house was sub-let to a separate individual tenant. The head tenant fell into arrears of rent. One of the sub-tenants applied to the Court of Chancery for relief. He was told he could have relief, but only if he paid off the arrears of rent under the head lease with respect to all 100 houses. I would imagine that was beyond his resources!)

20.6.4.1 **Section 146(4) of the LPA 1925**

Today, sub-tenants may seek relief under **s. 146(4) of the Law of Property Act 1925**. This provision applies to all breaches of covenants, **including** (unlike the rest of s. 146) **non-payment of rent**. (Mortgagees of leases can also seek relief under s. 146(4) where a mortgaged lease is threatened with forfeiture, and in modern conditions this is very important.)

The drafting of s. 146(4) is somewhat obscure. However the courts have managed to make sense of it. A good example is *Chatham Empire Theatre (1955) Ltd v Ultrans Ltd* [1961] 2 All ER 381.

Section 146(4) works in the following way. If the court decides that the head lease should be forfeited but that the sub-tenant should be protected, the head lease is destroyed by court order. The ex-sub-tenant is granted a new head lease for a period not exceeding that unexpired under the old sub-lease. If the old sub-lease was of part of the property, the new head lease will relate to that part only. The court has a discretion as to the detailed terms of the new head lease.

Where a mortgagee of a lease claims relief, and the court decides that the lessee himself does not deserve relief, the court orders the old lease to be destroyed. A new (head) lease is granted in its place to the **ex-mortgagee**. The mortgagee now becomes a lessee.

20.7 **Leasehold Property Repairs Act 1938**

This statute was passed because of a problem with 'shark' landlords in the 1930s who were inducing tenants to **surrender** long leases of poorly repaired property by threatening them with heavy claims for damages.

The landlord would first write to the tenant saying something like, 'Dear Tenant. Your house/shop is in shocking repair. We are going to sue you for £X,000 damages'. This terrified the tenant. (Many of the tenants affected were small businesses suffering from the effects of the Depression.)

A few weeks later another letter would arrive, in terms, 'Dear Tenant, if you agree to surrender your lease we will forget about our claim for damages'. The tenants were usually only too glad to accept the invitation. The practical outcome was that the landlord had succeeded in terminating the lease while by-passing the elaborate procedure laid down in s. 146 of the Law of Property Act 1925.

The 1938 Act applies to all leases for more than seven years with at least three years to run. Where the Act applies, a landlord cannot enforce a repairing covenant by forfeiture or **damages** unless he first serves a s. 146 notice.

In addition to the usual particulars, the warning notice must inform the tenant that he has 28 days in which to serve a 'counter-notice' claiming the protection of the Act. If this counter-notice is served (as usually it is), the landlord cannot take any further steps to enforce the repairing covenant unless he first gets the permission ('leave') of the court. This leave is generally given only if there is a pressing need for immediate repairs. Indeed the House of Lords has held that:

. . . save in special circumstances, the landlord must prove (on the balance of probabilities) that the immediate remedying of a breach of the repairing covenant is required in order to save the landlord from substantial loss or damage which the landlord would otherwise sustain (*per* Lord Templeman in *Associated British Ports* v *C H Bailey Plc* [1990] 1 All ER 929).

(If you get a chance to read this case, read first the **penultimate** paragraph of Lord Templeman's speech. You will then understand the real reasons underlying this very protracted litigation.)

20.7.1 *Sedac Investments* v *Tanner* [1982] 3 All ER 646

In this case a very bad tenant (a local Conservative Club!) covenanted to do the repairs but allowed the building to get into a dangerous state. The landlords (under pressure from the local authority) did the repairs themselves. The landlords then sued, but found their claim for damages blocked by the 1938 Act. There was no longer any pressing need for repairs!

A somewhat similar situation arose in *Jervis* v *Harris* [1996] 1 All ER 303, except that the lease expressly provided that if the landlord should carry out repairs the tenant would indemnify the landlord for the cost. It was held by the Court of Appeal that the 1938 Act did not prevent an action being brought on this **indemnity** clause.

 QUESTION 20.4

What is the moral for landlords of the decisions in *Sedac Investments* and *Jervis* v *Harris*?

When drafting new leases where the tenant will be liable to do the repairs, always include an indemnity clause similar to that in *Jervis* v *Harris*.

20.8 Reform of forfeiture of leases

The Law Commission, in 1986, proposed radical reform of this complex area of law. A recent (January 2004) consultation paper largely reaffirms these proposals.

 EXERCISE 20.4

Refer back to what I said about *Billson* v *Residential Apartments* at 20.6.2. In that case the House of Lords in December 1991 overruled a Court of Appeal decision made in February 1991. Also refer back to my remarks at 20.6.4.1 regarding s. 146(4) and in particular to the question of relief for mortgagees. Then consider the following questions, bearing in mind that 1991 was the depths of a recession and that a General Election was expected in the spring of 1992:

(a) What had less scrupulous landlords been doing from February to December 1991?

(b) Which wealthy organizations were particularly upset by these activities of these less scrupulous landlords?

(c) What would Parliament have been forced to do if the House of Lords had upheld the Court of Appeal decision in favour of the landlords?

My own answers would be as follows:

(a) What was happening was that landlords were staging 'dawn raids'; i.e., peaceably re-entering deserted buildings before the tenants arrived. The landlords thought that (courtesy of the Court of Appeal) they had thereby forfeited the lease(s) **and deprived the tenants, sub-tenants, and mortgagees** of their right to seek relief.

(b) The answer to this question lies in the answer to (a). Financial institutions (especially the big banks) had lent money to tenants who were now in severe financial difficulties because of the recession. The banks had taken mortgages of the tenants' leases to secure the loans, but these mortgages were being destroyed by the dawn raids.

(c) Had the House of Lords ruled the other way in *Billson*, the big banks would have been screaming at the government for immediate reform. With an election pending, the government would have been forced to dust off the 1986 Law Commission Report and tell Parliament, 'We do not have time to argue the details. We must immediately enact these proposals'.

 CONCLUDING REMARKS

The preceding paragraph, as well as relating to **Exercise 20.4**, is also the first part of my conclusion, so I will not repeat it.

The second part is to remind you of an examination question I asked a few years ago. Candidates were invited to discuss the following proposition:

A landlord who wants to forfeit a lease is often faced with a long and tortuous process. During that process he dare not collect any rent. And the proceedings for forfeiture may well end with the court forgiving the erring tenant.

I think you will have realized that I am in broad agreement with this proposition, and (as I hinted at 20.2) the law is arguably too protective of tenants. It is certainly not surprising that when the Court of Appeal in *Billson* appeared to open a door to landlords to circumvent one of the protections for tenants, many landlords rushed through only to find that door slammed shut by the House of Lords.

The House of Lords (led by Lord Templeman) took the heat off the government, but certainly did not eliminate the need for wholesale reform of this area of law.

■ SUMMARY

Termination of fixed-term leases. This can come about through:

natural expiry;
giving notice under a break clause;
merger;
surrender;
frustration;

(seemingly) repudiatory breach by landlord accepted by tenant;
forfeiture.

Forfeiture

The lease must contain a forfeiture clause.
The landlord normally forfeits by court proceedings; peaceable re-entry is a risky process.
The landlord must be careful not to waive the right to forfeit. In particular, once the landlord knows of the breach of covenant, the landlord must not demand or accept rent.

Forfeiture for non-payment of rent.

No special statutory procedure. The tenant can claim relief from forfeiture (by offering the arrears and costs) at any time up to six months after the landlord has retaken possession.

Forfeiture for breaches of covenant other than non-payment of rent.

The landlord must follow the procedure laid down in s. 146 of the LPA 1925:
Serve a notice; wait a reasonable time; then commence court proceedings.
Tenant can claim relief at any time up to when the landlord re-possesses; even after re-possession if the landlord re-enters without a court order.
The court can grant relief even though the breach is irremediable.

Position where sub-tenant's activities makes head lease liable to forfeiture

The head tenant should get rid of the sub-tenant as soon as possible, and then claim relief with respect to the head lease.

Position where a sub-tenant (or mortgagee) is prejudiced by head tenant's breach

The innocent party should claim relief under s. 146(4). The court awards the ex-sub-tenant (or ex-mortgagee) a new head lease.

The Leasehold Property Repairs Act 1938 restricts landlords who want to sue for damages (or forfeit) for disrepair. But only applies to leases for more than 7 years with at least 3 years to run.

CHAPTER 20: ASSESSMENT EXERCISE

In 1994 Letitia leased (by deed) a shop to Tamsin for 40 years. The lease includes a covenant under which the tenant undertakes to ensure that the shop is not used for illegal purposes. Rent is payable quarterly and in advance to Letitia's agent Rocky. The lease also includes a forfeiture clause which can be invoked if the tenant breaks any of the covenants.

In 2005 Tamsin lawfully assigned the lease to Ann. In early 2006 Dandy, one of Ann's shop assistants, took advantage of the fact that Ann did not normally arrive at the shop until 9.30 a.m. He started an early morning 'side-line' selling cocaine. After only a month Ann found out about the illegal trade. She immediately dismissed Dandy and reported his activities to the police. Last week Dandy was convicted of drug-trafficking.

Letitia has just read of Dandy's conviction in the local newspaper. She has decided to endeavour to forfeit the lease. She tells you, 'The rent under the existing lease is ridiculously low; if I can get Ann out a new tenant would be willing to pay three times as much.'

Advise Letitia.

See Appendix for a specimen answer.

■ FURTHER READING

For the Law Commission's 1986 proposals regarding reform of forfeiture, still very relevant today, see Law Commission report no. 142 'Forfeiture of Tenancies'. (The report includes a very clear summary.)

For an excellent compilation of cases and materials on forfeiture, see Maudsley and Burn's *Land Law Cases and Materials,* chapter eight, part IV.

PART VII

Loss of Ownership

21 Adverse possession and the Limitation Acts

21.1 Objectives

By the end of this chapter you should:

1 Appreciate the role adverse possession plays in English land law

2 Be able to explain the meaning of the concept

3 Appreciate fully the legal difficulties which arise where adverse possession is taken against land subject to a trust

4 Appreciate fully the legal difficulties which arise where adverse possession is taken against a leaseholder

5 Be able to understand the radically new rules introduced by the Land Registration Act 2002 which will in future govern adverse possession against a proprietor of registered land

21.2 Introduction

Adverse possession is a vital part of English land law. If the concept did not exist, then the English system of **unregistered** title would be impossible to operate.

The basic concept is not difficult to understand. Moreover, land lawyers have been greatly helped by a modern (1989) Court of Appeal decision, involving a very striking set of facts, which both clarified and simplified the law. Moreover that decision has been recently (2002) approved of and applied by the House of Lords.

Though I think you will find the early part of this chapter straightforward, I should warn you that difficulties will begin to mount when we consider, first, adverse possession against land which is subject to a lease and, secondly, adverse possession against land which is registered title.

Every few years we get a well-publicized case where an adverse possessor gains title to a quite large area of land. In *Bucks CC* v *Moran* [1989] 2 All ER 225, the defendant expanded his garden onto an area of land owned by the council and intended to be become part of a by-pass. He won the case.

EXERCISE 21.1

Most adverse possession cases are not nearly as spectacular. What do you think is the most common type of situation where the rules of adverse possession have to be applied?

The most common type of case for applying the adverse possession rules is a small encroachment between neighbours, e.g., where a boundary fence is moved perhaps a foot.

21.3 Possession gives a right to sue trespassers

First consider the following propositions:

(a) Ownership is often defined as 'the best right to possess'.
(b) Possession of land, or any other property, is itself evidence of ownership of that land or property. The longer the possession the better the evidence of ownership.

When a purchaser investigates title to unregistered land he is merely checking that the vendor and his predecessors have been in control of the land for a sufficiently long time to make his claim to ownership safe (see 2.5).

We all have heard the phrase 'Possession is nine-tenths of the law'. In the context of land law, this cliché is correct! A person in possession of land, though he has no title to it, can nevertheless defend that possession by legal proceedings against **anyone but the true owner**.

QUESTION 21.1

Suppose that Anthea is the owner in fee simple (unregistered title) of Wasteacre. In 2000 Bertram seized possession of Wasteacre and has remained in possession ever since. Now (2007) Charlotte (a total stranger with no connections to Anthea) is trying to interfere with Bertram's possession, or even to evict Bertram from Wasteacre. If Bertram sues Charlotte for trespass, who will win?

Bertram will win. It will be no defence for Charlotte to say, 'But it is not Bertram's land'.

21.4 The Limitation Act 1980

Section 15(1) of the Limitation Act 1980 replaces legislation dating back many centuries. The practical effect of this provision (and its predecessors) is to declare that in appropriate circumstances possession shall be ten-tenths of the law!

No action shall be brought by any person to recover any land after the expiration of twelve years from the date on which the right of action accrued to him or, if it first accrued to some person through whom he claims, to that person.

Under a provision which is now tucked away in Sch. 1, para. 8(1) of the 1980 Act, a 'right of action' accrues to the owner of a piece of land when a stranger takes 'adverse possession' of the land against him.

The practical effect of what I have said so far is as follows:

(a) Once adverse possession has started, the adverse possessor can defend his possession against all but the original owner.

(b) Once adverse possession has continued for 12 years, the adverse possessor can defend his possession against all **including** the original owner.

Question 21.1 has already illustrated proposition (a). Suppose now that Bertram remains in continuous adverse possession against Anthea for many more years. In the year 2012 proposition (b) will become operative and Bertram will have a title to Wasteacre which he can assert against the whole world, **including Anthea**. That title will be based on his long possession of the land.

Looked at from another angle, at the end of the 12 years' adverse possession the original owner's title (Anthea's title to Wasteacre in my example) is completely extinguished. The adverse possessor has a completely new (fee simple) title based on his long adverse possession. You should note, however, that it is not correct to say that in the year 2012 Anthea's title is transferred to Bertram.

Anthea may well, after 2012, retain title deeds to 'her' fee simple title to Wasteacre, but those deeds will be worthless scraps of paper.

21.4.1 'Squatters'

Unfortunately the word traditionally used by lawyers for any person who takes adverse possession is 'squatter'. This word, used in its time-honoured legal sense, is both broader in meaning and less emotive than the present-day colloquial usage.

21.4.2 Commencement of adverse possession

Adverse possession commences when the adverse possessor displaces the original owner. As was emphasized in *Bucks CC* v *Moran*, the adverse possessor **must take control of the land with the intention of excluding everyone else from the land**. As I have said already, the most common cases of adverse possession today are encroachments between neighbours, e.g., where a boundary fence is moved. However, periodically we do seem to get a (reported) case where an adverse possessor successfully 'annexes' to his own property a quite large chunk of land. *Bucks CC* v *Moran* is a good illustration of this type of case.

Another striking case is *Treloar* v *Nute* [1977] 1 All ER 230. In that case the plaintiff and the defendant were adjoining farmers. The plaintiff (an elderly lady) had about one-seventh of an acre of waste ground about which she totally forgot. The defendant and his father in effect took over the ground. They levelled it off (there had been a deep gully). They then used it for various purposes, such as an informal motor-bike trials course and as a rubbish dump.

Eventually the defendant started to build a bungalow on the ground. At that point Mrs Treloar woke up: 'Hey that's my land you're building on!'

The defendant and his father were able to prove that they had been using the ground for more than 12 years. Mrs Treloar's title to the land was extinguished. Nute (junior) had a new title based on adverse possession. The Court of Appeal therefore gave judgment for Nute.

21.4.3 **The 'adverse' in adverse possession**

For a long period of possession to extinguish an original owner's title, the possession must be 'adverse' to the original owner's title. This means that the possessor's occupation of the land must be **inconsistent** with the title of the original owner. Thus, during the running of a lease, a tenant cannot be in adverse possession against his landlord with respect to the land comprised in the lease. A tenant's possession is not in any way inconsistent with or in conflict with the landlord's ownership of the fee simple.

? **QUESTION** 21.2

What if a tenant fails to pay the rent? Does that make his possession 'adverse'?

Failure to pay rent does not make the tenant's possession 'adverse'. The tenant's lease is derived out of the landlord's freehold, and is not in conflict with that freehold, irrespective of whether or not the tenant pays rent. (However, the right to an instalment of rent is time-barred after a six-year delay in collecting that instalment.)

Trustees of land can never be in adverse possession against their beneficiaries. This is because there is no inconsistency between the trustees' **legal** title and the beneficiaries' **equitable** interests.

? **QUESTION** 21.3

Suppose A, B, C, D, and E are tenants in common of Highhouse, but only A and B are trustees of the legal title. A and B get nasty and shut C, D, and E out of the house. They keep C, D, and E locked out for more than 12 years. Are the rights of C, D, and E 'time-barred'?

Even if the unhappy state of affairs continues for 50 years or more, C, D, and E will never be 'time-barred'; their rights cannot be extinguished by the trustees' decision to keep possession of the house exclusively for themselves. See also *Earnshaw* v *Hartley* [1999] 3 WLR 709, [2000] Ch 155.

One other significant point is that a purchaser of land who takes possession prior to completion of the contract of sale is not in adverse possession unless and until the contract of sale is rescinded. A purchaser's 'estate contract' equitable interest is in no way inconsistent with the vendor's ownership of the legal fee simple: *Hyde* v *Pearce* [1982] 1 All ER 1029.

21.4.4 **The 'apparently abandoned plot' problem**

In *Treloar* v *Nute* (see 21.4.2) Mrs Treloar had totally forgotten about the land in dispute. The facts of that case are to be contrasted with the line of cases I am now going to discuss. I must mention this line of cases even though they have now been overruled by legislation.

These older cases held that where a landowner had a piece of land which he left vacant but for which he had future plans, a third party who occupied the land was not in adverse possession until either the owner abandoned his plans or the stranger did acts which rendered those plans impossible. The first case in the line appears to be *Leigh* v *Jack* (1879) 5 Ex Div 264. However, it was two mid-twentieth-century cases which caused considerable consternation.

In *Williams Brothers Ltd* v *Raftery* [1957] 3 All ER 593 the plaintiffs purchased in 1937 a piece of waste ground at the back of their factory. They hoped to expand their premises onto this ground, but they were prevented from doing so, first by the War, and then by the refusal of planning permission.

In 1940, the defendant came along, saw the waste ground, and started 'to dig for victory', that is he used the ground as a vegetable patch. Having helped to defeat Hitler, he then kept greyhounds on the land, erecting kennels and fencing. In 1957 the plaintiffs suddenly claimed possession of the ground. The defendant claimed he had gained a title to the ground by adverse possession.

A director of the plaintiffs testified that they had always retained their expansion 'plans', and that they had always hoped that the town planners would change their minds. (He did not produce any actual drawings, maps, or diagrams.) The Court of Appeal held that in view of the fact that the 'plans' for the ground had been 'retained' and that the defendant had done nothing to render them impossible, the defendant never had adverse possession of the land.

In *Wallis's Cayton Bay Holiday Camp* v *Shell-Mex* [1974] 3 All ER 575 the defendants acquired one and one-third acres of land in the middle of a field for the purposes of a new filling station. This one and one-third acres adjoined the site of a proposed new road, but neither the road nor the one and one-third acres were marked off by boundary markers. All a passer-by would see (looking from, say, the top of a double-deck bus) was an arable field no different from its neighbours. The remainder of the field belonged to Wallis's, which farmed both it and adjoining fields through a subsidiary company.

For eleven and a half years Wallis's farming activities extended to the one and one-third acres. Then the local authority abandoned the scheme for the new road. Shell promptly wrote to Wallis's offering to sell the one and one-third acres. Wallis's did not reply. (Why they did not reply relates to another point of adverse possession law with which we will deal with at 21.7.) Instead they carried on their farming for eight more months, and then claimed that they had got title through adverse possession.

The Court of Appeal ruled that as Shell had only recently abandoned their plans, there had been only a few months', not 12 years', adverse possession. Shell therefore won.

Lord Denning further confused matters by holding that people like Wallis's and Raftery were 'by a legal fiction' deemed to have had an implied licence to occupy the land. As they were there 'by permission', they could not be **adverse** possessors.

⚐ EXERCISE 21.2

The decisions in *Williams Brothers* and *Wallis's* cases were heavily criticized by many (including myself) as undermining the whole concept (and utility) of adverse possession. Consider why we said that.

The practical result of the *Williams Brothers* and *Wallis's* cases was that whether or not there was adverse possession depended not upon the activities of the alleged adverse possessor, **but upon the state of mind of the original owner.**

21.4.5 *Buckinghamshire County Council v Moran*

The following statutory provision (first enacted in 1980) was designed to overrule the *Williams Brothers* and *Wallis's* line of cases. (Now Sch. 1, para. 8(4) of the consolidating Limitation Act 1980.)

For the purpose of determining whether a person occupying land is in adverse possession of the land it shall not be assumed by implication of law that his occupation is by permission of the person entitled to the land merely by virtue of the fact that his occupation is not inconsistent with the latter's present or future enjoyment of the land.

This is not the clearest of statutory provisions, and it seems to aim only at Lord Denning's 'implied licence' idea. However the Court of Appeal in *Bucks CC v Moran* [1989] 2 All ER 225 held that this provision **did** overrule the broader principle 'recognized' in *Williams Brothers* and *Wallis's*. (This conclusion is now confirmed by the House of Lords decision in *Pye v Graham*, see 21.4.6 below.)

Moran extended his garden onto land which he knew was owned by the County Council; he knew they intended to build a road on it. In giving a judgment holding that Moran was an adverse possessor and that the County Council had lost their title, Slade LJ said:

If in any given case the land in dispute is unbuilt land and the squatter is aware that the owner, while having no present use for it, has a purpose in mind for its use in the future, the court is likely to require very clear evidence before it can be satisfied that the squatter who claims a possessory title has not only established factual possession of the land, but also the requisite intention to exclude the world at large, including the owner with the paper title, so far as is reasonably practicable and so far as the processes of the law will allow.

Thus, in cases where the owner of the original 'paper' title has retained plans for the land, it will be perfectly possible for his title to be destroyed by adverse possession. It will be a question of fact whether, despite the 'paper' owner retaining plans known to the alleged 'squatter', the latter has done sufficient to establish adverse possession.

21.4.6 *J A Pye (Oxford) v Graham*

In this case ([2002] UKHL 30, [2002] 3 WLR 221), the House of Lords approved and applied *Bucks CC v Moran*. The dispute related to a field which originally belonged to Pye, but which Graham had been using for many years for grazing and hay-making. Until 1983, these activities had been carried on by Graham under a licence granted by Pye. At the end of 1983, Pye wanting to develop the land, refused to renew the licence, and told Graham to vacate the field.

Graham did not vacate the field, but continued to use it for grazing and hay-making and similar activities until Pye started proceedings in 1997. Local inhabitants thought that the field belonged to Graham, and that it was part of the farm he owned ('Manor Farm'). The House of Lords held that Graham had acquired title to the land by virtue of adverse possession. He had had both factual possession of the land, and the necessary intent to exclude everyone from the land. Indeed Graham (or rather, his widow) won the case, even though it was clear that if Pye had at any time offered him a new lease or licence over the field, he would have gladly agreed to be a tenant or licensee.

21.5 Adverse possession and tenants

21.5.1 What if an adverse possessor displaces a tenant?

In the discussion so far we have assumed that the adverse possessor has displaced a fee simple owner. What, however, if the land in question has been leased to a tenant, and it is the tenant who is displaced by the adverse possessor? The principles applicable were restated by the House of Lords in *Fairweather* v *St Marylebone Property Co.* [1962] 2 All ER 288. (Note that in that case the lease was actually registered title. However, that fact is irelevant to the current discussion. Their Lordships (back in 1961) were of the view that the same principles applied whether the lease was unregistered or registered title.)

Back in 1893, a landlord (L) owned the fee simple in a house and an adjoining shed. In that year he granted a 99-year lease of the house and shed to T. T left the shed derelict. In 1920 a neighbour (M) took adverse possession of the shed. M and his successor, Fairweather, maintained the adverse possession until the dispute arose in 1959.

In 1959, St Marylebone bought from L the fee simple to the house and shed. By agreement between St Marylebone and T, the 99-year lease was 'surrendered', i.e., terminated by mutual agreement. This of course gave St Marylebone an immediate right to occupy the house. They then sued Fairweather, claiming possession of the shed.

Fairweather argued that because of the adverse possession he had acquired title to the rest of the term of the leasehold estate over the shed; the landlord (he said) could not claim the land until 1992! This neat, logical argument was not accepted by the House of Lords. Why not?

(a) A tenant's right to occupy land leased to him is lost after 12 years' adverse possession against him. Thus from 1932 onwards, T could not claim possession of the shed from M or (later) Fairweather.

(b) Where there has been 12 years' adverse possession it is wrong to say that the adverse possessor acquires the estate of the person he has displaced. Rather the adverse possessor has a completely new title. Thus Fairweather had **not** acquired T's leasehold estate over the shed lasting until 1992.

(c) Instead, Fairweather had a defective title to the land; defective in the sense that in certain circumstances (see (e) below) he could be ousted by the landlord.

(d) Where (under proposition (a) above) the tenant has lost the right to occupy the land to an adverse possessor, the lease is not totally destroyed. It continues to have a **notional existence** between landlord and tenant.

(e) When this 'notional lease' is terminated by agreement between the landlord and tenant, by forfeiture or by the expiry of the originally agreed period, the landlord gains an immediate right to claim possession of the land from the adverse possessor.

(f) The landlord will be 'time-barred' only if he allows 12 years to elapse from the termination of the notional lease without bringing proceedings against the adverse possessor.

In the *St Marylebone* case the plaintiffs sued almost immediately after the termination of the notional lease. Thus Fairweather, who thought he had got the shed until 1992, was evicted some 30 years earlier than he had anticipated.

I hope that you have already realized that anybody who (like Fairweather) maintains adverse possession against a tenant, even for well over 12 years, is going to be in a very insecure position. If the notional lease is terminated in any way, the adverse possessor can expect almost immediate eviction.

 EXERCISE 21.3

Consider the following situation. Suppose in 1984, Lawrence, the owner in fee simple of Dull Shack, leased Dull Shack to Terry for 99 years at a nominal rent. In 1986, Terry became a permanent invalid, and forgot all about his lease of Dull Shack. Lawrence did not bother to collect the nominal rent.

In 1992, Nina, a neighbour, took adverse possession of Dull Shack, using it for general storage purposes. She has continued in adverse possession ever since. Terry has recently remembered his lease of Dull Shack, and he also is informed that Nina is in adverse possession. What can he do to get Dull Shack back? (There are two, alternative answers.)

(a) Terry should approach Lawrence, and suggest the following 'deal'—
   (i) Terry surrenders the lease to Lawrence.
   (ii) Lawrence sues Nina for possession.
   (iii) Having got possession Lawrence grants a fresh lease to Terry.

I would expect Lawrence to charge a price for his co-operation.

(b) An alternative 'deal', which involves less trouble to Lawrence, is as follows:

   (i) Terry buys Lawrence's fee simple in reversion.
   (ii) This (seemingly) brings about a termination of the 'notional lease' by 'merger'. (The same person cannot be both landlord and tenant!)
   (iii) In his new capacity as owner of a fee simple, Terry sues Nina for possession. As this fee simple has not been extinguished by adverse possession, Terry should win.

I call the entering into one or other of these deals, 'Pulling the St Marylebone trick.'

21.5.2 **The problem of a tenant encroaching on adjoining land**

Figure 21.1

Consider the following scenario. In 1988, Leonora leased Centreacre to Thomas for 21 years. In 1990, Thomas moved both the eastern and western fences of Centreacre a few feet so as to encroach upon Westacre and Eastacre. The original fee simple in Westacre belongs to Leonora. The original fee simple in Eastacre belongs to Norman.

The fences have remained in their 1990 position. In effect Thomas has for the last umpteen years maintained adverse possession of two strips of land. Since 2002, no one will have been able to claim those strips from him. But what happens in 2009, when his lease expires?

The principles applicable in this kind of situation were restated in *Smirk* v *Lyndale Developments Ltd* [1975] 1 Ch 317, CA. Where a lessee encroaches upon other land, the encroachment is presumed to be an extension in the 'locus' of the lease. This means that the tenant is presumed merely to be expanding the area granted to him. This is so whether the land encroached upon belongs to a stranger or to the lessee's landlord.

 EXERCISE 21.4

Consider, therefore, what the answer is to our 'Thomas' problem. Remember that there are two separate strips of land to think about.

Applying the law set out in *Smirk* v *Lyndale* to our example of Thomas, the outcome is not favourable to him! When his lease expires in 2009 he will not be able to retain either of the two strips. Leonora will regain the strip Thomas 'pinched' from Westacre. She will also get the strip which Thomas 'pinched' from Norman's Eastacre.

Thomas's only hope of retaining one or both of the strips is if he can rebut the presumption that he is expanding the area of his lease. It seems that to rebut the presumption he would have to show that he was treating the land encroached upon as distinct from the land leased.

Suppose that the lease of Centreacre contained a covenant that Thomas would not keep dogs on the land. Suppose that on the strip 'pinched' from Westacre he has since 1990 kept kennels full of Alsatians, Rottweilers, etc., (or, if you like, Chihuahuas and Pekinese). I think that Thomas will be able to claim that he has a permanent title to the western strip. He will be able to tell Leonora that she cannot have this strip back. His dogs (of whatever breed) will not have to move to a new home!

21.6 Adverse possession where land is held in trust

The following rules apply whether land is held under a strict settlement, under a trust for sale, or under a new-style trust of land.

It is essential to consider the equitable interests under the trust separate from the legal estate:

(a) An equitable interest in possession is time-barred after 12 years' adverse possession of the land.

(b) An equitable interest in remainder or reversion is time-barred after—

(i) 12 years from the adverse possession starting; **or**
(ii) six years from the equitable interest coming into possession, **whichever is later**.

(c) The legal estate is not time-barred until all equitable interests under the trust have been time-barred.

Suppose Mauveacre has since 1988 been held in trust for Anthea for life, remainder to Bertram in fee simple. (It does not matter whether the trust is a strict settlement, a trust for sale, or new-style trust. It does not matter whether the legal title is vested in Anthea as life tenant or in independent trustees.)

Suppose that Squarm took adverse possession of Mauveacre in 1993 and has maintained adverse possession ever since. Anthea died in early 2007:

(a) Anthea's equitable life interest was 'time-barred' back in 2005. See rule (a) above.

(b) Bertram's equitable fee simple will not be time-barred until 2013. See rule (b)(ii) above.

(c) The legal estate (whoever has got it) will also be time-barred in 2013. See rule (c) above.

? **QUESTION** 21.4

Suppose now that Anthea had died in 1998, only five years after adverse possession had commenced.

(a) In what year was Bertram's equitable interest time-barred?
(b) In what year was the legal estate time-barred?

Bertram's equitable interest was time-barred in 2005, applying rule (b)(i). Applying rule (c), the legal estate was also time-barred in 2005.

21.7 Time starts running afresh by acknowledgement of title

If an adverse possessor, with time running in his favour, acknowledges the original owner's title, time stops running in his favour. A new 12-year period starts from the date of the acknowledgement of title.

By 'acknowledgement of title' is meant any direct or indirect recognition by the adverse possessor of the original owner's title, provided it is in writing and signed by the adverse possessor and addressed to the original owner.

In *Edginton* v *Clark* [1963] 3 All ER 468, the adverse possessor wrote to the original owner of the land offering to buy. The adverse possessor was held to have acknowledged title.

21.7.1 Acknowledgement of title made by person in whose favour time has already run is of no effect

Suppose that in 1994, Squirt took adverse possession of Greenacre, the original owner of which was Oswald. Squirt has maintained adverse possession ever since. In 2007, Oswald writes to Squirt offering to 'sell' Greenacre. Squirt immediately writes back, 'Dear Oswald, I am interested in buying Greenacre from you, I will go and see my solicitor'. What will the solicitor advise?

Squirt's solicitor will advise him that Oswald's title was time-barred in 2006. What about the letter? Fortunately for Squirt, it was sent too late!

Squirt's position must be contrasted with that of the defendant 'Tillson' in *Colchester Borough v Smith* [1992] 2 All ER 561. Tillson had been (apparently) in adverse possession of the plaintiff's land for well over 12 years. Despite that fact, the plaintiff began proceedings for possession against him. These **earlier** proceedings were **compromised** on the terms:

(a) that Tillson accepted that the plaintiff still owned the land;

(b) that the plaintiff granted Tillson a lease of the land.

In **later** proceedings for possession brought on the expiry of the lease, Tillson claimed that he had a freehold title by virtue of adverse possession. The Court of Appeal ruled that Tillson was bound by the earlier compromise and therefore was estopped from disputing the plaintiff's title to the freehold.

21.7.2 Nature of title acquired under Limitation Acts where title adversely possessed against is unregistered

When time runs out there is not an automatic 'statutory conveyance' of the original owner's title to the adverse possessor. In the Squirt-Oswald example in **Question 21.5**, Oswald's fee simple in Greenacre was destroyed in 2006. Squirt has a completely new fee simple based on his long possession of Greenacre.

An adverse possessor does, however, take 'his' land subject to third party rights such as easements, profits, and restrictive covenants. This was made clear in *Re Nisbet and Potts' Contract* [1906] 1 Ch 386, which also held that an adverse possessor was not a 'purchaser' for the purposes of the doctrine of notice. Neither will an adverse possessor be a purchaser for the purposes of modern legislation such as the Land Charges Acts.

21.8 Adverse possession where the title possessed against is registered land—the position under the Land Registration Act 1925

It will be best to begin with three preliminary comments. First, you may well be surprised that the law relating to adverse possession applies where the land is registered land. Many foreign lawyers familiar with continental systems of land registration would share your surprise. The very fact that adverse possession applies to registered land undermines the efficiency and accuracy of our system of land registration. Moreover, it appears that the rules regarding adverse possession in the Land Registration Act 1925 infringe Article 1 of the First Protocol to the European Commission on Human Rights. (*Pye* v *United Kingdom* The Times, 21 November 2005.)

Secondly, it is only in the last 35 years or so that there have been (outside London) large numbers of registered titles. This probably explains why there is very little case law on the impact of adverse possession on a registered title.

Thirdly, the Land Registration Act 2002 does NOT abolish adverse possession against registered titles. But it does introduce a radically different new set of rules which seemingly are compliant with the European Convention on Human Rights. These rules will be discussed in section 21.10. However, for the foreseeable future it will be necessary to know the basic principles of the 'old' 1925 Act rules.

21.8.1 The three crucial points when considering adverse possession against a registered title under the LRA 1925

21.8.1.1 Section 75(1) of the Land Registration Act 1925

This provided:

> The Limitation Acts shall apply to registered land in the same manner and to the same extent as those Acts apply to land not registered, except that where, if the land were not registered, the estate of the person registered as proprietor would be extinguished, such estate shall not be extinguished but shall be deemed to be held by the proprietor for the time being in trust for the person who, by virtue of the said Acts, has acquired title against any proprietor . . .

Dopey was the original owner in fee simple of Greyacre. In 1990 Squall took adverse possession and has maintained it ever since. Now if Dopey's fee simple in Greyacre was unregistered, that fee simple would have been destroyed in 2002. Squall gets a new fee simple based on his long possession.

?   **QUESTION** 21.6

What if (ever since he acquired the land in 1990) Dopey was registered proprietor of Greyacre?

Applying s. 75(1), if Dopey was registered proprietor in fee simple of Greyacre, his fee simple was not destroyed in 2002. Rather he held that fee simple under a 'bare trust' in trust for Squall, who had a new equitable fee simple.

21.8.1.2 Section 70(1)(f) of the Land Registration Act 1925

This provision made the rights of an adverse possessor an overriding interest. Therefore Squall's equitable fee simple would automatically bind a purchaser of Dopey's legal title. I do not think the purchaser would have been too happy!

21.8.1.3 **Rectification of the register**

Although s. 70(1)(f) of the Act gave him considerable security, an adverse possessor in whose favour time had already run could apply for rectification of the register. Provided there was sufficient proof of the adverse possession, the Registrar had to rectify the register. This rectification in effect transferred the legal fee simple from the original owner (Dopey) to the adverse possessor (Squall). The original owner (Dopey) was not compensated in any way.

21.9 **Adverse possession against the registered proprietor of a lease (old pre-2003 rules)**

This was a tricky area of law. The Land Registration Act 2002 has effectively solved the problems. Briefly, the position under the pre-2003 law if a 'squatter' maintained adverse possession against a registered lease for more than 12 years was as follows.

(a) The original registered lessee held the lease held in trust for the squatter.

(b) The squatter had the right to apply for the register to be rectified in his favour so that he became the registered lessee.

(c) Once the register was rectified the original lessee had no rights whatsoever in the land. Therefore. once the register was rectified, the original lessee could not defeat the (former) squatter's claim by 'pulling the St Marylebone trick' (i.e., entering into one of the 'deals' suggested at the end of 21.5.1). See the decision of Browne-Wilkinson J in *Spectrum Investments* v *Holmes* [1981] 1 All ER 6.

21.10 **Adverse possession under the Land Registration Act 2002**

As already hinted, the LRA 2002 completely revolutionizes the way adverse possession operates where adverse possession is taken against a registered estate. As from the commencement date of the new Act, s. 75 of the 1925 Act, the strange trust which arises under that section, and the s. 70(1)(f) overriding interest are all swept away. They are replaced by a (very different) new set of rules which, as we shall see, considerably strengthen the position of registered proprietors who find that some or all of their land has been adversely possessed. However, before looking at these new 'permanent' rules, some important 'transitional' rules must be considered.

21.10.1 **Adverse possessors who have already been 'squatting' for more than 12 years on 13 October 2003**

First remember that most adverse possessions are not spectacular cases like *Bucks CC* v *Moran* or *Pye* v *Graham* but rather are cases where one neighbour has encroached upon another neighbour's land. Such encroachments may go on for generations before the original (or current) registered proprietor of the strip encroached upon realizes that he may have 'lost' a piece of land which the register says belongs to him.

There can be no doubt that on 13 October 2003 (the commencement of the LRA 2002) there were many (perhaps thousands) of cases where an adverse possessor had already had **at least** 12 years' adverse possession against a registered proprietor—quite possibly a lot longer. In these cases, the following happened as the clock struck midnight on 13 October 2003 (see Sch. 12, para. 18):

(a) The trust which existed under LRA 1925, s. 75 disappeared.

(b) The adverse possessor therefore lost his interest under the now non-existent trust.

(c) The adverse possessor did NOT have an overriding interest under s. 70(1)(f). (That provision is repealed.)

HOWEVER:

(d) The adverse possessor is able to apply for the register to be rectified so as to make him the owner of the estate against which he has 'squatted'. The registered proprietor **will have no defence to this application**. (Contrast the discussion in 21.10.2.1.)

(e) This right to have the register rectified is a property right against the relevant registered estate. It is not automatically an overriding interest, but will normally be converted into an overriding interest by virtue of 'actual occupation' under Sch. 3, para. 2.

 EXERCISE 21.5

John became registered freehold proprietor of Yellow House in 1980. Keith became registered freehold proprietor of neighbouring Brown House in 1985.

Between the gardens of the two houses there is Grey Strip, about a metre wide. The Land Registry has Grey Strip registered as part of Yellow House. However in 1987, Keith erected a fence so that Grey Strip became part of the Brown House garden. Keith has cultivated Grey Strip ever since.

In 2007 John sells Yellow House to Laura. Laura, having looked closely at the Land Registry plan, claims that Grey Strip is hers, and sues to evict Keith. Keith counterclaims for rectification of the register. What will the court decide?

Keith should win the case. The legal analysis is as follows:

(a) From 1999 to 12 October 2003 LRA 1925, s. 75 applied. John held Grey Strip in trust for Keith.

(b) On 13 October 2003, Keith lost his equitable interest under the trust, but still retained a 'property right' to have the register rectified.

(c) That property right will be an overriding interest under Sch. 3, para. 2 binding on a purchaser such as Laura.

(d) Laura's claim to evict Keith will therefore fail, and Keith will have the register rectified so that Grey strip is now part of Brown House.

21.10.2 The new fundamental (post-2003) principle regarding adverse possession—the almost sacrosanct title of the registered proprietor

This new principle is that a registered proprietor cannot lose his estate to an adverse possessor, even if that adverse possession has lasted a very long time, say 50 years. (See LRA 2002, ss. 96–98 and Sch. 6.)

However, this principle that the registered title is sacrosanct from 'squatters' is subject to a number of exceptions, only two of which are significant. I will call these two exceptions:

(a) the Two Years' Inaction after Application exception;

(b) the Reasonably Believing Encroacher exception.

21.10.2.1 Two years inaction after application—the application stage

A fuller title for this exception would be 'Two years' inaction by the registered proprietor after application to be registered by the Adverse Possessor'. I will begin what is going to be a long discussion by quoting Sch. 6, para. 1(1) of the LRA 2002, a provision which, **at first sight**, appears to totally contradict my previous statement that 'a registered proprietor cannot lose his estate to an adverse possessor, even if that adverse possession has lasted a very long time, say fifty years'.

Paragraph 1(1) reads:

A person may apply to the registrar to be registered as the proprietor of a registered estate in land if he has been in adverse possession of the estate for the period of ten years ending on the date of the application.

This appears to be saying, '**Ten** years adverse possession and the adverse possessor wins ownership by simply asking the registry to change the register!' However, careful reading of the rest of Sch. 6 shows that this conclusion would be totally wrong. Paragraph 2 requires that notice of the application be given to the registered proprietor, and para. 5 (crucially) in effect provides that if the registered proprietor objects then **the application must automatically be rejected**. (For the moment, we can ignore the reasonably believing encroacher exception.)

 EXERCISE 21.6

In 1995, Bloggshire County Council became registered proprietor of a strip of land on which it intended to build a new road. It left the land derelict. In 1996, Moron, whose garden backed on to the strip, incorporated the strip into his garden. Like Moran in the real case of *Bucks CC v Moran*, Moron knew that the land belonged to the council.

In 2010, somebody tells Moron about Sch. 6, para. 1, so he applies to be registered as proprietor. What happens next?

(a) The registry gives notice to the council of Moron's application.

(b) The council will of course object.

(c) The registry must therefore reject the application.

But as we shall see in the next section, this is not necessarily the end of the story.

(If, through some oversight, the council—or any other registered proprietor—were not to object to the application under para. 1(1), the application by the adverse possessor would be granted; i.e., the (former) registered proprietor would lose ownership immediately, and what I say in the following sections would be irrelevant. However, I would imagine that almost all para. 1 applications will meet with objection from the registered proprietor.)

21.10.2.2 The two years to do something stage

Once an adverse possessor's application under Sch. 6, para. 1 has been rejected, the registered proprietor cannot just sit and do nothing saying to himself, 'the register gives me permanent protection from losing my land to the adverse possessor'. An idle registered proprietor will eventually be caught out by paras. 6 and 7 of Sch. 6.

Paragraph 6(1) provides 'Where a person's application under paragraph 1 is rejected, he may make a further application to be registered as the proprietor of the estate if he is in adverse possession of the estate from the date of the application until the last day of the period of two years beginning with the date of its rejection'.

Paragraph 7 then bluntly states, 'If a person makes an application under para. 6, he is entitled to be entered into the register as the new proprietor of the estate'.

What this means for the **adverse possessor** is that if, after having his first application rejected, he remains in adverse possession for a further two years, he can make a second application to be registered as owner—and this time **his application must succeed**.

What this means for the **original registered proprietor** is that he has two years in which to do something about the adverse possessor. In practical terms the proprietor will have two choices, either:

(a) take eviction proceedings against the adverse possessor or

(b) make an agreement with the adverse possessor that he can continue to occupy the land as a lessee.

? QUESTION 21.7

Facts as in Exercise 21.6. The Land Registry have just rejected Moron's application under Sch. 6, para. 1. What should Bloggshire County Council do next?

It should sue Moron for possession of the strip. However, it could offer to compromise the proceedings by granting him a periodic tenancy (say a monthly tenancy) of the strip. In that way Moron can keep the land until the planned road is actually built.

21.10.2.3 Summary of two years' inaction after application

The adverse possessor will gain title if all six of the following steps are completed:

1 The adverse possessor has at least ten year's adverse possession of the land;

2 The adverse possessor applies under para. 1 of Sch. 6 to be registered as proprietor;

3 The registered proprietor is given notice of the application;

4 The registered proprietor objects to the application, and it is therefore rejected;

5 The adverse possessor remains in adverse possession for a further two years;

6 The adverse possessor then makes a second application under para. 6.

(Exceptionally, if the registered proprietor does not object to the para. 1 application, the adverse possessor will gain title after step 3.)

21.10.3 **The reasonably believing encroacher exception**

This exception to the general rule that a registered title is sacrosanct as against an adverse possessor will be invoked (if it all) at step 4 in the analysis in 21.10.2.3. The 'Reasonably Believing Encroacher' rule is the one significant exception to the rule that if a registered proprietor objects to a para. 1 application, that application must be rejected. Indeed, if the adverse possessor proves (if need be to the Land Registry Adjudicator) that he is a 'Reasonably Believing Encroacher' he will 'win' the land, and the register will be immediately rectified in his favour.

The 'Reasonably Believing Encroacher' rule is to be found in sub-para. 4 of para. 1. If the adverse possessor can prove:

(a) the land to which the [para. 1] application relates is adjacent to land belonging to the applicant; and

(b) for at least ten years of the period of adverse possession ending on the date of the application, the applicant (or any predecessor in title) reasonably believed that the land to which the application relates belonged to him;

then the adverse possessor wins.

So land which he reasonably thought was his (but was not) actually becomes his!

The explanation for including this strange 'Reasonably Believing Encroacher' rule in the LRA 2002 lies in something I mentioned back in 9.9.1. There, I stated:

Another feature of English land registration strange to foreign eyes is that our system does not fix the exact boundaries of each plot. The Land Registry like to boast that their plans are **in fact** accurate to within a few inches. No doubt they usually are, but in *Lee* v *Barrey* [1957] Ch 251, there was a discrepancy of eight feet (2.5 m) between the plan and the actual boundary on the ground!

In other words, the lines on the registry's plans are only approximately correct. It follows that those plans will **not** be conclusive if a boundary dispute arises between neighbours. Moreover, it seems implicit in the LRA 2002 that a landowner might **reasonably** think that a boundary is in a different place from that marked on the registry's plans.

How then does this 'Reasonably Believing Encroacher' exception actually work?

EXERCISE 21.7

Mary became registered freehold proprietor of Red House in 2000. Norma became registered freehold proprietor of neighbouring Pink House in 2003.

Between the gardens of the two houses there is Grey Sliver, a strip about a metre wide. The Land Registry has Grey Sliver registered as part of Red House. However in 2004, Norma erects a fence so that Grey Sliver becomes part of the Pink House garden. Norma cultivates Grey Sliver as part of her garden.

In 2025 Mary sells Red House to Oliver. Oliver, having looked closely at the Land Registry plan, claims that Grey Sliver is his, and threatens Norma with proceedings to evict her from Grey Sliver. Norma applies under Sch. 6, para. 1, and when Oliver objects to her application, Norma invokes the 'Reasonably Believing Encroacher' exception. What will the Land Registry Adjudicator decide?

I am sure that he will reject Norma's claim. It was Norma who put up the fence thus 'annexing' Grey Sliver. I cannot see how she could say 'I reasonably believed this Grey Sliver strip was mine'.

 EXERCISE 21.8

Same facts as in Exercise 21.7, except that Norma sells Pink House to Queenie in 2010. Queenie, like most house purchasers, does not have a detailed survey of the property done for her. Neither she nor her solicitor compare the Land Registry plan with the situation 'on the ground'. (Even if they had, they may well have not spotted the discrepancy.) For 15 years Queenie cultivates her garden never realizing that a dispute might arise regarding the ownership of one of the edges of that garden. Then in 2025, Oliver buys Red House, and starts making threatening noises regarding the land he calls 'Grey Sliver'. Queenie applies under Sch. 6, para. 1, and when Oliver objects to her application, Queenie invokes the 'Reasonably Believing Encroacher' exception. What will the Land Registry Adjudicator decide?

I **think** that the Adjudicator will rule in Queenie's favour, and correct the register so that Grey Sliver appears as part of Pink House. But I am not 100 per cent sure. I can just hear Oliver's lawyer arguing, 'A reasonable woman would (in 2010) have had the garden measured up by a surveyor'.

I suspect that the 'Reasonably Believing Encroacher' exception will be productive of many (perhaps nasty) inter-neighbour disputes.

21.10.4 Adverse possession against a lease under the LRA 2002

It is clear from the wording of the legislation that where adverse possession is taken against a leasehold estate, any applications by the adverse possessor for registration under Sch. 6, paras. 1 and 6 will be with respect to that leasehold estate, not the freehold. So any estate acquired by an adverse possessor, whether under the 'Two Years' Inaction after Application' exception or under the 'Reasonably Believing Encroacher' exception, will be the lease, not the freehold. This will have the drawback for the (former) adverse possessor that he becomes subject to the covenants in the lease.

EXERCISE 21.9

In January 2000 Leonora leased Black House to Tamsin for 25 years. In January 2012 Squidge takes adverse possession of Black House. In February 2022, Squidge applies under Sch. 6, para. 1, but Tamsin objects, so his application is rejected. Nevertheless Tamsin makes absolutely no effort to evict Squidge. It is now late 2024. Is there any point in Squidge now making an application under Sch. 6, para. 6?

Not really. By the time the application has been processed, the lease will have expired.

CONCLUDING REMARKS

I hope you now see why at the beginning of this chapter I indicated that adverse possession is basically a simple concept which has always brought with it complex ramifications. The Land Registration Act 2002 has added to the complications. This chapter is now several pages longer than it otherwise would have been.

Should the concept of Adverse Possession simply be abolished? Many non-lawyers consider that Adverse Possession is absurd. 'It's legalized theft.' (Actually, land cannot be stolen.) What arguments are there in defence of the concept of Adverse Possession? As I have previously stated, the concept is essential to the proper operation of **unregistered** title. By destroying stale claims to ownership, the concept ensures that the person who (together with his predecessors in title) has been in control of unregistered land for a lengthy period is indeed the owner.

This argument cannot be applied to **registered** land. The only arguments which can justify applying adverse possession to registered land are socio-economic, and rather controversial. I would argue that land is a scarce commodity, and 'people' like Mrs Treloar, Williams Brothers Ltd, and Buckinghamshire County Council should not allow land to lie derelict. By contrast, people like Messrs, Nute (father and son), Raftery, Moran, and even Graham should be rewarded for their efforts.

The Land Registration Act 2002, by strengthening the position of the registered proprietor as against the adverse possessor, has largely rejected the socio-economic arguments in favour of the concept of adverse possession. However the 'Two Years' Inaction after Application' exception in effect allows the socio-economic arguments to prevail in favour of the adverse possessor where the registered proprietor, having received a clear warning of the adverse possessor's claim, cannot be bothered to take action against the adverse possessor.

■ **SUMMARY**

Adverse possession defined

There is adverse possession where somebody (the 'squatter')

(a) takes control of the land;

(B) with intent to exclude everyone else from the land;

(c) the squatter's claim to the land is inconsistent with ('adverse to') the title of the original owner.

Adverse possession against an unregistered freehold title

Once the adverse possession has lasted twelve years, the 'squatter' gains a new title based on long posses-sion and the title of the original freehold owner **is destroyed**.

Adverse possession against an unregistered leasehold title

Once the adverse possession has lasted twelve years, the squatter cannot be evicted by the lessee. But the lease remains valid between the lessee and the lessor, and time does not start to run against the lessor until this 'notional' lease has expired.

Adverse possession against a registered proprietor where the twelve years expired before 13 October 2003

The legal title remains with the registered proprietor, but the 'squatter' has a right to have the register rectified in his favour. This right to rectification is a property right, and (if Sch. 3, para. 2 is satisfied) it will be an overriding interest binding on a purchaser of the registered estate.

Adverse possession under the Land Registration Act 2002

No matter how long the adverse possession lasts, the squatter does not gain a property right against the registered estate.

After the 'squatter' (S) has been in possession for **ten** years, he can **apply** to be registered as proprietor. Notice is given to the current owner (C). If C does not object, S will be registered as owner in place of C.

If C does object, then subject to the 'Reasonably Believing Encroacher' exception, S's application must be rejected. If S's first application is rejected, then C has 2 years within which to evict S (or grant him some form of lease). If C does not act within two years, S can re-apply to be registered as proprietor, and this second application must be granted.

Reasonably believing encroacher

S will succeed in his first application, despite C's objections, if he can show:

 (i) S owns land adjacent to that in dispute; and
(ii) for at least ten years S reasonably believed the land in dispute was his.

 CHAPTER 21: ASSESSMENT EXERCISE

Edwina holds a freehold title to Redacre. She uses most of Redacre for her business as a scrap merchant. However she left vacant part of Redacre; this part is called the 'Grey Land'.

In 1987 Freda, the owner of nearby Blue House, started to cultivate Grey Land as an ornamental garden. Freda admits that, 'I have known all along that Grey Land belongs to Edwina'. Indeed in 2002 Freda wrote to Edwina offering to buy Grey Land. (Edwina did not reply to this letter.)

Advise Freda as to the legal position with respect to Grey Land:

(a) on the assumption that Edwina's title to the land is unregistered;
(b) on the assumption that Edwina has been registered proprietor of Redacre (including Grey Land) since 1970.

On the assumption that Edwina has been the registered proprietor since 1970, would your advice be different if Edwina had not started to cultivate the Grey Land until 1995, but had never written to Edwina offering to buy the land?

See Appendix for a specimen answer.

■ FURTHER READING

For an extended discussion of adverse possession (but not dealing with the Land Registration Act 2002), see *Megarry and Wade: Law of Real Property* (sixth edition by Charles Harpum) chapter 21.

For an even more detailed discussion, which does include the Land Registration Act 2002, see Gray and Gray, *Elements of Land Law* fourth edition, chapter six, pages 365–425.

For the thinking behind the provisions in the Land Registration Act 2002 regarding adverse possession, see Law Commission report no. 271, part XIV.

For a critical analysis of the provisions in the Land Registration Act 2002 regarding adverse possession, see Elizabeth Cooke, *The New Law of Land Registration* chapter seven.

22 Rectification of the register of title

22.1 Objectives

By the end of this chapter you should:

1 Be familiar with the situation where rectification of the register of title is likely to be claimed

2 Be able to explain the very limited circumstances in which rectification can be obtained against a registered proprietor in possession

3 Be able to advise on the circumstances in which a registered proprietor against whom rectification is ordered can be awarded compensation ('indemnity') from Land Registry funds

4 Be able to identify the circumstances in which a claimant for rectification who is refused rectification can be awarded compensation ('indemnity')

22.2 Introduction

Rectification of the register is a short but not unimportant topic. It is natural to deal with it immediately after adverse possession. As I indicated in the previous chapter, if somebody maintained adverse possession against a registered proprietor for the requisite period, usually under pre-2003 Law 12 years, he could apply to have the register rectified. On the register being rectified, the original owner ceased to have a legal title and the (former) adverse possessor acquired a legal title. Under post-2003 law, adverse possessors will still be able to obtain (in effect) rectification of the register **in certain circumstances** under Sch. 6 of the Land Registration Act 2002.

Rectification of the register is not, however, confined to adverse possession situations. The Land Registry is nowadays an enormous organization, so the occasional error is bound to occur. Moreover cases where crooks and fraudsters have got themselves registered as owners of land to which they are not entitled are not unknown.

Rectification of the register in situations other than adverse possession is now governed by the Land Registration Act 2002, Sch. 4. This schedule is not intended to change the substantive law on rectification, and reference to old pre-2003 cases will still therefore be very helpful. Schedule 4 does however clarify the terminology we should use when discussing making changes to the register.

Schedule 4 distinguishes between 'alteration' and 'rectification'. 'Alteration' is very broad in meaning, and covers every change made to the register whatever the circumstances. The concept 'rectification' is confined, by Sch. 4, para. 1, to an alteration 'which prejudicially affects the title of a registered proprietor'. I.e., a situation where an 'owner' loses land even though it is registered in his name.

22.3 The situations where rectification of the register may be appropriate

Put crudely, rectification of the register (by order of the court or of the registry) will be appropriate whenever a mistake has occurred which has resulted in somebody being registered as an owner when he should not really be entitled to the land. Experience indicates that these 'mistakes' usually fall into one of three categories:

(a) double conveyancing;

(b) some other mess-up which has resulted in the wrong person being registered as owner;

(c) fraud and/or forgery.

22.3.1 'Double conveyancing'

'Double conveyancing' occurs where somebody owns a piece of land, conveys that land to one person, and then later purports to convey **the same land** to somebody else.

? QUESTION 22.1

Consider the following example of 'double conveyancing' on the assumption that all the titles involved are unregistered. X owned the freehold to Greenfield; Greenfield included a small area known as Greypatch.

In 1980, X sold Greypatch to Y; the legal estate to Greypatch was conveyed to Y. It would be the normal practice for Y to ensure that the fact of the sale of Greypatch was endorsed upon the title deeds to Greenfield. Y (perhaps he was a 'do-it-yourself conveyancer') failed to do so. In 1987, X (purportedly) conveyed the whole of Greenfield, including Greypatch, to Z. Who owns Greypatch?

The answer is (of course) Y. X, having given up ownership of Greypatch to Y, cannot convey it to Z. What if compulsory registration intervenes between the two conveyances?

? QUESTION 22.2

Change (slightly) the facts of Question 22.1. Suppose in 1985 the district in which Greenfield is situated became an area of compulsory registration of title, and in 1987 Z applied for registration as proprietor of the whole of Greenfield. Z presented to the registry a perfect set of title deeds for the whole of Greenfield. What would the registry do?

The registry would of course grant Z an absolute title to Greenfield, including Greypatch. Z will therefore become legal owner of Greypatch. Y will lose his title to Greypatch, but is likely to seek rectification.

22.3.2 Other (possibly negligent) mess-ups

The facts of *Re 139 Deptford High Street*, [1951] 1 ChD 950 are instructive, even though, for reasons which will emerge later, the case would be decided differently today. Prior to 1948, No. 139 was unregistered title. In 1948, V sold No. 139 to P. The conveyance, which had no plan attached, described the land as 'all that shop and dwelling house situate and known as 139, High Street, Deptford in the County of London'. P applied for first registration.

It appears that V, P, their respective legal advisers, and the Land Registry all (reasonably) thought that No. 139 included a small piece of disused land at the back next to the railway. P was registered as proprietor of the dwelling house/shop **and the land at the back**. In fact this land really 'belonged to' British Railways. The registration thus deprived the railway of that small piece of land. When the railway found out, it sought and obtained rectification of the register on the basis that P (albeit innocently) had caused the error at the registry by submitting inaccurate documents.

22.3.3 Registration obtained through fraud and/or forgery

This is illustrated, firstly, by a story which happened at about the time of the First World War.

About the time of the First World War there was a notorious criminal at work in London. He operated in the following way:

(a) He would find a wealthy spinster who owned her own house.

(b) He would marry her.

(c) He would forge a conveyance or land transfer of her house in his favour.

(d) On the strength of the forgery, he got himself registered as proprietor of the house.

(e) He would murder the lady by drowning her in the bath.

And so on . . .

When he was caught, the personal representatives of the unfortunate ladies sought and obtained rectification of the register against the crook.

A second, very modern illustration are certain facts of a case which I discussed in **Chapter 10**, *Malory* v *Cheshire Homes* [2002] 3 WLR 1. You may recall that the case involved a derelict piece of land which had belonged to the claimants, 'Malory Enterprises (BVI)'. How Cheshire Homes (the well-known charity for the severely disabled) came to be registered proprietors of the derelict land is explained in para. 5 of the judgment.

In 1996 a company was dishonestly set up in the United Kingdom with the name Malory Enterprises Ltd ('Malory UK'). By deception this company obtained from [the] Land Registry a new land certificate in which the name of the proprietor was stated to be 'Malory Enterprises Ltd' of a new address. It then sold and executed a transfer of the [disputed] rear land to Cheshire, which was then registered as proprietor . . .

In effect Malory UK had impersonated Malory BVI, and fooled both the registry and Cheshire Homes. When Malory BVI discovered the fraud, they sought and obtained rectification of the register. (As we saw in **Chapter 10**, its claim to the derelict land was held to be an overriding interest by virtue of the fact that Malory BVI was still in actual occupation at the time of the 'transfer' to Cheshire.)

22.3.4 Rectification against a registered proprietor in possession

In the various situations like those discussed in 22.3.1 to 22.3.3 above, the parties who 'have lost their land' will claim rectification of the register, if need be, by litigation.

However, if a claim for rectification is brought against a registered proprietor who is in possession of the disputed land (and most defendants to a rectification claim will be in possession) then the claim is subject to restrictions now set out in Sch. 4, para. 6(2) of the 2002 Act. This provision states:

No alteration [rectification]of a registered estate in land may be made . . . without the proprietor's consent in relation to land in his possession unless—

(a) he has by fraud or lack of proper care caused or substantially contributed to the mistake, or

(b) it would for any other reason be unjust for the alteration [rectification] not to be made.

This provision, which reflects s. 82(3) of the Land Registration Act 1925 as amended in 1977, puts a registered proprietor in possession in a strong position. He can only lose the land registered in his name if:

(a) he was fraudulent; or

(b) he was negligent; or

(c) it is for some other reason unjust not to rectify the register.

22.3.4.1 Rectification against a fraudulent proprietor in possession

The murderer-cum-fraudster in the 'Brides-in-the-Bath' case in 22.3.3 would clearly (even in modern law) have no defence to a claim for rectification.

22.3.4.2 Rectification against a negligent proprietor in possession

 EXERCISE 22.1

What if a case like *Re 139 High Street, Deptford*, discussed in 23.3.2, were to occur today; would rectification be granted?

Rectification of the register would be refused. A registered proprietor in possession who had obtained registration by putting forward inaccurate document(s) would now be caught under Sch. 4, para. 6(2) only if either:

(a) he knew that the document(s) were inaccurate (that would be a case of fraud); or

(b) he ought to have known that the documents were inaccurate (that would be a case of 'lack of proper care').

22.3.4.3 **Rectification where it would be unjust not to rectify**

Three points should be made about the provision which is now Sch. 4, para. 6(2), formerly s. 82(3)(c) of the Land Registration Act 1925.

(a) It is clear from its context and wording (particularly the use of a double negative) that this provision should be used only in a case where it is absolutely clear that justice demands that the register be rectified.

(b) This provision (in substance) dates back to 1925. It was not changed in 1977.

(c) There has been only one case of real significance involving s. 82(3)(c) (*Epps* v *Esso* [1973] 2 All ER 465). In that case, Templeman J, applying the no-nonsense approach for which he (as Lord Templeman) became famous, refused rectification. The approach adopted by Templeman J in *Epps* is very much in line with the approach adopted by Parliament both in 1977 and 2002.

The figure below illustrates the area of land involved in *Epps* v *Esso*.

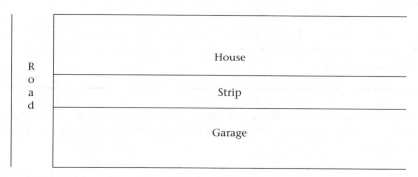

Figure 22.1 The land in dispute in *Epps* v *Esso.*

From **1935 to 1955**, C had owned the whole of the relevant area, situated in Gillingham, Kent.

In **1955**, C's personal representatives conveyed the house **and strip** to Edna Jones. She covenanted to erect a wall between the strip and the garage, but failed to do so. The existing fence between strip and house remained *in situ*. The strip therefore appeared to 'belong to' the garage.

In **1957** Gillingham became an area of compulsory registration.

In **1959**, C's personal representatives conveyed the garage and strip to Ball. Ball applied for first registration, and was registered as proprietor of both garage and strip. There was thus a 'double conveyancing' situation (see 22.3.1). But as Ball, the second purchaser, had become registered proprietor of the strip, he had legal title, and not the first purchaser, Edna Jones. (This is the same as Greypatch in **Question 22.2.**)

Since **1959** the strip has been in use as part of the garage. In **1964**, Ball sold the garage including the strip, to Esso; Esso became registered proprietor.

In **1968** Edna Jones's personal representatives sold the house **and purported to sell the strip** to Epps, but the Land Registry refused to register him as proprietor of the strip. He applied for rectification. Epps's only hope lay in s. 82(3)(c).

Templeman J regarded as totally irrelevant the following two arguments:

(a) Epps was a 'little man' claiming rectification against a huge organization. A strip 11 feet by 80 feet was a lot of land for Epps; to a multinational like Esso it was tiny.

(b) That the rules governing the grant of 'indemnity' (i.e., compensation) were much more generous to Esso than to Epps. If rectification had been granted against Esso, it would have got full compensation at a 1973 valuation. If rectification was refused, Epps would seemingly have got no compensation. (See 22.4.2.)

Templeman J was of the view that, 'Justice in the present case lies wholly with the defendants'. He applied what I call 'a comparative conveyancing care' approach. When Esso purchased the garage, both the register and the physical layout of the site indicated that the strip was part of the garage. When Epps purchased the house the title deeds said that the strip was part of the house. But the fact that no brick wall had been erected, and the physical appearance of the site, should have warned him that there was a problem. He should have raised the question of the boundaries with Esso before going ahead with his purchase. Templeman J summarized the situation by saying: 'Whereas the defendants bought the disputed strip, the plaintiffs bought a law suit'.

 EXERCISE 22.2

Consider again the sad situation of the Brides-in-the-Bath murderer/fraudster. Suppose the crook had sold one of the houses to a purchaser, who had moved in. Could the register be rectified, under modern law, against such a purchaser?

I would submit that the personal representatives would succeed in getting rectification only if they could show that the purchaser knew or ought to have known that the crook had gained title by criminal activities.

22.4 Indemnity

22.4.1 Indemnity for a registered proprietor where rectification is granted

This topic was previously governed by s. 83 of the Land Registration Act 1925, and is now governed by Sch. 8 of the 2002 Act.

In practice, rectifications of the register are not that common, and that is something which everyone concerned thinks should remain the case. As Templeman J pointed out in *Epps* v *Esso*, the whole purpose of land registration is to guarantee titles by making them secure.

In those cases where rectification is ordered, Sch. 8 of the LRA 2002 operates. **Prima facie**, a registered proprietor against whom rectification is granted is entitled to indemnity, i.e., compensation. He will get the value of the estate or interest he loses, valued as at the date of rectification. (See para. 6(a).)

A registered proprietor rectified against will, however, get no indemnity whatsoever if the rectification is to give effect to an overriding interest (*Re Chowood* [1933] Ch 574). This is clearly logical. A proprietor is in any event bound by an overriding interest. He thus loses nothing when the register is rectified against him. In *Re Chowood*, an adverse possessor had gained title to part of a piece of land of which Chowood Ltd was registered proprietor. The adverse possessor obtained rectification of the register. Chowood Ltd was held not to be entitled to any indemnity. The adverse possessor had an overriding interest under the Land Registration Act 1925, s. 70(1)(f), and Chowood lost nothing as a result of the rectification.

A registered proprietor rectified against will also get no indemnity whatsoever if he falls foul of what is now Sch. 8, para. 5(1):

No indemnity is payable under this Schedule on account of any loss suffered by a claimant—

(a) wholly or partly as a result of his own fraud; or

(b) wholly as a result of his own lack of proper care.

What then if the error which led to the rectification was partly as a result of a lack of proper care by the registered proprietor and partly the fault of someone else (perhaps the registry)? This is covered by para. 5(2):

Where any loss is suffered by a claimant partly as a result of his own lack of proper care, any indemnity payable to him is to be reduced to such extent as is fair having regard to his share in the responsibility for the loss.

There is here an analogy with the law of tort. Prior to 1945, a victim of (say) a road accident partly caused by the defendant's negligence but himself partly to blame, could not recover **any** damages. The Law Reform (Contributory Negligence) Act 1945 allows the court to award such a victim an appropriate percentage of the damages he could have recovered if he had been innocent of all blame.

22.4.2 Indemnity for a person who is refused rectification

Schedule 8, para. 1(b) of the 2002 Act, replacing s. 83(2) of the 1925 Act, is designed to provide for the payment of indemnity where the restrictive provisions regarding rectification against a proprietor in possession lead to rectification being refused despite some error in the registry. This form of indemnity is supposed to protect somebody like *Epps* (see 22.3.4.3). However, as Templeman J realized in *Epps* v *Esso*, there were two drawbacks for Mr Epps, or anybody in a similar situation:

(a) The land 'lost' is valued at the date the error occurred. (In *Epps* v *Esso* this would be 1959, not 1973.) This is still the law under the 2002 Act, see Sch. 8, para. 6(b).

(b) By what was s. 83(11) of the Land Registration Act 1925, this kind of claim for indemnity had to be brought within six years of the error in the register occurring. Epps did not bring his claim until 1971, so he was too late to claim any compensation. Epps was out of time!

However by Sch. 8, para. 8(b) of the LRA 2002, re-enacting a change first made by s. 2 of the Land Registration Act 1997, the six-year time limit now only starts running against a person in Epps's position from the date he knew or ought to have known that he had a claim against the registry. But the land 'lost' is still valued as of the date the error in the registry occurred.

Applying this new law to the facts of *Epps* v *Esso*, Epps only knew of his claim in 1968, when the registry refused to register him as owner of the strip. His claim for indemnity, brought in 1971, would therefore have been 'in time' under the new law. But the 'error' by the registry occurred in 1959, so he would have received only the 1959 value of the strip.

✖ CONCLUDING REMARKS

It does seem that a rectification of the register for reasons other than adverse possession is a relatively rare occurrence. This is fortunate. If rectifications were frequent, much of the purpose and value of registration of title would be lost. The whole purpose of land registration is to guarantee the security of titles. It is therefore not surprising that both Parliament and the courts (*Epps* v *Esso*, also *Norwich and Peterborough Building Society* v *Steed* [1993] Ch 116, CA) have reinforced the policy of limiting cases for rectification.

It may also be seen as encouraging that the Land Registry faces relatively few claims for indemnity. This is at least partly due to the efficiency of the registry. But the rules regarding the award of indemnity used to be too restrictive. Epps rightly lost his claim for rectification; but it was tough that he did not get any compensation either. The changes to the indemnity rules made by the Land Registration Act 1997 and now incorporated into the 2002 Act are therefore very welcome.

■ SUMMARY

Situations where rectification is likely to be claimed

1 Where there has been double conveyancing;

2 Where a registered proprietor has obtained registration by fraud;

3 Where a (perhaps negligent) mistake by the registry and/or landowner(s) has resulted in the worng person being registered.

Rectification against a registered proprietor in possession will only be granted if

A The registered proprietor has been fraudulent; or

B The registered proprietor was negligent; or

C It is for some other compelling reason unjust not to rectify the register.

Indemnity where rectification is ordered

The registered proprietor will normally get full compensation—the value of the land at the date of rectification.

The registered proprietor will get no compensation if he has been fraudulent, or if the registry's error was entirely caused by his negligence.

If the registry's error was partly the registered proprietor's fault, he will get reduced compensation.

Indemnity where rectification is refused despite an error at the registry

The victim who has 'lost' land will be compensated, but only at the value of the land when the error occurred.

CHAPTER 22: ASSESSMENT EXERCISE

The Aberconwy District (Llandudno, Conwy, Llanrwst, etc.) became an area of compulsory registration of title on 1 December 1988.

In early 1988 Geoffrey purchased a small piece of land 'Lomasacre' situated in Aberconwy. Lomasacre formed a small part of the vast 'Brooke Estate' owned by John. Geoffrey did his own conveyancing; as a result no indorsement referring to the sale of Lomasacre was placed on the deeds to the Brooke Estate.

Geoffrey has only visited Lomasacre on one occasion since he purchased it; on that occasion he dumped some rusting railings on part of the land.

Last week John sold the whole of the Brooke Estate to Malcolm; Malcolm believes that Lomasacre is part of the land he has purchased. He has successfully applied for registration as proprietor of the whole of the Brooke Estate.

Discuss.

See Appendix for a specimen answer.

■ FURTHER READING

(Remember that some changes were made to this area of law in 1977 and 1997, but the 2002 Act is not intended to make any substantive changes.)

For the thinking behind this area of law (and the decision to leave things as they were), see Law Commision report no. 271 part X.

However, for a highly critical analysis of the the current position, see Elizabeth Cooke, *The New Law of Land Registration* (Hart Publishing) chapter 6.

PART VIII

Easements

23

The essential characteristics of easements

23.1 Objectives

By the end of this chapter you should be able to:

1 Appreciate the wide variety of rights which can exist as easements

2 Explain the (somewhat ill-defined) limits on the type of right which can be an easement

3 Distinguish between dominant and servient land

23.2 Introduction

This chapter, and the two which follow it, deal with the law of easements. It will be rather short, but perhaps not very satisfying. In it we will be considering the question, 'What kinds of rights does the law recognize as easements?' As I hinted in the objectives set out above, we can give only a vague answer to that question.

23.3 Preliminary considerations

 EXERCISE 23.1

Re-read 1.4.3 on easements. Also re-read 1.4.2 on restrictive covenants and 1.4.4 on profits à prendre. You should note that quite a wide variety of rights can exist as easements, but be careful not to confuse easements with either restrictive covenants or with profits.

? **QUESTION** 23.1

What do a right of way, a right of support, a right of light, and a right to use a neighbour's toilet have in common?

They are all rights which English law recognizes as easements.

In continental legal systems the concept equivalent to easements is 'servitudes'. Modern continental systems, such as those in France and Germany, have a clear list of types of servitude, and no new types of servitude can be recognized. English law is more flexible. There is no exhaustive list of types of easement, and since the Second World War new types of easement have been recognized. In particular:

(a) the right of the occupants of one flat to use the toilet in a neighbouring flat: *Miller* v *Emcer Products* [1956] 1 All ER 237;

(b) the right of owners of houses situated around a 'private square' to use the private garden in the middle of the square for relaxation purposes: *Re Ellenborough Park* [1955] 3 All ER 667; recently applied in *Jackson* v *Mulvaney* [2003] 1 WLR 360.

(c) the right of owners of a factory to use a neighbouring airfield. The easement allowed visitors to the factory to fly their private aircraft in and out of the airfield: *Dowty Boulton Paul* v *Wolverhampton Corporation (No. 2)* [1973] 2 All ER 491.

Courts do not have a completely free hand to recognize (some would say 'invent') new easements. In *Phipps* v *Pears* [1964] 2 All ER 35, the Court of Appeal refused to accept as an easement the (alleged) right of one building to be protected from the weather by another building.

Any alleged easement (whether it is of a new type or one of the existing, well-recognized categories) must comply with the four broad principles which I am about to discuss in 23.4 to 23.7 below.

23.4 There must be a dominant and a servient tenement

As I explained in **Chapter 1** (1.4.3), an easement can exist only if it is attached to ('appurtenant to') a piece of dominant land. Suppose Gillian owns Wideviews Farm, situated in rural Derbyshire. She executes a deed in favour of Wendy (a keen walker) granting Wendy the right to use a path which crosses the farm. Wendy owns no land whatsoever. Though the right granted by the deed will give Wendy a lot of pleasure, it is certainly not an easement.

23.5 The easement must accommodate the dominant tenement

Suppose that in my Wideviews Farm example Wendy actually owns a house, but that house is situated in London, 150 miles away. The right to use the path across Wideviews is expressed to be for the benefit of Wendy's London house.

 QUESTION 23.2

Can Wendy's right be an easement?

It will not be an easement. A right to be an easement must 'accommodate' the dominant land; it must have some direct beneficial impact on the dominant land itself. It must not merely be for the grantee's personal benefit.

For an easement to accommodate the dominant land it is not essential that the dominant and servient land be contiguous, although they must be sufficiently near each other for the easement to be of direct benefit to the dominant land. In *Pugh* v *Savage* [1970] 2 All ER 353, there was a 'right of way' over one field to get to another field, but a third field lay between the servient and dominant fields. The right of way was held to be a valid easement.

In *Hill* v *Tupper* (1863) 159 ER 51 a rather different problem arose. The Basingstoke Canal Company owned the canal and some land on the banks of the canal. They leased the land on the banks of the canal to Hill for the purposes of a boatyard. The lease included a clause granting Hill the exclusive right to put pleasure boats on the canal. Tupper nevertheless started placing his pleasure boats on the canal.

Hill sued Tupper, claiming that his 'pleasure boat monopoly' was an easement. If the court had accepted that claim, it would have meant that the pleasure boat monopoly was a property right which could be protected by suing **anybody** who interfered with it. The court however held that the pleasure boat monopoly was **not** an easement. The monopoly did not 'accommodate' the land leased to Hill; rather it was for the benefit of Hill's business. (Hill's only remedy was to sue the canal company for breach of contract.)

? **QUESTION** 23.3

Suppose that in *Hill* v *Tupper*, the lease from the canal company granted Hill a right to cross the canal to get to and from his boatyard, but that right was being obstructed by Tupper's boats. Would Hill have been able to sue Tupper?

Yes, Hill will be able to sue Tupper. The right to cross the canal would be a right of way (albeit over water), and therefore Hill would have an easement, a property right which can be protected by suing **anybody** who interferes with it.

23.6 The tenements must not be owned and occupied by the same person

Gillian owns Stouttree Farm. Stouttree Farm includes Distantfield. To get to Distantfield from the public road, Gillian drives her tractor along a track across Nearfield, which is also part of her farm. Clearly in this situation there is no question of there being an easement. A landowner such as Gillian cannot have an easement over her own land!

Suppose, however, that Gillian leases Distantfield to Horace for 10 years. The lease includes a clause that Horace shall have a right of way across Nearfield to gain access to Distantfield. This clause will create a (leasehold) easement. The two fields are, of course, **still owned** (in fee simple) by the same person, but they are **not occupied** by the same person.

23.7 An easement must be capable of forming the subject matter of a grant

What this really means is that the law is rather cautious towards any claim for a new type of easement not previously recognized. A number of criteria may be applied if some new type of easement is claimed. (The court may also consider whether a new alleged easement is analogous to any established easement. In the 'right to use a toilet' case at **23.3** the Court of Appeal was influenced by an old case which had decided that a right to use a neighbour's kitchen could amount to an easement.)

23.7.1 An easement must be capable of reasonably exact definition

In *Harris* v *De Pinna* (1886) 33 ChD 238, the court, applying this principle, held that there could be no easement for a general flow of air to a timber-drying shed. Similarly, there cannot be an easement for 'a beautiful view'.

An easement of light, under which a dominant building is entitled to natural light coming across the servient land, is not an exception to this rule. Where a dominant building has an easement of light over servient land, the dominant building is not entitled to an unlimited amount of natural light coming across the servient land. The House of Lords made this point clear in *Colls* v *Home and Colonial Stores* [1904] AC 179, where it was held that where there is an easement of light, 'The light reaching the windows [of the dominant building] must be such as is sufficient according to the usual notions of mankind for the comfortable enjoyment of the building, bearing in mind the type of the building and its locality'. (For a modern case applying this test, see *Allen* v *Greenwood* [1979] 1 All ER 819.)

The existence of an easement of light over a piece of land restricts the kind of buildings which can be placed on that land. Putting a building upon the servient land does not infringe the easement of light provided the natural light which remains once the building is erected is still sufficient to satisfy the test laid down in *Colls* case.

23.7.2 An easement must not involve any expenditure by the servient owner

There appears to be one exception to this general rule. In rural areas you may come across the 'spurious easement' of fencing. Under this 'easement' the dominant farmer has the right to insist that the servient farmer maintain the boundary fence between their properties. Courts have repeatedly stressed that this fencing 'easement' is anomalous, and that no other exceptions to the 'no expenditure rule' will be tolerated.

The easement of **support** is not an exception to this rule. Easements of support are, of course, common, often existing where there are semi-detached or terraced buildings. Where an easement of support exists, it is the right of the dominant building not to have support from the servient building **deliberately withdrawn**. Thus, if the servient owner knocks down the servient building, with the result that the dominant building collapses, the dominant owner's rights have been infringed.

> **? QUESTION** 23.4
>
> What if the servient building simply falls down because of neglect by the servient owner?

The dominant owner has no claim for infringement of his easement. (He can, however, enter the servient land and, at his own expense, reconstruct the support he was getting!)

Where a private **right of way** exists, the servient owner is under no liability to maintain the way. However, the dominant owner has the right to carry out repair works.

23.7.3 An easement must not be so extensive as to amount to a claim to joint possession of the servient land

The essence of an easement is that it is a right to make use of somebody else's land, not a claim to joint possession of that land. In *Copeland* v *Greenhalf* [1952] 1 All ER 809 the alleged servient property was a long strip of land about 150 feet long and 20 feet wide. The servient owners used the strip to gain access to their orchard.

The alleged dominant owners were 'wheelwrights', i.e., vehicle repairers. For many years they parked vehicles awaiting repair on the strip. These vehicles often occupied a large part of the strip, but the wheelwrights were always careful to leave a gap through which the 'servient owners' could pass to get to their orchard.

The wheelwrights eventually claimed that they had a prescriptive easement to park their vehicles on the strip. The judge, Upjohn J, emphatically rejected the claim to an easement.

. . . in my judgment the right claimed here goes wholly outside any normal idea of an easement, that is, a right of the occupier of a dominant tenement over a servient tenement. **This claim really amounts to a claim to a joint user of the land by the defendant**. Practically he is claiming the whole beneficial user of the strip of land on the south-east side of the track so that he can leave there as many or as few lorries as he likes for any time that he likes and enter on it by himself, his servants and agents, to do repair work.' (Emphasis added.)

The claim was rejected because the wheelwrights were in effect claiming, not a right against someone else's land, but joint possession of the strip of land. Such a claim was (in effect) 'too big' to be an easement.

(Another interesting case is *Grigsby* v *Melville* [1973] 1 All ER 385, where, applying *Copeland* v *Greenhalf*, an alleged right to store goods in a cellar was held not to be an easement.)

In *Miller* v *Emcer Products* [1956] 1 All ER 237 (the right to use a toilet case), the Court of Appeal approved of, but distinguished, *Copeland* v *Greenhalf*. Romer LJ stated:

In my judgment the right had all the requisite characteristics of an easement. There is no doubt as to what were intended to be the dominant and servient tenements respectively, and the right was appurtenant to the former and calculated to enhance its beneficial use and enjoyment. It is true that during the times when the dominant owner exercised the right, the owner of the servient tenement would be excluded, but this in greater or lesser degree is a common feature of many easements (for example, rights of way) and does not amount to such an ouster of the servient owner's rights as was held to be incompatible with a legal easement in *Copeland* v *Greenhalf*.

23.7.3.1 Can there ever be an easement to park vehicles?

In *London and Blenheim Estates* v *Ladbroke Retail Parks* [1993] 1 All ER 307, the deputy High Court judge, Paul Baker QC (in *obiter dicta*) accepted that there could be an easement to park vehicles on a piece of (servient) land **provided the servient land was sufficiently large**. (This point was not considered when the case went to the Court of Appeal.) He said:

The essential question is one of degree. If the right granted in relation to the area over which it is to be exercisable is such that it would leave the servient owner without any reasonable use of his land, whether for parking or anything else, it could not be an easement though it might be some larger or different grant.

This *obiter dictum* has been accepted as correct in later cases, notably in *Batchelor* v *Marlow* [2003] 1 WLR 764. In that case the defendant garage owner claimed a (prescriptive) easement to park up to six cars on the servient land on Mondays to Fridays from 0830 to 1800. Six cars would cover the whole of the servient land. Unsurprisingly the Court of Appeal, applying *Copeland* v *Greenhalf*, held that there could be no easement. The Court rejected an ingenious argument for the defendant, which was in effect, 'I only want to use this land for forty-seven and a half hours of the week, the claimant can have it for the other one-hundred and twenty and a half'.

> **?** **QUESTION** 23.5
>
> Suppose you take a lease of one office in a large block, and that lease gives you the exclusive use of a numbered parking space in the basement car-park. Could this parking right be an easement?

Clearly not, but you could argue that you have 'exclusive possession' of the numbered space and that therefore you have a lease of the space.

23.7.4 New types of *negative* easements

The law is very cautious when it comes to a claim for a new type of *negative* easement.

It appears that easements can be classified as either **positive** easements, or **negative** easements. Easements such as rights of way or rights to use an airfield are **positive**. The essence of a positive easement is that the benefits of the easement are enjoyed by occupants of the dominant land performing some activity such as walking across the servient land or, in *Miller* v *Emcer Products*, using the toilet.

Rights of **light** and **support** are **negative** easements. The dominant land (or building) just sits there and passively enjoys the light or support it gets 'from' the servient land or building.

The effect of a negative easement is often severely to hamper the development of the servient land. The law is thus reluctant to recognize new types of negative easements. This was a major reason why the Court of Appeal, in *Phipps* v *Pears* [1964] 2 All ER 35, refused to accept as an easement the (alleged) right of one building to be protected from the weather by another building.

23.8 Access to Neighbouring Land Act 1992

I should briefly mention this Act. It is perfectly possible for an easement to exist granting the owners of the dominant property a right to go on the servient land in order to carry out maintenance and repairs to the dominant property. Such an easement is particularly useful where a building is constructed right up to the boundary with the servient property.

Unfortunately such easements for 'access for repairs' are not particularly common. Until recently a building owner who wanted to go on to neighbouring land to carry out repairs to his own building had (in the absence of an easement) to rely on getting permission from the neighbour. Some neighbours can be extremely unreasonable.

The 1992 Act was designed to solve this problem, but I must stress that it does **not** create a statutory form of easement. Rather, it allows a landowner, who needs access to a neighbour's land to carry out maintenance/repair work on his own property, to get a county court order authorizing him to go on to the neighbour's land. There is, however, no automatic right to an order for access. The court hearing an application may decide that making an order will cause too much hardship to the neighbour.

If the court does make an access order, then the court can (and probably will) impose conditions as to days/times, and as to other matters such as insurance.

 CONCLUDING REMARKS

The 1992 Act is a rare statutory intervention in an area of law which has otherwise been left to be developed by the courts.

The common law has not drawn up a fixed list of easements. This has the disadvantage of uncertainty, but has the great advantage of flexibility. The English law of easements can react to new technology, such as aircraft and computer cables, without the need to invoke the slow processes of the legislature.

■ SUMMARY

It is impossible to draw up an exhaustive list of easements. Common easements include:

Rights of way;
Rights of light;
Rights of support;
Rights to run drains or cables under adjoining land.

Less common easements include:

Right to use a neigbour's toilet;
Right to use a garden for relaxation purposes.

For a valid easement there must be a dominant and servient tenement. The dominant land must be benefited by the easement. Mere personal or business benefit (*Hill v Tupper*) is not sufficient.

An easement must not involve expenditure by the servient owner.

An easement is a subsidiary right against somebody else's land. An easement cannot give a right to (joint) possession of the servient land. An easement to park a vehicle can only exist if the servient land is so large that this rule is not infringed.

The Access to Neighbouring Land Act 1992 creates a statutory right between neighbours. This right is not an easement.

■ FURTHER READING

For a comprehensive consideration of the nature of easements (and profits) see *Megarry and Wade: Law of Real Property* (sixth edition by Harpum) chapter 18, pages 1078–1082.

For an even fuller consideration of the nature of easements and profits, see Gray and Gray, Elements of Land Law, fourth edition, pages 610–665.

24 Express and implied grant of easements

24.1 Objectives

By the end of this chapter you should be able to:

1 Explain the basic rule for interpreting express grants (and reservations) of easements

2 Recognize the situations in which implied grant of an easement is likely to be alleged

3 Explain **and distinguish between** the four different rules for the implied grant of easements

24.2 Introduction

This chapter (at 24.3 and 24.4) starts with some very straightforward 'black letter' law. But I must warn you that when we reach the question of implied grant of easements (24.5), matters become very complex. Some (arguably rather strange) rules have developed under which a vendor (or lessor) of land creates easements over land he retains in his possession even though those easements **are not expressly mentioned** in the conveyance (or lease).

24.3 Creation of easements (and profits)—legal or equitable?

An easement or a profit is a legal interest in land provided that:

(a) it is created (expressly or impliedly) by deed, by statute, or by prescription; **and**

(b) its duration is of a fee simple absolute in possession or a term of years absolute.

Please however re-read sections 10.3.3.1 and 10.3.3.2 regarding easements which are **created by express grant or express reservation AFTER the commencement of the Land Registration Act 2002**. LRA 2002, s. 27(2)(d) in effect requires that an expressly created easement or profit must itself be substantively registered where the servient land is registered title. If the new dominant owner fails to register his new easement or profit, that new easement or profit will only be equitable, and will only be a minor interest.

24.4 Express grant and reservation of easements (and profits)

There is an 'express reservation' of an easement in the following kind of situation. Bloggs owns the fee simple in Dominantacre and Servientacre. He sells Servientacre to Cluggs. Bloggs is anxious that he should have a right of way over Servientacre to get to Dominantacre. He thus includes a clause in the conveyance of Servientacre 'reserving' an easement of way over Servientacre to get to and from Dominantacre.

The interpretation of express grants and express reservations of easements sometimes gives rise to difficulties. In *St Edmundsbury and Ipswich Diocesan Board of Finance* v *Clark (No. 2)* [1975] 1 All ER 772 the Church of England originally owned a church and churchyard, and the adjoining rectory and rectory grounds. In 1945, the Church of England sold the rectory and its grounds to Clark.

The only access to the church building was across the rectory grounds, so the conveyance to Clark included an express reservation of an easement of way along an existing track across the rectory grounds to and from the church. Unfortunately this reservation did not make it clear whether this right of way was 'on foot only', or whether vehicles could use the track. Clark, to the great inconvenience of weddings, funerals, etc., insisted that the right of way was 'on foot only'.

Evidence established that in 1945 there had been at the churchyard end of the track two solid gateposts only about four feet apart. This fact proved fatal to the Church's claim.

The Court of Appeal held:

(a) When interpreting an express grant or reservation of an easement, the physical circumstances of the pieces of land at the time of the grant or reservation had to be taken into account.

(b) If, **but only if**, the doubts were not resolved by looking at the physical circumstances, the court should give the benefit of the doubt to the dominant owner and construe the grant in his favour.

The Court (applying rule (a) above) concluded that the narrow gap through the gateposts which existed back in 1945 meant that the right of way was on foot only. In view of the physical facts in 1945, rule (b) (which the Church was trying to invoke) was not applicable.

24.5 Implied grant of easements (and profits)

Implied grant of easements is a complex topic. This is largely because there are four separate headings (24.5.1 to 24.5.4 below) under which easements can be implied. The **common feature of all four headings is that originally the dominant and servient tenements were in common ownership; the dominant land is then sold off (or leased).** If certain conditions are satisfied then the grant of an easement over the servient land retained by the vendor/lessor is **implied** as one of the terms of the conveyance (or lease). As we shall see, such a result may be very convenient for the purchaser (or tenant), but very inconvenient for the vendor (landlord), who finds that he has 'impliedly' granted an easement over the land he retains.

24.5.1 **Ways of necessity**

Such an easement would arise on the sale of a 'land-locked' parcel of land, i.e., a vendor sells a part of his land which has no direct access to the public highway system. The purchaser of the isolated 'land-locked' plot acquires an implied easement to cross the vendor's retained land. The vendor can fix the route of the easement, but it must be a reasonably convenient route, and once selected it cannot be varied.

The way of necessity can be used only for those purposes for which the dominant land was being used at the time the necessity arose (i.e., at the time the land became isolated). In *Corporation of London* v *Riggs* (1880) 13 ChD 798, Riggs acquired a 'land-locked' piece of farmland in the middle of Epping Forest. Epping Forest was (and still is) the property of the City of London. Riggs started building 'tea-rooms' on his land. It was not disputed that Riggs had a 'way of necessity' to and from his land. However, he could use the way for farming purposes only. Neither contractors building the tea-rooms, nor his future clientèle, could use the way.

24.5.2 **Intended easements**

If dominant land is granted for a particular purpose known to the grantor, any easement over land retained by the grantor which is **absolutely essential** in order for that purpose to be carried out is implied into the grant. The leading modern case involved a situation where the dominant land was leased for a particular purpose, but the principle would equally apply where land was sold for a specific purpose known to the grantor.

In *Wong* v *Beaumont Property Trust* [1964] 2 All ER 119 a landlord had granted a lease of the basement of premises it owned to Blackaby. He covenanted:

(a) to run the premises as a 'popular restaurant';

(b) to comply with the Public Health Regulations;

(c) to eliminate 'all noxious smells'.

Blackaby's attempts to run the premises as an English restaurant were a miserable failure. He assigned the lease to Wong, who converted the restaurant to Chinese food, with resounding success. However, the tenant upstairs complained about the dreadful 'noxious smells' coming from the basement. Public Health Officers were called in. They told Wong that unless a ventilation shaft was run from the basement up the back of the above-ground floors of the building, Wong would have to close down.

The landlord refused to let Wong put up the ventilating shaft, so Wong commenced proceedings, claiming that he had an easement entitling him to put up a shaft. The county court judge found as a fact that, **at the time the lease was granted to Blackaby**, a ventilating shaft was necessary for the restaurant to function successfully and eliminate smells. The fact that neither of the original parties realized this need was irrelevant. Wong therefore was held entitled to his ventilation shaft. The Court of Appeal affirmed this conclusion.

24.5.3 **The rule in *Wheeldon* v *Burrows***

The two rules for implied grant of easements discussed at 24.5.1 and 24.5.2 involve creating an easement as if 'out of thin air'. Before the sale (or lease) of the dominant land there is not the slightest sign of there being an easement in favour of the dominant land. Remember that in *Wong* v *Beaumont*, before and at the time of the original lease, nobody had even dreamed of a ventilation shaft down to the basement.

The rule in *Wheeldon* v *Burrows* (1879) 12 ChD 31 operates in a very different way. The rule requires that before the dominant land was sold (or leased) by the person who originally owned both pieces of land, a 'nebulous right' already existed in favour of what became the dominant land. If certain conditions are fulfilled then, on the sale or lease taking place, the 'nebulous right' is converted into an easement.

There are two (rather different) types of nebulous right to which the *Wheeldon* v *Burrows* rule applies. These are called 'quasi-easements' and 'privileges'.

24.5.3.1 **Quasi-easements**

Two plots are in common ownership. The common owner exercises over one plot for the benefit of the other plot a right which could have been an easement had the two plots been in separate ownership. For example, Farmer Giles owns two fields, Closefield and Awayfield. Whenever he needs to go to Awayfield, he gains access to it by using a worn track across Closefield.

Or take another example. Bloggs owns a house and a large front garden to the south of his house. Underneath the garden there are drains, pipes, and cables, all leading out to the road. Bloggs also enjoys lovely sunshine streaming in over his garden to the windows of his house.

24.5.3.2 **Privileges**

Two plots are in the common ownership of L. L leases one of those plots to T. L later grants to T a revocable licence exercisable over the land he retained. That licence benefits the land leased, and could have been granted as an easement.

For example, L owns Smallhouse and (adjoining) Largefield. Smallhouse fronts on to a minor road. L leases Smallhouse to T. There is no mention in the lease of easements over Largefield. T originally used the minor road to get to and from Smallhouse, but this road is very circuitous. **As a friendly gesture**, L says to T, 'To save your shoe-leather take a short cut across my Largefield'. T gladly accepts the invitation.

Or take another example. L owns two terraced houses. L leases one of the houses, which has only an outside toilet right at the bottom of the garden, to T. L, some years after granting the lease, says to T, 'You can use my inside toilet if you like'.

(Note that in both of these examples L has granted a gratuitous licence **which he could revoke at any time**.)

24.5.3.3 **The almost magical conversion of 'nebulous rights' into easements**

Under the rule in *Wheeldon* v *Burrows*, three conditions must **all** be satisfied before a 'nebulous right' is converted into an easement upon the sale (or lease) of the dominant land:

(a) Immediately prior to the grant, the 'nebulous right' was used for the benefit of what becomes the dominant land.

(b) The 'nebulous right' was 'continuous and apparent'.

(c) The 'nebulous right' must be 'necessary for the reasonable or convenient enjoyment' of the (alleged) dominant land.

With respect to point (b) above, a 'nebulous right' is 'continuous and apparent' provided that it is regularly used and provided there is **physical evidence** on the plot of land involved of the existence of the right. For example, there might be a worn track leading across the 'servient' land towards the 'dominant' land. Even such matters as drains could be 'apparent' if there were such things as gratings and man-hole covers on the 'servient' land.

The simplest illustration of *Wheeldon* v *Burrows* is *Borman* v *Griffith* [1930] 1 Ch 49. In that case, James owned a sizeable country estate. The estate included a mansion leased to Griffith for the purposes of a school. Running across the estate from the mansion to the main road was a properly made up private driveway. On that private driveway was a smaller house known (somewhat confusingly) as 'The Gardens'.

In 1923, James agreed to lease 'The Gardens' to Borman, a poultry farmer. This agreement said nothing about access to 'The Gardens'. However, at the time of the agreement James was constructing an alternative access route to 'The Gardens'. In wet weather this alternative route proved impassable for the lorries which served Borman's business. The lorries therefore used the main driveway, despite opposition from Griffith.

The judge held, applying *Wheeldon* v *Burrows*, that an easement to use the driveway was to be implied into the 1923 agreement. He held that the three elements of the rule were satisfied. You should note in particular that for element (c), Borman had to show only that a right to use the driveway was 'necessary for the reasonable or convenient enjoyment' of the dominant land. He did not have to show the stricter standard of 'absolute necessity' which is required for an easement to arise under the 'intended easements' rule applied in *Wong* v *Beaumont* (see 24.5.2).

You should also note that Borman had only an agreement for a lease (i.e., an equitable lease) over 'The Gardens'. Fortunately for him, this did not matter. The rule in *Wheeldon* v *Burrows* is applicable not only to conveyances and legal leases, but also to contracts for sale and equitable leases.

In the Court of Appeal case of *Goldberg* v *Edwards* [1950] 1 Ch 247, the claim for an easement under *Wheeldon* v *Burrows* failed. Unlike *Borman* v *Griffith* (which involved a 'quasi-easement' type of nebulous right), *Goldberg* v *Edwards* involved a 'privilege'.

Edwards owned a main building, together with an annex at the back of the main building. He leased the annex to Goldberg. That lease included an express grant of a right of way permitting all visitors to the annex to gain access using an open yard at the side of the main building. While this first lease was still in force, Edwards gave permission for visitors to the annex to pass through the hallway of the main building. (That way, they did not get wet!)

The first lease expired, but Goldberg was granted a new lease, with the same express clause regarding using the open yard at the side. The new lease made no express mention of the hallway, but Goldberg claimed that the new lease impliedly granted him an easement to use the hallway.

Goldberg's claim under *Wheeldon* v *Burrows* failed, because the Court of Appeal ruled that a right to use the hallway, while it had its advantages, was not 'necessary for the reasonable or convenient enjoyment' of the annex.

In giving judgment on the *Wheeldon* v *Burrows* claim the Court of Appeal stressed two points rather ignored by certain textbooks:

(a) Implied grant under *Wheeldon* v *Burrows* can apply to 'privileges' as well as to 'quasi-easements'.

(b) All three conditions ((a), (b), and (c) above) must be satisfied before an implied easement can arise under *Wheeldon* v *Burrows*. (Some books **wrongly** suggest that it is sufficient to prove **either** condition (b) or (c).)

24.5.3.4 All three conditions must be satisfied for an easement to arise under *Wheeldon* v *Burrows*

Two almost simultaneous decisions of separate divisions of the Court of Appeal confirm that for an easement to arise under *Wheeldon* v *Burrows*, all three conditions must be fulfilled.

In both cases the (alleged) dominant owners bought a property in the country, and claimed an implied grant of a right of way across land retained by the vendor. In both cases there was an alternative means of access to the property. Both cases were 'quasi-easement' cases where prior to the sale the vendor had used the 'nebulous right' to gain access to the property. In both cases the 'right' (prior to the sale) was continuous and apparent. Both cases therefore turned on the 'necessary for reasonable or convenient enjoyment' point.

In *Wheeler* v *Saunders* [1995] 2 All ER 697 the alternative route was virtually just as convenient as the one being claimed by implied grant. A court presided over by Staughton LJ therefore rejected the claim to an implied easement.

In *Millman* v *Ellis* (1996) 71 P & CR 158, by contrast, the alternative route was dangerous and would involve making a detour. A court presided over by Sir Thomas Bingham MR held that a claim under *Wheeldon* v *Burrows* succeeded. Moreover the claim succeeded even though the (dangerous) alternative route was by virtue of an easement expressly granted by the vendor, in the conveyance of the dominant property, over other land which he retained.

24.5.4 Section 62 of the Law of Property Act 1925

The material part of s. 62 reads:

A conveyance of land shall be deemed to include . . . all . . . liberties, privileges, easements, rights and advantages whatsoever, appertaining or reputed to appertain to the land . . .

This statutory provision first appeared in the Conveyancing Act 1881. It is very probable that Parliament did not intend it to be a rule under which new easements could be **created**. Almost certainly the original purpose behind what is now s. 62 was simply to reaffirm the common law rule that where a parcel of land is 'dominant' to an existing easement or profit, a conveyance of that dominant land **automatically** passes the right to enjoy the easement or profit to the new owner.

The courts have, however, given s. 62 a strange interpretation, under which a conveyance or lease of land may convert an existing 'privilege' type of 'nebulous right' into a full easement. The best illustration of how s. 62 operates to create an easement is the decision of the Court of Appeal in *Wright* v *Macadam* [1949] 2 All ER 565.

Wright v *Macadam* concerned an apparently trivial matter which gave rise to a very important point of law. The defendant leased a top-floor flat to Mrs Wright. While this first lease was still running, Macadam gave Mrs Wright permission to store her coal in a coal-shed situated in the garden to the small block of flats.

When Mrs Wright's first lease ran out, it was renewed for a further period. At the time of renewal **nothing was said about the coal-shed**. Later, during the running of the second lease,

Macadam demanded that Mrs Wright pay one shilling and sixpence (7.5p) per week for the use of the coal-shed. She refused.

The Court of Appeal held that, on the renewal of the lease to Mrs Wright, there was implied into the renewed lease an easement to store coal in the coal-shed. The crucial point (fatal from Macadam's point of view) was the existence of the privilege **at the time the lease was renewed**. The statutory magic of s. 62 therefore converted Mrs Wright's privilege into a full easement.

If on the expiry of Mrs Wright's first lease, Macadam had leased the flat not to Mrs Wright but to a third party, s. 62 would have created an easement in favour of that third party.

> **?** **QUESTION** 24.1
>
> What if Macadam had sold the flat in fee simple to a third party?

The third party would have acquired an easement (in fee simple!) to store coal in the coal-shed. I think Macadam would have been very unhappy at such a result.

24.5.4.1 **The breadth of the s. 62 principle**

I should stress that for s. 62 to convert a 'privilege' into an easement, all that is necessary is that the 'privilege' exists at the time of the relevant conveyance (or lease). Under the s. 62 rule there is no requirement that the 'privilege' be 'continuous and apparent'. Neither is there any requirement that the privilege be 'necessary for the reasonable or convenient enjoyment' of the dominant land.

The facts of *Goldberg* v *Edwards* were set out at 24.5.3.3. The claim for an implied easement under *Wheeldon* v *Burrows* failed in that case.

> **?** **QUESTION** 24.2
>
> Goldberg also relied on s. 62. Did he win under that heading?

Despite losing on the *Wheeldon* v *Burrows* issue, Goldberg won the case; he was held to have acquired (on the renewal of his lease) an implied easement to use the hallway under s. 62!

> **?** **QUESTION** 24.3
>
> What is the moral for landlords of cases such as *Wright* v *Macadam* and *Goldberg* v *Edwards*?

(a) Do not ever give your tenants any friendly permissions to make use of land you retain in your possession.

(b) If you have been so foolish as to give such a friendly permission, revoke it (**in writing**) before the lease expires.

Either way, there will then be no 'privilege' on which s. 62 can work its statutory magic. (See also 24.7.)

24.5.4.2 The limits on s. 62

Although s. 62 appears as a rule very dramatic in its effects, there are two important limitations upon its scope.

(a) **Section 62 can operate only where there is a 'conveyance'.** A legal lease counts as a 'conveyance', but neither an equitable lease nor a contract for sale are 'conveyances' for the purposes of s. 62.

(b) **Section 62 applies only to convert 'privileges' into easements.** Unlike *Wheeldon* v *Burrows*, s. 62 cannot apply to 'quasi-easements'. The House of Lords made this point clear in *Sovmots Investments* v *Secretary for the Environment* [1977] 2 All ER 385, at 391, approving *Long* v *Gowlett* [1923] Ch 177 at 198.

? QUESTION 24.4

Why was s. 62 of no help to Borman in *Borman* v *Griffith*?

I hope you identified two reasons. First, Borman had only an equitable lease. Secondly (though this point is not expressly mentioned in the judgment), the case clearly involved a quasi-easement, to which s. 62 is inapplicable.

24.5.4.3 *Graham v Philcox*

This case, reported at [1984] 2 All ER 621, added a new way in which s. 62 can operate. This new way is in addition to what we have already discussed.

The material facts of the case were that L owned a large garden with a house at one end of that garden. In 1960, L leased the house to T. This lease included an express grant to T of a right of way over the garden **for the duration of the lease**. In 1975 (while T's lease was still running), L sold the fee simple reversion in the house to G. The 1975 conveyance made no mention of a right of way. The Court of Appeal held that s. 62 implied into the 1975 conveyance the grant to G of a fee simple easement of way over the garden.

The practical effect of this case appears to be that if the landlord of Blackacre grants to a lessee of Blackacre a full easement over Retainedacre for the duration of the lease, and then the landlord sells the freehold to Blackacre, there will be implied into the conveyance of Blackacre a freehold easement over Retainedacre!

24.5.4.4 Section 62 and profits à prendre

Unlike the other three forms of implied grant which we have been discussing, it appears that s. 62 could apply so as to imply a **profit** into a conveyance (or lease).

Suppose that Larry owns a house and an adjoining meadow. He leases the house to Teresa for 10 years. Teresa is a keen horsewoman, and when Larry discovers that fact he says to her, 'Seeing we are now good friends you can pasture your horse in my meadow'. Teresa accepts the invitation.

When the lease of the house runs out, Larry sells the fee simple in the house to Penny. The conveyance makes no mention of horses, but Penny now produces her horse and says to Larry, 'I have got the right to put my horse in your meadow'. It would appear that Penny is correct in this assertion. She has a fee simple **profit** to pasture one horse in the adjoining meadow.

24.6 Implied reservation of easements

This could occur only under the 'way of necessity' and 'intended easements' rules (see 24.5.1 and 24.5.2). (Section 62 and *Wheeldon* v *Burrows* cannot operate 'in reverse' to create easements by implied reservation.)

Suppose that Muggins owns Nearacre and Faracre. He foolishly sells Nearacre, with the result that Faracre becomes 'land-locked'. Muggins is lucky. He will have a 'way of necessity' over Nearacre to get to Faracre. (You must remember, however, the principle in *Corporation of London* v *Riggs* at 24.5.1.)

 EXERCISE 24.1

Suppose that Wang owns a building which includes a basement. He leases the above-ground floors to Bloggs on a 50-year lease, but he retains the basement. He opens a restaurant in the basement. The tenant of the upper floors complains, and the environmental health officers say that the restaurant has to have a ventilation shaft up the back of the above-ground floors. Can Wang claim an easement?

It would seem that Wang will be able to claim an easement for a ventilation shaft by implied reservation only if he can show that at the time the 50-year lease was granted **Bloggs** knew that Wang intended to run a restaurant in the basement: *Re Webb's Lease* [1951] 2 All ER 131 (see also 24.5.2). (See also *Peckham* v *Ellison* [1999] Conv 353.)

24.7 Exclusion of the rules providing for implied grant (and reservation)

The rules for implied grant (and reservation) which we have just discussed at some length depend upon 'the presumed agreement of the parties'. (You may, like me, find this surprising, but the point is an important one.)

It is perfectly permissible and indeed quite common for solicitors drafting contracts for sale (and contracts for leases) to include a clause in the contract excluding the rules relating to implied grant. Thus, in particular, a vendor or lessor of land who retains other land in the vicinity can, by careful drafting, avoid being saddled with easements which would otherwise arise 'by implication'.

? **QUESTION** 24.5

Refer back to *Graham* v *Philcox* discussed at 24.5.4.3. There L found himself saddled with a fee simple easement of way over the garden he retained. What should L's solicitor have done to avoid that result?

L's solicitor should have included in the contract for sale of the house in 1975 a clause to the effect, 'On the conveyance of the house, no easements over the garden shall be implied under s. 62, "the rule in *Wheeldon* v *Burrows*" or any other rule'. (Out of extreme caution, a similar clause should also be included in the conveyance itself.)

24.8 Compulsory purchase and the rules for implied grant

In *Sovmots Investments* v *Secretary for the Environment* [1977] 2 All ER 385, the House of Lords held that as the rules for implied grant and reservation of easements are founded on 'presumed agreement', the rules can have no application to land acquired under a compulsory purchase order.

24.9 Simultaneous sales or bequests

Suppose Alec owns Greenacre and Blueacre. He simultaneously grants Greenacre to Brian and Blueacre to Charles. It appears that *Wheeldon* v *Burrows* can operate in favour of Brian and/or Charles, but the other rules of implied grant, such as s. 62, can have no application.

24.10 Implied easements—legal or equitable?—overriding or minor?

The implied easement which arose in *Borman* v *Griffith* was (in effect) an implied term of the **equitable** lease which existed between James and Borman. The easement in that case was therefore only equitable.

In that respect, *Borman* v *Griffith* was an unusual case. Usually, when an implied easement (or profit) arises, that easement (or profit) is an implied term of a **deed** either transferring the legal freehold estate or granting a **legal** lease. Where (as in *Millman* v *Ellis, Wong* v *Beaumont*, and *Goldberg* v *Edwards*) an implied easement arises as an implied term of a deed, that easement will be legal.

Unregistered servient land

If an equitable implied easement arises against unregistered land, that easement will be registrable as a Land Charge, Class D(iii). However if a legal implied easement arises against unregistered servient land, that easement will of course be automatically binding on the whole world.

Registered servient land

Here the position gets even more complex.

Position of easements implied prior to the commencement of the Land Registration Act 2002

If a legal implied easement arises prior to the commencement of the 2002 Act, that easement is undoubtedly an overriding interest within Land Registration Act 1925, s. 70(1)(a). If an equitable implied easement arises prior to the commencement of the 2002 Act, that too will be overriding, assuming the decision in *Thatcher* v *Douglas* to be correct.

Position of easements implied after the commencement of the Land Registration Act 2002

If an equitable implied easement is created after the commencement of the 2002 Act on 13 October 2003, that easement cannot be an overriding interest. The relevant provision which replaces s. 70(1)(a) (Sch. 3, para. 3) refers only to **legal** easements. (See 10.3.3.3.)

If a legal implied easement is created after the commencement of the 2002 Act, it will normally be an overriding interest, but subject to the complex rules set out in 10.3.3.4 section (b).

CONCLUDING REMARKS

This whole chapter could be concluded in seven words: 'Make sure you draft your documents correctly'. As the Church of England discovered (*St Edmundsbury* v *Clark*, see 24.4), even an **expressly** created easement may prove to be incorrectly drafted. I would strongly suggest that the most important part of this chapter is 24.7, together with **Question 24.5** and its answer. The strange magic-like rules of implied grant benefit people such as Wong, Borman, Wright, and Goldberg, quite possibly in ways they did not really anticipate. Equally, people like Beaumont, Griffith (no doubt worried about the safety of his pupils), and the owners of the garden in *Graham* v *Philcox* find that they have 'impliedly granted' easements which may substantially depreciate the value of their land. Careful drafting of contracts, leases, and conveyances would have avoided such disasters.

■ SUMMARY

Where an easement is expressly granted or reserved it is crucial that the exact nature of the right is spelt out in the deed creating the easement. If there is doubt about the scope of an easement, the court can consider the physical features of the relevant land at the time of the grant/reservation.

There are four forms of implied grant of easements. All four have one common feature. Both the dominant and servient land must originally have been in common ownership.

1 **A way of necessity** arises where a landowner sells part of his land, with the result that either the land sold or the land retained is 'land-locked'. The way can only be used for those purposes for which the dominant land was being used at the time the land became isolated.

2 **An intended easement** arises where land is granted for a specific purpose, and the easement is absolutely essential if that purpose is to be carried out.

3 *Wheeldon* v *Burrows* A 'quasi-easement' is converted into a full easement provided

   (a) immediately prior to the sale of part of the land the 'quasi-easememt' was being used for the benefit of the part sold; and

   (b) the 'quasi-easement' was continuous and apparent; and

   (c) the right is reasonably necessary for the proper enjoyment of the part which has been sold.

4 **Section 62 of the Law of Property Act 1925** A privilege enjoyed by a tenant (such as Mrs Wright's licence to store coal) is converted into a full easement when a new lease is granted (or when the dominant land is sold).

Implied grant depends on the presumed intention of the parties. So a carefully drafted lease/conveyance can exclude the operation of the implied grant rules.

Impact of Land Registration Act 2002 In the past virtually all easements existing against a registered title have been overriding interests. But for easements created after 12 October 2003:

1 Any easement **expressly** granted out of a registered title will need to be substantively registered, otherwise it will be a minor interest;

2 Any legal easement **implied** into a deed will (normally) be an overriding interest.

▬ FURTHER READING

For a comprehensive treatment of implied grant of easements, see *Megarry and Wade: Law of Real Property* (sixth edition by Harpum) chapter 18, pages 1105–1118.

Alternatively, see Gray and Gray, *Elements of Land Law*, fourth edition, pages 671–692.

Prescription for easements (and profits)

25.1 Objectives

By the end of this chapter you should be able to:

1 Explain the general principles common to all forms of prescription, and in particular the concept 'user as of right'

2 Distinguish between the three forms of prescription

3 Appreciate why common law prescription is unlikely to be a very useful rule in modern conditions

4 Appreciate why the simple 'lost modern grant' rule can be used only as a last resort

5 Appreciate the complexities of the Prescription Act 1832

25.2 Introduction

The basic concept of prescription is not too difficult. Suppose John owns Remotehouse, situated next to Largefield, which is owned by Keith. The road from Remotehouse to the nearest shops is very circuitous. John therefore decides to take a short cut across Largefield. John **does not get any permission** from Keith. However, he uses 'his' short cut very regularly and in broad daylight, and Keith makes no attempt to stop John.

John's open and regular use of the short cut across Largefield does not alter the fact that every time he goes on Largefield he is a trespasser. At any time Keith could say to John, 'Stop crossing my field; if you don't stop I will sue you for an injunction and damages!'

Suppose, however, that John continues to use the short cut openly and without any objection from Keith for **20** years. Subject to some very complex rules, 20 years is the normal 'prescription period'. That means that (in principle) after 20 years' use of his short cut, John acquires an easement to cross Largefield. He ceases to be a trespasser, and Keith can no longer stop him. Put more crudely, John's use of the short cut (as a trespasser) for 20 years creates for himself (and for Remotehouse) an easement of way across Largefield.

25.3 The complexities of prescription law

The example given at 25.2, though a good way to start the discussion, rather oversimplifies the law of prescription. I wish the law was simply that '20 years' user gives you a prescriptive easement (or profit)'! But that is not the case. Unfortunately there are no less than three forms of prescription for easements and profits:

(a) common law prescription;

(b) lost modern grant;

(c) the Prescription Act 1832.

If somebody (such as John in my Remotehouse example) is claiming a prescriptive easement (or profit) he will succeed only if:

(a) he can satisfy certain important rules which are common for all three forms of prescription; **and**

(b) he can satisfy the specific rules governing **any one** of the three forms of prescription.

25.4 Rules common to all three forms of prescription

User, to be prescriptive, must be 'as of right'

I hope you noticed that in my Remotehouse example at 25.2 I said that John crossed Largefield openly, and without either permission or opposition from Keith. I said those things so as to ensure that John's user was 'as of right'. User is only 'as of right' if it is *nec vi, nec clam, nec precario*, i.e., 'without force, without secrecy, and without permission'.

25.4.1 Without force

If in my Remotehouse example John had had to force his way across Largefield, his user would not have been prescriptive.

In this context, 'force' has been given a very wide meaning, and the courts have ruled that user, to be prescriptive, must not be contentious in any way. Thus, fisticuffs man-to-man, the breaking down of barriers, and the climbing over of fences are all forceable user and therefore not prescriptive.

The courts have also held that user in face of express oral or written protests from the alleged servient owner should be deemed to be forceable, even though there is no actual violence. Thus if Keith constantly wrote to John saying, 'Get off my land!', John could not acquire a prescriptive easement.

25.4.2 Without secrecy

User, to be prescriptive, must be open; 'such that a reasonable person in the position of the alleged servient owner, diligent in the protection of his interests, would have a reasonable opportunity of discovering the right asserted'.

In *Lloyds Bank* v *Dalton* [1942] 1 Ch 466, Dalton owned the servient building, which was a large dye-works. The dominant building was a small outhouse which claimed a prescriptive easement of support against the dye-works. The outhouse had, for well over 20 years, leant against a wall of the dye-works. That wall was a blank wall without any windows.

The outhouse could therefore not be seen from the works, neither could it be seen from the public road. The court nevertheless rejected Dalton's contention that there was 'secret' user. A reasonable owner would surely go around his premises from time to time. A reasonable owner would therefore at some stage have discovered the outhouse.

Lloyds Bank v *Dalton* should be contrasted with *Liverpool Corporation* v *Coghill* [1918] 1 Ch 307. Coghill ran a chemical factory which worked 24 hours a day. For many years Coghill poured borax effluent into the corporation's sewers. Coghill always did so in the 'wee small hours'. This was not out of any deliberate intent to conceal what it was doing. Discharging effluent at night suited its 'production cycle'.

The Court of Appeal held that Coghill could not claim a prescriptive right. Its user was in law 'secret', even though there was no deliberate attempt at concealment.

25.4.3 Without permission

User must not depend on permission or consent. Even an oral permission is sufficient to negate prescription. Normally, once a user is permissive, it will always be permissive, i.e., a permission to use is normally regarded as lasting indefinitely. If, however, a permission were revoked but user still continued, the continued user would be 'as of right'.

Where the servient owner knows that user is going on, and simply tolerates such user without ever giving express permission, then that user is 'as of right': *Mills* v *Silver* [1991] 1 All ER 449.

25.4.4 User which is a criminal offence

As is shown by my Remotehouse and Largefield example in 25.2, the user as of right which eventually gives rise to a prescriptive easement will (until the easement is acquired) usually constitute the civil tort of trespass to land. Trespass to land is not **normally** a criminal offence.

If the alleged prescriptive user **necessarily** involves the commission of a criminal offence, then a prescriptive easement cannot arise. However, the recent (very welcome) decision of the House of Lords in the test case of *Bakewell Management Ltd* v *Brandwood* [2004] 2 WLR 955; [2004] UKHL 14 should be noted.

In that case the defendants, owners of houses on the edge of a common, had been for many years driving across the common to get from the public road to their homes. Section 193(4) of the LPA 1925 makes it an offence to drive across a common 'without lawful authority'. The claimants, the owners of the common, argued that the defendants' **'criminal'** conduct could not give rise to a prescriptive easement.

The House of Lords ruled in favour of the defendants. The defendant homeowners' conduct was not **necessarily** criminal; it would be perfectly lawful if they had had authority from the servient owners to drive across the servient land. Further, the whole essence of prescription is that if the appropriate conditions regarding user as of right exist, the law conclusively presumes that the servient owner has granted the dominant owner authority to use the servient land!

25.4.5 User must be continuous

In *Hollins* v *Verney* (1884) 13 QB 304, especially at 315, the alleged dominant owner had used the right of way only three times in the last 20 years. The Court of Appeal rejected the claim for a prescriptive easement. It held that user must be sufficiently regular so that a reasonable servient owner would know some right was being asserted. (You should note that this is in effect much the same rule as is applied in 'secrecy' cases.)

25.4.6 User must be by or on behalf of a fee simple against a fee simple

This is a peculiar rule which has become firmly embedded into English common law (see, for example, the case of *Simmons* v *Dobson* [1991] 4 All ER 25), though not into other versions of the common law (e.g., Irish law). English law insists that a prescriptive easement or profit **can be only of fee simple duration**. This apparently simple rule creates complications where either:

(a) the person carrying out the user as of right is a lessee rather than a fee simple owner; or

(b) the servient land has at any time been leased (or settled).

Four consequences flow from this rule:

 (i) A tenant cannot prescribe for an easement against his own landlord. For example, Leonard owns the fee simple in Blackacre and Whiteacre. He leases Whiteacre to Tamsin for 999 years. Tamsin immediately starts to cross Blackacre to get to Whiteacre. She and the successors to her lease continue to do so 'as of right' for hundreds of years. A prescriptive easement cannot arise.

 (ii) *A fortiori*, one tenant of a landlord cannot prescribe for an easement against another tenant of the same landlord. See *Simmons* v *Dobson*.

(iii) If a tenant prescribes 'as of right' against a third party, any resultant right enures to the benefit of the landlord's fee simple.

(iv) A period of user **entirely** against a lessee or life tenant of the servient land cannot be prescriptive. However, if user **commences** against a fee simple owner in actual possession, it does not matter if the servient land is subsequently leased.

 EXERCISE 25.1

Consider the old case of *Palk* v *Shinner* (1852) 118 ER 215, which illustrates the last two points above. Palk leased his land to various tenants. From 1820 onwards, the tenants crossed Shinner's land 'as of right' to reach the land leased to them. From 1821 onwards, Shinner's land was leased to X. User as of right by the tenants continued until the dispute broke out in about 1850. What do you think was the result of the case?

The court gave judgment for Palk, holding that his tenants were to be regarded as acting on his behalf (point (iii)). Palk thus acquired a fee simple easement. Moreover, as the user as of right had commenced against Shinner personally (a fee simple owner in actual possession) it did not matter that the servient land had **subsequently** been leased (point (iv)).

> **?**   **QUESTION** 25.1
>
> What would be the position if Shinner had leased his land to X in 1818?

The claim to a prescriptive easement would fail, as the user as of right would have been **entirely** against a lessee.

25.5 **Prescription at common law**

For reasons which will quickly become apparent, a claim for an easement or a profit by 'prescription at common law' is very rarely successful. The theory of this form of prescription is that once upon a time a deed was executed by the then servient owner in favour of the then dominant owner, granting the relevant easement or profit. However, this deed was granted so long ago that its execution is 'outside the scope of legal memory'.

Unfortunately legal memory is elephantine, and stretches back to 1189 (the year of the accession of Richard I). In effect, if you claim a prescriptive easement (or profit) at common law, you have boldly to assert that you and your predecessors have been exercising the right ever since 1189.

Fortunately you do not have to produce evidence of user covering the whole of the last 800 or so years. If 20 years' user is proved, user right back to 1189 will be presumed. But the presumption can be rebutted by showing any of the following facts:

(a) at some time since 1189 the right was not exercised; or

(b) at some time since 1189 the right could not have been exercised; or

(c) at some time since 1189 dominant and servient plots were in common ownership.

Thus a servient owner faced with a claim for prescription at common law will look round for rebutting evidence from elderly inhabitants or ancient records. Suppose the current owner of Westacre is claiming at common law a prescriptive easement of way over neighbouring Eastacre. The owner of Eastacre will be delighted if he can find some very senior citizen who says something like, 'When I was a little girl my mum worked at Westacre and nobody got to it by crossing Eastacre. They always used the track across Northacre'. Or perhaps it will be, 'When I was a little boy Eastacre was very swampy and impossible to cross. I remember because I once fell in; dad gave me a right walloping'.

Ancient records will be just as effective. Proof that for a few years *circa* (say) 1400 the same person owned both Westacre and Eastacre will be enough to defeat the common law claim.

25.6 **Prescription by lost modern grant**

The utility of common law prescription is largely destroyed by the absurd '1189 rule'. However, the old, pre-1875 courts invented a legal doctrine called 'lost modern grant'. This doctrine was designed to allow prescription for easements and profits where there was strong evidence of at least 20 years' 'user as of right' but it was clear that user had commenced 'in modern times'. Modern times was any date after 1189!

Lost modern grant is a 'legal fiction'. A legal fiction occurs where the court 'finds as a fact' something everyone knows is really not true, and then decides the case on the basis of that 'fact'. The essence of 'lost modern grant' is that the court 'finds as a fact' that a deed was executed 'in modern times' granting the easement (or profit) claimed, but that deed has been lost.

In the days when civil cases (including land disputes) were tried by juries, 'lost modern grant' caused judges (particularly trial judges) a lot of trouble. Suppose that the owner of Northacre was claiming a prescriptive easement of way across Southacre, and that it did appear that for many years the owners of Northacre had indeed been crossing Southacre to get to their land. The trial judge would have to direct the jury along the following lines:

Gentlemen; if you find that there is convincing evidence that the owners of Northacre have been 'as of right' crossing Southacre for at least 20 years, I **instruct** you to find as a fact that a deed was executed granting a right of way but that deed has somehow been mislaid.

Some nineteenth-century juries, sworn to 'well and truly try' the case, were understandably worried by this instruction. Nevertheless, in 1881 the House of Lords, in *Dalton* v *Angus* (1881) 6 App Cas 740, reaffirmed the validity of the lost modern grant rule.

Two developments in the twentieth century have greatly improved the situation. First, land law disputes are no longer tried by jury; they are tried by a judge alone. A judge is not going to be worried by the apparent absurdity of finding as a fact something no one really believes to be true. Secondly, this area of law has been much simplified by two modern Court of Appeal decisions, *Tehidy Minerals* v *Norman* [1971] 2 All ER 475 and *Oakley* v *Boston* [1975] 3 All ER 405.

Tehidy Minerals involved a claim for a prescriptive profit of grazing on a part of Bodmin Moor. In January 1920 a group of farmers started grazing their sheep on the servient land. They continued to do so 'as of right' until October 1941, when the land was requisitioned by the War Office for military training. The farmers continued to graze their sheep on the land, but it was conceded that this post-1941 grazing was by permission. (Permission came first from the War Office and then, after the land had been derequisitioned, from the servient owners.)

The farmers successfully claimed under 'lost modern grant' a prescriptive profit of pasture on the basis of their 1920 to 1941 user. The Court of Appeal held that a 'presumption' of lost modern grant arose where the claimant produced strong evidence of 20 years' user as of right. If there is such evidence then 'the deed which has got lost' is assumed to have been executed:

(a) at the earliest, immediately before user as of right commenced;

(b) at the latest, **20 years before** user as of right ceased.

The Court held that it is not sufficient to rebut the 'presumption' of lost modern grant for the servient owner to show that the grant never **in fact** took place. The presumption of lost modern grant can be rebutted (and the claim for the profit or easement therefore defeated) only by showing that **throughout the period (a) to (b)** ('the relevant period'), the grant was **legally impossible**. There would be 'legal impossibility' if, say, throughout 'the relevant period' the land had been requisitioned, or vested in a person who had no power to grant profits or easements.

In *Tehidy Minerals*, the relevant period for the presumed grant was January 1920 to October 1921. During those 21 months there was no question of a grant being legally impossible. Hence the farmers' victory.

In the later case of *Oakley* v *Boston*, a differently constituted Court of Appeal applied the rules in *Tehidy Minerals*, but held against the claimant for an easement. The evidence was that there had been user as of right of an alleged right of way from 1914 to 1962. After that there had been insufficient user.

? **QUESTION** 25.2

In *Oakley* v *Boston*, what was 'the relevant period' at some time during which the presumed grant would supposedly have taken place?

Applying *Tehidy Minerals* v *Norman*, the presumed grant would be some time between 1914 and 1942.

There was, however, one crucial fact in *Oakley* v *Boston* which I have not yet mentioned. The alleged servient land had been, until 1952, 'glebe land'. Glebe land is land vested in the local vicar (of the Church of England) not in his personal capacity but in his official capacity as an 'ecclesiastical corporation sole'.

The Court of Appeal first held (interpreting some very obscure nineteenth-century legislation governing the Church) that a vicar **owning land in his official capacity as an 'ecclesiastical corporation sole'** had no power to grant easements.

? **QUESTION** 25.3

What, therefore, was the result of the case?

As throughout 'the relevant period' when the supposed grant could have taken place it was 'legally impossible', the claim for a prescriptive easement invoking lost modern grant failed.

(See also now *Bakewell Management* v *Brandwood* [2004] UKHL 14 where the House of Lords, applying *Tehidy Minerals*, held that a claim for an easement under lost modern grant succeeded.)

25.7 Prescription under the Prescription Act 1832

Sections 1 and 2 of the Prescription Act 1832 are frighteningly complex. I set them out below, but do not (yet) try to make sense of them.

1. **Claims to right of common and other profits à prendre, not to be defeated after thirty years enjoyment by merely showing the commencement; after sixty years enjoyment the right to be absolute, unless had by consent or agreement**

... No claim which may be lawfully made at the common law, by custom, prescription, or grant, to any right of common or other profit or benefit to be taken and enjoyed from or upon any land of our sovereign lord the King ... or any land being parcel of the duchy of Lancaster or the duchy of Cornwall, or of any ecclesiastical or lay person, or body corporate, except such matters and things as are herein specially provided for, and except tithes, rent, and services, shall, where such right, profit, or benefit have been actually taken and enjoyed by any person claiming right thereto without interruption for the full period of thirty years, be defeated or destroyed by showing only that such right, profit, or benefit was first taken or enjoyed at any time prior to such period of thirty years, but nevertheless such claim may be defeated in any other way by which the same is now liable to be defeated; and when such right, profit, or benefit shall have been so taken and enjoyed as aforesaid for the full period of sixty years, the right thereto shall be deemed absolute and indefeasible, unless it shall appear that the same was taken and enjoyed by some consent or agreement expressly made or given for that purpose by deed or writing.

2. In claims of rights of way or other easement the periods to be twenty years and forty years
... No claim which may be lawfully made at the common law, by custom, prescription, or grant, to any way or other easement, or to any watercourse, or the use of any water, to be enjoyed or derived upon, over, or from any land or water of our said lord the King ... or being parcel of the duchy of Lancaster or of the duchy of Cornwall, or being the property of any ecclesiastical or lay person, or body corporate, when such way or other matter as herein last before mentioned shall have been actually enjoyed by any person claiming right thereto without interruption for the full period of twenty years, shall be defeated or destroyed by showing only that such way or other matter was first enjoyed at any time prior to such period of twenty years, but nevertheless such claim may be defeated in any other way by which the same is now liable to be defeated; and where such way or other matter as herein last before mentioned shall have been so enjoyed as aforesaid for the full period of forty years, the right thereto shall be deemed absolute and indefeasible, unless it shall appear that the same was enjoyed by some consent or agreement expressly given or made for that purpose by deed or writing.

I am sure you will agree that these provisions are very badly drafted. The House of Lords came to that conclusion in 1841, but nothing has ever been done to reform or repeal the Act.

The complexity of the 1832 Act is to be contrasted with the relative simplicity of the 'lost modern grant' rule as restated in *Tehidy Minerals* (see 25.6). I would like to be able to say to students, 'Forget the Prescription Act, rely on lost modern grant'. I cannot say that for two reasons:

(a) The courts have repeatedly held that lost modern grant, being a 'legal fiction', can be relied upon only if the other forms of prescription (common law and the 1832 Act) fail.

(b) The complexities of the Act produce the result that there are quite a few situations which the Act covers which are not covered by the other two forms of prescription.

25.7.1 Shorter and longer periods under the Act

 EXERCISE 25.2

Now study ss. 1 and 2 of the 1832 Act above and try to discern if there is some kind of pattern linking the two sections.

If you study ss. 1 and 2 of the Act, you will eventually realize that the Act makes some kind of distinction between 'shorter periods' and 'longer periods'. The shorter periods are 20 years' user as of right for easements, and 30 years for profits. The longer periods are 40 years' user as of right for easements, and 60 years for profits.

Where a claim for an easement or a profit is based on 20 or 30 years' user as of right, the claim will not 'be defeated or destroyed by showing only that such right, profit, or benefit was first taken or enjoyed at any time prior to such period of [twenty] thirty years, but such claim may be defeated in any other way by which the same is now liable to be defeated'.

Where a claim for an easement or a profit is based on 40 or 60 years' user as of right, 'the right thereto shall be deemed absolute and indefeasible'.

We will return to the differences between the shorter and longer periods at **25.7.3**. For the moment it is sufficient to say that most cases will be covered by the shorter periods. It will be relatively rare that a dominant owner will want to rely on the longer periods.

25.7.2 The 'next before action' and 'without interruption' rules

Section 4 of the 1832 Act introduces **for the purposes of the Act** (but not for the other forms of prescription) two very strange rules.

25.7.2.1 The 'next before action' rule

Each of the respective periods of years hereinbefore mentioned shall be deemed and taken to be the period next before some suit or action wherein the claim or matter . . . be brought into question.

What this really means is that the period of 'user as of right' relied on by the dominant owner for the purposes of the 1832 Act must be a period ending when the dispute between the parties arises. The dispute 'arises' when the writ or claim form in the court case is issued. (It does not matter whether it is the servient owner suing as claimant (plaintiff) claiming that there is no easement or profit or the dominant owner suing as claimant (plaintiff) claiming a prescriptive easement or profit.)

If there is a period (however long) of 'user as of right' **followed by a gap when there is no user**, and then after this gap the writ or claim form is issued, the Prescription Act 1832 is no help to the dominant owner. He will have to rely on one of the other forms of prescription.

This point is illustrated by the facts of *Oakley* v *Boston* (see 25.6). The judge found as a fact that regular user as of right ceased in 1962. The writ in the case was not issued until 1972. Because of the 10 year gap in activity the alleged dominant owner had no chance under the 1832 Act. Similarly in *Mills* v *Silver*, the dominant owners could rely only on lost modern grant, since the user as of right had been from 1922 to 1981 but the writ was not issued until 1987. (See also para. 29 of Lord Scott's speech in *Bakewell Management* v *Brandwood*.)

25.7.2.2 The 'without interruption' rule

No act or other matter shall be deemed to be an interruption within the meaning of the statute, unless the same shall have been or shall be submitted to or acquiesced in for one year after the party interrupted shall have had or shall have notice thereof and of the person making or authorising the same to be made.

This rule always reminds me of the children's riddle, 'When is a door not a door? When its ajar'. The riddle I pose to you is, 'When is an interruption not an interruption?' The answer is

'When we are dealing with the Prescription Act 1832 and the interruption has lasted less than a year'.

Suppose that in 1977, Tom, the owner of Greenacre, started (as of right) to cross Fred's Brownacre to get to and from Greenacre. In 1997, for about six months, the path across Brownacre was blocked by Fred. Fred then removed the blockage and Tom recommenced his user as of right. Fred has once again blocked the path.

> **? QUESTION 25.4**
>
> If Tom immediately issues a claim form claiming a prescriptive easement, will he win the case?

Yes, he will win. He will be able to show some 30 years' user 'next before action'. The six months' interruption is not an interruption for the purposes of the 1832 Act. (The result would be different if, back around 1997, Fred had blocked the path for 15 months.)

In **Question 25.4** I indicated that Tom immediately issued a claim when his path was blocked a second time. This was to avoid the (fatal for the dominant owner) gap between user as of right and commencement of legal proceedings.

Actually the immediate issue of a claim form is not essential. The 'without interruption' rule in effect creates an exception to the 'next before action' rule. Provided legal proceedings are commenced **within a year** of the date when the interruption first actually occurred, a dominant owner will be able to rely on user as of right continuing up to that date of actual interruption. (In our Tom and Greenacre example, Tom would lose if he delayed more than a year before issuing his claim.)

25.7.2.3 Interruption of user as of right in the twentieth year

The strange quirks of s. 4 were demonstrated as early as 1841 in the House of Lords case of *Flight v Thomas* (1841) 8 ER 91. In that case the dominant owner had enjoyed his easement as of right for 19 years and 11 months. He was then interrupted by an obstruction. He waited a few months before issuing his writ. Thus 20 years had elapsed from the commencement of his user as of right, but he had not yet been 'interrupted' for one year.

> **⚠ EXERCISE 25.3**
>
> What do you think was the result of the case?

The dominant owner was held to have a prescriptive easement. The practical result of this decision is that enjoyment for 19 years and a bit (even one day) will be sufficient to give a prescriptive easement under the 1832 Act, provided that the dominant owner times the issue of his claim form correctly. Similar principles would apply where one of the longer periods of prescription was being relied on and the interruption occurred in the thirtieth, fortieth, or sixtieth year of user as of right.

QUESTION 25.5

In January 1988, David started to cut across Greenacre to get to Yellowacre, and has done so ever since. Suppose it is now March 2007. What should Shane, the owner of Greenacre, do to stop David gaining an easement?

Shane should immediately issue a claim form against David. David will have only 19 years' (and a bit) user 'next before action', and therefore any claim for a prescriptive easement is bound to fail.

QUESTION 25.6

Suppose, in March 2007, Shane does not issue a claim form but instead puts up a fence barring David's way. What should David do?

David should 'lie low' until February 2008, and then issue a claim form claiming that he has a prescriptive easement. He should win, as the claim will be more than 20 years after user as of right commenced, but the 'interruption' will not have lasted one year.

25.7.3 Differences between longer and shorter periods under the Prescription Act 1832

25.7.3.1 Oral permissions

When enacting the longer periods of prescription, the 1832 Act (ss. 1 and 2) states that after 40 or 60 years' user, 'The right thereto [to the easement or profit] shall be deemed absolute and indefeasible, unless it shall appear that the same was taken and enjoyed by some consent or agreement expressly made or given for that purpose by deed or writing'.

User, to be prescriptive under the Prescription Act 1832, must (in principle) be 'as of right'. Thus the reference to 'consent . . . by deed or writing' seems very confusing. It would appear (though this has never been firmly decided by the courts) that for the longer periods of prescription the strange wording of the statute creates a small **exception** to the general rule that user to be prescriptive must be 'as of right'. It seems that if there has been 40 (or 60) years' user originally based on a purely **oral** permission, but that permission has not been renewed in the last 40 or 60 years, the user is prescriptive.

Suppose that in 1966 Stephen, the owner of Bluefield, gave oral permission to Daphne, the owner of Redfield, allowing Daphne to cross Bluefield to get to Redfield. That permission has never been renewed and Daphne has been crossing Bluefield for the last 40-something years. Although normally a permission lasts indefinitely (see 25.4.3), an **oral** permission **given more than 40 years ago is ignored**. Thus Daphne acquires a prescriptive easement of way under the longer period.

If Stephen had renewed the oral permission at any time in the last 40 years (say in 1977) Daphne would lose her claim for a prescriptive easement: *Gardner* v *Hodgson's Kingston Brewery* [1903] AC 229 and *Healey* v *Hawkins* [1968] 3 All ER 836.

25.7.3.2 Periods excluded from computation by s. 7 of the 1832 Act

Section 7 of the 1832 Act applies only with respect to the shorter (20- or 30-year) prescription periods:

Provided also, that the time during which any person otherwise capable of resisting the claim . . . shall have been or shall be an infant, idiot, non compos mentis, [feme covert], or tenant for life . . . shall be excluded in the computation of the periods hereinbefore mentioned . . .

This section creates a special rule designed to protect **servient** owners who are under a 'disability'. In effect a period of user against a person under one of the disabilities listed in s. 7 is not to count towards the 20 (30) years. The 'disabilities' are insanity, being under age, and being a life tenant. Being a 'feme covert' (married woman) was a disability until 1882!

? **QUESTION** 25.7

Suppose in 1981, W commenced user as of right of a pathway over X's land. From 1988 to 1996, X was insane. W (if he continues the user as of right) does not acquire any right under the Act until . . . ?

The answer is 2009. One way of looking at this is to say that the eight years of the insanity has to be added to the normal prescription period of 20 years to produce a total period of 28 years.

Suppose that, in the example in **Question 25.7**, between 1991 and 1995 (while X was insane) user as of right was prevented by a barbed wire fence. W's claim for a prescriptive easement will fail. Section 7 is purely for the protection of servient owners. An 'interruption' occurring during the period of the disability cannot be ignored!

25.7.3.3 Periods excluded from computation by s. 8 of the 1832 Act

This provision applies only to the 40-year period of prescription for easements. (It has no application to profits.)

To try to help make sense of the provision, I have split it into three parts below. (You will also see that I have written the word 'easement' in the second line, although in the official edition of the 1832 Act the word used is 'convenient'. The word 'convenient' makes no sense: it is thought that it is a misprint for 'easement'.)

Provided always, that when any land or water upon, over, or from which any such way or other [easement] watercourse or use of water shall have been or shall be enjoyed or derived hath been or shall be held under or by virtue of any term of life, or any term of years exceeding three years from the granting thereof,

the time of enjoyment of any such way or other matter as hereinbefore mentioned, during the continuance of such terms, shall be excluded in the computation of the said period of forty years,

in case the claim within three years after the end or sooner determination of such term be resisted by any person entitled to any reversion expectant on the determination thereof.

Section 8 operates in a way somewhat similar to s. 7 (see 25.7.3.2). However, notice carefully:

(a) that the 'disabilities' are that either the servient land has been leased for a period of more than three years, or that the servient owner was a life tenant. (See the last words of the first part of the section.);

(b) a servient owner can invoke the special protection given him by s. 8 only if proceedings disputing the easement are commenced within three years of the lease or life tenancy expiring. (See the third part of the section.)

 EXERCISE 25.4

Suppose Alf commenced user as of right of a path over Blackacre in 1961 and has continued ever since. From June 1964 to June 2004, the servient land was subject to a strict settlement under which Leonard was the life tenant.

What is the position under the 1832 Act if in March 2007 either Alf commences an action claiming an easement, or the (new) servient fee simple owner commences proceedings against Alf?

The servient owner would win in proceedings based on the 1832 Act; he would be able to invoke the protection of s. 8, and therefore a claim under the longer 40-year period would fail.

 QUESTION 25.8

What if legal proceedings (begun by Alf or the servient owner) were not commenced until July 2007?

The servient owner would be too late to invoke the protection of s. 8, as more than three years would have elapsed since the expiry of the life tenancy. Alf would win under the longer period provided by the 1832 Act.

25.7.3.4 The requirement that user be 'against a fee simple' does not apply to the longer periods of prescription

(See **25.4.5,** for the general rule.)

 EXERCISE 25.5

Continue the example I have been just discussing in **Exercise 25.4** and **Question 25.8**. Suppose the servient land was settled from June 1954 to June 2004, and that Alf's user as of right commenced (as before) in 1961. Further suppose that it is now March 2008, and Alf has just issued a claim form claiming a prescriptive easement under the 40-year period. Will he win?

Normally, the fact that user as of right commenced against a life tenant or lessee is fatal to a claim for a prescriptive easement. But when dealing with the 40-year period under the 1832 Act, the usual rule about 'user [commencing] against a fee simple' does not apply. So Alf will succeed in a claim under the 40-year period despite commencing his user against a life tenant.

? QUESTION 25.9

Use the same example as in **Exercise 25.5**, except that the servient (fee simple) owner issued a claim form against Alf sometime in 2007. Who will win this case?

Provided he issued his claim form before June 2007, the servient owner will win, as he will be protected by s. 8. If the servient owner delayed to the latter half of 2007 he would lose, as he would be outside the three-year period for 'resisting' given by the last part of s. 8 (see 25.7.3.3).

25.7.4 Prescription for easements of light

This is governed by s. 3 of the Prescription Act 1832. Section 3 was designed to make it easier to acquire a prescriptive easement for light. Unfortunately, it is, if anything, now too easy for a building to acquire a prescriptive easement of light over an adjoining vacant plot of land. The rules under s. 3 differ quite substantially from the normal rules governing prescription.

25.7.4.1 User under s. 3 need not be as of right

This was established in *Morgan* v *Fear* [1907] AC 425. The only aspect of user as of right applicable to s. 3 cases is that a **written** permission will debar a claim. Thus, if a dominant owner kept on demolishing obstructions to his light which appeared on the servient land, he could acquire a prescriptive easement! (He would, however, be liable for trespassing on the servient land when carrying out his demolition work.)

25.7.4.2 The normal rules about user 'by or on behalf of a fee simple against a fee simple' do not apply

Under s. 3 of the 1832 Act, a tenant can prescribe against his own landlord, or against a fellow tenant of his own landlord. (Yet apparently any easement which arises under s. 3 is in fee simple!)

25.7.4.3 Rights of Light Act 1959

In 1959, there were still some war-time bomb-sites which had not been redeveloped. It was suddenly realized that it had been nearly 20 years since 'the blitz', and that if there was not special legislation, prescriptive rights of light would be acquired over bomb-sites. Such rights of light would severely limit redevelopment.

The 1959 Act included temporary provisions which are now only of historic interest. The prescription period was extended to 27 years if the action related to an infringement occurring before 1 January 1963.

The Act also included permanent provisions (of an almost comical nature) which remain in force today.

Prior to the Second World War, if you owned land over which there was a risk that a neighbour would acquire a prescriptive easement of light, you erected enormous hoardings on your land to block out his light. With the advent of modern planning law, this is no longer possible.

The 1959 Act creates a procedure for erecting **imaginary** buildings on one's land. You do not need planning permission to erect your imaginary building, and you should make your imaginary building very large!

You, 'the potential servient owner', register an imaginary obstruction on your land in the **local** land charges register kept by the District Council. Registration is equivalent to an obstruction acquiesced in for one year, and the registration lasts only one year.

 EXERCISE 25.6

To be safe, how often should you register under the 1959 Act?

To be on the safe side, you should make a registration every **19** years. In that way your neighbour can never acquire a prescriptive easement of light.

If an imaginary obstruction is erected under the 1959 Act, the dominant owner may want to claim that he already has an easement of light and that the 'obstruction' has come too late. The 1959 Act allows him to sue as if his light were actually obstructed!

25.8 **Prescriptive easements and profits as legal interests**

Every prescriptive easement or profit which arises under the rules discussed in this chapter is

(a) of fee simple duration; and

(b) **deemed** to be created by deed.

It therefore follows that all prescriptive easements and profits are **legal** interests. Consequently, if the servient land is unregistered title, a prescriptive easement or profit will be good against the whole world. It will automatically be binding on a purchaser, whether or not that purchaser knew of the easement or profit.

25.8.1 **Prescriptive easements and profits—overriding interests?**

If a prescriptive easement or profit arises **prior** to the commencement of the Land Registration Act 2002, it will always be an overriding interest under s. 70(1)(a) of the 1925 LRA.

If, however, a prescriptive easement or profit first arises **after** the commencement of the Land Registration Act 2002, it will **usually**, but not always, be an overriding interest under the rules discussed in detail at 10.3.3.4.

CONCLUDING REMARKS

It has to be said that the English law of prescription is extremely complex, and is clearly in need of simplification and reform. Yet Parliament has, with the Land Registration Act 2002, added yet another complication. Perhaps our only consolation when we consider the complexities of the law is that (especially with the 1832 and 1959 Acts) there are aspects which are faintly comical.

There have been suggestions that the whole law of prescription should be abolished. Why should somebody, by trespassing for a long enough time, acquire a **property** right to do something which previously was unlawful? On the other hand, if you have been doing something for a very long time totally unchallenged, do you not feel that you have the right to do it?

My own personal view is that a very simple and effective reform would be for Parliament to repeal the 1832 and 1959 Acts (without replacement), to abolish prescription under the '1189' common law rule, and to abolish all prescription for easements for light. That would leave just 'lost modern grant' to govern all remaining cases. (In practice these remaining cases will involve rights of way, grazing, or (occasionally) support.)

■ SUMMARY

To claim a prescriptive easement (or profit), the claimant must show a long period (usually 20 years) of user as of right which comes within one of the three types of prescription.

User as of right means user which is open and is neither with the servient owner's express consent nor against his express objections.

Prescription at common law is presumptively established if the claimant can show twenty years' user as of right. However, that presumption can usually easily be rebutted by showing that user has not been (or cannot have been) continuous since 1189.

Prescription under the Prescription Act 1832 is (in principle) established if the claimant can show 20 years' user as of right (30 years for profits) which is 'next before action'.

Prescription under lost modern grant is established if the claimant can show strong evidence of 20 years' user as of right—this user does not have to be 'next before action'. The presumption of lost modern grant can only be rebutted by showing that the grant was legally impossible.

Prescription for an easement of light is governed by s. 3 of the 1832 Act. The light must have been enjoyed for at least 20 years 'next before action'. Potential servient owners should invoke the procedure in the Rights of Light Act 1959 to prevent the acquisition of an easement of light.

CHAPTER 25: ASSESSMENT EXERCISES

1. Last month Finnegan, owner of Blackacre and Whiteacre, two neighbouring farms, sold and conveyed Blackacre to Milligan. The conveyance contained no provision relating to easements and profits. Advise Milligan regarding the following:

(a) The only direct access to Blackacre is a narrow footpath insufficiently wide to accommodate motor traffic. Milligan wishes to make use of the private driveway which runs from Blackacre through Whiteacre and leads into the adjoining public highway.

(b) Some drains run from Blackacre under Whiteacre. Milligan wishes to make use of those drains.

(c) Cyrus, the owner of Redacre, an adjoining farm, claims that he can continue to graze his sheep on a hill-side forming part of Blackacre where sheep from Redacre have been grazed 'as long as anyone can remember'.

2. In 1984 Louise acquired the freehold to Grand House. Grand House adjoins West Field, the freehold to which was then owned by Nellie. Over the years Nellie has leased West Field to Olive for short periods.

On acquiring Grand House, Louise immediately leased it to Terry for 70 years. Soon after taking the lease, Terry started to pasture the five sheep he owned in West Field, and to take a short cut across West Field to get to the nearest station. He continued both of these activities until September 2006, without any objection from Nellie or Olive.

In September 2006 Gurinder acquired the freehold to West Field from Nellie, and immediately ordered Terry not to make any further use of West Field. Initially Terry complied with this demand, but now both he and Louise are threatening legal action.

It is now January 2007. Advise Gurinder.

See Appendix for specimen answers.

■ **FURTHER READING**

For a comprehensive discussion of prescription for easements, see *Megarry and Wade: Law of Real Property* (sixth edition by Harpum) chapter 18, pages 1118–1141.

Alternatively, see Gray and Gray, *Elements of Land Law*, fourth edition, pages 692–708.

For a discussion of the (complex) impact of the Land Registration Act 2002 on easements, see Battersby, 'Some thoughts on easements under the Land Registration Act 2002' [2005] Conveyancer 195–206.

Restrictive Covenants

26 Restrictive covenants— the basic principles

26.1 Objectives

By the end of this chapter you should be able to:

1 Distinguish **restrictive** covenants from positive covenants
2 Explain the rules which govern the running of the **burden** of restrictive covenants
3 Appreciate the true significance of s. 56 of the Law of Property Act 1925

26.2 Introduction

(Re-read 1.4.2 which deals with restrictive covenants.)

In this and the ensuing two chapters, we study a very confusing area of law. The material in this chapter (except perhaps the case of *Wrotham Park*, see 26.6) is relatively straightforward, but **Chapter 27** will be an entirely different matter. To help give you some confidence in this area, we start with another little story; one designed to give you some idea of the issues which we will be facing in this and the following chapters.

26.3 Restrictive and positive covenants distinguished

Suppose Alfred owns in fee simple two adjoining high-class residences, Blueacre and Redacre. He plans to retain Blueacre for his own home, and to sell Redacre to Bert. Alfred wishes to maintain 'the tone of the area'. In the conveyance of the fee simple in Redacre, Alfred induces Bert to covenant:

(a) that he will keep Redacre in good repair, and repaint every five years (a **positive** covenant);

(b) not to carry on any business in Redacre (a **negative** covenant).

These covenants are expressed to be for the benefit of Blueacre rather than just for Alfred's personal benefit. (We say that the covenants are 'annexed' to Blueacre.)

Suppose Alfred sells Blueacre to Charles. In principle Charles can enforce the covenants against Bert. He can enforce both the positive and the negative covenants against the **original** covenantor. (In *Smith* v *River Douglas Catchment Board* [1949] 2 All ER 179, the defendants promised a farmer, for the benefit of his farm, to maintain the banks of a river. A later purchaser of the farm was held entitled to enforce this promise.)

Suppose that Bert now sells Redacre to Donald. **Can Charles sue Donald on the covenants**?

With respect to the **negative** 'no businesses' covenant, the answer is (in principle) **yes**. This 'no businesses covenant' is a restrictive covenant, governed by the elaborate law which we are about to discuss.

With respect to the **positive** 'repair and repaint' covenant, the answer is **no**. It is a principle of English law that the **burden** of a positive covenant relating to a piece of land cannot 'run with the land'. The covenant to repair and repaint is enforceable only against the original covenantor, Bert. It cannot be enforced against Donald, a purchaser of the fee simple.

 This rule, that 'positive covenants cannot run with the burdened land', has been much criticized, but was reaffirmed by the House of Lords in *Rhone* v *Stephens* [1994] 2 All ER 65.

⥊ EXERCISE 26.1

Suppose that Alfred, instead of selling Redacre to Bert, had granted him a 999-year lease charging a large premium and a nominal rent. Bert later assigned the lease to Donald. Could Alfred enforce the repair and repaint covenant against Donald?

If you did not know the answer to this question, refer back to **19.3**. A repair and repaint covenant contained in the 999-year lease would be enforceable by Alfred against Donald under the doctrine of privity of estate.

26.3.1 Restrictive covenants law divides itself into three parts

(a) Issues relating to the running of the burden of covenants with the servient land.

(b) Issues relating to the running of the benefit of covenants with the dominant land.

(c) Developers trying to 'escape' from restrictive covenants burdening their land.

Issue (a) is straightforward and is discussed below. Issue (b), dealt with in **Chapter 27**, is notoriously complex: the courts (particularly in the last 50 years) created a total mess, though a recent Court of Appeal decision has somewhat simplified matters. Issue (c), dealt with in **Chapter 28**, is also quite complex, but has an element of excitement about it!

26.4 Passing the burden of a restrictive covenant

Three conditions must be fulfilled before the obligation to observe a restrictive covenant will pass to a successor in title to the servient land.

26.4.1 **The covenant must be negative in substance**

The test is that the observance of the covenant must not necessitate expenditure on the part of the servient owner. A covenant 'not to allow this building to fall into disrepair' is of course positive, and not a restrictive covenant. On the other hand, a covenant 'to keep Xacre as an open space uncovered by buildings' (the covenant involved in the 1847 case of *Tulk* v *Moxhay* (1848) [1843–60] All ER Rep 9 which in effect invented this whole area of law) is a restrictive covenant.

26.4.2 **The covenant must be made with an intent to burden the servient land**

The nineteenth-century lawyers who 'invented' restrictive covenants drew a distinction between:

(a) a covenant intended to bind only the covenantor; and

(b) a covenant intended to throw a continuing burden on the land itself and thereby bind all subsequent owners of the land.

Only the latter type of covenant is a valid restrictive covenant.

Nineteenth-century covenants usually included phraseology like, 'I Charley Farns-Barns covenant on behalf of myself and my successors in title . . .'. This long-winded phraseology is no longer necessary, as the point is now covered by a '**word-saving**' provision, s. 79(1) of the Law of Property Act 1925:

A covenant relating to any land of a covenantor or capable of being bound by him, shall, unless a contrary intention is expressed, be deemed to be made by the covenantor on behalf of himself his successors in title and the persons deriving title under him or them, and, subject as aforesaid, shall have effect as if such successors and other persons were expressed.

Section 79(1) in effect provides that covenants which relate to the covenantor's land are **deemed** to be made on behalf of his successors in title **unless** the contrary appears from the terms of the covenant. Thus anybody who makes a covenant about the use of his land is presumed to intend that the covenant will be a **permanent burden** on the land irrespective of its ownership. In the unlikely event that it is desired that covenant should bind only the original covenantor and not his successors, this will have to be expressly stated.

26.4.3 **The covenant must be made to protect dominant land retained by the covenantee**

In *London County Council* v *[Mrs] Allen* [1914] 3 KB 642 the LCC sold a large amount of land to Mr Allen, a builder. With respect to one small part of the land, Mr Allen covenanted not to build upon it. This small parcel was intended as an open space for the local residents. The LCC retained no other land in the vicinity.

Mr Allen sold the small parcel to his wife, who commenced building work. The LCC sought an injunction against Mrs Allen, which was refused. The Council had no dominant land, so it could not claim it had the benefit of a restrictive covenant. (Nowadays the Council would use town planning law to curb Mr and Mrs Allen's activities.)

A rather different problem arose in *Newton Abbot Co-operative Society Ltd* v *Williamson and Treadgold* [1952] 1 All ER 279. Originally, a Mrs Mardon owned two shops in the small central Devon town of Bovey Tracey. The shops were about 50 yards apart on opposite sides of the street.

In 1923, Mrs Mardon sold one of the shops. In the conveyance of that shop there was imposed a restrictive covenant which said that no ironmongery was to be sold from the shop. The restrictive covenant did not identify the dominant land. However, the shop across the road retained by Mrs Mardon sold . . . ironmongery!

The judge held that there was a valid restrictive covenant which bound a subsequent purchaser of the shop sold by Mrs Mardon in 1923. Although the dominant land was not expressly identified in the conveyance which contained the restrictive covenant, it could be identified by examining the geography of the locality. That, in the view of the judge, was sufficient.

 EXERCISE 26.2

What would have been the legal position if the shops had been 500 yards apart in a large city?

You might well argue that there would be no valid restrictive covenant, as it would not be possible confidently to identify the dominant land.

26.5 Restrictive covenants as equitable interests

Restrictive covenants were in effect first 'invented' in the mid-nineteenth century by the pre-1875 Court of Chancery. The common law courts never recognized them. Thus, historically, all restrictive covenants are equitable interests, and this was confirmed by s. 1 of the Law of Property Act 1925. It follows that:

(a) Where the servient estate is unregistered title, a pre-1926 restrictive covenant is still subject to the doctrine of notice.

(b) Where the servient estate is unregistered title, a post-1925 restrictive covenant is registrable as a land charge.

(c) Where the servient estate is registered title, the restrictive covenant is a minor interest which must be protected by entry on the register of a notice. (Prior to 2003 a caution might have been used.)

26.6 Remedies to enforce a restrictive covenant

The fact that a restrictive covenant is always only an equitable interest means that the principal remedy to enforce a restrictive covenant against a successor in title to the servient land is an injunction; there is no **automatic** right to damages.

In restrictive covenant cases the court has a discretion as to the remedy it can grant. The court may award damages instead of or in addition to an injunction. The discretion which the court has on matters of remedies is well illustrated by the decision in *Wrotham Park Estate* v *Parkside Homes* [1974] 2 All ER 321.

In 1935, the Wrotham Park Estate, then owned by the Earl of Strafford, extended to about 4,000 acres. In that year the Earl sold 47 acres out of the Estate. This land was subject to a restrictive covenant 'not to develop the . . . land for building purposes except in strict accordance with plans [approved by the owners of Wrotham Park Estate]'. The covenant was expressed to be for the benefit of the 'Wrotham Park Estate'.

This sort of restrictive covenant is quite common. The dominant owners do not want totally to prevent development of the servient land; they just want to ensure that the development is 'good class', not low grade, development.

The plaintiff company later acquired Wrotham Park Estate. The defendant, Parkside Homes, acquired a small part of the servient land. The defendant obtained planning permission **from the local authority** to build 13 'middle class' houses on this land. It did not, however, submit its plans to the plaintiff for approval. It believed (for reasons which will be explained at 27.3.1.3) that the plaintiff was not entitled to enforce the covenant.

In January 1972, the defendant started to lay foundations. On 14 February, the plaintiff issued a writ claiming an injunction to restrain building. The plaintiff, however, then made a mistake. It did not apply for an 'interlocutory', i.e., temporary, injunction to restrain the development pending a full trial of the dispute.

The defendant carried on building, and by the date of the trial before Brightman J (July 1973) the 13 houses were complete and 13 married couples had purchased them and moved in.

Brightman J held (for reasons which I will explain in the next chapter) that the plaintiff was entitled to enforce the restrictive covenant. The plaintiff, having won on that issue, took the attitude, 'The defendant has acted in defiance of our rights. There is a danger that the tone of the area will go down. The only way our rights can be protected is if the court makes an order (a "mandatory injunction") that the houses be demolished'.

Brightman J refused to grant such an order: 'It would, in my opinion, be an unpardonable waste of much needed houses to direct that they be pulled down'. He thus exercised his 'discretion' to refuse an injunction. But he also 'in his discretion' decided to award the plaintiff damages. How much damages should he award?

The houses themselves were of good quality, situated in an area (Potters Bar) which is prime 'commuter belt' for London. The existence of these houses did not in any way lower the tone of the area. There was every reason to suppose that if the defendant had complied with the covenant and submitted plans to the plaintiff, the plaintiff would have approved them.

You may be thinking that the judge therefore awarded nominal damages, but this would be allowing the defendant 'to get away with it'. Brightman J took note of a fact which you may find surprising but which is perfectly true. The dominant owner to a restrictive covenant is often willing to execute a deed releasing the servient land from the covenant. However, the dominant owner usually requires that he be paid a consideration (some would say 'bribe') for releasing the covenant. He often asks for a percentage of the profit the defendant will make from developing the (ex)-servient land.

Brightman J (correctly in my view) decided to award the plaintiff the 'price' it could **reasonably** have asked for releasing the covenant. The plaintiff suggested 50 per cent of the defendant's profits on the 13 houses. The judge awarded 5 per cent! The total profit was estimated at £50,000, thus the plaintiff got £2,500.

This award of damages by Brightman J in *Wrotham Park* was criticized in some quarters, but, in *Jaggard* v *Sawyer* [1995] 1 WLR 269, the Court of Appeal approved it and applied it to a situation where a single house had been built in a garden in breach of a restrictive covenant. As in *Wrotham Park*, damages were awarded on the basis of what a reasonable dominant owner could have asked for releasing the covenant. Moreover, in *Gafford* v *Graham* (1998) 77 P & CR 73, the Court of Appeal refused an injunction which would have demolished a riding school built in breach of a restrictive covenant, and again granted only damages.

26.7 The benefit of restrictive covenants—identifying the original covenantees

It is perfectly possible to enter into a restrictive covenant for the benefit of a number of original covenantees. For example, a restrictive covenant is entered into in favour of several landowners all with land adjacent to the servient land.

Suppose Ernest owned Centreacre and Eastacre. Centreacre is surrounded by Eastacre, Northacre, Westacre, and Southacre. Northacre is owned by Norman, Westacre by William, and Southacre by Stephen. All five parcels of land are farmland.

Ernest sells Centreacre to Celia. In the conveyance of Centreacre Celia covenants, for the benefit of Eastacre, Northacre, Westacre, and Southacre, that Centreacre will be used for agricultural purposes only. Thus clearly there are four parcels of dominant land and four original covenantees.

Prior to the Conveyancing Act 1881 there was a problem with the kind of arrangement just described. There was an old common law rule that only people who actually executed a deed could claim benefits under the deed. In our example only Celia and Ernest would execute the deed containing the restrictive covenant. Thus at common law only Ernest could claim to be an original covenantee and only Eastacre was dominant land. This, of course, was contrary to what Ernest and Celia intended.

The inconvenient old common law rule was abolished by what is now s. 56 of the Law of Property Act 1925. Under that section, any person identifiable at the time the deed is executed and intended to have the benefit of a covenant is an original covenantee, whether or not he executed the deed containing the covenant.

> **?** **QUESTION** 26.1
>
> In our example, under the modern law, who are the original covenantees, and what is/are the dominant land(s)?

I hope you deduced that Ernest, Norman, William, and Stephen are **all** original covenantees. Eastacre, Northacre, Westacre, and Southacre are separate parcels of dominant land.

CONCLUDING REMARKS

In this chapter you should have learnt three things of importance: the circumstances in which a restrictive covenant is enforceable against the servient land; the remedies available to a dominant owner when a restrictive covenant is infringed; the identification of the original covenantees. We are now in a position to move on to **Chapter 27**, in which we consider the various ways in which the right to enforce a restrictive covenant can pass from an original covenantee (in the example just considered, Ernest, Norman, William, and Stephen were all original covenantees) to a successor in title to that covenantee's land.

■ SUMMARY

For there to be a valid restrictive covenant, enforceable against successors in title to the servient land:

(a) the covenant must be intended to burden successors in title. This intention is normally presumed (LPA, s.79);

(b) the covenant must protect land retained by the covenantee;

(c) the covenant must be negative in substance.

A restrictive covenant is an equitable interest in land. The normal remedy for enforcing a restrictive covenant is an injunction. However, if a building has been completed in breach of covenant, the court is likely to award damages rather than order demolition of the premises.

A restrictive covenant may have several original covenantees (original dominant owners). An original covenantee (provided he is identified) need not sign the deed.

■ FURTHER READING

For a discussion of the House of Lords' decision in *Rhone* v *Stephens*, see John Snape, 'The burden of positive covenants' (1994) 58 Conveyancer 477.

27 The passing of the benefit of restrictive covenants

27.1 Objectives

By the end of this chapter you should be able to:

1 Explain how the concept of annexation of restrictive covenants operated prior to the controversial decision in *Federated Homes*

2 Understand the confusion created by the Court of Appeal decision in *Federated Homes* and how that confusion has now been largely resolved by the decision in *Crest Nicholson*

3 Explain the rules regarding assignment of restrictive covenants

4 Explain the concept 'building scheme'

5 Appreciate why the Law Commission is highly critical of the current state of the law

27.2 Introduction

I want you to think back to the law of easements for a moment. If an easement is appurtenant to a parcel of dominant land, then that easement automatically 'runs' with the dominant land. This means that anybody who acquires the dominant land can automatically enjoy the benefit of the easement.

I wish I could make a similar simple statement about the benefit of restrictive covenants. Unfortunately that is impossible. The law as to when a successor to dominant land acquires the right to enforce a restrictive covenant benefiting that land is extremely complex.

Indeed, there are three **alternative** sets of rules. If, but only if, a successor to the dominant land can bring himself within **one** of these sets of rules, he will be able to enforce the restrictive covenant. The sets of rules are:

(a) Annexation.

(b) Assignment.

(c) 'Building scheme'.

These sets of rules originally were developed in the nineteenth and early twentieth centuries. Until the Second World War the rules (though already quite complex) were clear and strictly enforced. Their strict enforcement sometimes meant that a purchaser of dominant land did not get the benefit of an existing covenant intended to benefit that land. But the law had the **great merit of certainty.**

That certainty was destroyed by some extremely short-sighted decisions of the courts, most notably the Court of Appeal decision in *Federated Homes Ltd* v *Mill Lodge Properties Ltd* [1980] 1 All ER 371. Those decisions showed an alarming trend to bend or change the old rules in favour of persons **claiming to be dominant owners.**

This trend made life very difficult for servient owners generally. If a person owns land which is subject to a restrictive covenant, it is sometimes very difficult to work out who the dominant owners are and thus who, if anyone, is entitled to sue if the covenant is broken. However, the recent Court of Appeal decision in *Crest Nicholson* v *McCallister* [2004] 1 WLR 2409 should make life easier for servient owners.

27.3 Annexation

The essence of annexation is easy to follow. If the benefit of a restrictive covenant is annexed to Blackacre then (*cf.* an appurtenant easement) the right to enforce the covenant passes on to all successors in title to Blackacre.

Unfortunately, considerable confusion was introduced into this area of the law by the judgment of the Court of Appeal in *Federated Homes Ltd* v *Mill Lodge Properties Ltd*, but the recent decision in *Crest Nicholson* largely ends that confusion.

In any event, *Federated Homes* (as it was interpreted between 1980 and 2004) could not apply to covenants entered into pre-1926. This was confirmed by the decision in *Sainsburys* v *Enfield Borough Council* [1989] 2 All ER 817. So we must first consider the law ignoring *Federated Homes*, as that 'old' law still applies to pre-1926 covenants. I must then endeavour to explain the effect of *Federated Homes* as it was interpreted between 1980 and 2004, and finally consider how *Crest Nicholson* has (largely) restored sanity to this area of law.

27.3.1 The traditional viewpoint on annexation (applicable to pre-1926 covenants)

According to the traditional view (ignoring *Federated Homes*), annexation can be achieved only by drafting the document containing the restrictive covenant to **express** an intention to benefit a defined piece of land, rather than merely to benefit the original covenantee.

To achieve annexation to (say) Blackacre, drafting using one of the following methods should be employed (even today competent solicitors always use one of these formulations):

(a) 'This covenant is entered into for the benefit of Blackacre'.

(b) 'This covenant is entered into for the benefit of Jones in his capacity as owner of Blackacre'.

(c) 'This covenant is entered into with Jones and his successors in title to Blackacre'.

The traditional approach to annexation is best exemplified by *Renals* v *Cowlishaw* (1879) 11 ChD 866. The conveyance of the servient land said that the restrictive covenant was entered into for the benefit of the vendors, 'their heirs, administrators and assigns'. That phrase implied the existence of dominant land, but the conveyance did not identify any dominant land. That omission was fatal. The Court of Appeal held that there had been no annexation.

A modern case, *Jamaica Mutual Life Assurance* v *Hillsborough* [1989] 1 WLR 1101, also involved a situation where the dominant land was not expressly identified. The Privy Council was applying Jamaican (**not English**) law, and held that in **Jamaica** annexation can be achieved only by an express clause in the document creating the restrictive covenants.

27.3.1.1 Annexation to the whole or to each and every part?

On the traditional view of the law, a restrictive covenant which is annexed to 'Blackacre' is presumptively annexed **only to the whole of Blackacre**. This presumption can be rebutted if the conveyance includes some phrase such as 'this covenant is annexed to Blackacre and each and every part thereof'.

When drafting a restrictive covenant for the benefit of a large piece of land, the solicitor acting for the dominant owner needs to decide whether:

(a) to annex the covenant only to the whole of the dominant land; **or**

(b) to annex the covenant to 'each and every part of the dominant land'.

Each alternative has its advantages and disadvantages.

27.3.1.2 The disadvantages of annexation only to the whole of the dominant land—the 'small plot-big plot' situation

Any annexation only to the whole may be ineffective if the servient land is small and the dominant land is (relatively) very large. This is because the dominant owner must prove that **the whole of the large** dominant land benefits from the covenant. The leading case is *Re Ballard* [1937] 2 All ER 691.

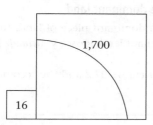

Figure 27.1 The dominant and servient land in *Re Ballard*

The then owners of the Childwickbury Estate sold 16 acres on the edge of the Estate, but subject to a restrictive covenant that the land sold should be used for agricultural purposes only. This covenant was expressed to be for the benefit of 'the whole of the Childwickbury Estate'. Childwickbury extended to 1,700 acres.

The judge held that there was no valid annexation. For annexation to be valid, the current owners of Childwickbury would have to have proved that **all 1,700 acres** were benefited by the 'agriculture only' covenant. In the judge's view, those parts of Childwickbury close to the 16 acres were benefited, but those further away were not.

If the covenant had been entered into 'for the benefit of Childwickbury and each and every part thereof', there would have been a valid annexation to those parts of Childwickbury close to the 16 acres, but not to those parts further away. There would have been a valid annexation to those parts south-west of the circular line in **Figure 27.1**, but not to those north-east thereof. (Where exactly the 'circular line' should be drawn, of course, might be subject to fierce dispute!)

27.3.1.3 The modern trend in 'small plot-big plot' cases

In the last 50 years the courts have been much more willing to find as a fact that a covenant on a very small piece of land does benefit the whole of a large plot. (Such findings of fact were made in *Marten* v *Flight Refuelling* [1961] 2 All ER 696 at 706; *Earl of Leicester* v *Wells-next-the-Sea UDC* [1972] 3 All ER 89, and in *Wrotham Park Estate* v *Parkside Homes* [1974] 2 All ER 321.)

You will recall that in *Wrotham Park Estate* v *Parkside Homes*, a covenant over 47 acres was annexed to the whole of a large estate extending to 4,000 acres. Was that annexation valid? The plaintiff called expert evidence from surveyors that the covenant over 47 acres could benefit all 4,000 acres. The defendant called expert evidence that the covenant could not possibly benefit all 4,000 acres. I am sure that judges from earlier generations would have laughed at the plaintiff's evidence and found that there was no valid annexation. Such judges would have dismissed the proceedings, and the issue of remedies discussed at 26.6 would not have arisen.

However Brightman J held:

> There can be obvious cases where a restrictive covenant clearly is, or clearly is not, of benefit to an estate. Between the two extremes there is inevitably an area where the benefit to the estate is a matter of personal opinion where responsible and reasonable persons can have divergent views.

In other words, if there is conflicting evidence as to whether the whole of the large plot benefits from the covenant, the decision should go in favour of annexation to the whole of the large piece of land. Thus the owners of Wrotham Park got the benefit of the doubt. The covenant was held to be validly annexed to the whole of their land and they could enforce the covenant.

27.3.1.4 Annexation destroyed on sub-division of the dominant land

If there is a valid annexation to (only) the whole of a dominant piece of land, then that annexation is destroyed on the subdivision of the dominant land: *Russell* v *Archdale* [1962] 2 All ER 305.

You should understand this principle if you consider **Figure 27.2** and the accompanying example.

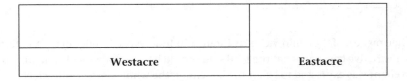

Westacre	Eastacre

Figure 27.2 Annexation destroyed where dominant land subdivided

Suppose the owner of Eastacre enters into a restrictive covenant expressed to be for the benefit of (only) the whole of Westacre. While Westacre remains all in one piece there is no problem; successive owners of Westacre can enforce the covenant. But if Wally, the current owner of Westacre, sells the northern half of the plot to (say) Norma, the right to enforce the covenant will **not** pass by virtue of annexation to Norma.

If Wally then sold the southern half of Westacre to Sally, Sally would not get the benefit of the covenant by virtue of annexation either. As I said before, the division of the land **destroys** the annexation.

> ### EXERCISE 27.1
>
> Consider what the position would be if the annexation had been to 'Westacre and each and every part thereof'.

The splitting of the land would **not** have been fatal to annexation. Both Norma and Sally would acquire the right to enforce the covenant.

27.3.1.5 **The disadvantage of annexation to each and every part**

When the dominant land is subdivided, the number of owners entitled to enforce the covenant is bound to increase; with a large dominant area the number of dominant owners could initially be one, but later be enormous. Consider the situation represented by the figure below.

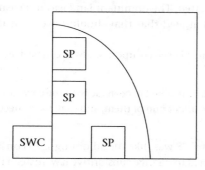

Figure 27.3 Annexation to each and every part of Bigpots Estate

The Duke of Dunstable owns the huge Bigpots Estate. He sells off 'south-west corner' (SWC), subject to a restrictive covenant banning building on the land. The covenant is annexed 'to the Bigpots Estate and each and every part thereof'. Subsequently the Duke sells off other small pieces of land (SP) near to south-west corner.

Sid, the current owner of south-west corner, asks the Duke to cancel the 'no building' covenant. The Duke agrees to do so 'for a consideration of £20,000'. Sid obtains planning permission, but the purchasers of the other small pieces near to south-west corner have acquired the right to enforce the covenant! Any one of them could enforce the covenant against Sid.

27.3.2 *Federated Homes* and 'statutory annexation'

It is possible to get tangled up in the facts of this case, so I am going to simplify the facts to their bare essentials. I will start by making two comments on those facts. First, the restrictive covenant involved was of a rather unusual type. You may well ask, 'Should these sorts of covenant be allowed?' I personally think they should be banned, but that is irrelevant! Under current law, they **are** allowed.

Secondly, it would appear that a large amount of money (profits from a large housing development) hung on the outcome of the case. The dispute arose because of bad drafting of the original restrictive covenant. One would think that solicitors acting for property developers would be punctilious in their drafting.

The story in the case starts with a firm called Mackenzie Hill Ltd owning a large amount of development land at Newport Pagnell (just north of Milton Keynes). It had outline planning permission to develop the land with 1,250 houses. It sold part of that land to Mill Lodge. The conveyance included a restrictive covenant:

In carrying out the development of the . . . land the purchaser shall not build at a greater density than a total of 300 dwellings so as not to reduce the number of units [i.e., houses] which the vendor might eventually erect on the retained land under the existing planning consent.

Mackenzie Hill later sold the land they retained in the area to Federated Homes. The Court of Appeal had (*inter alia*) to decide whether the above clause effected an annexation so that on the sale of the 'retained land' the right to enforce the covenant passed automatically to Federated Homes.

The Court in *Federated Homes* held that the clause quoted achieved a **valid annexation**.

I am sure nineteenth-century judges would have decided otherwise. They would have held, 'No annexation, the covenant was not correctly drafted. The dominant land was not clearly identified'. Many modern lawyers (including me) argued that that should have been the decision in 1980.

However, the Court of Appeal (led by Brightman LJ) seized upon s. 78(1) of the Law of Property Act 1925. This provides:

A covenant relating to any land of the covenantee shall be deemed to be made with the covenantee and his successors in title and the persons deriving title under him or them, and shall have effect as if such successors and other persons were expressed . . .

The Court rejected the commonly held view that s. 78 was (like the adjoining s. 79 considered at 26.4.2) a '**word-saving**' provision not designed to change substantive law. Instead the Court of Appeal put forward two alternative interpretations of s. 78.

(a) There is annexation where the covenant mentions the existence of dominant land, but that land can be identified only by looking at the surrounding circumstances.

or

(b) There is annexation whenever the covenantee retains land in the vicinity of the servient land, whether that land is mentioned in the restrictive covenant or not. (Annexation will then be to all the covenantee's land in the vicinity.)

Although the first view would have been sufficient to decide the case in favour of the plaintiffs, the Court appeared to favour the second view.

27.3.2.1 *Federated Homes* and 'each and every part'

Brightman LJ caused yet further confusion with an *obiter dictum* directed at the issue of whether annexation is only to the whole of a piece of dominant land, or is to 'each and every part'. Ignoring all past decisions (including his own in *Wrotham Park*, see 27.3.1.3) he was of the view that annexation is to be presumed to be to 'each and every part' unless the contrary is expressly stated.

27.3.2.2 The practical effect of *Federated Homes* between 1980 and 2004

The decision in *Federated Homes* apparently meant that whenever a restrictive covenant had been entered into after 1925 that covenant was automatically annexed to (each and every part of) **all** land which the covenantee retained in the vicinity of the servient land. It did not matter that the conveyance containing the covenant did not identify the dominant land.

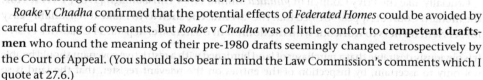

 EXERCISE 27.2

Consider the facts of the *Newton Abbot Co-op* case set out at 26.4.3. That case, as we shall see at 27.4.2, was decided on 'assignment' not 'annexation' principles. But try to apply the *Federated Homes* rule to the facts of *Newton Abbot Co-op*.

On the facts of *Newton Abbot Co-op* there would be **an annexation** to the ironmongers across the road (and each and every part of it), even though those premises were not even hinted at in the restrictive covenant.

27.3.2.3 Drafting of restrictive covenants in the light of *Federated Homes*

In *Roake* v *Chadha* [1984] 3 All ER 503, the judge specifically upheld the effectiveness of a clause **(drafted in 1934)** which made it clear that the benefit of a set of restrictive covenants was not to pass by annexation, but only by express assignment. The judge rejected an argument that the benefit of the covenants had nevertheless been annexed by virtue of s. 78. He held that careful drafting had excluded the effect of s. 78.

Roake v *Chadha* confirmed that the potential effects of *Federated Homes* could be avoided by careful drafting of covenants. But *Roake* v *Chadha* was of little comfort to **competent draftsmen** who found the meaning of their pre-1980 drafts seemingly changed retrospectively by the Court of Appeal. (You should also bear in mind the Law Commission's comments which I quote at 27.6.)

27.3.2.4 The Privy Council and the crucial importance of identifying dominant owners

Two fairly recent Privy Council decisions applied Jamaican and Trinidadian law respectively. They made no reference either to s. 78 or *Federated Homes*. However, both these cases were decided on policy grounds totally overlooked by *Federated Homes*. It is submitted that the reasoning in these two cases undermined *Federated Homes* as it was understood between 1980 and 2004.

Jamaica Mutual Life v *Hillsborough* [1989] 1 WLR 1101

In this case, the Privy Council held that, in Jamaica, annexation can be achieved only by an express clause identifying the dominant land. It seems that one of the reasons for the Privy Council's decision was the policy consideration that a person entering into a restrictive covenant ought from the outset to know for certain the identity of the dominant land(s). *Federated Homes* totally overlooked this enormously important consideration.

Emile Elias v Pine Groves [1993] 1 WLR 305

This case concerned an alleged building scheme. (Building schemes are discussed at 27.5.) The Privy Council (advising through Lord Browne-Wilkinson) reaffirmed a long-standing principle first stated in 1909, that for a valid scheme the area of land covered by the scheme must be fixed before any land is sold off by the common vendor: 'In order to create a valid building scheme, the purchasers of all the land within the area of the scheme must know what that area is'.

Thus, in a building scheme, owners of land know the full extent of the dominant land. By contrast, somebody who buys land subject to restrictive covenants annexed under the *Federated Homes* principle would be guessing at the identity of the dominant land.

27.3.2.5 Federated Homes emasculated—*Crest Nicholson* v *McCallister* [2004] 1 WLR 2409.

In *Crest Nicholson*, two brothers bought land at Claygate on the edge of London. Over a period from 1928 to 1936 they sold the land off in plots. Each conveyance was subject to a restrictive covenant in effect 'not more than one house per plot'. **The conveyances did not identify any dominant land.** There was certainly not a building scheme.

McCallister, who had acquired part of the land conveyed in 1936, claimed to be able to enforce the restrictive covenants in the earlier conveyances. He relied on the broad reading of the *Federated Homes* decision set out in **27.3.2.2.** He argued 'Under *Federated Homes* there is annexation to each and every part of all land which the covenantee retains in the vicinity. That land does not have to be identified in the covenant'.

Thankfully, the Court of Appeal rejected this wide reading of *Federated Homes* which had been adopted by most commentators since 1980. Rather, it held that for there to be a valid statutory annexation under s. 78, the dominant land must be either clearly spelt out in the conveyance itself, or the dominant land must be mentioned in the conveyance itself and be 'easily ascertainable' from looking at the surrounding circumstances.

Crucially, like the Privy Council in *Jamaica Mutual Life* v *Hillsborough* [1989] 1 WLR 1101, the modern Court of Appeal stressed that **the law must be such as to make it reasonably easy for servient owners to work out who the dominant owners are.** At para. 34 Chadwick LJ says:

It is obviously desirable that a purchaser of land burdened with a restrictive covenant should be able not only to ascertain, by inspection of the entries on the relevant register, that the land is so burdened, but also to ascertain the land for which the benefit of the covenant was taken—so that he can identify who can enforce the covenant. That latter object is achieved if the land which is intended to be benefited is defined in the instrument so as to be easily ascertainable.

To require a purchaser of land burdened with a restrictive covenant, but where the land for the benefit of which the covenant was taken is not described in the instrument, to make inquiries as to what (if any) land the original covenantee retained at the time of the conveyance and what (if any) of that retained land the covenant did, or might have, 'touched and concerned' would be oppressive. It must be kept in mind that (as in the present case) the time at which the enforceability of the covenant becomes an issue may be long after the date of the instrument by which it was imposed. [Paragraph break added for clarity.]

The one point not covered by the *Crest Nicholson* case is whether the annexation is presumed to be to each and every part of the dominant land. It is submitted that, bearing in mind the problems of the multiplication of dominant owners set out in **27.3.1.5**, annexation should be presumed to be to the whole of the dominant land unless the covenant expressly refers to 'each and every part'.

27.4 Assignment of the benefit of restrictive covenants

27.4.1 The rules for a valid assignment

These rules are important in two types of situation:

(a) Where the restrictive covenant has not been validly annexed to the dominant land.

(b) Where the restrictive covenant has been annexed only to the whole of the dominant land, and that dominant land is subdivided. (Remember that the subdivision destroys the annexation: see 27.3.1.4.)

Where assignment of the benefit of a restrictive covenant is under consideration, the rather elaborate rules in *Miles* v *Easter* [1933] Ch 611, especially at 632, apply. If a dominant owner is to be able to enforce a covenant under the assignment rules, four conditions must be satisfied:

(a) The covenant must be entered into for the benefit of 'ascertainable land'. It must be possible to identify the dominant land from the terms of the document containing the covenant, or (as in *Newton Abbot Co-op*) from the surrounding circumstances.

(b) This 'ascertainable land' must actually be benefited by the existence of the covenant. (In *Marten* v *Flight Refuelling* [1961] 2 All ER 696 and *Earl of Leicester* v *Wells-next-the-Sea* [1972] 3 All ER 77 it seems to have been assumed that where the 'ascertainable land' is a large area, the whole of that area must be benefited for the rules to operate. In each of these cases the judge found that a very large area was benefited by the restrictive covenants.)

(c) The assignee must have acquired at least part of the 'ascertainable land'. (In *Russell* v *Archdale* [1962] 2 All ER 305 and *Stilwell* v *Blackman* [1967] 3 All ER 514, it was held that a covenant annexed only to the **whole** of a piece of dominant land could be assigned on the sale of **part** of that dominant land.)

(d) Simultaneous with the conveyance of the land, the assignee must have been assigned the benefit of the restrictive covenant.

The basic idea underlying this last rule is that every time the dominant land is conveyed (or transferred in any way), the conveyance or other transfer document should include **an express clause** assigning the benefit of the restrictive covenant.

EXERCISE 27.3

Suppose I am contemplating buying Downacre. It appears that Downacre is dominant to a restrictive covenant over Slowacre, but that the covenant has not been annexed to Downacre. What will I insist be put into the conveyance of Downacre?

I will insist that the conveyance to me of Downacre includes a special clause assigning me the benefit of the covenant.

? QUESTION 27.1

If I later sell Downacre to Penny, what will she insist I put in the conveyance to her?

She will, of course, insist that I include in the conveyance to her a special clause assigning the benefit of the restrictive covenant.

27.4.2 **Exceptions to the rule that there must be an express assignment clause**

The courts have created two exceptions to the rule ((d) at 27.4.1) that every time the land which is dominant to an unannexed covenant is sold, the covenant passes only if there is an express assignment clause.

The first exception was recognized in *Northbourne* v *Johnstone* [1922] 2 Ch 309. In that case the contract for sale of the dominant land included a special clause promising that the vendor would assign to the purchaser an unannexed restrictive covenant. Somebody forgot to include the special assignment clause in the conveyance itself. The court nevertheless held that the purchaser had acquired the right to enforce the covenant. It applied the maxim 'equity looks on as done that which ought to be done' **to the contract**. The contract transferred to the purchaser the right to enforce the covenant.

The *Northbourne* exception is clearly correct. The same cannot be said of the second exception, which was created by the *Newton Abbot Co-op* case. At one stage in the history of the dominant ironmongers the current owner died, but her will made no mention of the unannexed covenant. Nor did the 'assent' of the shop signed by her executors. The judge nevertheless held that the current owners of the ironmongery could enforce the unannexed covenant.

In *Leicester* v *Wells-next-the-Sea* [1972] 3 All ER 77, the land dominant to the covenant was settled land. One life tenant died and was succeeded by another life tenant. The new vesting assent executed by the Settled Land Act trustees (the document required to transfer to him the legal estate) made no mention of the covenant, yet the new life tenant was held entitled to enforce the covenant.

The apparent effect of these two cases (on this point) is that if the dominant land devolves on death (rather than passing on sale) the new owner of the land can enforce the covenant without an express assignment in either the will, or the assent from the deceased's personal representatives.

These last two cases are a startling illustration of the sad trend I mentioned at 27.2, i.e., that modern courts tend 'to bend or change the old rules in favour of persons claiming to be dominant owners'. You should note, too, that in these two cases the dominant owners in whose favour the rules were 'bent' were donees, not purchasers!

27.5 Building schemes or schemes of development

If you go back to 1.4.2, you will see a modern example of what conveyancers have traditionally called 'a building scheme'. If a building scheme has been validly created then all properties within the scheme are both servient and dominant land. All the current owners are both obliged to observe the covenants and are entitled to enforce them.

27.5.1 The conditions required for a valid building scheme

To establish a building scheme a number of conditions must be satisfied. These conditions were laid down in *Elliston* v *Reacher* [1908] 2 Ch 374 at 384:

(a) At the outset the creator of the scheme (nowadays we would refer to him as 'the developer') sets up a scheme for a defined area of land. As the Privy Council reaffirmed in *Emile Elias* v *Pine Groves* [1993] 1 WLR 305 (see 27.3.2.4), the area of the scheme must be fixed before any selling commences.

(b) The creator of the scheme sells off the land in 'plots' subject to restrictive covenants. The covenants must form part of an organized scheme for the whole area decided upon before selling commenced. The 'plots' may be empty sites ripe for development, or they may already have been built upon. (In the nineteenth century the creator of a building scheme would usually sell off vacant plots on which the purchasers would arrange for the construction of their houses in compliance with the covenants. In the twentieth century the creators are usually firms like Barratt or Wimpey selling off houses they have already constructed.)

(c) The creator of the scheme must have intended the restrictions on each plot to be for the benefit of the other plots. (He must have intended 'mutual enforceability'.)

(d) The original purchasers from the creator of the scheme must have realized that the covenants were to be mutually enforceable between the purchasers.

27.5.2 Proving that the creator of the scheme intended mutual enforceability

Normally, the intention that the covenants should be mutually enforceable is apparent from documents drawn up when the scheme was first created.

In the nineteenth century the creator of a building scheme usually made his intentions clear by drawing up a 'mutual deed of covenant'. This was a document (often very long) which contained all the restrictive covenants and stated that the covenants were intended to be mutually enforceable. Each purchaser of a 'plot' was required to seal the 'mutual deed'. Thus, if there were 40 plots in the scheme, there would eventually be 41 seals on the mutual deed.

(For an example of such a 'mutual deed', read *Baxter* v *Four Oaks* [1965] 1 All ER 906.)

The enactment of s. 56 of the Law of Property Act 1925 (see 26.7) means that there is no longer any need to use this cumbersome 'mutual deed' device. What happens nowadays is that the developer (Wimpey, Barratt, etc.) sells off each house subject to restrictive covenants, and the conveyance (or land transfer) of each house makes it clear that the covenants are entered into for the benefit of all the other houses on the estate. This is undoubtedly sufficient to create a 'building scheme'. This is illustrated by *Eagling* v *Gardner* [1970] 2 All ER 838.

27.5.3 Proving intention from the circumstances surrounding the original sale

In *Elliston* v *Reacher* (the leading case on building schemes, see 27.5.1) the intention that there was to be mutual enforceability was proved not by reference to documents, but by reference to the manner in which the original plots of land were advertised and sold.

In that case the building scheme was created in 1861. The plots were sold from an office in Ipswich, but the scheme itself was on 10 acres of land at Felixstowe, 12 miles away on the Suffolk coast.

Anybody entering the office in Ipswich would have seen on the wall a large plan of the scheme, with the restrictive covenants endorsed prominently on the plan. Potential purchasers of a plot could buy a copy of this plan (with the covenants listed) for *1s 6d*. The covenants were of a kind designed to preserve the 'exclusive' nature of the area.

Now we all know that estate agents do their very best to sell properties. The prominent advertising of the restrictions was in effect saying to purchasers, 'Look what a high-class area you are buying into!' It was a natural inference from this advertising (drawn by all four judges who heard the case) that the creator of the scheme back in 1861 intended the covenants to be mutually enforceable.

The conclusion in *Elliston* v *Reacher* seems fair enough. But you should note that the dispute arose 45 years after the creation of the scheme; some of the original purchasers were still able to give evidence of what had happened. What if the dispute (which was over somebody wanting to build a hotel on one of the plots) had not arisen until 1990?

27.5.4 Modern cases expanding the building scheme principles

In *Elliston* v *Reacher* the courts perhaps 'stretched' the law a little bit in order to find the existence of a building scheme. (I think the judges should have insisted on the intent of mutual enforceability being spelt out in formal documentation.)

Two modern cases also betray this 'stretching' process. In *Baxter* v *Four Oaks* [1965] 1 All ER 906 there was a Victorian building scheme with one special feature. The common vendor had fixed the area of his scheme but had not divided his land into plots **before** commencing selling. Rather, he had sold each purchaser as much land as he (the purchaser) desired. (Remember that in those days the purchaser took a vacant site and then built his own house.)

Cross J held that the special feature of the case did not prevent there being a building scheme. (I am sure this is correct.) In *Baxter* there was an organized scheme of covenants for a defined area, and those covenants had been incorporated into a mutual deed of covenant.

The case which I think stretched things too far is *Re Dolphin's Conveyance* [1970] 2 All ER 664. In 1871, two sisters were tenants in common of the 30-acre 'Selly Hill Estate' on the (then) south-west edge of Birmingham. They started selling off sizeable parts of this estate. They then gave the remaining parts of Selly Hill to their nephew. He sold off further chunks of Selly Hill, until it had all gone by 1891.

As each chunk of Selly Hill was sold, restrictive covenants were imposed on the land. The purchasers (usually builders) promised to build only high class housing; each house was to have a minimum of a quarter of an acre of grounds.

On each sale the vendors (the sisters or the nephew) covenanted that if they sold further parts of Selly Hill, the same restrictive covenants would be imposed. The judge inferred from this promise by the vendors an intention that the covenants restricting the area to high-class housing were to be mutually enforceable.

The judge went on to hold that although:

(a) there had been no scheme of restrictive covenants for the whole area decided upon before sale commenced; **and**

(b) the selling of the estate had been spread over 20 years;

there was nevertheless in his view a situation within the building scheme principle. Thus current owners of large houses on Selly Hill could enforce the covenants against Birmingham Corporation, who had bought other parts of Selly Hill for high-density council housing.

 EXERCISE 27.4

Is *Re Dolphin* correct, in view of the Privy Council cases discussed at 27.3.2.4?

Re Dolphin would appear to be inconsistent with the principle reasserted by the Privy Council in *Emile Elias*, that the total area of the scheme must be fixed before selling commences. It might well therefore be overruled by the Court of Appeal or House of Lords.

27.6 The chaotic state of the law on the running of benefits of covenants

The Law Commission in its 1984 Report on Restrictive Covenants (Law Com. No. 127) summed up the situation at p. 30:

A traveller in this area of the law, old though it is, walks on ground which is still shifting. Particularly striking examples come from the same two topics: the *Federated Homes* case has made radical and controversial changes in what was thought to be the law about annexation, and successive court decisions in recent years [in particular *Re Dolphin*] have altered the conditions thought to be essential for the establishment of a building scheme.

Shifts in the law as interpreted by the courts may be wholly beneficial so far as future covenants are concerned, but they must of course apply equally to existing covenants and here their effects are much more mixed. If a landowner sought legal advice periodically about the enforcement of a particular covenant, he would have to be told different things at different times; and his lot would not be a happy one if he had acted in good faith on advice given one year only to find it invalidated the next.

Before leaving the subject of uncertainty we would mention one particular instance in which the law . . . is productive of uncertainty in practice. There is at present no requirement that the instrument creating the covenant shall describe the benefited land clearly enough to enable it to be identified without extrinsic evidence.

The Law Commission proposed to forbid the creation of new restrictive covenants. There would be a new type of right in land, 'land obligations'. 'Land obligations' would either be negative or (subject to certain limits) positive.

Land obligations would be of two types:

(a) Neighbour Obligations;

(b) Development Obligations (to be used in situations in which in the past a building scheme would have been created).

Whatever the form of the land obligation, one thing was crystal clear concerning the Commission's proposals. Any document(s) creating land obligations would have expressly to identify the intended dominant land. Thus, under the new law, there would be no room for decisions like *Newton Abbot Co-op*, *Re Dolphin*, or *Federated Homes* as it was understood prior to *Crest Nicholson*.

CONCLUDING REMARKS

Legislation in the area of restrictive covenants (though desirable) is perhaps not essential. (The Land Registration Act 2002, which has some effect on every other type of property right, has no impact on restrictive covenants.) What would be welcome would be cases in the House of Lords which

(a) overruled *Re Dolphin*;

(b) confirmed the Court of Appeal decision in *Crest Nicholson*;

(c) held that annexation was presumed to be to the whole of the dominant land, unless the covenant expressly referred to 'each and every part'.

■ SUMMARY

The right to enforce the restrictive covenants can pass in three different ways.

1 Annexation

For a restrictive covenant to be validly annexed, the dominant land must be easily identifiable applying the terms of the deed containing the covenant to the 'facts on the ground'.

Where a restrictive covenant is annexed to a parcel of land, the law is unclear as to whether annexation is to be presumed to be to the whole of the land only, or whether annexation to 'each and every part' is to be presumed.

2 Assignment

The dominant land must be identifiable from the documents or from the surrounding circumstances;
Every time the dominant land is sold, the benefit of the restrictive covenant must be expressly assigned to the new purchaser.

3 Building Scheme

For there to be a valid building scheme there must be:

(a) a common vendor with a defined area;

(b) the common vendor must have intended mutual enforceability;

(c) the original purchasers from the common vendor must have understood that mutual enforceability was intended.

■ FURTHER READING

Although over 20 years old (and pre-dating *Crest Nicholson!*) the 1984 Law Commission report no. 127 on Restrictive Covenants remains very interesting and informative reading.

Though just pre-dating the *Crest Nicholson* decision, '*Land Law*' by Pearce and Stevens contains an excellent and very clear chapter (chapter 16) on Restrictive Covenants.

(Of the two 'large' land law textbooks—*Megarry and Wade* and Gray and Gray—*Megarry and Wade* pre-dates *Crest Nicholson*. Gray and Gray, *Elements of Land Law* (fourth edition, pages 1372–1391 was published just after the *Crest Nicholson* decision, and has only a **brief** reference to the case.)

28 Escaping from restrictive covenants

28.1 Objectives

By the end of this chapter you should be able to:

1 Appreciate the problems which restrictive covenants and the highly complex law governing them can cause for developers

2 Explain how s. 84(2) of the Law of Property Act 1925 can be used by a servient owner to establish a conclusive list of all dominant owners

3 Explain why s. 84(1) of the 1925 Act is logically and conceptually totally distinct from s. 84(2)

4 Advise on and distinguish between the (quite complex) grounds set out in s. 84(1) for the discharge or modification of restrictive covenants

28.2 Introduction

If somebody buys a piece of land and obtains planning permission to develop it, his plans may still be obstructed by the existence of a restrictive covenant(s) burdening that land. **The granting of planning permission does not authorize the breaching of restrictive covenants.** The facts of *Re Dolphin* (considered at 27.5.4) neatly illustrate this point. The Corporation had planning permission for their council houses, but the restrictive covenants still prevented the development.

There are various courses of action open to the determined developer whose plans are obstructed by restrictive covenants. The main purpose of this chapter is to consider those various alternatives. You will see that I identify five (at 28.3 to 28.7) but notice that the alternatives do to some degree overlap. I should also warn you that the final alternative, proceedings under s. 84(1) of the Law of Property Act 1925, is by far the most complex.

28.3 Carry on regardless

Some developers may boldly say, 'Let's ignore those restrictive covenants', and start work hoping that no 'dominant owner' will come along and object. In some types of situation there is little risk in doing this. In particular, you will sometimes come across 'building schemes' where the covenants to maintain the 'poshness' of the area generally have been ignored.

 EXERCISE 28.1

If some 'dominant owner' in such an area tried to enforce the covenants by seeking an injunction, what do you think would probably happen?

The court would refuse an injunction, applying the maxim, 'He who comes to equity must come with clean hands'. In plain English, somebody who is in serious breach of the rules of the scheme is not entitled to enforce the rules against others.

 EXERCISE 28.2

In contrast to Exercise 28.1, suppose you are a dominant owner, 'your hands are clean', and the developer has just moved the bulldozers on to the servient land. Think back to the facts of *Wrotham Park*, at 26.6. Consider what you should do.

Like the plaintiff in *Wrotham Park* you should issue a writ (claim form) without delay. But (unlike in *Wrotham Park*) you should immediately seek a temporary 'interim' injunction pending a full trial of the dispute.

Obtaining such an injunction is now relatively easy as you have to show to a judge only that you have an **'arguable** case' that you are a dominant owner entitled to enforce the covenant. In view of the muddle and uncertainty in the law, it is not difficult for someone to put forward a plausible **claim** that he is a dominant owner.

28.4 'Doing a Parkside Homes'

This is merely a variant on the course of action already discussed at **28.3**, and is often adopted. In the *Wrotham Park* case the defendants believed (in my view, reasonably believed) that nobody was entitled to enforce the covenant against them. They did, however, have nagging doubts. (This is not an uncommon situation; it is yet another horrible side-effect of the chaotic law.)

Parkside Homes thus commenced their building work, **but took out an insurance policy** to protect themselves (and the purchasers of their houses) should anyone succeed in a claim that the covenant could still be enforced. As we know, a claim to enforce the covenant did (unexpectedly) succeed. The £2,500 damages awarded by Brightman J was paid (as his Lordship well knew) by the insurers.

28.5 **Attempt to buy out the dominant owners**

You must first realize that if there are (say) 10 dominant owners, then all 10 must be persuaded to give up their rights to enforce the covenant. If nine dominant owners say, 'OK, I will give up my rights,' but the tenth says, 'Over my dead body, even ten million pounds would not persuade me!', then that is enough to exclude this course of action.

You must also appreciate that as a result of the chaos caused by modern cases such as *Federated Homes, Wrotham Park,* and *Re Dolphin* (see **Chapter 27**), it is often impossible to be certain that you have 'persuaded' every dominant owner. Dominant owners have a habit of turning up and convincing sympathetic judges that they have a valid claim. It may therefore be necessary to insure against the possibility of other dominant owners appearing.

28.6 **Take proceedings under the Law of Property Act 1925, section 84(2)**

Section 84(2) is a ray of sunshine in the gloomy chaos created by ill-advised decisions of the courts. The relevant part of this subsection provides (emphasis added):

The court shall have power on the application of any person interested—

(a) To declare whether or not in any particular case any freehold land is or would in any given event be affected by a restriction imposed by any instrument; or

(b) To declare what, upon the true construction of any instrument purporting to impose a restriction, is the nature and extent of the restriction thereby imposed and **whether the same is [or would in any given event be] enforceable and if so by whom**.

Section 84(2) allows a servient owner to apply **to the High Court** for a declaration establishing a complete list of all the dominant owners. Any decision of the court produces a conclusive list which is binding on everyone in the whole world.

> **? QUESTION** 28.1
>
> Suppose Stephen is a servient owner of Blackacre. He takes proceedings under s. 84(2) with respect to Blackacre. The court makes a declaration that Tom, Dick, and Harriet (three close neighbours who were made parties to the court proceedings) are the dominant owners. Charley (a slightly more distant neighbour) turns up after the court's decision and says, 'Hey, I am a dominant owner as well!'. What will happen in any proceedings commenced by Charley?

Charley's claim must fail, **even though he was not a party to the s. 84(2) proceedings**.

Because the effect of an order under s. 84(2) is to destroy possible claims (like that of Charley) to be dominant owner, the courts have laid down a special procedure to be adopted in s. 84(2) cases: *Re Sunnyfield* [1932] 1 Ch 79 at 93, and *Re Elm Avenue* [1984] 3 All ER 632. The courts require that an applicant under s. 84(2) (Stephen in **Question 28.1**) circularizes all nearby owners, just in case any of them claim to be 'dominant'. The circular must tell the nearby owners that proceedings are pending, and that they have a right to join in as parties to those proceedings if they so wish. The circular will also warn that everyone is bound by the result of the proceedings whether or not they join in.

Having obtained a court order under s. 84(2) giving an exhaustive list of the dominant owners, the servient owner may well attempt to persuade those dominant owners to release their rights. If one or more refuse to be persuaded, then the servient owner may well then make an application to the Lands Tribunal under s. 84(1). (See 28.7 below.)

In *Re Dolphin*, Birmingham Corporation applied to the High Court for an order under s. 84(2). This application is the case which is reported and which we considered at 27.5.4. However, it is worth knowing that Birmingham Corporation, having established a (disappointingly long) list of dominant owners then applied to the Lands Tribunal for an order under s. 84(1). I believe that those proceedings were successful.

(Be wary of the confusing way in which the legislation is arranged. Section 84(2) is logically **anterior** to the rest of s. 84, including s. 84(1). Parliament, when amending s. 84 in 1969, should have removed 84(2) from its unnatural position and renumbered it s. 83A.)

28.7 Commence proceedings in the Lands Tribunal under section 84(1)

The essence of s. 84(1) of the Law of Property Act 1925, is that it gives to the Lands Tribunal the power to modify or discharge out of date restrictive covenants.

The Lands Tribunal is an important administrative tribunal, whose main role is to assess the compensation which should be paid when landowners are deprived of their land by a compulsory purchase order. (This is a function which bears little resemblance to dealing with restrictive covenants.)

The Lands Tribunal has no jurisdiction to decide disputes as to who is/are the dominant owners. Thus unless an order has already been obtained from the court under s. 84(2) of the 1925 Act, an applicant under s. 84(1) to the Lands Tribunal has to concede even questionable claims by neighbours that they are dominant owners. (In the case of *Re Bass* which we discuss at 28.7.2.2, it was questionable whether some of the objecting local residents were dominant owners. To speed things up, the applicants did not dispute the claims of these residents to be dominant owners.)

28.7.1 The big change in 1969

Prior to 1969, it was relatively difficult to get a restrictive covenant discharged or modified. In practice the introduction in 1969 of the new ground (aa) has considerably altered the law, and made life relatively easier for property developers.

Another quite substantial change made in 1969 is s. 84(1C). This makes it clear that 'modification' of a restrictive covenant includes removing one covenant and replacing it with a new one. Thus, for example, the Lands Tribunal could in appropriate circumstances remove a covenant saying 'agricultural purposes only' and replace it with one saying 'residential purposes only'.

28.7.2 The grounds for discharge or modification of restrictive covenants

Under the Law of Property Act 1925, s. 84(1), the grounds on which a restrictive covenant may be discharged or modified are as follows:

(a) that by reason of changes in the character of the property or the neighbourhood or other circumstances of the case, . . . the restriction ought to be deemed obsolete;

(aa) that . . . the continued existence [of the restrictive covenant undischarged/unmodified] would **impede some reasonable user** of the land for public or private purposes;

(b) that [the dominant owner(s)] . . . have agreed, either expressly or by implication, by their acts or omissions, to the [restrictive covenant(s)] being discharged or modified;

(c) that the proposed discharge or modification will not injure the persons entitled to the benefit of the restriction.

28.7.2.1 The old grounds (a), (b), and (c)

These are relatively straightforward. Ground (b) is virtually academic. If all the dominant owners agree to a restrictive covenant being discharged or modified, they will normally execute a deed to that effect. Applying to the tribunal in such a case would be a waste of time and money. The only possibility for a ground (b) case seems to be where the dominant owners indicated that they would agree to a discharge but then refused to execute the formal deed.

Ground (a) would be invoked, e.g., where there was a restrictive covenant 'agricultural purposes only', but all the surrounding land had been built upon. Or suppose there was one house in a street which was subject to a 'residential purposes only' covenant, but all the other houses had been converted into offices.

Ground (c) cases are relatively rare. In one case there was a restrictive covenant on a shop that no alcohol should be sold from the premises. The purpose of such a covenant was to keep the area free from the evil of 'the demon drink'. The applicants, however, already had an off-licence a few doors away. They wanted to transfer that off-licence to the servient shop. The covenant was discharged under ground (c). The 'demon drink' was already in the area; moving the outlet would not make things worse for the dominant owners.

28.7.2.2 New ground (aa)

This ground, introduced in 1969, may strike you as alarmingly vague. What on earth is 'some reasonable user'? However, this 'new' ground is further defined by s. 84(1A). Under ground (aa), two elements must be satisfied, though the first element consists of two alternatives:

(1) the restriction, in impeding 'some reasonable user', either—

(a) does not secure to [the dominant owner(s)] any practical benefits of substantial value or advantage . . . **or**

(b) is contrary to the public interest;

and

(2) ... money will be an adequate compensation for the loss or disadvantage (if any) which any [dominant owner] will suffer from the discharge or modification.

In determining these issues, s. 84(1B) provides that:

... the Lands Tribunal shall take into account the development plan and any declared or ascertainable pattern for the grant or refusal of planning permissions in the relevant area ...

In relation to element (1)(a) above, a dominant owner may find his right taken away by the Lands Tribunal even though the effect of removing the restrictive covenant will be to depreciate the value of his land **somewhat**.

In relation to the alternative element (1)(b) above, a dominant owner might lose his right even though the depreciation in the value of his land is **substantial**. Some might say that (1)(b) is a developers' charter. An applicant under ground (aa) will argue that the 'public interest' requires his development. He will make statements like 'much needed homes', or 'this factory if built will create X hundred jobs in an area of high unemployment'.

An applicant under ground (aa) must, however, always also satisfy element (2) above. So if his new factory, bus depot, or whatever is going to make life unbearable for the dominant owner(s), the application should be refused.

It is also important not to misunderstand s. 84(1B). That provision is **not** referring to the fact that the applicant has (presumably) obtained planning permission to develop his individual plot of land; rather it is telling the tribunal to consider the general planning picture for the area within which the applicant's plot is situated.

Town planners usually 'zone' areas for different purposes. One area may be zoned (i.e., designated) for housing, another for industry, a third for recreational activities, and so on. It is this 'zoning' which the Lands Tribunal has to take into account in applying s. 84(1B).

28.7.2.3 *Re Bass's Application* (1973) 26 P & CR 156

The seven-question analysis adopted by the Lands Tribunal in this well-publicized ground (aa) case is widely accepted as correct

The applicants had bought some land in 'inner-city' Birmingham which was 'zoned' for industrial use. They obtained planning permission to establish on the land what they called 'a trunker park'. In plain English, this meant a large depot for long-distance beer lorries. It was estimated that some 250 lorries a day would come in and out of the depot. The land was, however, subject to a 'residential purposes only' restrictive covenant. Local residents, claiming to be the dominant owners to this covenant, defeated Bass's application under ground (aa) to have the covenant removed.

The tribunal analysed the issues raised by ground (aa) applications into seven questions:

Q1 Is the proposed user reasonable?

Q2 Do the covenants impede that user?

Q3 Does impeding the proposed user secure practical benefits to the objectors?

Q4 If the answer to Q3 is yes, are those benefits of substantial value or advantage?

Q5 Is impeding the proposed user contrary to the public interest?

Q6 If no to Q4, would money be adequate compensation?

Q7 If yes to Q5, would money be adequate compensation?

Applying these questions to the facts the tribunal concluded:

Q1 Yes. Bass had obtained planning permission and the obtaining of such permission is usually conclusive proof that the user is a 'reasonable' one.

Q2 Clearly, yes!

Q3 Yes, the residents were spared all those lorries.

Q4 Yes, for the same reason. (I personally think that questions 3 and 4 will always go together.)

Q5 No! That was the crucial victory for the residents. Bass argued that if a landowner gets planning permission, this automatically proves that his plans are in the public interest. This argument was firmly rejected by the tribunal. The granting of planning permission merely indicates that the proposed development is **not against** the public interest.

Bass also argued that the establishment of their depot would benefit the economy of the area and create more jobs. The tribunal accepted this was true, but these benefits had to be balanced against the noise and congestion the lorries would cause. In the tribunal's view, these disadvantages outweighed the economic advantages.

The tribunal did not have to answer questions 6 and 7.

 EXERCISE 28.3

If the tribunal had had to consider questions 6 and 7, what do you think the tribunal would have decided?

I strongly suspect that the tribunal would have held that money was not adequate compensation for the residents for all the noise, stench, etc.

28.7.2.4 *Re Banks' Application* (1976) P & CR 138: a successful (aa) application

In this case the servient land adjoined the sea. The dominant land was a row of seven houses inland from the servient land and on a higher level than the servient land. The restrictive covenant prohibited building on the servient land, thus preserving a lovely view over the sea from the dominant houses.

The servient owner obtained planning permission to build a bungalow which would impinge **somewhat** on the view from the dominant houses. The application failed under s. 84(1)(c) but succeeded under ground (aa). The restrictive covenant was modified so as to allow the bungalow to be built, but the servient owner had to pay £2,000 compensation to each of the five dominant owners who had objected. (The case of *Gilbert* v *Spoor* [1982] 2 All ER 576, is also of interest.)

28.7.2.5 **The thin end of the wedge**

It often happens that a purchaser of a plot on a building scheme applies to the Lands Tribunal to have one of the covenants removed from his plot. 'Removing the covenant from my plot will not damage the area as a whole', he argues. 'Thin end of the wedge', say other owners of plots on the scheme.

In *McMorris* v *Brown* [1998] 3 WLR 971 at 979, the Judicial Committee of the Privy Council was faced in a Jamaican appeal with an application to discharge a restrictive covenant prohibiting the subdivision of plots within a building scheme. Lord Hoffmann, in giving the advice of the board, quoted the words of the Judge Bernard Marder QC, the then president of the English Lands Tribunal.

> It is, however, legitimate in considering a particular application to have regard to the scheme of covenants as a whole and to assess the importance to the beneficiaries of maintaining the integrity of the scheme. . . . In so far as this application would have the effect if granted of opening a breach in a carefully maintained and outstandingly successful scheme of development, to grant the application would in my view deprive the objectors of a substantial practical benefit, namely the assurance of the integrity of the scheme.

Lord Hoffmann then added, 'Their lordships adopt that approach as correct in principle under the English and Jamaican statutes alike'.

28.7.3 Compensation for dominant owners

Where the Lands Tribunal discharges or modifies a restrictive covenant(s), it has a discretion to award compensation to the dominant owner(s).

In practice compensation is hardly ever awarded in cases succeeding under the 'old' grounds (a), (b), and (c). However, the tribunal usually does award compensation in ground (aa) cases. When awarding compensation it has a choice between two, alternative measures of compensation:

(a) a sum to make up for any loss or disadvantage suffered by [the dominant owner] in consequence of the discharge or modification; **or**

(b) a sum to make up for any effect which the restriction had, at the time when it was imposed, in reducing the consideration then received for the land affected by it.

The first alternative is the 'natural measure of compensation' and is the one normally used.

You may find the second alternative difficult to follow. This second alternative recognizes the fact that when a covenant is placed upon a piece of land, that covenant depreciates the value of that land. Suppose that in 1960 Blackacre was sold for £20,000 subject to a covenant 'no buildings'. If that covenant had not been imposed the price for Blackacre would have been £25,000. The compensation payable under the second alternative will be £5,000.

? EXERCISE 28.4

What are the practical objections to this 'second alternative' for assessing compensation?

If you are objecting, 'It is difficult to prove what the land would have been worth without the covenant, particularly if the covenant was imposed a long time ago', and 'This measure of damages is not inflation proof', then I agree on both points. That is why the tribunal normally uses alternative (a) when awarding compensation (as it did in *Re Banks*).

EXERCISE 28.5

There are people who take the following attitude:

Restrictive covenants are a great nuisance to developers of land and bad for the economy of the country. They should all be abolished. We should trust the expertise of our town planners to protect us from undesirable developments.

Do you agree with these sentiments?

CONCLUDING REMARKS

I personally cannot agree. There is (perhaps regrettably) widespread distrust of town planners and planning law. This stems in part from the fact (emphasized in *Re Bass*) that planning permission for a development will be granted unless that development is **contrary** to the public interest. But there is also the widespread fear that town planners too often favour 'the public good' rather than the interests and anxieties of individuals who object to a particular development.

If you are a dominant owner in relation to a restrictive covenant banning or controlling development, you have a **private law** right which **you** can assert against the servient owner. You are not dependent for your protection on the whims of 'faceless' officials. However, in fairly limited circumstances, proceedings under s. 84(1) of the 1925 Act may deprive you of your right.

From time to time there are suggestions that there should be further reforms to s. 84(1) to make it easier for servient owners to have awkward covenants removed or modified. I have some sympathy with this suggestion. At minimum, ground (aa) needs simplifying and the provisions for compensation need clarification.

But perhaps the oddest feature of s. 84(1) is the fact that the powers given by the provision are **not** given to the courts. This means that developers are often involved in wasteful duplicate litigation. Like Birmingham Corporation in *Re Dolphin*, they have to go first to the court under s. 84(2) and then to the Lands Tribunal under s. 84(1). A simple reform would be to give the High Court (and for less valuable properties, county courts) jurisdiction to make orders under s. 84(1).

■ SUMMARY

Where a servient owner wants to carry out a development which would break a restrictive covenant, that owner has various options:

Carry on regardless. This is possible where there seems little chance that the covenant will be enforced. Where there is a **small** risk of somebody enforcing the covenants, it may be possible to insure against that risk.

Buy out dominant owners. The servient owner must be sure that he has bought out all possible claimants. If in doubt as to the identity of the dominant owners, he may take proceedings under s. 84(2) of the LPA.

Seek discharge of the covenants by the Lands Tribunal, on the grounds that the covenant is obsolete or (more likely) impedes 'some reasonable user' of the servient land. To succeed on the latter ground, he must show that money would be adequate compensation for the loss/disturbance suffered by the dominant owner(s).

Where a covenant is discharged, compensation is awarded for the depreciation in value of the dominant land(s).

 CHAPTER 28: ASSESSMENT EXERCISE

In 1870 Mark bought the fee simple in Broadacre. Broadacre was then 10 acres of poor quality farm land, so Mark decided to sell the land for high-class housing.

From 1871 to 1875 he sold off the whole of Broadacre in 40 plots of approximately a quarter of an acre each. In each conveyance he imposed restrictive covenants which (*inter alia*) prohibited the building of more than one house on each plot.

Luke has just purchased 'Redgables', a house built in 1873 on one of the plots sold by Mark. He has obtained planning permission to build a second house in the garden of 'Redgables'.

Luke's plans have caused alarm amongst some of his neighbours, and they are threatening proceedings for an injunction, claiming that they are entitled to enforce the 'one house per plot' restrictive covenant.

Other neighbours have indicated to Luke that they support him, and that they are also considering applying for planning permission to build a second house in their gardens. Advise Luke.

See Appendix for a specimen answer.

■ FURTHER READING

For an excellent collection of materials relating to s. 84 of the Law of Property Act 1925, see Maudsley and Burn's *Land Law Cases and Materials* eighth edition, pages 1001–1012.

For an extended textbook discussion of discharge of restrictive covenants, see Gray and Gray, *Elements of Land Law*, fourth edition, chapter thirteen, pages 1399–1410.

Mortgages

29 The creation of mortgages

29.1 Objectives

By the end of this chapter you should be able to:

1 Appreciate the historical development of the legal mortgage

2 Explain the way(s) in which legal mortgages can be created today

3 Explain how equitable mortgages can be created, both before and after 1989

29.2 Introduction

 EXERCISE 29.1

Re-read 1.4.1 on mortgages. Note carefully the correct terminology. Remember, too, that it is borrowers who grant mortgages, not banks and building societies!

The English law of mortgages has been the product of a historical evolution spread over many hundreds of years. Despite some quite drastic changes made in 1925, there is (as we shall see) still a large amount of law (and terminology) which is explicable only by reference to that long evolution.

Furthermore, because it is the product of a slow historical evolution, almost the whole of the law of mortgages has developed around mortgages of land which is **unregistered** title. It is easiest if we first look (in this chapter and the three ensuing chapters) at the law as it applies to unregistered titles. **Most** of that law applies equally to registered titles. There are, however, some important legal differences between mortgages of registered titles and mortgages of unregistered titles. Those differences particularly relate to 'formalities' and to 'priorities'. It is best if I leave these differences to the very last chapter (**Chapter 33**), even though nowadays most mortgages of land are of registered titles.

29.3 Form of a legal mortgage of a fee simple pre-1926

The pre-1926 standard way of mortgaging a fee simple may strike you as rather surprising. The mortgagor conveyed to the mortgagee the whole fee simple in the land, but subject to a **proviso for redemption**, i.e., a clause that if the debt was repaid with the appropriate interest on a named date, the mortgagee was obliged to reconvey the fee simple to the mortgagor.

(I should stress that even with this 'old' form of mortgage, the mortgagor (borrower) usually retained possession of the land. Remember that all a mortgagee normally requires is security for his loan. He normally does not want the bother of managing the land on which his loan is secured.)

If the mortgagor duly repaid on the named date (**the legal redemption date**) but the mortgagee did not reconvey the fee simple, the mortgagor could sue the mortgagee at common law for damages, or in equity for an order (of specific performance) that the property should be reconveyed.

What happened if the mortgagor failed to repay on the agreed legal redemption date? The attitude of the common law was 'Tough!'. The mortgagor lost all right to the property, even if the property was worth far more than the debt owed, and even if the failure to repay on time was due to some kind of accident.

Equity was much more sympathetic to mortgagors. The Court of Chancery ruled that if the mortgagor at any time **after the legal redemption date** repaid the loan with interest up to the date of actual repayment, the mortgagor was entitled to reclaim the land; if necessary equity would order (by a decree of specific performance) the reconveyance of the fee simple.

Lawyers came to realize that equity had created an **equitable right to redeem** continuing indefinitely after the legal redemption date. This equitable right to redeem was (and still is) the automatic right of every mortgagor; it can be terminated only by a **foreclosure order**, or by the mortgagee exercising his power of sale. (These concepts I will discuss in **Chapter 30**.)

29.3.1 The nominal legal redemption date

We now come to a point you may well find extremely strange. You may be thinking that the legal redemption date was (and is) fixed on the day when the parties anticipate that the loan will finally be repaid. So if Farns-Barnes borrowed £2,000 on 1 May 1900, the loan to be repaid in 10 years' time, you might expect the legal redemption date in any mortgage to secure the loan to be 1 May 1910.

However a very curious thing has happened to the legal redemption date. **The equitable right to redeem** (which always goes on indefinitely after the 'legal' redemption date) has become all important. It has consequently long been the practice to set the legal redemption date at some nominal date, usually six months after the date of the mortgage. In my Farns-Barnes example, the legal redemption date would normally be fixed on 1 November 1900, though nobody really expected Farns-Barnes to repay on that date.

Despite the fact that it is of such fundamental importance, the equitable right to redeem was (and still is) not normally mentioned in the mortgage deed.

29.3.2 **Mortgagor retaining possession**

It has long been the practice for mortgagees to allow mortgagors to remain in possession of the mortgaged property. Even today a mortgagee has **the right to take possession**. Mortgagees normally exercise that right only as a preliminary to enforcing their security by selling the property.

If a mortgagee did take possession, and held the property for a long period, equity would place on him a strict duty to 'account on the basis of wilful default'; a phrase which means that there is a duty to get the maximum income from the land. This rule (which I will explain more fully in **Chapter 30**), coupled with the fact that the mortgagee does not normally want the responsibility of looking after the land, effectively makes it not worth the mortgagee's while taking possession unless he wishes to enforce his security.

29.4 **Legal mortgages of fees simple after 1925**

The 1925 legislation banned the traditional form of mortgage, the conveyance of the fee simple with a provision for reconveyance on redemption. The 1925 legislators organized things so that the mortgagor retained the fee simple, but granted the mortgagee as security for the loan either a very long lease, or a 'charge by way of legal mortgage'. Thus the 1925 legislation provides two ways of mortgaging a fee simple.

29.4.1 **Mortgage by long lease ('mortgage by demise')**

The mortgagor grants to the mortgagee a lease for a very long period (usually 3,000 years) subject to a proviso for **cesser on redemption**, i.e., a provision that on the debt being repaid on a named date the lease should automatically terminate. This named date is the legal redemption date and is still usually fixed at a nominal six months from the date of the creation of the mortgage. The equitable right to redeem remains all important.

Any attempt after 1925 to create a mortgage by conveyance of the fee simple is converted by the Law of Property Act 1925, s. 85(2) to a mortgage by demise for 3,000 years, with a proviso for cesser on redemption.

Any legal mortgage existing on 1 January 1926 which had been created by conveyance of the fee simple was automatically converted into a mortgage by demise for 3,000 years. The fee simple was automatically revested in the mortgagor.

29.4.2 **Charge by way of legal mortgage**

For this form of mortgage (governed by s. 87 of the Law of Property Act 1925) a deed is necessary, identifying the land in question and expressly declaring it to be charged by way of legal mortgage. The mortgagee has the same rights, powers, and remedies **as if** he had taken a mortgage by 3,000-year lease, although strictly speaking he has no estate in the land, only a 'charge'. A legal redemption date is not necessary, although one is usually inserted providing for repayment at a nominal six months.

It is worth stressing that mortgages by long lease are virtually unknown today. All lenders nowadays use the modern 'charge by way of legal mortgage'. The mortgage deed is usually much more elaborate than the 'bare bones' form set out in Sch. IV of the 1925 Act.

29.4.3 Instalment mortgages

It should be borne in mind that the law of mortgages has largely developed around what is sometimes called the 'classic mortgage'. A classic mortgage is one where it is envisaged that the whole debt will be repaid in one lump sum, like the Farns-Barnes example at 29.3.1.

Many modern mortgages are, of course, instalment mortgages, where it is envisaged that the capital debt will be repaid in instalments over a long period of time. (25 years is the most common period, but there is no legal rule requiring that the period be 25 years.)

The general law of mortgages applies to instalment mortgages. An instalment mortgage must be by long lease or by charge by way of legal mortgage. It will in practice follow one of the following two patterns:

(a) The borrower covenants to repay the whole debt on a nominal redemption date (say six months); there are then clauses providing for repayment by instalments if (as, of course, will be the case) there is no repayment on the redemption date.

(b) There is no nominal redemption date; the borrower covenants to repay by instalments and there is a proviso that if he is a stated period in arrears (e.g., two months) the whole capital debt becomes repayable. Thus there is a 'floating' legal redemption date.

(If you are a mortgagor, it may at this stage be both interesting and useful to study the terms of 'your' mortgage. But be warned. In 1904, one of the greatest judges of the day, Lord Macnaghten, commented, 'No one...by the light of nature ever understood an English mortgage of real estate'. Despite the changes made in 1925, this remains true.)

29.5 The equity of redemption

'Equity of redemption' is the phrase used for the sum total of the mortgagor's equitable rights with respect to the mortgaged land. The 'equitable right to redeem' is by far the most important of those rights. Since 1925, a mortgagor owns both the legal estate and an 'equity of redemption'. The legal estate is of no intrinsic value, but the value of the equity of redemption is (roughly) the value of the property when unencumbered, minus the total debt outstanding. (Hence the expression, 'the equity in my house is £X,000'. Hence also the modern expression 'negative equity', where the amount of the debt exceeds the value of the property.)

An equity of redemption can be disposed of like any other interest in land. It can be sold, settled, leased, etc. It can itself be mortgaged, so as to create a second mortgage. Prior to 1926, as a first legal mortgage was normally created by conveyance of the legal estate, the mortgagor retained only an equitable interest, and therefore second and subsequent (3rd, 4th, etc.)

mortgages were necessarily equitable. After 1925, a series of legal mortgages is a quite normal phenomenon.

Pre-1926, a mortgagee, because he had the legal estate, had an automatic right to take possession of the deeds relating to that estate. Post-1925, a legal mortgagee has a statutory right to take possession of the title deeds, unless an earlier mortgagee has taken them. In practice a first mortgagee normally exercises the right to take possession of the deeds.

29.6 **Mortgages of leases**

29.6.1 **Pre-1926**

A legal lease was mortgaged either:

(a) by assignment of the lease with a proviso for re-assignment on redemption; **or**

(b) by sub-lease with a proviso for cesser on redemption.

 EXERCISE 29.2

Even before 1926, method (b) was normally used. Why? (The answer is to be found in the law of leases: see 19.3.)

If the mortgage were by assignment, then the mortgagee would come into privity of estate with the landlord and therefore be liable for the rent and to perform other covenants entered into by the tenant.

29.6.2 **Post-1925**

A mortgage of a lease now takes the form of either:

(a) a sub-lease with a proviso for cesser on redemption; **or**

(b) a charge by way of legal mortgage.

If form (b) is used (as is invariably the case nowadays) then the mortgagee is in the same position as if he had taken a mortgage by sub-lease to run out one day before the term mortgaged. (Any attempt to mortgage a lease by assignment is converted into a mortgage by sub-lease, the sub-lease to run out **10** days before the lease mortgaged expires.)

29.7 Equitable mortgages of legal estates

29.7.1 Equitable mortgages pre-1989

 EXERCISE 29.3

Refer back to 5.5.3.4, regarding the creation of equitable interests in land. Consider how that section may be applied to informal mortgages.

Equity treated any transaction (other than one by deed) carried through with intent to create a mortgage as a contract for a mortgage, and therefore as an equitable mortgage. In particular, if a borrower deposited title deeds with a lender with intent that the property to which they related should be security for the loan, the depositing of the deeds was sufficient to create an equitable mortgage **even though no new document was executed**.

The following scenario used to be quite common. Bloggs goes to his bank manager to see whether he can arrange an overdraft. 'What security can you offer us?' asks the manager. Bloggs produces the title deeds to his house. The manager looks at them: '35 Blogtown Way; that must be worth at least £90,000', he murmurs. 'Hand these deeds over to us and you can have an overdraft up to £70,000.' Bloggs hands over the deeds and the manager immediately authorizes the overdraft. **Before anything has been signed** Bloggs has created an equitable mortgage.

In practice an equitable mortgage 'by deposit of title deeds' was almost always immediately followed by a document **recording** the terms of the loan (interest rates, length of time for repayment, etc.). Moreover, because of the rules governing mortgagees' statutory powers and rights this document was usually a deed, referred to as a 'memorandum under seal'.

29.7.2 Comparison of legal and equitable mortgages pre-1989

With both a legal and an equitable mortgage the usual position was that a new deed was executed and the mortgagee took the existing title deeds to the property.

With a legal mortgage, the new deed was executed with the intent that it should **create** the mortgage; the existing title deeds were handed over for other reasons. (These reasons are to facilitate enforcement of the security should that be necessary, and to preserve the 'priority' of the mortgage.)

With an equitable mortgage, the new deed made it clear that it merely **recorded** a mortgage already created by deposit of the existing title deeds.

29.7.3 Equitable mortgages after 26 September 1989

Although some lenders did not in 1989 immediately grasp this point, equitable mortgages by deposit of title deeds are no longer possible. This is because under s. 2 of the Law of Property

(Miscellaneous Provisions) Act 1989, a contract to create an interest in land must be in writing. An equitable mortgage is technically such a contract. It is not now sufficient to have an oral transaction, such as a deposit of deeds, followed by a memorandum recording the transaction. Any post-1989 mortgages in this form are **void**; *United Bank of Kuwait* v *Sahib* (which actually involved a purported mortgage of a registered title by deposit of the land certificate) confirms this point.

To create an equitable mortgage after 26 September 1989, a written document will be required, signed by both parties, contracting to create or actually creating the mortgage. Thus, after 26 September 1989:

(a) A legal mortgage must be by deed.

(b) An equitable mortgage must be by a written document. This document will not be a deed, but must be signed by both parties and include all the terms of the mortgage.

(It seems that equitable mortgages of an unregistered title are now uncommon.)

CONCLUDING REMARKS

Although there are still four more chapters on the law of mortgages to be considered, I hope that you are already beginning to appreciate the emphasis I placed on historical evolution in the introduction to this chapter. Historical evolution explains why, even after 1925, the form of a legal mortgage with its legal redemption date and (unstated) equitable right to redeem, defies common sense and 'the light of nature'.

As will be confirmed by later chapters, the legal evolution of the law of mortgages most certainly did not end in 1925. Indeed, as we have just seen, Parliament made quite a drastic change to equitable mortgages in 1989. In the next chapter we will see further modern contributions to the evolution, not just from Parliament, but also from the courts.

SUMMARY

It is no longer possible to mortgage land by a conveyance of the freehold.

Legal mortgages since 1925 almost invariably take the form of a charge by way of legal mortgage. Such 'charges' usually still include a nominal 'legal redemption date' requiring repayment after only 6 months.

Nobody expects repayment on the nominal date. Once that date is past, the mortgagor has an 'equitable right to redeem' which continues indefinitely.

The 'Equity of Redemption' is the phrase used to cover all the rights which the mortgagor enjoys pending repayment of the mortgage.

An equitable mortgage by deposit of title deeds was possible prior to 1989, but this form of mortgage was abolished by s. 2 of the Law of Property (Miscellaneous Provisions) Act 1989. In modern law, an equitable mortgage has to be in a written document signed by both parties.

■ **FURTHER READING**

For a comprehensive discussion of the creation of mortgages, see *Megarry and Wade: Law of Real Property* (sixth edition) chapter 19, part 2, pages 1171–1185.

For proposals to reform this area of law see Law Commission report no. 204 'Transfer of Land— Land Mortgages' Part III, pages 12–17. (This report dating from 1991 is another excellent set of proposals from the Law Commission which, like those on Restrictive Covenants and Forfeiture of Leases, has been allowed to gather dust.)

30 The remedies of mortgagees

30.1 Objectives

By the end of this chapter you should be able to:

1 Explain and distinguish between the various remedies which mortgagees have to enforce their security

2 Appreciate why foreclosure (in its technical sense) is of limited significance today

3 Advise on the various restrictions which surround the mortgagee's power of sale

4 Explain the (limited) circumstances in which a mortgagee's claim for possession of a mortgaged property can be delayed

5 Appreciate the role receivers play in the law of mortgages

30.2 Introduction

In this chapter we meet another area of law, steeped in history, but ill-adapted to the economic realities of the twenty-first century. The continued existence of foreclosure (in its technical sense) can be explained only by history. The same is true of the **mortgagee's** (more or less automatic) right to take possession of the mortgaged property. As you read through this chapter you may well be surprised (perhaps indeed worried) by an apparent pro-mortgagee bias in the law. But the big 'institutional' lenders (banks, building societies, etc.) will argue that they need to have means of enforcing their security **quickly and cheaply**. They will argue that stricter limits on mortgagees' remedies might benefit individual mortgagors, but would be against the economic interests of the country as a whole.

30.3 Remedies of legal mortgagees—an overview

A mortgagee can always sue in contract to recover the debt owed, but there are four remedies for enforcing the security:

(a) foreclosure;.

(b) sale;

(c) taking possession;

(d) appointing a receiver.

The remedies of foreclosure and taking possession flow from the intrinsic nature of a mortgage. By contrast, the remedies of (b) sale and (d) appointing a receiver were originally conferred by express provision in the mortgage deed, but are now conferred on mortgagees by statutory provisions. Moreover, these remedies (unlike (a) and (c)) can be exercised without taking court proceedings. However, mortgagees who want to sell the property will (in modern economic conditions) almost certainly want to sell with vacant possession. They will therefore need a court order giving vacant possession before putting the property on the market.

A mortgagee can exercise any or all of the remedies (including an action in contract) in combination, provided the total amount recovered does not exceed the total capital and interest owed.

30.4 **Foreclosure**

I should stress that I am using the word 'foreclosure' in its narrow technical sense. (Sometimes the word is used by non-lawyers to mean **any action** taken by the mortgagee to enforce his security.) Understanding the concept of foreclosure is important to your understanding of the law of mortgages as a whole, even though, in modern conditions, foreclosures are relatively rare.

Foreclosure proceedings can be taken at any time after the legal redemption date is passed. The effect of a foreclosure order absolute **before** 1926 was that the legal estate already vested in the mortgagee was freed from the mortgagor's equity of redemption, which was destroyed by the order.

Since 1925, if a foreclosure order absolute is made it vests the legal estate in the mortgagee as well as destroying the equity of redemption. Thus the effect of foreclosure order is that someone who was a mortgagee becomes an outright owner.

 EXERCISE 30.1

Do you think that foreclosure will be an attractive remedy where there is substantial 'equity' in the property, for example where the property is worth £100,000 but the mortgage debt is only £50,000?

On what I have said so far, I will forgive you for answering this question 'Yes'. But now read on.

30.4.1 **The foreclosure process**

This will probably strike you as long and cumbersome, but the reason for the complexities is the desire to protect the mortgagor. Remember that if there is a foreclosure order absolute, the mortgagor loses **all** his rights. A foreclosure order is made in two stages. A foreclosure order *nisi* directs a Master (a senior court official) to prepare an account setting out exactly how much is owed. It further provides that if the money owed is not repaid within a specified period (usually six months) after the account has been drawn up, the foreclosure shall become **absolute**. The order absolute vests the property in the mortgagee free from the rights of the mortgagor.

Even a foreclosure order absolute may be 're-opened' in exceptional circumstances, and the equity of redemption thereby revived. This might occur, for example, where some last-minute accident prevented repayment of the debt within the time limit.

30.4.2 Judicial sale in foreclosure proceedings

I hope that you are already beginning to appreciate why foreclosure is not very common today. You may, however, be thinking, 'Despite it being a long-drawn-out affair, foreclosure will be attractive where the mortgaged property is worth substantially more than the total debt'.

You would be wrong in thinking in this way. In any foreclosure proceedings the mortgagor (or any persons deriving title through him, such as a second mortgagee or the owner of a constructive trust interest) may apply to the court for an order of judicial sale in place of foreclosure. Although there is a discretion, a sale will generally be ordered where the value of the property is noticeably **greater** than the mortgage debt. Hence the fact that foreclosure is not much resorted to nowadays.

> **? QUESTION** 30.1
>
> Foreclosure is sometimes resorted to in 'negative equity situations'. Why?

Although foreclosure is a slow process, where the value of the property is less than the mortgage debt there is seemingly no risk of an order for judicial sale. The mortgagee gets the property, and can sit and hope that (perhaps because of an improvement in the economy) the property will increase in value.

30.4.3 Foreclosure and dwelling houses

If the mortgaged property is or includes **a dwelling house**, there is a further safeguard protecting the mortgagor. The court may adjourn foreclosure proceedings if the mortgagor is likely to be able within a reasonable time to pay 'any sums' due under the mortgage. This flows from the Administration of Justice Act 1973, s. 8(3), which extended to foreclosure the rules I discuss at 30.6.2.2, restricting a mortgagee taking possession of a dwelling house.

30.5 The mortgagee's statutory power of sale

The relevant statutory provisions (Law of Property Act 1925, s. 101(1) and s. 103) draw a distinction between the statutory power of sale **'arising'** and the statutory power becoming **'exercisable'**. We will consider the significance of this distinction below.

30.5.1 **When does the statutory power arise?**

Two (very straightforward) conditions must be satisfied:

(a) the mortgage must be by deed; **and**

(b) the mortgage debt must be due, i.e., the legal redemption date must be past.

30.5.2 **When does the statutory power become exercisable?**

The power (having first arisen) becomes exercisable if **any one** of three conditions is satisfied:

(a) notice has been served on the mortgagor requiring repayment and three months have elapsed without the mortgagor repaying the whole debt; **or**

(b) interest is at least two months in arrears; **or**

(c) there has been a breach of a term of the mortgage other than one relating to repayment of capital and interest.

30.5.3 **Protection for purchasers in good faith from mortgagees**

If a mortgagee attempts to convey the property before the power of sale has even arisen, any conveyance will be completely invalid.

Once the power has **arisen**, a mortgagee can convey a good title to a purchaser free of the mortgagor's rights, **whether or not the power has become exercisable**.

A purchaser in good faith from a mortgagee need satisfy himself only that the power of sale has arisen; he is under no duty to enquire whether the power has become exercisable.

EXERCISE 30.2

What do you think is the rationale underlying the rule I have just stated?

The rule is eminently sensible from the point of view of the purchaser from the mortgagee. It is relatively easy for a purchaser to check if the power of sale has arisen; it would be very difficult for him to check whether the power has become exercisable.

It follows from this that if a mortgagee were to sell after the power had arisen but before it became exercisable, the mortgagor's only redress would be a claim for damages against the mortgagee. (Exceptionally, if a purchaser had actual knowledge of the fact that a power of sale had not become exercisable he would not be immune, as he would not be a purchaser in good faith.)

30.5.4 **Mortgagee's duties on selling the property**

First, a word of warning. The proposition in some textbooks and cases that a 'mortgagee is not a trustee of his power of sale' is not really accurate in view of modern developments, especially the decision in *Cuckmere Brick* (see below).

A mortgagee can sell either by auction or by 'private treaty'. (By 'private treaty' is meant negotiating with buyers individually.) Regarding the conduct of the sale by the mortgagee, the Court of Appeal in *Cuckmere Brick Co.* v *Mutual Finance Co.* [1971] 2 All ER 633 held:

(a) In deciding **when** to sell the mortgagee is entitled to consult his own interests to the total exclusion of the mortgagor's interests. Thus, he can sell at a time when the market for the type of property comprised in the mortgage is depressed. (This point is confirmed by recent decisions of the Privy Council, for example, *China and South Sea Bank* v *Tan* [1989] 3 All ER 839. Statements by Lord Denning and some textbooks that the mortgagee owes a duty of care to the mortgagor over the **timing** of the sale are undoubtedly wrong.)

(b) Having decided to sell at a particular time, in conducting the sale a mortgagee owes a duty of care to the mortgagor to take reasonable care to obtain the best price reasonably obtainable at that time. If the mortgagee fails to obtain that best price, he will have to account for the difference. The onus of proving that the mortgagee is in breach of this duty of care is **on the mortgagor**. (This duty of care is owed only to the mortgagor. It is not owed to a person who has an equitable interest in the property under a constructive or resulting trust: *Parker-Tweedale* v *Dunbar Bank plc* [1990] 2 All ER 577.)

In *Cuckmere Brick*, a property company owned a sizeable vacant site on the edge of Maidstone. The company had planning permission to develop the site for houses or flats. The mortgagees exercised their power of sale. They sold by auction. The adverts for the auction mentioned that there was planning permission for houses, but not the permission for flats. Because of this omission the site did not fetch as high a price as it should have. The mortgagees had to account for this difference in price.

? **QUESTION** 30.2

Under current law, can the mortgagee sell when the country is in the throes of a recession?

The answer is, of course, 'Yes'.

EXERCISE 30.3

Consider whether a mortgagee should be placed under a duty to take care as to the timing of sale.

I would argue 'No', for two connected reasons. First, a duty as to timing of sale would lead to endless litigation, with constant arguments like the following:

Mortgagor: 'You sold while the market was depressed; you should have waited for things to get better'.

Mortgagee: 'I was anxious to recover at least some of my money, and my economic advisers disagreed with the government's forecasts; my advisers said things would get worse'.

Secondly, 'a duty as to timing' would make lenders more cautious as to the **amount** they would be willing to lend on the security of a particular property. At the moment lenders often lend 80–90 per cent, or even 100 per cent, of the value of the property in the confident knowledge that they can enforce their security **at any time**.

30.5.5 **Can a mortgagee sell to his 'friends'?**

A mortgagee cannot sell to himself or to a nominee in trust for himself, or to his agent. He **can** sell to a company in which he has a substantial share-holding, but if the sale is challenged by the mortgagor **the onus of proof will be on the mortgagee** to show that reasonable efforts were made to obtain the best price: *Tse Kwong Lam* v *Wong Chit Sen* [1983] 1 WLR 1349.

30.5.6 **Position of purchasers and the question of price**

A purchaser from the mortgagee is under no duty to pay the best price. Provided he acts in good faith he will get a good title, even though the mortgagee should have obtained a higher price by taking greater care. It is not bad faith for a purchaser to consider that he has got a good bargain. It would be bad faith if the mortgagee and the purchaser conspired so that a deliberately low price was charged to the purchaser.

30.5.7 **The effect of sale**

The mortgagor's equity of redemption is destroyed as soon as the **contract** of sale is made; if the mortgagee has contracted to sell, the mortgagor cannot prevent completion by paying off the debt.

The conveyance by the mortgagee conveys the fee simple previously vested in the mortgagor free from the rights of the mortgagor and all subsequent mortgagees. These rights are all **overreached**. (I hope you noticed that we have here an exception to the ancient principle *nemo dat quod non habet* ('you cannot give what you have not got').) The conveyance is in principle subject to any mortgages having priority over that of the vendor, although an earlier mortgagee may permit a later mortgagee to sell free from the earlier mortgage.

Suppose that Messyacre is worth approximately £130,000. It is subject to a first mortgage for £70,000 in favour of Freda, and to a second mortgage for £50,000 in favour of Stephen. Any sale by Stephen would be (in principle) subject to Freda's first mortgage. Thus Stephen is unlikely to get more than £60,000 on such a sale. Freda might, however, allow the sale to take place free from her rights. Stephen would obviously then get a price in the region of £130,000. Freda (under the rules I am about to discuss) would still get 'first dip' into the proceeds of sale.

30.5.8 **Destination of proceeds of sale**

The mortgagee has always been regarded as 'trustee of the proceeds of sale'. Proceeds in the hands of a mortgagee must be applied in the following order:

(a) In paying off the total debt (capital and interest) owed to any mortgagee earlier in priority who permitted the property to be sold free from his mortgage (Freda in the example at 30.5.7).

(b) In discharging any costs of sale and any attempted sale.

(c) In discharging the total debt (capital and interest) owed to the mortgagee.

(d) The balance (if any) must be paid to the mortgagee next in order of priority or, if none, to the mortgagor.

If there is a mortgagee later in priority than the one selling, but the seller pays the balance to the mortgagor, then the seller is in principle liable for any loss suffered by a later mortgagee. There will be no such liability if the seller **had no notice** of the later mortgage. If the later mortgage has been registered as a land charge or entered on the register of title, the seller will automatically be fixed with notice of the later mortgage. A mortgagee should therefore search the Land Charges Register or the register of title (depending on whether the land is unregistered or registered) before paying surplus proceeds to the mortgagor.

If a later mortgagee receives surplus proceeds of sale from an earlier mortgagee, he must apply them as if they were proceeds of a sale effected by him.

30.6 Mortgagees taking possession

 QUESTION 30.3

Why does a mortgagee have the right to take possession immediately the mortgage is made; 'before the ink is dry', as one judge once put it?

You should remember that in the past (pre-1926) a mortgagee had an **estate** in the mortgaged land, while nowadays his 'charge by way of legal mortgage' gives him rights equivalent to an estate. He can assert those rights at any time and say, 'give me control of what is (in effect) my land'.

The Court of Appeal has recently reaffirmed the validity of the principle that a mortgagee is entitled to possession at any time he chooses. In two cases a mortgagee was held entitled to assert its immediate right to possession of the mortgaged property, notwithstanding substantial counterclaims for unliquidated damages brought by the mortgagors which, if valid, would totally extinguish the mortgagors' debts: *Ashley Guarantee* v *Zacaria* [1993] 1 All ER 254; *National Westminster Bank plc* v *Skelton* [1993] 1 All ER 242.

In practice, of course, mortgagees are content to allow the mortgagor to keep possession, and will take possession only if things start going wrong. Some textbooks still suggest that the usual reason a mortgagee takes possession is to recover arrears of **interest**. In modern conditions this is not correct. Today a mortgagee taking possession merely to recover arrears of interest is rare, though not unknown. The usual reason for taking possession is in order to sell with **vacant possession**. The desirability of selling with vacant possession is so great that if a mortgagee's court proceedings for possession are in some way delayed, the sale is (speaking from a practical point of view) also delayed.

30.6.1 Court proceedings for possession brought by a mortgagee

In order to avoid possible prosecution under the Criminal Law Act 1967, a mortgagee seeking possession in practice always seeks a court possession order. Proceedings are normally brought in the Chancery Division, and as a general principle the court has no jurisdiction to adjourn proceedings to give the mortgagor an opportunity to repay the loan. It must be stressed that as a general principle the mortgagee's right to possession is not in any way dependent on default by the mortgagor. It flows from the fact that a mortgagee has an estate in the land mortgaged, or rights equivalent to an estate.

30.6.2 Mortgagee taking possession of a dwelling house

Responsible lenders such as the big banks and building societies are reluctant to take possession proceedings. If such organizations took possession without good reason, it would be very bad for business! Less responsible lenders (some kinds of finance house and loan companies) do not worry so much about their reputations. In the late 1960s there was a rash of cases where less reputable mortgagees had taken possession of houses (with a view to selling with vacant possession), even though there had been no default (or certainly no serious default) by the mortgagor.

30.6.2.1 The 1970 'reform'

In my view, Parliament should have enacted a clear, unambiguous, and drastic reform applicable to all mortgages, and limiting mortgagees' rights to take possession to cases where there had been **serious default** by the mortgagor. Instead Parliament introduced special (but complex) rules applicable where the mortgaged property is **or includes** a dwelling house.

First, unless the house is within Greater London, a mortgagee's possession proceedings must be brought **in the county court**. This rule, which applies irrespective of the value of the house, is designed to avoid a provincial house-owner from being dragged off to London.

Secondly, and more importantly, s. 36 of the Administration of Justice Act 1970 gives the court a wide discretion to adjourn possession proceedings, or to make a possession order but suspend its operation. The idea is to give the mortgagor time to find the money and in the meantime protect him in his home.

Under s. 36, the power to adjourn or suspend exists if it appears to the court that it is likely that the mortgagor will be able to repay within a 'reasonable period', 'any sums due under the mortgage' (**i.e., the whole capital debt**). The adjournment or suspension can be made on conditions, e.g., 'the possession order is made but suspended for one year on condition that the mortgagor repays the debt at X pounds per month'; or 'I adjourn the proceedings for six months provided you repay half the debt in two months' time and the other half before the six months is up'.

30.6.2.2 A further 'reform' in 1973

Section 36 originally proved rather ineffective, because judges, even in instalment mortgage cases, initially interpreted the phrase 'any sums due' to mean the whole capital debt. Parliament therefore enacted s. 8 of the Administration of Justice Act 1973, which operates where the mortgage in question is an instalment mortgage. Under s. 8, an adjournment of possession proceedings or a suspended possession order can be granted if it is likely that within a reasonable period the mortgagor will be able to pay off arrears of instalments (if any) and meet any further instalments which fall due within that reasonable period.

> **EXERCISE** 30.4
>
> Could you express this point in another (perhaps clearer) way?

The mortgagee will not get an order for immediate possession if the mortgagor can show that he is (within a reasonable period) likely to catch up with the instalments.

Any clause making the whole capital debt repayable if instalments are in arrears (see clause (b) quoted at 29.4.3) is to be ignored when applying s. 8 of the 1973 Act.

But what is a 'reasonable' period for the court to allow the mortgagor to catch up with the instalments? Until 1996 the answer had been 'a year, two or three years at most'. The decision of the Court of Appeal in *Cheltenham and Gloucester BS* v *Norgan* [1996] 1 All ER 449 thus came as a considerable surprise, as it represented a substantial change in the law.

In *Cheltenham and Gloucester BS* v *Norgan* the Court of Appeal held that with an instalment mortgage a 'reasonable period' means **the full duration of the mortgage**. In *Norgan's* case the mortgage was an instalment mortgage created in 1986 and repayable over 22 years. The court in effect held that Mrs Norgan would be entitled to the protection of s. 8 provided she could show that she would have caught up with her instalments by 2008! To put it mildly, this case represented a considerable shift in the law in favour of mortgagors.

Possibly surprisingly, no building society or other institutional lender has tried to challenge *Norgan* in the House of Lords. I think this is because *Norgan* does have one advantage for institutional lenders. *Norgan* forces the borrower who gets into difficulties to consider his/her position **long term**. The borrower who wants to invoke the Administration of Justice Acts to prevent the mortgagee taking possession must now come to court armed with long-term financial plans.

Moreover, there are strong indications that the principle in *Norgan* does not apply where there is negative equity or (seemingly) a risk of negative equity. See *Cheltenham and Gloucester BS* v *Krausz* [1997] 1 All ER 21, and an article in the New Law Journal by District Judge Nic Madge ((1997) 147 NLJ 459), an acknowledged expert in this field.

The same article discusses the situation where there is substantial positive equity in a house, the mortgagor is in arrears with instalments and will not be able to catch up within 'a reasonable time', but the mortgagor wants to sell the property. (He may well think that he can get a better price than the building society.) In this situation the lower courts are willing to make a suspended possession order against the mortgagor thus enabling him to conduct a sale during the period of the suspension. It seems that the suspension is likely to be between three and 12 months, depending on the exact circumstances of the case. (See the Court of Appeal decision in *National and Provincial Building Society* v *Lloyd* [1996] 1 All ER 630.) The Court of Appeal in *Krausz* appears to approve of this development.

30.6.2.3 **Protection for persons deriving title from the mortgagor**

A person deriving title from the mortgagor of a dwelling house can ask the court to adjourn or suspend possession proceedings. In particular, this will include a spouse of the mortgagor with Class F rights of occupation.

EXERCISE 30.5

Who else would count as 'deriving title' for the purposes of this legislation?

A cohabitee who had a constructive trust interest would certainly derive title, but so would a tenant of the mortgagor.

It should be stressed, however, that the spouse/cohabitee/tenant will have to show that she/he can within a reasonable period find the money to catch up with the instalments. Mrs Goddard, in *Hastings and Thanet Building Society* v *Goddard* [1970] 3 All ER 954, found out about her husband's arrears only when it was far too late for her to do anything about them.

30.6.2.4 A possible lifeline to mortgagors with negative equity?

In *Palk* v *Mortgage Services Funding plc* [1993] 2 All ER 481 the Palks owned a house encumbered with a debt amounting to £358,000. They had found a prospective purchaser willing to pay just £283,000, and they wanted to sell the property and make up the difference out of their personal resources.

The mortgagee refused to agree to this, and took proceedings for possession. It was the mortgagee's intention not to sell the house until 'the market improved', and in the meantime to let the house to a tenant. It was clear that the rent obtainable **would be substantially less** than the interest continuing to accrue. Thus the amount owed by the Palks would steadily increase, as would the amount of 'negative equity'.

The Palks thus faced an ever-increasing debt and (presumably) eventual bankruptcy. They therefore applied for and obtained an order of sale under the **Law of Property Act 1925, s. 91(2)**, a hitherto little known provision of the 1925 Act which gives the court **a discretion** to order the sale of mortgaged property. In making the order for sale the Court of Appeal stressed that a mortgagee must not exercise its various powers in a manner wholly unfair to the mortgagor.

Palk's case, which was decided during the property recession of the early nineties, received wide publicity, and was warmly welcomed. But the facts of the case—a mortgagee seeking possession of a house but not intending to sell—were very unusual. *Palk's* case was, moreover, distinguished in *Cheltenham and Gloucester BS* v *Krausz. Krausz* stands for the, arguably obvious, proposition that where the mortgagee in a negative equity situation is seeking possession of the property **to sell with vacant possession**, then an application by the mortgagor for an order of sale under s. 91(2) will be refused.

30.6.3 Duty of mortgagee in possession to account strictly

The rules below apply only in those cases (relatively rare nowadays) where a mortgagee takes possession **on a long-term basis**.

A mortgagee who takes long-term possession must use any income gained from the land (e.g., in particular rents from tenants) to pay off interest on the debt. Any surplus income is (at the mortgagee's option) either paid to the mortgagor, or put to reducing the capital debt.

One rule I have already mentioned (at 29.3.1) I must now explain more fully. I have already said that if a mortgagee takes possession on a long-term basis, the mortgagee must account 'on the basis of wilful default'. This means that the mortgagee must manage the property to get the maximum income obtainable by reasonable methods. If he fails to get that maximum income, he will nevertheless be deemed to have received it. (The amount owed by the mortgagor will thus be reduced by the amount of extra income the mortgagee should have obtained.)

The leading case on this point is still *White v City of London Brewery* (1889) 42 ChD 237. (Note that a lot of cases concerning mortgage law arose around the turn of the nineteenth/twentieth century, and quite a few of them involved public houses. When considering these cases, remember that in some respects economic conditions were different over a century ago; in particular, interest rates were much lower.)

In *White v City of London Brewery* a pub, originally a 'free' house, was mortgaged to a brewery, the mortgage (surprisingly) not containing a tie clause. The brewery took possession and leased the pub as a 'tied house'.

In those days a tied house was confined to one brewery's products and fetched a **lower** rent than a 'free' house, which can sell whatever brands of beer it wishes. In finalizing the amount which White owed the brewery, the court ruled that the brewery had to account on the basis of the higher rent which a 'free house' would then have commanded. (The tie in the lease was to the mortgagees, but that is irrelevant.)

30.7 **Power to appoint a receiver**

This remedy (governed by s. 109 of the Law of Property Act 1925) is in practice exercised only where the mortgaged land is subject to leases, and the mortgagee wishes to intercept rent payable under those leases. It is a particularly attractive remedy where the mortgaged property is a block of flats or offices, or a row of shops.

Where a mortgagee appoints a receiver, the rents payable by the tenants must be paid by them to the receiver and not to the mortgagor. The power to appoint a receiver **arises** when the power of sale **arises**; it becomes **exercisable** when the power of sale becomes **exercisable** (see 30.5). If there were a purported appointment of a receiver before the power arose, any payment of rent to the receiver would not discharge the tenant's obligations.

> **? QUESTION** 30.4
>
> Bearing in mind what was said at 30.5.3, what do you think would be the position if a receiver were appointed after the power to appoint had arisen but before it had become exercisable. Would rent paid to the receiver discharge the tenant's obligations?

The tenant would be in the clear. If the power to appoint has arisen, any payments by the tenant to the receiver are valid, whether or not the power has become exercisable.

Any money received by the receiver must be applied in the following order:

(a) To pay rents, rates, etc. payable with respect to the mortgaged estate.

(b) To pay interest on any mortgages having priority over the appointor's mortgage.

(c) To pay the receiver's commission (usually 5 per cent of the gross receipts).

(d) To pay insurance on the property.

(e) To pay for repairs on the property, if the mortgagee so directs.

(f) To pay the interest due to the appointing mortgagee.

(g) If the mortgagee so directs, to reduce the capital debt (otherwise any surplus goes to the mortgagor).

In practice it is heads (f) and (g) which really matter from the mortgagee's point of view.

30.7.1 Receiver deemed to be the mortgagor's agent

The mortgagee, exercising the power to appoint a receiver given by the Law of Property Act 1925, can choose whoever he likes to act as a receiver. He does not have to choose a professional person such as an accountant or surveyor. Yet the receiver is **deemed to be the mortgagor's agent**. Consequently, as the Court of Appeal held in *Medforth* v *Blake* [1999] 1 All ER 97, where a receiver takes over management of a mortgaged property, he owes a duty of care to the mortgagor to take care in looking after the property.

> **? QUESTION** 30.5
>
> If a receiver defaults by, say, running off to Latin America with the rents he has collected, who bears the loss?

Although it is the mortgagee who appoints the receiver, it is the **mortgagor** not the mortgagee who will bear the loss.

This harsh rule, that the mortgagor takes the risk of the receiver's dishonesty or incompetence, is to be contrasted with the very strict 'wilful default' rule which operates if the mortgagee personally takes long-term control of the land (see 30.6.3). Moreover, in *Downsview* v *First City Corporation* [1993] 3 All ER 626, the Privy Council has held that while the power to appoint a receiver must be exercised in good faith **only** for the purposes of enforcing the mortgagee's security, the mortgagee owes the mortgagor **no duty** to be careful in selecting the receiver appointed.

It is therefore not surprising that mortgagees rarely take long-term personal possession of mortgaged property. In cases where the capital of the debt is well-secured but there have been problems with interest payments, appointing a receiver may be a much more attractive remedy!

There is, however, one (arguable) advantage if a mortgagee takes personal possession of the land rather than appointing a receiver. If a mortgagee personally takes possession and remains in possession for 12 years without either acknowledging the mortgagor's title or receiving any payment from the mortgagor towards capital or interest, the mortgagor's rights are extinguished by the Limitation Acts. The mortgagee acquires an unencumbered title by virtue of adverse possession. If a receiver's appointment lasts more than 12 years (or even 112 years), this cannot affect the mortgagor's title. The receiver is agent of the mortgagor, and therefore cannot be in adverse possession against him.

30.8 Remedies of an equitable mortgagee

30.8.1 Foreclosure

Nowadays this remedy operates exactly as with a legal mortgage (see **30.4**).

30.8.2 Sale and appointing a receiver

A pre-1989 equitable mortgage by deposit of title deeds accompanied by a memorandum under seal was 'made by deed' for the purposes of the statutory power of sale and other statutory powers, such as the power to appoint a receiver.

Where an equitable mortgage is not 'made by deed' there will be no statutory powers of sale or appointing a receiver. The mortgagee can apply to the court for an order of judicial sale, or for the court to appoint a receiver.

The Law Reform (Miscellaneous Provisions) Act 1989, s. 2, in effect requires all equitable mortgages to be made by a formal document. To incorporate the statutory powers of sale and appointing a receiver, that document will have to be a deed.

30.8.3 Taking possession

It seems that an equitable mortgagee has no right to take possession of the property, unless the memorandum under seal (or other document) gives him the right, which it usually does.

 CONCLUDING REMARKS

The decisions of the Court of Appeal in *Norgan*, *Palk*, *Krausz*, and *Lloyd* all demonstrate that modern judges are striving valiantly to shape the law to fit in with current economic realities.

It is very easy to advocate statutory reform, but it is far more difficult to agree what those reforms should be. Most critics agree that nothing valuable would be lost if foreclosure were abolished and the mortgagee's right to possession restricted to cases where the mortgagor is in serious default. But other questions are more difficult. For example:

(a) Should the mortgagee be under a duty as to the **timing** of sale?

(b) Should (in the light of *Downsveiw*) restrictions be placed on who can be appointed a receiver?

(c) Should (strengthening the rule in *Palk*) a mortgagor who has negative equity have an automatic right to cut his losses by having the property sold?

In considering these questions, remember that mortgagees (including the big institutional lenders) will argue that restrictions on their remedies to enforce mortgages will reduce their willingness to lend amounts up to almost the full value of the mortgaged property. If loans secured by a mortgage cease to be readily available, the whole economy of the country will suffer.

■ SUMMARY

The remedies of a mortgagee in order of practical importance:

Sale Once the power of sale has arisen, the mortgagee can sell at any time, even when the market is depressed. However, the mortgagee will be liable to the mortgagor if he sells before the power of sale has become exercisable, or if he is negligent in the way the sale is conducted.

Normally, if allegations are made that the sale has been conducted negligently, the onus of proof is on the mortgagor. But if a mortgagee sells to 'an associated person', the onus will be on the mortgagee.

Possession Nowadays normally exercised as a preliminary to selling the property. If the property **includes** a dwelling house, the Administration of Justice Acts restrictions apply. The mortgagor will be able to (effectively) prevent possession if he can show that he can catch up with his repayments within 'a reasonable time'. Unless there is negative equity, 'reasonable time' means the full duration of the mortgage.

(If there is negative equity, and the mortgagor wants to cut his losses by selling, the court may delay a mortgagee's claim to possession for up to a year, at most.)

Appoint a receiver This is only relevant where the mortgaged property is leased out to tenants. Anybody can be appointed as a receiver, and any losses caused by the receiver are borne by the mortgagor. (The mortgagor can sue the receiver for negligence.)

The rent collected by the receiver is used to pay off interest owed. Any rent remaining after interest has been paid goes to the mortgagor, unless the mortgagee asks for it to be used to reduce the capital debt.

Foreclosure This is very rarely ordered today. The mortgagor's rights are destroyed by court order, and the mortgagee becomes outright owner. If there is any positive equity and the mortgagee seeks foreclosure, the mortgagor should ask for a court order of sale.

 CHAPTER 30: ASSESSMENT EXERCISE

In 1999 Bertha borrowed £60,000 from the Doorway Building Society. The loan is secured by a first legal mortgage of Bertha's freehold house 'Arkwrite Towers'.

In 2001 Bertha borrowed a further £30,000 from Princewest Finance Ltd secured by a second legal mortgage on Arkwrite Towers. The interest on this loan is 23%, and Bertha has fallen into arrears with her repayments to Princewest.

(a) Explain whether it will be possible for Princewest to take possession of and sell Arkwrite Towers, and how such a sale would affect the position of the Doorway Building Society.

(b) If Princewest sells Arkwrite Towers at less than its open market value, consider whether Bertha would have any remedy against either:

(i) Princewest, or

(ii) the purchaser from Princewest.

(c) How must Princewest apply the proceeds of any sale of Arkwrite Towers?

See Appendix for a specimen answer.

■ FURTHER READING

For a comprehensive discussion of mortgagees' enforcing their security, see *Megarry and Wade: Law of Real Property* (sixth edition by Harpum) chapter 19, pages 1187–1215.

On *Norgan* and the related cases, see Nic Madge (1997) 147 NLJ 459.

For proposals for reform of this area of law, see Law Commission report no. 204, 'Transfer of Land—Land Mortgages', Part VII, pages 49–66.

31 Special legal rules governing mortgages

31.1 Objectives

By the end of this chapter you should be able to:

1 Explain the (inadequate) statutory rules regarding insurance of mortgaged premises

2 Explain the statutory rules regarding the leasing of mortgaged land, and the position if that power of leasing is excluded

3 Understand the rules applicable where a mortgage granted by joint mortgagors is affected by undue influence.

4 Appreciate the limits the law puts on mortgagees' attempts to delay redemption of a mortgage

5 Appreciate the concept of 'collateral advantages', and be able to distinguish between (i) the rules governing the validity of such advantages prior to redemption, and (ii) the rules governing their validity after redemption

6 Explain consolidation of mortgages

31.2 Introduction

The contents of this chapter are (inevitably) something of a miscellany. But there is one general point which I can usefully make at this stage. Much of the law discussed in this chapter dates from the first 40 years of the twentieth century. This is true not just for the relevant legislation, which is still largely in its 1925 form, but also for much of the case law. Consequently, a law, developed for the economic conditions which prevailed at the beginning of the twentieth century, has to be applied to the very different conditions (in particular much higher interest rates) which prevail at the beginning of the twenty-first century.

31.3 Fire insurance of the mortgaged property

A mortgagee whose mortgage is 'made by deed' has a statutory power (Law of Property Act 1925, ss. 101 and 108) to take out fire insurance on the mortgaged property and add the premiums to the capital debt. The policy must be for an amount specified in the mortgage deed, but in the absence of a specific provision the amount **must not exceed two-thirds** of the cost of restoring the building in the event of total destruction.

The statutory power is excluded if:

(a) the mortgage deed specifically provides that there shall be no fire insurance;

(b) the mortgagor maintains a policy in accordance with the express terms of the deed;

(c) the mortgage deed says nothing about fire insurance, but the mortgagor with the mortgagee's consent keeps up a policy for at least two-thirds of the cost of restoration in the event of total destruction.

As you may already have guessed, the statutory power relating to insurance is totally inadequate for modern conditions.

 EXERCISE 31.1

How do institutional lenders such as banks and building societies deal with this problem?

I hope you realized that they invoke exclusion (b). Most modern mortgages specifically require the mortgagor to maintain insurance cover (against all catastrophes, not just fire) to the **full value** of the property. Alternatively, they provide that the mortgagee will insure the property for its full value and add the premiums to the mortgage debt.

31.4 Leasing of the mortgaged property

Prima facie there is in every mortgage executed post-1881 a statutory power of granting a lease binding upon both parties to the mortgage (Law of Property Act 1925, s. 99).

This statutory power belongs to the mortgagee if he has taken possession, or if he has appointed a receiver; otherwise the power belongs to the mortgagor. **In practice modern mortgages usually exclude the mortgagor's power to grant leases, but not the mortgagee's.**

 EXERCISE 31.2

Why do you think that modern mortgages usually exclude the mortgagor's statutory power to grant leases?

Because, despite the restrictions set out at 31.4.2 of this chapter, mortgagees fear that mortgagors will lease the property on terms which (particularly as to rent) will reduce the value of their security.

31.4.1 Position where the statutory power is excluded

If a mortgagor who remains in possession of the mortgaged property grants a lease, **it will not be binding on the mortgagee**. But the mortgagee could estop himself from claiming that the lease is not binding on him by words or conduct which would lead a reasonable man in the position of the tenant to conclude that the mortgagee does regard the tenant's rights as binding upon him.

Appointing a receiver does not give rise to an estoppel, as the receiver is deemed to be the mortgagor's agent. However, creating the impression that the mortgagee is now the landlord and the receiver is his agent would raise the estoppel. For example, in *Chatsworth Properties* v *Effiom* [1971] 1 All ER 604, the mortgagee wrote to the tenants saying, 'Do not pay your rent to your *former* landlord, but to the receiver we have appointed'. The mortgagee was held to be estopped, and bound by the tenants' leases.

31.4.2 Position where the statutory power applies

Where the statutory power to grant a lease applies, the following restrictions are imposed:

(a) No mining or forestry leases are allowed.

(b) Building leases may be granted for up to 999 years; otherwise the lease must not exceed 50 years.

(c) The lease must take effect in possession within 12 months.

(d) The lease must be at the best rent reasonably obtainable. A premium ('fine') must not be charged.

(e) The tenant must covenant to pay the rent. There must be a forfeiture clause for non-payment of rent if the rent is 30 days in arrear. (A lesser period of grace may be fixed.)

(f) The lease need not be by deed. The tenant should execute a counterpart, but failure to do so does not invalidate the lease.

31.5 Mortgages voidable for undue influence

Over the last fifteen years, the courts have been troubled by cases with the following fact pattern.

H and W (who may or may not be married) jointly own their home. H wants to raise money, usually to finance a business enterprise. H wants to be able to mortgage the house to secure a bank loan, but to do that he needs W's agreement. H puts emotional pressure on W to execute the deed, and she, wanting to please her husband, signs. The business venture fails, and the bank, who did not actually know of the pressure H had put on W, wants to enforce its mortgage.

There is usually little doubt that as between H and W, the transaction is voidable because of H's undue influence. But that is of little value to W. What she really wants is for the court to rule that H's undue influence (albeit not known to the bank) makes the mortgage **void against the bank**.

There have been two leading House of Lords cases involving this pattern of facts. The first was *Barclays Bank v O'Brien* [1993] 4 All ER 417. The legal principles applicable to this fact situation were laid down in a 'summary' which occurs almost at the end of Lord Browne-Wilkinson's speech. Before I set out that summary, I would make three points. First, the emphasis is mine. Secondly, to aid readability I have divided up a long paragraph into several short ones. Thirdly, his Lordship refers to W as 'the surety' and the lender bank as 'the creditor'.

Where one cohabitee has entered into an obligation to stand as surety for the debts of the other cohabitee, and the creditor is aware that they are cohabitees:

(1) the surety obligation [the mortgage] will be valid and enforceable by the creditor [against W] unless the suretyship was procured by the undue influence, misrepresentation or other legal wrong of the principal debtor [H];

(2) if there has been undue influence, misrepresentation or other legal wrong by the principal debtor, **unless the creditor has taken reasonable steps to satisfy himself that the surety entered into the obligation freely and in knowledge of the true facts, the creditor will be unable to enforce the surety obligation [i.e. mortgage] because he will be fixed with constructive notice of the surety's right to set aside the transaction;**

(3) unless there are special exceptional circumstances, a creditor will have taken such reasonable steps to avoid being fixed with constructive notice if the creditor warns the surety (**at a meeting not attended by the principal debtor**) of the amount of her potential liability and of the risks involved and advises the surety [W] to take independent legal advice. ([1993] 3 WLR 786 at 800G and H)

Put more briefly, W will be able to have the mortgage set aside if the bank has constructive (or actual) notice of H's undue influence on her. The bank will have constructive notice of that influence unless it has (in the absence of H) warned W of the risks she is taking in signing the mortgage. (The Bank in *O'Brien* had not taken any steps to warn W, so W, who had been pressurized into signing by her husband, was entitled to have the mortgage set aside.)

31.5.1 O'Brien—a very, very different doctrine of notice

In Chapter 6 (and especially the story about 'High Chimneys') I explained the 'equitable doctrine of notice'. In that chapter we were concerned with an issue of **property law**—whether an equitable **property** interest existing against land which is **unregistered title** can bind somebody who subsequently acquires the land or rights in the land. for example, was Mrs Tizard's constructive trust interest binding on the later mortgagee, Kingsnorth Finance? This doctrine of notice (which in principle applies only to unregistered land) should perhaps now be referred to as 'proprietary doctrine of notice'.

O'Brien concerns a very different doctrine of notice. This doctrine concerns whether W's **contractual** right to have the agreement with H set aside for undue influence (and/or misrepresentation) can also be asserted against the bank to invalidate the mortgage. Moreover, as *O'Brien* and all the later cases such as *Etridge* involve a **contractual** right not a property right, it does not matter whether the land involved is registered or unregistered. (Indeed in almost all cases, the home has been registered title.)

31.5.2 How does the bank protect itself from constructive notice of H's undue influence?

Despite what Lord Browne-Wilkinson said in the section of his summary he numbered three, the decision in *O'Brien* has given rise to a flood of litigation on the kind of precautions banks should take to avoid having constructive notice of H's undue influence. Put another way, what exactly should a bank do to ensure that its mortgage is valid and cannot be challenged by W on the grounds that she was pressured into signing?

This question is answered by the House of Lords' decision in a group of cases usually referred to as *Royal Bank of Scotland v Etridge (No.2)* [2002] 2 AC 773; [2001] 3 WLR 1021. In *Etridge* all five Law Lords delivered reasoned speeches, but that of Lord Nicholls of Birkenhead is the clearest. At paragraph 79 of his speech his Lordship gives detailed guidance as to how banks should ensure that any mortgage granted to them cannot be challenged. The essence of this guidance is that W should receive independent advice, not from the bank, but from a solicitor. (Emphasis is in the original, paragraph breaks added.)

Since the bank is looking for its protection to legal advice given to the wife by a solicitor who, in this respect, is acting solely for her, I consider the bank should take steps to check **directly with the wife** the name of the solicitor she wants to act for her. To this end, in future the bank should communicate directly with the wife, informing her that for its protection it will require written confirmation from a solicitor, acting for her, to the effect that the solicitor has fully explained to her the nature of the documents and the practical implications they will have for her.

She should be told that the purpose of this requirement is that thereafter she should not be able to dispute she is legally bound by the documents once she has signed them. She should be asked to nominate a solicitor whom she is willing to instruct to advise her, separately from her husband, and act for her in giving the necessary confirmation to the bank. She should be told that, if she wishes, the solicitor may be the same solicitor as is acting for her husband in the transaction. If a solicitor is already acting for the husband and the wife, she should be asked whether she would prefer that a different solicitor should act for her regarding the bank's requirement for confirmation from a solicitor.

The bank should not proceed with the transaction until it has received an appropriate response directly from the wife.

The bank must give to the solicitor advising the wife full financial details of the proposed transaction:

. . . it should become routine practice for banks, if relying on confirmation from a solicitor for their protection, to send to the solicitor the necessary financial information. What is required must depend on the facts of the case. Ordinarily this will include information on the purpose for which the proposed new facility has been requested, the current amount of the husband's indebtedness, the amount of his current overdraft facility, and the amount and terms of any new facility.

In brief, a bank to be sure that the mortgage of the jointly owned home is valid, must do three things:

(a) get written confirmation from W as to the identity of the solicitor acting **for her**;

(b) ensure that that solicitor has full financial details of the proposed transaction;

(c) get a written certificate from the solicitor that he has fully explained the transaction to W.

31.6 The rules of equity protecting the equitable right to redeem

The equitable right to redeem cannot be excluded by the terms of the mortgage. In order to escape from this rule, attempts have been made from time to time to disguise a mortgage as some other transaction. However, equity treats any transaction which **in substance** is the grant of security for a loan as a mortgage.

For example, suppose Andrea conveys Greenacre to Betty for £w, but Betty immediately grants Andrea an option to repurchase the property in x years' time for £y. £y appears to be £w plus interest for x years. Equity will treat the transaction as a mortgage, with an equitable right to redeem continuing **after** x years have expired.

31.6.1 No irredeemable mortgages

A mortgage granted by a human being cannot be made irredeemable. Moreover, it is the essence of a mortgage that having repaid the debt the mortgagor must get his property back free from all rights of the mortgagee. As the older cases say, there must be no 'fetters' or 'clogs' on redemption. One consequence of this is that it is impossible to include, **as a term of the mortgage**, a provision giving the mortgagee an option to purchase the mortgaged property. But if, after the land has been mortgaged, the mortgagor **as a completely separate transaction** grants an option to the mortgagee, the option is valid.

It would also appear that, as a completely separate transaction, a mortgagor can sell or lease the land to the mortgagee: *Alec Lobb (Garages) Ltd* v *Total Oil* [1985] 1 All ER 303.

31.6.2 Postponement of redemption

Occasionally a mortgage is created which deliberately postpones the legal redemption date from the traditional six months, and in effect provides that the debt **cannot** be repaid until x years have run.

Most mortgagees are, of course, very pleased when the debt is repaid, so you may well be asking, why should a mortgagee want to postpone the right to redeem? There are two possible answers to this question. In some cases the mortgagee, who is in effect investing his money in the loan, may want to be sure that his investment continues for a longish period. He may not want the bother of finding a new investment if the mortgage debt is repaid.

The second answer lies in the well-known fact that when a brewery lends money to a publican, the mortgage will include a tie clause tying the publican's pub to the brewery. (A similar thing happens, of course, with petrol companies and filling stations.) By postponing the right to redeem, the brewery (or petrol company) hopes to prolong the duration of the tie as long as possible.

A postponement of redemption is valid only if on all the facts the postponement is not 'unconscionable or oppressive' to the mortgagor. If the postponement is void under this rule, the mortgagor can redeem at any time.

Where there is a mortgage of a **lease**, and the postponement is so great that the right to redeem is of very little value, the postponement is undoubtedly void. In *Fairclough* v *Swan Brewery Ltd* [1912] AC 565, a lease of a hotel with 17 years to run was mortgaged to a brewery, redemption being postponed until there was just six weeks to run on the lease. (The mortgage of course included a 'tie' to the brewery.) The Privy Council had no difficulty holding the postponement invalid.

Where there is a mortgage of a **fee simple** there is no set rule that a postponement for greater than *x* years is void, but for less than *x* years is valid. Whether the postponement is oppressive or unconscionable depends on the circumstances of each case. The relative economic strengths of the parties is all important. In *Esso* v *Harpers* [1966] 1 All ER 725, the Court of Appeal held a postponement for 21 years in the mortgage of a filling station to be void. (I am sure you have guessed that the mortgage included a 'tie' to Esso petrol. As the postponement of redemption was held invalid, Harpers could repay the mortgage and thereby free themselves from the 'tie'.)

Esso v *Harpers* should be contrasted with *Knightsbridge Estates* v *Byrne* [1938] 4 All ER 618. In that case a London property company mortgaged land to an insurance company (a 'big man' to 'big man' transaction). A postponement of redemption for 40 years was held to be valid. It was in all the circumstances perfectly fair that the insurance company stipulate that the mortgage continue as a long-term investment.

31.7 **Collateral advantages**

A collateral advantage arises where a mortgagee stipulates that in return for his loan he shall get **as well as a normal rate of interest**, some other additional benefit.

The most common example of a collateral advantage is, as you may have guessed, a 'tie' to a mortgagee brewery, petrol company, etc. For other kinds of more unusual collateral advantages, see the cases of *Multi-Service Bookbinding* v *Marden, Bradley* v *Carritt*, and *Kreglinger* v *New Patagonia Meat Company Ltd*, all of which we consider below.

Collateral advantages give rise to two distinct problems:

(a) Validity of the advantage while the loan remains outstanding.

(b) Validity of the advantage after redemption of the mortgage.

31.7.1 **Validity while the mortgage subsists**

A collateral advantage is in principle valid as long as the mortgage remains unredeemed. It is void only if:

(a) it is oppressive or unconscionable in nature; or

(b) it is in unreasonable restraint of trade; or

(c) it infringes the Consumer Credit Act 1974, ss. 137 to 139.

'Ties' are generally not oppressive or unconscionable, nor it seems are they in unreasonable restraint of trade, provided they cease on redemption and the right to redeem is not postponed beyond the traditional six months.

In *Multi-Service Bookbinding* v *Marden* [1978] 2 All ER 489, there was a rather interesting 'collateral advantage'. A clause provided for the capital repayments to increase proportionate to the decrease in value of the pound sterling against the Swiss franc ('the Swiss franc uplift'). This clause was held to be valid. Notice, however, that in this case the lender was a private individual anxious to preserve the capital value of his investment. An unscrupulous money-lender might not receive such sympathetic treatment.

The more simple device of index-linking capital repayments would also seem to be valid. See *Nationwide Building Society* v *Registrar of Friendly Societies* [1983] 1 WLR 1226. In any event, the Building Societies Act 1986 now specifically empowers **building societies** to grant index-linked mortgages (see ss. 10 to 23).

Where one party to a mortgage is an individual, the mortgage could fall foul of the Consumer Credit Act 1974, ss. 137 to 139. If an agreement is an 'extortionate credit bargain', the court can modify or set aside the terms of the agreement. A credit bargain is 'extortionate' if it:

(a) requires the debtor to make payments which are grossly exorbitant; or

(b) otherwise grossly contravenes ordinary principles of fair dealing.

These provisions apply even to building societies and other lenders exempted from the general provisions of the Consumer Credit Act 1974. They apply whatever the size of the loan. In *Davies* v *Directloans Ltd* [1986] 2 All ER 783, the terms of a loan granted to a cohabiting couple to enable them to buy a house were held valid, even though the rate of interest charged was 21.6% as against a (then) market rate of approximately 17%. The couple's income was very uncertain (they were artists by profession), and they were therefore unable to borrow from institutional lenders. The high rate of interest was not therefore 'extortionate'.

(I should stress that details of the Consumer Credit Act 1974 go way beyond what I have just told you and are outside the scope of traditional land law syllabuses, and therefore outside the scope of this text.)

31.7.2 Collateral advantages after redemption

A collateral advantage which forms **part of the terms of the mortgage** ceases to have effect on the redemption of a mortgage, even though it was intended that the advantage should continue after redemption.

> **?** **QUESTION** 31.1
>
> What happens, on redemption of the mortgage, to a 'tie clause' tying the borrower to the lender's beer, petrol, or whatever?

A tie clause in a mortgage must cease on redemption: *Noakes* v *Rice* [1902] AC 24. (This rule regarding collateral advantages applies whether the collateral advantage (tie clause or whatever) is contained in the mortgage deed, or in some other document contemporaneous to the mortgage.)

The case of *Bradley* v *Carritt* [1903] AC 253, given prominence in most textbooks, is quite tricky. The mortgagor was the controlling shareholder of a tea company. The mortgagor was not the tea company itself, which of course is in law a separate person. The property mortgaged was the shares themselves. (Shares in companies are often mortgaged.)

The mortgagee was a tea-broker. The mortgage included a collateral advantage under which the mortgagor promised that the mortgagee should always remain broker to the company.

The mortgagor, having paid off the mortgage, was held, by the House of Lords, to be released from this promise of permanent employment for the mortgagee.

> **EXERCISE** 31.3
>
> If the collateral advantage had been allowed to continue after redemption, what would have been the position of the mortgagor and his shareholding?

He would never have been free to dispose of his shares. He would have had to have kept them so as to keep control of the company, and whom it employed!

31.7.3 A collateral advantage as an independent agreement

A collateral advantage, even one appearing in the mortgage deed, may on occasion be treated as an **independent agreement** separate from the mortgage. If a collateral advantage is held to be an independent agreement it has continuing validity after redemption of the mortgage.

In *Kreglinger* v *New Patagonia Meat Company* [1914] AC 25 the meat company were mortgagors, while the mortgagees were a firm of woolbrokers. It was what we might call a 'big man' mortgaging to 'big man' situation. (Contrast the facts of *Esso v Harpers*.) The mortgage contained a provision that for the next five years the company should not sell any sheepskins to any other person without first offering them to the woolbrokers at the best price obtainable elsewhere.

The idea of this clause was (in effect) to guarantee to the woolbrokers (the mortgagees) a supply of sheepskins for the next five years. The woolbrokers accepted a slightly reduced rate of interest in return for this guarantee. (2.5% instead of 2.75%—interest rates were much lower in those days!) The mortgagor repaid the debt after only two years. The House of Lords held that the 'sheepskins clause' remained valid for the full five years, even though the mortgagors had redeemed the mortgage.

The distinction drawn by the House of Lords in *Kreglinger* between advantages which 'form part of the terms of the mortgage' and advantages which are 'independent agreements' is often criticized as very artificial. I agree with the critics. The 'independent agreement' rule is in reality a convenient way of distinguishing collateral advantages such as 'ties' imposed by the 'big man' on the 'small man', from fair advantages agreed to by parties of equal bargaining strength. *Kreglinger* was a case falling into the latter category.

31.8 Redemption of mortgages

31.8.1 When may redemption take place?

A mortgage may be redeemed:

(a) on the legal redemption date;

(b) at any other time expressly permitted by the terms of the mortgage;

(c) on the expiry of six months' notice of intention to repay;

(d) at any time, without notice, if the mortgagee is demanding repayment or attempting to enforce the security, or if the loan was intended to be temporary.

Notice, therefore, that unless situations (a), (b), or (d) apply, a mortgagor is not entitled as a matter of law suddenly to turn up at the mortgagee's door and say, 'Here is all the money I owe you'. Unless one of those situations apply, the mortgagee is entitled to six months' notice, or six months' interest in lieu of notice.

Having said that, I should mention that in practice institutional lenders such as banks and building societies are usually flexible in their approach to redemption, and are **usually** happy to accept repayment at less than six months' notice.

31.8.2 Who may redeem?

The original mortgagor may redeem, together with any persons who derive title through him.

 EXERCISE 31.4

What sort of people 'derive title' through a mortgagor?

Undoubtedly this concept covers a spouse with matrimonial home rights under the Family Law Act, or anybody (e.g., a cohabitee) with a constructive trust interest in the property. It would also include a tenant of the mortgagor, even if his lease is not binding on the mortgagee.

31.8.3 The effect of redemption

If a mortgage is repaid by the mortgagor himself, it is simply discharged. If it is repaid by a third party entitled to redeem then the mortgage is transferred to that third party; that (in effect) means that the third party assumes the role of mortgagee.

31.8.4 Machinery of redemption

 Where a mortgage is redeemed, the parties could execute a new deed discharging or transferring the mortgage (as the case may be). However, it is the normal practice to invoke Law of Property Act 1925, s. 115, under which the mortgagee indorses on or annexes to the mortgage deed a receipt for the debt, indicating who is paying the money. If the person named is the mortgagor, the mortgage is simply discharged; if the person named is a third party, the receipt will transfer the mortgage to him.

On redemption the title deeds should be handed back to the mortgagor or handed to the transferee (as the case may be). If the loan is repaid by the mortgagor, then before handing the title deeds back the mortgagee must search the Land Charges Register. If he thereby discovers a subsequent mortgagee, he must hand the title deeds to that subsequent mortgagee.

31.9 **Consolidation of mortgages**

Consolidation of mortgages occurs where a mortgagee has two mortgages created by the same mortgagor, and insists that if one mortgage is redeemed the other mortgage is redeemed as well. This right of consolidation is of practical value where the mortgagor proposes to repay a well-secured loan, but to leave a poorly-secured loan outstanding. For example, Bloggs owns Blackacre and Whiteacre, both worth £50,000 and both mortgaged to the Muggtown Bank. The debt secured on Blackacre is £70,000; the debt secured on Whiteacre is only £15,000. Bloggs proposes to repay the £15,000 secured on Whiteacre.

The following conditions must be satisfied for consolidation to be effected:

(1) At least one of the two mortgages must confer a right of consolidation. (Modern mortgages always include a clause entitling the mortgagee to consolidate.)

(2) The legal redemption date on each mortgage must be past.

(3) Both mortgages must have been made by the same mortgagor.

(4) At some point of time (however long or short) both mortgages were in common ownership, and both equities of redemption were in common ownership.

Consider the following examples of condition (4) (assuming the first three conditions are satisfied):

(a) X mortgages Brownacre to A and Greenacre to B. C acquires both mortgages. C is entitled to consolidate. He would no doubt wish to do so if the loan secured on Greenacre was for £70,000 but Greenacre is now worth only £50,000, while Brownacre is worth considerably more than the loan secured on Brownacre.

(b) C would still be entitled to consolidate if subsequently the equity of redemption in Brownacre was sold to Y, and the equity in Greenacre was sold to Z. If (say) Y was compelled to pay off the mortgage on Greenacre, he would take the mortgage on Greenacre by transfer (for what it's worth!).

(c) If (say) X had sold the equity in Blackacre to Y before C had acquired both mortgages, there could be no consolidation by C.

This consolidation rule is often criticized, and I agree with those (including now the Law Commission) who say that it should be abolished. The consolidation rule is a major reason why, in modern conditions, people are reluctant to buy a property subject to a mortgage which will **not** be discharged out of the proceeds of sale.

? QUESTION 31.2

Why is consolidation a risk to somebody who buys an equity of redemption, i.e., a property subject to an outstanding mortgage?

A person who buys land subject to a mortgage always runs the risk that the mortgage on his land will be consolidated with a mortgage of which he has never even heard. (Y, in our recent example, may never have heard of Greenacre!)

CONCLUDING REMARKS

In the introduction to this chapter I stressed that the law has not kept pace with economic realities. I hope, however, that you have noticed that some of these rules, for example those relating to insurance and leasing, can and **often are** avoided by careful drafting of the mortgage. The parties 'contract out' of the awkward rules.

The parties cannot (of course) contract out of the rules regarding undue influence. Nor can the parties contract out of the arguably outmoded and largely judge-made rules regarding delaying redemption and collateral advantages. In an era when the phrase 'consumer protection' had not been even thought of, the judges realized that borrowers needed protection from oppressive terms which lenders might otherwise impose.

However, as the *Kreglinger* case perhaps demonstrates, these judge-made rules lack the flexibility of modern legislation such as the Consumer Credit Act or the Unfair Contract Terms Act. Moreover, these judge-made rules apply to all borrowers, whatever their wealth or status.

■ SUMMARY

Fire insurance and leasing of mortgaged property
The Law of Property Act 1925 contains quite elaborate rules on these issues, but the parties can (and usually do) 'contract out' of these rules.

Rules protecting mortgagors
These cannot be contracted out of.

Undue influence
Where there are joint mortgagors (H and W) and H pressurizes W into signing the mortgage, W is entitled to have the mortgage set aside if the mortgagee has constructive notice of the undue influence. In practice, the mortgagee will have constructive notice of such undue influence unless it receives a 'certificate' from a solicitor named by W that he has given W independent advice about the nature of the transaction.

Collateral advantages
These are benefits to the mortgagee going beyond the usual right to payment of capital and interest.

Pending redemption
A collateral advantage is valid unless it is either:

(a) unconscionable/oppressive; or

(b) in unreasonable restraint of trade; or

(c) an extortionate credit bargain.

After redemption

After redemption the collateral advantage ceases, unless it is a rare case of the advantage being construed as an 'independent agreement'.

Redemption of mortgages

The right to redeem belongs not just to the mortgagor, but also any person deriving title from the mortgagor. Unless the mortgagee is pressing for repayment, anybody intending to redeem a mortgage may have to give six months' notice or pay six months' interest in lieu of notice.

If someone other than the mortgagor redeems the mortgage, then (normally) the mortgage is transferred to that person.

Consolidation of mortgages is a possible trap for mortgagors. The mortgagor wanting to pay off one loan may find himself having to pay off two loans.

■ FURTHER READING

Megarry and Wade: Law of Real Property (sixth edition by Harpum) deals with the various rights and duties of mortgagors and mortgagees (including the *O'Brien* problem) in chapter 19, pages 1215–1255.

The Law Commission, in its report no. 104, discusses reform of rights and duties in Part VI (pages 34–48) and Part VIII, pages 67–68. Part VIII is entitled 'Jurisdiction to set aside or vary terms of the mortgage'.

32 Priority of mortgages of unregistered titles

32.1 Objectives

By the end of this chapter you should be able to:

1 Identify which mortgages are registrable as land charges and which are not

2 Appreciate the problems centred on s. 97 of the Law of Property Act 1925

3 Advise as to when a further advance may be 'tacked'

32.2 Introduction

As you know, a parcel of land can be (simultaneously) subject to several mortgages. Problems of priority will arise if the borrower defaults and it transpires that the total amount of money secured on the land exceeds its value.

Suppose Tom, Dick, and Harriet have each lent Mathew £40,000. Each has taken a mortgage of Mathew's house, Mudstacks, to secure their loan. Mathew is in financial difficulties and Mudstacks is worth only £60,000. It follows that the mortgagee who comes first in priority will get paid in full. The mortgagee who comes second will get (roughly) only £20,000 from Mudstacks. The mortgagee who comes third in priority . . .

As you may have already guessed, the 'natural order' of priority between mortgages is order of creation. The mortgage which was created first has first claim, the mortgage created second has second claim, and so on. But as we shall see, that 'natural order' of priority between mortgages can be upset.

Priority of mortgages is one topic where it makes a considerable difference whether the land mortgaged is unregistered or registered title. The rules applicable where the land is unregistered are complex, and (in this respect at least) it is perhaps fortunate that unregistered titles are in quite rapid decline.

32.3 Priority of mortgages where an unregistered legal estate is mortgaged

Very little depends nowadays on whether the mortgage(s) is (are) legal or equitable. The vital distinction (nowadays) is between mortgages registrable as land charges and mortgages which are not so registrable.

If a mortgagee **does** take possession of the title deeds to the land at the time the mortgage is created, the mortgage is **not** capable of registration as a land charge. (Remember that **normally** the mortgagee whose mortgage is created first takes possession of the title deeds. He is not, however, absolutely obliged to do so.)

If a mortgagee (whether legal or equitable) does **not** take possession of the title deeds to the land at the time the mortgage is created (probably this will be because another mortgagee already has them), the mortgage **is** registrable as a land charge. If legal, it will be a class C(i) 'puisne mortgage'; if equitable it will be a form of 'general equitable charge', class C(iii).

(If at the date of the mortgage the mortgagee takes the deeds but returns them to the mortgagor for any reason prior to redemption, this does not make his mortgage registrable as a land charge. Equally, if a mortgagee did not take the deeds at the outset, but obtained them later, his mortgage remains registrable.)

32.3.1 Position of a legal mortgagee whose mortgage is not registrable

A legal mortgagee whose mortgage is not registrable can lose priority to a later mortgagee in limited circumstances only:

(a) By allowing the mortgagor to retake possession of the title deeds, thus enabling the mortgagor fraudulently to represent to a new lender that the property is not mortgaged. It seems, however, that this rule applies only if the mortgagee knew of the fraudulent intent, or where he was 'grossly negligent' in his caring for the title deeds (for example he left them lying around and enabled the mortgagor to 'steal' the deeds).

(b) If an earlier mortgagee prematurely endorses a receipt for the debt on the mortgage deed before he has in fact been repaid, and a later mortgagee therefore assumes the earlier mortgage has been discharged, the earlier mortgagee will be estopped from claiming priority.

32.3.2 Position of an equitable mortgagee whose mortgage is not registrable

(You should remember that the old-fashioned, pre-1989 equitable mortgage by deposit of title deeds will fall into this category.)

An equitable mortgagee whose mortgage is not registrable could lose priority to a later mortgagee (legal or equitable) under the rules just discussed with respect to legal mortgagees.

In addition, you may recall that an equitable mortgage where the mortgagee **has** taken the title deeds is an example of an equitable interest not registrable as a land charge but still subject to the doctrine of notice. Therefore, such an equitable mortgagee could **theoretically** lose priority to a later **legal** mortgagee who took his mortgage without notice of the earlier equitable mortgage.

If an equitable mortgagee remains in possession of the title deeds, the fact that the mortgagor does not have them will be notice to any subsequent mortgagee of the existence of the prior equitable mortgage.

32.3.3 Mortgages registrable as land charges

If a registrable mortgage is in fact registered as a land charge then it is bound to have priority over subsequently created mortgages. If it is not registered, then by s. 4(5) of the Land Charges Act 1972, it 'shall be void as against a purchaser of the land charged therewith, or any interest in that land'. (This is the usual rule which operates when there is a failure to register **any type** of land charge.)

B will have priority. Moreover it is crucial to realize that (applying the Land Charges Act rules) B has priority:

(a) whether B's mortgage is legal or equitable;

(b) whether B's mortgage is registrable or not;

(c) whether or not, if registrable, B's mortgage has been registered;

(d) whether B knew of A's mortgage or not.

32.3.4 Section 97 of the Law of Property Act 1925

This provision creates a difficulty when considering the priorities between mortgages which are registrable as land charges. It provides:

Every mortgage affecting a legal estate in land . . . shall rank according to its date of registration as a land charge pursuant to the Land Charges Act.

Read literally, this appears to lay down a special rule for a series of mortgages all of which are registrable; viz. that priority depends upon the order in which the mortgages are entered onto the register.

EXERCISE 32.1

Apply s. 97 literally to the following example:

1 April X grants a registrable mortgage to A, who does not register.

1 May X grants a registrable mortgage to B, who does not register.

1 June A belatedly registers.

1 July B belatedly registers.

Whose mortgage gets priority?

Applying s. 97 **literally**, you should have worked out that A gets priority.

 EXERCISE 32.2

Apply the usual Land Charges Act rule to the example just given.

Applying the usual Land Charges Act rule, B has priority. So here we have two statutory rules which produce conflicting results. Which is the correct rule? No one is sure, as there is no relevant case law.

32.3.4.1 Arguments for applying the Land Charges Act rule

Most commentators seem to think that s. 97 of the 1925 Act should not be construed literally. Where s. 97 says 'pursuant to the Land Charges Act', that phrase (it is argued) should be taken as incorporating the principles of the Land Charges Act, including s. 4(5). If the literal interpretation of s. 97 were adopted, there would be a special rule for registrable mortgages operating by way of exception to the general rules for priority which apply to all other registrable interests. That could be very awkward.

32.3.4.2 Arguments for taking s. 97 literally

There are two arguments in favour of construing s. 97 literally:

(a) A literal reading of s. 97 produces a simple rule that 'first on the register is first in priority'. Moreover this rule is the one which (in effect) operates where the mortgaged land is registered title. (We will examine this point in **Chapter 33**.)

(b) If the normal Land Charges Act rules apply to priorities of mortgages, we could end up with a 'vicious circle' of priorities.

EXERCISE 32.3

Try to apply the Land Charges Act 1972, s. 4(5) to the following example:
1 September Z grants a registrable mortgage to D, who does not register.
1 October Z grants a registrable mortgage to E, who does not register.
1 November D belatedly registers.
1 December Z grants a registrable mortgage to F.

Applying s. 4(5), you might conclude that D has priority over F, F has priority over E, and E has priority over D. This is clearly nonsense.

32.3.4.3 Will these problems ever be solved?

Do we construe s. 97 literally? If not, what do we do about the vicious circle just described in **Exercise 32.3**?

These questions have now existed for 80 years, and, despite the large number of mortgages of unregistered titles since 1925, the courts have never had to answer them.

 EXERCISE 32.4

Do you think that these questions will ever be answered? If not, why not?

My personal guess is that they will never be answered. I suspect that if these questions ever arise, the competing mortgagees (all commercial enterprises of one kind or another) choose to settle out of court rather than engage in expensive litigation where the costs are almost certain to exceed the amount at stake.

You should also remember that with the extension of registration of title, the chance of these problems arising is much reduced.

32.4 Tacking of further advances

(Note that the word used here, 'tacking', has nothing to do with sailing! Rather 'tacking' is used in this context in a sense similar to 'nailing together', or 'sewing together'. Under the 'tacking' rules, a mortgagee is allowed to join together two or more loans.)

Tacking is in effect a qualification upon the rules of priority already discussed. Tacking is of importance only where one person (call him A) has lent two or more loans secured on the same property, while some other person (call him B) has also lent money secured on the same property. If under the general rules for priority the order would be A–B–A, but the conditions for tacking are fulfilled, A can amalgamate his two loans, and thus gain priority for his second loan over that of B.

32.4.1 The economic significance of tacking of further advances

A further advance is any additional loan secured on a piece of property made by a lender who has already lent money secured on that property. It is worth noting immediately that mortgagors often borrow money from an 'institutional lender' and then later go back to that same lender for a 'further advance' to finance (say) an extension to the house, or to raise money for a business enterprise, or even to finance their education! Moreover, most modern mortgages are expressed in terms such as: 'This mortgage secures a loan of £X0,000 and any further advance which the mortgagee chooses to make'.

 EXERCISE 32.5

Consider how the current discussion applies to a secured overdraft.

The mortgage to secure the overdraft will always contain a clause similar to that just quoted. Every time the bank honours a cheque drawn on the overdraft it in effect makes a further loan (a 'further advance') to the customer.

The rules as to 'tacking' are thus important to institutional lenders, and absolutely crucial for banks.

32.4.2 When can a further advance be tacked?

A further advance may be tacked:

(a) where the intervening lender has agreed that the further advance should have priority; or

(b) where the further advance was made without notice of the intervening mortgage (whether legal or equitable).

If the intervening mortgage was registrable, and has been registered, then as registration equals notice tacking is normally impossible. This is subject to the exception that where a mortgage is expressly made to secure not only the original loan but any further advance which may be made subsequently, the rule that registration of a land charge equals actual notice does not apply. The mortgagee is able to tack unless he has 'notice' of the intervening mortgage in the pre-1926 sense.

 This special rule (Law of Property Act 1925, s. 94(2)) was enacted to benefit banks. If there were no such rule, a bank might have to search the land charges register every time it was considering honouring a cheque drawn on a 'secured overdraft' account.

32.4.3 Mortgage containing an obligation to make further advances

Where a mortgagee is under an obligation to make further advances up to a given figure should the mortgagor ask for them, there is an **automatic right to tack** which cannot be lost by any form of notice of the intervening mortgage, provided that the total amount lent does not exceed the figure agreed on. This is another rule of importance to banks; banks often promise a customer to lend money up to an agreed limit, should the customer ask for the money.

QUESTION 32.3

Quentin executed a first legal mortgage of Blackacre in favour of his bankers, Bloggs Bank plc. The bank took possession of the title deeds. The mortgage is to secure Quentin's overdraft. The bank promised, in any event, to lend up to £100,000; the mortgage also secures 'any further overdraft facilities as the Bank in its discretion shall see fit'.

Suppose that six months ago the overdraft stood at £80,000. Quentin then took a further loan of £40,000 from Blue Dragon Securities Ltd secured by a legal charge on Blackacre.

Quentin is now in financial difficulties. His overdraft stands at £120,000. By agreement between the parties Blackacre has been sold, and the net proceeds after deducting the costs of sale are £110,000. To how much of that sum is the bank entitled?

Under the rule just discussed the bank can, in any event, claim £100,000 out of the proceeds of sale. Whether it can claim the other £10,000 (in whole or part) ahead of Blue Dragon will depend upon whether (rule (b) above) it had notice of the second mortgage before making further payments from the overdrawn account.

QUESTION 32.4

In a situation like that in Question 32.3, what should a lender like Blue Dragon do to preserve its priority against tacking of further advances by the bank?

It is not enough for Blue Dragon to register its mortgage as a land charge (Law of Property Act 1925, s. 94(2)). Blue Dragon should write a formal letter to the bank informing it of the second mortgage. Remember, however, that no action by Blue Dragon can prevent tacking **up to** £100,000.

CONCLUDING REMARKS

I think you will agree that this chapter, while relatively short, has been full of complications. In one crucial respect (s. 97 of the 1925 Act) the law is in need of clarification, either by the courts or by Parliament.

Unfortunately, the problems are unlikely to be resolved in the near future. However, and this is fortunate, the problems will gradually fade away with the reduction in the number of unregistered titles. Moreover, the rule introduced by the Land Registration Act 1997 that a first legal mortgage of an unregistered title triggers compulsory registration of that title will accelerate the disappearance process.

SUMMARY

If the mortgagee of an unregistered title takes possession of the title deeds, then the mortgage (legal or equitable) will have priority over all subsequent mortgages.

Mortgages of an unregistered title where the mortgagee does not have the deeds

A legal mortgage where the deeds are not taken is registrable as a land charge, 'puisne mortgage'—class C(i).

An equitable mortgage where the deeds are not taken is registrable as a land charge, 'general equitable charge'—class c(iii).

If the mortgagee fails to register the mortgage as a land charge, then that mortgage is void against later 'purchasers'—that includes mortgagees—of the land.

Section 97 of the LPA 1925 confuses matters by apparently laying down a special rule for mortgages registrable as land charges—'first mortgage on the register is first in priority, second on the register is second, etc.' It is however submitted that s. 97 should not be construed in this very literal way.

Tacking of further advances

A first mortgagee can 'tack on' further advances in priority over a later mortgagee provided either:

(a) the further advance is made in pursuance of an obligation to lend up to a certain figure; or

(b) the first mortgagee had no notice of the later mortgage. (In this context, registration of the second mortgage as a land charge does not constitute notice to the first mortgagee.)

(To protect its position, a second mortgagee should inform the first mortgagee of the second mortgage.)

FURTHER READING

Megarry and Wade: Law of Real Property (sixth edition by Harpum) deals with priority of mortgages of unregistered land in chapter 19 at pages 1270–1287. See particularly the treatment of the problems thrown up by s. 97 of the Law of Property Act and s. 4(5) of the Land Charges Act.

For proposed reform of this area of law, see Law Commission report no. 204 (Land Mortgages) part III, pages 17–24 (priority generally) and Part IX, pages 69–70 (tacking).

33 Mortgages of registered land

33.1 Objectives

By the end of this chapter you should be able to:

1 Understand the various ways of mortgaging a registered title

2 Explain the priority and tacking rules for mortgages by registered charge

3 Explain equitable mortgages of a registered title, both under past and modern law

33.2 Introduction

Mortgages of registered titles are really quite a different animal from mortgages of unregistered titles. I can illustrate this by referring back to the preceding four chapters. The only part of **Chapter 29** directly applicable to mortgages of registered title is the concept of 'legal redemption date' and 'equity of redemption'. **Chapters 30 and 31 do apply** to mortgages of registered titles, but **Chapter 32** has no **direct** application to registered title.

There are (and were prior to the Land Registration Act 2002) two basic types of mortgage of registered land:

(a) Mortgage by registered charge;

(b) Equitable mortgage (or charge).

33.3 Mortgage by registered charge

This is the standard way of mortgaging a registered title, both under the Land Registration Act 1925 and the Land Registration Act 2002. It is the direct equivalent of the 'charge by way of legal mortgage' used for unregistered titles. The mortgagor executes a deed charging the land; the land must be identified by reference to the register. (In practice the title number(s) is given.) While a nominal legal redemption date is not necessary for a mortgage by registered charge, old practices die hard, and one usually is inserted.

Under the Land Registration Act 1925, the mortgagee presented the mortgage deed and the land certificate to the registry, and the charge was registered. The land certificate was kept at the registry (not taken by the mortgagee). Under the Land Registration Act 1925 the mortgagee was issued with a 'charge certificate'.

The Land Registration Act 2002 slightly simplifies matters. As under the 1925 Act, the mortgagee must register the charge to gain a legal title. (See *Mortgage Corporation* v *Nationwide Credit Corporation* discussed in 33.3.3.) However:

(a) the mortgagee will not have to produce the land certificate to the registry; and

(b) charge certificates will **not** be issued.

Some people may be surprised at point (b), but it is a logical corollary to the abolition of land certificates. Mortgagees will have to rely on the accuracy of the registry's records.

33.3.1 Priorities of mortgages by registered charge

If there is a series of registered charges, they rank for priority in the order they are entered on the register, not in the order of creation.

(Compare this simple statement (one sentence of 27 words) with the pages of discussion at 32.3 and 32.4.)

33.3.1.1 Tacking prior to the LRA 2002

(Re-read the discussion on tacking at 32.5 and compare it with the following discussion.)

If a registered charge was expressed to secure further advances, the mortgagee had the usual right to 'tack' further advances on to the original loan. However, if there was any application by a third party to make an entry on the register with respect to the land (e.g., a third party applies to register a charge in his favour), the registrar had to send a formal warning of that application to the mortgagee. Any further advances made after the date on which the warning notice should have been received did not have priority over the third party's rights, unless there was an obligation to make those further advances.

Where a mortgagee by registered charge was under an obligation to make further advances up to an agreed limit, the existence of this obligation should have been made clear in the mortgagee's application to register his charge. Provided that had been done, the existence of the obligation would be entered on the register and the mortgagee could 'tack' up to the agreed limit; i.e., further advances up to the agreed limit would have priority over later entries on the register.

> **?** **QUESTION** 33.1
>
> Use the same example as in Questions 32.3 and 32.4 at the end of the previous chapter, except that Blackacre is registered land and both mortgages are by registered charge. What should have happened in the period immediately after the second mortgage executed in favour of Blue Dragon, and with what consequences?

Blue Dragon would apply to register its charge. The registry would send a formal warning to Bloggs Bank. The bank would no longer be able to tack further advances, **except** it could tack up to the agreed limit of £100,000, provided the existence of the obligation to lend up to £100,000 had appeared in its application to register its charge. (In practice, it would undoubtedly be included in the bank's application.)

33.3.1.2 **Tacking after the LRA 2002**

It appears that 'secondary lenders' such as Blue Dragon did not like the procedure just outlined. In particular, if a 'secondary lender' takes a registered charge on a property already mortgaged to a bank or building society, the secondary lender will write direct to the first lender informing it of the second charge. In other words, it adopts the same procedure as it would if the mortgaged property were unregistered title. (See 32.4.3.)

The Land Registration Act 2002 therefore abolishes the rules outlined in 33.3.1.1. Section 49(1) in effect provides that the first mortgagee (Bloggs Bank in my example) can go on tacking further advances until it has received notice from the second mortgagee (Blue Dragon in my example). Even after it has received this notice, the first mortgagee can go on tacking further advances if either:

(a) the first mortgagee was under an obligation to make the further advance(s) or

(b) the first mortgage fixed a **maximum** amount for which the mortgage was to be security, and the further advance(s) do not take the amount lent over that agreed maximum.

Rule (a) corresponds of course to current rules for both registered and unregistered land. Rule (b) is new. It is to cater for the situation where a bank says to a customer, who has a secured overdraft, 'We may be willing to lend up to £X0,000, but we are not promising that'. (See Land Registration Act 2002, s. 49(4).)

33.3.2 **The pre-1989 equitable mortgage by deposit of the land certificate**

This form of mortgage was popular with banks and other similar lenders when granting short-term finance to trusted customers. Provided no need arose to enforce the mortgage, this form of mortgage was cheaper than a mortgage by registered charge. In particular, the bank avoided paying the fee required for a mortgage by registered charge.

This form of mortgage was the (rough) equivalent to the pre-1989 equitable mortgage by deposit of title deeds. The land certificate was handed to the lender, and that created a 'lien' over the registered land. To preserve his priority the mortgagee entered a special 'notice of deposit' with the registry.

Mortgages by deposit of the Land Certificate were effectively abolished by s. 2 of the Law of Property (Miscellaneous Provisions) Act 1989. See *United Bank of Kuwait* v *Sahib* [1996] 3 All ER 215.

33.3.3 **Post-1989 equitable mortgages of a registered title**

It seems that a new form of equitable mortgage of a registered title has come into use where a bank lends money to a trusted customer. This new form of equitable mortgage involves three stages, though stage (b) is not essential:

(a) a written contract signed by both parties setting out all the terms of the mortgage. This contract will include a promise by the mortgagor to execute a mortgage by registered charge should the mortgagee so require;

(b) the mortgagor hands the land certificate to the lender;

(c) the lender enters a notice to protect its priority against later mortgagees.

Again this new form of equitable mortgage, sometimes referred to as an equitable charge, saves on Land Registry fees.

This new form of mortgage does, however, have one drawback. In *Mortgage Corporation* v *Nationwide Credit Corporation* [1993] 4 All ER 623, X mortgaged a property to A by executing a charge. However A neither registered the charge nor protected it in any other way. A's mortgage was therefore an (equitable) minor interest. X then executed a charge in favour of B, which 'protected' its interest **by entering a notice**. Both A and B wanted to enforce their security. Which had priority?

The Court of Appeal ruled in favour of A. If B had actually substantively registered its charge so as to acquire a **legal** charge, B would have undoubtedly gained priority. But the Court of Appeal ruled that entering an ordinary notice, while guaranteeing that the (equitable) mortgage **binds later purchasers or mortgagees**, does not give the (equitable) mortgage priority over an earlier created right, even though that earlier right has not been protected by entry on the register. A had priority, applying the general principle, 'first in time, first in right'.

33.3.4 Equitable mortgages after the commencement of the Land Registration Act 2002

The Land Registration Act 2002 makes no provision for an equitable mortgage of a registered title—but nor does it ban them! So it seems that equitable mortgages of the type just described in **33.3.3** may still be used. But they will still suffer from the weakness identified in *Mortgage Corporation* v *Nationwide Credit Corporation*. An equitable mortgage/charge, though properly protected by a notice, will not gain priority over an earlier **unprotected** equitable mortgage/charge.

 CONCLUDING REMARKS

Compared with most of the other chapters in this book, I hope that you have found this one short and relatively straightforward. Mortgages of registered land is a good topic to end with, as it illustrates two important facets of English land law.

First, one of the weaknesses of the English system of registration of title, unaffected by the Land Registration Act 2002, is that it still allows transactions (such as equitable mortgages) to take place with 'registered' land even though those transactions are not fully recorded on the land register. To lawyers from at least three of our partners in the European Union (Germany, Austria, and Sweden) this is totally absurd.

Secondly, for many purposes England (and Wales) has two systems of substantive land law; there is the unregistered title system and the registered title system. The first of these two systems will gradually fade away, but it will be a long time before it totally disappears.

■ SUMMARY

The standard form of legal mortgage for registered land is the mortgage by registered charge.

Priorities of mortgages by registered charge: first on the register has first priority, second on the register has second priority, etc.

Tacking A first mortgagee by registered charge can 'tack on' further advances in priority over a later mortgagee provided either:

 (i) the further advance is made in pursuance of an obligation to lend up to a certain figure; or

 (ii) the further advance is made in pursuance of a provision in the mortgage which allows the mortgagee to lend up to a certain figure if it so wishes; or

 (iii) the first mortgagee had no notice of the later mortgage.

Equitable mortgages of registered land. It seems that such a mortgage is possible. But it has one major drawback. Unlike a mortgage by registered charge, it will **not** gain priority over any existing rights which have **not** been protected by entry on the register.

 CHAPTER 33: ASSESSMENT EXERCISE

'The rules governing the priority of mortgages of an unregistered title are both complex and uncertain. The rules governing the priority of mortgages of a registered title are by comparison straightforward.'
 Discuss.
 See Appendix for a specimen answer.

■ FURTHER READING

For the thinking behind the provisions in the Land Registration Act 2002 governing mortgages ('charges') see Law Commission report no. 271, part VII, pages 118–137. Note, however, that very little is said about equitable mortgages/charges of registered land.

APPENDIX

Assessment Exercises—Specimen Answers

Chapter 4 Assessment Exercise—Specimen Answer

On 8 June 1989 the Law Commission published a report titled 'Transfer of Land: Trusts of Land' (Law Com. No. 181). The report considered entailed interests and modified fees simple. It recommended that no new entailed interests should be created, but it did not recommend the prohibition of new modified fees. Although fees tail are now very few in number, and modified fees are virtually non-existent, it can still be argued that the Law Commission did not go far enough in its proposals for reform of these estates.

The fee tail is a strange legal relic which has somehow survived into the late twentieth century. Fees tail were first recognized as estates in land in 1285. Until the nineteenth century land (particularly the large country estate) was often subject to a fee tail. Very few exist today. A fee tail is an estate of inheritance, i.e. it can pass from generation to generation within the same family and lasts as long as the original grantee or any of his lineal descendants are alive. However, there are strict rules governing which of the descendants may inherit the fee tail. When an owner of the fee tail dies the rules ensure that the land must pass to the 'heir' of the deceased owner. Thus the land will pass first to the eldest male descendant and only if there is no male descendant will the land pass to the eldest female descendant. A fee simple is different. As the word 'simple' informs us, it may be left to anybody, whether or not they are the 'heir'.

Before 1833 the fee tail was a useful device for keeping land within the family, but since the Fines and Recoveries Act 1833 the person who owns the fee tail estate in possession (known as the 'tenant in tail') may, if they are of full age, 'bar' the entail by the relatively cheap and simple process of executing a disentailing assurance. Barring the entail converts the fee tail into a fee simple which can be sold or given away to persons outside the family. Consequently, there can be no good reason for creating a fee tail today.

In its 1989 report the Law Commission acknowledged the irrelevance of fees tail to modern land ownership by recommending legislation to prevent the creation of any new fees tail (para. 16.1) and this proposal has now been enacted in the Trusts of Land and Appointment of Trustees Act 1996 (Sch. 1, para. 5). However, in making this recommendation, the Law Commission did not go far enough. The working paper which preceded the report had recommended that existing fees tail should be converted into fees simple. It is regrettable that this recommendation did not appear in the final report; it could have saved future tenants in tail the trouble of having to bar the entail. Further, the very concept of inheritance by the 'heir' might be thought of as unsuitable to modern society, providing as it does for inheritance by males in preference to females.

The vast majority of fees simple in existence today are 'absolute', which means that, in principle, they will last for ever. An almost negligible minority of fees are said to be 'modified'.

The determinable fee simple is a fee simple which is modified in such a way that it will terminate automatically upon the occurrence of a specified event which may never happen. Examples include: 'to John Smith in fee simple until he marries Fanny Bloggs' and 'to Ann Green in fee simple during the time that she remains a faithful Protestant'. The essence of the modification is that it is of a temporal nature, using words such as 'until', 'while', and 'during'.

The fee simple upon condition subsequent can be defined as a fee simple where the grantee is given an apparently absolute fee simple to which a clause is added to the effect that if a stated condition is broken, the estate shall be liable to forfeiture. For example: 'To John Smith in fee simple provided that he never marries Fanny Bloggs' and 'to Ann Green in fee simple unless she forsakes the Protestant religion'. The essence of the modification is that it is of a conditional nature, using words such as 'provided that', 'on condition', 'unless', and 'but not if'.

In its 1989 report the Law Commission considered modified fees (para. 17.1) and had the opportunity to recommend their abolition. The Commission did not take this opportunity and today it is still possible to create modified fees simple.

One argument in favour of their abolition is that they are out of line with modern ideas of freedom, particularly religious freedom. As recently as 1975, the House of Lords unanimously upheld a condition subsequent which provided for forfeiture on the grantee becoming a Roman Catholic (*Blathwayt* v *Baron Cawley* [1975] 3 All ER 625). Lord Wilberforce, delivering the leading speech, acknowledged that 'conditions such as this are, or at least are becoming, inconsistent with standards now widely accepted' but upheld the condition because in 1936, when the fee had been granted, the condition had been added through the exercise, not of discrimination, but of choice. The Law Lords upheld the donor's freedom to give away his property on such conditions as **he chose**.

Both the Law Lords in 1975 and the Law Commission in 1989 in effect sidestepped the application of the European Convention on Human Rights to modified fees. It is at least arguable that since the enactment of the Human Rights Act 1998, modified fees which restrict choices as to religion or marriage are no longer valid.

.Whether or not that is the case, it is submitted that fees tail, determinable fees, and fees upon condition subsequent are totally anachronistic, and should be abolished by legislation.

Chapter 5 Assessment Exercise—Specimen Answer

Part A

Section 52 of the LPA 1925 requires, subject to certain exceptions not applicable here, that grants (and transfers) of legal rights be made by deed. The agreement of two months ago is not in the form of a deed, and therefore cannot be a legal lease.

Matthew has, however, almost certainly got an equitable lease. A line of nineteenth-century cases, culminating in *Walsh* v *Lonsdale* (1882) 21 ChD 9 (decided just after the Judicature Acts) held that any contract for a lease (or informal grant of a lease) is regarded by equity as creating an equitable lease. In equity the parties to the contract or informal transaction have the same rights and duties they would have had, had a deed been executed.

Subject to certain points raised below, Matthew will be able to invoke the principle in *Walsh* v *Lonsdale* and claim that the written agreement confers on him an equitable lease.

One possible initial stumbling block for Matthew is that for an agreement to create an equitable lease, it must be a legally valid contract. Contracts for the sale or transfer of rights in land (unlike most contracts) are subject to special requirements as to form. Section 2 of the 1989 Law of Property (Miscellaneous Provisions) Act requires land contracts to be in a written document signed by both parties, including all the agreed terms. Thus if (say) Matthew did not sign the agreement, or some of the agreed terms did not appear in the document, the agreement would be VOID. Consequently Matthew would not have an equitable lease.

Assuming that the agreement did comply with s. 2, then Matthew has an equitable lease, but the continued existence of that lease is under threat from another direction.

Matthew's right to an equitable lease depends upon his right to claim the equitable remedy of specific performance of the agreement. If Matthew is in substantial breach of his agreement he will lose the right to specific performance ('He who comes to equity must have clean hands') and thus destroy his equitable lease. Matthew does not want to suffer the fate of the tenant farmer in *Coatsworth* v *Johnson* [1886–90] All ER Rep 547, who lost his equitable lease because he failed to comply with the obligation to farm 'in a husbandlike manner'. Matthew must abandon his plan to run a bike-repair business from the house.

Part B

The first point to make is that if the 'contract' between Henry and Teresa does not comply with section 2 of the 1989 Act, then the contract is void, and Henry can repudiate the 'arrangement' without fear of being sued by Teresa.

Assuming the contract complies with section 2, then in principle an ancient rule of equity will operate on that contract. Applying the maxim 'Equity looks on as done that which ought to be done', somebody who has contracted to buy a piece of land is regarded in equity as owner of that land even though the legal estate has not yet been conveyed to him. This means that the 'risk' of anything untoward happening to the property passes to a purchaser when the contract is signed, not (at the later stage) when the legal estate is conveyed to the purchaser.

Thus if a building is destroyed by fire or some other calamity between contract and completion, the (unfortunate) purchaser must complete the deal. Applied to Taylor Cottage, this principle would mean that Henry would have to accept a conveyance of the badly damaged building and pay the full price.

The principle that 'the risk passees on contract not completion' has been heavily criticized, and in 1990 the Law Society drew up a new set of standard conditions for the sale of land, clause 5 of which is crucial. Clause 5 provides that the seller of land must 'transfer the property in the same state as it was at the date of the contract', and also that if between contract and completion 'the physical state of the property makes it unusable for its purpose' the buyer can rescind the contract.

Thus, provided the contract signed last week incorporated clause 5, Henry can certainly claim compensation from Teresa, and (alternatively) if the property is uninhabitable, rescind the contract.

If the contract did not include clause 5, then Henry must complete the deal. He will have to hope that his solicitor arranged insurance for the cottage from the date of the contract.

The point regarding the outhouse is only relevant if Henry cannot rescind the contract because of the bus damage. Another consequence (more beneficial to purchasers) of the theory that a purchaser becomes owner in equity on contract not completion is the rule that the vendor must take managerial decisions with respect to the land only in consultation with the purchaser. In *Abdullah v Shah* [1959] AC 124 the vendor immediately relet part of the property which had fallen vacant between contract and completion. The purchaser, who would have preferred the property empty, was awarded a reduction in price by the Judicial Committee of the Privy Council.

In the same way Henry (if forced to complete the deal despite the bus damage) can claim a reduction in price to compensate for the demolition of the outhouse.

Chapter 8 Assessment Exercise—Specimen Answer

(a) There are two types of right which Martin can claim against Grand Villa. The first is his 'matrimonial home rights' granted by the Family Law Act 1996. These rights automatically arise from the fact that he is Ruth's spouse and she had sole title to the matrimonial home.

The matrimonial home rights are classed as an equitable interest, but are not subject to the doctrine of notice; they are registrable as a Land Charge 'Class F'. Almost certainly Martin did not know that he needed to register his Class F charge, and thus it is almost certain that his rights of occupation will not bind William.

Martin's second right is the constructive trust interest which he obtained in Grand Villa through paying £200,000 for a total reconstruction. Cases such as *Lloyds Bank v Rosset* hold that substantial contributions to the cost of purchasing or reconstructing a property will give rise to a constructive trust interest in the contributor's favour.

A constructive trust interest is subject to the equitable doctrine of notice. Thus Martin's interest will bind William unless William can prove that he is a bona fide purchaser for value of a legal estate (or interest) without notice of Martin's interest. It is reasonably clear that William is a bona fide purchaser for value of a legal estate. Thus William will take Grand Villa free from Martin's interest if he can prove that at the time of the conveyance he was without notice of Martin's claim.

'Notice' comes in three forms, actual, constructive, and imputed. It would appear that at the time of the purchase William had no actual knowledge (i.e. actual notice) of Martin's constructive trust interest. However Martin will probably contend that William had constructive notice of Martin's interest.

Under the constructive notice rule a purchaser of land must make all those enquiries which a reasonable purchaser makes. In particular he must inspect the land for signs of occupiers other than the vendor and investigate the title deeds. If a purchaser fails to make a reasonable enquiry which would have revealed an equitable interest, he will be stuck with constructive notice of that interest.

Martin's interest is not the sort which is revealed in title deeds. But it is the sort which may gain protection from the rule in *Hunt v Luck* [1902] 1 Ch 428. If on inspecting the land the (potential) purchaser sees signs of a person other than the vendor occupying the land, then the purchaser must seek out that other person and enquire of him what claim he has to the land.

We must hope that William made a proper inspection of Grand Villa, and that when he made that inspection there were no signs that Martin lived there.... Only if that is the case will William be without notice of Martin's interest.

If William employed a surveyor to inspect the land, we must hope that there were no signs of Martin when the surveyor called to inspect. This is because of the imputed notice rule. If a purchaser employs an agent then any (actual or constructive) notice which comes to that agent is automatically attributed to the purchaser with the result that he is bound by the relevant equitable interest.

(b) As the document granting the lease is not a deed, David has only got an equitable lease. Post-1925 such a lease is not subject to the doctrine of notice. It is registrable as an 'Estate Contract' land charge. It is unlikely that David (who probably did not take legal advice) will have registered. If he has not registered then his equitable lease will be void against William, as William is (apparently) a purchaser for money or money's worth of a legal estate. Moreover it will be void against William even if he actually knew of the equitable lease. (See *Hollington Brothers* v *Rhodes* [1951] 2 All ER 578.)

(c) Whether the restrictive covenant benefiting Blackview binds William may well depend upon the date it was entered into. The deed produced by Harry must be carefully examined to see whether or not it was executed after 1925.

If it transpires that the 'residential purposes' only covenant was entered into after 1925, then it will be registrable as a land charge. It will only bind William if it was correctly registered as a land charge against the name of the owner of Grand Villa who (back in the 'twenties') entered into the restrictive covenant. If the covenant was not correctly registered it will be void against William, even if he knew about the covenant through looking at the title deeds.

If the covenant was entered into before 1926 then it will not be registrable as a land charge; it will be subject to the old doctrine of notice.

As mentioned earlier, the purchaser of land is expected to investigate the title deeds. If William inspected the deeds and saw the restrictive covenant mentioned, he would have actual notice. If his solicitor inspected the deeds and saw the covenant, William would have imputed notice.

If William (or his solicitor) failed to investigate title properly, with the result that the covenant ought to have been discovered from the deeds but wasn't, then William will have constructive (or constructive imputed) notice.

The duty to investigate deeds is not however a duty to investigate documents back to time immemorial. It is a duty to go back to the 'root of title'; the root is the most recent conveyance which is at least fifteen years old. When William purchased Grand Villa the root would have been the conveyance to Ruth in 1960. If (as is possible) the 'residential only' covenant is not mentioned in that conveyance (nor in any later document such as a mortgage of Grand Villa produced by Ruth to William or his solicitor), then William will not have notice of the covenant and will not be bound by it.

Chapter 10 Assessment Exercise—Specimen Answer

The right to use the toilet granted to Ursula is an easement—see *Miller* v *Emcer Products*. However, as there was no deed, the easement cannot be a legal easement. Nevertheless, provided the agreement complies with s. 2 of 1989 Law of Property (Miscellaneous Provisions) Act Ursula will have an equitable easement. To comply with s. 2 the written agreement must be signed by both parties and contain all the terms they agreed on.

Schedule 3, para. 3 of the Land Registration Act 2002 makes **legal** easements **overriding** interests automatically binding on purchasers of the registered title. However, under the new law, **equitable** easements are not overriding interests. Ursula's toilet right is therefore a minor interest and will only be binding on Ahmed if she has 'protected' it by entering a 'notice' on the register. It is unlikely that she would know of this requirement, and therefore her easement is likely to be void against the purchaser, Ahmed.

Ursula has two equitable rights with respect to the garden—an equitable lease under *Walsh* v *Lonsdale* and an option. In principle both rights are minor interests which need protection by entry of a notice on the register. Again, it is unlikely that Ursula will realize this.

However, these two rights may be upgraded to an overriding interest if Land Registration Act 2002, Sch. 3, para. 2 is satisfied. For Ursula to satisfy this provision:

(1) She must be in actual occupation;

(2) That occupation must be 'obvious on a reasonably careful inspection'.

While Ursula was presumably occupying 'her' part of the garden by cultivating it, it is probable that her occupation would not be obvious on reasonably careful inspection. Anybody visiting the land would imagine that the cultivation was being done by the landowner (Seema). **Ursula's** occupation would only be obvious if she had (say) erected a notice proclaiming 'Ursula's garden'. Ursula's rights are probably not overriding under Sch. 3, para. 2.

If Ursula is within Sch. 3, para. 2, then her equitable lease will be an overriding interest. Her option would also be an overriding interest (*Webb* v *Pollmount*) but only with respect to the part of the garden which she was occupying. (The decision in *Ferrishurst* has been overruled by new statutory wording.)

Pritesh clearly does not have a constructive trust interest (see *Lloyd's Bank* v *Rosset*—like Mrs Rosset, he has not contributed substantially to either the purchase or the improvement of the property). He will, though, have a matrimonial home right under the Family Law Act. But the latter is a minor interest which cannot be upgraded to overriding under Sch. 3, para. 2. It only binds a purchaser if it has been protected by entry of a notice on the register. It is unlikely that Pritesh would know of the need to enter a notice to protect his right. So that right will be void against our client Ahmed.

Chapter 13 Assessment Exercise— Specimen Answer

Black House

Samantha should set up a 'trust of land' governed by the 1996 Act. The trustees of a 'new-style' trust of land are expressly granted all the powers of an absolute owner of land (s. 6(1)). However, the following points should be made.

First, s. 8(1) of the Act allows the settlor to reduce or remove the powers of the trustees. So under s. 8(1) Samantha could expressly provide that the trustees shall have no power of sale during Thomas's lifetime. Inserting such a clause is (from an economic point of view) definitely not a good idea as it prevents the trustees from responding to changed circumstances. Samatha is therefore advised not to insert a 'takeaway clause'.

Secondly, Samantha should instead make use of s. 8(2), which provides that the exercise of the trustees' power of sale and the exercise of the trustees' other powers can be made expressly subject to the consent of any named person or persons. She might, for instance, wish to make any sale subject to Thomas's consent, with a view to keeping Black House unsold during Thomas's lifetime. However, if she is concerned that Thomas might consent to a sale, she could make the trustees' power of sale subject to the consent of another trusted friend. She should choose a friend whom she is confident will not consent to a sale in Thomas's lifetime unless circumstances are such that a sale becomes necessary for the welfare of the beneficiaries.

Thirdly, Samantha should include a clause expressly making Thomas's occupation of Black House a purpose of the trust; he will then be entitled to occupy the house unless the land becomes unsuitable for him or unavailable to him (s. 12). However, if Thomas occupies the land by reason of his entitlement under s. 12 the trustees can subject him to certain reasonable conditions of occupation (s. 13(3)). He might, for example, be required to keep the premises in a good state of repair.

Finally, one crucial general point should be made. If Thomas, Luke, and John are all adults and have capacity (that is, do not suffer from a legally relevant disability) and together agree, they can bring the trust to an end under the rule in *Saunders* v *Vautier* [1825–42] 1 All ER Rep 58 and do what they like with the trust land. Neither Samantha nor her trustees can do anything to prevent this possibility happening.

White House

As with Black House, Samantha should be advised that her proposed disposition can only be effected by a new-style trust of land. The issues are whether Samantha can ensure that the house will be sold at Norman's request, and whether the proceeds will be reinvested to meet Norman's needs.

As to the first issue, it is worth noting that under the traditional Settled Land Act 'strict settlement' Norman, as tenant for life, would have had the power to sell the land. After the Trusts of Land etc. Act 1996 it is no longer possible to create a trust of this type. Section 6(1) of the 1996 Act vests the power of sale in the trustees of the new-style 'trust of land' and s. 4(1) grants the trustees the power to postpone sale of the land indefinitely, the length of postponement lying entirely within the trustees' discretion (s. 4(1)). This statutory power to postpone cannot be excluded by contrary expression in the trust instrument. Thus, the trustees cannot be placed under a duty to sell, and consequently Samantha cannot ensure that the house will be sold at Norman's request. Accordingly, Samantha should be advised to choose trustees who are likely to respond favourably to Norman's request. To this end she could, of course, appoint Norman himself to be one of the trustees if she so wishes (members of our firm of solicitors could be appointed to be the other trustees).

As to the second issue, Samantha should be advised that if the trustees sell White House, they are authorized to reinvest the proceeds of sale in new land (ss. 6(3) and 17(1)); that includes the purchase of a lease. Samantha should also be informed that, before selling and reinvesting the proceeds of sale, the trustees will be obliged to consult Norman, as the beneficiary in possession, and to give effect to his wishes so far as his wishes are deemed by them to be consistent with the general interests of the trust (s. 11(1)).

We should also advise Samantha that if her trustees refuse to accede to Norman's reasonable request for a sale and/or reinvestment in appropriate property, all is not lost. Norman could apply under s. 14 for a court order requiring the trustees to sell and reinvest the proceeds of sale in, say, a smaller house nearer to the shops! According to s. 15 the court must have regard to, *inter alia*, the intentions of Samantha, and the purposes for which the trust land is held.

(If the trustees sell White House, and the 'new' smaller house does not exhaust the proceeds of sale, the surplus proceeds will be invested by the trustees—Norman will get the income from these investments.)

Chapter 16 Assessment Exercise— Specimen Answer

The Legal Ownership of the Retreat

As the friends were co-owners, a trust for sale was imposed on them in 1990. However, only Steven, Julia, and Mark became trustees, as Tracey was under 18 and only adults can be appointed trustees. Tracey would NOT become a trustee on her attaining the age of 18.

The only event after 1990 to affect the trusteeship of the legal title is the death of Steven and Julia. This event (as a result of the survivorship rule) leaves Mark as the only trustee, though not (as we shall see) the sole beneficiary.

Can Mark Sell Without a Court Order?

In theory, yes, in practical reality, no. Mark appears to be a sole surviving joint tenant, so he might try and take advantage of the Law of Property (Joint Tenants) Act 1964. Alternatively, to give added reassurance to the purchaser, he could appoint a friend as co-trustee, and the two of them convey The Retreat to the purchaser. Either way a sale would overreach the equitable interests of Tracey and any other beneficiary.

The practical reality is, however, that no purchaser, even a very keen one, is going to buy with Tracey in permanent occupation. Undoubtedly Tracey has the right to occupy the property until it is sold (see *Bull* and *Boland*). On the sale by two trustees taking place, her rights will be overreached (*Flegg*) and she will become a trespasser vis-à-vis the purchaser. But the purchaser will 'acquire' the problem of taking proceedings to evict Tracey. No sane purchaser (particularly one keen to move in quickly) is going to buy in these circumstances.

Thus Mark will be forced to take proceedings under s. 14, Trusts of Land and Appointment of Trustees Act 1996. (See below.)

The Equitable Ownership of The Retreat

The initial position

There appears to be nothing to rebut the initial presumption of joint tenancy. Note in particular that the four contributed equally to the cost. However, there might be a tenancy in common (in equal shares) if the court found there was a business element to the arrangements, e.g. if they envisaged holiday lettings of The Retreat when none of them wanted to use it themselves.

Current Position if Parties Initially Tenants in Common

An equitable interest as tenants in common can be left by will. Therefore after the car crash Violet and Karen would become tenants in common in equity alongside Mark and Tracey.

Current Position if Parties Initially Equitable Joint Tenants

The Effect of Julia's Mortgage

This clearly severs her equitable interest, converting it into a one-quarter share as tenant in common. On her death this equitable interest will pass by her will (subject to the mortgage) to Karen.

The Effect of Steven's Frequent Arguments

It is possible to sever by informal agreement, or by conduct which indicates that the parties are treating the joint tenancy as at an end (*Burgess* v *Rawnsley*). As the outbursts were ignored by the other three it seems that there has been no informal severance by conduct/agreement.

However, Lord Denning was of the view in *Burgess* that an oral unilateral statement would effect a severance. This rather impractical view is unsupported by authority, but if it were correct then presumably the outbursts would effect a severance. As a result Violet would inherit a quarter share.

If (as is probably the case) Steven has not severed, then Violet does not inherit any interest in The Retreat. The 'survivorship' rule operates between joint tenants; the law of succession has no application to a joint tenancy interest. The current equitable ownership would be Julia one-quarter with the other three-quarters belonging to Mark and Tracey as joint tenants.

Mark's prospects of getting an order of sale

Violet's support is probably irrelevant, as she only has an interest if either the parties were initially tenants in common or if Steven has severed. If Violet has no interest and Karen comes out against a sale then a majority by value would be against sale.

But it is submitted that Mark has the trump card. The purpose for which the property was acquired has clearly failed, and that normally means that the court in its discretion will order a sale under s. 14, Trusts of Land etc. Act 1996. (See *Jones v Challenger*, contrast *Re Buchanan-Wollaston* and see, now, s. 15, Trusts of Land etc. Act 1996.)

A refusal of sale would be very unfair on Mark, as he would be left with his money locked up in an asset he no longer has any use for. In *Dennis v McDonald* the Court of Appeal adopted a compromise whereby a sale was refused but the co-owner in occupation had to pay a rent. However, that was a case of a broken-down cohabitation, very different from this one!

A much more sensible compromise, **and one which can be reached without the expense of litigation**, is for Tracey to buy out the interests of the other parties involved. Mark should propose this in '*Calderbank*' letters sent to Tracey and Karen. (A '*Calderbank*' letter is a letter sent 'without prejudice except as to costs'.)

Chapter 17 Assessment Exercise— Specimen Answer

The Basic Test of Exclusive Possession

The first major case to discuss the *way* in which a lease should be distinguished from a licence was *Wells v Hull Corporation*. The facts of this 1875 case are very far removed from modern cases, which usually involve residential properties.

Hull Corporation owned a dry dock which it 'let' for short periods (usually a week) to shipowners for the purposes of carrying out repairs. The court held that whether the transaction constituted a lease or a licence turned on whether the grantee shipowner had been given 'exclusive possession' of the dock. The grantee would have 'exclusive possession' if he had been granted the **overall general control** of the dock.

On the facts the shipowners were held only to have licences as they lacked the necessary control of the dock. Under the terms of the standard form used by the Corporation, the Corporation continued to operate the dock gates, the pumps, and also supervised the cleaning out of the dock at the end of each day's repair work. These clauses meant that the shipowners did not have exclusive possession.

Moving forward more than a hundred years it can be said that nowadays the most obvious type of licensee in modern conditions is the traditional lodger. His 'landlady' (in the colloquial sense) retains control of his room, cleaning out, tidying up and changing bed linen. In *Marchant v Charters*, a case in 1977 which presumably survives *Street v Mountford*, the grantee was not a lodger in the time-honoured sense but the occupant of a service flat. The grantor provided daily cleaning and regular changes of bed linen; the grantee was held to have only a licence.

Possessory Licences from 1945 to 1985

After the Second World War there were a number of cases which seemed to indicate that if a transaction (which was not a service occupancy) granted exclusive possession, a licence not a lease would arise if it could be proved that 'the intent of the parties' was that there should only be a licence.

This problematic line of cases possibly started with *Marcroft Wagons v Smith* in 1951. There the existing tenancy of a house had terminated, but the grantors allowed the daughter of the ex-tenants to continue to live there for six months while she sought alternative accommodation. They charged her the same rent as before, but refused to give her a rent book or any other documentation. The daughter was held to be only a licensee. The Court of Appeal held that a lease had not been 'intended'.

As a result of this and other cases grantors thought, 'If we draft our grants so that they are **called** possessory licences we are on to a winner. We will escape all the restrictions of the Rent Acts'.

Things come to a head in Street v Mountford

In this case Street granted Mountford the exclusive possession of a flat. The document they both signed included the kind of provisions you would expect in a residential lease, but it also explicitly stated that the transaction was not a lease, only a licence. The Court of Appeal held that the subjective 'intent of the parties' was decisive, and that Mountford only had a licence.

When *Street* reached the House of Lords, the House overruled the Court of Appeal. In particular the House held that the test for whether a transaction was a lease or a licence was NOT the subjective 'intent of the parties'.

The House of Lords held (in effect reverting to the nineteenth-century position) that it was the objective test of exclusive possession which determined whether a transaction was a lease or a licence. A transaction which granted exclusive possession created a lease unless it fell within certain exceptions.

The exceptions recognized by the Lords were four in number. Service occupancies and occupation by virtue of an office (e.g. a vicar in his vicarage) were two. The other two exceptions are where a purchaser of premises is allowed into possession ahead of completion and where somebody allows friend(s) to occupy his premises as an act of generosity.

The 1974 case of *Heslop* v *Burns* is a clear illustration of this last exception. There an impoverished couple lived rent free in the house of a wealthy benefactor. They were held only to be licensees. Whether *Marcroft* v *Smith* comes within this exception is more debatable. The grantors had some understandable sympathy for the daughter, but they did charge her rent!

Non-exclusive Licences

Another trick adopted by residential grantors even prior to *Street* was examined by the House of Lords in *Antoniades* v *Villiers*. There the two partners to a cohabitation had each signed a separate 'non-exclusive' licence over a very small flat. One of the clauses of each agreement read 'The licensor shall be entitled at any time to use the rooms together with the licensee and permit other persons to use all of the rooms together with the licensee.'

The House of Lords held that the documents had to be read together as creating one lease, and that the clause just quoted had to be rejected as a 'pretence'.

A case decided at the same time as *Antoniades, AG Securities* v *Vaughan*, has however shown a way forward for grantors still determined to give only licences over their property. The grantors had granted four non-exclusive licences over a four-bedroom flat, each licence commencing on a different day, for a different duration, and at a different rent. The House of Lords held that there were four licences, overruling a Court of Appeal decision that the four documents should be read as creating one lease.

Grantors retaining Rights over the Premises

It is quite clear that if a grantor retains keys to premises the use of which he has granted to other(s), that does not prevent the transaction from giving exclusive possession and therefore being a lease. But what if the grantor inserts into a grant a clause deliberately designed to negate exclusive possession? In *Aslan* v *Murphy* Aslan granted to Murphy the use of a tiny basement flat, but with a strange looking clause inserted that Murphy had no right to use the premises between 1030 and 1200 every day. The licensor also had 'the right' to introduce into the flat another occupant.

In practice these clauses were never enforced and the Court of Appeal in effect held that they were 'pretences' (*cf. Antoniades* v *Villiers*). Murphy was held to have a lease.

This robust approach of in effect deleting from transactions clauses inserted by grantors which **on paper but not in reality** negate the granting of exclusive possession calls into question the 1971 decision of the Court of Appeal in *Shell-Mex* v *Manchester Garages*.

Shell granted the use of a filling station to the defendants for one year. The grant included a strange clause under which Shell could alter the layout of the premises. The clause even entitled Shell to move the very extensive underground storage tanks. The Court of Appeal held that the defendants only had a licence.

It is submitted that if this case were to recur the courts would apply (in the commercial field) the same approach as has been applied to dwellings. The artificial clauses about layout would be ignored as 'pretences'; the garage would have exclusive possession and therefore a one year lease protected by the Landlord and Tenant Act 1954, Part II.

Chapter 19 Assessment Exercise— Specimen Answer

The lease omits a forfeiture clause, thus limiting the remedies Lisa can seek for breach of covenant. She can sue for damages, and also an injunction to restrain non-residential user, but she will be unable to reclaim possession, even if the breach is extremely serious.

A second preliminary point is that if Tommy assigned or sub-let to Percy without even asking for Lisa's consent, that would be a breach of covenant. Lisa could claim damages, but the transaction would be valid (*Peabody* v *Higgins*). If Percy was a man of excellent character to whom no reasonable objection could have been taken the damages might be nominal.

Assuming that Tommy asks (in writing) for consent to assign or sub-let to Percy, then the Landlord and Tenant Acts 1927 and 1988 apply to covenant (iii), a 'qualified covenant' against assignment etc. The 1927 Act (s. 19) implies into covenant (iii) a proviso that Lisa must not unreasonably withhold her consent.

The 1988 Act is even more significant, placing on Landlords (like Lisa) a series of duties if they receive from a tenant with respect to a qualified covenant a written request for consent to an assignment or sub-letting. First, Lisa must give an answer within a 'reasonable time'. Secondly she must give consent, unless there are reasonable grounds for refusing. Thirdly, if she says 'no' then she must give written reasons. Moreover, if she breaches any of these duties, Tommy can sue for damages.

The 1988 Act also establishes that in any dispute over a landlord's actions where there is a qualified covenant, the onus of proof will be on the landlord to show that (s)he is being reasonable.

Thus Lisa is advised to say 'yes' to any written request from Tommy, unless she has good grounds for objecting which she can prove to the satisfaction of the court. Case law (particularly the *Louisville Investments* case) indicates that purely personal objections (e.g. 'I cannot stand accountants') will not suffice. The landlord's objections must relate to the character of the assignee/sub-tenant or his proposed use for the premises. If Percy were of proven bad character, e.g. a convicted criminal or male prostitute, that would be good grounds for objection.

More importantly, if Lisa could prove that Percy intended to use the premises for inappropriate purposes, e.g. that he was definitely going to use the house as an office, that would be good grounds for saying 'no'.

It follows from this discussion that the answer to part (i) largely depends on whether Lisa is confident that she has reasonable grounds of objection provable in court. If this is so, then she will win any litigation commenced by Tommy. She might even consider herself seeking an injunction to restrain the proposed sub-letting/assignment.

If, in response to Tommy, she advances inadequate reasons, she may be lucky. Tommy may not want to risk litigation, and may abandon his proposed transaction. Lisa will have bluffed her way out. But Tommy may well call Lisa's bluff, and when told 'no' go ahead and assign or sub-let without consent. Proceedings then commenced by Lisa would fail.

Tommy might alternatively claim a declaration that Lisa is withholding her consent unreasonably and/or claim damages under the 1988 Act. Tommy would win. Moreover, if because of delay caused by litigation Percy lost interest in the premises, the damages could be substantial.

With respect to part (ii) of the question, if Lisa wishes to enforce covenants (a) or (b) against Tommy, then the position is the same, whether Tommy has sub-let or assigned. Tommy, being the original tenant, is liable for the duration of the lease. (The lease is prior to the enactment of the Landlord and Tenant (Covenants) Act 1995.) Tommy contracted for forty years, so he (or his personal representatives after his death) remain liable for that period. This will be so, whether the breach about which Lisa is complaining is actually committed by Tommy, Percy, or an assignee from Percy.

With respect to enforcement against Percy, it matters whether the transaction is an assignment or sub-lease. If an assignment, then Lisa and Percy will come into a relationship known as 'privity of estate'. Such privity exists where two parties are in a direct landlord and tenant relationship. Where parties are in privity of estate, then covenants which 'touch and concern the land' are enforceable between them.

Covenants to pay rent and relating to user of the premises touch and concern the land. Thus if rent arrears build up, Lisa will have the choice of suing Tommy (contract) or Percy (privity of estate). She can only recover one lot of damages. She should sue whoever has the most money.

If the house is used for purposes other than a private dwelling, she can again sue either Tommy or Percy, though if she wants an injunction preventing the user she should sue Percy.

If the transaction is a sub-letting, then there is no privity of estate between Lisa and Percy, as there is no direct relationship of landlord and tenant. (Tommy, as it were, stands between them.) Thus the covenant to pay rent would only be enforceable against Tommy.

Covenant (c) is special. It is a restrictive covenant, which can be enforced by a landlord (Lisa) against a sub-tenant (Percy), not by invoking landlord and tenant law, but by invoking restrictive covenants law. If the lease is registered title, then the covenant automatically binds a sub-tenant. (Land Registration Act, s. 23). If the lease is unregistered, then Percy is only bound if he has notice of the covenant. Lisa can ensure this by consenting to the sub-letting on condition that Tommy tells Percy about the covenant. (Case law and the 1988 Act allow consent on conditions, providing they are reasonable. Clearly this condition is reasonable.)

Chapter 20 Assessment Exercise—Specimen Answer

There is one point of which Letitia should be warned almost the moment she has sat down in the office. As she wishes to forfeit the lease she should be careful not to do anything which might be construed by a court as 'waiver'.

Demanding/accepting rent is always a waiver of forfeiture even if done by an agent of the landlord who is ignorant of the landlord's intent to forfeit. (See *Belgravia* v *Woolgar*.) Letitia should immediately insist that Rocky marks his file relating to the shop 'No rent to be collected'. If Rocky uses a computer system to send out rent demands/reminders, the computer must be reprogramed immediately.

The forfeiture process instituted by Letitia should proceed in two stages.

(1) Serve a notice under s. 146 of the LPA, and then (after waiting a reasonable time)

(2) Issue a claim form claiming forfeiture of the lease and possession of the property.

(It is still theoretically possible to forfeit a lease without court proceedings, using 'peaceable re-entry'. Letitia might be tempted to do what the landlords did in *Billson* v *Residential Apartments*; sneak in very early one morning when no one is at the shop.)

However, the House of Lords decision in *Billson* makes peaceable re-entry an undesirable course. Under the Lords' decision a tenant can claim relief from forfeiture after the landlord has peaceably re-entered, perhaps quite a long time after. Thus after the peaceable re-entry no new tenant would be keen to take a lease of the property for fear that Ann would reappear claiming relief.

The s. 146 notice should be served on Ann (the current tenant, see *Old Grovebury*). Extreme care should be taken in drafting the notice. If the notice is not correctly drafted, any court proceedings for forfeiture commenced after the notice will be abortive, and Letitia will have to start all over again.

The notice should give full details of the breach of covenant, and if Letitia wants monetary compensation the notice should contain a demand for such compensation.

If Ann's breach is 'capable of remedy' the notice should include a demand that the breach be remedied. This 'capable of remedy' point is notoriously tricky.

Normally a breach by a tenant of a covenant against illegal user is irremediable. The damage has been done; the property has been besmirched; everyone knows that the house is a brothel or the shop a drug den.... However, Letitia's case looks slightly like the problematic case of *Glass* v *Kencakes* where Paull J (not a specialist land lawyer) held that illegal user by a sub-tenant in breach of the head lease had been remedied by evicting the sub-tenant before the property became tainted.

Letitia is therefore advised to play safe. She should include in the s. 146 notice a clause, 'Remedy this breach if capable of remedy'. Moreover she should wait at least three months between serving the notice and issuing her claim form. (A fortnight wait would be sufficient if the breach were irremediable.)

Having got to court (and getting there is clearly going to take at minimum a few months) Letitia should be warned that Ann will probably apply (by way of counterclaim) for relief from forfeiture. Although relief from forfeiture is in the discretion of the court, Ann's case for relief is strong. (The breach may be technically incapable of remedy, but the Court of Appeal in *Woolgar* and now the Lords in *Billson* have made it clear that relief can be granted with respect to an irremediable breach.)

Ann has a strong case for relief as the breach was not committed by her personally but by her employee. She sacked Dandy the moment she found out. To grant forfeiture would be to deprive Ann of a very valuable asset—a lease with many years to run at (seemingly) a cheap rent. When Ann acquired the lease in 2005 she presumably had to pay quite a substantial price to Tamsin.

Probably Letitia's only hope is to come to court in a state of righteous indignation, fuming, 'I will not have my shop used as an emporium for HARD drugs such as Cocaine. Ann should have been careful whom she employed, and should have been at the shop every day when it opened.'

It would be fatal to her chances of forfeiture for Letitia to let on that she only wanted Ann out in order to get in a tenant who was willing to pay a much higher rent (*cf. Woolgar*). Moreover, if Ann proves that Letitia already has a new tenant lined up, that would destroy any claim that the property had been tainted.

It would thus appear that Letitia is likely to spend a lot of money, time, and energy pursuing forfeiture proceedings which will probably end with relief from forfeiture being granted. It is probably not worth all the effort, particularly when it is remembered that Letitia will not be able to collect any rent while the forfeiture proceedings are pending.

Letitia may feel confident that she can relet the property at a much higher rent. In the current economic climate her confidence may be misplaced. We see a lot of empty shops, even in the (relatively) prosperous South-East. If the shop was left unlet for any length of time Letitia might even have a problem with 'shop squatters'.

Letitia might, as an alternative to forfeiture, consider suing for damages. She has the choice of suing Tamsin (privity of contract) or Ann (privity of estate). However, as Letitia's reversion is not due to come into possession until 2034, it is difficult to see her recovering anything more than nominal damages.

Chapter 21 Assessment Exercise— Specimen Answer

Freda would first have to establish that she was in adverse possession of Grey Land since 1987. Adverse possession is defined by cases such as *Moran* as the taking control of the relevant land with intent to exclude everyone else from the land. It does not matter that the 'squatter' knows that the land in question is not hers.

It seems that Freda satisfies the *Moran* test. Her offer to buy made in 2002 is (fortunately) irrelevant. Had it been made in 1998, it would have been an acknowledgement of Edwina's title which would have stopped time running in Freda's favour.

But an offer/acknowledgement made after time has already run in favour of the squatter is of no effect. It cannot revive rights which have already been destroyed.

If Edwina's title was unregistered

This title was destroyed when the 12 years ran out some time in 1999. Freda has a new title based on her long possession. She will have no title deeds, but she will be able to defend her ownership (the correct word) by legal proceedings against anybody who tries to interfere with that ownership. For example, she will be able to defend her right to Grey Land against somebody who buys Redacre from Edwina.

To help secure her position against possible future challenges, Freda should voluntarily register her title. In her application she should admit that she has been an adverse possessor. The Land Registry will initially only grant her a possessory title, but that will be upgraded to absolute title after a further 12 years.

If Edwina's title was registered

Edwina remains legal owner of Grey Land, as the register is conclusive as to legal ownership. From (some time) 1999 to October 2003, Edwina held the Grey Land on trust for Freda. The transitional provisions of the Land Registration Act 2002 abolished this trust. Edwina now holds Grey Land subject to Freda's property right to apply to be registered as proprietor of Grey Land.

Freda should apply for rectification of the registration, which is bound to succeed. (Contrast what will be said in the next section.)

Should Edwina try to sell the Grey Land before Freda obtains rectification, then Freda should be able to assert against any purchaser an overriding interest within Sch. 3, para. 2. (Her right to apply for rectification is a property right.) To be absolutely sure of her position under Sch. 3, para. 2, she should:

(a) remain firmly in actual occupation of the Grey Land;

(b) ensure that her occupation is obvious on a reasonably careful inspection; e.g. Freda should put up a sign board proclaiming her ownership;

(c) answer any question posed by strangers regarding her right to be on Grey Land.

If Freda only started cultivating in 1995

This situation is radically different—it is governed by Sch. 6 of the Land Registration Act 2002. However long Freda goes on cultivating, even 50 or more years, she will not gain a proprietary right to Grey Land. At any time Edwina (or her personal representatives) could 'wake up' and bring proceedings to evict Freda.

Freda has a stark choice. Either she carries on cultivating hoping that Edwina has forgotten about Grey Land, or she takes a chance and applies to the registry under Sch. 6 of the Land Registration Act 2002 to be registered as owner of Grey Land. If she follows the latter course, the registry will give notice of her application to Edwina, who is likely to be stirred into action.

In the unlikely event of Edwina ignoring the notice from the registry, Freda will win ownership—she will be registered as owner of Grey Land and Edwina will lose all her rights—and without compensation.

But if Edwina does object to Freda's application, this first application is bound to be rejected. Freda's only remaining hope is that Edwina, having secured the rejection of Freda's first application, takes no further action for another two years. The chances are that Edwina will bring eviction proceedings against Freda within two years, but if she does not, then Freda should make a second application to be registered as owner of Grey Land. This time, Freda's application will succeed.

(As Freda knew all along that the land 'belonged' to Edwina, there is no possibility of her relying on the 'reasonably believing encroacher exception'.)

Chapter 22 Assessment Exercise— Specimen Answer

The problem scenario describes a 'double conveyancing' situation. John sold Lomasacre to Geoffrey in early 1988, before it became compulsory to register Lomasacre with a separate title. In these circumstances Geoffrey should have ensured that the sale of Lomasacre had been endorsed on the deeds of the Brooke Estate. He failed to do so. Recently John sold the whole of the Brooke Estate to Malcolm, with the result that Lomasacre has been conveyed twice. On these facts it is clear that Geoffrey has a claim to Lomasacre. However, to the scenario must be added the fact that Malcolm has been registered successfully as proprietor of the whole of the Brooke Estate, including Lomasacre.

Now Geoffrey's only hope of asserting his title to Lomasacre is to obtain rectification of the register.

The court's power to order rectification is set out in Sch. 4 of the Land Registration Act 2002, replacing s. 82 of the Land Registration Act 1925. If, as in the present case, rectification of the register is sought against a 'registered proprietor in possession', the claim to rectification is subject to the limitations set out in para. 6(2) of Sch. 4, which provides as follows:

No alteration affecting the title of the proprietor of a registered estate in land may be made under paragraph 5 without the proprietor's consent in relation to land in his possession unless—

(a) he has by fraud or lack of proper care caused or substantially contributed to the mistake, or

(b) it would for any other reason be unjust for the alteration not to be made.

It is unlikely that para. 6(2)(a) will apply. There is nothing in the facts of the instant case to suggest that Malcolm (the registered proprietor) acted fraudulently—on the contrary, we are informed that he **believed** Lomasacre to be part of the land he had paid for. Neither is there any evidence that Malcolm lacked care or substantially contributed to the mistaken registration—quite the opposite, it is Geoffrey who has committed the substantial mistake. Certainly the presence on Lomasacre of 'rusting railings' cannot be said to have indicated to Malcolm (or anyone else for that matter) that Geoffrey might have a claim to beneficial ownership of the land. In fact, the presence of 'rust' on the railings suggests, if anything, that the land has not been used for some time.

Geoffrey's only hope is that rectification (or 'alteration of the register', as it is described in the 2002 Act) will be ordered on the broad ground that it would be unjust to leave the register unaltered. However, it is clear from the wording of para. 6(2)(b) (particularly the use of a double negative) that this provision should only be used in a case where it is absolutely clear that justice demands that the register should be rectified.

One question the courts will ask is whether, if Geoffrey is refused rectification, cash compensation at the market value of his lost land will be adequate compensation (*Epps* v *Esso* (1973)). Considering the infrequent and uneconomic use to which Geoffrey has put his land the answer to that question is almost certainly 'yes', and the conclusion seems inevitable that justice will not demand a rectification, so that rectification will be refused. Of course Geoffrey's argument that justice is on his side is not helped by his failure to follow normal conveyancing practice.

The question of compensation remains. According to Sch. 8, para. 1(1)(a) of the 2002 Act a person is **presumed** entitled to be indemnified by the registrar if he suffers loss by reason of rectification of the register but in the present case there is no doubt that the presumption in favour of compensation will be rebutted. Geoffrey's compensation will be dramatically reduced, or even disallowed, due to his own serious lack of care, for, according to para. 5 of the schedule:

(1) No indemnity is payable under this Schedule on account of any loss suffered by a claimant—
    (a) wholly or partly as a result of his own fraud, or
    (b) wholly as a result of his own lack of proper care.

(2) Where any loss is suffered by a claimant partly as a result of his own lack of proper care, any indemnity payable to him is to be reduced to such extent as is fair having regard to his share in the responsibility for the loss . . .

Chapter 25 Assessment Exercises—Specimen Answers

Question 1

Regarding (a) and (b) Milligan will have to try and rely on the (rather complex) rules for implied grant of easements. There are no less than four separate rules in which an easement can arise by implied grant.

The first rule is 'way of necessity'. This rule is relevant only to (a). It only applies if land is sold which is completely 'land-locked', i.e. there is absolutely no way in and out except over the vendor's land. This does not appear to be the case with Blackacre, as there is the 'narrow footpath'. This path may not be adequate for farming purposes, but its existence is sufficient to prevent there being a way of necessity.

The second rule is the rule of 'intended easements'. If land is granted by a vendor or lessor to be used for a particular purpose **known to the vendor/lessor**, then there is implied into the conveyance/lease any easement over land retained by the vendor/lessor which is ABSOLUTELY ESSENTIAL in order to carry out that 'particular purpose'. (See the ventilation shaft case of *Wong* v *Beaumont*.)

With respect to (a) Milligan must argue:

(i) that Finnegan knew that Milligan intended to use Blackacre as a farm; AND
(ii) that a right to use the private driveway was absolutely essential to carry on a farm business.

Milligan should have no difficulty proving point (i), but point (ii) is very problematic. Finnegan would probably successfully contend that there were possible alternatives (e.g. widening and surfacing the narrow footpath to take motor traffic) and that therefore using the driveway was not **absolutely essential**.

With respect to (b) Milligan will have to argue that it is absolutely essential that he use the existing drains under Whiteacre. But Finnegan is likely to respond that alternative drains could be always laid not passing under Whiteacre. If that is the case, then Milligan has no chance under the intended easements rule.

Milligan's best chance would appear to be with the third rule of implied grant, the rule in *Wheeldon* v *Burrows*. Under this rule pre-existing nebulous rights known as 'privileges' and 'quasi-easements' can be magically converted into easements on the conveyance of the dominant land.

A 'privilege' would arise if the owner of two plots had leased one of them and then later granted the tenant some licence over the land he retained. There appears no evidence of Finnegan having done this. A quasi-easement would exist where the owner of two plots makes use of one plot for the benefit of the other in circumstances where had the plots been in separate ownership the 'use' could have been granted as an easement. It seems very likely that prior to the sale of Blackacre Finnegan made use of quasi-easements over the driveway and the drains.

If the following three conditions were satisfied one or both of these quasi-easements would be converted into full easements in favour of Blackacre the moment Blackacre was conveyed to Milligan:

(1) The quasi-easement was 'continuous and apparent', i.e. regularly used, and detectable by inspection of the plots of land.

(2) The quasi-easement was used for the benefit of the dominant land immediately prior to its being conveyed.

(3) The quasi-easement was necessary for the reasonable or convenient enjoyment of the dominant land.

Element (2) is presumably satisfied with respect to both (a) and (b). (1) is clearly satisfied with respect to the driveway, but whether the drains are 'apparent' will depend upon whether there was evidence **on the surface** (man-hole covers, gratings, etc) of their existence.

It is submitted that element (3) is satisfied with respect to both (a) and (b). While the driveway and drains are probably not 'absolutely essential', they probably do satisfy the lesser test of necessity laid down for *Wheeldon* v *Burrows*.

The fourth rule for implied grant, s. 62, can apply only to 'privileges'; and is therefore seemingly of no help to Milligan's claims.

With respect to (c) Cyrus is going to claim a profit of pasture by prescription. The basic idea underlying prescription for easements and profits is that if the dominant owner has been exercising his claim **'as of right'** for the past twenty years he thereby acquires an easement/profit to exercise his claim permanently.

For user to be 'as of right' it must be open ('without secrecy'), without force, and without permission. Cyrus's user has clearly been open, but if his user depended upon a permission (even an oral one) granted by Finnegan or one of his predecessors, there could be no prescription. (Exceptionally, if there was a purely oral permission given more than sixty years ago and never repeated, a claim under s. 1 of the Prescription Act 1832 would apparently succeed.)

If Cyrus's user was in the face of active opposition from Finnegan (protests or more obstructive behaviour), then user would be forceable and not prescriptive. Assuming Cyrus's user was as of right he would not *ipso facto* acquire a prescriptive profit. He must also satisfy one of the three alternative prescription periods, common law, or the Prescription Act 1832, or lost modern grant.

Cyrus probably will not succeed under the common law rule, as he has to assert that he and his predecessors have been grazing sheep on the hillside since 1189. But the Prescription Act, s. 1 will almost certainly be available, which requires thirty (not twenty) years' user as of right 'next before action'.

If Cyrus can only show between twenty and thirty years' user as of right he will probably be able to rely on the presumption of lost modern grant. This presumption could only be rebutted by showing that throughout the relevant period the grant of a profit was a legal impossibility.

Question 2

For reasons which will emerge, there is no need to treat the claims of Louise and Terry separately. Louise will claim that a prescriptive easement of way and a prescriptive profit of pasture have been acquired over West Field, and that those rights are 'appurtenant' to the freehold in Grand House. Terry will claim that, as current Tenant of Grand House, he is automatically entitled to the benefit of those rights appurtenant to Grand House.

There are two stages to the establishing of a claim for a prescriptive easement or profit. First, the dominant owner must show that certain general rules common to all three forms of prescription are satisfied. Secondly, he/she must show that the 'user as of right' satisfies the rules specific to one of the three forms of prescription.

The General Rules

Louise and Terry will firstly have to show that there has been continuous user as of right, i.e. open user without permission from the servient owner and without force or dispute in any form.

For user to be 'open' it must be such as would indicate to a reasonable servient owner that a right was being exercised (*Lloyds Bank* v *Dalton*). The grazing was obviously 'open', as presumably was the crossing the field to get to the station, unless Terry only used the short cut at night-time, which is highly unlikely.

We are told that user was 'without any objection', so there is no question of 'forcible user'. Gurinder's only hope under the 'user as of right' heading would be to prove that Nellie gave express permission to Terry for his activities. An oral permission would be sufficient, but it must be stressed that mere acquiescence in the prescriber's activities, which seems to be the case here, does not equal permission.

Louise and Terry must also satisfy the general rule that user be 'by or on behalf of a fee simple against a fee simple'. A prescriptive easement is always in fee simple, and is (theoretically) a grant from the servient freeholder to the dominant freeholder.

The application of this rule has two aspects. First, any prescriptive user by a lessee such as Terry is deemed to be as agent for his landlord. Thus Terry could not have prescribed against land owned by Louise, but any prescriptive right which he establishes against a third party such as Nellie is appurtenant to her freehold, though he gets the benefit for the seventy years of his lease.

Secondly, user as of right to be prescriptive must commence against a freeholder in physical possession. Thus if the commencement of the grazing and the 'short cutting' was during one of the 'short periods' when Nellie had let the field to Olive, Gurinder will be able to defeat the claims for prescriptive rights.

The Forms of Prescription

Assuming that Gurinder is unable to defeat the prescriptive rights under the general rules just discussed, Terry and Louise will invoke the Prescription Act 1832 for the (alleged) right of way, and lost modern grant for the profit of grazing. (Any claim under the third form of prescription, common law, is bound to fail as user evidently commenced long after 1189.)

Under the Prescription Act 1832 Louise and Terry will have to show user as of right for twenty years 'next before action'. Accordingly, their claim will succeed despite the fact that for about seven months Terry complied with the demand not to exercise his 'rights'. Provided Louise and Terry issue their claim form before the break in user has lasted one year, they should win. Section 4 of the 1832 Act requires the user to be 'next before action', i.e. (normally) immediately preceding the issue of the claim form in the case in which the easement is disputed. But it then provides that an 'interruption' of user for less than twelve months shall not count as an interruption to defeat the claim.

Louise and Terry will not be able to rely on the 1832 Act for their claim to a prescriptive profit. This is simply because s. 1 of the Act lays down a minimum period of 30 years' user for profits. Louise and Terry (like the farmers in *Tehidy Minerals* v *Norman*) will thus have to fall back on the 'last resort' form of prescription, 'lost modern grant'.

To succeed under this heading they will have to show strong evidence of at least twenty years user as of right. If they can do so (and it seems they can) the court will, by way of legal fiction, presume that a deed was executed 'in modern times' but that deed has been mislaid . . . .

In lost modern grant cases nobody really believes that a deed existed. Yet recent cases rule that the presumption of lost grant cannot be rebutted by factual proof (however convincing) that there was no deed. The presumption can only be rebutted by showing that the grant was throughout 'the relevant time' impossible as a matter of law.

The 'relevant time' begins when user as of right commenced, and ends twenty years before user as of right ceased. If throughout that time the granting of a valid profit would have been legally impossible because (say) the land was requisitioned or because Nellie was under some special legal disability like the vicar in *Oakley* v *Boston*, then Gurinder would defeat the claim to a profit. But it should be stressed that cases where the alleged servient owner can show legal impossibility are rare.

Chapter 28 Assessment Exercise—Specimen Answer

Prima facie there would appear to be a building scheme here, in which the restrictive covenants are mutually enforceable between the current owners of the plots. See the conditions laid down in *Elliston* v *Reacher*. The objectors would have to prove that back in the 1870s the covenants formed part of an organized scheme for a defined area, that Mark intended the covenants to be mutually enforceable, and that the **original purchasers** understood that that was his intention.

Assuming that each plot on Broadacre is subject to a building scheme, the question arises whether Luke can escape from the covenant restricting him to building one house on his plot. A number of possible avenues of escape may be available to him.

First, he might carry on regardless and build a second house on his plot. Although, with neighbours threatening to seek an injunction against further building on his land, this would appear to be inadvisable. Normally it will not be difficult for Luke's neighbours to obtain an interlocutory injunction, all they need to show is an 'arguable case' against Luke's plans. However, an injunction is an equitable remedy granted in the discretion of the court and it will not be awarded if the applicant has 'unclean hands'. Thus, if the neighbours who oppose Luke can be shown to have breached (substantially) any of the scheme covenants, they will be unlikely to obtain an injunction against him.

Secondly, he might carry on regardless, but take out insurance against the possibility that he might be subjected to an injunction. However, in the light of the threats he has received it is likely that insurance cover will be prohibitively expensive, or even refused altogether.

Thirdly, Luke might seek to identify all the 'dominant' owners (neighbours who are able to enforce the restrictive covenant) and attempt to persuade them to support him, perhaps by 'buying them out', although he is unlikely to be able to buy them all out without the financial support of those neighbours who support his plans.

But how will Luke know that he has persuaded all the dominant owners? The answer is that under s. 84(2) of the Law of Property Act 1925 the High Court can declare a definitive list of the dominant owners. Once such a declaration has been made Luke need not fear the claims of any dominant owner not appearing on the list. The High Court will only make a declaration under s. 84(2) if Luke has first circularized all his neighbours informing them that proceedings are pending, that they can be joined as parties, and that they will be bound by the result (*Re Sunnyfield* [1932] 1 Ch 79).

If Luke is unable to persuade all the dominant owners to release him from the restrictive covenant he may commence proceedings in the Lands Tribunal under s. 84(1) of the Law of Property Act 1925. The Lands Tribunal has the power, on such an application, to modify or discharge out of date restrictive covenants.

Under s. 84(1) there are a number of grounds on which a restrictive covenant may be discharged or modified. Luke is most likely to succeed under ground s. 84(1)(aa), which was introduced in 1969. The ground is that: 'the continued existence [of the restrictive covenant undischarged/modified] would impede some reasonable user of the land for public or private purposes'.

Section 84(1A) provides that two elements must be satisfied in order to succeed under s. 84(1)(aa). First, the restrictive covenant must (a) 'not secure to [the dominant owner(s)] any practical benefits of substantial value or advantage . . .'**or** (b) must be 'contrary to the public interest'. Secondly, money must be 'an adequate compensation for the loss or disadvantage (if any) which any [dominant owner] will suffer from the discharge or modification'. In determining these issues '. . . the Lands Tribunal shall take into account the development plan and any declared or ascertainable pattern for the grant or refusal of planning permissions in the relevant area . . .' (s. 84(1B)). Thus Luke may be able to rely on the development plan for his area if it suggests that there is a shortage of local housing. But it will not satisfy s. 84(1B) for Luke to point, merely, to the **individual** planning permission that has been granted to him.

If, the geography of Broadacre is such that Luke could build a second house without depriving his neighbours of a 'substantial' practical benefit (perhaps his plot is on the edge of the estate and

obscured by trees) he might just succeed under ground (aa) (*Re Banks' Application* (1976) P & CR 138). If such is the case the restrictive covenant will be modified or discharged, but only if money would be an adequate compensation to the dominant owners for the loss of the restriction. If the covenant is discharged and compensation is awarded, it will be awarded to each objecting dominant owner. Each objector should (normally) receive the amount by which his property is reduced in value by the presence of the extra house.

It is, however, submitted that Luke is unlikely to win under s. 84(1)(aa). The objectors will argue that a pleasant environment is worth more than money can buy, and that Luke's application is the 'thin end of the wedge'. They will rely heavily on the Judicial Committee decision in *McMorris*, which stressed that discharge/modification of a covenant should not be allowed where it would be 'the thin end of the wedge'.

Chapter 30 Assessment Exercise—Specimen Answer

(a) In order to take possession under the Criminal Law Act 1967, a mortgagee seeking possession in practice always seeks a court possession order. In the case of residential property repossession is always illegal unless it takes place by order of the court. Thus, assuming that 'Arkwrite Towers' is a dwelling house, Princewest will need to apply to court for a possession order under s. 36 of the Administration of Justice Act 1970.

Section 36 gives the court a wide discretion to adjourn possession proceedings, or to make a possession order but suspend its operation. The intention is to give the mortgagor time to find the money to pay off the mortgage. Possession will only be suspended or adjourned if it appears that the mortgagor will be able to repay the loan within a 'reasonable period'. Further protection is given to mortgagors of instalment mortgages by s. 8 of the Administration of Justice Act 1973 (most mortgages of dwelling houses are paid off by instalments).

Section 8 authorizes the court to suspend or adjourn possession in cases where it appears likely that the mortgagor will, within a reasonable period, be able to pay off instalments that are in arrears and catch up with current instalment payments. A reasonable period was thought to be around two years at most (depending upon the economic climate) but in *Cheltenham and Gloucester*

Building Society v *Norgan* [1996] 1 All ER 449, the Court of Appeal held that the court should take the full term of the mortgage (usually 25 years) as its starting point in determining the 'reasonable period' for repayment. Waite LJ stated that courts should ask at the outset the question: would it be possible for the borrower to maintain payment-off of the arrears by instalments over that period?

Assuming that the building society has gained possession of the house it will now be able to sell, provided that the power of sale has arisen and has become exercisable. It will **arise** if the mortgage is by deed and if the legal redemption date has passed (the mortgage is five years old, and so the power of sale will almost certainly have arisen). The power to sell is **exercisable** if (*inter alia*) interest repayments are at least two months in arrears, as appears to be the case in the present scenario. Accordingly, it appears from the facts that sale will be possible once possession has been secured.

The effect of a sale on the first mortgagee, Doorway, depends upon whether Doorway had allowed the sale to take place free from its rights. If it did, Doorway will be entitled to recover its share from the sale proceeds. If Doorway refused to allow the sale to continue free from its rights, the sale could still go ahead, but the house would yield greatly reduced sale proceeds, as any purchaser would be bound by the first mortgage.

(b)(i) The Court of Appeal in *Cuckmere Brick Co.* v *Mutual Finance Co.* [1971] 2 All ER 633 held that in deciding **when** to sell the mortgagee is entitled to consult its own interests to the total exclusion of the mortgagor's interests. However, having decided to sell at a particular time, in conducting the sale a mortgagee owes a duty of care to the mortgagor to obtain the best price reasonably obtainable at that time. If the mortgagee fails to obtain the best price he will have to account for the difference. The onus of proving that the mortgagee is in breach of this duty is on the mortgagor, unless the purchaser from the mortgagee has a personal connection with the mortgagee, in which case the onus is on the mortgagee to show that reasonable efforts were made to obtain the best price (*Tse Kwong Lam* v *Wong Chit Sen* [1983] 1 WLR 1349).

(ii) If a mortgagee attempts to convey the property before the power of sale has arisen, any conveyance will be completely invalid. Once the power of sale has arisen, a mortgagee can convey a good title to a purchaser free of the mortgagor's rights, whether or not the power of sale has become exercisable. A purchaser in good faith from a mortgagee need satisfy himself only that the power of sale has arisen; he is under no duty to enquire whether the power has become exercisable.

A purchaser from the mortgagee is under no duty to pay the best price. Provided he acts in good faith he will get a good title, even if the mortgagee should have obtained a higher price by taking greater care. It would be acting in bad faith if the purchaser conspired with the mortgagee to purchase at an undervalue.

(c) Princewest is treated as 'trustee of the proceeds of sale'. Proceeds from the sale must be applied in the following order: First, in paying off the total debt owed to the prior mortgagee, Doorway Building Society, if Doorway had permitted the sale to proceed free from its mortgage. Secondly, in discharging any costs of sale and any attempted sale. Thirdly, in discharging the total debt (capital and interest) owed to Princewest. Finally, the balance (if any) must be paid to Bertha. If Princewest departs from this strict order it may be liable for breach of its trust.

Chapter 33 Assessment Exercise—Specimen Answer

Mortgages of Unregistered Titles

Where the mortgagee takes possession of the title deeds at the time the mortgage is created (usual in the case of a first mortgage)

A mortgage of this nature will not be registrable as a land charge. If the mortgage is legal the mortgagee can lose priority to a later mortgagee in limited circumstances only. Namely, (a) by deliberately (or in gross negligence) permitting the mortgagor to retake possession of the title deeds, thus allowing the mortgagor fraudulently to represent to a new lender that the property is not mortgaged; or (b) by prematurely endorsing a receipt on the mortgage, thereby giving later mortgagees the impression that the first mortgage has been fully paid off.

If the mortgage is equitable the same principles ((a) and (b)) apply. In addition, an equitable mortgage where the mortgagee has taken the title deeds is an example of an equitable interest not registrable as a land charge but still subject to the doctrine of notice. Therefore, such an equitable mortgagee could theoretically lose priority to a later legal mortgagee who took without notice of the earlier equitable mortgage. The risk is purely theoretical, however, because the absence of title deeds in such a case would give any later mortgagee notice of the first mortgage.

Where the mortgagee does not take possession of the title deeds at the time the mortgage is created

In such a case the mortgage will be registrable as a land charge. If it is a legal mortgage it will be a 'puisne' mortgage registrable as a class C(i) land charge. If it is an equitable mortgage it will be a general equitable charge registrable as a class C(iii) land charge. If a registrable mortgage is in fact promptly registered as a land charge then it is bound to have priority over subsequently created mortgages. The real 'complexity and uncertainty' in this area of law arises if a registrable mortgage is not registered, or is registered late (after the creation of a second mortgage of the land). In such a case s. 4(5) of the Land Charges Act 1972 and s. 97 of the Law of Property Act 1925 will apply.

Section 4(5) provides that if a registrable mortgage is not in fact registered it 'shall be void as against a purchaser of the land charged therewith, or any interest in that land'. Accordingly, in the normal course of events, if X grants a registrable mortgage to A which A omits to register, and then X grants a mortgage to B, it is B's mortgage which will have priority.

The picture becomes more confused if we now imagine that B's mortgage is also registrable, but has not been registered. According to s. 4(5) of the Land Charges Act 1972 nothing turns on whether B's mortgage has been registered, but s. 97 of the Law of Property Act 1925 could change the situation entirely. Section 97 provides that 'every mortgage affecting a legal estate in land . . . shall rank according to its date of registration as a land charge pursuant to the Land Charges Act'. If s. 97 is read literally, A, in the example given above, could regain priority over B by registering his mortgage after B has obtained her mortgage, but before B has registered her mortgage as a land charge. In short, there is a conflict in the results which flow from a literal application of ss. 4(5) and 97.

Which section should be followed? The conflict has existed for about 80 years and has not yet been resolved by any decided case. A literal reading of s. 4(5) suggests that an unregistered mortgage is rendered 'void' against the holder of a subsequent mortgage, and the usual rule is that once an interest in land is void against a purchaser (or mortgagee) subsequent registration cannot make it valid again. In further support of s. 4(5) it could be argued that where s. 97 says 'pursuant to the Land Charges Act' it means 'pursuant to the Land Charges Act **and the rules contained therein**'.

On the other hand, a literal reading of s. 97 leads to the clear conclusion that priority between registrable mortgages is to be determined only according to the date of registration. Perhaps s. 97 will ultimately be favoured, but it would make mortgages distinct from other land charges (which would not be ideal). However, it would be a simple rule to apply, and it would make the rule for unregistered title similar to that for registered title.

Mortgages of Registered Titles

In contrast to the above, the rule for determining priority of mortgages of a registered title is very straightforward. If there is a series of registered charges, they rank in priority in the order they are entered on the register, not in the order of their creation. The rule is not dissimilar to the rule in s. 97 interpreted literally, and lends support to a literal application of s. 97. As the rule is first on the register has first priority, it is imperative for a mortgagee of registered land to get its charge substantively registered as soon as possible.

Equitable mortgages of a registered title do present a problem. The Land Registration Act 2002 does not ban such mortgages. However, in *Mortgage Corporation Ltd* v *Nationwide Credit Corporation Ltd* (1993) it was held that an equitable mortgage of a registered title will **not** gain priority over an earlier unregistered mortgage or other unprotected right. The entering of a notice 'protecting' the equitable mortgage (which can now under the 2002 Act be done without the agreement of the mortgagor) secures the equitable mortgage against later transactions, but does not give it priority over earlier unprotected transactions.

It is submitted that Parliament should solve the problem thrown up by the *Mortgage Corporation* case by banning equitable mortgages of registered titles.

GLOSSARY

Administrators In the property law context, administrators wind up the affairs of a deceased person who has died intestate (or who made a will but there are no executors).

Assent The document used by personal representatives to transfer the deceased's property to whoever is entitled under the deceased's will or the rules of intestacy.

Assignment A general word meaning 'transfer of a property right'. In the context of land law, the word is often used with respect to leases, the landlord's reversion to a lease, and with respect to the benefit of restrictive covenants.

Bona vacantia Latin phrase translating as 'ownerless property'. Bona vacantia arises if someone dies without making a will and without leaving any 'statutory next-of-kin' (close relatives).

Building Scheme (Sometimes referred to a scheme of development.) A housing development where all the properties are subject to an organized system of restrictive covenants. Every property will be servient land, but every property will also be dominant land to the other properties on the development.

Class F land charge Phrase often used by lawyers when referring to matrimonial home rights (see below). Strictly speaking, it should only be used if the home in question is unregistered title.

Commonhold A new form of land ownership—in effect a new form of tenure—which became available in 2004. It is envisaged that this new tenure will be used for blocks of flats. A special type of company, a 'Commonhold Association', will hold the block in fee simple. A flat-owner will hold his flat **in fee simple** off the association under Commonhold tenure.

Constructive trust interest A constructive trust interest (or constructive trust share) arises in favour of Y where X owns a piece of land ('Whiteacre') and Y either pays a large part of the price of Whiteacre, or substantially contributes to the repayment of the mortgage on Whiteacre, or pays for or personally undertakes substantial improvements to Whiteacre. (Note that there are various other forms of 'constructive trust' which are relevant only to the law of trusts.)

Conveyance The document (in the form of a deed) which transfers a legal estate in unregistered land from one person to another.

Co-ownership of land A situation where two or more people are simultaneously entitled to enjoy the benefits of a piece of land. Co-ownership may take the form of either a joint tenancy or a tenancy in common.

Copyhold A form of tenure derived from medieval feudalism which existed until 1925. The 1925 legislation converted all copyholds into freeholds.

Dominant land The name given to land benefited by an easement, restrictive covenant, or appurtenant profit.

Easement A right of one landowner (the 'dominant owner') to make use of nearby land (the 'servient land') for the benefit of his own land (the dominant land). Typical easements are private rights of way, and the right to run a drain under someone else's land.

Equity of redemption Where property is mortgaged, the mortgagor (since 1925) retains ownership. However it is still customary to refer to the rights of the mortgagor as the 'equity of redemption'. Hence people saying, 'the equity in our house is £X0,000.

Estate In its technical sense, to own an 'estate' means to have the right to enjoy land for a defined period or indefinitely. At common law, there were four estates: fee simple, fee tail, life estate, and lease.

Estate contract Where somebody has contracted to buy a piece of land, but that land has not yet been transferred to him, the purchaser is said to own an 'estate contract'.

Estate contract has a wider meaning in the context of registration of land charges. See 8.3.3.1.

Estate 'pur autre vie' A type of life estate. A right to enjoy land for a period measured by the lifetime(s) of some other person(s). For example, to John Smith for the lifetime of Jane Brown.

Executors The people appointed by a deceased's will to wind up his/her affairs.

Fee simple The person who owns the fee simple in Blackacre is in practical reality the owner of Blackacre. A fee simple can be freely bought and sold.

In technical terms a fee simple is an 'estate' in land which (post-1926) gives its owner the right to enjoy the land for ever. If the owner of a fee simple dies, it passes according to the terms of his will, or the rules for intestacy.

Fee tail A virtually obsolete estate in land (no new ones can be created after 1996). In contrast to a fee simple, a fee tail only lasts so long as the original grantee of the estate or any of his lineal descendants are still alive. Since 1833, it has usually been possible to convert a fee tail into a fee simple by 'barring the entail'.

Fine In the context of land law, an old word for 'premium', i.e. a capital payment made either for the grant of a new lease or the assignment of an existing lease.

Foreclosure A process (almost obsolete) under which a mortgagee of land enforces his security by obtaining a court order which makes him outright owner of the mortgaged land.

Freehold Has two meanings; which is correct depends on the context.

(i) As synonymous with fee simple, e.g. when a layperson says 'I own the freehold to my house.'

(ii) 'Freehold tenure': the relationship under which every owner of a fee simple (technically) holds his land off the Crown.

General equitable charge This in practice can take two forms.

(i) An equitable mortgage of an unregistered title where the mortgagee does not take possession of the title deeds.

(ii) An unpaid vendor's lien (see below).

Heir When an owner of land died prior to 1926, his real property passed to his heir—usually his eldest son. The concept 'heir' is of little relevance today, but would have to be applied if someone died owning a fee tail which he had not barred.

Incorporeal hereditament Phrase used by some of the larger textbooks (e.g. *Megarry and Wade*, chapter 18) to cover easements, profits, and rentcharges (but not more modern rights such as restrictive covenants or constructive trust interests). 'Hereditament' because the property right is capable of being inherited; 'incorporeal' because the right does not give its owner possession of the relevant land.

Intestacy (or 'to die intestate') An intestacy arises where a person dies without having made a will. His property (both real and personal) passes to his statutory next-of-kin.

Joint tenancy A form of co-ownership (which may relate to a fee simple, a lease, or any other property) where

(a) each co-owner has an equal right to enjoy the land;

(b) there is a right of survivorship. When one joint tenant dies, his interest passes to the remaining joint tenants.

A joint tenancy may exist with respect to a legal estate or with respect to an equitable interest under a trust. Contrast tenancy in common.

Land transfer Where a registered estate is being transferred from A to B, the document (in the form of a deed) which is executed by A in B's favour. But B does not become legal owner until he has registered his title at the registry.

Lease In practice there are two types of lease:

(i) Fixed term. The lease has a fixed **maximum** duration, e.g., a 99-year lease of a flat.

(ii) Periodic tenancy. A lease for one (usually relatively short) period which goes on automatically renewing itself until either landlord or tenant gives one period's notice to terminate the relationship. (For example, weekly, monthly, or quarterly tenancies.)

Letters of administration Where a person has died intestate (or made a will but not appointed executors) letters of administration authorize administrators to wind up the deceased's affairs.

Licence by estoppel Where a landowner (L) encourages a third party (T) to expend money and/or effort on L's land, and T reasonably assumes that he will have some degree of permanency on the land, T acquires some sort of property right in the land. The extent and size of that right is (in effect) in the discretion of the court.

Life estate/life interest The right to enjoy land (or other property) either for one's own lifetime or for a period measured by the lifetime(s) of some other person(s).

Life tenant The name given to the beneficiary under a strict settlement who is currently entitled to enjoy the land. The life tenant hold the legal title to the land in trust for himself and the other beneficiaries.

Matrimonial home rights Where one spouse has sole title (freehold or leasehold) to the matrimonial home, the other spouse automatically has matrimonial home rights; in effect a right to live in the matrimonial home until evicted by the court. This right can be made binding on third parties (such as purchasers or mortgagees) by entering a notice on the land register, or if the title to the home is unregistered, entering a Class F land charge on the Land Charges Register.

This right now also applies to registered partners.

Minor interest A property right existing against a registered title which will only bind a third party purchaser if it has been protected by an entry on the register.

Mortgage A right over the borrower's land granted by the borrower (mortgagor) to the lender (mortgagee) which gives security for a loan. If the borrower fails to repay, the lender can enforce the security, usually by taking possession of and selling the mortgaged land.

Option The holder of an option can at any time within a fixed period insist that the land subject to the option be sold to him. (Contrast right of pre-emption.)

Overreaching Where land is subject to a trust, then, provided the purchase price is paid to the trustees, the equitable interests of the beneficiaries do not bind the purchaser but transfer to the purchase price. (The purchase price should be invested by the trustees.)

Overriding interest A property right existing against a registered title which binds third party purchasers even though it does not appear on the register.

Premium In the context of land law, a capital payment made either for the grant of a new lease or the assignment of an existing lease.

Privity of estate Privity of estate exists where two parties are in a direct landlord and tenant relationship. It does not matter whether they were the original parties to the lease.

Probate Where a deceased has made a will appointing executors, the executors obtain a grant of probate authorizing them to wind up the deceased's affairs.

Profit (or profit á prendre) The right to go on somebody else's land (the servient land) and remove from that land something which exists naturally. A profit may be 'in gross', i.e. the owner of the profit does not have any dominant land; e.g. fishing rights or the right to extract gravel or some other mineral. Alternatively, a profit may be 'appurtenant' to dominant land (as with an easement), e.g. (in particular) the right of one farm to graze its sheep on neighbouring land.

Proprietary estoppel See licence by estoppel.

Puisne mortgage A legal mortgage of an unregistered title (in practice a second or later mortgage) where the mortgagee has not got possession of the title deeds.

Receiver Broadly defined, a receiver is somebody (X) who is appointed to take control of somebody else's (Y's)

property. In the narrow context of land law, a receiver is either

(i) somebody appointed by the mortgagee to take control of the mortgaged land;

(ii) (in the context of leases) somebody appointed by the court or the Leasehold Valuation Tribunal to take control of premises which the landlord has allowed to fall into disrepair.

Remainder Where a trust is created and the settlor creating the trust creates a life interest, any interest or interests which only take effect after the first interest has ended are said to be 'in remainder'.

Rentcharge (Not to be confused with rent under a lease payable to a landlord.) The right to receive a regular sum of money (usually annual) from the owner for the time being of a particular fee simple estate. If the fee simple in Blackacre is subject to a rentcharge of £100 per annum in favour of Y, the current owner of that fee simple must pay the £100 per year to Y.

Restrictive covenant A promise by one landowner for the benefit of neighbouring landowner(s) that he will not do certain activities on his land. The land (permanently) restricted is known as the 'servient land', while the land benefited is known as the 'dominant land'. Note that with any one restrictive covenant there may be several (or even many) pieces of dominant land. See also building scheme.

Reversion In the specific context of leases, the landlord's rights are often referred to as 'the reversion'. In a different context, an estate in reversion arises where the owner of a fee simple grants a life estate/interest, but does not stipulate what is to happen when the owner of the life estate/interest dies.

Right of entry (or right of re-entry) In its technical land law sense, the owner of a right of entry has (if the appropriate conditions are fulfilled) a right to forfeit a legal estate and reclaim possession of the land.

In more colloquial terms, a landlord's right to forfeit a lease if the tenant breaks the terms of the lease.

Right of pre-emption A right of first refusal. If the owner of the relevant land decides he wants to sell, he must offer it to the person who holds the right of pre-emption before he puts it on the open market.

Right of survivorship See joint tenancy.

Servient land The name given to land which is subject to an easement, restrictive covenant, or profit. (Derived from the Latin word 'servus' = slave.)

Settlement In modern law, another name for a trust.

Settlor A person who creates a trust of land or other property.

Statutory next-of-kin Where a person dies intestate his property passes to his statutory next-of-kin. Usually it is the spouse and/or children of the deceased. If no children it is the parent(s). If no parent(s), it is the siblings. If no siblings, it is other close relatives, especially first cousins and their descendants.

Strict settlement An almost obsolete form of trust of land where the settlor's intention is that land should stay in the family from generation to generation. The legal title to the land is held by the life tenant, not by independent trustees.

Tenancy in common A form of co-ownership (which may relate to a fee simple, a lease, or any other property) where the co-owners have (physically) 'undivided shares'. On the death of a tenant in common, his share passes to his successors under his will or the law of intestacy.

Since 1925, a tenancy in common cannot exist with respect to a legal estate, but only with respect to the equitable interests under a trust for land.

Tenant

(i) In its colloquial sense, somebody who holds land under (any type) of lease.

(ii) In its technical sense it has a wider meaning—anybody who has a right to any estate in land. For example, if Jack owns the fee simple in Blackacre, one could say, 'Jack is tenant in fee simple of Blackacre.'

Tenure Of limited significance today. Technically a landowner's tenure indicated the type of conditions under which he held his land. Originally (in medieval times) there were many different tenures. Since 1925 there have been only two tenures, freehold and leasehold. However, commonhold is best understood as a new form of tenure.

Title deeds In unregistered land, the documents which record the various past transactions with the land. They are produced by the current owner of the land to show that his title to the land cannot be disputed.

Trust for sale A form of trust of land, popular prior to the Trusts of Land etc. Act 1996, under which the legal title was vested in trustees who were **theoretically** under a duty to sell the land and invest the proceeds for the benefit of the beneficiaries. **In reality**, the trustees often postponed the sale indefinitely.

Undivided shares An alternative name for a tenancy in common. So called because each co-owner has a share in the land which has not been geographically partitioned off.

Unpaid vendor's lien A property right which arises in favour of the seller of Blackacre if he transfers Blackacre to the purchaser but some or all of the purchase price remains unpaid.

■ INDEX